DEUTERONOMY
AND THE
DEUTERONOMIC
SCHOOL

DEUTERONOMY AND THE DEUTERONOMIC SCHOOL

Moshe Weinfeld

OXFORD
AT THE CLARENDON PRESS

Oxford University Press, Walton Street, Oxford OX2 6DP
London Glasgow New York Toronto
Delhi Bombay Calcutta Madras Karachi
Kuala Lumpur Singapore Hong Kong Tokyo
Nairobi Dar es Salaam Cape Town
Melbourne Auckland

and associated companies in
Beirut Berlin Ibadan Mexico City Nicosia

Oxford is a trade mark of Oxford University Press

Published in the United States
by Oxford University Press, New York

ISBN 0 19 826626 X

First published 1972
Reprinted 1983

Printed and bound in Great Britain by
Biddles Ltd, Guildford and King's Lynn

לאמי זכרונה לברכה

PREFACE

The process that has led to the publication of this book began with my M.A. thesis (in 1957) on the 'Dependence of Deuteronomy upon Wisdom Literature' (published in *Y. Kaufmann Jubilee Volume*, Jerusalem, 1960, pp. פט–קח.) The conclusions there drawn that Deuteronomy had been composed by scribes and wise men (cf. Jer. 8: 8) brought me to the investigation of two other aspects of this book: the homiletic framework of Deuteronomy and its school and the liberal rationalistic vein of the deuteronomic Code. Analysis of the sermons in the three branches of deuteronomic composition—Deuteronomy, the editorial framework of the Former Prophets, and the prose sermons in Jeremiah—and of the legal material in Deuteronomy, tended to confirm these conclusions.

Further support was provided by the publication of the vassal treaties of Esarhaddon (= *VTE*). A close study of these treaties, the longest ever discovered in Mesopotamia, revealed a great number of parallels to the covenant form of the book of Deuteronomy (which is not surprising in view of the fact that the vassal treaties of Esarhaddon were written in 672 B.C., that is, close to the time of composition of the book of Deuteronomy). The similarity in the formulation of the deuteronomic Covenant and the Assyrian treaties led me to infer that trained scribes of the Judean court transferred literary patterns from the political sphere, with which they were intimately familiar, to the religious sphere in which they began to be active during the Hezekian–Josianic reign. In fact, the evidence from contemporaneous Assyrian literature adds a new dimension to de Wette's hypothesis about dating Deuteronomy.

My treatment of all these questions was elaborated during the years 1960 to 1963 and presented in the form of a dissertation submitted to the Hebrew University in 1964—supervised by Prof. I. L. Seeligmann. During the years 1965–7 I revised the material extensively. At this stage I added the Appendix on Deuteronomic Phraseology, which I consider a vital part of the work, since style is the only objective criterion for determining whether a biblical passage is deuteronomic or not; it is arranged so as to show the occurrence of the phrases in the three main branches of deuteronomic composition and the theological doctrines on which they centre (see Introduction).

The progress of the work, as outlined above, is not reflected in the present form of the book. Its structure is thematic: Part I—Typology (speech and treaty formulation); Part II—The Law and its ideology; Part III—Affinities to wisdom literature. Part Two could be elaborated and treated more extensively, but in the framework of the present study I had to be brief (I hope to discuss the problem of the relationship between the various codes of the Pentateuch in the future; for the time being see my article 'Pentateuch' in the *Encyclopedia Judaica*).

Though the thesis underlying this book is that Deuteronomy originated in the scribal circles of Hezekiah–Josiah, I do not consider this as central in my work, which treats the *Sitz im Leben* of deuteronomic creation rather than its historical setting. This is also the reason for not discussing here the problem of Josiah's reform which, although crucial from the historical point of view, does not further the understanding of Deuteronomy *per se*. The accounts of the discovery of the Book of the Torah and Josiah's reform in 2 Kgs. 22–3 and their historical evaluation are treated briefly in my article 'Josiah' in the *Encyclopedia Judaica* and I plan to treat the subject at greater length elsewhere.

In acknowledging my gratitude to different persons who have contributed to the accuracy of this work I begin with Professor I. L. Seeligmann, who supervised the dissertation and whose valuable comments were most useful for the present study. I am also indebted to Professors A. Malamat, S. Loewenstamm, H. L. Ginsberg, and M. Greenberg, who read the work in its thesis form and made very helpful suggestions. Substantial parts of the work were read by Professors W. W. Hallo, W. L. Moran, and M. Tsevat, and I am most grateful for their comments and observations.

Mr. M. Freundlich translated from Hebrew the first draft of the study, for which I am very thankful. I am deeply indebted to Mr. I. Zarbib for his painstaking efforts in the preparation of the various indexes and glossaries to the book. I would also thank the librarians of the Hebrew University and the National Library here and especially Mr. Zand and his assistants, as well as the librarians of the Jewish Theological Seminary of America,

Columbia University, and Union Theological Seminary in New York during my stay there, for their devoted help.

I am deeply indebted to the Delegates of the Oxford University Press and to members of their staff for their patient and conscientious work in every stage of the preparation of this material.

Last but not least, I owe a great debt to my wife for her help and encouragement during all the stages of this work. She has typed a considerable part of the work and undertaken many different tasks in connection with it.

M. WEINFELD

Jerusalem
June 1971

CONTENTS

ABBREVIATIONS

COMMENTARIES ON THE BIBLE—SERIES

ATD	Das Alte Testament Deutsch, Göttingen.
BK	Biblischer Kommentar, Neukirchen.
CB	Cambridge Bible for Schools and Colleges, Cambridge.
EH	Exegetisches Handbuch zum Alten Testament, Münster.
HAT	Handbuch zum Alten Testament, Tübingen.
HKAT	Handkommentar zum Alten Testament, Göttingen.
ICC	The International Critical Commentary, Edinburgh.
KAT	Kommentar zum Alten Testament, Leipzig, Gütersloh.
KeH	Kurzgefasstes exegetisches Handbuch zum Alten Testament, Leipzig.
KHC	Kurzer Hand-Commentar zum Alten Testament, Tübingen.
OTL	The Old Testament Library, London.
SAT	Die Schriften des Alten Testaments, Göttingen.

OTHER ABBREVIATIONS

BC	Book of the Covenant (Exod. 21: 22–23: 33).
BH	*Biblia Hebraica*, 3rd edn., ed. R. Kittel.
BT	Babylonian Talmud.
CH	Codex Hammurabi (see *BL*).
Dtr	Deuteronomist (= Editorial framework of the Former Prophets).
EA	El-Amarna letters: J. A. Knudtzon, *Die El-Amarna Tafeln*, Leipzig, 1915.
F	J. Friedrich, *Staatsverträge des Hatti Reiches*, treaties 1–3, *MVÄG* 31, 1 (1926); treaties 4–6, *MVÄG* 34, 1 (1930), cited by treaty no.
HL	Hittite Laws: see A. Goetze, *ANET*, 2nd edn., pp. 188–97.
JPS	The Jewish Publication Society of America.
KS	*Kleine Schriften*.
MT	Massoretic Text.
NF	Neue Folge.
Q	Qumran.
W	E. F. Weidner, *Politische Dokumente aus Kleinasien*, *BoSt*, 8–9, Leipzig, 1923, cited by treaty no.

TEXTS AND LITERATURE

ABL	R. F. Harper, *Assyrian and Babylonian Letters*, Chicago, 1892–1914, cited by number. For transcription see *RCAE*.
AfO	*Archiv für Orientforschung*, Berlin: Graz.
AHw	W. von Soden, *Akkadisches Handwörterbuch*, Wiesbaden, 1965– .
AJSL	*American Journal of Semitic Languages and Literatures.*
ANET	*Ancient Near Eastern Texts relating to the Old Testament*, 2nd edn., ed. J. B. Pritchard, Princeton, New Jersey, 1955.
AO	*Der Alte Orient*, Leipzig.
ARM	*Archives Royales de Mari*, Paris, 1950– , cited by letter no.
ARu	J. Kohler and A. Ungnad, *Assyrische Rechtsurkunden*, Leipzig, 1913, cited by document no.
AS	*Assyriological Studies*, Chicago.
AT	D. J. Wiseman, *The Alalakh Tablets*, Occasional Publications of the British Institute of Archaeology at Ankara 2, London, 1953, cited by text no.
BA	*The Biblical Archaeologist*, New Haven, Conn.
BASOR	*Bulletin of the American Schools of Oriental Research*, New Haven, Conn. & Baltimore, Md.
BBSt	L. W. King, *Babylonian Boundary Stones*, London, 1912, cited by number, column, and line.
BL	G. R. Driver and J. C. Miles, *The Babylonian laws*, vol. I 1952, vol. II, Oxford, 1955.
BO	*Bibliotheca Orientalis*, Leiden.
BoSt	*Boghazköi-Studien*, Leipzig.
BWL	W. G. Lambert, *Babylonian Wisdom Literature*, Oxford, 1960.
BZ	*Biblische Zeitschrift*, Freiburg & Paderborn.
BZAW	*Beihefte zur Zeitschrift für die alttestamentliche Wissenschaft.*
CAD	*Chicago Assyrian Dictionary*, Chicago, 1956– .
CBQ	*Catholic Biblical Quarterly*, Washington.
CT	*Cuneiform Texts from Babylonian Tablets in the British Museum*, London, 1896– .
EI	*Eretz Israel*, Israel Exploration Society, Jerusalem (Hebrew).
FRLANT	*Forschungen zur Religion und Literatur des Alten und Neuen Testaments*, Göttingen.
GAG	W. von Soden, *Grundriss der Akkadischen Grammatik*, Rome, 1952.

GKC	Gesenius' *Hebrew Grammar*, ed. and enlarged by E. Kautzsch. 2nd English edn., trans. and revised in accordance with the 28th German edn., 1909, by A. E. Cowley, Oxford, 1910.
HAB	F. Sommer and A. Falkenstein, *Die hethitisch-akkadische Bilingue des Hattušili I*, Abhandlungen der Bayer. Akad. der Wiss., Phil.-histor. Abt. NF 16, München, 1938.
HIR	Y. Kaufmann, *History of the Israelite Religion*, 4 vols., 1938–56, Tel-Aviv & Jerusalem (Hebrew). See *The Religion of Israel*, Y. Kaufmann, trans. and abridged M. Greenberg, Chicago, 1960.
HUCA	*Hebrew Union College Annual*, Cincinnati.
IAK	*Die Inschriften der Altassyrischen Königen*, Altorientalische Bibliothek, vol. i, Leipzig, 1926.
IEJ	*Israel Exploration Journal*, Jerusalem.
JAOS	*Journal of the American Oriental Society*, New Haven.
JBL	*Journal of Biblical Literature*, Philadelphia.
JCS	*Journal of Cuneiform Studies*, New Haven.
JEA	*Journal of Egyptian Archaeology*, London.
JJS	*Journal of Jewish Studies*, London.
JNES	*Journal of Near Eastern Studies*, Chicago.
JSS	*Journal of Semitic Studies*, Manchester University Press.
KAH	*Keilschrifttexte aus Assur historischen Inhalts*, Leipzig, vol. I, 1911; II, 1922.
KAI	H. Donner & W. Röllig, *Kanaanäische und Aramäische Inschriften*, 3 vols., 1964, cited by inscription no.
KB	Köhler–Baumgartner, *Lexicon in Veteris Testamenti Libros*, 1953.
KBo	*Keilschrifttexte aus Boghazköi*, vol. I, Leipzig, Berlin, 1916, cited by text no.
KUB	*Keilschrifturkunden aus Boghazköi*, Berlin, cited by text no.
MAL	G. R. Driver and J. C. Miles, *The Assyrian Laws*, Oxford, 1935.
MDOG	*Mitteilungen der Deutschen Orient-Gesellschaft*, Berlin.
MGWJ	*Monatsschrift für Geschichte und Wissenschaft des Judentums*, Breslau.
MIO	*Mitteilungen des Instituts für Orientforschung*, Berlin.
MVÄG	*Mitteilungen der Vorderasiatisch-Ägyptischen Gesellschaft*, Leipzig.
NKZ	*Neue Kirchliche Zeitschrift*, Erlangen & Leipzig.
OIP	*The Oriental Institute Publications*, Chicago.
OLZ	*Orientalistische Literaturzeitung*, Berlin.
PEQ	*Palestine Exploration Quarterly*, London.

PRU	*Le Palais Royal d'Ugarit*, 5 vols., Paris, 1955– .
RA	*Revue d'Assyriologie et d'Archéologie Orientale*, Paris.
RB	*Revue Biblique*, Paris.
RCAE	L. Waterman, *Royal Correspondence of the Assyrian Empire*, 4 vols., 1930–6, cited by letter no.
RE	Pauly–Wissowa, *Realencyclopädie der classischen Altertumswissenschaft*, Stuttgart.
RHA	*Revue Hittite et Asianique*, Paris.
RSR	*Recherches de Science Religieuse*, Paris, 1910– .
SAK	F. Thureau-Dangin, *Die sumerischen und akkadischen Königsinschriften*, Leipzig, 1907.
SVT	*Supplement to Vetus Testamentum*, Leiden.
ThLZ	*Theologische Literaturzeitung*, Leipzig & Berlin.
ThZ	*Theologische Zeitschrift*, Basel.
UM	C. H. Gordon, *Ugaritic Textbook*, Rome, 1965, cited by text no.
VT	*Vetus Testamentum*, Leiden.
VTE	D. J. Wiseman, *The Vassal Treaties of Esarhaddon*, *Iraq* 20, 1958, 1–99, cited by line.
YOS	Yale Oriental Series, Babylonian Texts, New Haven, 1915– .
ZA	*Zeitschrift für Assyriologie*, Berlin.
ZAW	*Zeitschrift für die alttestamentliche Wissenschaft*, Berlin.
ZDPV	*Zeitschrift des Deutschen Palästina Vereins*, Wiesbaden.
ZNW	*Zeitschrift für die neutestamentliche Wissenschaft*.

INTRODUCTION

THE seventh century B.C. marks a turning-point in the history of Israelite literary composition. In the latter half of this century a new and unique literary style emerged which was to dominate most of the Israelite literature composed during a period of approximately 150 years (650–500 B.C.). It first appears in the book of Deuteronomy discovered in the year 622[1] and is afterwards encountered in the historical books and in prophetic literature (especially Jeremiah).

This style is distinguished by its simplicity, fluency, and lucidity and may be recognized both by its phraseology and more especially by its rhetorical character.

The main characteristic of deuteronomic phraseology is not the employment of new idioms and expressions, because many of these could be found in the earlier sources and especially in the Elohistic source. Indeed, it would be nonsense to say that all of a sudden in the seventh century a new vocabulary and new expressions were created. Language grows in an organic and natural way and is not created artificially. What constitutes the novelty of the deuteronomic style therefore is not new idioms and new expressions, but a specific jargon reflecting the religious upheaval of this time. The deuteronomic phraseology revolves around a few basic theological tenets such as:[2]

1. The struggle against idolatry
2. The centralization of the cult
3. Exodus, covenant, and election
4. The monotheistic creed
5. Observance of the law and loyalty to the covenant
6. Inheritance of the land
7. Retribution and material motivation
8. Fulfilment of prophecy } Deuteronomist[3]
9. The election of the Davidic dynasty }

What makes a phrase deuteronomic is not its mere occurrence in Deuteronomy, but its meaning within the framework of

[1] See 2 Kgs. 22. [2] See Appendix A. [3] Cf. p. 4 n. 1.

deuteronomic theology. Neutral phrases such as:[1] לא תוכל 'you are not allowed'; לא תחוס עינך 'you must show not pity'; איכה 'how'; גדל 'greatness'; היטב 'thoroughly'; קרב 'the midst'; מעשה ידים 'work of the hands'; אבה 'to be willing'; השמיד 'to destroy'; אכל ושבע 'to eat and be satisfied'; אלהים אחרים 'foreign gods'; אות נפש 'the desire of the soul', although they occur in Deuteronomy very frequently, are part and parcel of the common Hebrew vocabulary and cannot be considered specifically deuteronomic phrases. Their more frequent appearance in Deuteronomy than elsewhere may be explained by the special context in which they appear. Thus, for example, the phrase אות נפש occurs four times in Deuteronomy (12: 15, 20, 21; 18: 6) and twice in other parts of the Old Testament (1 Sam. 23: 20; Jer. 2: 24).[2] But the distribution of this phrase does not permit us to draw any conclusions as to its origin. By employing it, the author intends to make clear that things which have hitherto been prohibited (secular slaughter, 12: 15 and 20, and the right of the Levite to officiate at the central sanctuary, 18: 6 and 8) are now permissible without restriction: 'wherever one desires'.

The phrase לא תחוס עינך likewise arises from the special context. Whenever there is a danger that the punisher would be lenient or even unwilling to perform the punishment the author uses לא תחוס עינך 'you must show (him) no pity'. Examples are to be found in the case of the total extermination of the Canaanites (7: 16), the executing of one's relative or friend (13: 9), the killing of a person brought back from the city of refuge (19: 13), the executing of a false witness who has not actually committed the crime (19: 21), and the cutting off of the hand of a woman accused of immodesty (25: 12).

Similarly, the expression לא תוכל, in the sense of 'you may not', has been regarded as deuteronomic,[3] because it occurs very often in Deuteronomy, although it is found in other sources.[4] But the frequency with which it occurs in Deuteronomy is to be explained in the light of the context. Whenever it would seem that people might ignore a specific commandment or law because of its novelty or apparent peculiarity, the author adds לא תוכל 'you are

[1] See, e.g., the list of S. R. Driver, *Deuteronomy*, ICC, lxxviii–lxxxiv.

[2] Very close to אות נפש is תאות נפש in Isa. 26: 8; Ps. 10: 3. As a verb (אוה with נפש as subject) this phrase occurs in various books of the Old Testament.

[3] Cf. no. 44 in Driver's list.

[4] Gen. 43: 32; Exod. 19: 23.

forbidden'.[1] In no case can the occurrence of such phrases in a text be used as evidence of deuteronomic origin. Only those recurrent phrases that express the essence of the theology of Deuteronomy can be considered 'deuteronomic'.

The most outstanding feature of deuteronomic style is its use of rhetoric. This is true of all forms of deuteronomic writing. In the book of Deuteronomy itself the rhetorical style is manifest, not only in the introductory discourses but also in the law code and particularly in the laws which reflect the religious reform (chs. 12–18). Klostermann[2] has, indeed, rightly observed that Deuteronomy is not a 'law-book' but rather 'a collection of material for the public recital of the law'. The laws themselves are presented in a rhetorical parenetic framework, and their sole purpose is to foster the didactic aims which underlie the book. Thus, for example, the legal content of the ordinances concerning the year of release and the manumission of slaves in Deuteronomy is contained in six brief verses (15: 1–3, 12, 16–17), or about a third of the total space devoted to the subject. It is not the law itself, then, which is of primary concern to the author of Deuteronomy but its inherent religio-moral force, as he so amply elucidates.

The deuteronomic editor of Joshua–Kings makes similar use of oration to unfold the principle of divine retribution acting in Israelite history.[3] By employing these speeches and pragmatic discourses to link together the diverse narratives and chronicles he gives them a wider historical meaning. This is especially evident in the deuteronomic redaction of the books of Kings, where they are generally put into the mouths of prophets and so endowed with religious authority. The function of these speeches is to emphasize the role of the divine factor in Israelite history, in other words to furnish the ideological grounds of theodicy. The crucial events in that history, such as the division of the united kingdom (1 Kgs. 11: 31–9), the end of the Jeroboam dynasty (14: 7–11 and 13–16), the fall of the kingdoms of Israel (2 Kgs. 17: 7–23) and Judah (21: 10–15; 22: 15–20), are all theologically justified in the speeches of God's servants, the prophets. Sermons of a similar tendency are ascribed to Jeremiah, the herald of Judah's doom (see below).

[1] Compare לא יכהל in Aramaic inscriptions and papyri. See recently Y. Muffs, *Studies in Aramaic Legal Papyri from Elephantine*, Studia et Documenta ad Iura Orientis Antiqui Pertinentia, vol. 8, 1969, p. 36 n. 2.

[2] A. Klostermann, *Der Pentateuch*, NF, 1907, 344.

[3] Cf. M. Noth, *Überlieferungsgeschichtliche Studien*, 1943, 5 ff.

The use of oration is equally characteristic of all branches of deuteronomic writing—the book of Deuteronomy, the editorial framework of Joshua–Kings (= Dtr) and the prose sermons in the book of Jeremiah (source C)[1]—and was adopted by the deuteronomic circle as a literary device throughout the entire period of its activity. The deuteronomic historian and the author of the prose sermons in the book of Jeremiah did not merely emulate the style of Deuteronomy, as is commonly assumed, for this style was as much an inherent feature of their literary creativeness as it was of the 'author' of Deuteronomy. The fact that the Deuteronomist and the editor of the prose sermons in Jeremiah used idioms and expressions not found in the book of Deuteronomy proper points to a continuous ideological and literary development within the deuteronomic circle and attests to the dynamism of the school. Indeed, an examination of the linguistic and ideological fabric of the deuteronomic movement shows that its development progressed from Deuteronomy through deuteronomic historiography to the prose sermons in the book of Jeremiah.

The concept of the chosen 'place' המקום in the book of Deuteronomy, which underlies the law of cult centralization, is developed in the deuteronomic historical literature in terms of the chosen 'city'/Jerusalem העיר/ירושלים and the 'temple' הבית. In connection with this concept we meet not only those idioms which occur in Deuteronomy proper, such as 'the place which Yahweh will choose to make his name dwell there' המקום אשר יבחר יהוה לשכן שמו שם, or 'to put his name there' לשום שמו שם (Deut. 12: 5, 11, 21, etc.), but also such expressions as 'that my name *might be* there' יהיה שמי שם (1 Kgs. 8: 16 and 29; 2 Kgs. 23: 27); 'the house that Yahweh's name is called upon' הבית אשר שם יהוה נקרא עליו (1 Kgs. 8: 43, compare Jer. chap. 7, *passim*); 'the house which I have consecrated for my name' הבית אשר הקדשתי לשמי (1 Kgs. 9: 7, cf. 3).

A similar terminological development is encountered in connection with the monarchy. The book of Deuteronomy speaks only in a general manner of selecting a king: 'set a king over you whom Yahweh your God will choose' שים עליך מלך אשר יבחר יהוה

[1] By 'the Deuteronomist' I mean the editor of the historical books (Dtr), by 'the deuteronomic editor' either the Deuteronomist or the editor of the prose sermons of Jeremiah. (Mowinckel's source C, see below, p. 27). Both are to be distinguished from 'the author of Deuteronomy'.

אלהיך בו (17: 15), and promises the chosen king, if he will observe the law, that his dynasty will be perpetuated: 'that he may continue long in his kingdom, he and his children in Israel' למען יאריך ימים על ממלכתו הוא ובניו בקרב ישראל (v. 20). The Dtr treats of these ideas in a more concrete manner. He specifies the chosen king David דוד עבדי אשר בחרתי (1 Kgs. 11: 34). He attaches the promise of the perpetuation of the dynasty to the Davidic dynasty in particular: 'there shall not fail you a man on the throne of Israel' לא יכרת לך איש מעל כסא ישראל (1 Kgs. 2: 4; 8: 25; 9: 5); provided that the Davidic house observe the law.

The book of Deuteronomy commands the king to read the law *all his days* and to observe its teaching (17: 18–19).[1] The Dtr repeats this commandment with respect to Joshua but strengthens it by requiring the leader to meditate upon the law *day and night* והגית בו יומם ולילה (Josh. 1: 8, cf. Ps. 1: 2). The idioms 'be strong and resolute' חזק ואמץ, which occur in the book of Deuteronomy only in the context of the *conquest of the land* (Deut. 31: 7–8, cf. 1: 38; 3: 28) are employed by the Dtr with respect to the general *observance of the Torah*: 'Only be strong and resolute to observe and do according to all the law which Moses my servant commanded you' (Josh. 1: 7). A similar use of these idioms is encountered in the Dtr's interpretation of David's testament to Solomon (1 Kgs. 2: 3–4): though the term חזק in the original testament referred to brutal daring in executing dynastic vengeance, the Dtr relates it to the observance of the Torah.[2]

In connection with the idea of cult centralization the book of Deuteronomy refers to the Israelites sacrificing 'at every place that you see' בכל מקום אשר תראה (12: 13), or 'at one of your city gates' באחד שעריך (16: 5). The Dtr, however, employs the more concrete term: 'the high places' במות in this context, and the *pi'el* formation of the stems זבח and קטר when referring to the illegitimate cult.[3]

The book of Deuteronomy speaks of worshipping foreign gods only in the most general terms: 'to go' (or: 'to turn aside after and') 'serve foreign gods and worship them' ללכת (לסור) אחרי אלהים

[1] These verses are interpolated and mar the continuity of the law. Verse 20 follows naturally after v. 17 and explains why the king is warned not to increase his wealth, referred to in v. 17 (for a similar warning and explanation, cf. Deut. 8: 13–14; cf. below p. 367). The interpolation nevertheless antedated Josh. 1: 8, which has re-worked the concept expressed in Deut. 17: 18–19 by extending and developing it.

[2] For discussion see below, p. 11.

[3] See Appendix A, II. 9.

אחרים לעבד ולהשתחוות להם (17: 3; 11: 16; 13: 3, 7, 14). The Dtr and the deuteronomic editor of Jeremiah, however, speak more concretely of Baal and Ashtoreth worship and of burning incense to Baal and the Queen of Heaven.

It seems that the author of Deuteronomy, in putting his speech into the mouth of Moses, purposely avoided mentioning concrete names and objects such as Jerusalem, the city, the house, David, *bamōt*, Baal, and Ashtoreth, which might sound anachronistic.

Just as there are expressions in Dtr which do not occur in the book of Deuteronomy, so we find expressions in the prose sermons of Jeremiah which occur neither in Deuteronomy nor in Dtr. This fact led Bright[1] to conclude that these Jeremian sermons were composed independently of Dtr and, in fact, much earlier. To our mind, however, this difference in idiom points to the contrary. The fact that the prose sermons in Jeremiah contain idioms—which, as Bright concedes, are of deuteronomic character—yet are not met with elsewhere in deuteronomic literature, indicates rather that the sermons date after Dtr and constitute a new stage in the development of deuteronomic composition. As the Deuteronomist had developed and given a more specific sense to the general expressions of the book of Deuteronomy, so the deuteronomic editor of Jeremiah developed the terminology of the Deuteronomist. Thus, while Dtr speaks of 'burning incense to foreign gods' קטר לאלהים אחרים (which is not mentioned in Deuteronomy), the deuteronomic editor of Jeremiah also refers to 'pouring libations to foreign gods' הסך נסכים לאלהים אחרים (7: 18; 19: 13; 32: 29; 44: 17). Dtr speaks of the king 'sitting upon the throne of *Israel*',[2] whereas the deuteronomic editor of Jeremiah speaks more specifically of the king 'sitting upon the throne of *David*'.[3]

The arguments that Bright adduced are valid in disproving the assertion that Deutero-Isaiah and late Israelite prophecy influenced the book of Jeremiah, but they do not demonstrate that the deuteronomic sermons in Jeremiah antedate the Dtr passages in Joshua–Kings.[4]

[1] J. Bright, 'The Date of the Prose Sermons of Jeremiah', *JBL* 70 (1951), 15 ff.

[2] See Appendix A, IX. 8.

[3] See Appendix A, IX. 6.

[4] Of the twenty-three expressions of Jeremiah's prose sermons pointed out by Bright (ibid., p. 25) as not occurring elsewhere in deuteronomic literature thirteen expressions: דבר שקר, נבא שקר, בטח על שקר, לקח מוסר, ערי יהודה וחוצות ירושלים, פקד על, נחם על הטובה/הרעה, אדם ובהמה, ה׳ צבאות אלהי ישראל, דבר חרב ורעב הנביאים הנבאים (Bright's 27a and b) occur in the

We may therefore describe the course of the formation and historical development of the school in the following manner:

1. The book of Deuteronomy, composed in the latter half of the seventh century B.C.

2. The deuteronomic edition of Joshua–Kings, which received its fixed form in the first half of the sixth century.

3. The deuteronomic prose sermons in Jeremiah, which were apparently composed during the second half of the sixth century.[1]

Though the book of Deuteronomy quite probably consists of different editorial strands, no established criterion exists by which we can determine either the extent of each strand of its composition or its ideological teaching.[2]

poetic passages of Jeremiah and elsewhere, as Bright himself admits. Is it not natural to expect that the editor of the prose sermons would adopt phraseology from the authentic prophecies of Jeremiah which he was editing, just as he adopted phraseology from Dtr which antedated him? A case in point is the expression 'in the cities of Judah and the streets of Jerusalem', which Bright regards as characteristic of the prose sermons in Jeremiah. Actually, the phrase is a combination by the deuteronomic editor of two authentic Jeremian expressions: 'the cities of Judah' (4: 16) and 'the streets of Jerusalem' (5: 1; 11: 13; 14: 16).

Two expressions: שוב איש מדרך הרעה, ישב על כסא דוד are expansions of original deuteronomic clichés (see Appendix A, IX. 6, 8 and VIII. 7), and two others: מבקש נפש, נביאיכם are common Hebrew words which can by no means be seen as clichés.

Two other idioms: נפל תחנה, היתה נפשו לשלל actually belong to the biographical narratives of Jeremiah (= source B of Mowinckel) (38: 2; 39: 18; 45: 5; 37: 20; 38: 26; 42: 2), which influenced the prose sermons in 21: 9 (on the dependence of this verse on 38: 2, see Commentaries) and 36: 7; 42: 9 respectively. Two other expressions peculiar to the Jeremian prose sermons: היטיבו דרכיכם ומעלליכם, השכם ושלח / ודבר reflect the Judean consciousness of sin and the vindication of the divine judgement upon Israel, which gradually took root in the mind of the people during the years after the fall of Judah. It is also possible that these are genuine Jeremian expressions which had by chance been preserved in the deuteronomic circle and not in the poetry and biography of Jeremiah. The phrases קול ששון וקול שמחה קול חתן וקול כלה, הבאים בשערים האלה, which likewise occur only in the prose sermons, may be rhetorical clichés especially liked by the deuteronomic editor of Jeremiah.

[1] The opening sermon of Zachariah (1: 4–6), who prophesied in 520 B.C., is of the same type as the prose sermons of Jeremiah (cf. 25: 4–5; 26: 3 and 5).

[2] C. Steuernagel attempted to do so in the second edition of his commentary on Deuteronomy (*Das Deuteronomium*, HKAT², 1923), but not with great success. Noth's view that chs. 1: 1–4: 40, 31*, and 34* belong to Dtr (cf. *Überlieferungsgeschichtliche Studien*, 12 ff.) is more convincing, though it cannot be accepted without qualifications. The linguistic relationship between these chapters and chapters 5–30 is very strong, in any case much stronger than that between 1: 1–4: 40, 31*, 34* and the Dtr, cf. Driver, *Deuteronomy*, ICC, lxxii.

Many scholars assert that two editorial strands may be discerned in the deuteronomic history,[1] which is not improbable, considering that it contains different literary strata. But again we have no fixed criterion by which we may differentiate between two editorial stages.[2]

The three major branches of deuteronomic composition, on the other hand, i.e. Deuteronomy, Dtr, and the Jeremian prose sermons—each of which is composed or incorporated in a different literary genre: law, history, and prophecy—have a distinct character of their own, although, as we have shown, they exhibit signs of linguistic and ideological interdependence.

The question that arises in the light of all this is: what circle is responsible for these rhetorical compositions? Some scholars have suggested identifications and put forward views on the *Sitz im Leben* of the homiletic style of the deuteronomic composition. Klostermann,[3] for example, believed the homiletic style of Deuteronomy to be that employed by the public reciters of the law; Bentzen[4] and von Rad[5] identified it with that employed by the Levitical instructors of the law; Weiser,[6] on the other hand, claims that, both in Deuteronomy and in the Jeremian prose sermons, it is predominantly cultic in character. The basic premiss underlying these views is that deuteronomic homiletics ultimately derives from some actual reality and that orations of this type had been delivered in circumstances of one sort or another, before they were written down.

But do we need to accept this *a priori* hypothesis, or are we justified in dispensing with the question of their supposed *Sitz im Leben* and viewing these orations as programmatic compositions drafted by scribes? The orations might have been used in a cultic

[1] Cf. recently F. M. Cross, 'The Structure of the Deuteronomic History', *Perspectives in Jewish Learning*, III (Chicago), 9–24.

[2] A. Jepsen (*Die Quellen des Königsbuches*², 1956) contends that the book of Kings underwent two redactions, one by a Priestly redactor, which he designates as K (= R^{I}), and the second by a deuteronomic redactor, Dtr (= R^{II}). He appears, however, not to have realized that the diction and ideology of his K source is distinctly deuteronomic in character. The recurring expressions in Kings which Jepsen assigns to K, such as אהב את יהוה, הלך בדרכי יהוה, עשה הישר בעיני יהוה, עשה הרע בעיני יהוה, על כל גבעה גבהה ותחת כל עץ רענן, הלך עבד . . . והשתחוה, דבק . . . לא סר are all deuteronomic. See Appendix A.

[3] *Der Pentateuch*, 154 ff.

[4] A. Bentzen, *Die Josianische Reform und ihre Voraussetzungen*, 1926.

[5] G. von Rad, *Studies in Deuteronomy* (tr. by D. Stalker), 1953.

[6] A. Weiser, *Einleitung in das Alte Testament*, 6th edn., 1966, pp. 68, 121, 196–7.

situation, but they did not necessarily originate in one before being committed to writing.

The thesis of the present study is that deuteronomic composition is the creation of scribal circles which began their literary project some time prior to the reign of Josiah and were still at work after the fall of Judah. We shall try to demonstrate this thesis in three ways: by a typological analysis of the literary form employed by the authors, by an investigation of the religious ideology of deuteronomic composition, and by a study of its didactic aims and methods.

PART ONE

THE TYPOLOGY OF DEUTERONOMIC COMPOSITION

I

THE ORATIONS

1. THE VALEDICTORY ADDRESS

THE book of Deuteronomy, the archetype of all deuteronomic literature, is presented in its entirety[1] as a valedictory oration delivered by Moses shortly before his death. Such addresses are to be found in pre-deuteronomic literature also but in the form of a song (Deut. 32: 1–43)[2] or a blessing (Deut. 33).[3] The author of Deuteronomy, however, has found these old poems unsatisfactory. In their stead he placed in the mouth of Moses a long prose valedictory which treats of both history and law. The earlier traditions of the valedictory were included or rather appended to the book,[4] but were overshadowed by the long prose oration.

This deuteronomic practice of ending the narratives about major national leaders with their delivery of a didactic valedictory

[1] Moses appears as a speaker not only in the introductory and epilogue chapters but also in the legal sections of the book. Cf. Deut. 18: 15–17.

[2] The Song (Deut. 32: 1–43) had been preceded by an Elohistic introduction: Deut. 31: 16–22 (see S. R. Driver, *Deuteronomy*, ICC, pp. 336 ff.) which presented the Song as a written 'witness' עד for the next generations when troubles might befall them as a result of violating the covenant. This stimulated the author of Deuteronomy to present also the deuteronomic Torah as a witness for the future generations (31: 26 ff.). Both the Song and the Torah were said to be written by Moses (cf. 31: 9 with 22) and taught by him to Israel (31: 22; 32: 46). Ideologically also the Song had great influence on Deuteronomy (compare, e.g., verse 7 of the Song with 4: 32, v. 11 with 1: 31, vv. 13–18 with 8: 11–18), see also Appendix A and the references there to Deut. 32.

[3] On the relationship between the Song and the Blessing see K. Budde, *Das Lied Moses*, 1920, pp. 42 f.

[4] See M. Noth, *Überlieferungsgeschichtliche Studien*, p. 40.

oration is also encountered in the historical works redacted by the deuteronomic school. Thus the deuteronomic edition of the book of Joshua had similarly ended with a composed valedictory which the Deuteronomist had put in the mouth of Joshua (Josh. 23).[1] It was only a later compiler who apparently thought fit to attach Joshua's covenant with the people (ch. 24) which the national mind had come to regard as his last testament.[2]

A late editorial addition having closer affinity with that met with in the book of Deuteronomy is David's swan-song (2 Sam. 22) and prophetic blessing (23: 1–7),[3] both of which—though ancient traditions—have been incorporated in the chapters appended to the book of Samuel only after it had assumed its basic structure.[4] The original deuteronomic redaction of the book ended the account of David's life with a didactic valedictory ascribed to the king (1 Kgs. 2: 3–4) and incorporated into the ancient tradition of David's last testament. The editor's purpose in inserting the speech in this place was to obscure the original import of the ancient tradition of David's last testament (vv. 1–2 and 5–9) and to reduce it to secondary significance. According to the older tradition David charged Solomon to muster courage for a stronghanded destruction of his enemies (see v. 2: 'Take courage and acquit yourself like a man' וחזקת והיית לאיש and 1 Sam. 4: 9: 'Take courage and acquit yourselves as men, O Philistines' התחזקו והיו לאנשים פלשתים).[5] The deuteronomic editor, however, interrupted the testament in the middle[6] and inserted a didactic speech (vv. 3–4) which completely altered the original import of the testament. The strength which in the original Davidic charge referred to brutal daring has been transfigured by the interpolated speech to denote the religio-spiritual force with which Solomon was to apply himself to the observance of God's laws (see Josh. 1: 7).

[1] See M. Noth, op. cit., p. 9 and particularly n. 1; Y. Kaufmann, *The Book of Joshua*, 1959, p. 244 (Hebrew).

[2] The correspondence between the concepts 'covenant' and 'testament' finds expression in the Greek term διαθήκη. See below, p. 12 n. 3.

[3] See M. Mowinckel, 'Die letzten Worte Davids, II Sam. 23, 1–7', *ZAW* 45 (1927), 30–58.

[4] See J. Wellhausen, *Die Composition des Hexateuchs*, 1899, pp. 260–3; M. Noth, op. cit., p. 62 n. 3; O. Eissfeldt, *Einleitung in das Alte Testament*³, pp. 358–9.

[5] Cf. the expression *lu-ú a-wi-la-at* ('acquit yourself as a man') in a like military context (*ARM* I, 69: 13') and 2 Sam. 13: 28: 'Strike Amnon then kill him . . . be courageous (חזקו) and be valiant (והיו לבני חיל).'

[6] See J. A. Montgomery, *Kings*, ICC, p. 87.

Ancient tradition, then, ascribed both to Moses and to David a farewell song, blessing, and testament. The deuteronomic school, in contrast, attributed to them instead parenetic farewell addresses (designed to serve as guides for the future generations) in the centre of which stands the book of the Torah and its perceptions.

The deuteronomic valedictory addresses are particularly encountered in contexts that describe a change in national leadership occurring at the end of an historical period.[1] The Mosaic discourses, for example, terminate the era of the desert wandering. The period of conquest, which according to the deuteronomic historian was successfully completed during Joshua's time, closes with Joshua's brilliant parenetic address (Josh. 23). The prophet Samuel, living at the close of the period of the judges, similarly bids farewell in a comprehensive historical address (1 Sam. 12)[2] designed so as to serve as an instruction for future generations. David's testament to Solomon also opens, as we have noticed, with a brief exhortation intended for the future kings of the dynasty.[3]

The deuteronomic editor, however, did not always find a suitable opportunity of introducing his ideological message by means of such eminent mouthpieces as Moses, Joshua, Samuel, or David. Consequently we find that significant historical periods not dominated by great prophetic leaders are summarized by the editor himself as part of his exposition. We meet with these editorial summaries in the passage prefacing the period of the judges (Judg. 2: 6 ff.) and in the editor's description of the fall of the Northern Kingdom (2 Kgs. 17: 7 ff.),[4] the former anticipating the general

[1] See M. Noth, op. cit., p. 5.

[2] The chapter is substantially of pre-deuteronomic origin (see K. Budde, *Die Bücher Samuel*, KHC, 1902; Eissfeldt, *Einleitung*, pp. 361 ff.) but was redacted and placed in its present context by the deuteronomic editor. The deuteronomic clichés in this chapter are: 'to fear the Lord, to worship Him and obey Him' ירא את יהוה עבד אתו ושמע בקולו (v. 14), 'to turn aside from behind the Lord' סור מאחרי יהוה (v. 20), 'to worship the Lord wholeheartedly' עבד את יהוה בכל לב (v. 20), 'to make for himself as a people' עשה לו לעם (v. 22), 'to fear the Lord to worship Him truly, wholeheartedly' ירא את יהוה עבד אתו באמת בכל לב (v. 24). For these clichés see Appendix A.

[3] In their valedictory addresses the departing leaders charge the people or their dynastic successors to observe God's covenant. On the reaffirmation of covenants in situations where a new personage succeeds to leadership, see K. Baltzer, *Das Bundesformular*, 1960, pp. 71 ff., see also below, p. 61 n. 6.

[4] Cf. the editorial summary of the history of the Judean kingdom in 2 Kgs. 21: 11–16 in connection with the reign of Manasseh, whose religious policy is described as having irrevocably sealed the doom of Judah (cf. 23: 26, 24: 3).

course of the historical period about to commence, the latter reviewing the period that had just terminated. These anticipatory and retrospective summaries are found only in deuteronomic literature, and have no parallel in any of the other literary strands of the Bible.[1] This type of historical summary is already met with in Deuteronomy proper: the prologue (especially chs. 1–3,[2] 5–9) reviews the historical period that had just come to an end, whereas the epilogue surveys Israel's historical future (chs. 29–31). Though the impersonal editorial expositions in the books of Judges and Kings naturally do not make use of the direct mode of address (i.e. אתה, אתם), as do the historical discourses in the book of Deuteronomy, the two are nevertheless identical both in their form and essence.[3] Like the deuteronomic orations, the same editor's own expositions were intended to replace the earlier traditions, which were only subsequently restored as an appendage to the deuteronomic redaction by a later compiler. Thus alongside the deuteronomic introduction to the book of Judges (2: 6 ff.) we meet with a pre-deuteronomic historico-theological introduction[4] (1: 1–2: 5) which was appended to the book by a later compiler.[5]

The purpose of the editorial expositions of the Deuteronomist was to summarize the decisive periods of Israelite history, in effect dividing the history of Israel (starting with the conquest) into three distinct parts: the period of the conquest, which is reviewed in Joshua's valedictory address (Josh. 23); the period of the judges, which is outlined in the deuteronomic introduction in Judg. 2: 11 ff. and summarized in 1 Sam. 12; and the monarchy summarized in 2 Kgs. 17: 7 ff. and 21: 10–15.

Y. Kaufmann has argued that this three-fold division of Israelite

[1] See M. Noth, *Überliefer. Studien*, p. 6.

[2] The question whether Deut. 1: 6–3: 29 constitutes the original or (as M. Noth contends) a later introduction to the book is immaterial. We here refer only to the literary *Gattung* common to all deuteronomic composition early or late.

[3] See H. W. Hertzberg, *Josua, Richter, Ruth*, ATD, 1959, p. 162.

[4] See G. F. Moore, *Judges*, ICC, 1895; K. Budde, *Richter*, KHC, 1897; G. A. Cooke, *Judges*, CB, 1913; C. F. Burney, *The Book of Judges*, 1920.

[5] See E. O'Doherty, 'The Literary Problem of Judges 1, 1–3, 6', *CBQ* 18 (1956), pp. 1–7. On the appending of ancient material to fixed independent literary units, see I. L. Seeligmann, 'Hebräische Erzählung und biblische Geschichtsschreibung', *ThZ* 18 (1962), 323. I concur with O'Doherty's view that the original position of Josh. 24: 28–31 (= Judg. 2: 6–9) was in Judges and that a later compiler duplicated it in Joshua after he added ch. 24 as a conclusion to Joshua and Judg. 1: 1–2: 5 as an introduction to Judges, thus marking a distinct division between the two books.

history is ancient and finds literary expression in the military narratives met with in Num. 21–2 Sam. 23. He distinguishes three types of wars in these narratives: (1) wars of conquest, (2) defensive wars, and (3) imperial wars.[1] Kaufmann is, of course, correct in maintaining that pre-deuteronomic traditions similarly distinguished between wars of conquest and defensive wars. But these traditions do not conceive the two types of warfare as characterizing two distinct historical periods. Judg. 1, for example, alludes to wars of conquest (vv. 1–26) and defence (vv. 27–36; see particularly v. 34) as being waged in the same period. The period of Joshua is not depicted as one of conquest alone, nor is the post-Joshua period only one of defensive wars against Canaanite pressure. The pre-deuteronomic traditions refer both to Canaanite pressure during Joshua's lifetime (Josh. 17: 14–18) and to campaigns of conquest not undertaken under his leadership (Judg. 1: 1–26).

The deuteronomic historian, in contrast, sharply differentiates between the period of conquest, completed in Joshua's lifetime, and that of Canaanite oppression and defensive wars following upon his death. He sees the period of Joshua as a golden age of ideal religious devotion to Yahweh (Judg. 2: 7), thanks to which Israel won sweeping victories within the area of the conquest.[2] The period of the judges, on the other hand, is depicted as the nadir of Israelite history, the period in which the Israelites worshipped 'the gods of the peoples round about them' and were therefore delivered into their hands and oppressed (Judg. 2: 11 ff.).[3]

[1] Y. Kaufmann, *The Book of Judges*, 1962, pp. 1–14 (Hebrew).

[2] Cf. Josh. 24: 31. This verse and especially the notion of worshipping God 'all the days of Joshua' contradicts the ancient tradition of Shechem (Josh. 24: 1–28), according to which the Israelites of Joshua's time worshipped 'foreign gods' before the conclusion of the covenant. The deuteronomic cliché in this verse (Judg. 2: 7 = Josh. 24: 31) is 'to experience/see the great work of God which he performed for Israel' ידע/ראה את מעשה יהוה הגדול אשר עשה לישראל, Cf. Deut. 11: 7, and see Appendix A, III. 17a.

[3] The Deuteronomist regarded the conquest as having been completed in Joshua's lifetime so that Canaanite pressure on Israel could have come only 'from the enemy round about' (Judg. 2: 14). The references to the tributary status of the remaining Canaanite peoples in Judg. 1 and the parallel sections in Josh. 15–19 are from non-deuteronomic sources and openly contradict both the law of the Canaanite ban in Deut. 20 and the deuteronomic account of the Israelite campaigns in Josh. 10–11 according to which no Canaanite was left alive in the land. For a discussion of the two conceptions of the conquest see my article 'The Period of the Conquest and of the Judges as Seen by the Earlier and the Later Sources', *VT* 17 (1967), 93–113.

2. THE PROPHETIC ORATION

(*a*) *In Joshua–Kings*

Von Rad has demonstrated that the focal point of deuteronomic historiography is the prophetic word of God fulfilled in Israelite history.[1] It is centred, in other words, on the belief that the fateful events in the life of the nation happen as a consequence of the divine word which foreordained them. The idea that God reveals his designs (i.e. the historical events that are to take place) by means of a prophetic word is, to be sure, an ancient one; however, what distinguishes the deuteronomic concept is that the divine *dabar* is conceived as an 'acting force which begets future events'[2] rather than a mantic word of God which merely reveals the future. Thus, unlike the pre-deuteronomic concept of the word of God reflected in the popular prophetic narratives and relating only to present and actual events, the deuteronomic word of God relates to all periods and generations and blends with the long-range divine historical scheme. It is by means of the prophetic sermons, that the Deuteronomist presents his clear-cut scheme of Israelite history, beginning with the settlement, and culminating with the destruction of the Judean state. Every national achievement or failure in this scheme is the result of the prophetic word of God which foreordained it. Joshua's conquest of the land, on the one hand (Josh. 1: 1–9) and Israel's inability to dispossess the remaining peoples, on the other (Judg. 2: 20–1),[3] the election of Saul[4] and his rejection (1 Sam. 15: 28),[5] the promise of everlasting kingdom to David

[1] G. von Rad, *Studies in Deuteronomy*, pp. 78 ff.

[2] As phrased by I. L. Seeligmann, 'Aetiological Elements in Biblical Historiography', *Zion* 26 (1961), 167 (Hebrew with English summary).

[3] Cf. M. Weinfeld, 'The Period of the Conquest etc.', *VT* 17 (1967), 99–103.

[4] The Deuteronomist relied on early traditions for the narrative of Saul's and David's election to the throne and so did not need to supply his own prophetic word of God to account for these events. He may nevertheless have introduced his own phraseology here and there as he had, for example, in 2 Sam. 7: 13. See D. J. McCarthy, 'II Samuel 7 and the Structure of the Deuteronomic History', *JBL* 84 (1965), 131–8 and the following note.

[5] This verse may also be a deuteronomic prophecy, cf. the phrase קרע ממלכה 'rending of the kingdom' which occurs only here and in other deuteronomic prophetic compositions (1 Kgs. 11: 11, 13, 31; 14: 8; 2 Kgs. 17: 21). A. Weiser has shown that vv. 25–30a are secondary ('I Samuel 15', *ZAW* 54 [1936], 5 f.) and to my mind are of deuteronomic origin. See also R. Kittel, *Die heilige Schrift, übersetzt von Kautzsch*[4], 1922, pp. 430–1. 1 Sam. 28: 17, which relates to this verse, also seems to be an editorial accretion (see K. Budde, *Samuel*, KHC, 1902, p. 182 and A. Schulz, *Die Bücher Samuel*, EH, 1919/20, I, 392).

(2 Sam. 7)[1] and the secession of the northern tribes from the everlasting kingdom (1 Kgs. 11: 11–13), the promise of kingship over Israel to Jeroboam (vv. 31–9) and the extinction of his dynasty (14: 7–11 and 13–16), the establishment and rejection of the Baasha dynasty (16: 1–4, 7), the destruction of the house of Ahab (21: 20b–9) and the establishment of the house of Jehu (2 Kgs. 9: 7–10), the fall of the northern kingdom (1 Kgs. 14: 15–16; 2 Kgs. 17: 7–23) and finally, the destruction of Jerusalem and the Judean state (2 Kgs. 21: 10–15; 22: 16–17), all occur as a consequence of the power of the word of God uttered by his servants the prophets. This long chain of prophecies embodies the view of history of the Deuteronomist who began his work under the shadow of the fall of Samaria and concluded it after the fall of Jerusalem, giving it a pattern that was to demonstrate that the divine word acted in all stages of Israel's history and that the national catastrophes were the consequences of the sins of Israel and Judah and their kings, or in brief, that God had acted justifiably.

These prophetic orations are generally ascribed to prophets known to us from the popular prophetic tradition which was woven into the historical work of the Deuteronomist, and in which such personages as Ahijah the Shilonite, Jehu son of Hanani, Elijah, Elisha, and Huldah the prophetess figure as mantic prophets. The original *dabar* of God uttered by these prophets relates to the personal fate and future of the kings. The divine punishments which these prophecies foretell generally concern the violent death of the king or the death of his infant son (2 Sam. 12: 13–14; 1 Kgs. 14: 12; 2 Kgs. 1: 16; 8: 10) or, conversely, that he is to become king (2 Kgs. 8: 13; 9: 3) or will succeed in battle (see 2 Kgs 3: 16–19; 13: 17; 14: 25) or will die a peaceful death (2 Kgs. 22: 20) and so forth. In contrast, the deuteronomic word of God, which is appended to the words of these prophets deals, not with the individual and personal fate of the king, but with the fate of his 'house', i.e. his dynasty; in other words, it concerns his historical destiny—his place in the divine historical scheme.

We can convey this more concretely by considering the prophecies individually.

1. The wife of Jeroboam visits Ahijah the Shilonite to inquire of the fate of her ailing son (1 Kgs. 14). The prophet, who discerns the identity of Jeroboam's wife despite her disguise, informs her

[1] See p. 15 n. 4.

that her son shall die (v. 12). According to the earlier prophetic narrative,[1] then, the death of the son constitutes Jeroboam's punishment (see 2 Sam. 12: 13–16). The Deuteronomist, however, finding both the substance of the prophetic word and the punishment entirely unsatisfactory, put into the mouth of Ahijah a programmatic prophetic oration which largely treats of the destruction of the house of Jeroboam (vv. 7–11) and the eventual exile of Israel to the lands beyond the Euphrates (vv. 14–16). The immediate fulfilment of the mantic prophecy which concerns the personal punishment of Jeroboam was of little importance to the Deuteronomist. He was more interested in the fulfilment of the divine word concerning the extinction of the Jeroboam dynasty and the execution of the punishment resulting from his historico-national sin. The authentic prophecy of Ahijah was certainly motivated by a transgression reflecting the specific circumstances of the time and not just the deuteronomic typical sins (vv. 9, 15) relating to the kingdom of Israel as a whole.[2] Indeed, it has been already indicated that the relationship between Ahijah the Shilonite and Jeroboam has to be seen against the rivalry between Jerusalem and Shiloh and the tension between Zadok the Jerusalemite chief priest and Ebiathar, the descendant of the house of Eli, who was removed by Solomon (1 Kgs. 2: 26). A Caquot[3] plausibly suggests that Ahijah supported Jeroboam against Jerusalem in the hope that Jeroboam would rebuild the sanctuary of his native town Shiloh, but Jeroboam greatly disappointed him when he turned instead towards Beth-El and Dan (1 Kgs. 12: 29 f.) and this is what

[1] Verses 1–6, 12, 17. The deuteronomic character of the remaining verses of this prophecy may be identified by their rhetorical style and by expressions reflecting the deuteronomic doctrines: 'rend the kingdom from the house of David', 'my servant David', 'walk after me wholeheartedly', 'observe my commandments', 'to do that which is right in my eyes' (v. 8); 'go and make foreign gods and molten images to vex me' (v. 9); 'make their Asherim vexing Yahweh' (v. 15); 'for the sins of Jeroboam which he committed and caused Israel to sin' (v. 16); 'him who dies . . . in the city shall the dogs eat and him who dies in the country shall the birds of heaven eat' (v. 11); 'he shall pluck Israel from off this good land' (v. 15). For these expressions see Appendix A.

[2] The golden calves established by Jeroboam are not to be considered as idols which might have given rise to the doom prophecy of Ahijah because, as has already been indicated (see Albright, *From Stone Age to Christianity*, pp. 228–30; Kaufmann, *HIR*, II, 259–61), like the cherubs in Jerusalem the calves were conceived as *the* throne or pedestal of God. Indeed, none of the prophets preceding Hosea reprove the Israelites for worshipping the golden calves, see H. L. Ginsberg, *JBL* 80 (1961), 344 f.

[3] 'Ahiyya de Silo et Jeroboam Ier', *Semitica* 11 (1961), 17–27.

caused the prediction of the punishment in 1 Kgs. 14. It stands to reason, then, that the genuine cause of the conflict between Ahijah and Jeroboam was repressed by the Deuteronomist in favour of a wide national historical explanation.

2. Elijah seeks out Ahab to admonish him for the murder of Naboth the Jezreelite (1 Kgs. 21: 17 ff.). The original admonition is addressed boldly and poignantly: 'Have you killed, and also taken possession. . . . Thus says the Lord: In the place where dogs licked up the blood of Naboth shall dogs lick your own blood' (v. 19). The punishment, then, was to correspond to the crime measure for measure, Ahab's blood being shed in the very place where he had shed Naboth's blood. The deuteronomic editor, however, did not remain content with the description of Ahab's sin and punishment as related by the earlier prophetic narrative. The sin—to his mind—was not merely the murder of Naboth, but also included the cultic pollutions which Ahab had introduced into Israel through the influence of his wife Jezebel, and his propagation of the sins of Jeroboam (1 Kgs. 16: 30–3; 21: 20b–6). The punishment, again according to the Deuteronomist, was also not to be merely personal (i.e. the shedding of his blood), but was to include his house and dynasty. He therefore added to Elijah's original prophecy a programmatic prophetic speech (vv. 20b–6)[1] which largely consists of stereotyped[2] maledictions of the type already encountered in connection with Jeroboam (14: 10 ff.) and Baasha (16: 3–4). Its conclusion is drawn up in indirect speech and is the editor's own summary remarks on the religious policy of Ahab (vv. 25–6).

In the sequence of the original prophetic narrative Ahab is said to have expressed his regret at the crime (v. 27),[3] and as a result the divine sentence is transferred to his son (vv. 28–9), as was David's punishment in 2 Sam. 12: 13–14 and Jeroboam's in 1 Kgs. 14. However, as we shall see below,[4] the prophecy concerning the

[1] The deuteronomic character of this passage may be recognized by the phrases: 'sold himself to do evil in the sight of Yahweh' (vv. 20 and 25); 'Behold, I shall bring evil upon you' (v. 21); 'sweep out' (בער אחרי) (v. 20); 'the anger which you provoked' (הכעס אשר הכעסת) (v. 22); 'you caused Israel to sin' (v. 22); and 'to follow the fetishes' (v. 26). Cf. Appendix A.

[2] See below, p. 131.

[3] Cf. Kittel's commentary (HKAT 1902) and Eissfeldt in Kautzsch's *Heilige Schrift*[4] (1922). The narrative phraseology of this verse also indicates its authenticity.

[4] p. 24.

transference of Ahab's punishment has come down to us only in a deuteronomic redaction and not in its original version. Elijah's original prophecy must surely have dealt with the transference of Ahab's divine punishment incurred by the murder of Naboth: not Ahab's blood, but that of his son was to be shed in Naboth's field. Thus the popular prophetic narrative in 2 Kgs. 9 relates that after Jehu slew Joram the son of Ahab he said to his aide Bidkar, 'Take him up and cast him on the plot of ground belonging to Naboth the Jezreelite; for remember, when you and I[1] rode side by side behind Ahab his father, how the Lord uttered this oracle against him: "... I will requite you on this plot of ground"! Now therefore take him up and cast him on the plot of ground in accordance with the word of the Lord' (2 Kgs. 9: 25–6). According to the original prophecy, then, the curse of Elijah was fulfilled, not on the person of Ahab but on the person of his son. Indeed, Ahab's blood was not shed in the same place as Naboth's blood (1 Kgs. 22: 35 and 37).

The deuteronomic editor altered the prophecy concerning the transference of Ahab's punishment to his son in accordance with the purpose which he intended these prophecies to serve. In his version the punishment that was to be transferred to his son was not the punishment incurred by the murder of Naboth, but that resulting from Ahab's historical sin, whereas Naboth's blood and the curse of Elijah were to devolve on Ahab himself.[2] This indeed was the Deuteronomist's purpose in describing Ahab's death in 1 Kgs. 22: 38: 'and the dogs licked his blood and the harlots washed themselves [in it] according to the word of the Lord which he had spoken.' It has been pointed out[3] that both this verse and verse 35b[4] were interpolated by the editor who wished to connect this incident with Elijah's prophecy in 21: 19.

To depict graphically the fulfilment of the prophetic curse concerning the dogs lapping up Ahab's blood, the Deuteronomist alludes to the blood of Ahab's wound flowing on to the floor of the chariot, and to the washing of the chariot in Samaria.[5] In doing so,

[1] את after ואתה is to be omitted as dittography, see *BH*³.

[2] This fits well the concept of individual retribution which characterizes the deuteronomic literature, see below, pp. 318 f.

[3] See Montgomery, *Kings*, ICC, p. 341; J. Gray, *Kings*, OTL, p. 405.

[4] The secondary character of the clause is attested by both its logical flaw in relating the fact of Ahab's death before giving the detail of his blood flow, which the LXX rectifies by reversing the sequence—and by the omission of this clause in the parallel narrative in 2 Chron. 18: 34.

[5] On the schematic character of this curse, see below, p. 134.

however, he removed the very sting of Elijah's prophecy. The emphasis in Elijah's oracle is on the *place* where Naboth's blood was spilt, and it is in this sense that the fulfilment of the word of God is described—as has been shown in 2 Kgs. 9, whereas the Deuteronomist relates that Ahab's blood was licked by dogs in Samaria, and not in Jezreel where the crime was committed.

3. In the pre-deuteronomic strand of the book of Kings we meet with a word of God revealed to Elijah concerning the anointing of Hazael as king of Aram and of Jehu as king of Israel (1 Kgs. 19: 15–16). Its fulfilment and execution are described in 2 Kgs. 8: 7–15 and 9: 1–13. However, as the Deuteronomist was only concerned with the historico-national perspective of the prophecies, he took no interest in the prophecy regarding Hazael, king of Aram, and consequently left it untouched. But he did attach great importance to the prophecy concerning the anointing of Jehu, the purpose of which, to his mind, was the foreordainment of the destruction of the house of Ahab. Here also, then, as in previous instances, he interrupted the prophetic narrative to put a corresponding sermon into the mouth of the prophet-disciple (vv. 7–10a)—according neither with the instructions given the disciple nor with the haste with which his task was to be performed (v. 3)—calling upon Jehu to destroy the house of Ahab. Thus, whereas the purpose of the earlier prophetic narrative was to relate how the word of God to Elijah concerning the anointment of Jehu was fulfilled, the object of the Deuteronomist was to show how the act of Jehu's anointing as king was to advance the divine historical plan. As in the deuteronomic prophetic orations against Jeroboam, Baasha, and Ahab (1 Kgs. 14: 10; 16: 11; 21: 21–2), so also in this speech we find the stereotyped curse concerning the total extermination of the royal family and the bodies consumed by dogs (Jezebel). These stereotyped curses derive, as we shall see,[1] from the conventional descriptions of retributive punishments encountered in ancient Near Eastern treaties, and unlike the description of the divine punishment in the original prophetic narrative (2 Kgs. 9: 25–6) the deuteronomic curse is a set form. In the prophetic narratives and in the annalistic sources we find no mention of the fulfilment of a curse of this sort. The curse on Jezebel, which is inserted into the deuteronomic word of God (1 Kgs. 21: 23; 2 Kgs. 9: 10) the fulfilment of which is recounted in the deuteronomic passage in

[1] p. 131.

2 Kgs. 9: 36–7, also belongs to the class of stereotyped curses. The original prophetic story (2 Kgs. 9: 30–5) tells of Jezebel being cast through the window and being trampled underfoot by the horses below, which tore her body to pieces and scattered her limbs in all directions, no more than 'the skull and the feet and the palms of her hands' being recovered for burial (v. 35). The Deuteronomist, however, regarded this as the fulfilment of his stereotyped curse of dead bodies being eaten by dogs and therefore added vv. 36–7 to explain that Jezebel's body was not found because it was eaten by dogs.[1]

It has been shown, then, that while the authentic prophecies treat primarily of matters personally affecting the king or the royal family, the deuteronomic prophecies treat of matters of historico-national significance. The admonitions and maledictions in the deuteronomic prophecies all bear a schematic stamp and generally have no reference to the circumstances of the time and place in which they are uttered. They are applicable to all the kings of Israel and could have been addressed to each and any one of them. The sin theme, for example, is identical in each one of these orations: the sin of Jeroboam I, i.e. his repudiation of Jerusalem's supremacy and his institution of the cult of the calves, a sin for which all the kings of Israel were held accountable. The punishment of this sin is also the same for almost all of the Israelite dynasties: the corpses of the royal house shall be consumed by dogs and the birds of heaven. The genuine prophecies, on the other hand, are integrally connected with the historical circumstances in which they are uttered and arose from the actual situation reflected by them.

The concept of the prophetic *dabar* as an active force begetting future events is, of course, already encountered in the early strands of Pentateuchal literature. Thus, for example, the divine promise to the Patriarchs that their descendants shall inherit the land is, in effect, a prophetic word of God, fulfilled at the time of the Israelite conquest. However, the Deuteronomist's innovation was to make this prophetic word of God the focal point of his history. Every event of religio-national significance must occur as a result of the

[1] R. Kittel has pointed out that if dogs had actually devoured Jezebel's corpse then their first prey would have been her primary limbs, such as the hands and feet, yet it was precisely these limbs that were ultimately recovered for burial (HKAT ad loc.).

word of God which foreordained that event and to which historical reality must exactly conform, so that in the phraseology of the Deuteronomist 'nothing shall fall to the earth of the word of the Lord' (cf. Josh. 21: 43; 23: 14; 1 Sam. 3: 19; 1 Kgs. 8: 56; 2 Kgs. 10: 10). Should the word of the Lord fail to be substantiated in whole or in part then he constructs a second word of God, or alters the preceding one so as to harmonize it with historical fact.[1] In his discussion of this 'negative prophetic cycle' in the prophetic pericopes in Joshua–Kings, Y. Kaufmann[2] defined this editorial phenomenon in the following manner: 'When a word of God fails to materialize or does not completely materialize, then a second word of God appears which nullifies or qualifies the former so that it is the second word of God which is fulfilled.' This editorial phenomenon is characteristic only of deuteronomic history and stands in contrast to the method and approach of the Chronicler, who deleted all the negative prophetic cycles and based his work solely on the positive cycles. The singularity of the Deuteronomist's treatment of the word of God is particularly evident in his account of the ancient word of God concerning the conquest of Canaan to which we have referred above. The Patriarchs were promised that their posterity would inherit the land whose borders were to extend from the river of Egypt to the Euphrates (Gen. 15: 18; Exod. 23: 31), a promise which is reaffirmed in the divine word to Joshua met with in deuteronomic literature (Josh. 1: 1–9; 13: 1–6a). According to the deuteronomic account, however (Josh. 10–11), the promise was only partially fulfilled, for Joshua had only conquered the land 'from Mount Halak, that rises to Seir, as far as Baal Gad in the valley of Lebanon' (11: 17; 12: 7). The remaining territory (Josh. 13: 1–6a) was therefore, according to Joshua's command, to be conquered after his death (Josh. 23); but this was never carried out. To save the credit of the first promise, the Deuteronomist reconstructed a second word of God which nullified the first one: 'So the anger of the Lord was kindled against Israel; and he said, "Because this people have transgressed my covenant which I commanded their fathers, and have not obeyed my voice, I will not

[1] A similar attitude is attested in the ancient Greek prophecies. See, e.g., H. W. Parke–D. E. W. Wormell, *The Delphic Oracle*, Vol. II, 1956, p. xiv: 'It was a traditional motive to suppose that when an oracle had appeared at one time to be imperfectly fulfilled, a later and exact accomplishment would some day be found'.

[2] *HIR* IV, 458.

henceforth drive out before them any of the nations that Joshua left when he died . . ." ' (Judg. 2: 20–1).[1]

This editorial use of the 'negative prophetic cycle' runs through the whole of deuteronomic literature and we shall consequently discuss it only briefly.

1. According to an ancient prophetic vision (2 Sam. 7) David is promised eternal kingship over Israel (v. 16). This oracle was never entirely fulfilled. After Solomon's death the northern tribes rebelled and established their own independent kingdom. To nullify the previous oracle a prophecy was therefore added which again explained the inconsistent turn of events as a consequence of sin, in this instance the sins of Solomon (1 Kgs. 11: 11–13).

2. Ahijah the Shilonite in a prophetic *dabar* promises Jeroboam kingship over the northern tribes. This promise is given full expression in a prophetic programmatic speech which the Deuteronomist puts in the mouth of Ahijah (1 Kgs. 11: 31b–9).[2] However, as the dynasty of Jeroboam died with the son of its founder, a second prophetic *dabar* had to be supplied to nullify the first. This second *dabar* was—as has been noted above—inserted into the episode concerning the death of Jeroboam's son (1 Kgs. 14) and foretells the extinction of the house of Jeroboam, and the eventual exile of the tribes of Israel to the lands beyond the Euphrates. We are carefully informed of the complete fulfilment of these prophecies. Upon seizing the throne, Baasha massacred the entire house of Jeroboam: 'He left to the house of Jeroboam not one that breathed, until he had destroyed it, according to the word of the Lord which he spoke by his servant Ahijah the Shilonite' (1 Kgs. 15: 29). We are reminded of it yet again in the Deuteronomist's summary of the history of the kingdom of Israel: 'And Jeroboam drove (read וידח) Israel from following the Lord . . . until the Lord removed Israel out of his sight, as he had spoken by all his servants

[1] See M. Weinfeld, 'The period of the conquest, etc.', 99 f.

[2] The deuteronomic phrases in this speech are: 'rending of the kingdom' (v. 31); 'for the sake of my servant David' (vv. 32 and 35); 'Jerusalem the city which I have chosen' (v. 32); 'to put my name there' (v. 36); 'because they forsook me and bowed down to Ashtoret', etc. (v. 33); 'did not walk in my ways' (v. 33); 'to do what is right in Yahweh's eyes' (v. 33); 'keep my commandments and my statutes/ordinances' (vv. 34 and 38; compare v. 33); 'David my servant whom I have chosen' (v. 34); 'that there may be a lamp for David my servant' (v. 36). These expressions revolve around four main deuteronomic ideas: (1) The election of Jerusalem and the Davidic dynasty. (2) The observance of God's commandments. (3) The struggle against idolatry. (4) The centralization of cult.

the prophets' (2 Kgs. 17: 21–3). This desire of the Deuteronomist to harmonize the prophecy with historical reality is especially evident in verse 13 of this oration. According to the deuteronomic prophecy the sons of the house of Jeroboam will die a violent death and their corpses will be eaten by dogs—one of the typical stereotyped curses employed in the prophetic maledictions of the Deuteronomist (1 Kgs. 14: 10–11; 16: 3–4; 21: 24; 2 Kgs. 9: 9–10). This curse does not, however, conform with the pre-deuteronomic mantic prophecy appearing in the same chapter according to which Jeroboam's son was to die a natural death. To avoid the contradiction the Deuteronomist adds to his prophecy: '. . . for he only of Jeroboam shall come to the grave, because in him there is found something pleasing to the Lord, the God of Israel, in the house of Jeroboam' (v. 13).

3. The deuteronomic speech appended to the word of God pronounced by Elijah (1 Kgs. 21: 20b–6) foretells the annihilation of the house of Ahab in phraseology identical with that in the stereotyped maledictions concerning Jeroboam and Baasha (14: 10–11; 16: 3–4). Nevertheless the house of Ahab continued to reign, and his two sons ruled for some fourteen years after his death. To resolve the difficulty, another oracle—grounded on a more ancient prophecy[1] —is added to soften the previous one: '. . . because he has humbled himself before me, I will not bring the evil in his days, but in his son's days will I bring the evil upon his house' (1 Kgs. 21: 28–9).[2]

4. Jehu did indeed destroy the house of Ahab and extirpate the Baal cult, but he did not turn from the sins of Jeroboam, nor was he careful to observe the laws of Yahweh, the God of Israel (2 Kgs. 10: 31). How, then, are we to account for the fact that his dynasty lasted for approximately a century? This difficulty was also resolved by a second [prophetic] word of God to Jehu: 'And the Lord said to Jehu, "Because you have done well in carrying out what is right in my eyes, and have done to the house of Ahab

[1] Cf. above, p. 18.

[2] The deuteronomic expressions are 'subdue before the Lord' כנע מפני יהוה (not found outside the deuteronomic and chronistic literature, see S. Japhet, *VT* 18 [1968], 359) and 'bring evil upon' הביא הרעה על, a typical opening formula of the deuteronomic oracle of punishment (see Appendix A, p. 350). A. Jepsen (*Die Quellen des Königsbuches*[2], 1956, pp. 27–8) ascribes 1 Kgs. 21: 29 to the Chronicler, but the view is groundless. The postponement of the divine punishment because of repentance or correct religious conduct substantially accords with the ideology of the Deuteronomist and there is no warrant in ascribing it particularly to the Chronicler.

according to all that was in my heart, your sons of the fourth generation shall sit on the throne of Israel"' (2 Kgs. 10: 30).[1] The Deuteronomist informs us of the eventual fulfilment of this word of God after he has recounted the events of the assassination of Zechariah, the son of Jeroboam, the fourth descendant of Jehu: 'This was the promise of the Lord which he gave to Jehu, "your sons shall sit upon the throne of Israel to the fourth generation". *And so it came to pass*' (2 Kgs. 15: 12).

5. The prosperity and greatness of the kingdom of Jeroboam son of Joash of the house of Jehu, who, like his predecessors, did not turn from the sins of Jeroboam (2 Kgs. 14: 24), also demanded a special explanation. This is provided in a word of God ascribed to Jonah, the son of Amithai of Gath-hepher (vv. 25–7). Jonah, like the other popular prophets, was a historical personage but the Deuteronomist nevertheless expanded his prophecy and harmonized it with his own views. Unlike Amos, Jonah the son of Amithai—who was apparently a mantic prophet—prophesied greatness for Jeroboam the son of Joash. As the Deuteronomist regarded Jeroboam as a sinful king who propagated the evil ways of his ancestors he could not ascribe a favourable prophecy of this sort to Jonah; so he obscured its original import with the rationalization that it was the divine desire to prevent Israel from being obliterated from under the heavens (v. 27). He thus divested the prophecy of its true significance and at the same time cast a pallor upon the lustre of this flourishing period.

6. According to the word of God uttered by Huldah (2 Kgs. 22: 16–17,) Judah's doom was irrevocably sealed because of the worship of foreign gods which reached its peak in the period of Manasseh (2 Kgs. 21: 2–16). This prediction found confirmation

[1] The deuteronomic phrases are: 'did well in doing what was right in my eyes' and '(sons to the fourth generation) shall sit upon the throne of Israel' ישבו לך על כסא ישראל (בני רבעים). For this phrase see the Nerab inscription (*KAI* 226: 5): 'and with my eyes, what do I see? Children of the fourth generation' ובעיני מחזה אנה בני רבע which is almost identical with the phrase: *adi 4 lipīya balṭūssunu āmurma* = 'I saw my descendants to the fourth generation, all in full health' in the inscription of Nabonidus' mother (*Anatolian Studies* 8 (1958), 50 II: 33–4) and compare Job 42: 16. See, however, in the Mesopotamian omina literature (YOS X, Text 31, col. v: 48–vi: 3): *šar-ru-um* [*ù*] *še-er-ri-šu a-di ḫa-am-ši-*[*šu*] *i-na* ^{giš}GU. ZA-*im* [*uš*]-*ša-ab* = 'the king and his offspring will sit on the throne until the fifth generation', which is parallel in respect to dynasty to 2 Kgs. 10: 30 but differs in the number of the generations (five instead of four).

in the Book of the Torah, which was discovered in the temple at that time and concerning which a delegation was sent to question the prophetess (2 Kgs. 22). The kingdom of Judah, however, continued to exist for many decades; a second prophecy was consequently necessary to qualify the threat of the divine punishment. This second prophecy was woven into the words of Huldah the prophetess, and declared that Josiah's pious submissiveness had led the punishment to be postponed until a later time (2 Kgs. 22: 19–20).

This prophecy had apparently undergone the same editorial treatment as the similar prophecy on Ahab in 1 Kgs. 21: 28–9.[1] The clause 'Regarding the words which you have heard' in 2 Kgs. 22: 18, can be reconciled with its context only with difficulty, and scholars have therefore justifiably postulated a deletion in Huldah's prophecy. It is possible, however, that the prophecy concerning Josiah's being gathered peacefully to his ancestors (v. 20) still reflects part of the original content of Huldah's oracle. Huldah may have reacted to Josiah's weeping and rending of his garments in the same way as Elijah had reacted to Ahab's expression of regret and rending of his garments and have prophesied that the divine punishment would be transferred to his children (cf. 2 Kgs. 20: 18–19). In that case the Deuteronomist would have intentionally obscured the sense of the prophecy and reshaped it so as to make it assume a national import. Its principal message, in his view, was the postponement 'of the evil which was to come upon this place' (v. 20) and not the transference of the personal adversities that were to befall Josiah.

We see, therefore, that the Deuteronomist put prophetic sermons of his own composition into the mouths of authentic historical figures, just as he did with the valedictory addresses that he had composed. Indeed where the subject-matter in question was prophecy he had no recourse but to embody his ideological views in the words of a prophetic figure or an oracle emanating from the Godhead itself, though he ascribed oracles to the Deity himself (Judg. 2: 20; 1 Kgs. 11: 11) only when no prophet of traditional renown was at hand. The interpolative character of these prophecies is none the less apparent, and the artificiality with which the Deuteronomist appended his prophetic compositions to the ancient and authentic words of God may still be discerned.

[1] Cf. above, pp. 18–19, 24.

Similar methods of redaction are also evident in the deuteronomic sermons in the book of Jeremiah.

(*b*) *In Jeremiah*

Duhm was the first to call attention to the prose sermons in the book of Jeremiah and to assign them to a deuteronomic editor.[1] Mowinckel took up the thesis and carried it further with an analysis of the sermons in which he demonstrated their distinctive features.[2] We cannot go along with Duhm and Mowinckel in totally rejecting the authenticity of the prose sermons, for as Bright has shown,[3] the biographical narratives (source B) whose authenticity is unquestioned very often provide the setting or the framework for a prose oracle. But even Bright admits that these oracles are not the *ipssisima verba* of the prophet and that they have been enormously expanded by the circle which transmitted them to us. These expansions, and especially those occurring at the end of the prose accounts which Bright terms A^1,[4] swarm—as Bright rightly indicated[5]—with C or deuteronomic clichés, and they are therefore less genuine than the accounts themselves. Indeed, it is mainly these clichés[6] which enable us to distinguish between the genuine and the non-genuine in the prose oracles, although admittedly one must base the distinction on such philological criteria as disruption of context,[7] contradictions,[8] etc. It seems therefore that in Jeremiah as in Kings, homiletic passages were appended to the

[1] B. Duhm, *Jeremia*, KHC, 1901, pp. xvi–xx.

[2] S. Mowinckel, *Zur Komposition des Buches Jeremia*, 1914. In a later book (*Prophecy and Tradition*, 1946, pp. 62 f.) Mowinckel modified his view by referring not to a source (C) but to a circle. According to his modified position, which seems more reasonable, the C strand represents a tradition of deuteronomic scribes who transmitted the oracles of Jeremiah in their own way.

[3] J. Bright, 'The Date of the Prose Sermons of Jeremiah', *JBL* 70 (1951), 15–35, and 'The Prophetic Reminiscence: its Place and Function in the Book of Jeremiah', *Proceedings of the ninth meeting of Die Ou-Testamentiese Werkgemeenskap in Suid-Afrika*, held at the University of Stellenbosch, 26–9 July 1966, pp. 11–39. See also his *Jeremiah* in the Anchor Bible, 1965.

[4] Art. cit. in the *Proceedings of the ninth meeting of Die Ou-Testamentiese Werkgemeenskap in Suid-Afrika*, pp. 18 f.

[5] Ibid., pp. 20 ff.

[6] Mostly those found in Deuteronomy and in the deuteronomic framework of the Former Prophets. Other C clichés which occur only in Jeremiah are less reliable for this purpose. They may reflect the vocabulary and style of the prophetic circle transmitting the prose oracles but might also have been used by the prophet himself. The passages in the C source which also Bright considers unauthentic, e.g. 19: 2b–9; 32: 17–23 and 28–35 (see *Jeremiah*, Anchor Bible, ad loc.) are indeed full of deuteronomic clichés.

[7] Like 19: 2b–9 (see below), 32: 17–23 and 28–35; 35: 14b–15.

[8] See below, pp. 28 f.

original by an editor whose vocabulary and system of work justify our referring to him as deuteronomic.

Like the deuteronomic orations in Joshua–Kings, the prophetic sermons in Jeremiah are programmatic in character, their purpose being to demonstrate that the fall of Judah and the destruction of the temple, the most horrifying and overwhelming of catastrophes in Israelite history, occurred, like the fall of the kingdom of Israel, by force of the prophetic word of God. Just as the deuteronomic prophecies in Joshua–Kings were attributed to well-known prophets active in their respective periods, so the prophecies concerning the doom of Jerusalem were ascribed by the deuteronomic circle to the prophet living and active during the period of the fall and destruction of the state—Jeremiah of Anathoth. As the deuteronomic editor of Joshua–Kings appended his prophetic orations to original authentic prophecies, so the author of source C attached his sermons to the brief but genuine prophecies of Jeremiah.

We may bring as an example the deuteronomic sermon in Jer. 19, which is typical both in diction and content. In the authentic passage of this chapter we are informed that the prophet was commanded to buy an earthen flask, and to proceed with some of the elders of the people and some senior priests (v. 1), to the entrance of the Potsherd Gate (v. 2a), where he was to smash the flask before their eyes (v. 10) and to declare in the name of the Lord, 'So will I break this people and this city, as one breaks a potter's vessel, so that it can never be mended' (v. 11).[1] Between the verses on the procession (v. 2a) and those on the breaking of the flask (v. 10) the deuteronomic editor introduced a long sermon treating of the national sins which were to be the cause of Jerusalem's destruction and enumerating stereotyped punishments typical of the maledictions in Deut. 28 and the deuteronomic historiography.[2] This sermon deprives the symbolic act which Jeremiah is about to perform of all its potential drama and is reminiscent of the speech

[1] The sequence 11b–13 was added by the deuteronomic editor who was principally interested in the *tophet*, see Rudolph's commentary, HAT[2], 1958, ad loc.

[2] The deuteronomic clichés are: 'I shall bring evil upon this place' (v. 3); 'that the ears of everyone who hears it will ring' (v. 3); 'because they have forsaken me' (v. 4); 'to make incense to foreign gods' (v. 4); 'whom they did not know' (v. 4); 'to fill . . . with innocent blood' (v. 4); 'to burn their sons in the fire' (v. 5); 'to make their corpses food for the birds of the heaven and for the beasts of the land' (v. 7); 'to make an astonishment and hiss, all who pass by shall be appalled and will whistle' (v. 8); 'to eat the flesh of sons and daughters' (v. 9); 'in the straits and in the distress to which their enemies shall reduce them' (v. 9).

which the Deuteronomist had put in the mouth of an anxious prophet-disciple who wished only to anoint Jehu's head with oil and flee (2 Kgs. 9: 7–10).[1] Both these primary narratives told of some impressive, dramatic act (the pouring of oil or the smashing of a flask) accompanied by a brief and poignant message ('I anoint you king over Israel' or 'So will I break this people'); in both the oration is a later deuteronomic insertion which only weakens the dramatic quality of the act.

The introduction to the sermon: 'Hear the word of the Lord, O kings of Judah and inhabitants of Jerusalem' (v. 3)—which recurs in the deuteronomic oration in ch. 17, 19 ff.—is very strange. Not only does it contradict the original prophecy (vv. 1 and 10) according to which Jeremiah was to deliver his message only before the group of senior priests and the elders of the people, but it also contains the illogical suggestion that the prophet could in reality have addressed several 'kings of Judah' at one and the same time.[2]

The sins which are mentioned in this sermon (the burning of incense to foreign gods, the shedding of innocent blood, the building of high places to Baal, the burnt offerings of child victims) recur in stereotyped formulations in other deuteronomic sermons in Jeremiah.[3] They are the sins of which the deuteronomic editor accuses Israel and Judah throughout their history from the time they left the land of Egypt until the 'present day' (Jer. 7: 25; 11: 7; 32: 30–1, see also 1 Sam. 8: 8; 2 Kgs. 21: 15), the sins which Yahweh's servants perenially inveighed against but to no avail (7: 13, 25; 11: 7; 25: 3, 4, etc.). It is highly improbable that these sins ever flourished in Judah after the Josianic reform. The Tophet, for example, was destroyed by Josiah (2 Kgs. 23: 10) and is most unlikely to have been reintroduced after his death. It is likewise difficult to suppose that Baal worship, which was characteristic of the northern kingdom (see Jer. 23: 13), ever took root again in Judah after the radical extirpation of foreign worship in the days of Josiah. It would appear therefore, that most of these sins, and particularly the sins of the Tophet and the burning of incense to foreign gods, are those past offenses which the Deuteronomist accused Manasseh of encouraging and which he regarded as having inevitably sealed

[1] See above, p. 20.

[2] Compare the genuine verse in Jer. 4: 9 where the king (in singular) is mentioned with the princes, the priests, and the prophets.

[3] Cf. 7: 6, 9, 31; 11: 12–13; 32: 29–35; 44: 2–10 and 20–5.

Judah's doom (2 Kgs. 21: 1–16, see also Jer. 15: 4). Had Jehoiakim and his successors also been guilty of such sins there would have been no need for the Deuteronomist to blame Manasseh in particular for the fall and destruction of Judah. The book of Kings, moreover, refers to these cultic aberrations when describing the reigns of the Israelite and Judean kings but makes no allusion to them when describing the reigns of the kings who ruled Judah after the death of Josiah, and as Kaufmann has perceptively observed[1] the same is true of the sin of the high places. We may infer then that not only was idolatrous worship not reintroduced after the reform but the cult of the high places was also never restored. Other considerations also militate against the view that the religious reforms were abolished after the death of Josiah.

1. Both Jeremiah (31: 29) and Ezekiel (18: 2) quote the popular adage: 'The fathers have eaten sour grapes and the children's teeth are set on edge'—a conception which is met with in the book of Lamentations: 'Our fathers sinned and are no more; and we bear their iniquities' (5: 7). We may infer then that the contemporaries of Jeremiah and Ezekiel were aware of the sinful character of the preceding generation but believed themselves to be innocent.

2. In Jer. 44: 18, the Judeans complain that their political and economic adversities (which commenced with the death of Josiah) began when they had ceased to worship foreign gods, i.e. during the Jehoiakim–Zedekian period.

3. The Jeremian admonitions against the kings (21: 11–23: 8) and prophets (23: 9–40) of Judah make no allusion whatever to the worship of foreign gods. In fact the Jeremian admonition against the prophets carefully distinguishes between the religious sins of the prophets of Samaria (Baalism, 23: 13) and the moral sins of the prophets of Jerusalem (adultery, lying; v. 14). Jeremiah moreover compares the Judean prophets of his own time, whom he accuses of having caused the people to forget Yahweh because of their prophetic dreams, with their *ancestors* who caused Yahweh to be forgotten because of Baal (23: 27). We may conclude from this that Baal prophecy had been discontinued in Judah and no longer existed as a religious factor during the time of the prophets contemporary with Jeremiah.[2]

[1] *HIR* III, 385 ff.

[2] Cf. J. Milgrom, 'The Date of Jeremiah, Chap. 2', *JNES* 14 (1955), 68.

The admonitions in the deuteronomic accretions in the book of Jeremiah must therefore be taken as retrospective religious surveys and not as admonitions arising from or reflecting the reality of the historical contexts in which they were incorporated. The notion expressed in them that the historical sins of Israel began with the Exodus is the pessimistic conception of the Deuteronomist, who lived in the period following the fall of Judah. Jeremiah himself, however, did not share this conception. Both he and his mentor Hosea[1] regarded the time of Israel's desert-wandering as a period of obedience and grace and not one of sin and rebellion against God. One cannot say that Jeremiah and Hosea were not aware of or ignored completely the Pentateuchal tradition about rebellion in the desert, for the divergence from the Pentateuchal presentation could be explained 'as a literary variation rather than as a case of deliberate reassessment of history'.[2] However, although they could have accepted the JE traditions on *sporadic* sin and punishment in the desert, they could in no way accept the deuteronomic and Ezekelian approach (Ezek. 20)[3] which sees the history of the desert-wandering as constant rebellion. In contrast to Deuteronomy and deuteronomic literature (Deut. 9: 6 f., 24; 10: 16; 29: 3; 31: 27; 2 Kgs. 21: 15 = Dtr, the prose sermons in Jeremiah and Pss. 78, 106), Jeremiah and Hosea say explicitly that Israel in the desert was as pure and fresh as first fruits (Hos. 9: 10; Jer. 2: 2).[4] and that it was only after reaching the verge of the Land[5] that they started to sin.[6]

The maledictions and the punishments met with in the prose sermons of Jeremiah also bear a schematic stamp[7] and do not

[1] For Hosean influence on Jeremiah see K. Gross, 'Die literarische Verwandtschaft Jeremias mit Hosea', 1930 (unpublished dissertation); idem, 'Hoseas Einfluss auf Jeremias Anschauungen', *NKZ* 42 (1931), 241–65, 327–43.

[2] See S. Talmon, 'The Desert Motif in the Bible and in Qumran Literature', *Biblical Motifs, Studies and Texts*, vol. iii, Brandeis University, ed. A. Altmann, 1966, pp. 31–63 and espec. 49–53.

[3] Ezekiel goes even further and traces back the rebellion to Egypt (vv. 5–10, compare Deut. 29: 15–16).

[4] Compare 'as the first ripe in the fig tree at her first season' כבכורה בתאנה בראשיתה in Hosea with 'his first yield' ראשית תבואתה in Jeremiah.

[5] 'As soon as they came to Baal Peor they dedicated themselves to shame' (= בשת which is a euphemism for Baal), Hos. 9: 10.

[6] Cf. Jer. ch. 2 where after referring to the grace of the desert period (vv. 2 and 6), the prophet states: 'and I brought you into the land of Carmel . . . and you came and defiled my land' (v. 7). On Hosea's and Jeremiah's outlooks in this respect, see H. L. Ginsberg, 'Hosea's Ephraim, More Fool than Knave', *JBL* 80 (1961), 345 ff.

[7] See below, pp. 138 ff.

necessarily reflect the historical reality of Jeremiah's time. Like the deuteronomic maledictions in the book of Kings they are equally applicable to each and every one of the kings (cf. the 'kings of Judah') and to each and every dynastic period, since they contain no specific allusion to any actual event. These sermons in general bear no dates and make no reference to the life of the prophet (as opposed to the Baruch source). What principally determined their inclusion was, therefore, as Mowinckel had pointed out,[1] the general import of the admonition itself and not its specific relevance to actual circumstances.

3. THE LITURGICAL ORATION

The oratorical style of the deuteronomic school also invaded the domain of cult and divine worship. Deuteronomy is indeed the only book in the Pentateuch which prescribes the recitation of prayers in ritual ceremonies[2] (Deut. 21: 8; 26: 3b–10a; 15). These prayers, appended to very specific cultic rites, are very stylized and could be applied to any circumstances. The prayer of expiation, for example, used by the elders in the ceremony of unsolved murder (Deut. 21: 8) does not relate to the guilt or innocence of the inhabitants of the city nearest the scene of the crime and for whom the ceremony is performed, but rather to all the people of Israel in their corporate responsibility for the crime. The prayer for expiation is, in effect, a stylized parenetic formula[3] crystallized and attached to the ancient law by the compiler of Deuteronomy.[4] Originally it was unrelated to the earlier quasi-magical ceremony. By incorporating this prayer the author of Deuteronomy modified its magical element and converted the ceremony into only a symbolic act.[5]

The short prayer appended to the confession associated with the removal of the tithes (Deut. 26: 15) also follows a fixed liturgical

[1] In his book *Zur Komposition des Buches Jeremia*.

[2] As opposed to P in which the rites are conducted in complete silence, see Y. Kaufmann, *HIR* II, 476-8.

[3] עמך ישראל is a phrase beloved of the deuteronomic liturgies. Outside our text it is found in the prayer after the removal of tithes (26: 15), in David's prayer in 2 Sam. 7 (vv. 23 and 24 Dtr., see below), in Solomon's dedication prayer (1 Kgs. 8, *passim*), and in Jeremiah's (deuteronomic) prayer (32: 21). עמך . . . אשר פדית is also attested in a liturgical context in Deut. 9: 26 and in 2 Sam. 7: 23.

[4] See A. Roifer, 'The 'Egla 'Arufah', *Tarbiz* 31 (1962/3), 141–3, (Hebrew, with English summary).

[5] See below, p. 211.

pattern and bears no relation to the circumstances of the ceremony. The Israelite does not pray for a good harvest as a reward for his faithful observance of the sacral dues but beseeches God, by recalling his promise to the Patriarchs, to look down from his holy abode and bless the people and land of Israel.[1]

The same is true of the thanksgiving prayer in the rite of the first fruits (26: 3–10). It would have been more in keeping with the circumstances if the farmer presenting the first crops of his soil had expressed his gratitude to Jahweh for the fecundity and bounty with which his plot had been blessed.[2] Instead he is ordered to repeat a set form of thanksgiving recalling the great religio-historical events (the Exodus and the inheritance of the land of Canaan) in Israelite history, in which the blessing of the farmer's produce, there being ceremonially offered, receives but scant attention.[3] By this recitation of a religious affirmation lacking specific relevance to the presentation of the farmer's own crops the author of Deuteronomy transformed a ceremony into a liturgical oration. It is this liturgical oration giving national and historical significance to the ritual act that is of central importance to the author.

G. von Rad argues[4] that Deut. 26: 5–9 constitutes an ancient credo, but this can hardly be accepted. Although there are in this declaration some affinities to older literature (Num. 20: 15–16) and to ancient formulae[5] the declaration as it stands is stylized in typical deuteronomic language, as von Rad himself admits.[6] Moreover, by comparing it with Num. 20, we are able to discern in it features which characterize the specific theology of Deuteronomy:

Deut. 26: 6–8	Num. 20: 15–16
וירעו אתנו המצרים . . .	וירעו לנו מצרים ולאבותינו
ונצעק אל יהוה אלהי אבתינו וישמע יהוה את	ונצעק אל יהוה וישמע קולנו
קלנו . . . ויוציאנו יהוה ממצרים ביד חזקה	וישלח מלאך ויציאנו ממצרים
ובזרע נטויה ובמרא גדול ובאתות ובמפתים	

1 See C. Steuernagel, *Deuteronomium*^{2}, HKAT, 1923, p. 145.

2 Cf. M. Buber, *Israel und Palästina*, 1950, pp. 157 f.

3 Cf. A. Jirku, *Die älteste Geschichte Israels im Rahmen lehrhaften Darstellung*, 1917, p. 49.

4 'The Form-Critical Problem of the Hexateuch', *The Problem of the Hexateuch and Other Essays*, 3 ff.

5 Compare v. 5b with Exod. 1: 7 and 9; v. 6 with Exod. 1: 12–14; v. 7 with Exod. 3: 7 and 9.

6 'The deuteronomic phraseology of the latter half of this prayer in particular is quite unmistakable' (ibid., p. 4).

The deuteronomic style is evident in unmistakably deuteronomic expressions: 'with a mighty hand and outstretched arm, with great terror and by signs and portents' ביד חזקה ובזרע נטויה ובמרא גדל ובאתות ובמפתים,[1] whereas the deuteronomic ideology can be seen in the omission of the role of the angel in the redemption of the people (a tradition which is known to us from the Elohistic source, Exod. 14: 19a; 23: 20; 32: 34, on which D relies upon in other respects). This same tendency can also be found in Deut. 7 which —as we shall see later—takes up most of the motifs of Exod. 23: 20–33 but omits that of the angel.[2] Deut. 4: 32 f. is yet another example: 'He led you out of Egypt by himself [with his presence][3] with his great might' ויציאך בפניו בכחו הגדול ממצרים corresponding to Isa: 63: 9 which (according to LXX) reads: 'Not a messenger or an angel—his presence (פניו) saved them.'[4] Clearly the idea of the angel as mediator is alien to the deuteronomic concept of the nature of God.[5] We may then conclude that the author of Deuteronomy reworked ancient formulae and incorporated them in his own liturgical composition (26: 5–10), and not with von Rad that the passage is an ancient liturgy.

A liturgical declaration of a distinctly didactic character is to be found in Deut. 6: 20–5,[6] which illustrates how the author transformed a collocution attached to a ritual ceremony into a liturgical oration irrelevant to the ceremony. The son–father collocution occurs in the Tetrateuch[7] only against a cultic background (Exod. 12: 26–7; 13: 8 and 14–15).[8] The son's question belongs to the

[1] Cf. B. S. Childs, 'Deuteronomic Formulae of the Exodus Traditions', *Hebräische Wortforschung, Festschrift for W. Baumgartner, SVT* 16 (1967), 30–9.

[2] Cf. most recently A. Rofé, 'Israelite Belief in Angels in the Pre-Exilic Period, as evidenced by Biblical Traditions', Dissert. Hebrew Univ., Jerusalem, 1969 (Hebrew with Engl. summ.), pp. 289 ff.

[3] Cf. Exod. 33: 14–15 for this meaning.

[4] Read: (ויהי להם למושיע בכל צרתם. לא צִר ומלאך, פניו הושיעם).

[5] The objection to the idea of redemption by an angel may be traced back to Hosea, see H. L. Ginsberg, *JBL* 80 (1961), 339 ff.

[6] Von Rad also finds an ancient credo in this passage (op. cit., pp. 13–14), but this is highly improbable, since the diction throughout is characteristically deuteronomic. The passage, moreover, as von Rad himself concedes (p. 13), is part of a larger parenetic section and should not therefore be regarded as a separate unit.

[7] Compare also Josh. 4: 6–7 and 21–2, where it relates to sacral objects intended to symbolize the miraculous nature of the crossing. See J. A. Soggin, 'Kultätiologische Sagen und Katechese im Hexateuch', *VT* 10 (1960), 341–67.

[8] Cf. J. A. Soggin, art. cit.

strange ritual of the paschal sacrifice (daubing the door frames and lintel with blood, etc.) and the first-born (sacrifice, beheading, redemption). The father's reply concerns the particular miracle in the rite. The didactic purpose of the author of Deuteronomy necessitated the inclusion of the son–father collocution, though divorced from its actual setting and converted into an instruction. It no longer has any reference to the paschal sacrifice, nor does it centre on any particular set of religious prescriptions, but relates to *all the testimonies, the statutes and laws* (v. 20), and includes a declaration of the national credo stated in terms of the Exodus and Israel's inheritance of the promised land.[1]

Liturgical oratory reached its height in the prayer of Solomon in 1 Kgs. 8. The original prayer is summarized in the ancient song of vv. 12–13[2] apparently recited by Solomon during the temple inauguration ceremonies. In it he solemnly announces that he has built a permanent abode for God: 'I have built thee an exalted house, a place for thee to dwell for ever.' A similar dedicatory prayer was recited by Gudea ensi of Lagash upon the completion of the Ningirsu temple. After extolling the prowess of his god, Gudea declares: 'I have built thy temple for thee . . . into a good dwelling thou shalt go',[3] a statement apparently introducing his request for god's blessing in return for having constructed the temple. We are then told that Gudea's request was granted—the land was filled with brightness and splendour and blessed with plentitude. A similar request occurs in an Esarhaddon inscription which record's the king's restoration of the Esagila temple in Babylon and his installation of the gods in the sanctuary.[4] The building

[1] I. L. Seeligmann, 'Aetiological Elements in Biblical Historiography', *Zion* 26 (1961), 155 ff. correctly sees in Deut. 6: 20–3 and other passages of similar background homiletic addresses which appear only in the more developed stages of Biblical historiography, as against the school of Alt, which does not distinguish between primitive legends and the homiletic sermon.

[2] Note the LXX conclusion of the song: 'For it is written in the Book of the Song (= השיר)' (read perhaps: The Book of Jashar (ספר הישר)).

[3] See G. A. Barton, *The Royal Inscriptions of Sumer and Akkad*, 1929, p. 239 (Cylinder B. II: 21–III: 1). For a discussion of Gudea's prayer see A. Falkenstein–W. von Soden, *Sumerische und akkadische Hymnen und Gebete*, 1953, pp. 148 and 174.

[4] See R. Borger, *Die Insvhriften Asarhaddons*, 1956, § 11: Bab. A–G, Episode 32, pp. 23–4. Cf. especially Ep. 32*b*: 39–41: 'I restored the images of the great gods and caused them to dwell in their sanctuaries as a *dwelling forever*' (*šubat darâti*, compare מכון לשבתך עולמים in 1 Kgs. 8: 13). Cf. also below, pp. 195 f.

completed, Esarhaddon uttered a long prayer[1] beseeching the gods to bless his kingdom with prosperity and his people with affluence in return for the pious deeds done on behalf of the god.

This type of prayer is replaced in the deuteronomic tradition by a lengthy liturgical oration, extolling the temple as a house of prayer, attached to the dedicatory Song,[2] and containing no

[1] See R. Borger, *Die Inschriften Asarhaddons*, 1956, § 11: Bab. A–G, Episode 39, pp. 26–7.

[2] The deuteronomic phraseology of this litany may be classified as follows (see above p. 1):

(*a*) *The centralization of the cult*

'to choose a city from all the tribes of Israel' / 'the city which you have chosen' (vv. 16, 29, 44); 'that my name be there' (vv. 16 and 29); 'to call my name upon this house' (v. 43); 'to build a house to the name of Yahweh' (vv. 17, 18, 19, 20, 44, 48).

(*b*) *The Davidic dynasty*

'to choose David to be over my people Israel' (v. 16); 'to sit upon the throne of Israel' (vv. 20 and 25); 'no man shall be cut off from before me who may sit upon the throne of Israel' (v. 25).

(*c*) *Exodus, covenant and election*

'your people and your inheritance whom you brought out from Egypt from the midst of the furnace of iron' (v. 51); 'mighty hand and outstretched arm' (v. 42).

(*d*) *Inheritance of the land*

'the land which you gave to our/their fathers' (vv. 34 and 40); 'the land which you gave to your people as an inheritance' (v. 36); 'who has given rest to his people Israel' (v. 56).

(*e*) *Observance of the laws and loyalty to the covenant*

'with all the heart and with all the soul' (v. 48); 'to walk before Yahweh with all the heart' (v. 23, cf. 25); 'wholeheartedly with Yahweh' (v. 61); 'to walk in all his ways' (v. 58); 'to keep his commandments, statutes and judgements' (v. 58, cf. v. 61); 'to fear Yahweh all the days' (vv. 40 and 43).

(*f*) *The monotheistic creed*

'there is none like you, O God, in heaven above or earth below' (v. 23); 'Yahweh is God there is none other' (v. 60).

(*g*) *Fulfilment of prophecy*

'Yahweh has established his word which he spoke' (v. 20); 'spoke with his mouth and fulfilled it with his hand' (vv. 15 and 24); 'let the word which you spoke be confirmed' (v. 26); 'not a single word has fallen of all the words that he has spoken to Moses' (v. 56).

(*h*) *Other formulae showing influence of Deuteronomy*

'when the heavens are shut up and there is no rain' בהעצר שמים ולא יהיה מטר (v. 35, cf. Deut. 11: 17); 'condemning the wrong . . . and vindicating the right' להרשיע רשע . . . להצדיק צדיק (v. 32, cf. Deut. 25: 1); 'all the days that they live upon the face of the earth' כל הימים אשר הם חיים על פני האדמה (v. 40, cf. Deut. 4: 10; 12: 1; 31: 13); 'if his enemy besieges him in the land of his cities' כי יצר לו אויבו בארץ שעריו (v. 37, cf. Deut. 28: 52, 55, 57); 'the foreigner . . . who comes from a distant land' נכרי . . . בא מארץ רחוקה (v. 41, cf. Deut. 29: 21); 'to lay it to heart' השיב אל לב (v. 47, cf. Deut. 4: 39; 30: 1).

allusion to the function of the temple as a place of domicile for God. We shall see[1] that the omission of this reference is intentional, in order to emphasize that God's dwelling place is in heaven. The prayer of Solomon in 1 Kgs. 8: 15 ff. is in fact not a prayer but a discourse on the function of prayer in Yahweh's chosen place, which sees the temple as an immense house of prayer with its doors open equally to foreigners coming from distant lands (vv. 41–3; cf. Isa. 56: 6–7). Whereas the primary function of the chosen place in the book of Deuteronomy is to serve as the exclusive place of sacrifice, the Deuteronomist here conceives of it solely as a house of prayer.[2]

It has been shown that the deuteronomic liturgical declarations, although attached to cultic ceremonies, constitute, from the literary point of view, independent units. At the heart of them lie the great events of Exodus–Election–Promised Land formulated in the typical deuteronomic style.[3] The contents of these declarations are very ancient (cf. Josh. 24) and thus do not reflect any novelty in the deuteronomic literature. However, a new element is introduced, the doctrine of the uniqueness of God, which generally accompanies the deuteronomic Exodus–Election doctrine.

Let us, then, glance at these liturgical formulae and their constituents:

1. In Deut. 3: 23–5 a prayer of Moses, to which no allusion is made in the earlier sources of the Pentateuch, opens with a statement proclaiming God's mighty deeds in the Exodus coupled with his uniqueness: 'O Lord God, you have begun to show your servant your greatness (גדלך) and your mighty hand (ידך החזקה), since *what God is there in heaven or on earth* that can do like your deeds and mighty acts?' (כמעשיך וכגבורתיך).

2. A similar statement appears in the deuteronomic section of David's prayer in 2 Sam. 7: 22b–24,[4] beginning not with the mighty

[1] pp. 193 ff.

[2] The incipient stages of this conception are, however, already evident in Deuteronomy proper, see below, pp. 193 ff.

[3] The characteristic phraseology of these declarations consists of the following phrases: 'redeem from the house of bondage' פדה מבית עבדים (in P גאל); 'by trials, signs and portents' במסות באתות ובמופתים; 'with mighty hand and outstretched arm' ביד חזקה ובזרוע נטויה: 'with great terrors' ובמראים גדולים; 'deeds and mighty acts' מעשים וגברות; 'great and awesome deeds' גדלות ונוראות.

[4] The deuteronomic character of this passage has been recognized by L. Rost, *Die Überlieferung von der Thronnachfolge Davids*, 1926, p. 49, and M. Noth,

deeds of God in the Exodus but with the monotheistic credo: 'there is none like you and there is no God besides you' אין כמוך ואין אלהים זולתך and only then goes on to the Exodus–Election idea phrased in a manner similar to that of Deut. 4: 33–5[1] to which we shall return later.

3. Solomon also opens his litany (the character of which has already been discussed) with a proclamation of the uniqueness of God (1 Kgs. 8: 23) 'there is none like you, O God, in heaven above or on earth below' אין כמוך אלהים בשמים ממעל ועל הארץ מתחת, but he adds the principle of retribution: 'who keeps the gracious covenant to your servants' שמר הברית והחסד לעבדיך which is rooted in the liturgic formula שמר הברית והחסד לאהביו (Deut. 7: 9, see

Überliefer. Studien, pp. 64–5. Besides the outstanding deuteronomic phrases found in the passage: 'your people Israel' עמך ישראל; 'the greatness and the awesome (deeds)' הגדולה ונוראות; 'to redeem for himself as a people' לפדות לו לעם; 'and you, Yahweh, became a God for them' ואתה יהוה היית להם לאלהים; 'and you established your people Israel for you as a people' ותכונן לך את עמך ישראל לך לעם (cf. Deut. 26: 17–18; 29: 12), one can identify the deuteronomic character of the passage by its particular ideology. The prayer of David (except vv. 22b–24) and so God's promise preceding it (vv. 8–17) revolve around the 'great name' and 'greatness' of David (vv. 9 and 21), i.e. his dynasty and renown (compare 2 Sam. 8: 13) (see my article in *'Oz le-David, Biblical Essays in Honor of D. Ben-Gurion*, 1964, p. 400 [Hebrew]) whereas the whole concern of the deuteronomic interpolation is 'the great and awesome deeds' (גדולות ונוראות) done by God to Israel at the time of Exodus (v. 23). In the authentic part of the chapter what is to be established for ever is the house of David (vv. 13b, 16, 25), while in the deuteronomic passage it is the people of Israel (v. 24a = election). This shifting of 'greatness' from David to Israel could have been made by David himself as a token of gratitude to God but taking into account the deuteronomic nature of the passage—both from the ideological and stylistic point of view—we must surely conclude that we have here as in the case of Solomon (1 Kgs. 8: 14 ff.) an ancient prayer supplemented by a deuteronomic declaration of faith.

[1] 'According to that we have heard with our ears' ככל אשר שמענו באזנינו (v. 22) refers to the voice of God at Sinai and corresponds to Deut. 4: 33: 'Has any people heard the voice of a god . . . as you have?' . . . השמע עם קול אלהים כאשר שמעתה (see below, pp. 207 f.). 2 Sam. 7: 23 has to be read (according to A. Geiger, *Urschrift und Übersetzungen*, 1857, p. 288, see too: S. R. Driver, *Notes on the Hebrew Text of the Books of Samuel*, 1913, ad loc.) ומי כעמך ישראל גוי אחר בארץ אשר הלכו אלהים לפדות לו לעם ולשום לו שם ולעשות להם גדלות ונוראות לגרש מפני עמו גוי ואלהיו 'Is there another people on earth which a god went to redeem for himself as a people, to make himself a name, and to do for them great and awesome deeds in driving out a people and its gods before his people?' The idea is based upon Deut. 4: 34: הנסה אלהים לבא לקחת לו גוי מקרב גוי . . . ובמראים גדולים ככל אשר עשה לכם . . . במצרים 'Has a god ever attempted to take himself a nation out of the midst of another nation (= redeem) . . . through great terrors as he has done to you in Egypt?'

below) and which becomes dominant in the later liturgy (Dan. 9: 4; Neh. 9: 32).

4. Hezekiah's prayer (2 Kgs. 19: 15–19) also opens with a declaration on God's unity and exclusive sovereignty: 'You alone are God for all the kingdoms of the earth' אתה הוא האלהים לבדך לכל ממלכות הארץ, which is here supplemented with a new element, viz. the creation motif: 'You made heaven and earth' אתה עשית את השמים ואת הארץ (v. 15). This prayer, of which nothing is heard in the parallel account of Sennacherib's besieging of Jerusalem (2 Kgs. 18: 17–19: 9a) reflects the deuteronomic style[1] and cannot be considered as a part of the authentic prophetic story.[2] The cosmogonic element found here which is not attested in the previous prayers constitutes, as we shall see, an important element in the exilic and post-exilic liturgy (Jer. 32: 17; Neh. 1: 5 [אלהי השמים], 9: 6, see 1 Chr. 29: 11; 2 Chr. 2: 11; 20: 6; 3 Macc. 2: 3; Enoch 84: 2–6) and in the doxologies of Second Isaiah.

5. The deuteronomic prayer[3] in Jer. 32: 17–23 opens with the phrase: 'You have made heaven and earth with your great strength and outstretched arm' אתה עשית את השמים ואת הארץ בכחך הגדול ובזרעך הנטויה. The interesting thing in this opening formula is that the 'stretched-out arm' (זרע נטויה) which is found in the other deuteronomic liturgies in an Exodus context occurs here and in Jer. 27: 5 in a cosmogonical context, a novelty which may stem from the development of the liturgy.[4] A similar universalizing tendency may be found in the continuation of this prayer, in v. 20. The 'signs and portents' אתות ומופתים which occur in previous liturgies only in an Exodus context, appear here for the first time in connection with Israel and humanity in general: בישראל ובאדם. Similarly the principle of retribution 'extends kindness to the thousandth generation' עשה חסד לאלפים (v. 18), originally relating to the grace of God towards his people,[5] is here expanded by the

[1] מעשה ידי אדם עץ ואבן (v. 18) is found only in Deut. 4: 28. Compare 27: 15 (see below, p. 277); 28: 36 and 64; 29: 16. Polemics against idolatry is a characteristic feature of Deuteronomy, see Appendix A, pp. 320 f. Burning the idols in fire (v. 18) is likewise commanded only by Deuteronomy (7: 5 and 25).

[2] See B. S. Childs, *Isaiah and the Assyrian Crisis*, Studies in Biblical Theology, 1967, pp. 99 f.

[3] See Rudolph, *Jeremiah*², HAT, ad loc.

[4] Cf. 1 Chr. 29: 11 where גדלה וגבורה which in the deuteronomic liturgies are usually connected with Exodus, occur in the context of God's rule in the world (בשמים ובארץ). The same applies to 2 Chr. 20: 6 where כח וגבורה expresses the power of God's sovereignty and rulership among all the nations.

[5] Cf. Deut. 7: 9.

principle of individual retribution (v. 18) rooted in the wisdom (= universalistic) sphere.[1] We also find here the attributes האל הגדול הגבור (v. 18) which appear in the declaration of Deut. 10: 17 (see below) and which become later an opening formula of liturgies (Dan. 9: 4; Neh. 1: 5; 9: 32).

We see thus that the liturgies which the deuteronomic scribes put into the mouths of the great national heroes: Moses, David, Solomon, Hezekiah, and Jeremiah contain, besides the motif of Exodus–Election, new elements, viz.: the uniqueness of God, creation, and the idea of retribution which actually expresses the notion of providence. As in the case of other deuteronomic orations, however, so also in the liturgical oration, the editor did not always put the oration in the mouth of the hero. In many instances the liturgy is uttered by the author himself. Such is the proclamation of Deut. 6: 4 which sounds like a solemn enunciation of a credal statement and indeed was accepted later as an obligatory confession of faith (the *Shema'*). It is no mere chance that next to this verse comes the command to teach the children the words of God (v. 7). But this proclamation although very impressive, is too laconic and not joined by other themes (Exodus–Election–Creation) as other deuteronomic liturgies would lead one to expect.

1. Deut. 4: 32 ff. urges the listeners to inquire (כי שאל נא) whether such a thing has ever happened since the creation of man: namely, a people experiencing the revelation of its God and its redemption by 'signs and portents' (vv. 33–4). Then comes the response: 'You have been shown (all this) in order to know *that the Lord alone is God* כי יהוה הוא האלהים, *there is none beside Him*' אין עוד מלבדו (v. 35). That the wonders at the time of Exodus had been done in order to proclaim Jahweh and his omnipotence, is known to us from the earlier sources, e.g. Exod. 8: 6; 9: 14 and 29; 10: 2, etc.[2] The new element is the emphasis on exclusiveness especially emphasized at the end of the passage under consideration: 'Know therefore this day and keep in mind *that the Lord alone is God in heaven above and on earth below, there is no other*' כי יהוה הוא האלהים בשמים ממעל ועל הארץ מתחת אין עוד (v. 39).

2. Deut. 7: 6 f. opens with the ideas of Election and Exodus and ends with the proclamation: 'Know, therefore, *that only the Lord*

[1] Cf. Jer. 17: 10, a verse incorporated in a passage of proverbial sayings.

[2] See C. J. Labuschagne, *The Incomparability of Yahweh in the Old Testament*, 1966, pp. 92 ff.

your God is God, כי יהוה הוא האלהים, the steadfast God *who keeps his gracious covenant to them that love him,* שמר הברית והחסד לאהביו and repays them that hate him to their face.' To the monotheistic principle there is added the doctrine of retribution which we have seen to characterize the later deuteronomic liturgies.

3. In the context of a 'military speech' the question is posed about defeating the Canaanites the answer being given in the deuteronomic stereotyped form: 'Bear in mind (זכר תזכר) what the Lord your God did to Pharaoh and all the Egyptians: the great trials (המסת הגדלת) that you saw . . . the signs and the portents והאתות והמפתים . . . for the Lord your God is in your midst, a great and awesome God אל גדול ונורא' (Deut. 7: 18–21).

4. Deut. 10: 17 ff. opens with the affirmation of God's sovereignty in heaven and earth, and then passes on to the ideas of Election and Exodus. These are couched in a language characteristic of the deuteronomic liturgies. So, for example, the phrase 'the heavens and the heaven of heavens' השמים ושמי השמים in v. 14 is found in the Solomonic liturgy in 1 Kgs. 8: 27, and likewise in the litany in Neh. 9: 6. The epithets 'the great, the mighty, and the awesome' (הגדול הגבור (והנורא—as already indicated—occur in the liturgy in Jer. 32: 18, in the formalized prayers in Dan. 9: 4; Neh. 1: 5; 9: 32, and finally found their way into the Benediction of *Shemoneh Esreh.* In this passage the mighty deeds of God are declaimed in the stereotyped language characteristic of the deuteronomic literature:

He is your glory הוא תהלתך[1] and he is your God who has done *with you these great and awesome deeds* את הגדולות ואת הנוראות האלה that you saw with your own eyes. . . . And know this day that it was not your children who neither experienced nor witnessed the lesson (מוסר) of the Lord, *His greatness, His mighty hand, His outstretched arm, His signs and His deeds* that He performed in Egypt את גדלו את ידו החזקה וזרעו הנטויה. ואת אתתיו ואת מעשיו אשר עשה בתוך מצרים . . . but that it was you who saw with your own eyes *all the great deeds that the Lord*

[1] In the light of this phrase and the liturgic formula in Ps. 109: 1 (אלהי תהלתי) we may retain ('my glory') תהלתי in the prayer of Jer. 17: 14 and should not necessarily emend to תחלתי ('my hope') as proposed by Duhm. (*Jeremia*, KHC, 1901, ad loc.). The following phrase in our verse 'he is your God' הוא אלהיך is also attested in a Jeremianic prayer: 'bring me back and I shall come back *for you, Yahweh, are my God'* השיבני ואשובה כי אתה יהוה אלהי (31: 17).

performed כי עיניכם הראת את כל מעשה יהוה הגדל אשר עשה (Deut. 10: 21–11: 7).

All these proclamations are directed towards deepening the monotheistic conscience, as is evident from the form of address normally preceding the proclamations: 'Hear' שמע; 'Know' וידעת; 'Bear in mind' זכר תזכר; 'recall to mind' והשבת אל לבבך, etc. This strengthening of the monotheistic belief goes hand in hand with the polemic against paganism frequently found in Deuteronomy (4: 28; 12: 31; 27: 15; 28: 36 and 64; 29: 16)[1] and is strongly developed in Second Isaiah.[2]

To summarize, these conclusions may be drawn:

1. In Deuteronomy we find for the first time the command to recite liturgies (Deut. 21: 8–9; 26: 1–11 and 12–15).

2. In the framework of Deuteronomy proclamations of faith are made which, in addition to the old doctrine of Exodus–Election, contain the idea of uniqueness of God and his exclusive sovereignty (4: 32–9; 6: 4; 7: 9–10; 10: 14).

3. Beginning with Deut. 3: 23–5, thence to the deuteronomic historiography (2 Sam. 7: 22–4; 1 Kgs. 8: 23; 2 Kgs. 19: 15–19), the deuteronomic stratum in Jeremiah (32: 17–23), and closing with Daniel, Nehemiah, and Chronicles, prayers are ascribed to the national leaders opening with the proclamation of the uniqueness of God, and supplemented (especially in the later texts) by the theme of world creation.

[1] See above, p. 39 n. 1.

[2] One wonders if some of the central religious ideas of Second Isaiah such as: the uniqueness of God, the Exodus tradition (here interrelated with the restoration of Israel), and the Creation may not have their roots in deuteronomic theology. Moreover, the exclusiveness of God is expressed in language reminiscent of Deut. 4: 39 (אני יהוה אין עוד), and the doctrine of Election (בחר) of Israel, which is peculiar to Deuteronomy among the Pentateuchal literature, is also most prominent in Second Isaiah. The deuteronomic litany in 1 Kgs. 8 also has much in common with Deutero- (or Trito-)Isaiah. (The distinction between Deutero-Isaiah and Trito-Isaiah, which was introduced by B. Duhm, has been recently questioned by many scholars; Kaufmann, *HIR*, IV, M. Haran, בין ראשונות לחדשות 1963 (Hebrew, see also his article in *SVT*, vol. 9, 1963), and most recently F. Maass, 'Tritojesaja', *Festschrift L. Rost*, *BZAW* 104 (1967), 153–63.) The latter prophet speaks about foreigners (בני נכר), who are given the right to participate in worship and prayer in the Israelite sanctuary (Isa. 56: 1–7), an idea expressed in 1 Kgs. 8: 41–3. Another feature of Deutero-Isaiah's theology, which seems to be rooted in deuteronomic thinking, is the notion of the sanctuary's functioning as a 'prayer house' which is mentioned in Isa. 56: 7 and which pervades the whole deuteronomic litany.

4. These liturgies setting forth the ideas of uniqueness of God, Election of Israel, God as the creator and provider, have their origins in the style of the book of Deuteronomy.

As we have seen, most of these declarations are connected with worship and prayer and indeed are found to be the essential elements of the Jewish liturgy at the time of the second Temple.

Indeed, the basic ideas and form of the deuteronomic liturgy prevail in the Jewish liturgy of later times. Thus, the *Shema'* liturgy which—according to the Rabbinic interpretation—declares the acceptance of the exclusive Kingship of God[1] is preceded by a benediction which proclaims God's love to Israel especially in the election of his people (cf. the formula: הבוחר בעמו ישראל באהבה), an idea taken from the deuteronomic liturgical orations.[2] This is followed by the *Ge'ullah* Benediction centred on the redemption from Egypt, which is also one of the basic tenets in the liturgies of Deuteronomy. As a matter of fact, the deliverance from Egypt, the main theme of the *Ge'ullah* prayer, is closely related to the idea of the incomparability of God (cf. מי כמוכה) in the prayer of the morning and evening. The relationship between the deliverance from Egypt and the incomparability of God already exists in the Exodus traditions (cf. Exod. 15: 11) and in the credal statements of the book of Deuteronomy.

The first benediction in the series of the *Shema'* benedictions, on the other hand, is related to the theme of God's creation (especially to the creation of lights and changing seasons) which, as we have seen, is attested in the later deuteronomic liturgies.

The association of the individual with the community in the liturgies of Deuteronomy is one of the corner-stones of the prayer

[1] Cf. the valuable work of M. Kadushin, *Worship and Ethics: A Study in Rabbinic Judaism*, 1964, pp. 78 ff.

[2] Cf. Deut. 4: 37; 7: 7; 10: 15.

In the Rabbinic literature the concept of election is tied to the concept of acceptance of 'the yoke of the Kingship of God' עול מלכות שמים (see Kadushin, *Worship*, pp. 90 ff.). God's love and grace are being expressed by the fact that he gave Israel the Torah (cf. the blessing before the recital of the Torah 'who chose us from among all peoples by giving us His Torah' אשר בחר בנו מכל העמים ונתן לנו את תורתו) a concept appearing for the first time in the liturgy in Neh. 9: 13–14 where the giving of the Torah is part of God's grace to Israel. In Deuteronomy as in the earlier sources the law is an obligation which has to be observed because of God's grace to Israel, whereas in Nehemiah and in the Rabbinic literature the giving of the law to Israel is itself a great privilege.

of the Second Temple. Like the farmer in Deuteronomy who associates himself in his prayer with the whole people of Israel (Deut. 26: 3–10 and 15) so also the individual in the later Jewish prayer never prays on his own behalf but always on behalf of the whole community;[1] or even the whole of mankind.

Finally, we have seen that the principle embodied in the Daily *Tefillah* (שמונה עשרה) of praise preceding supplication[2] operates also in the deuteronomic prayers of Moses, David, Solomon, Hezekiah, and Jeremiah.[3]

In the light of these observations we may safely conclude that it was Deuteronomy, or the Josianic reform, which paved the way for the institution of the synagogue.[4] The abolition of the scattered holy places created a religious vacuum. This vacuum was filled by liturgy, which, as we have seen, was a kind of formalized prayer based on the basic religious tenets of Israel. A new means of worship was thus established: prayer replaced sacrifice, which, until now, had constituted the basic medium of communion with God. Thus the religion of Israel underwent a metamorphosis: from a religion of cult to a religion of prayer and confession. Undoubtedly the Exile, during which no cultic worship was maintained, must have contributed very much to this important turning-point in Israelite religion. Nevertheless, a consideration of the evidence of Deuteronomy and of the interrelationship between the book and the Josianic reform suggests that the beginning of the change took place at the time of the reform.[5] The very fact that Deuteronomy is

[1] Cf. Kadushin, op. cit., pp. 117 f. The phrase עמך ישראל which is so characteristic of the deuteronomic prayer (see p. 32, n. 3 above) is very prominent in the 'short Tefillah' which is to be said instead of the regular *Tefillah* (Mishnah Berakhoth, iv: 4; Tosefta Berakhoth, iii: 7, ed. S. Lieberman, pp. 13 f.).

[2] The *berakhoth* characterized as a 'praise' were already the fixed elements of every *Tefillah* in the days of the Second Temple. (See e.g. Mishnah Rosh-Hashanah, iv: 5).

[3] In contrast with the other ancient prayers like those of Jacob (Gen. 32: 10–13), Moses (Num. 12: 13), Joshua (7: 7–9), Samson (Judg. 16: 28), Hannah (1 Sam. 1: 11) where no praise occurs.

[4] That the synagogue arose out of the reform of Josiah has been argued by J. Weingreen, *Hermathena* 98 (1964), 68 ff. For a thorough and valuable discussion of the rise of the synagogue see H. H. Rowley, *Worship in Ancient Israel*, 1967, pp. 213 ff.

[5] L. Finkelstein ('The Origin of the Synagogue', *Proceedings of the American Academy for Jewish Research*, 1 (1930), 49–59) suggested that the synagogue has its roots at the time of Manasseh, when the temple was polluted and the pious men looked for a new kind of worship, which could be conducted easily in secret. This suggestion seems highly plausible.

the only book in the Pentateuch which imposes upon the Israelite the duty to recite liturgies speaks for itself.

4. THE MILITARY ORATION

In addition to the three types of orations thus far discussed we also meet the military oration in deuteronomic literature.[1] Thus Deut. 20, for example, contains an inspiring oration by a priest to the Israelite warriors before their departure for battle.[2] Speeches of this type are common in the framework of the book of Deuteronomy (1: 29–33; 2: 24–5[3] and 31; 3: 21–2; 7: 17–24; 9: 1–6; 11: 22–5; 31: 1–6) and undoubtedly voice the patriotism and national fervour that swept through Judah during the Josianic period.

Military addresses are, to be sure, evident in earlier Biblical traditions[4] where they are directly related to specific and concrete situations and are marked by a variety of styles, whereas in the book of Deuteronomy they are of a general and stylized character, applicable to any military situation.

These orations are punctuated by short recurring rallying cries such as: אל תירא ואל תחת 'do not fear or be dismayed', אל תירא ואל תערץ 'do not fear or be in dread', אל תחפזו ואל תערצו 'do not tremble or be in dread', חזק ואמץ 'be strong and of good courage',[5]

[1] See G. von Rad, *Studies in Deuteronomy*, pp. 51–2.

[2] Von Rad (ibid.) assigns this oration to the deuteronomic strand, and the officers' declaration in the same section to an earlier strand, which he believes reflects an early Israelite custom that obtained during the period of the holy wars.

[3] v. 25b is modelled on Exod. 15: 14, see W. L. Moran, 'The End of the Unholy War and the Anti-Exodus', *Biblica* 44 (1963), 340.

[4] See, for instance, Exod. 14: 13–14; Judg. 4: 14; 7: 15; 2 Sam. 10: 12.

[5] The *Sitz im Leben* of the formulae חזק ואמץ and אל תירא is not, as N. Lohfink (*Scholastik* 37 (1962), 32 f.) and H. Graf Reventlow (*Liturgie und prophetisches Ich bei Jeremia*, 1963, pp. 58 ff.) contend, the leader's appointment to office but the occasion of war and confrontation with a difficult task that must be performed (cf. Josh. 10: 25; 2 Sam 2: 7; 10: 12; 13: 28; 1 Kgs. 2: 2; Isa. 7: 4; 35: 4; Hag. 2: 4–5; 2 Chr. 32: 7, etc.) and particularly upon a new and inexperienced leader (cf. Jer. 1: 8 and 17; Ezek. 2: 6; 3: 9). The formulae are also met with in contexts which have no reference whatever to a leader's appointment to office (cf., e.g., Deut. 1: 29–30; 7: 18 and 21; 20: 1 and 3; 31: 6; Josh. 10: 25), as Lohfink himself concedes (op. cit., p. 38), and are consequently to be viewed against a background in which the established or new leader and his people are charged to perform a difficult task (the Deuteronomist also conceives the charge of observing the Law as a task which requires strength and courage, cf. Josh. 1: 7; 1 Kgs. 2: 2–3). For the employment of like formulae in ancient Near Eastern literature to inspire and encourage kings confronted by enemies see the oracles to Esarhaddon and Ashurbanipal (in *ANET*[2], pp. 449–51) and the Zakir Inscription (*KAI* 202: 12 ff.). The phrase in Assyrian is *lā tapallaḫ* and in Aramaic אל תזחל, both meaning: 'do not fear'.

etc., the purpose of which was to dispel the fear of the people and fortify their spirits and confidence: 'No man shall be able to stand against you לא יתיצב איש בפניכם, the Lord your God will lay the fear of you and the dread of you upon all the land that you shall tread' (Deut. 11: 25; cf. Josh. 1: 5). Such rallying cries go back of course to the period of Israel's ancient wars (cf. 2 Sam. 10: 12: '*Be of good courage* (חזק ונתחזק) . . . for our people, and for the cities of our God') and were apparently employed in prophetic oracles designed to encourage the leader-warriors of Israel.[1] In Deuteronomy, however, these rallying cries were developed into stirring military addresses. This method of military rhetorical development is particularly evident in Deut. 7. At the core of this chapter lie several verses which occur in the brief epilogue of the Book of the Covenant (Exod. 23: 20–33).[2] Yet while the verses in the Book of the Covenant contain only briefly formulated promises, treating of Israel's inheritance of the land of Canaan as a reward for observing God's covenant, in Deuteronomy these sayings have been reworked and expanded into a military oration of consummate construction.[3] The address opens with a warning against forming contacts with the vanquished peoples of Canaan (1–5), then proceeds to the subject of Israel's mission (6–11), the

[1] J. Begrich ('Das priesterliche Heilsorakel', *ZAW* 52 (1934), 81–92) has pointed out that the formula אל תירא derives from the *Heilsorakel*, i.e. the salvation oracle, cf. also recently H. M. Dion, 'The Patriarchal Traditions and the Literary Form of the "Oracle of Salvation"', *CBQ* 29 (1967), 198–206. We do now know, on the other hand, of the affinities between this formula and prophetic oracles (see references to Assyrian and Aramaic documents in the previous note; cf. Jer. 1: 8 and 19). The provenance of these formulae should consequently be sought for in prophetic composition and perhaps in court prophecy. Assyrian and Aramaic parallels do indeed point to a court background of such formulae. The fact that these formulae are also encountered in Deutero-Isaiah may be explained in the light of the royal terminology employed by the prophet and his description of Israel and the Servant of Yahweh in royal imagery (on this point see, S. Paul, 'Deutero-Isaiah and Cuneiform Royal Inscriptions', *JAOS* 88 (1968), 180–5).

[2] Cf. Exod. 23: 23 with Deut. 7: 1; v. 24 with v. 5a; vv. 25–6 with vv. 11–15; v. 27 with v. 23; vv. 28–30 with vv. 20–2; v. 32 with v. 2; v. 33 with v. 16 and 25 (compare מוקש with תוקש). Only the reference to the angel in the epilogue of the Book of the Covenant (vv. 20–23a) has no analogue in the deuteronomic passage and the omission may be due to the specific theology of the book (see above, p. 34).

[3] Von Rad, *Studies*, pp. 53–4, regards vv. 16–26 as a separate literary unit, arguing that in contrast to the preceding passages this one does not allude to the Law, to which we may reply that the subject of the passage does not require any reference to the Law. The homogeneity of the chapter is further demonstrated by the integration of its opening and concluding verses, cf. vv. 2 and 24; 5, and 25–6, cf. also N. Lohfink, *Das Hauptgebot*, p. 183.

blessing (12–15), and concludes with inspiring and encouraging remarks concerning the conquest (16–24) which in turn end with warnings similar to those in the introduction (note particularly v. 25 and v. 5). The principal purpose of the oration is to encourage the people about to embark upon the conquest by allaying their natural apprehensions ('These nations are greater than I; how can I dispossess them?' (v. 17)) with fortifying assurances: '. . . remember what the Lord your God did to Pharaoh and to all Egypt . . . so will the Lord your God do to all the peoples of whom you are afraid . . . you shall not be in dread of them, for the Lord . . . is in the midst of you, a great and awesome God' (vv. 18–21).

The epilogue of the Book of the Covenant makes almost no mention of the fact that it is *Israel* who will dispossess the peoples of Canaan: it is *God* who will dispossess the Canaanites (vv. 29 and 30).[1] Consequently there is no particular need to encourage the people with rallying slogans. Not so the book of Deuteronomy which places the task of dispossessing the Canaanite peoples directly upon the Israelites themselves, and thus finds it necessary to fortify the spirit of the people and eradicate their fear of waging war against the outnumbering enemy. The deuteronomic oration has accordingly shifted the focal point from the warring Deity to the warring Israelites. Thus while in the Book of the Covenant the Deity is described as saying of the enemy '*I will* not drive them out from before you in one year lest the land become desolate and the wild beast multiply against you' (v. 29), in the deuteronomic passage Moses says, '*You will* not make an end of them quickly, lest the wild beasts grow too numerous for you' (v. 22). Whereas, in the Book of the Covenant God promises Israel that he will send hornets to drive Israel's enemy out of the land (v. 28, see also Josh. 24: 12), the deuteronomic passage states that God will send the hornets to destroy the hidden survivors of the enemy (v. 20): the unconcealed enemy will presumably be dealt with by the Israelites themselves. The oration finally ends with the encouraging announcement: 'Not a man shall be able to stand against you, until you have destroyed them' (v. 24) which is frequently encountered

[1] Read v. 31b with LXX and Vulgate: וגרשתים מפניך. The suffix form מו in the third person plural occurs only in Biblical poetry (twenty-two times, cf. GK § 58g) and in view of the different orientations of the Exodus and deuteronomic passages in question the Massoretic reading is probably corrupt.

in other deuteronomic military orations (Deut. 11: 25; Josh. 1: 5; see 10: 8).

The briefly formulated promises concerning the conquest and inheritance of the land in Exod. 23 have, then, been converted into a stirring oration suffused with profound national patriotism.

We can recognize the deuteronomic author's stress on the military element when we compare the literary material of Deuteronomy with its underlying traditions in Numbers.

1. In Num. 14: 40 f. we are told that after the sin of the spies, the people insisted 'to go up' הננו ועלינו to the land and were commanded 'not to go up' אל תעלו because God was not with them. Deut. 1: 41–2 quotes this very tradition but adds to the concept of 'going up' the concept of 'fighting': 'we will go up *and fight*' אנחנו נעלה ונלחמנו and correspondingly 'Do not go up *and do not fight*' לא תעלו ולא תלחמו. The deuteronomic author even adds details about the military preparations: 'and everyone of you girded himself with war gear', about which nothing is said in the original tradition of Numbers.

2. The generation whose census was taken in the desert and thus was supposed to be the army invading the land of Canaan (cf. Num. 14: 29) is called in Deut. 2: 14 and 16 and in the deuteronomic passage in Josh. 5: 4 and 6: 'the men of war' אנשי המלחמה,[1] an expression not found in Num. 14, upon which the deuteronomic account is based.[2] The expression is used, on the other hand, to describe the men fighting under the command of Joshua in the wars of the Conquest (Josh. 6: 3; 8: 1, 3, 11; 10: 7 (עם המלחמה), and 24).

3. Deut. 3: 18 and Josh. 1: 14 (= Dtr) refer to the חלוצים of the eastern part of the Jordan as 'warriors' בני חיל and גבורי חיל

[1] The 'camp' המחנה and the 'men of war' in Deut. 2: 14–16 may have been used tendentiously as an inversion of the Holy War motif (see Moran, 'Unholy War, etc.' pp. 334 f.) but their use might also be explained as an aspect of the military dimension within the deuteronomic framework. The explicit references to weapons in 1: 41 and to 'warriors' in 3: 18 are not 'exceptional' as Moran contends (ibid., p. 335) but rather point to the preoccupation of the deuteronomic author with the military aspect of the conquest.

[2] In P the expression is found in connection with the battle with Midian (Num. 31: 28) but significantly enough never in connection with the wars of conquest which were considered the wars before God לפני יהוה, see Num. 32: 20, 21, 27, 29.

respectively, terms not mentioned in the original account of Numbers, but again found in the descriptions of the expeditions of Joshua (8: 3; 10: 7).

The deuteronomic military orations, concentrated into the prologue and epilogue of the book, centre on the theme of the conquest, and are twice ascribed to Moses when addressing the people (7: 17–24; 9: 1–6) and twice when addressing Joshua (3: 31–2; 21: 7–8).

The deuteronomic redactor of the book of Joshua continued this tradition of military rhetoric. We find stirring military speeches such as God's address to Joshua (Josh. 1: 1–9) and Joshua's address to the Israelite warriors (10: 25)[1] incorporated into his own composition.

At the heart of these speeches lies the firm conviction in victory over the enemy; hence, we find the constant call for boldness on the part of the people to go up to conquer and possess the land: 'The Lord your God has set the land before you; go up, take possession as . . . God . . . has told you' (Deut. 1: 21) 'Begin to take possession, that you may occupy his land' (2: 31) and the like.[2] The orations similarly emphasize the vast numerical supremacy of the Canaanite peoples facing Israel (גוים גדולים ועצומים) (Deut. 4: 38; 7: 1 and 17; 9: 1; 11: 23; Josh. 23: 9), hence the need for Israel's stalwart faith and firm spirit.

The patriotic tone of the military orations also underlies the deuteronomic description of the conquest in Josh. 1–12. Although the individual narratives concerning the conquest of the various cities are, of course, ancient, the framework in which they are incorporated is late and substantially deuteronomic in origin. As opposed to chs. 14–19, which have markedly tribal characteristics, these deuteronomic chapters carry a distinct national stamp. Whereas in chs. 14–19 and Judg. 1, the wars and Israelite settlement are described as tribal affairs, the conquest in chs. 1–12 is seen as a national war waged in swift and total campaigns against which no resistance is possible ('Their heart melted, and there was

[1] The military orations in the deuteronomic strand of Joshua differ from those in Deuteronomy proper only in that the deuteronomic editor of Joshua combines religio-Torah motifs with military motifs and consequently also takes the formula חזק ואמץ in the religious sense of constant readiness to observe God's law (cf. Josh. 1: 6–9 with Deut. 31: 7–8; see also 1 Kgs. 2: 2–4).

[2] See M. Buber, *Israel und Palästina*, 1950, p. 41.

no longer any spirit in them, because of the people of Israel', Josh. 5: 1; 'There was no courage left in any man because of you' 2: 11; 'Not one of all their enemies had withstood them', 21: 42) and which left no enemy alive in their wake ('... and he utterly destroyed every person ... he left none remaining', 10: 28 and 30, etc.; 'they did not leave any that breathed', 11: 14, etc.).

The national resurgence of the Josianic period[1] thus led not only to a reassessment of the traditions of the conquest but also altered the concept of the personality of the leader conqueror. It is only in the deuteronomic strand of the book of Joshua that Joshua figures as a national-*military* leader (see particularly Josh. 10: 40–2; 11: 16–20; 21: 41–3) who conquers 'all the land' 'at one time'. In the earlier traditions he appears (like Moses) as a national-*religious* leader: he leads the Israelites across a dry Jordan (chs. 3–4), establishes a covenant (24), circumcises the Israelites (5: 2–8), dispatches spies (2), and divides the country by lot before the Lord (particularly in the P traditions). The wars of Joshua, according to these latter traditions, are locally fought battles in which the sacral factor plays a dominant role (for example, the conquest of Jericho, the Achan episode). In the deuteronomic strand, on the other hand, Joshua figures as a typical military national leader who wages lightning and sweeping campaigns (chs. 10–12) and in which the sacral element is completely absent but is replaced by a pervasive and fervent national feeling. Thus Josh. 10–12, manifestly deuteronomic in character (especially 10: 25–43; 11: 10–12: 24), are imbued with an ardent national fervour which finds expression both in the redactor's own remarks (10: 40–2; 11: 16–20) and in the orations ascribed to Joshua (10: 19 and 25).

The deuteronomic authors appear to have been influenced in this type of composition by non-Israelite sources particularly Assyrian war descriptions. We meet with the same sort of military psychological phraseology and atmosphere[2] in contemporaneous royal Assyrian inscriptions. The construction לא תירא ולא תחת prevalent in deuteronomic military orations is also encountered in the form *ḫattu puluḫtu* ('fear and dread') in the neo-Assyrian

[1] See below, pp. 166 f. For detailed discussion see my paper, 'The Awakening of Israel's National Consciousness in the Seventh Century B.C.', in *'Oz le-David, Biblical Essays in Honor of D. Ben-Gurion*, 1964, pp. 396–420.

[2] See H. W. F. Saggs, 'Assyrian Warfare in the Sargonid Period', *Iraq* 25 (1963), 149 f.

inscriptions.[1] We similarly encounter military rallying cries of the type found in deuteronomic literature such as, for example, לא תירא ולא תערוץ.[2] Such expressions as 'he did not leave a survivor' לא השאיר שריד, 'he did not leave a soul' לא השאיר נשמה, met with in deuteronomic literature are also found in royal Assyrian inscriptions.[3] The public exhibition of the executed bodies of the enemy described by the Deuteronomist in Josh. 10 (see. Deut. 21: 22–3) appears to have been a conventional part of Assyria's military psychological strategy.[4]

The military orations and the picture of total war described in the deuteronomic strand of the book of Joshua reflect, therefore, the military reality of the eighth and seventh centuries B.C. which has been turned back to conditions prevailing during the period of the conquest.

5. THE *SITZ IM LEBEN* OF THE ORATIONS

These orations then are, as we have seen, literary programmatic creations and do not convey the actual content of speeches once delivered in concrete circumstances. On the contrary, the early speech forms arising from some specific reality have been converted by this school into orations of an idealizing character. We have seen, for example, that the original valedictory, testament, and blessing have been replaced by a lengthy parenetic valedictory and

[1] Cf. *ḫattum u puluḫtum elišunu ittabikma* = 'terror and fear were poured out over them'. See R. Borger, *Die Inschriften Asarhaddons*, p. 58, l. 29, cf. *OIP* II, p. 82, l. 41.

[2] *lā tapallaḫma niqittu lā taraššu.* 'Do not fear and have no anxiety' in an unpublished letter from Nimrud quoted by Saggs, 'Assyrian Warfare', p. 150.

[3] Cf. the expressions: *ēdu amēla lā īzib* 'he did not leave out a single man'; and *napištum ul ēzib* 'I did not spare a single soul', for references cf. *CAD* vol. 4 (E), p. 37 (c), 1′; 422–3 (e), 1′–2′. Cf. also the expression *ēdu ul ipparšid* 'no man escaped', M. Streck, *Assurbanipal* II, p. 36, iv: 62; p. 74, ix: 40.

[4] Cf. Saggs, 'Assyrian Warfare', p. 149: 'This represented a definite conscious use by the Assyrians not of terrorism for sadistic purposes, but of psychological warfare.' (See also W. von Soden, *Herrscher im Alten Orient*, pp. 83 f.) Cf. especially the hanging of the rebel leaders of Ekron by Sennacherib who were guilty of *ḫiṭīti u gullulti* 'crime or sin' or 'who caused a crime to be committed' *ša ḫiṭītu ušabšû* (*OIP* II, p. 32, iii: 7–14) and the Biblical expression in connection with impalement חטא משפט מות 'a sin worthy of death' and קללת אלהים 'an affront of God' in Deut. 21: 22–3. The Akkadian *ana ili qullulum* 'to commit a sin against God' refers particularly to the violation of oaths sworn in the name of a deity and the violation of treaties and agreements. See H. C. Brichto, *The Problem of the Curse in the Hebrew Bible*, 1963, p. 178.

that genuine military formulae have been supplanted by politico-military programmatic addresses. In place of the prayer, predicated by its concrete circumstances, we encounter a stereotyped religious declaration in the language of deuteronomic religio-national ideology. Instead of the authentic word of God expressed through concrete events or circumstances[1] we have a stereotyped prophetical admonition, applicable to all events and historical periods.

These orations, then, are literary compositions uttering the thoughts and mood of their authors. These authors put into the mouths of such national leaders as Moses, Joshua, Samuel, David, Solomon, in addition to priestly (Deut. 20) and prophetic personages (in Kings and Jeremiah), that which conformed with their own ideology.

A similar literary method is to be found in Greek historical writings. The numerous orations cited in the works of Herodotus and Thucydides, supposedly delivered by national heroes and figures are rightly considered by scholars to be literary creations.[2] Thucydides himself states, moreover, that it was his habit to make the speakers say what in his opinion was demanded of them by the various occasions (I. 22. 1).[3]

Typologically speaking, therefore, we may say that the orations in deuteronomic writings are similar to those of the Greek

[1] See H. Gressmann, *Der Messias*, 1929, pp. 65–148 (Prophetische Gattungen).

[2] See W. Schmid, *Geschichte der Griechischen Literatur* I. 2, 1934, pp. 643 f.; I. 5, 1948, pp. 161 f.; and A. Deffner, *Die Rede bei Herodot und ihre Weiterbildung bei Thukydides*, *Diss.*, 1933, Munich.

[3] *ὡς δ' ἂν ἐδόκουν ἐμοὶ ἕκαστοι περὶ τῶν αἰεὶ παρόντων τὰ δέοντα μάλιστ' εἰπεῖν, ἐχομένῳ ὅτι ἐγγύτατα τῆς ξυμπάσης γνώμης τῶν ἀληθῶς λεχθέντων, οὕτως εἴρηται.* Scholars are divided as to the exact meaning of the term *τὰ δέοντα* employed by Thucydides. Most take it to mean '*ideal* truth', i.e. that Thucydides had the speaker say that which *should have* conformed with the *ideal* truth (see, e.g., E. Meyer, *Forschungen zur alten Geschichte* II, 1899, p. 380), while other scholars point to the next part of the passage—in which Thucydides states that he adhered 'as closely as possible to the general sense of what they really said'—as demonstrating their own view that Thucydides has approximated the *factual* truth of what was said and that the orations are not his own gratuitous inventions, see A. W. Gomme, *Essays in Greek History and Literature*, 1937, pp. 156 ff.; L. Fuchs, *The History of the Peloponnesian War*, 1959, pp. 32–3 (Hebrew); D. Rokeach, 'A Note on Thucydides 1: 22: 1', *Eranos* 9 (1962), 104–7.

The same question applies of course to the deuteronomic orations and a distinction must apparently be made between the orations of those prophets who were contemporaries of the Deuteronomist (as Jeremiah and perhaps Huldah) and those of the earlier national figures such as Moses, Joshua, David, and Solomon. The latter are undoubtedly fictional throughout, whereas the former may contain the original nucleus of what was said.

historians, the essential difference lying only in the thematic character of the orations. The Greek historians wrote political histories, hence the orations relate to the political aspects of the narrative, whereas the Judean historians wrote religious history and the orations consequently centre on religious, not political matters.

The Greek and Israelite orations also differ in that the former harmonize with the contexts in which they occur and are consequently of a variegated sort, whereas the latter, though they occur in varying contexts, are nevertheless of a stereotyped kind. This difference is also due to the religious tendentiousness of Judean historians, who in an effort to convey their religious ideology by indoctrination, incorporated their ideological beliefs into each and every oration.

The orations *as they have come down to us in Deuteronomy*, are undoubtedly the product of speculative thought and do not derive from cultic reality. Such complex and speculative oratory was not delivered orally before being committed to writing and the speeches, if ever delivered in public, were as recitations from a written text—as Josiah's from the discovered book (2 Kgs. 23: 1–3). Indeed, the orations in Deuteronomy are delivered in clear consciousness of the fact that they had already been written down before delivery (Deut. 28: 58; 29: 19–20 and 26).[1] It was only after they were set down in writing and incorporated in the literary frame called 'the Book of the Torah' that they were entrusted to the charge of *the priests the Levites*, 'the guardians of the Law' (Deut. 31: 9). This specific function of *the priests the Levites* is mentioned only in Deuteronomy and always in reference to a written and fixed Torah (Deut. 17: 18; 31: 9 and 26). The book of the Law then was *entrusted* to the Levitical priests but it did not *originate* with them. The book of Deuteronomy, which frequently refers to the writing of the Torah, does not so much as once associate the Levitical priests with the writing of it. Moses writes the Torah and entrusts it to the Levitical priests (31: 9). The king writes a copy of the book of Deuteronomy (presumably by means of his scribes) 'from that which is in charge of the Levitical priests' (17: 18), but they themselves do not act as writers or copyists. In chapter 27 Moses, not the Levites, is commanded to inscribe the

[1] See Driver, *Deuteronomy*, p. 316: 'The expression ["this book"] betrays the fact that from the first Deuteronomy was a *written* book.'

Torah on stones; the Levites are present but act only as the administrators of the oath. We cannot, therefore, agree with Bentzen[1] and von Rad[2] who assert that the deuteronomic orations have their origin in Levitical discourses and sermons. The Levites 'who taught the people' in the days of Ezra (Neh. 8; 2 Chron. 17: 7–9), a function which von Rad attributes to them in pre-exilic times as well,[3] are in fact functioning within the framework of a new institution which owes its concept to the author of Chronicles. It was he who invested the Levites with the robes of the teacher-priests in keeping with his purpose of glorifying the Levites at the expense of the priests.[4] It is indeed surprising that though von Rad himself states in another connection that 'the central concern of the Chronist is the position of the Levites in the organization of post-exilic Israel'[5] he nevertheless does not hesitate to identify these Levites—whose didactic and exhortative functions are alluded to only by the Chronicler—as the circle from which the book of Deuteronomy originated. As a matter of fact, in the pre-exilic period it was the priests who functioned as teachers of the people; it was of them that people inquired of the divine word; it was they who instructed the people in matters regarding the sacred and the profane, the ritually clean and unclean, and so forth. The priests, then, were the guardians and teachers of the oral law in the pre-exilic period, whereas the Levites became the interpreters and teachers of the written law only in the post-exilic period and were, moreover, assisted in this task by Israelites who of course had no sacral status (Neh. 8: 4 and 7; 2 Chron. 17: 7).[6]

[1] A. Bentzen, *Die Josianische Reform und ihre Voraussetzungen* 1926, pp. 95 ff.

[2] *Studies in Deuteronomy*, pp. 66 f.

[3] G. E. Wright contends that according to Deuteronomy there were Levites whose sole function was to give instructions in the Torah ('The Levites in Deuteronomy', *VT* 4 (1954), pp. 325–30). But J. A. Emerton ('Priests and Levites in Deuteronomy', *VT* 12 (1962), 129–38) rightly argues that Deuteronomy recognizes the right of all Levites to participate in the cult and that there is no evidence in Deuteronomy indicating that the role of some Levites was confined to instruction.

[4] Cf., e.g., 2 Chr. 29: 34; 30: 3, 17, 22, etc. See W. Rudolph, *Chronikbücher*, HAT 1955, pp. xv–xvi.

[5] *Das Geschichtsbild des Chronistischen Werkes*, 1930, p. 119.

[6] Rudolph (*Chronikbücher*, pp. 250–1) argues that 2 Chr. 17: 8 (in which Levites appear as instructors of the Torah) is unauthentic and that it is the Chronicler's retrojection of circumstances true of his own period. His thesis seems convincing in view of the fact that the names enumerated in v. 8 are typical of the later period while those in vv. 7 and 9 are typical of earlier periods.

The whole theory about the Levites standing behind Deuteronomy can be refuted on other grounds. First of all, it is inconceivable that the Levites, who were deprived of their office through the centralization of the cult and as a result of which are considered in Deuteronomy as a part of the *personae miserabiles*,[1] could be identified with the circle which stands behind Deuteronomy. The Levites, as composers of Deuteronomy, would be comparable to one cutting off the branch upon which he sits. Von Rad saw this difficulty[2] but tried to do away with it by arguing that the demand for centralization in Deuteronomy rested upon a very narrow basis and could be considered a late stratum in the book. Such an answer seems hardly satisfactory; after all, centralization serves as the guiding principle for chs. 12–19, the nucleus of the code, and therefore cannot be simply discounted.[3]

Secondly, Deuteronomy, as is well known, combines material of cultic with national and political institutions: similarly the deuteronomic work comprises a vast body of literary material, including historical memoirs, popular narratives, historical annals, chronicles, administrative lists, etc. Are we to suppose, then, that so insignificant a provincial class as the Levites could possibly have preserved or have at its disposal such a rich variety of material?[4] In order to solve this problem, and to explain the strange combination of cultic and national-political institutions which we find in Deuteronomy, von Rad[5] assumes a connection between the Levites and the עם הארץ, which constituted the national military

[1] Deuteronomy is the only book which adds the Levite to the *personae miserabiles* known from the Tetrateuch: the poor (עני), the resident alien (גר), the orphan, and the widow. (Cf. Exod. 22: 20–4; 23: 9; Lev. 19: 10; 23: 22.) The rise of this new social stratum in Deuteronomy comes without doubt as a result of the abolition of the provincial cult rites. The Levite existed side by side with the priest (כהן) from very old times, but he became destitute only after the reform.

[2] *Studies in Deuteronomy*, p. 67.

[3] The laws about sacrifices, tithes, firstlings, holidays, and the cities of refuge, incorporated in this collection, are based on the principle of centralization and reflect clearly the change these institutions underwent following the reform, see below, pp. 213 ff.

[4] A. Bentzen (*Jos. Reform*, pp. 95 ff.) regarded the Levites as the authors of all deuteronomic literature, whereas von Rad does not allude to the role of the Levites in the composition of deuteronomic historiography. His failure to investigate the question of the Deuteronomist's identity is strange, as the Levites, in his opinion, functioned as instructors from pre-exilic days until the restoration; therefore, it would be natural for him to regard them as playing an influential role in all deuteronomic literature.

[5] *Studies in Deuteronomy*, pp. 60 ff.

movement in Judah.[1] But this supposition is necessary only if we take for granted that the Levites were the composers of Deuteronomy. If we reject this hypothesis would it not be more reasonable to see in the composers of Deuteronomy a neutral circle which has access to different types of literary material rather than a provincial circle whose access to various literary sources is limited?

Von Rad himself has justifiably observed that only persons holding public office could have had such a wide range of literary material at their command.[2] Why, then, do only the Levites qualify for this public office? Again, it is von Rad who maintains that we know less concerning the functions and the history of the Levites today than we ever did.[3] Indeed, except for what is told of them in Chronicles (admittedly an especially unreliable source in matters concerning the cult and cultic classes) we know nothing of the Levites as teachers and instructors of law in the pre-exilic period.[4]

As a matter of fact, one can trace the history of the birth of von Rad's theory about the Levites. In 1934, analysing the sermons in the book of Chronicles,[5] he came to the conclusion that these sermons reflect the instruction of the Levites of the post-exilic period who built their sermons on quotations from ancient authoritative texts. Asking himself about the 'situation in life' of the Levite sermon style, he said that it would be conceivable that the Levites who had been deprived of office through the centralization of the cult found a new sphere of activity in religious instruction.[6] This means, then, that the Levite sermon is the outcome of the reform while, in his *Deuteronomium Studien* (1947) he considers the Levites a religious order from old times, responsible for the composition of Deuteronomy. This change of attitude was caused apparently by von Rad's discovery, in the meantime, i.e. in 1938, of the covenantal structure of Deuteronomy.

Struck by the peculiar structure of the book of Deuteronomy: homily, laws, sealing of covenant, blessings and curses, von Rad

[1] See especially E. Würthwein, *Der 'am ha'areṣ im A.T.*, 1936, see also below, pp. 88 f.

[2] *Theologie*, 80.

[3] Ibid., p. 79 n. 5.

[4] See Noth's review of von Rad's *Deuteronomium Studien*, in *ThLZ* 75 (1948), cols. 537 ff.

[5] See 'The Levitical sermon in I and II Chronicles', in *The Problem of the Hexateuch*, 1966, pp. 267–80.

[6] Ibid., p. 279.

rightly observed[1] that such a strange combination of different literary genres could hardly be invented. He assumed therefore that the complex literary structure must have been rooted in a cultic ceremony in which God's laws were recited by clergy. Traces of an old cultic ceremony could indeed be found in Deut. 27, and in Josh. 24, traditions connected with Shechem. According to von Rad, Deuteronomy renews the cultic tradition of the old Shechem amphictyony, a theory which accords with the prevalent opinion about the affinities of Deuteronomy to northern traditions.[2] As a matter of fact, already in the nineteenth century A. Klostermann[3] had conjectured that the homiletic style of Deuteronomy reflects a public recital, but he could not yet, of course, base his thesis on form-critical observations, as did von Rad, and therefore did not connect it with the cult.

Now, if Deuteronomy really reflects a cultic ceremony, it is reasonable to suppose that the clerics who took part in the ceremony were responsible for the composition of the book.

But the whole problem was changed when attention was drawn to the structure of the treaties in the ancient Near East. Investigation of the structure of the political treaties current in the ancient East during the latter half of the second and the first half of the first millennium B.C. has shown that the combination of elements encountered in the covenant of the plains of Moab was already to be found in such treaties. There was consequently no need for the authors of Deuteronomy to search about for the various literary genres and combine them in order to create the type of composition that they had in mind—a point von Rad wonders about—since they could already find them combined in the treaty forms of the surrounding area. There is reason to suppose, then, in view of the strong resemblance that exists between the covenant in the book of Deuteronomy and the political treaties prevalent in the surrounding area, that the structure of the covenant in the book of Deuteronomy is a literary imitation and not the reflection of a cultic ceremony which is still unattested. And if it is unnecessary to assume a cultic ceremony for understanding the structure of Deuteronomy, then the assumption that the Levites preserved this

1 'The form-critical problem of the Hexateuch', *The Problem of the Hexateuch*, pp. 26–40.

2 See, e.g., A. Alt, 'Die Heimat des Deuteronomiums', *KS* II, 250–75.

3 *Der Pentateuch*, NF 1907, pp. 154 ff.

cultic tradition becomes dubious too, for if a literary pattern lies behind the form of Deuteronomy, then it would be much more reasonable to assume that a literary circle which was familiar with treaty writing composed the book of Deuteronomy. The next chapter will, therefore, be devoted to the clarification of this aspect of deuteronomic composition.

II

TREATY FORM AND PHRASEOLOGY—AFFINITIES WITH THE ANCIENT NEAR EASTERN TREATY FORMULAE

I. THE COVENANT OF THE PLAINS OF MOAB

(*a*) *Structure*

G. E. MENDENHALL[1] was the first to draw attention to the resemblance between the pattern of the Israelite covenant and that of ancient Near Eastern treaties, particularly the Hittite vassal-treaties. As the Hittite treaties date from the fourteenth and thirteenth centuries B.C.—the period in which the Israelite tribes began to settle in Canaan—Mendenhall arrived at certain conclusions with respect to the Sinai and Shechem covenants (Exod. 19–24) which also relate to this period. He did not, however, investigate whether a similar resemblance might exist between the structure of the Hittite treaties and that of the Covenant of the Plains of Moab. Since he assumed that the classical structure of state treaties (in the form that had solidified in the Hittite kingdom) obtained only in the latter part of the second millennium B.C.[2] and as the book of Deuteronomy was composed in the following millennium when—as he believed—the original treaty structure was no longer known,[3] he concluded that it could not possibly reflect the original treaty pattern. He seems, however, to have disregarded the state treaties dating from the ninth to the seventh centuries B.C.[4] which clearly show that similar treaty forms were also prevalent in the first millennium, perhaps because of their very

[1] G. E. Mendenhall, 'Covenant Forms in Israelite Tradition', *BA* 17 (1954), 50 ff.; cf. K. Baltzer, *Das Bundesformular*, 1960. More recent treatments are D. J. McCarthy, *Treaty and Covenant*, Analecta Biblica 21, 1963 and D. R. Hillers, *Treaty Curses and the O.T. Prophets*, Biblica et Orientalia 16, 1964.

[2] Mendenhall, 'Covenant', pp. 56–7.

[3] Cf. his remarks, ibid.: 'Even in Israel, the writer submits that the older form of covenant was no longer widely known after the united monarchy'!

[4] (*a*) The Aramean treaty between Bir-Ga'yah King of KTK and Matîʿel of Arpad (A. Dupont-Sommer, *Les Inscriptions araméennes de Sfiré*, 1958; J. A. Fitzmyer, *The Aramaic Inscriptions of Sefîre*, Biblica et Orientalia 19, 1967). (*b*) The treaty of Aššurnirāri V (754–745 B.C.) of Assyria with the Mati'ilu

fragmentary condition he did not regard them as being on the same level with the Hittite treaties. But his conclusions have been seriously undermined by the discovery of a group of treaties made between Esarhaddon and his eastern vassals in 672 B.C.[1] which were found some two years after the publication of his article. On the basis of these treaties, which are identically formulated, D. J. Wiseman published a restored version of the treaty made with Ramataia the Median,[2] the longest treaty text thus far discovered, justifiably concluding that there was a continuity of tradition in the formulation of state treaties in Mesopotamia and Asia Minor, and that this traditional formulation remained substantially unchanged from the time of the Hittite Empire down through the neo-Assyrian period.[3]

There is no justification, then, for regarding the formulation of the Hittite treaties as being unique, nor is there any basis for Mendenhall's supposition that only Hittite treaties served as the model and archetype of the Biblical covenant. The pattern of the Hittite state treaties is, without doubt, reflected in the covenant forms of the early biblical sources (Ex. 19–24; Jos. 24), but the discovery of state treaties formulated in the traditional pattern and dating from the same period of Deuteronomy militates against the view that the author of Deuteronomy has imitated ancient treaty forms. It is more likely, as will become apparent later on, that the author of Deuteronomy formulated the Covenant of the Plains of Moab on the pattern of political treaties current in his own time which propagated the tradition of the Hittite treaty. Furthermore, it is in Deuteronomy rather than Exodus or Joshua that the original pattern

of Bit-Agusi (E. Weidner, *AfO* 8 (1932–3), 17 ff.). (*c*) The treaty of Šamši-Adad V the Assyrian (823–811 B.C.) with the Babylonian Marduk-zākir-šumi I (cf. E. Weidner, ibid., pp. 27–9). (*d*) Esarhaddon's (680–669 B.C.) treaty with Baal of Tyre (R. Borger, *Die Inschriften Asarhaddons*, 1956, pp. 107–9).

[1] M. A. Mallowan, 'Excavations of Nimrud (Kalḫu) 1955', *Iraq* 18 (1956), 12–14.

[2] 'The Vassal-Treaties of Esarhaddon', *Iraq* 20 (1958), 1–100, hereafter also quoted as *VTE*.

[3] Ibid., p. 28. J. M. Munn-Rankin ('Diplomacy in Western Asia in the Early Second Millenium B.C.', *Iraq* 18 (1956), 68–110) is of the opinion that the tradition goes back to the eighteenth century B.C. McCarthy would date it as early as the third millennium and sees a fundamental unity in the treaty forms from the third to the first millennium B.C.: 'In spite of variations in different times and places, variations even of some importance, there is a fundamental unity in the treaties. And this unity goes back beyond the Hittite examples unto the third millennium' (*Treaty and Covenant*, p. 80), and see below, pp. 73–4.

has been preserved. The major sections of the Hittite state treaties, such as the preamble, the historical prologue, the stipulation of undivided allegiance,[1] the clauses of the treaty, the invocation of witnesses, the blessings and curses, together with other features which appear in the Hittite treaty, such as the oath-imprecation, the deposit of the treaty, and its periodic reading, are all found in the book of Deuteronomy, whereas many of them are lacking in Exod. 19–24 and in Josh. 24. Let us briefly consider some of these sections, especially those missing in Exodus and Joshua.

1. *The curses and blessings*

The curses and blessings constitute the sanctioning paragraph of all ancient Near Eastern treaties. It is by their means, and particularly through the curses,[2] whose efficacy is guaranteed by the gods, that the provisions of the treaty are supposedly ensured. Sanctions of this kind were included not only in treaty texts but in all types of official legal settlements: judicial arrangements in connection with border conflicts,[3] grants and land transactions,[4] the imposition of a system of laws upon the people,[5] imposing an oath in connection with succession,[6] and assuring the loyalty of officials,[7] soldiers,[8]

[1] The paragraph is so designated by K. Baltzer (*Bundesformular*, pp. 22–3). As opposed to McCarthy (*Treaty and Covenant*, p. 32) I believe there are grounds for distinguishing between the general demand for allegiance and the specific detailed demands which, in effect, constitute the stipulations of the treaty. Instead of this paragraph, V. Korošec (*Hethitische Staatsverträge*, 1931) and Mendenhall cite the paragraph pertaining to the deposit and the reading of the treaty. This section, however, relates to the manner of the treaty's presentation and its technical implementation, but does not constitute a part of the treaty itself. I therefore find Baltzer's classification of the treaty paragraphs more acceptable.

[2] Cf. M. Noth, 'For All Who Rely On Works of the Law are under a Curse', *The Laws in the Pentateuch*, etc., 118 ff.

[3] Cf. especially the Stele of the Vultures (F. Thureau-Dangin, *Die Sumerischen und akkadischen Königsinschriften* [hereafter *SAKI*], pp. 10 f., for partial recent translation see S. N. Kramer, *The Sumerians*, 1963, pp. 310 f.), the cones of Entemena of Lagash (*SAKI*, pp. 36 ff., S. N. Kramer, op. cit., pp. 313 f.).

[4] Cf. the Mesopotamian boundary (*kudurru*) stones in L. W. King, *Babylonian Boundary Stones* (hereafter quoted as *BBSt*), 1912; see also F. X. Steinmetzer, *Die babylonischen Kudurru als Urkundenform*, 1922.

[5] See especially the epilogues of the Hammurabi and the Lipit-Ishtar codes.

[6] The main purpose of the vassal treaties of Esarhaddon is to assure fidelity to Ashurbanipal, Esarhaddon's successor. Cf. also the oath of fealty to Ashurbanipal (L. Waterman, *Royal Correspondence of the Assyrian Empire* (hereafter quoted as *RCAE*), 1930–1, no. 1105, 1239).

[7] Cf. Einar von Schuler, *Hethitische Dienstanweisungen*, 1957, see also A. Goetze, *ANET*², pp. 207 f.

[8] Cf. J. Friedrich, *ZA*, NF 1 (1924), 161–92; A Goetze, *ANET*², pp. 353 f.

and craftsmen.[1] In the epilogue of the book of Deuteronomy we do in fact find an elaborate and detailed formulation of curses and blessings (ch. 28) which, in both structure and content,[2] correspond to those met with in Mesopotamian texts, but which are, on the other hand, entirely lacking in the covenant in the book of Exodus and in Josh. 24.[3]

2. *The witnesses of the covenant*

In Hittite, Aramaic, and Neo-Assyrian treaties the gods and other mighty forces of nature such as Heaven and Earth are invoked as witnesses and serve as guarantors that punishment will be executed should the treaty be violated. In the Biblical covenant, on the other hand, the Deity could not be called upon as a witness, inasmuch as he constituted a party to the covenant, and so only the forces of nature could be invoked for this purpose. (Heaven and Earth, for instance, in Deut. 4: 26; 30: 19; 31: 28.)[4] We find no such invocation of cosmic witnesses, however, in the books of Exodus and Joshua. In Josh. 24 the Israelites serve as their own witnesses, i.e. they are to testify against themselves should they violate the covenant,[5] and the great stone which Joshua had erected in the Shechem sanctuary[6] is to act as a second witness.

3. *The oath-imprecation*

The oath sworn at the scene of the covenant gave it binding validity. This oath included a conditional imprecation: if the party swearing fails to observe the treaty then may the curses and all their terrors befall him.[7] Now it is only in the deuteronomic

[1] See D. B. Weisberg, *Guild Structure and Political Allegiance in Early Achaemenid Mesopotamia*, 1967.

[2] See below, pp. 116 ff.

[3] Exod. 23: 20–33 is not a blessing but a promise made with regard to the inheritance of the land (see above pp. 46–7 f.). The passage, furthermore, makes no mention whatever of a curse; nor is Josh. 24: 20 a malediction. For discussion see McCarthy, *Treaty and Covenant*, pp. 152 ff.

[4] See M. Delcor, 'Les attaches littéraires, l'origine et la signification de l'expression biblique "Prendre à témoin le ciel et la terre"', *VT* 16 [1966], 8–25.

[5] See Baltzer, *Bundesformular*, p. 35.

[6] On the Shechem sanctuary in early biblical tradition, see G. E. Wright, *Shechem*, 1965, pp. 123 ff.

[7] See V. Korošec, *Staatsverträge*, p. 97 and J. M. Price, *The Oath in Court Procedure in Early Babylonia and the Old Testament*, p. 23. (For a recent discussion of the term אלה and its connection with שבועה and ברית, see H. C. Brichto, *Curse*, 1963, pp. 25 ff.). In his opinion the original meaning of the word אלה is

covenant that we meet with a sworn imprecation (אלה) of this sort (29: 9–28). Though the covenant of Sinai in Exod. 19 (v. 8) and 24 (v. 7) and that of Shechem in Josh. 24 (v. 24) have the obligation to heed and observe the terms of the covenant, no mention whatever is made of a *sworn* imprecation of the type that we would expect to find accompanied by curses and blessings. The covenant in Exod. 24 (vv. 4–8) and Josh. 24 (cf. Deut. 27: 5–7 = E, see below) receives its binding validity not from a sworn imprecation but through ritual ceremony (cf. Ps. 50: 5), i.e. building an altar, erecting stone pillars, sacrificing, and in Exod. 24 also sprinkling the sacrificial blood upon the altar and the people. The deuteronomic covenant, on the other hand, and the Hittite and Assyrian state treaties receive their validity by virtue of the oath-imprecation (the Akkadian *māmītu*) and not by ritual ceremony.[1]

4. *The deposit of the treaty text*

Treaty texts in the ancient Near East were customarily deposited in sanctuaries, at the feet of the gods.[2] Again, it is not in Exod. 24 nor in Josh. 24, but in Deuteronomy that we meet with this practice. There the ark is regarded as the receptacle of the tablets of covenant[3] (לחות הברית)[4] and the book of the Torah (= the book of the covenant) is to be placed at its side to serve as a witness against the children of Israel (31: 26).

5. *The copies*[5]

In addition to the original sealed duplicates which were

'curse' and the construction ברית ואלה in Deut. 29: 11 and 13, etc., is a hendiadys which denotes a treaty that includes, or is based on, a curse. The Akkadian expression *adê māmīt* which is equivalent to the Hebrew אלות ברית (see below) is also a hendiadys which means 'pact adjuration'. See E. A. Speiser, 'An Angelic Curse', Ex. 19: 20', *JAOS* 80 (1960), p. 198 n. 1.

[1] See below, pp. 102 f.

[2] See V. Korošec, *Staatsverträge*, 100; N. H. Tur-Sinai, *The Language and the Book*, III, 60–1 (Hebrew).

[3] In the previous sources the role of the ark is mainly that of the throne and footstool of the Deity (see M. Haran, 'The Ark and the Cherubim', *IEJ* 9 [1959], 30–8 and 89–94) whereas in Deuteronomy the only function of the ark is that of a receptacle for the covenant, see below, pp. 208 f.

[4] Deut. 9: 9–10; 10: 1–5.

[5] There is also a possibility that Deuteronomy preserved in its structure the notion of the duplicate. We learn from Hittite treaties that treaty texts were generally written in duplicate, one for each of the parties of the treaty, and that each party deposited its copy in its respective sanctuary. (See E. Weidner,

deposited in the respective sanctuaries of the two parties to the covenant,[1] it was customary to prepare unsealed copies for state use.[2] Reference to the making of such additional treaty copies is also found in Deuteronomy. According to Deut. 17: 18, the king is commanded to write '*a copy of the law* from that which is in charge of the Levitical priests'. In other words, he was to have a copy made of the original covenant document which lay at the side of the ark and was delivered to the safe-keeping of the Levitical priests (Deut. 31: 9).

6. *The periodic reading of the treaty*

This stipulation, which occurs in the Hittite treaties,[3] is again found only in Deuteronomy (31: 9–13; see 17: 19). Like the Hittite treaties, the deuteronomic law specifies that the Book of the

Politische Dokumente aus Kleinasien, BoSt, 8–9 (1923): the treaty between Šuppiluliuma and Mattiwaza (no. 1) Rs. ll. 35 ff.; the treaty between Mattiwaza and Šuppiluliuma (no. 2) Rs. l. 7. In the following discussion the Hittite treaties in Akkadian published by Weidner and those in Hittite published by J. Friedrich, *Staatsverträge des Hatti Reiches* will be referred to according to the numerical listing given them there, e.g., W(eidner) 1, W2, etc., or F(riedrich) 1, F2, etc. The treaties numbered 1–3 by Friedrich were published in *MVÄG* 31 (1926) and treaties 4–6 in *MVÄG* 34 (1930).) It seems to us that there is a reference to this practice in Deut. 29: 28—the passage which closes the section dealing with the covenant and oath-imprecation (see below, pp. 100 ff.). The verse reads: 'The secret *one* belongs to the Lord our God, but the revealed *one* (read *hanisteret* and *haniglēt* respectively) belongs to us and our children forever that we may all do the words of this law.' G. Grimme (*OLZ* 10 (1907), 612 f.) took the obscure verse to refer to the long-concealed Book of the Torah which was discovered in the days of Josiah. Tur-Sinai (*Language and Book*, III, 59 ff.) argues more cogently, however, that the verse refers to the two copies of the covenant, i.e. one open and one sealed, which were made in conformance with the custom prevailing in the Ancient East of preserving purchase deeds in open and sealed copies (cf. Jer. 32: 14). Be this as it may with respect to purchase deeds, however, there is no reference to the preservation of treaty documents in this twofold manner. It is more likely, therefore, that the verse refers to the duplicate copies of the covenant, each of which was to be retained by the respective parties according to the practice referred to in the Hittite treaties. Since the Deity who dwells in secret abode is in this case one of the parties of the covenant, his copy of the covenant would consequently be hidden and concealed from us; the copy possessed by Israel, on the other hand, is open and revealed and intended 'for us and our children'.

[1] Korošec, *Staatsverträge*, pp. 16 f.

[2] The Hittite tablets that have come down to us are, in Korošec's opinion, copies from the royal archives, ibid., p. 3.

[3] W1, Rs. 36–7: '*always and constantly* let them recite it before the king of Mittani' (this reminds us of the commandment in Deut. 17: 19: 'and let him (= the king) read in it *all the days of his life*') 'and before the men of the land of Ḫurri'. Compare F5, § 19: 73–5; 'let this tablet be recited before you three times a year'.

Covenant is to be read periodically in the presence of the leader[1] and his subjects so that they may know and observe it.[2] The Deuteronomist even recounts the execution of this ordinance. During the ceremony of the blessings and curses on Mt. Ebal (Josh. 8: 30–5) Joshua reads 'all the words of the law . . . according to all that is written in the book of the law' (v. 34), and obeying the command of Moses his master he reads the law 'before all the assembly of Israel, and the women, and the little ones' (v. 35; cf. Deut. 31: 12). Josiah also reads—according to the Deuteronomist —(2 Kgs. 23) the 'Book of the Covenant' before all the people small and great (vv. 2–3).

7. *The stipulations*

(1) The conditions of the treaty which are the essential part of every contract are elaborately treated in the book of Deuteronomy (chs. 12–26), but are entirely lacking in Josh. 24. (2) In the Assyrian treaties the clauses or stipulations of the treaty are termed *adê* and in the Aramaic treaty of Sefire עדיא, עדן, words (always in the plural) which both etymologically and in meaning are the counterparts of the term עֵדוֹת employed in Deuteronomy[3] and in deuteronomic literature.

The structure of the state treaty prevalent among the peoples of the ancient Near East has, therefore, been preserved in its original form in Deuteronomy and not in the Biblical sources antedating it.

[1] The instructions 'assemble the people', 'you shall read this law . . . in their hearing' pertain to Joshua who is here deemed to be the successor of Moses, and are not directed to the priests and elders mentioned in v. 9. The ordinance regarding the reading of the Torah, in fact, follows Moses' address to Joshua (vv. 7–8), but the editor was compelled to introduce the detail concerning the writing of the Torah before Moses could command Joshua regarding its recitation. Verses 11–12 are indeed addressed in the singular: 'to appear before the Lord *thy* God (אלהיך)', '*thou* shalt read (תקרא) this law', 'assemble (הקהל) the people'. Because of the interpolation of v. 9 original אותו was turned into אותם, (v. 10) For these verses compare also E. Nielsen, *Shechem*, 1959, p. 49.

[2] Compare Deut. 31: 12–13 with F3, § 30: 3 which also deals with the reciting of the treaty (cf. also F5, § 19: 75, and see above, p. 64, n. 3). 'They will observe to do all the words of this Torah' (ושמרו לעשות את כל דברי התורה הזאת) in Deut. 31: 12 is paralleled by AWĀTE^MEŠ *paḫši* = 'observe the words' in F3, § 30: 3 (*paḫš*- = Akkadian *naṣāru* = Hebrew שמר).

[3] See Wiseman *VTE*, p. 81 (note) and J. Fitzmyer, *Sefîre*, pp. 23–4. The priestly term '*edût*, though etymologically and functionally identical with *adê* and עדיא (compare ארון/לוחות העדת with ארון/לוחות הברית and cf. B. Volkwein, *Bibl. Zeitschrift* 13 (1969), 18–40) is never formed in plural, nor is it synonymous with 'laws' חוקים, 'judgements' משפטים, etc., as in deuteronomic literature.

It is only in Deuteronomy[1] that we encounter all the elements which characterize the Hittite and Assyrian treaties—a fact which, as we shall demonstrate below, is highly revealing with respect to the nature and manner of the book's composition. We may perhaps demonstrate this more concretely by listing the covenant features in Deuteronomy and in other Biblical sources side by side:

	Exod. 19–24	*Josh.* 24	*Deut.*
Preamble	19: 3b; 20: 2a	2aα	1: 1–6a; 5: 6a
Historical prologue	19: 4; 20: 2b	2–13	1: 6b–3: 29; 5; 9: 7–10: 11
The basic stipulation of allegiance	19: 5–6a; 20: 3–5a	14	4: 1–23; 6: 4–7: 26; 10: 12–22
Covenant clauses	21–3; 20: 7–17	..	12–26
Invocation of witnesses	..	..	4: 26; 30: 19; 31: 28
Blessings and curses	..	..	28
The oath-imprecation	..	..	29: 9–28
The deposit	..	..	10: 1–5; 31: 24–6
The periodic reading	..	..	31: 9–13
Duplicates and copies	..	..	17: 18–19; 31: 25–6

The table clearly shows that only Deuteronomy has preserved the classic structure of the political treaty. It is, moreover, interesting to note that it is particularly those formal elements which alone give the treaty its binding judicial validity—the blessings and curses, the invocation of witnesses, the oath-imprecation, the deposit, the periodic readings, the duplicates and copies—that are completely lacking in the covenants in Exodus and Josh. 24.

V. Korošec[2] has pointed out that the Hittite and Mesopotamian[3] treaty consisted of two major sections: (1) The *riksu* which comprises the demands and stipulations which the overlord presents to his vassal (or ally in a parity treaty). (2) *The māmītu* which comprises the vassal's (or ally's) acceptance of the stipulations and obligations of the treaty clauses.

[1] The entire book, comprising all its strata, is the work of a group who had a common working method. Typologically speaking, therefore, it is immaterial whether the text occurs in an earlier or later strand of the book.

[2] *Staatsverträge*, pp. 26 ff., 34 ff.

[3] The *riksu* and the *māmītu* are both found already in the 'Babyl. Synchronistic History', see E. Schrader, *KB* I, 194 (Kol. i: 3–4).

It is the latter, or *māmītu*, section which gives the treaty its binding validity, for the rejection of the *māmītu* on the part of the vassal or ally would, perforce, deprive the treaty of any validity. The author of Deuteronomy, who was apparently familiar with the structure of political treaties,[1] has here supplied the formal validating part of the covenant lacking in the earlier sources: what is new in the deuteronomic formulation of the covenant is the addition of the *māmītu* part to the covenant elements already encountered in the earlier Biblical sources. The 'Book of the Torah', on which the Covenant of the Plains of Moab centres, is actually 'a (book of the) covenant and oath-imprecation', ברית ואלה (Deut. 29: 11, 13, 20), as are the Mesopotamian and Hittite state treaties, which in Akkadian were designated by the term *ṭuppu ša rikilti* (or *riksi*) *u ša māmīti* during the second millennium,[2] and (*ṭuppu*) *adê māmīti* or *adê tāmīti* during the first millennium.[3]

Although all the elements of the deuteronomic covenant are found in the Hittite treaty, one element at least points to the later neo-Assyrian and Aramean treaty pattern. The Hittite treaty has very short and generalized curse formulae, while Deuteronomy like the Assyrian treaties and the Sefire steles contains a series of elaborate curses.[4] On the other hand, we must admit that Deuteronomy includes the 'historical prologue' which is not found in the treaties of the first millennium. However, this can hardly prove that Deuteronomy belongs to a pattern which differs from that of the Assyrio-Aramean treaty type. First of all, the lack of the historical prologue in the Assyrio-Aramean treaties may be simply due to a gap in our documentary evidence. Of the five treaties preserved from the first millenium, three (Šamši-Adad V with Marduk-zākir-šumi I, Aššurnirāri V with Mati'ilu of Bīt Agusi, and Esarhaddon with Baal of Tyre) have been mutilated at the beginning just where the historical prologue ought to be.[5] In the fourth text, the Esarhaddon vassal treaty, since it is concerned with

[1] See below, pp. 116 ff.

[2] W2, Rs. 63; W9, Vs. 24.

[3] See J. J. Gelb, *BO* 19 (1962) 161 for references. Gelb contends that the expression *riksu u māmītu* denotes a parity or vassal treaty whereas *adê māmīte* only denotes the oath of allegiance sworn by the vassal.

[4] See McCarthy, *Treaty and Covenant*, pp. 98 f.

[5] E. Weidner (*AfO* 8, p. 17) suggests that the big gap at the beginning of Aššurnirāri's treaty may be filled up by some of the unpublished historical fragments in the British Museum. It is, then, not impossible that this treaty had a historical introduction.

succession, an introduction surveying the previous relations between the sovereign and the vassal would have been out of place. The fifth treaty, the Sefire steles, cannot be of much help for two reasons: (1) it reflects provincial political arrangements whose background and character are unknown to us;[1] (2) the order of the texts is uncertain.[2] It is difficult, therefore, to reach conclusions concerning structure from such problematic documents. On the other hand, in a recently published fragment of a neo-Assyrian treaty there does seem to have been a remnant of a historical prologue.[3]

Secondly, from the neo-Assyrian royal grants we learn that the Assyrian kings availed themselves of the literary pattern called 'historical prologue' and used in its framework the same phraseology which they used in the treaties.[4] If then, we do not find the historical prologue in the treaties, the reason is not that it was unknown to the Assyrians but, more likely, a matter of principle. As Professor A. Goetze has suggested,[5] the Assyrian emperor who saw himself as king of the world seems to have felt that it would have been both unnecessary and humiliating to justify his demand for loyalty by referring to his gracious acts on behalf of the vassal in the manner of the Hittite kings. This assumption may also explain the lack of blessings in the Assyrian treaty.[6] The Hittites felt it necessary not only to justify their demands for loyalty but also to give promises of help in time of danger, as well as to bestow divine blessings for loyal service. The Assyrians neither gave promises to the vassal nor bestowed blessings but, on the contrary, increased and expanded the list of threats and curses in order to terrorize him.

The arrogance of the Assyrian king may also explain the lack of

[1] e.g. whether the treaty between Matî'el and Bir-Ga'yah preceded or followed that of Mati'ilu with Aššurnirāri V (754 B.C.); whether the Sefire treaty represents a vassal treaty or, as M. Noth argues (*ZDPV* 77 (1961), 138–45), a parity treaty.

[2] See J. Fitzmeyer, *Sefîre*, pp. 2–3.

[3] Cf. A. F. Campbell, *Biblica* 50 (1969), 534–5.

[4] Cf., e.g. J. Kohler–A. Ungnad, *Assyrische Rechtsurkunden*, 1913 (hereafter quoted as *ARu*), no. 15, 16, 18, 20, 21, see below, pp. 75 f. Compare especially: *iṣṣuru maṣṣarti šarrūtiya* (*ARu* 15: 17, 16: 17, 18: 20, 20: 9) with *u maṣ[ṣartu ša] ipqidu ninaṣṣaru* in the oath of the Assyrian officials to Assurbanipal (Waterman, *RCAE* no. 1105: 11–12); *ša libbašu gummuru ana bēlišu* (*ARu* 15: 13, 16: 13, 18: 16) with the Esarhaddon treaties (*VTE*) ll. 53, 169, 310. In *ARu* 20: 11 there is explicit reference to a treaty.

[5] In a private conversation.

[6] In the Sefire treaties there are some short blessing formulae, I, C: 15–16, II, B: 4.

any sign of affection from the sovereign to his vassal. In the Hittite treaties and in the Israelite covenant, along with the demand for love and loyalty on the part of the vassal come expressions of affection from the side of the sovereign.[1] The Assyrians, however, demand scrupulous love and loyalty from their vassals (see below, p. 81), but no sign of affection from their side is indicated anywhere.

The formal resemblance between Deuteronomy and Mesopotamian and Hittite state treaties finds expression not only in the structure of the treaty but also in its detail and formulation. We may take the historical prologue as an example.

The prologue in the book of Deuteronomy, in both its versions (1: 1–4: 40; 4: 45–11: 32), recalls to a great extent the historical prologue met with in state treaties. This section of the Hittite treaties recounts the political relationship between the ancestors of the vassals and the kings of the land of Hatti. It is in this context that the promise made to the ancestors of the vassal is mentioned. Muršiliš II tells Duppi-Tešup of Amurru:[2] 'When your father died, in accordance with your father's word, I did not drop you. Since your father had mentioned to me your name . . . I have sought after you. To be sure, you were sick and ailing, but although you were ailing, I . . . put you in the place of your father and took your brothers and sisters and Amurru in oath for you.' In a similar manner the author of Deuteronomy says: 'And because he loved your fathers and chose their descendants after them and brought you out of Egypt . . . to drive out nations before you . . . to give you their land for an inheritance . . . as at this day' (4: 37–8; cf. 7: 15); '. . . it is because the Lord loves you, and is keeping the oath which he swore to your fathers . . .' (7: 8); and 'Not because of your righteousness or the uprightness of your heart . . . but . . . that he may confirm the word which the Lord swore to

[1] Cf. W2, Vs. 24: *anāku ul anassukka ana māruttiya eppuškami* = 'I shall not reject you, I shall make you my son'. See also *PRU* IV, 17.132: 17–18 (p. 36): *tammar dumqa ša šarru . . . udammiqakku* = you will enjoy the favour which the king . . . will bestow upon you'. For the Israelite covenant, see Exod. 19: 4–6 (סגלה), Lev. 25: 42 and 55 (עבדי הם), Deut. 14: 1 (בנים אתם לה') and the frequent indications of God's love to Israel in Deuteronomy. Compare the letter from the Hittite king to 'Ammurapi King of Ugarit (*PRU* V, no. 60: 11–12) 'Now [you belong] to the Sun your lord. You are [his ser]vant his property (*sglt* = סגלה)'. See Huffmon-Parker, *BASOR* 184 (1966), 36 f. Cf. below, p. 226 n. 2.

[2] F1, §§ 7–8: 11–18, English translation according to A. Goetze, *ANET*², pp. 203–4.

your fathers . . .' (9: 5). The detail regarding the sickness and affliction of the vassal also occurs in Deuteronomy—because of the virtue of the Patriarchs the Lord had redeemed Israel from the land of Egypt, a place where they knew '. . . sickness . . . and evil diseases . . .' (7: 15).

A great deal of space is allocated in the Hittite treaties to a description of the benevolent acts the overlord had performed on behalf of his vassal: rescuing him from distress,[1] smiting his enemies,[2] raising him from his lowly state and making him a man of importance.[3] The historical prologue of Deuteronomy similarly describes the gracious acts of God performed on behalf of Israel: God had redeemed the children of Israel from the house of bondage, smitten their enemies, and from a handful of seventy persons had made them a great nation (10: 22).

The historical prologues recall not only the virtue of the vassal's ancestors but also their rebelliousness and obduracy. Thus, in the treaty between Muršiliš II and Kupanta-Kal the former relates how Mašḫuiluwaš had quarrelled and incited the people against the sovereign and how, as a result, he was deposed and his heir Kupanta-Kal took possession of the land.[4] In another treaty Tudḫalyaš IV dwells upon the rebellion of Amurru in the time of his father's predecessor Muwatalliš[5] and warns Ištarmuwa from Amurru not to behave like Mašturiš, the king of the Šeḫa riverland, who betrayed the Hittite king Muwatalliš.[6] This last example has nothing to do with the history of Amurru; its author's apparent purpose was to illustrate a moral principle regardless of the immediate relevancy of the incident cited.[7] In like manner, the historical introduction to Deuteronomy recalls the rebelliousness of the fathers of the children of Israel and their vexation of God during the entire period of the desert wanderings (Deut. 1: 26–8; 9: 7–24). As in the Hittite treaty, the author employs a description

[1] W9, Vs. 11 ff.; F3, §§ 2–3.

[2] F3, § 3: 14.

[3] F6, §§ 1–2 and notes on pp. 137–8.

[4] F3, §§ 4 ff.; the verb used for quarrelling is *šullāi-*, the equivalent of the Akkadian *ṣâlu* (see Friedrich, *Heth. Wörterb.*), which is rendered in Hebrew by ריב, a common verb in the context of the desert rebellion.

[5] Cf. O. Szemerényi, 'Vertrag des Hethiterkönigs Tudḫalija IV mit Ištarmūwa von Amurru', *Acta Societatis Hungaricae Orient.*, 9 (1945), col. i: 28 f.; compare I. Suqi, *Orient* (Society for Near Eastern Studies in Japan), 1, 1960, 1–22.

[6] Szemerényi, op. cit., col. ii: 15 f.

[7] See I. Suqi, art. cit., p. 19.

bearing a general admonitory character. Like Muršiliš, the author of Deuteronomy is eager to warn the people not to try God as they did before (6: 16).

In the Hittite treaties the historical prologue generally ends with a declaration granting land and rule to the vassal. This declaration is very often accompanied by a description of the land and its boundaries.[1] In the first of the deuteronomic prologues we find a territorial survey of the Trans-Jordanian area (3: 8 ff.) structurally similar to the boundary descriptions in the Hittite,[2] Babylonian,[3] neo-Assyrian,[4] and Aramean documents.[5] In the second (chs. 5–11) we find an inventory of the land's resources similar to those found in the gift documents of the Hittite,[6] Ugaritic,[7] and Assyrian kings.[8] These inventories include landed properties: cities, houses, cisterns, vineyards, and olive trees (6: 10–11); the land's natural gifts: brooks of water, fountains, underground springs, valleys,

[1] See F3, §§ 8–9, F5, § 4, and cf. the Abban treaty (Wiseman, *JCS* 12 (1957), 124 ff.) with the border descriptions in the historical prologue. It is uncertain whether the border descriptions constitute part of the historical prologue, as Baltzer believes (*Bundesformular*, p. 22), or whether they are essentially part of the treaty stipulations, as McCarthy contends (*Treaty and Covenant*, pp. 58–9, 132). The important point is that in Deuteronomy the border descriptions occur in the historical prologue (chs. 1–3) and that in state treaty documents they occur in connection with it (see also the Šuppiluliuma-Niqmadu treaty, *PRU* IV. 17.340, pp. 48–52 and the treaty with Ulmi-Tešup, E. Cavaignac, *RHA* 10 (1933), 68 ff.).

[2] In addition to the treaties mentioned in the previous note see the sources quoted in J. Garstang–O. R. Gurney, *The Geography of the Hittite Empire*, 1959, pp. 59, 66–7, 121, 124–215.

[3] Cf. the Babylonian *kudurrus* (see above, p. 61 n. 4) and especially F. Steinmetzer, *Eine Schenkungsurkunde des Königs Melišichu*, Beiträge zur Assyriologie, vol. 8, Heft 2, 1910, pp. 4 f.

[4] See the Esarhaddon treaty with Baal of Tyre iii, 18–22, (Borger, *Asarh.*, p. 109) a passage which is nothing but a border delineation of the vassal's territory.

[5] See the Elephantine deeds of gifts (A. Cowley, *Aramaic Papyri of the Fifth Century* B.C., 1923, nos., 6, 8, 13, 25). While these are private documents, typologically they represent the same pattern as the royal grant, see below, p. 78.

[6] Cf. the deed for Šaḫurunuva's descendants, *KUB* XXVI. 43, and the duplicate XXVI. 50 (see translation of the list of places, fields, sheepfolds (?), and vineyards in J. Garstang–O. R. Gurney, *Geography*, pp. 124–5). For a juridical analysis of this document see V. Korošec, 'Einige Juristische Bemerkungen zur Šahurunuva-Urkunde', *Münchener Beiträge zur Papyrusforschung und antiken Rechtsgeschichte* 35 (1945), 191–222.

[7] *PRU* III. 15.155, 16.204, 16.138, 16.139, 16.269, 16.160, 16.353, 15.122, etc.; compare K. Baltzer, *Bundesformular*, p. 30.

[8] J. Kohler–A. Ungnad, *ARu*, no. 1–30: houses, fields, and vineyards (*passim*). For a new edition of these texts see J. N. Postgate, *Neo-Assyrian Royal Grants and Decrees*, Studia Pohl: Series Maior 1, 1969.

and hills (8: 7); its soil produce: wheat, barley, grape, fig, pomegranate, olive trees, and honey, and the land's underground resources, such as iron and copper (8: 8–9).

In the Hittite treaties, as in the book of Deuteronomy, the land is given to the vassal as a gift and he is urged to take possession of it: 'See, I gave you the Zippašla mountain land, occupy it';[1] 'See, I have given the land before you, go take possession' (Deut. 1: 8 and 21). The granting of the land in the Hittite treaties is very often mentioned together with the explicit warning not to trespass beyond the boundaries set by the overlord.[2] In the historical prologue of Deuteronomy we similarly read: 'Do not contend with them, for I will not give you any of their land, no, not so much as for the sole of the foot to tread on' (2: 5; cf. vv. 9 and 18–19). The overlord could just as well have given the land to another, since the vassal had no natural right to it (cf. Deut. 9: 4–5); and he must therefore remain content with what was granted him. Thus Muršiliš II says to Manapa-Dattaš:[3] 'Behold, I have given you the Šeḫa-River-Land and the Land Appawiya. But unto Mašḫuiluwaš I have given the Land Mira and the Land Kuwaliya, whereas unto Targašnalliš have I given the land Ḫapalla . . . and you, Manapa-Dattaš . . .' (gap). In the historical prologue of Deuteronomy we similarly hear: 'Behold, I have set the land before you' (1: 8); 'I have given Mount Seir unto Esau' (2: 5); 'I have given Ar to the sons of Lot for a possession' (2: 9); 'I have given (the land of Ammon) to the sons of Lot for a possession' (2: 19). The purpose of these reminders is to justify the command forbidding trespassing and acts of hostility against these peoples.[4] So it is likely that the gap after the words: 'And you, Manapa-Dattaš' in the treaty of Muršiliš II similarly contained a command not to trespass upon the neighbouring territories, just as in the treaties of Muršiliš II with Targašnalliš[5] and with Kupanta-Kal,[6] which also deal with the regulation of affairs between the three above countries,[7] there are explicit warnings against war and mutual acts of hostility.

[1] A. Goetze, *Madduwattaš*, *MVÄG* 32. 1 (1927), Vs. 19, 43–4.

[2] F3, §§ 9–10; F4, § 5; W1, Rs. 23; *Madduwataš*, Vs. 20, 44.

[3] F4, §§ 10–11; cf. F3, § 3.

[4] The basic structure of these injunctions goes back to the sources utilized by the author of Deuteronomy, see W. A. Sumner, 'Israel's Encounters with Edom, Moab, Ammon, Sihon and Og according to the Deuteronomist', *VT* 18 (1968), 216 ff.

[5] F2, § 9.

[6] F3, § 27.

[7] See Friedrich, *MVÄG* 31 (1926), 50.

This notion of not trespassing beyond the fixed boundaries goes back to the Sumerians[1] and actually constitutes the origin of the treaty form in the ancient Near East.[2] Indeed, the city states of Sumer were the ones which consolidated for the first time the formula of a written legal arrangement between states. The basic elements of the treaty are already found in the stele of Eannatum of Lagash.[3] Here we find the preamble,[4] the historical prologue, stipulations, the oath of the covenant made in the framework of a ritual ceremony,[5] and the curses.[6] The connection between boundary arrangements and the 'treaty' is clearly shown by the 'Synchronistic History',[7] which is nothing more than a survey of political relations, especially border regulations, between Babylonia and Assyria apparently aimed to prepare a treaty or a legal settlement.[8] The closest link, however, between the 'treaty' and the

[1] Cf. the sources mentioned above, p. 61 n. 3.

[2] This has been pointed out to me by Professor Th. Jacobsen (in a private conversation).

[3] See also McCarthy, *Treaty and Covenant*, pp. 15 ff.

[4] Compare the beginning of the Stele of the Vultures (first five sections) in which the divine call of Eannatum is presented (cf. E. Sollberger, *Corpus des inscriptions 'royales' présargoniques de Lagaš*, 1956, see translation in S. N. Kramer, *The Sumerians*, 1963, p. 310).

[5] Cf. Stele of the Vultures, xviii. 2 f.; 'Two doves on whose eyes he had put spices (and) on whose heads he had strewn cedar (?) he caused to be eaten for Enlil at Nippur (with the plea): As long as days exist . . . if the Ummaite . . . breaks his word, etc.' (translation according to S. N. Kramer, *The Sumerians*, p. 311). An offering of a similar kind although in a different context is to be found in Lev. 14: 4 and 49, where two birds (cf. Gen. 15: 9) are taken together with cedar wood, crimson stuff (שני תולעת), and hyssop. The word translated by Kramer 'spices' is šim/šimbi (= Akk. *guḫlu*, Hebr. כחל) (full form: šim-bi-zi-da), which is actually antimony. Another ritual or sacred meal accompanying the oath is to be found in Rev. i: 37–40: [d] Utu lugal nì-sig$_{10}$-ga-ra larsam [ki] é-babbar NINDÁ+GUD-še an-kú which is translated by E. Sollberger, (*Le Système verbal dans les inscriptions 'royales' présargoniques de Lagaš*, 1952, example 161): 'à Utu le roi étincelant à Larsa dans l'Ebabbar, j'y ai fait le sacrifice (alimentaire).' NINDÁ+GUD equals Akk. *bîru* which is bull or young cattle, in many cases three years old. Compare the covenant with Abraham (Gen. 15: 9) where we find a three-year-old heifer and two doves (תור וגוזל), see also below, p. 102.

[6] The most salient curse is the hurling of the šušgal net of the gods (*passim*). It may not be without significance that in Ezek. 17: 19 f. the punishment for violating the oath by the Judaic king is God's net being spread upon him. (See D. R. Hillers, *Treaty Curses*, pp. 69–70.) Another curse mentioned there is that of the serpent fanging the foot of the transgressor of the border (Rev. v: 34 f. translation according to Kramer) which may have its parallel in Eccl. 10: 8: 'And who breaks down the fence a serpent shall bite him.'

[7] See E. Schrader, *KB* I, 194 f.

[8] Ibid. 194 n. 1.

border settlements is represented by the boundary stones, the so-called *kudurru* inscriptions which were common in Babylonia from the middle of the second millenium onwards. Their structure preserves the same elements as are found in the 'treaty': the preamble, the historical prologue, border delineations, stipulations, witnesses, blessings, and curses.[1] To be sure, the *kudurri* do not constitute treaty documents but royal grants, and, as we shall see, a distinction must be made between the treaty and the grant. Nevertheless, there certainly is a functional and formal overlap between these two types of documents. While the grant is mainly a promise by the donor to the recipient, it presupposes the loyalty of the latter. By the same token the treaty, whose principal concern is with the obligation of the vassal, presupposes the sovereign's promise to protect his vassal's country and dynasty. This close similarity of treaty and grant is most clearly demonstrated in the Hittite treaty, which is based on the suzerain's bestowal of land to his vassal. It is met with likewise in the covenant of Deuteronomy, whose introduction also combines the gift of the land to the Patriarchs with the covenant between God and the people.

The historical prologue in Deuteronomy, in fact, adds to the treaty form inherent in the structure of Deuteronomy the grant formulation taken from the ancient patriarchal traditions in Genesis. To understand properly the 'promise of the land' which is so salient a feature in the prologue of Deuteronomy, we must clarify the meaning of this motif in its original setting by looking at the covenant with the Patriarchs, the central idea in the Genesis traditions.

The covenant with Abraham, like the covenant with David, belongs to the 'grant' type, which differs from the 'vassal' type of covenant. While the 'grant' constitutes an obligation of the master to his servant,[2] the 'treaty' constitutes an obligation of the servant, the vassal, to his master the suzerain. In the 'grant' the curse is directed towards the one who violates the rights of the king's *servant*,[3] while in the treaty the curse is directed towards the vassal

[1] See F. X. Steinmetzer, *Die Babyl. Kudurru, etc.*, pp. 257 f.

[2] As long as he maintains his service; the moment he betrays his master and follows another he, of course, forfeits the gift. Cf. D. J. Wiseman, 'Abban and Alalaḫ', *JCS* 12 (1958), 126. 47 f., compare A. Draffkorn, *JCS* 13 (1959), 94 ff.

[3] Cf. the *kudurru* inscriptions in L. W. King, *BBSt*, and the neo-Assyrian grants in Kohler–Ungnad, *ARu*, nos. 1–30. For the Hittite grants cf. H. Güterbock, *Siegel aus Bogazköy*, *AfO* Beiheft 5 (1940), esp. pp. 47–55 dealing with the

who violates the rights of his *king*. In other words, the 'grant' serves mainly to protect the rights of the *servant*, the treaty to protect the rights of the *master*. While the grant is a reward for loyalty and good deeds *already performed*, the treaty is an inducement to future loyalty.

The promise of land and progeny to Abraham is indeed unconditional, and it comes as a reward for his faithfulness (Gen. 22: 26 and 28; 26: 5). Likewise the promise of a 'house' to David is unconditional (2 Sam. 7: 15–16); it comes as a reward for his loyalty (1 Kgs. 3: 6; 8: 25; 9: 7; 11: 4 and 6; 14: 8, etc.). The terminology used in this context is very close to that used in the Assyrian grants. Thus in the grant of Aššurbanipal to his servant Balṭāya we read:[1] 'Balṭāya . . . whose heart is devoted (lit. is whole) to his master, served me (lit. stood before me) with truthfulness and acted perfectly (lit. walked in perfection) in my palace, grew up with a good name[2] kept the charge of my kingship.' Similar formulations are to be found in connection with the grants to Abraham and David. Thus we read in Gen. 26: 4–5: 'I will give to your descendants all these lands . . . inasmuch as Abraham obeyed me (שמע בקולי)[3] and kept my charge (וישמר משמרתי), my commandments, my laws, and my teachings',[4] a verse preserving verbally the

Landschenkungsurkunden, and see also the treaty with Ulmi-Tešup, Rev. ii: 20–7 (E. Cavaignac, *RHA* 10 (1933) pp. 68 ff.). Cf. also the gift deed of Abban to Yarimlim (Wiseman, *AT** 1: 16–20) complemented by the tablet ATT/39/84 (see the text cited in the previous note) in which Abban takes the following oath: *šum-ma ša ad-di-nu-ki-um-mi e-le-eq-qú-*[*ú*] = '(May I be cursed) if I take back what I gave you.' (For the conditional oath sentences see von Soden, *GAG* § 185 g, i.). The oath of Abban reminds us of the oath of God to Abraham in Gen. 15. As in the Alalaḫ text, so here it is the donor (= God) who takes the pledge and passes between the pieces, as though he would invoke the curse upon himself (see my article *JAOS* 90 (1970), 196 f.). Compare also the formulation of the Abban grant: 'On that day (*ina ūmišu*) Abban gave the city' (*AT** 1, line 5) with the formulation in Gen. 15: 18: 'on that day (ביום ההוא) Yahweh concluded a covenant with Abraham saying: "to your offspring I give this land" '.

1 *ᵐBal-ṭa-a-a* . . . (*ša*) *libbašu gummuru ana bēlišu; ina maḫrīya ina kināti izzi-*[*zuma*], *ittallaku šalm*[*iš*]*qirib ekalliya, ina šumi damqi irbû*[*ma*], [*iṣ*]*ṣuru maṣṣarti šarrūtiya*. Cf. J. N. Postgate, *Neo-Assyrian Royal Grants and Decrees*, Studia Pohl: Series Maior 1, 1969, nos. 9: 11–20, comp. 10: 11–20, 11: 11–20. (=*ARu*, numbers 15, 16, 18).

2 The translation of Y. Muffs, *Aramaic Legal Papyri*, 134, 203, who joins *qirib ekalliya* with *ittallaku šalmiš*. *CAD*, vol. 3 (D), p. 69 reads: *qirib ekalliya ina šumi damqi irbûma* = 'he grew with a good name in my palace'. Cf. p. 76 n. 2 below.

3 Cf. in the Amarna letters: *ša išme ana bēlišu* (74: 38, 147: 51).

4 There is nothing deuteronomic in this verse. שמע בקול along with other terms expressing obedience is very frequent in the deuteronomic literature which stresses loyalty to the covenant, but, as we already indicated, this does not mean

notion of keeping guard or charge (*iṣṣuru maṣṣarti*) found in the Assyrian text. The notion of 'serving perfectly' found in the Assyrian grants is also verbally paralleled in the patriarchal and the Davidic traditions. Thus the faithfulness of the patriarchs is expressed by 'walked before me' התהלך לפני (24: 40; 48: 15 = JE; 17: 1 = P), which is the equivalent of the expression: *ina maḫrīya ittallak/izziz* in the Assyrian grant.[1] The P source adds to התהלך לפני the phrase והיה תמים (17: 1), which conveys the idea of perfect or loyal service expressed in the Assyrian document by (*ittallaku*) *šalmiš*.[2] According to P not only Abraham but also Noah was rewarded by God (Gen. 9: 1–17) for his loyalty, which is expressed by the very phrases used of Abraham's devotion: התהלך עם האלהים, תמים היה (6: 9). The pledge of God to keep his promises in connection with Noah and Abraham is expressed in P by זכר[3] 'deliberate' (recall),[4] which is equivalent to *ḫasāsu*[5] also found

that the terms as such were coined by the deuteronomic movement. The combination of חקים ותורות 'laws and teachings' is never found in the deuteronomic literature. (Deuteronomy always uses Torah in singular and usually with the definite article [התורה] see below, p. 338.) On the other hand, the combination is attested in JE (Exod. 18: 16 and 20). On שמר משמרת see Appendix A, p. 335.

[1] Cf. Y. Muffs, *Aramaic Legal Papyri*, p. 203.

[2] Compare Mal. 2: 6, בשלום ובמישור הלך אתי which means 'he served me with integrity and equity', see Y. Muffs, op. cit., pp. 203–4. This phrase occurs in connection with the grant of priesthood to Levi: 'that my covenant might be with Levi ... my covenant was with him of life and peace' ...להיות בריתי את לוי בריתי היתה אתו החיים והשלום., which recalls the grant of eternal priesthood to Phinehas in Num. 25: 12–13: 'I grant him my pact of friendship. It shall be for him and his descendants after him a pact of priesthood for ever' הנני נותן לו את בריתי שלום. והיתה לו ולזרעו אחריו ברית כהונת עולם, which was also given because of profound loyalty. Compare also 1 Sam. 2: 30 where the dynastic succession of the priesthood of Eli is dealt with: 'I said indeed that your house and the house of your father should walk before me for ever (יתהלכו לפני עד עולם)'. See M. Tsevat, 'Studies in the Book of Samuel, III', *HUCA* 34 (1963), 76. Grants of priestly revenues are also known from the *kudurru* documents, see the discussion of Thureau-Dangin, 'Un acte de donation de Marduk-zākir-šumi', *RA* 16 (1919), 117 ff. For the interpretation of *ittallaku šalmiš* as 'served with integrity' and not as Kohler–Ungnad translate 'in good or peaceful condition (wohlbehalten)', see Y. Muffs, *Aramaic Legal Papyri*, p. 203. *alāku/atalluku šalmiš* is equivalent also to הלך בתום 'walk with integrity' (Prov. 10: 9), and to התהלך בתום (לב) which in Ps. 101: 2 is connected with בקרב ביתי (within my house/palace') as in *ARu* 15: 18–19; 16: 18–19; 18: 18–19.

[3] This is expressed in Deut. and the Dtr by שמר, cf. שמר הברית והחסד (Deut. 7: 9 and 12; 1 Kgs. 8: 23). Compare Exod. 20: 8 (זכר) with Deut. 5: 12 (שמר).

[4] On the verb זכר, cf. P. A. H. de Boer, *Gedenken und Gedächtnis in der Welt des Alten Testaments*, 1962; B. S. Childs, *Memory and Tradition in Israel*, 1962; W. Schottroff, '*Gedenken*' *im Alten Orient und im Alten Testament*², 1967.

[5] See *EA* 228: 18 f.: *liḫsusmi* glossed by *yazkurmi*.

in the above Assyrian grants:[1] [*ṭā*]*btašu aḫsusma ukîn šeri*[*ktašu*] = 'I took favourable thought for him[2] and established his gift . . .'. For the establishing of the grant, P and also D use הקים, which is equivalent to *ukîn* in the Assyrian grant.

David's loyalty to God is couched in phrases that are even closer to the grant terminology: 'who walked before you in truth, righteousness, and loyalty' הלך לפניך באמת ובצדקה ובישרת לבב (1 Kgs. 3: 6); 'walked . . . with wholeheartedness and loyalty' הלך בתם לבב ובישר (9: 4); 'walked after me with all his heart' הלך אחרי בכל לבבו (14: 8); 'a whole heart (like the heart of David)' לבב שלם (כלבב דוד) (15: 3).[3] These are the counterparts of the Assyrian terms: 'with his whole heart' *libbašu gummuru*; 'stood before me in truth' *ina maḫrīya ina kinātí izzizuma*;[4] 'walked with loyalty (perfection)' *ittallaku šalmis*.[5] Similar language is also used both in the Old Testament and in the Assyrian grants, to describe the reward for this loyalty. Thus 'who returns kindness to the one who serves in obedience and who guards his royal command'[6] in the Assyrian grants is identical with 'who keeps his gracious promise to those who are loyal to him (lit. who love him) and guard his commandments' (שמר הברית והחסד לאהביו ולשמרי מצותיו) in the framework of a patriarchal tradition (Deut. 7: 9, see v. 12) and to 'who keeps his gracious promise to your servants who serve you wholeheartedly' (שמר הברית והחסד לעבדיך ההלכים לפניך בכל לבם) in a Davidic context (1 Kgs. 8: 23, see 3: 6). The grant *par excellence* is an act of royal benevolence arising from the king's desire to reward his loyal servant.[7] It is no wonder, then, that the gift of the land to

[1] Cf. Postgate, *Neo-Assyrian Grants*, 9: 22, 10: 22, 11: 22. (= *ARu*, numbers 15, 16, 18).

[2] For the correspondence of this phrase to זכר ברית/חסד cf. *JAOS* 90 (1970), 187 f.

[3] Cf. also 2 Kgs. 20: 3.

[4] As in Hebrew, so also in Akk. התהלך/הלך לפני (*ina pāni alāku*/*atalluku*) is similar in its connotation to עמד לפני (*ina pāni uzuzzu*), but the latter seems to have a more concrete meaning (praying, intercession, worshipping, serving) whereas the former is more abstract. For discussion of the above see F. Nötscher, '*Das Angesicht Gottes schauen*', *nach biblischer und babylonischer Auffassung*, 1924, pp. 83 f., 112 f.

[5] The close affinities to the neo-Assyrian phraseology in these verses may be understood in the light of an identical chronological and cultural background. All of these verses appear in a deuteronomic context, which means that they were styled in the seventh century, a period in which the above-mentioned documents were written.

[6] *ana pāliḫi nāṣir amāt šarrūtišu utirru gimilli dumqi* (Postgate, *Neo-Assyrian Grants*, 9: 9–10, 10: 9–10, 11: 9–10).

[7] Cf. Thureau-Dangin, 'Un acte de donation', 118: 'Ces titres de propriété

Abraham[1] and the assurance of dynasty to David[2] were formulated in the style of grants to outstanding servants.

It goes without saying that the legal formulations expressing the gift of land and dynasty are identical with the grant formulations. So, for example, the formulae 'for your descendants for ever' לזרעך עד עולם (Gen. 13: 15) and 'your offspring after you throughout their generations' זרעך אחריך לדרתם (Gen. 17: 7 and 9 = P) are found in donation texts from Ugarit[3] and Elephantine.[4] A very important part of the grant document is the depiction of the borders of the given land,[5] an element found in the Covenant with Abraham (Gen. 15: 18–21) and in the other passages referring to this covenant (Exod. 23: 31; Deut. 1: 7–8; 3: 8 ff.), as we have shown above.

Land and 'house' (= dynasty), the objects of the Abrahamic and Davidic covenants, are indeed the outstanding gifts of the sovereign in the Hittite and Syro-Palestine political reality. Thus we read in the treaty of Ḫattušiliš III (or Tudḫalyaš IV) with

sont généralement des actes royaux de donation dont le bénéficaire est, soit un enfant du roi, soit un prêtre ou temple, soit quelque serviteur que le roi veut récompenser.'

[1] The gift of Hebron to Caleb (Josh. 14: 6 ff.; Judg. 1: 20) is also a reward for loyalty and obedience: 'because he filled up after the Lord' מלא אחרי יהוה (Num. 14: 24; 32: 11 and 12; Josh. 14: 8, 9, 14; Deut. 1: 36), i.e. 'followed with undivided allegiance'. Semantically the expression is very close to תמים שלם עם יהוה, i.e. 'wholly devoted to the Lord'. מלא אחרי יהוה is found only in connection with Caleb and, in our opinion, reflects the original formulation of the grant tradition of Caleb.

[2] The rights of the priests and the Levites were also guaranteed by a grant (cf. p. 76 n. 2 above): the Holy donations given to them are a gift for ever and 'a salt covenant' (Num. 18: 19). The tithe which, according to Num. 18: 21 f. belongs to the Levites, was also given to them as a grant for their service: 'in return for the services that they perform' חלף עבדתם אשר הם עבדים. Grants of the tithe of a city to royal servants are known to us from Ugarit (*PRU* III, 16.153: 10–12, p. 147; 16.244: 5–7, p. 93).

[3] Cf. e.g. *PRU* III, 16.132: 27–8 (p. 141) *u ittadinšu ana* ^{m}*Adalšeni* [*u*] *ana mārēšu adi dārīti* = 'and gives it to Adalšeni and his sons for ever'. As in Hebrew so also here we have variants in the formulation: *adi dāriš* = (עד עולם) and *ana dārīti* (or *ana dāriš* [לדורות]). The formula in Ugaritic is *wlbnh 'd 'lm* (*PRU* II, 16.382, pp. 20–1).

[4] Cf. A. Cowley, *Aramaic Papyri*, no. 8: 9 (p. 22): 'you have rights over it from this day for ever and your children after you' אנתי שליטה בה מן יומא זנה ועד עלם ובניכי אחריכי, compare no. 25: 9 (p. 85). On the preservation of ancient legalistic formulae in Elephantine see Y. Muffs, *Aramaic Legal Papyri*, pp. 179 ff.

[5] See *BBSt* and also Cowley, *Aramaic Papyri*, no. 8: 3 ff., 13: 13 f., 25: 4 f.

Ulmi-Tešup of Dattaša:[1] 'After you, your son and grandson will possess it, nobody will take it away from them. If one of your descendants sins (*uašta-*), the king will prosecute him at his court. Then when he is found guilty . . . if he deserves death he will die. But nobody will take away from the descendant of Ulmi-Tešup *either his house or his land* in order to give it to a descendant of somebody else.'[2] In a similar manner Muršiliš II reinforces the right of Kupanta-Kal to the '*house* and the *land* in spite of his father's sins'.[3] This conception lies also behind the promise of 'the house' to David and his descendants in 2 Sam. 7: 8–16 (cf. 2 Sam. 23: 5; Ps. 89: 4–5 and 20–38), a conception changed afterwards by the Deuteronomist who made this promise conditional (1 Kgs. 2: 4; 8: 25; 9: 4 f.; compare Ps. 132: 11–12).[4] The promise of the dynasty in the Davidic covenant is connected with the image of the son of God, a feature found also in the promise of dynasty in the Hittite treaties. Šuppiluliumaš says to Mattiwaza,[5] 'I will make you my son[6] . . . on the throne of your father I will cause you to sit', a promise found in connection with David also in Pss. 2: 6–7; 89: 31. The continuation of the Hittite passage: 'the word which comes out of his mouth will not turn back'[7] is parallel to the version of the dynastic promise in Ps. 132: 11: 'Yahweh *swore* to David in truth *from which he will not turn away*: I will set one of your issue on your throne.'

[1] See E. Laroche, *RHA* 48 (1948), 40–8, who discusses the date of this treaty. Its connection with the Davidic covenant has been seen by R. de Vaux, 'Le roi d'Israel, vassal de Yahvé', *Mélanges E. Tisserant* I, 1964, 119–33.

[2] Compare the deed for Šaḫurunuva's descendants, *KUB* XXVI. 43 and 50, (see V. Korošec, 'Bemerkungen zur Šaḫurunuva-Urkunde') ll. 60–7.

[3] F3, §§ 7–8 (pp. 112–15), §§ 21–2 (pp. 134–7).

[4] The conception of the conditionality of the dynasty may be as old as that of the unconditional promise of dynasty and even older (cf. M. Tsevat, 'Studies in Samuel, III', 75 f., though I cannot accept his opinion that 2 Sam. 7: 13b–16 is a gloss), cf. Ps. 132 which seems to be very ancient (cf. Tsevat, op. cit., p. 78). What is peculiar to the deuteronomic work is the transformation of this concept of conditionality into the dominant factor in the history of the monarchy, and its linking not only to the covenant ברית and עדות but also to 'the law of Moses' תורת משה (cf. 1 Kgs. 2: 4, compare 2 Kgs. 21: 7–8).

[5] W2, Vs. 23 f.

[6] *ana māruttiya eppuškami*; *ana mārūti epēšu* means to adopt as a child (compare the Nuzi material, for references see *CAD*, vol. IV (E), p. 231) and so is the formula 'I will be for him as a father and he will be for me as a son' אני אהיה לו לאב והוא יהיה לי לבן a formula of adoption. For the clarification of the whole verse, see my article, *JAOS* 90 (1970), 191 ff.

[7] *amātu ša ina pīšu uṣṣu ana kutallišu ul itâr.*

The covenants with Abraham and David are thus based on a common pattern, and their literary formulation may have the same historical and literary antecedents.[1] The promise of the land to Abraham is preceded by the promise of progeny (Gen. 15: 4–5) and the latter is formulated in the same way as the promise of the dynasty in 2 Sam. 7: 12: אשר יצא ממעיך.[2] Similarly the promise of a great name to Abraham (ואגדלה שמך, Gen. 12: 2) resembles 2 Sam. 7: 9: 'David will have a name like the name of the great ones of the earth' כשם הגדולים אשר בארץ.[3] As I have shown elsewhere,[4] the greatness of the name has a political significance, a thing which comes to expression also in the Genesis traditions, which apparently crystallized under the impact of the United monarchy.[5]

The Priestly source in Genesis goes even further and combines the promise of the Land with the promise of dynasty. To the promise of progeny he adds that 'kings shall come out from you' (17: 6 and 16; 35: 11), which sounds like a promise of dynasty.

Moreover, like the covenant with David (2 Sam. 7: 16; 23: 5; Ps. 89: 29 f.), the covenant with Abraham in P is given eternal validity. The term ברית עולם, applied to David's dynasty in the ancient testament of David (2 Sam. 23: 5), is employed by P in reference to Abraham (Gen. 17: 7, 13, 19), as well as Noah (Gen. 9: 16) and Aaron (Num. 18: 19; 25: 13).

The formulation of the priestly covenant with Abraham 'to be unto you a God' להיות לך לאלהים (Gen. 17: 7 and 8) and the priestly formulation of the covenant with Israel, 'I will be your God and you shall be my people' והייתי לכם לאלהים ואתם תהיו לי לעם (Lev. 26: 12; Exod. 6: 7; compare Deut. 29: 12), also has its counterpart in the Davidic covenant, 'I will be for him as a father and he will be for me as a son' אני אהיה לו לאב והוא יהיה לי לבן (2 Sam. 7: 14; compare Ps. 89: 27–8). In both the formula is taken

[1] The covenant itself, i.e. the obligation of God sanctioned by cutting the animals (Gen. 15), is very ancient and reflects the covenant customs in Mari and Alalaḫ (see *JAOS* 90, 196 f.), but the literary formulation of it by JE is later and seems to be from the time of the United Monarchy, see R. E. Clements, *Abraham and David*, Studies in Biblical Theology, 1967.

[2] See Carlson, *David the Chosen King*, p. 122.

[3] Ibid., pp. 114–15.

[4] Cf. M. Weinfeld, 'Awakening of National Consciousness', *'Oz le-David*, pp. 399–400.

[5] The extent of the promised land in Gen. 15: 19–21 also points to a Davidic background.

from the legal terminology[1] used in connection with marriage and and adoption.

The author of Deuteronomy, then, assimilated in his introduction the patriarchal covenant-grant pattern, and this is why the 'oath of the fathers', the Land, and its borders play so important a role here. In its original setting the promise of the Land was unconditional, although it presupposed—as we have indicated—loyalty[2] and the fulfilment of some obligations and duties (see Gen. 18: 19; Ps. 132: 12); the covenant of promise itself was never formulated as conditional (cf. Gen. 15; 2 Sam. 7). But Deuteronomy and the deuteronomic school made both the grant of the Land and the promise of dynasty conditional on observance of the Law—in their view the most dominant and fateful factor in the history of Israel (cf. 4: 1, 25–6, 40; 5: 33; 6: 17–18; 7: 12, etc.).

(*b*) *The stipulation of undivided allegiance*

W. L. Moran[3] has recently demonstrated that the concept of 'the love of God' in the book of Deuteronomy is actually borrowed from the political life of the ancient Near East. Political loyalty was generally expressed by the term 'love'. Thus, the king, demanding loyalty of his subjects, enjoins: 'Love me as you love yourselves'.[4] Political loyalty tolerates no compromise. Hence the suzerain demands the vassal's love of heart and soul or wholehearted love.[5] Loving the king with one's entire heart signified the severance of all contact with other political powers: we find in the state treaties that the suzerain frequently warns the vassal not to transfer his allegiance to other kings nor to serve their wishes.

This expression, then, which served a political need in the ancient Near East, came to serve a religious need in Israel. It should be noted that the religious use of this expression was especially possible in Israel. The religion of Israel was the only religion that demanded exclusive loyalty; the God of Israel was a jealous God, who would suffer no rival.[6] The religion of Israel therefore

[1] See Y. Muffs, 'Studies in Biblical Law IV (The Antiquity of P)', Lectures in the Jewish Theological Seminary, 1965.

[2] Cf. the gift of Abban to Yarimlin, see above, p. 74 n. 2.

[3] W. L. Moran, 'The Ancient Near Eastern Background of Love of God in Deuteronomy', *CBQ* 25 (1963), 77 ff.

[4] Wiseman, *VTE*, l. 268.

[5] See references cited by Moran, 'Love of God in Deuteronomy', note 35.

[6] Cf. אל קנא in Exod. 20: 5; 34: 14; Deut. 4: 24; 5: 9; 6: 15; אל קנוא in Josh. 24: 19, Nahum 1: 2. The identical root קנא is used in Numb. 15: 14 in the

precluded the possibility of dual or multiple loyalties, such as were permitted in other religions where the believer was bound in diverse relationships to many gods. So the stipulation in political treaties demanding exclusive loyalty to one king corresponds strikingly to the religious belief in one single, exclusive Deity.

The concept of the Kingship of God seems also to have contributed to the concept of Israel as the vassal of Yahweh the King. It is true that the idea of the Kingship of God was prevalent all over the ancient Near East.[1] There was, nevertheless, an important difference between the Israelite notion of divine kingship and the corresponding idea in other nations.[2] Israel adopted the idea of the Kingship of God a long time before establishing the human institution of kingship. As a result, for hundreds of years the only kingship recognized and institutionalized in Israel was the Kingship of God. During the period of the Judges Yahweh was actually the King of Israel (cf. Judg. 8: 23; 1 Sam. 8: 7; 10: 19)[3] and was not,

sense of a husband who is jealous of his wife. On the basis of this and other marital formulae describing Israel's relationship to God, e.g. והייתי לכם לאלהים ואתם תהיו לי לעם (Lev. 26: 12; cf. Hos. 1: 9; 2: 4 and 25; see Y. Muffs, 'Studies in Biblical Law IV'), זנה ('to whore', see especially Exod. 34: 15–16), G. Cohen ('The Song and Songs and the Jewish Religious Mentality', *The S. Friedland Lectures 1960–1966*, The Jewish Theological Seminary of America, New York: 1966, pp. 4 ff.) traced back the metaphor of God as the husband of Israel to the Pentateuch. This seems quite reasonable and may moderate somewhat our notion of love as mere loyalty, especially in so far as Deuteronomy stresses also the love of God for Israel, which cannot be taken as loyalty. On the other hand, it must be observed that, while in Hosea and Jeremiah the husband–wife metaphor is explicit, no explicit reference to such a metaphor is to be found in the Pentateuch. In both the Pentateuch and the covenantal documents from the ancient Near East one find the father–son and master–servant metahpors, but never the husband–wife metaphor. We must conclude, therefore, that the prophets were responsible for the development of the idea of marital love between God and Israel, although the idea may have been latent already in the covenant traditions of the Pentateuch (cf. also J. J. Rabinowitz, *JNES* 18 (1959), 73). Certainly the expressions of loyalty and disloyalty (אהב and זנה) lend themselves to such affectionate poetic interpretation. Nevertheless, it seems that they were not so intended in the original covenant formulations.

[1] See H. Frankfort, *Kingship and the Gods*, 1948.

[2] See F. Rothschild, 'The Idea of God's Kingship in Jewish Thought' (unpublished dissertation, Jewish Theological Seminary of America, 1967), ch. 3.

[3] See M. Buber, *Königtum Gottes*[3], 1956. The anti-monarchic attitude expressed in these texts has nothing to do with the Deuteronomist (see below, pp. 168 f.). On the contrary, it seems to reflect the opposition to the establishment of the monarchy at the time of Saul, when a monarchical regime was still but a possibility and not, as in later times, the existing form of government, to which no alternative could even be imagined. Even the great prophets could not conceive the ideal future without a king.

as in the other religions of the ancient Near East, the image of the earthly king.

Because of the concept of the Kingship of God the relations between the people and their God had to be patterned after the conventional model of relations between a king and his subjects, a written treaty. It is no wonder, then, that the pattern of the state political treaty found a permanent place in the Israelite religion, nor is it a coincidence that this treaty pattern was adopted in its entirety precisely by the Book of Deuteronomy. The pattern of a state treaty based on the demand for exclusive allegiance is well suited to a book in which the concept of the unity of God reaches the apogee of expression. Thus, we find that Deuteronomy and deuteronomic literature abound with terms originating in the diplomatic vocabulary of the Near East. Such expressions as: 'to go after . . . others' ללכת אחרי (אלהים) אחרים;[1] 'to turn to . . . others'[2] פנה אל (אלהים) אחרים;[3] 'to serve . . . others' עבד . . . אחרים;[4] 'to love, to cleave' אהב, דבק;[5] 'to fear' ירא;[6] 'to

[1] Akk. *alāku arki*; see, e.g. the El-Amarna Letters (= *EA*) 136: 11 ff.; 149: 46; 280: 20. Cf. also *ARM*, IV, 11: 18 f.

[2] Cf. Deut. 31: 18 and 20 (cf. Hos. 3: 1). These verses are embedded in a passage (vv. 16–22) bearing an Elohistic stamp, which serves as an introduction to the Song (see Commentaries). Deuteronomy proper prefers the term הלך אחרי אלהים אחרים. By the same token the verb זנה, which occurs here and in the Elohistic strand (Exod. 34: 15–16, cf. Hosea, *passim*), never appears in Deuteronomy, perhaps because of Deuteronomy's reservation towards the conjugal understanding of the relationship between God and his people (see p. 81 n. 6 above). Cf. Moran, 'Ancient Near Eastern Background', 82 n. 35. One must admit, however, that הלך אחרי as well as *alāku arki* in Akkadian also have a conjugal connotation, cf. Jer. 2: 2 and 25; Hos. 2: 7 and 15, and for the Akkadian idiom see P. Koschaker, *JCS* 5 (1951), 107–8; Yaron *JSS* 8 (1963), 9–16.

[3] In Akk. *saḫāru ana*, cf. W7, Vs. 6–7: *māt* *āl* *Ki-iz-zu-wa-at-ni a-na māt* *āl* *Ḫa-[at-t]i ip-ṭu-ur a-n[a m]āt Ḫur-ri iš-ḫu-ur* = 'the country Kizzuwatna seceded from the Ḫatti country and turned to the Ḫurri country'. Cf. also ll. 27–8 there. (On the š in *išḫur* instead of the s, see A. Goetze, *Kizzuwatna and the Problem of Hittite Geography*, 1940, p. 37 n. 146.) Cf. also the Sefire treaty III: 7 ואל תפנו באשרה, which should be rendered 'do not turn to him'. See J. Greenfield, 'Stylistic Aspects of the Sefire Treaty inscriptions', *Acta Orientalia* 29 (1965), 7. Greenfield's interpretation finds support in Ezek. 29: 16 (בפנותם אחריהם), which is said in connection with the alliances with Egypt: 'And it (Egypt) shall be no more the confidence of the House of Israel . . . when they turn after them.'

[4] Cf. *arādu, ardūtu*, especially in the El-Amarna letters, cf. also W2, Vs. 29–30: *u anāku ana tērte ardūtišu luzzizma* = 'and I will put myself under the command of his service.'

[5] See Moran, 'Love of God in Deuteronomy', for references.

[6] *palāḫu* see, e.g., *ARM* I, 3: 4 (*waradka u pāliḫkama*); *VTE*, l. 396. Cf. above, p. 77 n. 6 (*ana pāliḫi nāṣir amat šarrūtišu*).

swear' נשבע;[1] 'to hearken to (or obey) the voice of' שמע בקול;[2] 'to be perfect תמים with (blameless before) him', 'to act in truth', באמת,[3] all of which are encountered in the diplomatic letters and state treaties of the second and first millennia B.C., and especially in the vassal treaties of Esarhaddon, in which they have particular political significance, found their way into Deuteronomy (and eventually into deuteronomic literature) as terms expressing religious loyalty.[4] Conversely, idioms which originally expressed political treason came in Deuteronomy to express religious treason.

It might seem that the borrowing of these terms was merely formal and extrinsic: that terms and expressions that were once

[1] *VTE* l. 129: 'if you swear an oath to another king, another master', cf. l. 72. Cf. Deut. 6: 13; 10: 20 (see also Josh. 23: 7 = Dtr), Jer. 12: 16, Isa. 45: 23.

[2] *VTE*, ll. 194–6: 'if you do not observe all that he commands, if you do not perform his command'.

[3] *VTE*, ll. 96–9: 'If you do not act in complete truth (*kittu šalimtu* [i.e. justly], if you do not answer [*apālu*, see Borger, *ZA* 20 (1961), ad loc. and compare 1 Kgs. 12: 7: ועניתם] him in truth and uprightness, if you do not speak sincerely (*ina kitti ša libbikunu*) with him', cf. ll. 51–2 and 236; *AfO* 8, Vs. iii: 15, p. 20; cf. Deut. 18: 13 and 1 Kgs. 3: 6; 9: 5 (both Dtr). See above, p. 76.

[4] Actually, however, the word 'king' itself is never used in Deuteronomy to refer to God, even in places where one would expect it, as in Deut. 10: 17 (compare Dan. 2: 47). It is reserved in Deuteronomy for the earthly king (Deut. 17: 14 f.; 28: 36) and its use in reference to God seems intentionally to be avoided. (This has been suggested to me by Professor H. L. Ginsberg.) It is also possible that the avoidance was due to the association of the word with 'Molech' which is so strongly condemned in deuteronomic literature. In post-exilic times, however, 'Kingship of God' became a very important term in the liturgy (cf. especially in the benedictions: מלך העולם 'King of the Universe' [King of eternity?], see E. J. Wiesenberg, 'The Liturgical Term Melekh Ha-'olam', *JJS* 15 (1964), 1–56, and the *Malkuyot* in the New Year prayer) and in religious doctrine. The Rabbinic term קבלת עול מלכות שמים 'the acceptance of the yoke of the Kingship of God' actually belongs to the set of the covenantal terms expressing loyalty to the sovereign. Cf., for example, in the El-Amarna letters: GIŠ *nīri* (gloss: *ḫullu*) *šarri bēlīya ana kišādiya u ubbalušu* = 'the yoke of the king my lord is upon my neck and I carry it' (*EA* 296: 37–9, compare 257: 15, compare Jer. 27: 11; 28: 14.). Compare also the expressions *nīra emēdu*, *abšāna emēdu* in the neo-Assyrian documents, which correspond to Hebrew שים עול, שים מוסרות (put a yoke, put bands) respectively, and actually mean to impose the king's subjection upon the vassal, see *CAD*, vol. IV (E), p. 41, 3a, pp. 142–3, 1; vol. I (A), pp. 65–6. 'Carrying the yoke' in the sense of being loyal and obedient is not found in the Pentateuch but is indicated in Jer. 2: 20; 5: 5. In Jer. 30: 8–9, the idea of serving God and David stands in clear contrast to serving foreigners by carrying their yoke. In the neo-Assyrian inscriptions we also find the idea of carrying the yoke of God explicitly expressed. Thus we read in the annals of Aššurbanipal: *yâti arad pāliḫka kurbannima lašūṭa abšānka* = 'be gracious toward me, your loyal servant, and let me bear your yoke' (M. Streck, *Assurbanipal II*, p. 22, ii: 125).

part of the political vocabulary were stripped of their political content and passed into religious usage and came to have only a theological significance. This, however, is not the case. Even after these expressions were adapted to religious needs they did not lose their original import. Political faithlessness had from earliest times been identified in Israel with religious faithlessness, and the ties between religion and politics there, as throughout the entire ancient world, were very strong. We have pointed out elsewhere[1] that the Hezekian and Josianic Reforms were a vigorous expression of both political and religious emancipation, in which the political factor was even more decisive than the religious one. A similar fusion of religious and political factors is also encountered among the surrounding peoples. Thus, in the treaty between Šuppiluliumaš[2] King of Ḫatti and Šunaššura King of Kizzuwatna, we meet the statement:[3] 'if the land shall act with hostility . . . against Šunaššura and (or) against his gods'.[4] When Aššurbanipal said of Gyges King of Lydia that 'because he did not observe *the command of the god Aššur, my begetter*, but trusted in his own power and hardened his heart . . .',[5] he meant that Gyges did not remain politically loyal to him. This congruence of political and religious loyalty is more pronounced, however, in Israel than elsewhere.

The covenant made by Jehoiada at the time of Jehoash's coronation (2 Kgs. 11: 17) is very instructive in this respect.[6] Its major object was to guarantee the loyalty of the ministers and the people to the new king. Jehoiada presents the prince to the centurions of the Carites and the guards of the temple and makes a covenant with them, to which he binds them by an oath (2 Kgs. 11:4). Afterwards

[1] See my article, 'Cult Centralization in Israel in the Light of a neo-Babylonian Analogy', *JNES* 23 (1964), 202–12.

[2] That he was the partner of Šunaššura in this treaty and not Muwatalliš, as Weidner suggested, see A. Goetze, *Kizzuwatna*, p. 36 n. 141.

[3] W7, Vs. ii: 42–3.

[4] Weidner, basing his translation on the *omina* texts, renders *šanîš* (*ilimšu*) 'beziehungsweise, oder' (loc. cit., n. 5).

[5] M. Streck, *Assurbanipal II*, 1916, p. 21, ii: 112–13: *aššu ša amat* (*ilu*) *Aššur ilu bāniya la iṣṣuru ana emūq ramānišu ittakilma igpuš libbu* (cf. Deut. 8: 12–18).

[6] The covenant mentioned in v. 4 is different from the covenant in v. 17. In v. 4 Jehoiada imposes on the soldiers and other officials taking part in the *coup d'état* a sworn obligation similar to the Hittite soldiers' oath (see above, p. 61 n. 8). See also, most recently, J. A. Soggin, 'Akkadisch TAR BERĪTI', *VT* 18 (1968), 210 ff. In v. 17 the covenant is with the king and the whole people. For the soldier's oath cf. also E. von Schuler, *Hethitische Dienstanweisungen* (*AfO*, Beiheft 10 [1957]), 8–35 and S. Alp, 'Military Instructions of the Hittite King Tutḫaliya IV (?)', *Belleten* 11 (1947), 388 ff.

he brings the king's son out before the people and 'puts upon him the crown and the עדות'. Amid rejoicing and acclamations Jehoash is made king, anointed (vv. 11 and 19), and escorted to the royal palace where he takes his seat upon the throne (v. 19). Von Rad[1] finds Egyptian features in this ceremony in the reference to עדות, which he takes to be the coronation protocol prevalent in Egyptian coronation ceremonies. G. Widengren,[2] however, has already observed that the word עדות is the Hebrew cognate of the Akkadian *adê*, and, as we have noted above, also the Aramaic עדן, both of which denote a treaty and its stipulations. It is likely, therefore, that the עדות here also refers to a covenant document.[3] The Biblical ceremony referred to here has salient Mesopotamian features, with a particularly marked similarity to the enthronement ceremonies of the Assyrian kings. As in Assyria,[4] so here the priest conducts the coronation ceremony. Jehoiada presents the royal insignia (? עדות, נזר) and the sanctified weapons[5]—a procedure well known to us from the Assyrian ritual.[6] As in Assyria, so here, it is the priest who sets the crown upon the king's head.[7] It is also possible that the Assyrian king was anointed[8] as was the King of Israel. After the ceremony the Assyrian king is led to his palace, accompanied by the sound of music; he is then seated on his throne[9]—a procedure identical with the description of the

[1] G. von Rad, 'The Royal Ritual in Judah', *The Problem of the Hexateuch*, pp. 222–31.

[2] G. Widengren, *Sakrales Königtum im A.T. und im Judentum*, 1955, p. 94 n. 69.

[3] According to K. A. Kitchen (*The Ancient Orient and the O.T.*, 1966, p. 108 n. 84) this word occurs as an oath also in Egyptian. See also Ps. 89: 40, where the 'crown' is mentioned alongside the 'covenant' ברית, which is identical with the עדות (Ps. 132: 12). We must, nevertheless, take into consideration Wellhausen's emendation: הצעדות (for עדות), not only because it appears together with נזר as the insignia of Saul (2 Sam. 1: 10), but also because both occur in the Assyrian coronation ritual (K. F. Müller, *Das Assyrische Ritual* I, *MVÄG* 41 (Fasc. 3) (1937), p. 12, l. 26; there is no basis for Müller's completion according to which the *šemēru* (= the bracelet) is to be given to the priest rather than the king).

[4] See Müller, loc. cit.

[5] The shield and the spears of David (v. 10), which David consecrated (2 Sam. 8: 7 and 11–12), were used for ceremonial purposes, and so are equivalent to the *miṭṭu*, i.e. the divine weapon in Assyria.

[6] Müller, op. cit. p. 10, ii: 15, cf. F. Thureau-Dangin, *Rituels accadiens*, 1921, p. 144, ll. 415–19.

[7] Müller, op. cit. p. 12, ii: 27–8.

[8] Müller, op. cit., p. 21, ll. 32 f. Cf. also B. Meissner, *Babyl. u. Ass.* I, 1920, pp. 63–4, but see E. Kutsch, *Salbung als Rechtsakt im Alten Testament und im alten Orient*, 1963, pp. 40–1.

[9] [*ina kus*]*sê ša šarrūte ušēšubūšu* (Müller, op. cit. p. 14, iii: 1), cf. 2 Chr. 23: 20: ויושיבו את המלך על כסא הממלכה.

ceremony in 2 Kgs. 11. Similarly, Aššurbanipal recounts in his annals[1] that Esarhaddon 'had gathered the people of Assyria, the great and the small ... made them swear by the gods, made a treaty and validated the covenant[2] to retain me as the *king's son* ... (amid) rejoicing and acclamations[3] I entered the king's palace'[4] or in another version:[5] 'and as I entered the palace the entire camp resounded ... and the princes rejoiced'. Like Esarhaddon, who binds his subjects by an oath of fidelity to Aššurbanipal the king's son (*mār šarri*) and makes a covenant with them, Jehoiada also makes a similar covenant with the people, after which *'am ha'areṣ* 'rejoices' as the king passes from the temple to the royal palace. Aššurbanipal is similarly escorted amid rejoicing and acclamations to the *bīt-redūti*[6] following the covenant ceremony, which takes place in the temple. It was the custom also in Assyria, as in 2 Kgs. 11, to display the new king in his royal attire before he entered the palace.[7]

What is surprising is that the description of the coronation ceremony, whose central concern we should expect to be a covenant between the king and the people, should give priority to a covenant between God and the people and the king and only refer secondarily to a covenant between the king and the people (2 Kgs. 11: 17).[8] It is likely, therefore, as Baltzer contends, that the verse

[1] M. Streck, *Assurbanipal II*, p. 4, i: 18–23: *upaḫḫir nišē māt Aššur ṣiḫir u rabi ... ana nasir* (for *naṣār*) *mār šarrūtiya epēš adê niš ilāni ušazkiršunuti udannina riksāte ... ina ḫidâte rišāte ērub ina bīt redūti.*

[2] *udannina riksāte* means: he made the covenant valid or binding, compare *riksātim dannātim nišakkan* = we will establish a binding agreement (*RA* 36, 51: 10), cf. *CAD*, vol. III (D), 94–5. *ṭuppu dannu*, as well as ברית נאמנה in Hebrew (Ps. 89: 29), means a valid and therefore lasting document. Similarly *māmītu* (NAM ERÍM) *danna* in Idrimi l. 50 means a binding oath. 'Mighty oath', as translated by S. Smith, does not make any sense. Neither does 'mighty document' for *tuppu dannu*. In *VTE*, ll. 23 and 65: *ša adê udanninūni* also means: validated the treaty (and see Addenda).

[3] On *ḫidâte rišāte* and *ulṣi rišāte*, which may be hendiadystic expressions, see M. Streck, *Assurbanipal III* (Glossary), 570.

[4] *Bīt-redūti* should be taken to mean the place of coronation; it particularly denotes the palace of Sennacherib and his successors (Esarhaddon and Aššurbanipal), see Streck, op. cit. III, 569.

[5] Streck, op. cit. 258, ii: 7–8: *ekallu ina erebiya irâš* (?) *gimir karāši ... ḫadû rubê.*

[6] See above, n. 3.

[7] See B. Meissner, *Babyl. u. Ass.* I, 63–4.

[8] Contradictory emendations have been suggested for this verse. G. von Rad (*Studies* p. 64 n. 1) suggests deleting v. 17b: 'and between the king and between the people'. M. Noth contends that the passage 'covenant between Yahweh and between the king and between the people' is unauthentic ('Old Testament Covenant-Making in the Light of a Text from Mari', *The Laws etc.*, pp. 115–16). More probably correct is the view of R. Kittel (HKAT ad loc.) that the

refers to a covenant ceremony involving a double oath-taking of the sort described in Hittite treaties.[1] There the sovereign, on the one hand, makes the vassal and the people swear fealty to him while, on the other hand, he makes the people swear fealty to their king/vassal. It appears that the persons who pledged themselves to observe this double covenant in the Biblical passage were the *'am ha'areṣ*, the body which played an active role in the enthronement of Jehoash and which was later to support Josiah's accession to the throne (2 Kgs. 21: 24).[2] In fact, the policy of this body was based on a twofold loyalty—to the throne and dynasty on the one hand and to Israel's ancient heritage on the other (2 Kgs. 11: 18; cf. Lev. 20: 2 and 4). The religious loyalty of the *'am ha'areṣ* stemmed from the covenant between God and Israel, its political allegiance to the throne and the dynasty from the covenant between the king and the people. Let us investigate the stipulations of this double covenant.

The Bible, which is primarily concerned with the relationship

passage refers to a double covenant, i.e. a religious one between the Deity and the king and the people, and a political one between the king and the people. The latter view obviates the need for deletions. The Chronicler (2 Chr. 23: 16) has omitted the reference to the political covenant in the parallel passage for theological reasons.

[1] See Baltzer, *Bundesformular*, pp. 85–7. McCarthy (*Treaty and Covenant*, p. 142 n. 4) rejects 2 Kgs. 11 as a true parallel, for he argues that 'in Ḫatti the relations ran between sovereign and vassal, then between the vassal and the nation', while 'in Kings it is sovereign and nation, king and nation'. The passage, however, refers explicitly to the king's and the nation's together making a covenant with God, while McCarthy himself cites (op. cit.) a Hittite parallel in which the sovereign makes a treaty (the Ḫuqqanaš Treaty) with the vassal and nation together.

[2] The *'am ha'areṣ* is identical with the 'people of Judah' עם יהודה, who placed Azariah on the throne after the assassination of his father (2 Kgs. 14: 21, see E. Würthwein, *Der 'am ha'areṣ im A.T.*, 1936), and it appears to be identical with the 'men of Judah' איש יהודה referred to in connection with the Josianic Reforms (2 Kgs. 23: 2; cf. Jer. 11: 2 and 9, which refer to the reform). The expressions 'people' or 'men of Judah' are generally contrasted with the 'inhabitants of Jerusalem' ישבי ירושלם (Jer. 25: 2; 2 Kgs. 23: 2; Isa. 5: 3; Jer. 7: 4; 11: 2 and 9; 17: 25, etc.). It may be inferred, therefore, that in these contexts the expression איש יהודה denotes the general citizenry or rather its representatives as opposed to the ישבי ירושלם, who apparently constituted the official body of Jerusalem. There is no basis for Alt's distinction (A. Alt, 'Die Stadtstaat Samaria', *KS* III, 300) between עם הארץ and איש יהודה as Judeans and ישבי ירושלם as the people of Jerusalem. (See recently G. Buccellati, *Cities and Nations of Ancient Syria*, Studia Semitica 26 (1967), 224 f.) For the word יושב denoting 'judge' or 'ruler' see F. M. Cross and D. N. Freedman, *JNES* 14 (1955), 278 f., and the Akkadian passages referred to by Brichto, *Curse*, pp. 160–1.

between God and Israel, has preserved details only concerning the covenant made between God and the people. But there must have been specifically formulated covenants between the king and the people in Israel, as among the surrounding peoples. This may be inferred from the vassal-treaty of Esarhaddon concluded during Aššurbanipal's enthronement ceremony. Most of its stipulations deal with homage to the king. For our discussion, however, the most instructive clauses are those commanding the people actively to oppose all acts of rebellion and assassination attempts and to preserve the dynasty, for example:

(You swear) that should Esarhaddon, king of Assyria, die during the minority of his sons (and) either an officer or a courtier[1] put Aššurbanipal, the crown prince, to death (and) take over the kingship of the land of Assyria. That you will not make common cause with him, that you will not become his servant (but) you will break away and be hostile. . . . You will seize him and put him to death and will then cause a son of Aššurbanipal, the crown prince, to take the throne of Assyria. (You swear) that you will (if necessary) await the woman pregnant by Esarhaddon, king of Assyria (or) the wife of Aššurbanipal the crown prince. That, after (the son) is born you will bring him up and will set (him) on the throne of Assyria. That you will seize and slay the perpetrators of rebellion. You will destroy their name and their seed from the land. That by shedding blood for blood, you will avenge Aššurbanipal, the crown prince. That you will neither feed Aššurbanipal . . . nor give him to drink, nor anoint him with a deadly (poisonous) plant . . .' (ll. 237–63).

Similarly we read in the Sefire treaty:[2] 'If anyone of my brothers . . . of my officers or anyone of my officials seeks my head to kill me[3] and to kill my son and my offspring—if they kill me, you must come to avenge my blood from the hand of my enemies.'

These obligations to preserve the dynasty find bold expression in the official Hittite documents where high officials demonstrate

[1] LÚ.SAG (Akk. *ša rēši* = eunuch, Heb. סריס) and *ša ziqni* (from the elders) convey the idea 'all the officials, the bearded and unbearded alike'.

[2] והן מן חד אחי . . . או מן חד נגדי או מן חד [פ]קדי . . . יבעה ראשי להמתתי ולהמתת ברי ועקרי, הן אי[ת]י יקתלן את תאתה ותקם דמי מן יד שנאי (III: 9–11). For פקד, נגד cf. Jer. 20: 1.

[3] Compare the Hittite treaty from Kizzuwatna: *šumma ardu sa Paddatiššu ana qaqqad bēlišu ippalas*, 'if a servant that belongs to Paddatiššu sought the head of his master' (G. R. Meyer, 'Zwei Neue Kizzuwatna Verträge', *MIO* 1 (1953), p. 114, ll. 6–7), cf. *PRU* IV, p. 126, 17.159: 7: *maruṣ qaqqadišu ubta''i*, 'she sought the sickness of his head'. Cf. J. Greenfield, 'Stylistic Aspects', p. 7.

their profound loyalty to their kings by describing their own efforts to put the right successor on the throne. One of the officers says, 'Had there been descendants, I would not have passed over them. I would, rather, have protected them. Since there were no offspring of his [i.e. of the king], I inquired concerning a pregnant woman, but there was no pregnant woman.'[1] From the Esarhaddon vassal treaties we learn that the vassals were actually sworn to await the deceased king's pregnant woman in order to secure legitimate succession (cf. above).

If we trace the political activity of the *'am ha'ares* in the books of Kings, we shall discover that this circle carefully complies with these procedures. Thus the *'am ha'areṣ* co-operate with Jehoiada in installing the seven-year-old prince Jehoash as king (2 Kgs. 11). They apparently[2] support Amaziah son of Jehoash in consolidating his position on the throne after the assassination of his father, and they execute the assassins[3] (12: 21–2; 14: 5–6). After the assassination of Amaziah they install his son, the sixteen-year-old Azariah, as king (14: 21).[4] It is they who execute the assassins of King Amon[5] and bring his eight-year-old son, Josiah, to the throne (21: 24), and again it is they who enthrone Jehoahaz as king after his father's death (23: 30). It may be assumed, then, in the light of the above, that the covenant between the king and the people in Israel contained clauses similar to those encountered in the Esarhaddon treaty. It is not certain, however, whether such a covenant was made anew with each individual king or whether there was one permanent and abiding statute, whose stipulations applied to all kings of the Davidic dynasty and which was renewed only in the event of an interruption in the continuity of the dynastic rule as in the days of Athaliah.[6]

[1] E. Laroche, 'Suppiluliuma II', *RA* 47 (1953), 70, ii: 3 f. Cf. H. Otten, *MDOG* 94 (1963), 3–4.

[2] See J. A. Soggin, ''Am Ha'areṣ und Königtum', *VT* 13 (1963), 192–3.

[3] In contrast to the Esarhaddon treaty, which commands the vassal to destroy also the progeny of the conspirators, the deuteronomic editor points out that in compliance with the (deuteronomic) law (24: 16) the sons of the assassins were not executed.

[4] עם יהודה is identical with עם הארץ, see p. 88 n. 2 above.

[5] Soggin, ''Am Ha'areṣ', 194, remarks in this respect: 'warum der 'a.h. sich an der Mördern geracht habe, wird vor den Quellen nicht gesagt'. We, however, would view the matter as an obligation stipulated by the covenant between the people and the king.

[6] G. Fohrer, 'Der Vertrag zwischen König und Volk in Israel'. *ZAW* 71 (1959), 13.

In the northern kingdom, where there was no enduring dynastic rule comparable to the Davidic dynasty, the covenant between king and people was even more essential than in Judah. A reference to this covenant has been preserved in Hos. 10: 3–4: 'For now they will say: 'We have no king, for we fear not the Lord, and a king, what could he do for us?' They pledged agreements;[1] with false oaths they make covenants; so judgement springs up like poisonous weeds in the furrows of the field.' These verses undoubtedly reflect the chaotic political situation that prevailed on the eve of Samaria's fall, and they refer to the frequent assassinations of the kings of Israel to which Hosea alludes in ch. 7. The prophet apparently accuses the people of dishonouring the covenant and oath-imprecation which bound the king and the people.[2]

(*c*) *The covenant between God and the people*

In Deut. 13 we encounter laws permeated with an atmosphere of conspiracy of the sort that characterizes the political sphere. They deal with instances in which a person who holds an office of divine authority (13: 2–6), a relative or friend (vv. 7–12), or a group of citizens (vv. 13–19) incites an Israelite or group of Israelites to worship foreign gods. The idolatrous suggestion is made secretly v. 7); knowledge of it spreads by rumour (v. 13); it is to be verified

[1] So correctly, Professor H. L. Ginsberg (orally). Compare דברו דבר in Isa. 8: 10, which Professor Ginsberg translates 'agree on action'.

The Akkadian equivalent to דבר *dabābu* has also, among others, the meaning 'to come to an agreement' (*CAD*, vol. III (D), p. 8b) as well as 'to pledge' (W. L. Moran, *JNES* (1963), p. 173 n. 19). Cf. also *dabābu dibbātu* in Akkadian, which means 'to come to an agreement' (*CAD* vol. III (D), p. 131). Professor H. L. Ginsberg called my attention to Judg. 11: 11 וידבר יפתח את כל דבריו לפני יהוה במצפה, which the new JPS translation renders as 'He affirmed his terms' (fixed in the negotiations between him and the elders), and also to Gen. 24: 33 לא אכל עד אם דברתי דברי, which also means 'I will not eat until I transact my business'.

[2] The ראש mentioned in this passage is the bitter and poisonous root (cf. Jer. 8: 14; 9: 14; Lam. 3: 15 and 19) from which the regicides would prepare the potion to poison the king (cf. Jer. 8: 14; 9: 14). Cf. the section of the Esarhaddon treaty quoted above for an allusion to the manner in which they did away with the kings.

In the Phoenician inscriptions and in the Prophets the legitimate king is called צמח צדק (צדקה) (*KAI* 43: 11, 16: 1 [בן צדק], Jer. 23: 5; 33: 15; cf. Isa. 11: 1; Zech. 6: 12), an epithet which signified for the prophets the proper function of the king and especially that of the young crown prince: the performance of משפט וצדקה (see below, pp. 153 f.). It seems that Hosea and also Amos (5: 7; 6: 12) were making use of the idea of צמח צדקה in paronomasia by saying that instead of the sprout of justice there comes out the sprout of poison.

by judicial investigation[1] (cf. 17: 4).[2] The Israelite to whom the suggestion is made is required to disclose the *provocateur*. He is to have no compassion for him, even if he is a relative or the most intimate of friends (v. 9).

The religious treason here is described and combated just as if it were political treason. Inciting an entire community to adopt foreign worship (13: 13–19) implies no less than its delivery into the hands of the enemy. It is precisely for this reason that the punishment for this offence is so severe. F. Horst has observed that indeed 'if the instigators succeed in drawing to their side the population of an entire city, then it should be considered a public act, which could not be imagined as free from political consequences.'[3]

Warnings of the type found in Deut. 13 are encountered in Hittite, Aramean, and neo-Assyrian political treaties; indeed they constitute the principal subject-matter of these treaties. Conspiracies and seditious agitation being the initial stages of all plots to overthrow a political regime, it is no wonder that the suzerains were careful to have their vassals swear fidelity particularly in matters of this sort.

In the ancient political treaties, as in Deut. 13, the vassals are commanded to disclose and to act against all seditious activities or attempts to incite rebellion, whether by individuals or groups. Let us cite some examples:

If a man or a city shall rebel against the Sun and alienate himself,[4]

[1] Verse 15: 'You shall investigate and inquire and interrogate thoroughly' (translation of this verse follows *The Torah*², JPS, 1967). For an inquisition in connection with rumours about the king, cf. an Assyrian letter (*ABL* 472, see R. H. Pfeiffer, *State Letters of Assyria*, no. 66, p. 59, rev. 2–3) *dibbi ibaššû ša šarri ša ašmû, mār šipri luṣamma lišâlāni* = 'There is some talk about the king, which I have heard; may the messenger of the king come (and) question me'. See also *ABL* 656, rev. 19. Mark the verb *šemû* שמע in connection with the rumour and *ša'ālu* שאל concerning the investigation.

On the political significance of our passage in Deuteronomy see the remarks of F. Horst (*Das Privilegrecht Jahwes*, 1930, p. 19): 'Politische Organe, das angeredete "Du", stellen ein profanrichterliches Ermittlungsverfahren an, das die Grundlage zu einen strafrechtlichen Einschreiten bildet. Auch das mag wohl ein Hinweis sein, dass der religiöse Abfall zugleich eine politische Loslösung bedeutete, der die politischen Organe nicht gleichgültig zusehen konnten.'

[2] Deut. 17: 2–7 is related both in contents and in phraseology to ch. 13. Most of the scholars agree that Deut. 16: 21–17: 7, which is out of place in the context of Deut. 16: 18–18: 22 (laws on the judges, the king, the priest, and the prophet), has been displaced from its original position, viz. from before 13: 2. On the reason for the displacement see K. Budde, *ZAW* 36 (1916), 193 ff.

[3] *Das Privilegrecht*, 17.

[4] *itti šamši bartam ippuš inakkir.*

when Šunaššura shall hear this, he shall report it to the Sun ... If a man from Kizzuwatna shall hear anything slanderous from the mouth of an enemy concerning the Sun, he shall report this to the Sun.

(Treaty between Šuppiluliumaš and Šunaššura)[1]

If a man shall quarrel[2] with the Sun and speak defection[3] against it, whether he be a prince (DUMU LUGAL), a great noble (BE-LU RA-BU-U) ... an official (LÚ KI-BI-DU)[4] of the palace ... or any other man etc. ... and you will not deliver him but shall conceal him ... (then) you have violated the covenant. If you shall hear words of rebellion[5] rising[6] in the land of Hatti, then you shall rally to the side of the Sun.... Because men are corrupt (base)[7] and rumours shall be discharged and a man shall come to you and shall say secretly[8] such and such ... write it to the Sun. And when it is true ...[9]

(Treaty between Muršiliš II and Targašnalliš of Ḫapalla)[10]

[And whoever will come to you] or to your son or to your offspring or to one of the Kings of Arpad and will s[pea]k [ag]ainst me or against my son or against my grandson or against my offspring ... and utters evil words[11] ... you must hand them over into my hands ... and if you [do] not [do] so, you will have been false to all the gods of the treaty, which is in [this] inscription.

(Sefire treaty)[12]

[1] W7, Vs. ii: 16–18, Rs. iii: 25–7. For the identity of the parties in this treaty, see above, p. 85 n. 2.

[2] *idalaṷešzi*. The verb equals Akk. *mašiktu bašû*, 'to alienate, to rebel', cf. W9, Vs. 32 and G. Smith, *Idrimi*, l. 4: [*nukurtu*] *mašiktu ittabši* (restored according to A. Goetze, *JCS* 4 (1950), 227), which means that there was a rebellion. Cf. *EA* 92: 11.

[3] *za-am-m*[*u-ra-iz-zi*], 'slander'. See the discussion of Friedrich, *MVÄG* 30 (1926), 71–2.

[4] Taken from Akk. *amēl qīpti* (= *qēpu*) (Friedrich, ad loc.), which means commissioner or governor.

[5] *idaluš memiịa*[*š Š*]*Á BAL*, 'bad talk of rebellion' (*BAL* = *nabalkutu*).

[6] *šarā išparzazi*. Cf. the discussion of Friedrich, *MVÄG* 30 (1926), 38.

[7] See Friedrich, notes ad loc., cf. Deut. 13: 14 בני בליעל.

[8] *taštašịịāizzi*, 'will whisper', cf. *VTE*, ll. 500–2; *mušadbibūt liḫšu*, 'who speak secrets' = 'who spread rumours'.

[9] *nu man memiịaš ašanza*, 'and when the thing is established'. *ašant-* is a participle from *eš*, 'to be', and means literally 'existent' and 'established' like Hebr. נכון, אמת, אמן, and Akk. *kânu, kēnu, kittu*. Cf. Deut. 13: 15 והנה אמת נכון הדבר, 'if it be true, the fact is established'. Cf. also in a Kizzuwatna treaty (*MIO* 1 (1953), 112 ff.), ll. 3, 8: *šumma awātum kittum*, 'if it be true', or 'if the fact be established'.

[10] F2, §§ 2–6.

[11] מלן לחית means 'bad words' (see H. L. Ginsberg, *JAOS* 59 (1939), 105), a term equivalent to the Hitt. *idaluš memiịaš* (bad word), which appears in the Hittite treaties and Instructions in the context of seditious agitation. See J. Greenfield, *Acta Orientalia* 29 (1965), 8–9.

[12] III: 1–4.

Similar warnings occur in the Hittite instructions for functionaries,[1] which are closely related to the treaties[2] in both form and content, for example:[3] 'If a noble, a prince, or a relative . . . brings up seditious words . . . (saying): "Come let us join another (king),"[4] but the one to whom it is said does not denounce him, that one will be under oath.'

In the Esarhaddon treaty and in the Assyrian officials' oath of loyalty to Aššurbanipal[5] most of the stipulations deal with conspiracies against the crown prince and we shall see later how close they are in style to the warnings against sedition in Deuteronomy.

Similar injunctions are reflected in the loyalty oaths of the royal craftsmen in Mesopotamia. In these oaths the craftsmen swear that they will report whatever they may see or hear and that they will not conceal anything.[6]

The analogies to be found in the Hittite, Aramean, and Assyrian treaties can help us to grasp the real meaning of Deut. 13: 10. It has long been recognized[7] that Deut. 13: 10 should be emended to read with LXX הגד תגידנו instead of the Masoretic הרג תהרגנו.[8] F. Horst has rightly observed[9] that only the reading of the Septuagint can properly account for the use of the adversative כי at the beginning of v. 10: 'nor shall you conceal him' (= end of verse 9) '*but* you shall report him'.

The reading of the Septuagint can be substantiated by additional factors. First, it would be hard to explain how the verb הרג, which is so well attested in the Pentateuch, was misread into הגד, which

[1] See Einar vonSchuler, *Hethitische Dienstanweisungen*, *AfO*, Beiheft 10 (1957), 8–33, and especially the introduction there (pp. 1–7), where other Hittite instructions are dealt with.

[2] Cf. A. Goetze, 'State and Society of the Hittites', *Historia, Zeitschrift für alte Geschichte*, Einzelschriften, 7 (1964), 32–3; von Schuler, ibid. 45–9.

[3] E. von Schuler, *Dienstanweisungen*, p. 26, § 16, cf. p. 14, §§ 24 and 25.

[4] Cf. Deut. 13: 3, 7, 14: 'let us follow and worship another god'. The direct speech in warnings of this kind is to be found in the Esarhaddon treaty also (ll. 323, 333, 341, 365, etc.), accompanied by the introductory formula: *ma-a*, which is equivalent to לאמר 'saying' in Deut. 13: 3, 7, 14.

[5] See L. Waterman, *RCAE*, letter no. 1105.

[6] D. B. Weisberg, *Guild Structure*, Text I: 25–6 (pp. 6, 8). See also pp. 35 ff. These oaths refer to someone who does work in another temple without the king's permission.

[7] Klostermann, *Pentateuch*, NF. 1907, p. 277. This view was presented convincingly by K. Budde, *ZAW* 36 (1916), 187–97, though he did not refer to Klostermann.

[8] Cf. too J. Hempel in *BH*[3].

[9] *Privilegrecht*, pp. 33–4.

only very rarely occurs in the sense of denunciation.[1] Secondly, vv. 9–10 are addressed to the seduced as an individual, so that הרג תהרגנו would appear to imply the application of lynch-law; but this is contradicted by 10b, which presupposes a public trial (cf. 17: 6–7). Thirdly, the הרג תהרגנו would seem to be superfluous in the light of v. 11 וסקלתו באבנים; in fact, the parallel passage 17: 5 f., which is verbally close to ours, mentions only stoning.

The restored verb הגד תגידנו in this context may only mean 'to report', since the disclosure of the agitator's name would, in effect, lead to his apprehension by the authorities.[2] It may be no coincidence, then, that in the same context in the Aramaic treaty from Sefire[3] we meet with the expression הסכר תהסכרהם 'you shall deliver them up',[4] which corresponds morphologically and functionally to the expression הגד תגידם. Furthermore, in an identical context in the political treaties we find the verb *qabû*,[5] which literally corresponds to the verb הגד and which here also connotes disclosure and deliverance to the authorities. The Akkadian term *mašāru*[6] (*bašāru*?),[7] which occurs in the Hittite treaty (written in

[1] It is much easier to explain how הגד תגידנו was turned into הרג תהרגנו. According to K. Budde (article cited on p. 94, n. 7) the transposition of 17: 2–7 (see p. 92 n. 2) is responsible for the scribal emendation. In the original context, i.e. when 17: 2–7 preceded 13: 2, the ideas of denunciation (cf. והגד לך ושמעת in 17: 4) and that the accuser was to be the first to take part in the execution (v. 6) were quite clear. The moment this passage was removed (see Budde's article for the reason for transposition) the connection between הגד תגידנו and ידך תהיה בו seemed loose. Therefore the former expression was emended into הרג תהרגנו, which ostensibly added to the understanding of what followed.

[2] For הגד in the sense of 'to report' see Lev. 5: 1; Prov. 29: 24.

[3] Stele III: 1–2.

[4] Cf. Fitzmyer, *Sefîre*, pp. 105–6; J. Greenfield, *Acta Orientalia* 29 (1965), 9.

[5] Cf. *VTE* ll. 81–2, 120–2; *MIO* 1 (1953), 114, ll. 15, 16. In the treaties written in the Hittite language the verb is *mema-* (= say), cf. E. von Schuler, *Dienstanweisungen*, p. 14, § 24, l. 52.

[6] W7, Vs. ii: 18, Rs. iii: 24, 27. Weidner reads in all these instances: *i-ma-aš-ša-ar* from *mašāru* (see p. 97 n. 3) incorrectly deriving it from *muššuru wuššuru*. A verb (מסר) is attested, in the sense of denouncing, only in Syriac (cf. C. Brockelmann, *Lexicon Syriacum*) and in the Talmudic sources (cf. J. Levy, *Wörterbuch über die Talmudim und Midrashim*). Very instructive in this respect is the Midrash on Job. 16: 11: יסגרני אל אל עויל (compare הסכר ביד in the quoted text of Sefire III: 1–2) which is interpreted by מסרני ביד השטן (Shemot Rab. 21, 7).

[7] Dr. S. Kaufman (Chicago Oriental Institute) called my attention to the fact that the sign read *ma* in the quoted lines (see note 6) looks like *ba*. This might provide us with a verb found in a similar context in Alalaḫ (*tubassarāni*, Wiseman, *Alalaḫ*, 2: 18, 28) and in neo-Assyrian texts (cf. *CAD*, vol. II (B), 347, 2), though there as elsewhere in Akkadian the D stem only.

Akkadian) quoted above, actually denotes disclosure that leads to the arrest of the accused. As in the state treaties, the object of the deuteronomic command to inform the authorities of the conspirator's action is that he be brought to trial and convicted (and not, as may be inferred from the MT, that the Israelite in question is to kill the guilty party without delivering him to the authorities). We may compare Jer. 20: 10. 'For I hear many whispering: "Terror is on every side! Denounce him! Let us denounce him (הגדו ונגידנו)", say all my familiar friends, watching for my fall. "Perhaps he will be deceived; then we will overcome him and take our revenge on him."' Jeremiah's relatives and close friends watch for an unguarded word by him, for which they may denounce him as an incendiary and deliver him up to the authorities.[1] It should be noted that the character of the deuteronomic law of incitement is extremely unusual as compared with other Pentateuchal laws, for it is the only one that carries the death penalty for mere incitement to sin. This anomalous law may be best understood only through considering the political implications of this particular malefaction.

The warnings against yielding to incitement to treason in the Hittite and Assyrian documents are usually interspersed with demands for unreserved loyalty to the overlord. Thus the vassal is instructed in the Esarhaddon vassal-treaties to love the king,[2] to speak to him in good faith,[3] to serve him wholeheartedly,[4] to hearken unto his voice, and to obey his commands.[5]

This combination of warnings against incitement to sedition, on the one hand, with expressions of utmost loyalty and fidelity, on the other hand, is especially conspicuous in the oaths of the Hittite and Assyrian officials to their rulers. For example, we read in the oath of the Assyrian officials to Aššurbanipal: 'If any guard . . . or plotter who speaks a word that is not good[6] against Aššurbanipal . . . in fetters we shall bring him to Aššurbanipal. . . . From this day, as long as we live, Aššurbanipal king of Assyria is the man we love. . . . Another king and another lord . . . we shall never seek.'[7]

[1] Cf. recent commentaries. This verse recalls the manner in which the inciter is accused and brought to trial according to the Mishnah (Sanhedrin vii: 10).

[2] ll. 266–8; see above, p. 81.

[3] ll. 51–2 and 96–9.

[4] l. 152.

[5] ll. 194–6.

[6] *a-mat la ṭa-ab-ti*; this might be the Akkadian equivalent of מלין לחית in Aramaic and *idaluš memii̯aš* in Hittite (see p. 93 n. 11 above and cf. W. L. Moran, *JNES* 22 (1963), 173–6).

[7] L. Waterman, *RCAE* no. 1105, obv. 12–35.

Similarly we read in the Hittite military instructions:[1] 'And as you love[2] your own wives, your own children, your own houses, just so love the rules of the king and practise them well.'[3]

As in the vassal-treaties of Esarhaddon and in the oaths of loyalty of the Hittite and Assyrian officials, so in Deuteronomy the demand for fidelity is found in the context of laws dealing with incitement and defection, for instance: 'You shall walk after the Lord your God, and fear him, and keep his commandments, and obey his voice, and you shall serve him and cleave to him' (Deut. 13: 5).[4]

The similarity between Deut. 13 and the loyalty clauses in state treaties finds its fullest expression, however, in the Esarhaddon treaty, which chronologically and in many other respects[5] is closer to the book of Deuteronomy than the other treaties. Thus, in the Esarhaddon treaty we repeatedly encounter the phrase: 'If you listen to, conceal[6] and do not report . . .',[7] which corresponds word for word to the commands in Deut. 13.[8] There are, however, other analogies:

1. Deut. 13: 2 warns against the prophet and the prophetic

[1] S. Alp, *Belleten* 11 (1947), ll. 30–1.

[2] Alp translates *genzu ḫarteni* 'have affection', but as *genzu* is equated with Akk. *rêmu* (F. Sommer, *HAB* 49: 81), we may be justified on the basis of the Assyrian parallels in translating 'have love'.

[3] Cf. also the expressions of fidelity in E. von Schuler, 'Die Würdenträgereide des Arnuwanda', *Orientalia* 25 (1956), p. 226, col. ii, ll 16 ff. The Assyrian and Hittite demands of loyalty differ in that the former stress loyalty to the king and the palace (see E. Weidner, 'Hof- und Harems- Erlasse assyrischer Könige aus dem 2. Jahrtausend v. Chr.', *AfO* 17 (1954–6), 257 ff.) while the latter emphasizes the general duties of the officials and not just those related directly to the person of the king. Thus, for example, in the last example cited in the text from the military instructions the officials are called to be loyal to the *rules* of the king and not just to the king himself as in the Assyrian examples, which we cited. On the authoritative approach of the Assyrians also see above, pp. 68–9. See also E. von Schuler, *Dienstanweisungen*, p. 6.

[4] Verses 4b–5 are generally taken to be editorial because of their plural address. In light of the evidence presented here and in view of the frequent shifting from singular to plural in the treaties and in the Phoenician inscriptions (see W. L. Moran, *Biblica* 73 (1962), 103), we should be more sceptical about the distinction between singular and plural styles. Even if we accept this distinction as a criterion for discerning different strata in Deuteronomy (see recently C. H. Cazelles, *CBQ* 29 (1967), 207–19), we may say that the editor framed this material in accordance with the conventional treaty formulae.

[5] Cf. below, pp. 116 ff.

[6] Cf. F6, § 4: 27–30, § 18; F3, § 15: 17–25; W10, Rs. 23 (*la tupazzaršu*).

[7] *šum-ma ta-šam-ma-ni tu-pa-za-ra-a-ni* . . . *la ta-qab-ba-a-ni* ll. 108–22, 500–12, compare 130–46, 336–52, 368–9.

[8] See vv. 9–10: ולא תשמע אליו . . . ולא תכסה עליו . . . כי הגד תגידנו.

dreamer who may attempt to incite the people to worship foreign gods. In the Esarhaddon treaty the Assyrian king also warns against agitators who hold mantic offices: the *rāgimu*, the *maḫḫû*,[1] and the *šā'ilu*[2] (ll. 116–17)—agitators of a type not mentioned in the Hittite and Aramean treaties.[3]

2. As in the Esarhaddon treaties, so in Deuteronomy besides the warnings against agitating officials we find warnings against plots originating in family circles. There is even a correspondence in the way the members of the family are specified. Where the Esarhaddon treaty has: 'If you listen to or conceal any word . . . from the mouth of your brothers, your sons, your daughters',[4] we find in Deut. 13: 7: 'If your brother, your own mother's son,[5]

[1] See A. Malamat, 'Prophecy in the Mari Documents', *EI* 4 (1956/7), 75 ff. (Hebrew with English summary). In Malamat's view the *maḫḫû* is a sort of ecstatic prophet and is 'phenomenologically closer to the Biblical prophet than other cultic personages known to us from Akkadian literature'. Wiseman is inclined to believe, following H. W. Saggs ('The Nimrud Letters', *Iraq* 17 (1955), 135), who in turn has taken up the suggestion of W. J. Martin (*Tribut und Tributleistungen bei Assyria*, pp. 26–7) that the *maḫḫû* in this context is an official and not necessarily a sacral personage. The fact that he is here mentioned, however, between two sacral functionaries: the *rāgimu* and the *šā'ilu* would lead to the inference that the *maḫḫû* is a prophet and not an official, and so von Soden in his article, '*maḫḫû*' in *AHw*.

[2] Following Borger's restoration (*ZA* NF 20 (1961), 178) read: DUMU *šā'ili amāt DINGIR* (.MEŠ), which brings to mind the person who consults the word of the Lord in Biblical accounts; cf. 2 Sam. 16: 23: כאשר ישאל בדבר האלהים 'as one consults the oracle of God'. The *šā'ilu* in the Akkadian literature was generally involved in the interpretation of dreams, although this was not his only function; see L. Oppenheim, *The Interpretation of Dreams in the Ancient Near East*, 1956, pp. 221 f. It is possible then that the נביא represents the types of *maḫḫû* and *rāgimu* while חלם חלום equals the *šā'ilu* type.

[3] Deut. 13: 2 speaks about a prophet or a dreamer, who acts by a sign or a portent (אות or מופת), oracular devices attested in contemporaneous Assyrian literature. Thus, for example, in Aššurbanipal's annals: '*ina IZKIM.MEŠ* (*idāte* = אותות, see *ittu* II, *AHw*, p. 406) MÁŠ.GE$_6$ (*šuttu*) INIM.GAR (*egirrû*) *šipir maḫḫê*' = by portents (given) through dreams and omens received by prophets', M. Streck, *Assurpanipal II*, p. 120, v: 95; cf. *CAD*, vol. IV (E), p. 45a. For *egirrû* see: L. Oppenheim, *AfO* 17 (1954), 49 ff.

[4] ll. 115–16.

[5] LXX and Samaritan add: 'the son of your father', but this seems to be a harmonizing gloss. The legislator tries to stress in this context the very close relationship to the relative or the friend (cf. אשת חיקך and רעך אשר כנפשך). With 'your mother's son' בן אמך he wants to make clear that even if it be your uterine brother, you must report him for treason. The specially close relationship to the uterine brother is expressed too in the Esarhaddon treaties in speaking about loyalty to Aššurbanipal's brother(s): 'his brother(s)', 'son(s) by the same mother', ll. 94, 171, 270, 504. In the Hittite instructions the reference is mostly to brother by the same father (E. von Schuler, *Dienstanweisungen*, p. 1,

or your son or daughter or the wife of your bosom or your closest friend[1] entices you secretly saying 'Come let us worship other gods . . .'.

3. The expression 'to speak defection or rebellion' דבר סרה encountered in Deut. 13: 6 occurs literally in the Esarhaddon treaty —*dabab surrāte*[2]—and appears to be an expression taken from the political vocabulary of the period.[3]

Finally there is a striking verbal similarity between the deuteronomic law of incitement and punitive command in the Sefire treaty to be applied if an entire city is won over by conspirators. Deut. 13: 16 commands: 'You shall surely put the inhabitants of that city to the sword . . .' הכה תכה את ישבי העיר ההוא לפי חרב, while the Sefire treaty says: 'And if it be a city then you shall smite it by the sword' והן קריה הא נכה תכוה בחרב.[4]

§ 2, ll. 9 f. [according to Goetze's reading in *JCS* 13 (1959), 66], p. 14, § 26, l. 58 [cf. Goetze, op. cit., p. 67]), but sometimes a distinction is made between the legitimate brother and the brother from a concubine (Schuler, ibid., p. 23, §§ 4–5). It should be added that in *VTE* the brothers are mentioned along with Aššurbanipal as the ones to whom loyalty must be kept, while in the Hittite instructions the brothers appear among the potential instigators of rebellion.

[1] Wife and friend are not mentioned in the Esarhaddon treaties. The friend, however, appears in the oath of loyalty to Aššurbanipal (*ABL* 1239, rev. 22): *lu-u bēl ṭa-ba-te-ku-nu* = or (from) your friends. Cf. also the reconstruction of Goetze in the Hittite instructions (*JCS* 13 (1959), 67 to Text no. 1, ii: 43–6): 'Nobody must say, "he is my [friend], [I shall not] denounce [him]".'

[2] l. 502.

[3] See M. Streck, *Assurbanipal II*, p. 12: 120, (*da-bab-ti*, var. *da-bab*), 64: 91, 70: 68; A. C. Lie, *Sargon*, l. 79 (*da-bab-ti sar-ra-ti*); cf. too M. Schorr, 'Einige hebr. babylonische Redersarten', *MGWJ* 53 (1909), 432.

[4] Sefire III: 12–13 in accordance with Fitzmyer's (*Sefîre*) reading: תכוה instead of תפוה. J. Greenfield (*Acta Orientalia* 29, p. 5) considers the annihilation of the priestly city of Nob by Saul (1 Sam. 22: 19), which is described in language similar to that of Deut., an example of a rebellious city. On the other hand, R. Frankena has surmised ('The Vassal Treaties of Esarhaddon and the dating of Deuteronomy', *Oudtest. Studiën* 14 (1965), 143) that Saul's wrath toward his officials in this story (v. 8) was provoked by their concealing from him the treaty between David and Jonathan, which constituted a breach of their obligations to report every conspiracy to the king. Frankena's view may have some support in the parallel between the phraseology ואין גלה את אזני employed in 1 Sam. 22: 8 and '[*uz-ni*] *lā tu-pat-ta-a-ni*', which appears in the oath of loyalty to Aššurbanipal (Waterman, *RCAE* 1239, rev. 6–7). Cf. *VTE* ll. 143–4. As in the Hittite and Assyrian Kingdoms so in Israel the king used to put his officials under oath (see above, pp. 89 f.). In our case Ahimelek and his kin, the priests of Nob, who, like the other officials, had presumably been put under obligation (cf. v. 8 with v. 13), not only broke their obligation to report treachery but also gave bread and assistance to the fugitive traitor. This last violation constituted an outstanding breach of the covenant (cf. Sefire III: 5 ff. and

The religious import of the ordinances met with in Deut. 13, then, is fused with political import, which accounts for their resemblance to the clauses of the political treaties of the ancient Near East. It would appear that Deut. 13 constituted an important section of the covenant which Josiah made with the people. As we have already noted, it reflects the revolutionary atmosphere that prevailed during his period.

The laws against sedition in Deuteronomy preserve ancient material[1] pertaining to the ancient covenant between God and Israel, but the form in which these laws now lie before us cannot be earlier than the seventh century B.C. The present style of the laws and their affinities with political documents from the seventh century prove their connection with Josianic times.

Frankena's[2] suggestion that Josiah's covenant with God was considered as a substitute for the former treaty with the King of Assyria and that it thereby expressed vassalship to Yahweh instead of vassalship to the King of Assyria is very plausible, and it explains the similarity between the warnings against sedition in the political treaties and in Deut. 13. Political and religious aspects, particularly in the Israelite covenant, were fused to such an extent, however, that it is sometimes difficult to distinguish between them. Therefore it must be said that, although the passage in Deut. 13 seems to be concerned only with religious loyalty to the God of Israel, the laws actually served to guarantee the political-national allegiance of the people no less than their religious allegiance—a fact exemplified by the law of the rebellious city.[3]

(*d*) *The scene of the covenant and the oath-imprecation*

Deut. 29: 9–28 is a kind of protocol summarizing the section on

esp. ותסך להם לחם, which means 'you will provide them with food' (see J. Greenfield, *Acta Orientalia* 29, p. 8) and the treaties with the Kaskeans (see E. von Schuler, *Die Kaskäer*, 1965, p. 119 § 14, cf. p. 139, § 3), where the vassal is also commanded not to put the enemy on the right way, a service which Ahimelek may have offered David by giving the oracle (vv. 10 and 13 שאל לו ביהוה, cf. Judg. 18: 5–6). The vassals of Esarhaddon were also sworn to 'set a fair path at the feet of Aššurbanipal (KASKAL SIG_5 *ina* GÌR-*šu la ta-ša-kan-a-ni*), a phrase identical with one in the Hittite treaties: *nu tu-uz-zi-im* SIG_5-*an* KASKAL-[*a*]*n u-i-da-at-tin* = 'bring the army upon a fair path' (see E. von Schuler, op. cit., pp. 127–8, § 14).

[1] See, for instance, J. L'Hour, 'Une législation criminelle dans le Deutéronome', *Biblica* 44 (1963), 1–15.

[2] R. Frankena, *Oudtest Studiën*. 14 (1965), 122–54.

[3] See above, p. 92.

the covenant and oath-imprecation,[1] and it, too, is permeated with motifs and scenes characteristic of the ancient Near Eastern treaties. We have already analysed[2] the concept of the covenant and oath-imprecation in this section in the light of the Akkadian *adê māmīt*, but what is most instructive is the covenant scene (vv. 9–14) and its parallel in the conventional treaty documents prevalent during the eighth and seventh centuries B.C. We cite below some of the more striking similarities between them:

1. Treaty ceremonies in the ancient Near East, and especially during the neo-Assyrian and neo-Babylonian periods, were generally conducted in the presence of a large group of people including men, women, and children,[3] and also of all classes of the population:[4] scribes, diviners, priests, physicians and augurs. A similar representation of all classes of Israelite society is met with in the covenant ceremonies depicted in Deut. 29: 9–14 and in other parts of deuteronomic literature: 'You stand this day all of you before the Lord your God; your heads, your judges,[5] your elders, and your officers, all the men of Israel, your little ones, your wives, and the sojourner who is in your camp, both he who hews your wood and he who draws your water' (Deut. 29: 9–10; see Josh. 8: 33 and 35). And similarly in the Josianic covenant: 'All the men of Judah and all the ישבי ירושלם,[6] and the priests and the prophets, all the people, both small and great (למקטן ועד גדול)' (2 Kgs. 23: 2). The same expression 'the small and the great', occurs verbatim in connection with the treaty ceremony in the Esarhaddon treaty (l. 5)[7] and in the annals of Aššurbanipal.[8]

[1] Cf. N. Lohfink, 'Der Bundesschluss im Land Moab', *BZ* 6 (1962), 38: 'Das sich anschliessende Stück 29, 9–14 ist ein fast juristisch gemeinter, präzis formulierter Text, eine Art *Protokoll*' (emphasis added). To my mind the 'protocol' compromises all of vv. 9–28 which are thematically related and appear to constitute a homogeneous unit.

[2] Above, pp. 66 f.

[3] Cf. L. Waterman, *RCAE* 202, Rev. 10–13: *ṣābē mārēšunu u aššātišunu.*

[4] L. Waterman, *RCAE* 33: 13–14: *ṭupšarrē, bārê, mašmašē, asê, dāgil iṣṣūrē.*

[5] Read שפטיכם for שבטיכם with LXX, compare Josh. 8: 33; 23: 2; 24: 1. See S. R. Driver, *Deuteronomy*, ICC, ad loc., and com. 2 Sam. 7: 7 with 1 Chr. 17: 6.

[6] Cf. above, p. 88 n. 2.

[7] *gabbu* TUR GAL (*ṣiḫir* [*u*] *rabi*) *mala bašû*='young and old, as many as there are'.

[8] *upaḫḫir nišē māt aššur ṣiḫir u rabi* (M. Streck, *Assurbanipal* II, p. 4, i: 18), see above, p. 87.

2. Treaties of the third and second millenium were ratified by sacrifices. Thus, in the treaty between Naram Sin and the Elamites (2300–2250 B.C.)[1] we find sacrifices offered and statues erected at the Elamite sanctuary. The stele of the vultures also tells us about sacrificing a bull and two doves.[2] In the Mari documents we even meet with two different traditions of covenantal sacrifices:[3] the provincial tribes seem to prefer a goat[4] and a puppy for the ritual ceremony of the covenant, whereas the King of Mari seems to insist on killing an ass.[5] In the Alalaḫ documents the covenant involves cutting the neck of a lamb[6] and in one instance there is an explicit reference to 'cutting the neck of a *sacrificial* lamb'.[7] A later Alalaḫian covenantal text[8] mentions an offering[9] and a brazier[10] in connection with the oath that the parties had taken. Similar features characterize the ancient Israelite covenants. The animals that are involved in the covenant with Abraham in Gen. 15 seem to have a sacrificial role assigned to them.[11] The covenant in Exod. 24 is based wholly upon sacrifice. The secular patriarchal covenants are also ratified by sacrifices (Gen. 21: 27; 31:54).[12]

[1] Cf. Hinz, 'Elams vertrag mit Naram Sin von Akkade', *ZA* 24 (1967), 66–96.

[2] See above, p. 73.

[3] Cf. *ARM* II, 37.

[4] *ḫazzum* (compare *ḫanzum* and *enzum*) is Hebrew עֵז (see *AHw*).

[5] *ḫayaram qatālum*, *ARM* II, 37: 6, 11.

[6] D. J. Wiseman, *JCS* 12, p. 126, rev. l. 41: *kišād 1 immeru iṭbuḫ*.

[7] *AT** 54: 16–18: GÚ SILÁ *a-sa-ki* IGI PN UGULA UKU.UŠ *ṭa-bi-iḫ* 'the neck of a sacrificial lamb was cut in the presence of PN the general' (see Draffkorn, *JCS* 13, p. 95, n. 11). The presence of the general at this transaction may be paralleled with Gen. 21: 22 f. and the Yahwistic counterpart in 26: 26 ff. See JAOS 90 (1970), p. 97, n. 119.

[8] S. Smith, *The Statue of Idrimi*, 1949, cf. the review by A. Goetze, *JCS* 4 (1950), 226–31.

[9] Read in l. 55 with Goetze (ibid., p. 228) SISKUR instead of GAZ, compare in l. 89 the same sign (SISKUR) with *ni-iq-qi* ḪI.A.

[10] *kinūnu* in l. 55.

[11] See S. E. Loewenstamm, 'Zur Traditionsgeschichte des Bundes zwischen den Stücken', *VT* 18 (1968), 500 ff. We cannot, however, accept his view that the sacrifice is a late element in the tradition of Gen. 15. As we have seen, the sacrificial element in the covenant is very ancient and if it is true that two motifs are combined here, as Loewenstamm argues, sacrifice on the one hand and symbolic dramatization on the other, we would be inclined to say—following the history of the covenant form—that sacrifice antedates the symbolic act. The three-year-old bull in 1 Sam. 1: 24 (cf. LXX and Q) and the three-year animals in Gen. 15 do not necessarily reflect a Shilonite tradition because these are also known from the Mesopotamian sacrificial tradition, see *CAD*, vol. 2 (B), bīru B, p. 266 for references, and see my article in *JAOS* 90 (1970), p. 198, n. 131.

[12] We are also told there that Abraham gave seven lambs to Abimelech as a 'witness' (עדה) or, as Speiser (*Genesis*, Anchor Bible, ad loc.) translates, a 'proof' for his rights to the well. A similar procedure is found in an old Babylonian act of partition where one of the partners gives to the other two lambs as a proof of

The 'killing of a lamb' is also attested in a Hittite treaty,[1] and covenantal sacrifices were likewise common in Greece.

In the deuteronomic covenant, however, as in other treaties of the first millenium, the sacrificial element is completely absent. The Assyrian treaty becomes binding and valid, not by virtue of the treaty ritual, but by the oath-imprecation (the *māmītu*)[2] that accompanies the ceremony. The ritual itself—if it is performed—serves only a symbolic and dramatic end: to impress tangibly upon the vassal the inevitable consequences of infringing the covenant. The treaty between Aššurnirari V and Mati'ilu of Bit-Agusi[3] even states explicitly that the ram is brought forward in the treaty ceremony not for sacrificial purposes, but to serve as an example of the punishment awaiting the transgressor of the treaty (= Drohritus):

This ram was not taken from its flock for sacrifice . . . if Mati'ilu (shall violate) the covenant and oath to the gods, then, as this ram, which was taken from its flock and to its flock will not return, and at the head of its flock shall not stand, so Mati'ilu with his sons, [ministers], the men of his city, shall be taken from their city, and to his city he shall not return, and at the head of his city he shall not stand . . . if he who is specified by name shall violate this covenant . . . as the head of this ram shall be struck off so shall his head be struck off.[4]

Like Saul, who cut a yoke of oxen into pieces and proclaimed: 'Whoever does not come after Saul and Samuel, so shall it be done to his oxen' (1 Sam. 11: 7),[5] so Bir Ga'yah declared in his treaty with Matî'el: '(As) this calf is cut into two, so may Matî'el be cut into two.'[6] Zedekiah's covenant with the people on the manumission of the slaves (Jer. 34: 8–22) is to be understood in an analogous way; those passing between the two parts of the calf (v. 18) must have accepted the consequences ensuing from a violation of the oath-imprecation in this manner: 'so may it befall me if I shall not observe the words of the covenant.'[7] Dramatic acts of this sort

the agreement (see E. Szlechter, *JCS* 7 (1953), p. 92, § 5, ll. 16–17). Compare also A. Goetze, *JCS* 4 (1950), p. 228, n. 20.

1 Cf. H. Otten, *Istanbuler Mitteilungen* 17 (1967) p. 56, Vs. 15′.

2 Cf. above, pp. 66–7.

3 See E. Weidner, *AfO* 8 (1932–3), 16 ff.

4 Weidner, ibid., col. i: 10 ff.

5 Compare the Mari letter (*ARM* II, no. 48) where it is proposed to cut off the head of a criminal and circulate it among the cities of Ḫana that the troops may fear and quickly assemble.

6 The Sefire treaty I, A: 39–40; compare *VTE*, ll. 551–4, 576–8.

7 Cf. W. Rudolph, *Jeremia*², HAT, 1958, p. 205.

were not, however, performed only with animals. In the Sefire treaty,[1] in the *VTE*,[2] and in Hittite military oath-taking ceremonies[3] similar acts were performed with wax images and other objects.[4] Generally speaking, however, it appears that they were not a requisite part of the ceremony. Many Hittite and Assyrian treaties make no mention of them, nor does the book of Deuteronomy. Apparently the oath-imprecation, recorded in the treaty document was believed to be enough to deter the treaty party from violating its stipulations.

3. The emphasis on the perpetual validity of the treaty as binding all the generations to come is met with both in the *VTE* and in the deuteronomic covenant. Thus the Esarhaddon treaty opens: 'The treaty . . . with Ramatia . . . with his sons . . . his grandsons . . . young and old . . . with all of you, your sons, your grandsons *who will exist in the days to come after the treaty* . . . the treaty (which) Esarhaddon, King of Assyria, had made with you *in the presence of the gods* . . .'[5] and similarly stipulates at the close of the section containing the treaty conditions: 'You swear that you, *while you stand at this place* of this oath swearing . . . wholeheartedly[6] . . . you will teach (the oath)[7] to your sons *who shall be after the treaty*.'[8] In the Covenant of the Plains of Moab Moses likewise declares: '*You stand this day all of you before the Lord* your God . . . all the men of Israel, your little ones, your wives . . . that you may enter into the sworn covenant of the Lord your God . . . Nor is it

[1] I, A: 35–42.

[2] ll. 608–11.

[3] J. Friedrich, 'Der hethitische Soldateneid', *ZA* NF I (1924), 161–92, i: 41–5; ii: 1–3.

[4] This type of symbolism was also employed in Babylonian magic ceremonies (see E. Reiner, *Šurpu*, ll. 60–112).

[5] ll. 1–7.

[6] *ina gu-mur-*[*ti*] *ŠÀ-ku-nu* (= 'wholeheartedly') occurs only in the parallel texts (4337; cf. 4348b) but not in the major text (4327). Wiseman, and so Borger, is of the opinion that it was omitted by mistake. Cf. the similar expression employed in connection with the Josianic covenant: 'And the king . . . . made a covenant . . . *with all his heart* . . .' (2 Kgs. 23: 3), see also Frankena, *Oudtest. Studiën*, p. 14 (1965), 141.

[7] As against Wiseman's reading: *tu-šal-laṭ-a-ni* read with R. Borger (*ZA* 20): *tu-šal-mad-a-ni* (*mad* and *lat* have the same phonogram).

[8] ll. 385–90, compare ll. 288–93: If you will not relate (them) *to your sons and to your grandsons*, *to your seed and to your seed's seed* which shall be in the future, that you will order them as follows: 'Guard this treaty, do not transgress your treaty (*or*) *you will lose your lives*', which sounds similar to Deut. 4: 9–10: 'Only take heed and *preserve your soul* lest you forget the things . . . *make them known to your children and your children's children*' (cf. 4: 40; 6: 2, etc.).

with you only that I make this sworn covenant, *but with him who is not here with us . . . as well as with him who stands here this day*' (Deut. 29: 9–14; cf. 5: 2–4).[1] In the same chapter Moses refers to the generations to come as 'your children who will come up after you' בניכם אשר יקומו מאחריכם (vv. 21–2). This expression also occurs in the Aramaic treaty of Sefire in connection with the treaty commitments devolving upon the future generations: 'And with his (Matî'el's)[2] sons who will come up after him . . .'.[3]

However, in addition to these parallels, we also meet in this section a great many expressions and moods adopted from the sphere of treaties in the ancient Near East. Like ch. 13 this chapter reminds us of the Josianic covenant scene[4] in which the people and their leaders participated (2 Kgs. 23: 1–3), though, in place of the priests and the prophets in the Josianic covenant scene we meet with the tribal chieftains and officers (29: 9 and 10), the leaders of the desert congregation. Like ch. 13, this chapter also contains a warning against individuals or groups harbouring treasonable thoughts in their minds. In this instance, however, they do not disclose these thoughts to anyone, i.e. they do not attempt to incite or arouse others to rebellion, but keep their seditious thoughts to themselves. These persons delude themselves in thinking that since they are committing no actual transgression no harm will befall them: שלום יהיה לי כי בשרירות לבי אלך (29: 18), i.e. 'Since I intend to keep my evil thoughts to myself[5] no one will know and none will

[1] As in *VTE* so in Deuteronomy this section of the validity of covenant comes twice, before the stipulations and after them.

[2] The word בנוה relates to Matî'el (cf. F. Rosenthal, *ANET*², p. 504) compare I, B: 1–3 and I, C: 1–4 and see: H. Tadmor, *Yeivin Festschrift* (Jerusalem) 1970, 397 ff. (Hebrew).

[3] I, A: 5: זי יסקן באשרה, cf. I, B: 3; I, C: 4. The word באשרה = באתרה (בתרה), and means 'after him'. See J. Fitzmyer, *Sefire*, ad loc., and cf. Dan. 2: 39: . . . ובתרך תקום מלכו. The expression יקומו מאחריכם in Deut. 29: 21, corresponds therefore to יסקן באשרה in the Sefire treaty.

[4] The concluding verse of the section (v. 28) which is formulated in the first person plural constitutes the commitment of the treaty party. Cf. the vassal's pledge in the Esarhaddon treaty which is also formulated in the first person plural (ll. 494–512).

[5] The expression 'stubbornness of heart' (שרירות לב) denotes obstinate thought or reflection, cf. Jer. 18: 12: 'We will follow our own plans (מחשבותינו) and everyone will act according to the stubbornness of his evil heart (שרירות לבו)', where the word מחשבה parallels שרירות לב. See also Targum Onkelos's translation of Deut. 29: 18: 'for in the reflections of my heart will I go', see also D. Hoffman, *Deuteronomium*, ad loc. The phrase שרירות לב in Ps. 81. 13 which parallels the word מועצה (counsel) apparently must be similarly rendered as

punish me.' Only this interpretation seems to give any plausible meaning to the verse. Some scholars render the phrase שלום יהיה לי כי בשרירות לבי אלך in the *concessive* sense: 'There will be peace unto me, even though I walk in the stubbornness of my heart.' This is not a plausible interpretation. Apart from the difficulty of ascribing an unusual meaning to the particle כי, the verse fails to account for the defector's sense of security as it does if we take the word in its usual sense, 'because'.

Now eventualities of this sort are also referred to in the political treaties of the ancient Near East:

If a Hittite man will do evil against me . . . and you will not report it, and you will even say: 'I have sworn an oath-imprecation, I shall not speak and I shall not act but he may do as his heart desires' . . . (then) these curses will destroy you.

(Treaty between Šuppiluliumaš and Ḫuqqanaš)[1]

If somebody acts treacherously and says the following: 'I am bound by the covenant[2] but if the enemy kills him or he kills the enemy I cannot (or will not) know' . . . he violates the oath.

(Treaty between Šuppiluliumaš and Tette)[3]

And [if one of my sons says: 'I shall sit upon the throne] of my father' . . . or if my son seeks [my head to kill me and you say in your soul]: 'let him kill whomever he would kill'[4] . . . you will have been false to all the gods of [the treaty].

(Sefire treaty)[5]

The Hittite and Aramaic treaties, then, like Deut. 29 also deal with the eventuality of tacit rebellion. However, as the authorities cannot act as they do in ch. 13 against such passive violators of the covenant, their punishment must consequently be left to Heaven:

'obstinate deliberation', cf. Prov. 20: 18: 'Plans (מחשבות) are established by counsel (בעצה).' Ehrlich's rendering of Deut. 29: 18 (*Randglossen*, ad loc.) is highly conjectural and cannot be demonstrated. After writing the present chapter my attention was called to L. Kopf's article in *VT* 9 (1959) (p. 283) in which he similarly renders the expression שרירות לב 'reflection, thought', taking the stem שרר to be the Hebrew cognate of the Arabic سرّ.

1 F6, §§ 15–16; cf. F5, § 17; F1, § 9. Friedrich, *MVÄG* 34, p. 117 n. 4.

2 *anāku ša mām[īti] u ša riksime* = 'I am (a man) of the oath and the covenant'.

3 W3, Vs. ii: 26 f., compare W4, Vs. 15 f.

4 יקתל מן יקתל which conveys the idea found in the just-mentioned Hittite treaty: 'if the enemy kills him or he kills the enemy I won't know.'

5 II, B: 7–9. The restorations are based on III: 11 and 17. See Fitzmyer, ad loc.

'The Lord will not pardon him, *but rather the anger of the Lord and his passion will rage against the man and the curses written in this book will settle upon him and the Lord will blot out his name from under heaven*' (Deut. 29: 19).

Similar formulations are repeatedly encountered in the epilogue sections or on the seal impressions of the ancient Near Eastern treaties:

If you will not observe these words . . . and in the days that come you, your sons, your sons' sons, with your leaders will not remain loyal . . . *according to all that is written in this tablet . . . then* (*these curses*) *will destroy you and* your sons . . . and your house *from the face of the earth.*
(Treaty between Muršiliš II and Manapa-Dattaš)[1]

These are the *words of the covenant and imprecation written in this tablet.*[2] If Duppi-Tešup will not observe the words of the covenant and oath-imprecation (then) *these curses will destroy* Duppi-Tešup, his wife, his son, his son's son, his house, his city, his land, and all his possesions.
(Treaty between Muršiliš II and Duppi-Tešup)[3]

Whoever will not observe the words of the inscription which is on this stele and will say: 'I shall efface some of his words' . . . *may the gods overturn th*[*at m*]*an and his house and all that* (*is*) *in it . . . let his sci*[*on*] *inherit no name.*
(Sefire treaty)[4]

This type of malediction is to be found already in the epilogue of the Code of Hammurabi:[5]

If a man has not heeded my *words which I wrote on my stele* . . . has effaced my name, may he (Enlil) order . . . *the destruction of his city*, the dispersion of his people . . . the *extinction of his name and memory from the land.*

The curse of blotting out of one's name seems to derive from the genre of curses originally laid on those who erased or mutilated

[1] F4, § 19.

[2] *awāte ša riksi u ša māmīti ša ina libbi ṭuppi annīti šaṭrat*; cf. Streck, *Assurbanipal II*, p. 76, ix: 60: *arrāti mala ina adêšunu šaṭrā*, 'as many curses as there are written in their treaties'; the Sefire steles (*passim*): עדיא זי בספרה זנה 'the oaths which are in this inscription' and ככל אלות הברית הכתובה בספר התורה הזה 'in accordance with the oaths of the covenant written in this book of the Torah' (Deut. 29: 20, cf. v. 19).

[3] F1, § 20, cf. W3, Rs. iv: 46–52, W4, Rs. 12–16; cf. also the treaty between Muršiliš II and Niqmepa (*PRU* IV, 17.338: 6′–13′ (pp. 86–7); 17.353: 9′–17′ (p. 90); 17.357: 7′–11′ (p. 93)).

[4] I, C: 16–25 (cf. II, C).

[5] xxvi b: 18–80; cf. xxviii b: 45–9 (see Driver–Miles, *BL* II, 100–1, 104–5).

the words of an inscription, as may be learned, for example, from the seal impression of the Esarhaddon treaty:[1] 'He who erases (my) written name or alters this, . . . erase his name and his seed from the land.' The punishment was to be measure for measure.[2] Whoever expunged the name of the inscriber of the stone would suffer the fate of having his name erased (from the Book of Life?).[3] Thus, for example, Azitawadda, king of the Danunites, wrote:[4] 'If there be a king among kings and a prince among princes or a man . . . *who shall wipe out the name of* Azitawadda from this gate . . . may Ba'al-šamem and El, the Creator-of-the-Earth . . . wipe out that ruler and that king and that man . . .'.[5] Kilamuwa similarly threatened in his inscription: 'He who smashes this inscription, may Ba'al-Ṣamad smash his head.'[6] However, this formulation was sometimes divorced from its original limited context (in which it referred to the damaging of an inscription) and was employed as a malediction against potential infringers of the treaty stipulations.

The treaty curses are likewise described as possessing an independent power of their own to pursue those who violate the treaty. Thus, in the Hittite treaties we repeatedly encounter the formula: 'And the curses shall pursue you relentlessly.'[7] Similarly we read in the epilogue of the Code of Hammurabi: 'May they (the curses) quickly overtake him',[8] and in the Esarhaddon annals: 'the oaths of the great gods which they violated overtook them'.[9]

This conception also finds expression in various passages in the deuteronomic covenant, for instance: 'and every oath written in

[1] Seal Impression A, ll. 13–15: *šá* MU [*šaṭ*]-*ru i-pa-aš-ši-ṭu* . . . *an-nu-u ú-nak-ka-ru* MU-*šú* NUMUN-*šú ina* KUR *pi-šiṭ* (p. 15).

[2] Compare also the curses treated by G. Offner, 'À propos de la sauvegarde des tablettes en Assyro-Babylonie', *RA* 44 (1950), 135 ff.: *ša ṭuppa šuatu itabbalu* ^{d}*Šamaš litbalšu* = whoever will carry away this tablet may Šamaš carry him away; *šā šumī šaṭru ipaššiṭu šumšu išaṭṭaru* ^{d}*Nabu ṭupšar gimri šumšu lipšiṭ* = whoever shall erase my written name and will write down his name may Nabu the universal scribe erase his name (pp. 136 and 138).

[3] Cf. Ps. 69: 29.

[4] See *KAI* 26, A iii: 12 f.

[5] אש ימח שם אזתוד . . . ומח בעל שמם . . .

[6] *KAI* 24: 15 f. ומי ישחת הספר ז ישחת ראש בעל צמד. Cf. also the Nerab inscription (*KAI* 225): 'Whoever (you are) removes (תהנס) this statue . . . from its place may the gods . . . remove (יסחו) your name and place from the living ones . . . and if you guard (תנצר) this statue . . . may your offspring be guarded (תנצר).'

[7] F5, § 9: 56–7 (*parḫieškandu*), § 16: 30.

[8] *errētim dannātim* . . . *arḫiš likšudāšu* (CH xxviii b: 84–91, compare xxvii b: 33).

[9] *māmīt ilāni rabûti ša ētiqu ikšudanni* (R. Borger, *Asarhaddon*, 103: 23).

this document will come upon him' ורבצה בו כל האלה הכתובה בספר הזה (Deut. 29: 19), 'all these curses shall come upon you and overtake you' ובאו עליך כל הקללות האלה והשיגוך (28: 15), or 'all these curses shall come upon you and pursue you and overtake you' ובאו עליך כל הקללות האלה ורדפוך[1] והשיגוך (28: 45).

The Esarhaddon inscriptions and the *kudurru* also contain a divine jealousy and wrath motif similar to that found in Deut. 29: 19: 'the anger of the Lord and his passion will rage . . .'. Thus, we read in the Esarhaddon inscription: '(And whosoever will not preserve this inscription then) *may the god Aššur . . . look down upon him in anger* (*ezziš likkilmešu*), *let him overturn his kingdom, and cut off his name and seed from the land*.'[2] The Sefire treaty similarly refers to יום חרון 'a day of wrath' (II, B: 12), which is to befall those who violate the covenant.

Thus, the four motifs occurring in Deut. 29: 19: (*a*) the divine wrath, (*b*) the curse which settles upon and pursues the malefactor, (*c*) the oath-imprecation inscribed in a document, (*d*) the obliteration of the malefactor's name and memory, are also met with in treaties and legal documents of the ancient Near East where, as in Deuteronomy, they form part of the closing section of the treaty or document.

These formulae all threaten annihilation of the violator's seed and possessions by divine agencies if he himself eludes apprehension by men. The punishment of the covert transgressors of the treaty by total annihilation through divine agency corresponds to the punishment inflicted by human agencies upon overt violators. A city that was incited to idolatrous worship and received its punishment at the hands of mortal agents was, according to deuteronomic law, to be destroyed together with its inhabitants, beasts, and all objects found therein, to be razed and burnt and turned into an eternal heap never to be rebuilt (13: 16–17). The city or land that violates the covenant but is punished by God is described as suffering a similar fate: 'brimstone and salt, and a burnt-out waste, unsown, and growing nothing, where no grass can

[1] The Hittite verb *parḫ-* (p. 108 n. 7), means also 'to pursue', 'drive', etc.

[2] R. Borger, *Asarhaddon*, Ass. A, viii: a–f (p. 6), and in Esarhaddon's Nippur inscription: 'He who will destroy in mischief the inscription containing my name, or will change its place, may the Great-Mistress of Nippur, the great lady, frown upon him in anger and annihilate his name (and) his seed in all the lands.' See A. Goetze, 'Esarhaddon's Inscription from Nippur', *JCS* 17 (1963), 130–1, ll. 20–1.

sprout, an overthrow like that of Sodom and Gomorrah, Admah and Zeboiim which the Lord overthrew in his anger and wrath' (Deut. 29: 22). The razing and burning of a city and its sowing with salt and brimstone seem to have been the conventional punishment for breach of treaty. Thus Aššurbanipal boasts that he destroyed Elam and had it strewn with salt and cress (*saḫlû*).[1] Tiglath-Pileser I recounts that he turned the city of Ḫunuša into a city of rubble and had it strewn with *ṣīpu*;[2] and like Deut. 29: 22 the Sefire treaty states that if Matî'el will violate the treaty then Arpad will be burnt to the ground and sown with salt and cress.[3] The use of these harmful substances (salt, cress, *ṣīpu*) with respect to treaty violators is met with in other Biblical passages besides Deut. 29: 22. Abimelech is described as having sown the rebellious city of Shechem with salt (Judg. 9: 45).[4] In a doom oracle on Ammon and Moab (Zeph. 2: 8–10) in addition to salt[5] mention is also made of nettles (חרול), which like its counterparts (קמוש, סירים, חוח)[6] is equivalent to cress (= *saḫlû*) and *kudimmu*. A woe oracle on Edom (Isa. 34: 9 ff.) describes the destroyed Edom[7] as being overgrown with thistles (קמוש), as well as being covered with brimstone and pitch (v. 9), which appears to be the equivalent of the Akkadian *ṣīpu*.[8] Another passage

[1] Streck, *Assurbanipal II*, p. 56, vi: 78–80: *nagē māt Elam* [ki] *ušaḫrib ṭābta* [šam] *saḫlê usappiḫa ṣīruššun*. See also R. Thompson, *The Prisms of Esarhaddon and Ashurbanipal*, 1931, pl. 17, col. v: 7–8, p. 84; Shalmaneser I (*KAH* I. 13: 2) speaks of having strewn the city of Arinna with *kudimmu* which in Gevirtz's opinion is identical with *saḫlû* ('Jericho and Schehem', *VT* 13 (1963), p. 57, n. 3).

[2] L. W. King, *The Annals of the Kings of Assyria* I, 1902, p. 79, col. vi, 14: NA4 (.MEŠ) *ṣi-pa* . . . *azru*. (cf. p. 119 : 14).

[3] I, A: 35–6. איך זי תקד שעותא זא באש כן תקד ארפד . . . ויזרע בהן הדד מלח ושחלין.

[4] See Gevirtz, 'Jericho'.

[5] Cf. another oracle on Moab (Jer. 48: 9 ff.) which contains an imprecation (v. 10) and was apparently uttered during a war resulting from a breach of treaty (see below): 'Give ציץ to Moab for she would fly away; her cities shall become a desolation with no inhabitant in them.' The word ציץ means 'salt' as in Ugaritic, see W. L. Moran, *Biblica* 39 (1958), 69–71.

[6] Like cress (*saḫlû*) and *kudimmu* these are likewise noxious weeds which grow among the rubble, cf. Prov. 24: 31; Job 30: 7. Compare also Hos. 9: 6 where קמוש and חוח are mentioned as overgrowing the homes of the Ephraimites.

[7] For a recent discussion of this oracle see Hillers, *Treaty curses* 44 f. in which he demonstrates that it contains imprecations of the type encountered in political treaties and believes that they belonged to the group of imprecations that appeared in the treaty between Judah and Edom. Hillers has, however, only dealt with the imprecations in vv. 11 ff., but in the light of our above remarks, vv. 9–10, which refer to the land turning into pitch and brimstone, should also be taken as imprecations connected with this treaty.

[8] Like *ṣipu* (see *CAD* vol. 16 (Ṣ), *ṣipu* B) brimstone and pitch are mineral substances; see the article חמר, *Encyclopedia Miqra'it* III.

in Isaiah (33:7–12)[1] which refers to covenant violation describes the devastated land as being filled with burnt thorns (קוצים כסוחים) and lime (שיד), which, like pitch and *ṣīpu*, is an inflammable material.

The common property of these substances: salt (= *ṭābtu*), lime, brimstone, pitch (= *ṣīpu*?), cress, nettles, and thistles (= *saḫlû*, *kudimmu*) is their capacity to turn an area into a perpetual wasteland. This waste and desolation is depicted in Biblical literature either as a desert and wilderness or as a saltland (ארץ מלחה) (Jer. 17: 6; Job 39: 6) and is generally compared to the destruction of Sodom and Gomorrah (Deut. 29: 22; Isa. 13: 19; Jer. 49: 18; 50: 40; Amos 4: 11; Zeph. 2: 9) which God laid waste by raining fire and brimstone upon them (Gen. 19: 24) and turning them into saltfields (cf. v. 26). In view of the fact that the passages referred to above occur in connection with breach of treaty[2] we may legitimately assume that the overthrow of Sodom and Gomorrah was conceived as the classic punishment of breach of covenant with the Deity (Gen. 13: 14; 18: 20; 19: 20)[3] and that the Deity was conceived as employing the conventional means of punishing treaty violators (i.e. by destroying the land with brimstone and salt). This may also be inferred from the phraseology employed by the author of Deut. 29. The verb הפך in the sense of 'to destroy', 'to devastate' in reference to the punishment of breach of treaty is also used in the Sefire treaty (I, C: 21),[4] as is the verb שחת (I, A: 32), and is frequently employed in the Biblical descriptions of the overthrow of Sodom and Gomorrah (Gen. 19: 13, 14, 21, 25, 29).

[1] The reading עדים instead of the MT ערים in v. 9 (= I Q Is.[a]) was already suggested by Duhm in his commentary on Isaiah (HKAT[3]). However, in his time the terms *adê* and עדן as denoting 'treaty' were still unknown and he consequently took the word as a reference to the witnesses of the treaty. The word עדים would, therefore, constitute an exact parallel of the word ברית which occurs in the second colon of the verse and is thus identical in meaning with the term עֵדוֹת, see above, p. 65 n. 3. Cf. also H. L. Ginsberg, *H. Yalon Jubil. Vol.* 1963, pp. 171–2 (Hebrew). For the term מאס עדים cf. Assyrian: *adê mēsu* (A. G. Lie, *Sargon, The annals* 1929, 68).

[2] On the relationship between the passages in the oracles on the various nations (Isa. 13; Jer. 49–50; Zeph. 2) and treaty imprecations, see Hillers, *Treaty Curses*, pp. 52–3. On Amos 4: 11 and its connection with the treaty, see W. Brueggemann, *VT* 15 (1965) 1–15.

[3] For חטא, עון as denoting the violation of a treaty, cf. Ezek. 21: 28–9; on these verses see M. Tsevat, *JBL* 78 (1959), 199 ff.

[4] 'So may the gods overturn (יהפכו) that man and his house.' As in Gen. 19: 25, the 'overthrow' refers not only to the place where the transgressors of the treaty live (*house*, and in Gen. 19 *cities*) but also the persons themselves (*man*, and in Gen. 19: 25 *the inhabitants of the cities*).

Like the Sefire treaty the Biblical descriptions of the destruction of Sodom and Gomorrah also refer to the destruction of all vegetation (Gen. 19: 25; cf. Deut. 29: 22).

The principal object of strewing a destroyed city with brimstone, salt, and nettles was to prevent its resettlement. The city was to remain a wasteland, never to be resown or resettled (cf. Jer. 17: 6), or, as Deuteronomy phrases it (13: 17), it was to be turned 'into an everlasting heap' תל עולם. The act of strewing the destroyed area with salt was, of course, accompanied by the pronouncement of imprecations of a sacral nature which were intended to inflict harm on whoever would restore it,[1] but these imprecations no more reduce the political significance of the act than the imprecations which accompany the state treaties detract from the political character of the treaties.[2]

A detailed description of a settlement destroyed in a similar manner is met with in Job 18: 8–21, a passage which depicts the frightful end of the dwellings of the ungodly:

For he sends (?) his feet into a net and he walks upon a snare. The trap shall grip his heel . . . The snare is laid for him in the ground and a trap for him in the way. Horrors frighten him on every side, and chase him at his heels. His strength (= his firstborn)[3] is hunger-bitten, and calamity is ready for his rib (= wife).[4] He shall eat the strips of his hide, the starving firstborn[5] shall eat his own flesh-strips. He is torn from the tent in which he trusted, and horrors make him go to the king.[6] In his

[1] Josh. 6: 26; on the problem in general see Gevirtz, 'Jericho'.

[2] As against Gevirtz (ibid.), who regards the procedure as a preparatory act in the consecration of the city.

[3] אונו here means the 'firstborn' as in Gen. 49: 3; Deut. 21: 17; Ps. 78: 51; 105: 36. See N. H. Torczyner, *Job*, ad loc.

[4] Rashi explains צלעו here as the evildoer's *wife* (cf. Gen. 2. 21 ff.), and so Torczyner, op. cit. This seems quite logical in view of the parallelism with son (cf., e.g., Ps. 109: 9).

[5] בכור מות is the son who is doomed to death like בן מות (cf. Torczyner, op. cit.). *bukru* in Akkadian (used mainly in poetry) means son or child and not necessarily firstborn (cf. *CAD*, vol. 2 (B), pp. 309–10). It seems that in Hebrew poetry also the word בכור sometimes means simply son, cf. Isa. 14: 30. N. Sarna ('The mythological Background of Job 18', *JBL* 72 (1963), 315) following Cassuto takes בכור מות as son of Môt, the ruler of the Canaanite nether world, who, in his opinion, is here depicted as devouring the evil man's skin. This idea, however, does not fit the context which deals with the hunger of the evil man and his sons (see the preceding verse) and not with the hunger of Môt and his son.

[6] As Moran has demonstrated ('*taqtul—Third Masculine Singular', *Biblica* 45 (1964), 80–2) there is no reason to say that the subject of ותצעדהו is בכור מות

tent dwells Lilith;[1] brimstone is scattered upon his habitation. His roots dry up beneath, and his branches wither above. His memory perishes from the earth, and he has no name in the street. He is thrust from light into darkness, and driven out of the world. He has no offspring or descendant among his people, and no survivor where he used to live. They that come after him shall be astonished at his day, and horror seizes them that were before him. Surely such are the dwellings of the ungodly, such is the place of him who knows not God.

The image of being caught in the trap is very common in treaty maledictions.[2] The terrors which haunt the evildoer are the horrors which accompany the destruction of his dwelling place (cf. Ezek. 26: 21; 27: 36; 28: 19; Ps. 73: 19).[3] The king mentioned in this context is the king who, besieging the city, places his horrors 'round about' as does the king mentioned in Job 15: 24: 'Distress and straits[4] terrify him; they prevail against him, like a king prepared for battle' (לכידור). The word כדור[5] is known to us from Isa. 29: 3, where it occurs in connection with a siege: 'And I will encamp against you round about (כדור) and will besiege you with towers and I will raise siegeworks against you.' The siege will cause a severe famine so that the children will eat strips of skin,[6] a description reminding us of the depiction of the siege of Babylon

and that we have a rare masculine form with a t-preformative (so Sarna, op. cit.). I am inclined rather to accept Moran's (op. cit., p. 82 n. 1) suggestion of vocalizing *w^e taṣ'idūhū* = 'they march him' [with] בלהות as the subject (see Torczyner, *Job*, ad loc.). The translation should then be 'Horrors make him go to the king (= for judgement'; compare 2 Kgs. 25: 6).

[1] Read '*Lilith* dwells in his tent' as suggested by several scholars (cf. *BH*³). Isa. 34, an oracle which contains many treaty imprecations (see above), refers to *Lilith* as finding a resting place among the ruins of Edom (cf. the Sumerian epic 'Gilgamesh, Enkidu and the Nether World' where it is said that Lilith built her house in the midst of the desolated tree (Kramer, *Sumerians*, 200). There are grounds therefore for reading לילית instead of the MT מבלי לו, which is not easily reconciled with the general import of the verse. For the curse of demons choosing the houses of the perfidious cf. *VTE*, l. 493.

[2] Cf. above, p. 73 n. 6.

[3] The horror of destruction is expressed here also by the words: בלהות (v. 11), שמם, שער (v. 20), expressions connected with the fear of the ghosts living in the desolation (cf. the Lilith in v. 15). בלהות is always used in connection with destruction but not necessarily with the nether world as N. Sarna ('The Mythological Background of Job 18') contends. Its occurrence with צלמות in Job 24: 17 does not make it characteristic of Sheol since צלמות as such does not denote the darkness of Sheol, but darkness in general. Cf. D. Winton Thomas, 'צלמות in the Old Testament', *JSS* 7 (1962), 191–200.

[4] For the terms צר, מצוק in curses that relate to the siege of a city, see below, pp. 127–8.

[5] The word may be a cognate of the Akk. *dūru*, 'wall'.

[6] That is, strips of their own skin, see Torczyner, *Job*, ad loc.

in the days of Šamaššumukin.[1] The besieged finally fell into the hands of the king, who devastates their land and strews זרה[2] it with brimstone (v. 15). Then an imprecation follows which was current throughout the ancient Near East. The malediction: 'His roots dry up beneath, and his branches wither above' (v. 16) also occurs in the inscription of Eshmun'azar of Sidon[3] while the curse concerning the blotting out of the name and memory of the malevolent (vv. 17–19) was, as we have seen, an almost stereotyped motif in ancient Near Eastern imprecations.

The passage concludes (v. 20) by describing the astonishment of the former and later generations[4] at the catastrope and the utter destruction of the evildoer. This theme is also treated in Deut. 29 and was later adopted by deuteronomic historiography (1 Kgs. 9: 8–9) and in the deuteronomic prose sermons of the book of Jeremiah:[5] 'And the generation to come . . . and the foreigner that shall

[1] *ana būrišunu šêrē mārēšunu mārātešunu ēkulū, iksusū kurussu* (Streck, *Assurbanipal II*, p. 36, iv: 44–5), 'in their hunger they ate the flesh of their sons and daughters and chewed skin' (see *AHw*, *kurussu*). A similar motif is to be found in the curse of Agade where it is said: 'the strips of the door of his father's house . . . he will grind with his teeth' (A. Falkenstein, 'Fluch über Akkade', *ZA* NF 23 (1965), 120: 254–5). After this curse comes, similarly to our passage in Job and the passage in Isa. 34: 11 ff., a description of desolation breeding demons and wild birds (ibid., ll. 257–61).

[2] The same verb *zerû* is met with in a Tiglath-Pileser I text, see above, p. 110 n. 2.

[3] *KAI* 14: 11–12: אל יכן לם שרש למט ופר למעל. Compare Isa. 37: 31 (= 2 Kgs. 19: 30, Amos 2; 9), for further parallels see Gevirtz, *VT* 11 (1961), p. 150 n. 2. For the understanding of פרי see H. L. Ginsberg, ' "Roots below and fruit above" and related matters', *Hebrew and Semitic Studies*, presented to G. R. Driver, 1963, pp. 72–6.

[4] The phrase concerning the קדמונים and אחרונים is an ossified poetic formula which need not be submitted to logical analysis, since it is only the future generations yet to come which will be astonished and not the earlier generations who have already passed away. Thus, the prose text of Deut. 29 which depicts the original conception of the scene of destruction refers to the reaction of the future generations (v. 21). Similarly literary usage is met with in the phrase מעתה ועד עולם employed in Biblical poetry. The phrase originates from legal documents in which it denoted the date when a transaction was to go into effect. In poetic texts, however, the term is only used as a literary idiom and is not to be taken literally as meaning 'from this moment on' (cf. Mic. 4: 7; Ps. 113: 2). For discussion see S. E. Loewenstamm, 'From This Time and Forevermore', *Tarbiz* 32 (1963), 313–16 (Hebrew with English summary).

The words קדמונים and אחרונים are the equivalents of the Akkadian *maḫrûti* and *arkûti*, which, when occurring together, express totality (cf. below, p. 140 n. 3). The fact that the two Hebrew words appear in *parallelismus membrorum* softens in a way the difficulty in the logic of the verse.

[5] Jer. 16: 10–11; 22: 8–9; see below, pp. 138 ff.

come from a far land will say, when they see the afflictions of that land . . . And all the nations will say:[1] "Why has the Lord done thus to the land?" . . . And they will say, "It is because they forsook the covenant of the Lord, the God of their fathers . . ."' (vv. 21–4). This motif of self-condemnation is also encountered in neo-Assyrian texts in connection with a breach of treaty. Thus we read in the annals of Aššurbanipal: 'Whenever the people of Arabia asked one another saying: "Why is it that such evil has befallen Arabia?" (they answered themselves) saying: "Because we did not observe the solemn treaty of the god Aššur."'[2] In the treaty of Aššurnirari V with Mati'ilu of Bit-Agusi[3] a similar self-condemnation by Mati'ilu's people is encountered in the conclusion of the imprecation section: "And they shall say, 'Woe (to us), we have violated the treaty of Aššurnirari, king of the land of Aššur."'[4] The cuneiform signs preceding this line are unclear, and Weidner[5] has rightly observed that these must have surely included the introductory remarks to the line containing the self-condemnation.

In conclusion we cite below a number of passages from the Esarhaddon inscriptions[6] which contain descriptions of national catastrophes similar to that met with in Deut. 29: 19–27:

The Esarhaddon Inscriptions	Deut. 29
And the anger of Enlil kindled . . . he has proposed to do evil to destroy the land and annihilate its inhabitants (Epis. 5, Fass. a). In the anger of his heart he was determined to destroy the land and annihilate its inhabitants. *A mighty curse was in his mouth* (Epis. 5, Fass. b).	*The anger of the Lord was kindled against this land*, bringing upon it all *the curses* written in this book (v. 26). But the *anger* of the Lord and his passion will rage (v. 19) (cf. 2 Kgs. 22. 16–17 = Dtr).

[1] ואמרו כל הגויים resumes ואמר הדור האחרון in v. 21 so that at the end the question is asked by the Israelites, the foreigners, and all the nations together and answered by them too. This goes well with the Assyrian parallel text where the vassals ask themselves and answer for themselves, whereas in the secondary texts the question is put and answered by the foreigners passing by only (1 Kgs. 9: 8–9; Jer. 22: 8–9) or in another case it is asked by the people and answered by the prophet (Jer. 16: 10–11, v. 19).

[2] Streck, *Assurbanipal II*, p. 79, ix: 68–72, see W. Moran, 'The Ancient Near Eastern background of the love of God', *CBQ* 25 (1963), 84.

[3] E. F. Weidner, *AfO* 8 (1932), 22, Rs. v: 14–15: *u liqbiū mā aḫūla mā ina adê ša Aššurnirāri šar* (*māt Aššur*) *niḫtiṭi*.

[4] The phrase *ina/ana adê ḫaṭû* is the equivalent of the Hebrew הפר ברית; cf. W. von Soden, *AHw, adû* I, where he renders *ina adê ḫaṭû* as 'Eid brechen'.

[5] Ibid., p. 22 n. 42.

[6] R. Borger, *Asarhaddon* § 11, Bab. A–G, pp. 12–15.

The Esarhaddon Inscriptions	Deut. 29
Upon Babylon and Esagila *did his heart anger and his wrath kindle* (Epis. 5, Fass. c).	
A swollen stream . . .*as the Deluge* . . . flooded the city, its inhabitants, its temples, and made it a wasteland (Epis. 7, Fass. 2). Esagila and Babylon were a desert, *a land unploughed* (Epis. 7, Fass. b).	. . . the whole *land unsown growing nothing* . . . *an overthrow like that of Sodom and Gomorrah* (v. 22).
And the people who dwell in her *have fled to another place* and have taken shelter *in a land they did not know* (Epis. 9, Fass. a). The people who dwell in her . . . were distributed among strangers (mob)[1] and have become slaves (Epis. 9, Fass. c).	And the Lord uprooted them from their land in anger and fury and great wrath and cast them *into another land*, as at this day (v. 27). [I will hurl you out of this land *into a land* which *you have not known* . . . (Jer. 16: 13); you will serve strangers in a land which is not yours (Jer. 5: 19).]

The vindication of divine punishment met with in the closing chapter of the deuteronomic covenant is therefore akin to the *topos* prevalent in the Assyrian political documents of the eighth and seventh centuries B.C. and may have been adopted by deuteronomic literature as a result of foreign influence.

THE CURSES

(*a*) *In Deuteronomy 28 and the Near-Eastern state treaties*[2]

The similarity between the imprecations in Deut. 28 and those in ancient Near Eastern treaties has been pointed out by several scholars.[3] This resemblance is at times so striking that it is difficult to escape the impression that Deuteronomy borrowed directly from outside sources. D. J. Wiseman[4] and R. Borger,[5] for example, have called particular attention to the resemblance between Deut. 28: 23 and the vassal-treaties of Esarhaddon ll. 528–33:

[1] The Akkadian text reads: *ana ṣi-in-di ù bir-te* and is translated by *CAD*, vol. 16, (Ṣ) p. 172: 'riffraff', cf. Lambert, *BWL* 34: 99, 286 f.

[2] This study in its basic form has been published in *Biblica* 46 (1965), 417–27.

[3] McCarthy, *Treaty and Covenant*, pp. 122–3; D. R. Hillers, *Treaty Curses*; R. Frankena, *Oudtest. Studiën* 14 (1965).

[4] *VTE*, p. 88 (ll. 528–9).

[5] 'Zu den Asarhaddon-Verträgen aus Nimrud', *ZA*, NF 20 (1961), 191–2.

Deut. 28: 23

And the heavens over your head shall be brass, and the earth under you shall be iron.

VTE 528–31

May they [the gods] make your ground like iron so that no one can plough [cut] it. Just as rain does not fall from a brazen heaven, so may rain and dew not come upon your fields and pastures.

This striking similarity led Borger to assume that the authors of Deuteronomy borrowed the imagery from Assyrian treaty formulations, even perhaps from a treaty between Assyria and Judah.[1] Moran[2] suggested the possibility that maledictions of the type found in the *VTE* might have been included in the treaty between Aššurbanipal and Manasseh King of Judah (cf. 2 Chron. 33: 11–13). It would be reckless, however, to make assertions solely on the basis of this isolated example.[3] We must look for further evidence.

In *VTE* 419–30 we encounter a series of imprecations identical with those of Deut. 28: 26–35:[4]

Deut. 28: 27: The Lord will smite you with Egyptian inflammation (שחין מצרים). . . . and with scars (גרב)[5] from which you shall never recover.

VTE 419–20: May Sin . . . the light of heaven and earth clothe you with leprosy;[6] may he not order your entering into the presence of the gods or king.

[1] Ibid., pp. 191–2.

[2] 'The Ancient Near Eastern background of the love of God', *CBQ* 14 (1963), p. 84 n. 2.

[3] The fact that the same malediction is found in Lev. 26: 19, which appears to be free from Assyrian influence and which has no sign of dependence on Deuteronomy (see below, pp. 180 f.) may perhaps indicate that this metaphor could not be considered characteristically Assyrian. D. R. Hillers (*Treaty Curses*, p. 38) argues that Deut. 28: 23 is an authentic fragment of ancient poetry, which is quite possible. Even if we do not go along with Hillers, the appearance of this same curse in many different forms should warn us against hasty conclusions as to its origin. Thus, in the Esarhaddon version, unlike that in Deuteronomy, the ground appears before the heaven, and the curse is styled in prose rather than poetry. On the other hand, in Deuteronomy and in *VTE* the brass occurs as a simile for sky and the iron for the ground while in Leviticus the order is reversed. See Hillers, pp. 41–2.

[4] This has been observed independently by R. Frankena, *Oudtest. Studiën* 14, pp. 148 ff., but he included in the parallel series only vv. 28–34.

[5] The Hebr. גרב is some type of leprosy (cf. Syriac and Middle Aram. גרבא), and it corresponds to the Akk. *garābu*, which in the Igituh short version (*AfO* 18 [1957], 83, 172) is equated with saḫar-šub-ba, the term used in *VTE* 419; cf. *AHw* s.v. *garābu*; *CAD* vol. 5 (G), p. 46a. For the clarification of *garābu* cf. J. V. Kinnier-Wilson, *RA* 60 (1966), 47–58.

[6] Cf. also the treaty between Aššurnirari V and Mati'ilu: 'May they (the gods) clothe his (Mati'ilu's) nobles (and) the people of his country with leprosy like

Deut. 28: 28–9: The Lord will smite you with madness and blindness and confusion of mind, and you shall grope at noonday as the blind gropes in the darkness, and you shall not prosper in your ways, and you shall only be oppressed and robbed continually, and there shall be none to help you.

VTE 422–4: May Shamash . . . not render you a just judgment (not give you a reliable decision); may he deprive you of the sight of your eyes (so that) they will wander about in darkness.[1]

V. 26: Your corpses shall be food for all birds of the heaven and for beasts of the earth.

VTE 425–7; May Ninurta . . . fell you with his swift arrow; may he fill the steppe with your corpses; may he feed your flesh to the vulture (and) the jackal.

V. 30a: You shall betroth a wife, and another man shall lie with her.

VTE 428–9: May Venus, the brightest of stars, make your wives lie in your enemy's lap while your eyes look (at them).

V. 30 b: You shall build a house, and you shall not dwell in it. V. 32: Your sons and your daughters shall be given to another people.

VTE 429–30a: May your sons not be masters of your house.

V. 33: A nation which you have not known shall eat up the fruit of your ground and of your labours. . . .

VTE 430b: May a foreign enemy divide all your goods.

Not only are the curses of leprosy, blindness, exposure of the slain, sexual violation of the wife, pillage, and the enslavement of children common to both. They occur in almost identical order, with the single exception of the curse of pestilence and unburied corpses, which in the *VTE* follows the affliction of blindness while in Deuteronomy it precedes the imprecation concerning leprosy.

a garment', *AfO* 8 (1932) 20, Rs. iv: 5. saḫar corresponds to Akk. *epru*, 'earth, dust'; šub to Akk. *nadû*, 'to throw'; the idea of throwing earth actually lies behind the description of the שחין among the ten plagues (Exod. 9: 8 ff.): Moses throws soot toward the sky. This becomes dust throughout Egypt and causes the שחין. In the light of this one should reconsider the meaning of ויזרקו עפר על ראשיהם השמימה 'and they threw dust upon their heads toward heaven' in Job 2: 12, which is reminiscent of וזרקו משה השמימה in Exod. 9: 8. Does this have to do with some kind of sympathetic magic?

[1] For the basis of this translation see my article, *Biblica* 46 (1965), 419 n. 1; cf. also *ABL* 1105, r. 8–11; for interpretation see R. Borger, *ZA* NF 20 (1961), 187 and K. Deller, *Orientalia* 34 (1965), 271–2.

This imprecation, however, has no fixed position in the *VTE* either: in text ND 4329, for example, it occurs after the curse of pillage.[1]

Although the order of curses in Deuteronomy seems to have no plausible explanation, the sequence in the *VTE* is based on the hierarchy within the Assyrian pantheon.[2] Ashur, Ninlil,[3] Sin, and Shamash, who begin the series of maledictions in the Esarhaddon treaty, appear almost invariably at the head of every Assyrian catalogue of gods. Sin and Shamash (also major deities in the Babylonian pantheon), who are juxtaposed here, almost always appear together in other texts as well; in the Esarhaddon inscriptions, for example, these gods are even referred to as twins.[4] The plague of leprosy mentioned in the Assyrian curse is the plague always associated with the god Sin,[5] while the curse of darkness, which here symbolizes the absence of law and justice and which follows the curse of leprosy, is the punishment inflicted by Shamash, the sun god as well as the god of law and justice. Indeed, it is the very nature of the Shamash curse that enables us to comprehend the meaning of the curse of blindness and wandering in darkness mentioned in Deut. 28: 28–9. The darkness and blindness here signify anarchy and social lawlessness: 'And you shall be only oppressed and robbed continually, and there shall be none to help you. . . .'[6] The

[1] See Wiseman's remark (p. 61) on *VTE* 425–7. It is possible that Deut. 28: 26 is not in its original place and that, like the malediction in the Assyrian treaty, it originally occurred after the curse of darkness in v. 29. Since enemy pillage usually follows in the wake of military defeat, it is plausible to assume that vv. 30 ff., which deal with pillage and capture by the enemy, originally followed immediately after the curse of defeat in v. 26. The removal of v. 26 from its original position in the list may result from the editor's wish to join two related maledictions (vv. 25a and 26), which originally occurred in separate passages. The imprecation in v. 25a, which is the exact antithesis of the blessing in v. 7, constitutes the chiastic close of the two thematically parallel groups of blessings (vv. 7–12a) and curses (vv. 20–5; vv. 43–4 correspond to 12b–13).

[2] Cf. Hillers, *Treaty Curses*, p. 13: 'Where curses by individual gods occur in series they are usually listed in strict order of the god's rank within the pantheon.'

[3] In duplicates ND 4329 and ND 4335 the curse of Ninlil is followed by the curse of Anu, who generally appears at the head of the divine hierarchy.

[4] *d[Sin u dŠam]aš ilāni maššūte*; see R. Borger, *Asarhaddon*, p. 2, i: 31, and note.

[5] Cf. J. Nougayrol, 'La Lèpre, arme redoutée du dieu-lune', *JCS* 2 (1948), 205.

[6] Cf. Isa. 59: 9: 'Therefore justice is far from us, and righteousness does not overtake us; we look for light, and behold darkness, and for brightness, but we walk in gloom.' The expressions 'madness and blindness and confusion of mind' mentioned in v. 28 denote a state of panic and disorganization and are also employed in this sense in Zech. 12: 4 (in connection with war). They are, consequently, not to be taken as physical afflictions. See M. Held, *JCS* 15 (1961), 15.

saviour (מושיע) to which this verse makes reference is undoubtedly the judge who saves[1] the oppressed from the hands of his oppressor.[2] Now the curse of darkness and lawlessness has no logical connection with the curse of leprous diseases, which immediately precedes it. Their proximity remains inexplicable, therefore, unless it be understood in the light of the Sin–Shamash relationship in Mesopotamian religion. The close association of the two is also encountered in other treaty texts[3] and in execrations inscribed on Babylonian *kudurru* stones. In a *kudurru* stone inscription dating from the reign of Marduk-nādin-aḫḫē we read: 'May Sin, who dwells in the bright heavens, clothe his body with leprosy as with a garment; may Shamash, the chief justice of heaven and earth, be his opponent in court (?) and stand up against him.'[4] A boundary stone from the time of Nabû-mukīn-apli similarly reads: '[May Sin, the eye] of heaven and earth, [clothe] his body with leprosy [as with a garment].[5] . . . May Shamash, the judge of heaven and earth, not decree his judgement and his decision.' The curses are likewise found in close sequence in the Code of Hammurabi: 'May Shamash, the great judge of heaven and earth . . . not render his judgement. . . . May Sin, the lord of heaven, lay upon him heavy guilt (and, in consequence) with his great punishment which will not disappear from his body.'[6] The expression 'great punishment', *šērtu rabītu*, refers to the plague of leprosy, as may be inferred from another text which reads: 'May Sin, the lord of the crown . . . the father of the great gods make him bear leprosy [which

[1] It is well known that the concepts judge (שופט) and saviour (מושיע) are identical in meaning in the Old Testament, and there is no need to dwell on the subject.

[2] Targum Jonathan (M. Ginsburger's edn., Berlin, 1903) translates v. 29b in the same sense: 'And you will seek good counsel for respite from your adversities, but there will be none among you to show the truth.'

[3] Cf. *ABL* 1105, r. 8–12; A. T. Clay, *Babylonian Records in the Library of J. Pierpont Morgan*, vol. IV, no. 50: 16–17.

[4] L. W. King, *BBSt* no. 8, iv: 7–11; for this interpretation see *CAD* vol. 3 (D), pp. 140–1 (s.v. *dikuggallu*) and p. 137a (s.v. *dikkuldû*).

[5] L. W. King, *BBSt* no. 9, i: 46–ii: 3; for the restoration of ll. 46–7 cf. also the Babylonian *kudurru* inscription: ^{d}XXX IGI!^{in} AN^{e} ù KI^{tim} SAḪAR·ŠUB·BA-a *i-na zu-um-ri!-šu li-šab-šu-ma*, H. V. Hilprecht, *The Babylonian Expedition of the University of Pennsylvania*, series A, vol. I, pt. II (Philadelphia, 1896), 149, iii: 6–7.

[6] CH xxvii b: 14–63. It is interesting to note that the curses in the Marduk-zākir-šumi I and Šamši-Adad V treaty (*AfO* 8, pp. 17 ff.) have been directly borrowed from the Code of Hammurabi; see R. Borger, *Orientalia* 34 (1965), 168–9, especially ll. 27–31.

cannot be healed], his *great punishment* (*šērtašu rabīta*)'.[1] The same phrase, '(of) which (you) cannot be healed' is encountered in Deut. 28: 27 and 35. The motif 'to clothe with leprosy' also occurs in Deut. 28; v. 35, which repeats the malediction of v. 27 and which closes this particular section of the imprecations, reads: 'The Lord will afflict you . . . with a severe inflammation (בשחין רע)[2] . . . from the sole of your foot to the crown of your head', a phrase which also describes Job's leprosy (Job 2: 7) and which implies a leprous condition covering the entire body. The same condition is implied in the reference to the 'clothing with leprosy' that occurs in the treaty between Aššurnirari V and Mati'ilu of Bit-Agusi[3] and in the *kudurru* stone inscriptions cited above.

The peculiar association of the curses of leprosy and judicial blindness in Deut. 28: 27–9 cannot, therefore, be satisfactorily explained unless we assume that the pairing of these two concepts, which is comprehensible only in the light of Mesopotamian religion, was transferred from a copy of a Mesopotamian treaty to the book of Deuteronomy.

The coupling of these two maledictions does not in itself necessarily prove neo-Assyrian influence since, as we have seen, the same association is also encountered in Babylonian texts, which go back to the Old-Babylonian period. The fact, however, that both the subject-matter and the sequence of maledictions in this section of Deuteronomy are identical with the parallel series of curses in *VTE* attests that there was a direct borrowing by Deuteronomy from

[1] C. J. Gadd–L. Legrain, *Ur Excavation Texts* I, 1928, 165, ii: 23–5; for the restoration of l. 24, see J. Nougayrol, *JCS* 2 (1948), 207 n. 12.

[2] In the Aramaic 'Prayer of Nabonidus' discovered at Qumran (J. T. Milik, *RB* 63 (1956), 405–11, cf. the comprehensive study of R. Meyer, *Das Gebet des Nabonid*, 1962) we are told that Nabonidus was afflicted with שחנא באישא (= Hebrew שחין רע). As is well known, Nabonidus became a patron of the cult of Sin, which caused much bitterness among Marduk's priests. J. Tigay from the University of Pennsylvania (an unpublished study) suggests that behind the tradition of Nabonidus' leprosy is hidden a polemic to the effect that even Sin, his own beloved god, turned against him. Sin's punishment of Nabonidus may also be reflected in the tradition of Dan. 2–5, the influence on which by the stories of Nabonidus has long ago been recognized; see, e.g., W. von Soden, *ZAW* 53 (1935), 81–9. According to Dan. 5 the king lived in the steppe like a wild ass (ערוד, Dan. 5: 21)—a common motif in Sin's curse of leprosy; cf. the continuation of the Sin-curse in *VTE* 421: 'Roam the steppe like a wild ass (*kīma sirrime*)'; *sirrimu* is the equivalent of ערוד; see J. Greenfield, *JSS* 11 (1966), 98–100.

[3] *kīma naḫalapti liḫa*[*llipū*]; cf. above, p. 117 n. 6.

Assyrian treaty documents. Apart from the *VTE* and Deut. 28 no such series of maledictions has as yet been discovered. Since this is the case and since the order of the curses is explicable only against a Mesopotamian background, we may conclude that a Judean scribe transposed an entire and consecutive series of maledictions from Assyrian treaty documents to the book of Deuteronomv (Deut. 28: [26] 27–35).

The principal curses (vv. 27–35) of this section have been incorporated in an independent literary unit, which opens with curses of leprosy and darkness (vv. 27–9) and closes chiastically with imprecations of darkness[1] and leprosy (vv. 34–5).[2] Therefore this entire sequence of maledictions paralleling the series of curses in ll. 419–30 of the *VTE* would seem to constitute a separate and distinct group of inprecations, which in substance was borrowed from Assyrian treaty forms.[3] Indeed scholars have long regarded the group as an anomalous unit in so far as it mars the symmetry of the entire section comprising Deut. 28: 1–45.[4] In view of the fact that Deuteronomy received its fixed form during the reign of Manasseh[5] it may be conjectured that the maledictions in question, though formulated in the Israelite spirit and style,[6] were adopted

[1] Note the same phrase 'the sight of your eyes' in v. 34 and *niṭil ēnēkunu* in *VTE*, l. 425.

[2] On vv. 27–35 as an independent unit see D. Hoffmann, *Deuteronomium* II, 1923, ad loc.

[3] If we are right in assuming that v. 26 is correctly placed after v. 29 (cf. above, p. 119 n. 1), then we may regard all of the maledictions in this group as having been directly copied from an Assyrian treaty with Judah.

[4] Cf. above, p. 119 n. 1. Vv. 26–36 constitute the only section of the curses in which one can find no correspondence to the blessings of vv. 1–14. This section is further characterized by its depiction of political disasters brought about by an enemy of imperial stature, while the rest of the verses in 1–45 refer to natural calamities. Even when war is mentioned as in v. 25, it is a war with an enemy with whom Israel can fight—i.e. a local enemy as opposed to a world-wide empire against which combat is inconceivable. (See, e.g., v. 32 ואין לאל ידיך 'you shall be helpless'.) Throughout the entire passage Israel's helplessness is stressed: the pillage is done before its eyes (v. 31 לעיניך), and nothing can be done to prevent it. The gravity of the enemy is described by terms like 'a nation unknown to you and your fathers' גוי אשר לא ידעת אתה ואבותיך; cf. also vv. 49 ff.

[5] Or some time during the Hezekian–Josianic period, in any case before the year 622 B.C.

[6] Cf. especially the so-called 'futility' curses in vv. 30 ff. and their parallels in prophetic literature: Amos 5: 11; Mic. 6: 14–15; Zeph. 1: 13, Hag. 1: 6 pointed out by Hillers, *Treaty Curses*, pp. 28 ff. See also Frankena, *Oudtest. Studiën* 14, p. 179.

in substance from the political treaties of Esarhaddon or Aššur-banipal.[1]

According to Frankena[2] vv. 36–7 may also have been included in Manasseh's treaty with the Assyrians. But unlike the previous curses, which were ascribed to the appropriate Assyrian deities, the curse of deportation was apparently ascribed to Yahweh. This conclusion can be deduced from Esarhaddon's treaty with Baal of Tyre, where the deportation curse is ascribed to the native gods Melqart and Esmun (iv: 14 f.) in order to stress the idea that the native gods will abandon their own people for failure to abide by an oath—a notion prevalent in the theology of the ancient Near East. As in the *Vorlage* of our passage, so also in Esarhaddon's treaty with Baal of Tyre a series of curses sanctioned by the Assyrian gods precedes the curses ascribed to the native deities. Like the curses in Deut. 28: 26–35, the Assyrian curses in Esarhaddon's treaty with Baal of Tyre parallel an identical sequence in *VTE* (cf. Baal, iv: 1–5 with *VTE* 457–65).[3]

The curses in the following paragraphs (vv. 38–42) may also have been included in the Assyrian treaty with Manasseh, but, unlike vv. 26–35, they have a more local character. Presumably they were sanctioned by the national God, as were the curses in Baal iv: 10–13, which, directed against the characteristic interests of a seafaring state, were to be effectuated by the gods of Tyre and not by the Assyrian gods.[4] Indeed, we meet here with agricultural references typical of Syria and Palestine, such as olives[5] as well as various agricultural blights peculiar to these lands, such as the grape worm (תולעת) and the casting of olives (vv. 39–40).

[1] The curse of pillage in vv. 30 ff. is paralleled not only in *VTE* but also in other Assyrian literature. See, e.g., *ana niṭli ēnīšu māssu lišpur*, 'let him rule his land before his eyes' (*IAK* p. 126), and in a form parallel to Deut. 28: 30: *bīt ippušu libêl šanûmma*, 'the house which he builds let another person take over' (*BBSt* no. 6, ii: 53).

[2] *Oudtest. Studiën* 14, pp. 130–1 and 150.

[3] Cf. Borger, *ZA* 20 (1961), ad loc. He restores the curses of both texts with the help of each other.

[4] The same applies to the curse of the devouring lion in iv: 6 ff., which, also bearing a provincial character, was attributed to the native gods—Bethel and Anath-Bethel. B. Mazar sees a connection between the tradition of the lions' killing the Samaritans, in consequence of which a priest was brought to Beth-El (cf. also the story in 1 Kgs. 13 concerning the lion and the prophet in Beth-El), and the curse in the treaty with Baal.

[5] The Mesopotamians usually made oil of sesame (see Herodotus, *Hist.* I. 193; cf. also Meissner, *Babyl. u. Ass.* I. 198–9).

These imprecations also have affinities with extra-Biblical sources. Curses of this type, however, refer strictly to the agricultural *realia* of the area in question. Thus, for example, we read in the Sefire treaty:[1] 'For seven years may the locust (ארבה) devour (Arpad), and for seven years may the worm (תולעה) eat, and for seven [years may] תוי[2] come upon the face of its land. May the grass not come forth so that no green may be seen,[3] (and may its) vegetation not be [seen].'

These provincial features, however, find only a small place in Deut. 28. As a rule it is the punitive imagery derived from the Assyrian suzerainty treaties that predominates here. A comparison with the imprecations found in Lev. 26 should bring this into greater relief. The setting of the curses and blessings in Lev. 26 is distinctly provincial. We hear of threshing, of the vintage, of sowing (v. 5), of wild beasts attacking people (חית השדה or חיה רעה) and preying upon domestic animals (vv. 6 and 22),[4] of deserted roads

[1] I, A: 27–8.

[2] Since this malediction occurs in connection with crop failure, it may be assumed that תוי is some sort of agricultural pest, which may perhaps be synonymous with the Biblical צלצל (v. 42; cf. Isa. 18: 1). If this supposition be correct, then Deut. 28: 38–42 may very well prove to be a striking parallel to Sefire I, A: 27–8 (in Deut. ארבה, תלעת, צלצל; in Sefire ארבה, תולעה, תוי). The description of the locust in Exod. 10: 14–15 as coming up and covering the face of the land is identical with the description of the תוי in the Sefire treaty, and it appears to support our interpretation of the Aramaic term. Cf. Exod. 10: 14–15 ויעל הארבה . . . ויכס את עין כל הארץ . . . ויאכל את כל עשב . . . ירק and Sefire: [יס]ק תוי על אפי ארקה ואל יפק חצר וליתחזי ירק. J. Greenfield (*JBL* 87 (1968), 241) proposed to restore תוי into תהוי. He assumed a noun in the fem. sing. before it. If this were correct, this noun might still refer to some kind of blight, and, in the light of the following observation, it might even be possible that a word like סק should be restored before the proposed verb: the word צלצל is translated in Targum Onkelos by סקאה (quoted in BT, Tractate Baba Qama 116b), a noun, which also occurs in Sifre Deut. 42 as סקי ('the late rain brings the סקי = cricket?').

[3] Cf. Deut. 29: 22 ולא יעלה בה כל עשב and the treaty of Aššurnirari V, Rs. iv: 20; *urqīt ṣēri lū lā uṣṣâ* dUTU *lū lā immar*, 'may the green of the field not come forth and see the light of the sun' (for the reading, cf. *CAD* vol. 16 (Ṣ), p. 143) and see below, p. 141.

[4] Cf. Gen. 9: 5 (=P); 37: 33, 1 Kgs. 13: 24 f.; 2 Kgs. 17: 26, and for the references to wild animals in the prophets see Hillers, *Treaty Curses*, 54–6. The threat of attack by wild beasts occurs only in Deut. 32: 24 and in P. Ezekiel drew upon P when he included the חיה רעה among the calamities which were to befall Israel (cf. especially Ezek. 14: 15 and 21), and thus added the vicious beast (חיה רעה) to the three known calamities: famine, sword, and pestilence רעב, חרב, דבר (cf. 2 Sam. 24: 13 and especially Jer.). On the devouring lion in the Esarhaddon treaty with Baal, see above, p. 123 n. 4.

(v. 22; cf. Isa. 33: 8; Lam. 1: 4), of the rural populace's crowding into cities to escape the approaching enemy (v. 25; cf. Jer. 8: 14), of pestilence (vv. 25b and 30; cf. Amos 4: 10; Isa. 9: 7),[1] of the search for food (v. 26; cf. Amos 4: 6), of the destruction of sanctuaries and cultic places (vv. 30–1; cf. Amos 7: 9) and of the eventual devastation of the land (vv. 32 ff.). The order of the maledictions follows a general development of subject, which is accompanied by an exhortative refrain similar to that found in the punitive oracles of Amos 4: 6–11.[2] The curses employ the conventional numerical typology of seven (vv. 18, 21, 24, 28) and ten (v. 26).

None of these descriptions, which reflect realistic conditions of adversity and which have something of a provincial colouring, are found in Deut. 28. They *are* encountered, on the other hand, in the Aramaic Sefire treaty, which, as we have seen, reflects a provincial setting similar to that of Palestine. Like Lev. 26 and Amos 4 (cf. also Isa. 9: 7 ff.), the Sefire treaty also employs repetitive phrases[3] and also uses the typological number seven (I, A: 21–4). Similarly it speaks of beasts preying upon people (I, A: 30–2), of pestilence (I, B: 30;[4] cf. II, B: 11), search for food,[5] eating and not

[1] In all these places the phrase is שלח דבר. (Isa. 9: 7 has to be vocalized *deber šillaḥ* with the LXX.)

[2] On the similarity between the imprecations in Amos 4: 6–11 and Lev. 26 see H. Graf Reventlow, *Das Amt des Propheten bei Amos*, 1962, pp. 86 ff. and W. Brueggeman, 'Amos 4, 4–13, and Israel's Covenant Worship', *VT* 15 (1965), 1–15.

[3] Cf. I, A: 14, 24 (והן ישקר מתעאל); I, B: 23, 27–8, 33, 36, 38; II, B: 9, 14, 18; III: 4, 7, 9, 14, 17, 19, 20, 23, 27 (שקרתם בעדיא זי בספרא זנה).

[4] ופגר ארבא מעל פגר 'and I shall heap (literally, 'multiply') corpse upon corpse in Arpad'. Cf. Lev. 26: 30: ונתתי את פגריכם על פגרי גלוליכם 'and I will heap your carcasses upon your (lifeless, *JPS*) fetishes' (*pgr* in Ugaritic means 'stela' or 'monument', UT 69: 2, 70: 1). Cf. also Amos 8: 3 רב הפגר.

[5] I, A: 24 ושבע בנתה יהכן בשט לחם ואל יהרגן, 'And may his seven daughters go looking for food, but not . . . (?).' I tend to accept Hillers's (*Treaty Curses*, pp. 71–4) reading (בנתה instead of בכתה; the other readings and the interpretations which follow from them are unreasonable: see, e.g., Fitzmyer ad loc.) but I am sceptical about his interpretation of יהרגן. The image here seems to be that of members of the family roving about in search of food—a picture very common in the Bible (Pss. 37: 25; 109: 10; Job 15: 23, etc.). We should therefore expect at the end of the Sefire curse something like 'they will not find' as in Amos 8: 11–13: ישוטטו ולא ימצאו (note the juxtaposition of דבר ה׳ with לחם ומים), but ואל יהרגן does not lend itself to this kind of interpretation unless the text be in error. On the other hand, it is possible to hold to the interpretation of יהרגן as 'seduce' and still to keep our notion of 'seeking food' in so far as the

being sated (I, A: 21–4),[1] and the devastation of the land (I, A: 32–3).[2]

The difference in the character of the priestly and the deuteronomic maledictions leads us to infer, then, that the deuteronomic covenant, by contrast with the priestly covenant, was drafted by scribes who were chiefly influenced by Assyrian treaty formulae.

. . . . .

It is generally assumed that the imprecations in Deut. 28: 48 ff. are later interpolations, reflecting the siege conditions and the destruction of Judah.[3] But comparison with the maledictions found in the Esarhaddon and the Aššurnirari V treaties suggests that this is not so,[4] for the Assyrian treaties contain similar curses relating to

prostitution is carried on as a device for getting food and not for its own sake (Hillers's suggested parallel from Tel Ḫalaf, p. 72, therefore misses the point; see Fitzmyer, pp. 43–4). Prostitution carried on to acquire sustenance seems to be implied in Prov. 6: 26: כי בעד אשה זונה עד ככר לחם. At any rate, the context of Sefire I, A: 21–4 is hunger and famine very much like Lev. 26: 26 but unlike Isa. 4: 1, in which the point is the lack of men. There is, then, no justification for putting the curse of Sefire I, A: 24 under the title of 'lack of men', where Hillers places it.

[1] 'and should seven nurses . . . nurse a young boy, may he not be satiated; and should seven mares suckle a colt, may it not be sa[ted, and should seven] cows give suck to a calf, may it not be sated, and should seven ewes suckle a lamb, [may it not be sa]ted.' Cf. the annals of Aššurbanipal: 'when the camel foals, the donkey foals, calves or lambs would suckle seven times on their dams, they could not fill up their stomachs with milk' (Streck, *Assurbanipal II*, pp. 76–8, ix: 65–7), which appears in a provincial context, i.e. in connection with the Arab tribes. The animals mentioned there—camels and donkey foals—indeed reflect a nomadic background. As in Lev. 26: 26, so in Sefire I, A: 21–4 the search for food and the eating without satiation are coupled. Cf. also Amos 4: 6–8.

[2] [יש]תחט לישמן אחוה ותהוי ארפד תל ..... 'May its vegetation (or grass) be destroyed (but see J. Greenfield, *JBL* 87 [1968], 241) unto desolation, and may Arpad become a mound.' Cf. the treaty of Aššurnirari V with the same Mati'ilu: *mātaka ana tūšari, nišēka ana riḫṣi, ālānika ana tilê, bītaka ana ḫarbāti lûtēr*, 'your land may be turned into a steppe, your inhabitants into a flood, your cities into mounds, your house into ruins' (*AfO* 8, Rs. v: 5–7). Cf. also the treaty of Esarhaddon with Baal: *mātkunu ana ḫapê* (see Borger, *ZA* 20, p. 183 n. 3) *nišēkunu ana šalāli liddinū*, 'may they give your land unto destruction, your people to be carried off' (iv: 14–15). These last two received the sanction of the provincial gods Melqart and Esmun. Cf. the same threat mentioned in the clause section of *VTE*: *mātkunu ana ḫapê nišēkunu ana šalāli la taddanā*, 'so that you will not turn your land to destruction, your people to be carried off (ll. 294–5). This curse is not linked to any Assyrian god—a fact which may indicate that it belongs to the native part of the curses. See above, p. 123.

[3] See e.g., M. Noth, 'For all who rely on Works of the Law etc.', *The Laws in the Pentateuch*, p. 120.

[4] For cogent arguments against the presence of late insertions in Deut. 28 see Hillers, *Treaty Curses*, pp. 30 ff.

the enemy's invasion and onslaught. This fact implies that maledictions of this type do not necessarily reflect a real situation but belong rather to the typology of the political documents current in the eighth and seventh centuries B.C. We cite below several parallel maledictions as illustrations of this point:

VTE 448–50: A mother [will lock her door] against her daughter.[1] In your hunger eat the flesh of your sons! In the famine and want may one man eat the flesh of another.[2] (Cf. ll. 547–50 and 570–2).

Deut. 28: 53–7: And you shall eat the offspring of your body, the flesh of your sons and daughters ... in the straits and in the distress.[4] ... The most tender ... woman will grudge to her son and to her daughter ... she will eat them secretly for want of all things ... in the straits and distress. ... (cf. Jer. 19: 9).

Treaty of Aššurnirari V, Rs. iv: 8–11: May Hadad, the canal inspector of heaven and earth, destroy Mati'ilu's land and the people of his land through constant want, hunger, and famine. May they eat the flesh of their sons and daughters, and may it taste as good to them as the flesh of a ram or sheep.[3]

We hear of the materialization, as it were, of this category of curses in the annals of Aššurbanipal, for instance, in the Rassam Cylinder: 'Famine broke out among them, and they ate the flesh of their children to satisfy their hunger. Ashur, Sin, Shamash ... quickly inflicted upon them as many curses as there are written in their treaty',[5] and in another passage: 'In famine and want they ate each other's flesh.'[6] In the passages treating of these catastrophes

[1] On the basis of related texts (quoted *CAD*, vol. 4 (E), pp. 25–6) R. Borger, *ZA* 20 (1961), 188, suggests the restoration AMA UGU DUMU.MÍ-*šá* [KÁ-*šá ed-dil*].

[2] Read with Borger (op. cit.) *ina būrikunu šēr mārēkunu aklā. ina bub*[*ūti*] (*ḫušaḫḫu*) *amēlu šēr amēli līkul*.

[3] Cf. E. Weidner, *AfO* 8, p. 20.

[4] The words מצור ומצוק in this context mean 'straits', 'distress', coming as a result of siege.

[5] Streck, *Assurbanipal II*, p. 76, ix: 58–60.

[6] Ibid. viii: 36–7.

we generally encounter such terms as *sunqu*, *bubūtu*, *ḫušaḫḫu*,[1] which denote famine and general want. So it appears that the expressions: מצוק, מצור, חוסר כל which occur in an identical context in Deut. 28 (cf. Jer. 19: 9) are the equivalents of these Akkadian terms.[2]

A salient parallel to the *VTE* malediction may be found in the use of the word בסתר in Deuteronomy to designate the manner in which the mother stealthily eats the flesh of her children—an eventuality which is also mentioned in the Esarhaddon curse.[3] Although Lev. 26 also contains a curse of cannibalism (v. 19), the subject is nevertheless only briefly mentioned, and it lacks the political background that characterizes the parallel maledictions in Deuteronomy and in the Assyrian treaties.

The structure and composition of the Esarhaddon treaty are no less helpful than its subject-matter in understanding Deut. 28. The repetitions and the lack of integration that characterize Deut. 28 have led scholars to assume that the chapter underwent several stages of redaction.[4] Thus, for example, even the moderates among the scholars argue that vv. 45–6 are the original conclusion of the list of curses and that vv. 47–68 represent a post-exilic addition. Moreover, their argument continues, the addition is not a unity in itself, since it contains a conclusion in the middle (vv. 58–61); therefore, according to this reasoning, Deut. 28 reflects two stages of editorial activity. The very basis of this supposition is destroyed, however, by an examination of the Esarhaddon treaty, the original copy of which has survived and bears an exact date (the 16th day of the month of *Iyyar*, Eponym of Nabû-bēl-uṣur, or May 672 B.C.), for this treaty is also repetitive, and it leaps from subject to subject, perhaps even more than does Deut. 28. For instance, after the individualized curses of lines 414–71 comes a conclusion (472–5) similar in content to Deut. 28: 45.[5] This is followed by a list of

[1] Cf. *VTE* 480 and the references quoted in *AHw* (s.v. *bubūtu*, *ḫušaḫḫu*) and *CAD* vol. 6 (H) pp. 260–1 (s.v. *ḫušaḫḫu*); both *bubūtu* and *ḫušaḫḫu* have the common logogram SU.KU; for *sunqu* cf. E. Weidner, *Die Inschriften Tukulti-Ninurtas I*, 1959, 7, vi: 2; *ARu* 44: 20 and *passim*.

[2] *ḫušaḫḫu* also means 'scarcity' and may parallel the Biblical חסר; *sunqu* may, similarly, correspond to צוק, מצוק, and צנוק.

[3] On the subject of siege famines, see A. L. Oppenheim, *Iraq* 17 (1955), 69–89, compare also 2 Kgs. 6: 28–9.

[4] See in Hillers's discussion, *Treaty Curses*, pp. 30 ff.

[5] The text in Deuteronomy reads: 'All these curses shall befall you; they shall pursue you and overtake you until you are wiped out' while the parallel

anonymous curses (476–93), a statement of the vassals (494–512), and another series of individualized curses (513–25), which actually belong to the previous section, i.e. 414–71.[1] Next comes another concluding passage (526–9), which forms the transition to a section of curses based upon similes (530–668). In fact, this last apparently homogeneous section is not a unity, for it also includes individualized curses (545–6, 649–51, 662, 663–4) and generalized curses without similes. Moreover, the same imprecations recur again and again in the *VTE* in different formulations without any logical or systematic progression: the curse of cannibalism recurs in three different places (ll. 448–50, 547–50, 570–2), the locust occurs twice (ll. 442–3 and 599–600), and so on. There is no doubt, then, that both the *VTE* curses and Deut. 28 are composite literary creations, but—as Hillers has already indicated[2]—'not because of late redactional activity but because the scribes have combined a variety of traditional curses'.

(*b*) *In deuteronomic literature*

The deuteronomic authors also incorporated in their work maledictions like those customarily included in the treaties discussed above. They are to be found mostly in the deuteronomic prophetic orations in the books of Kings and Jeremiah.

It is true that the curses found in the treaties have a history behind them and had been drawn from different sources, such as epic literature,[3] incantation texts,[4] and especially boundary stones.[5] So when we find similar curses in the deuteronomic literature this might be just a coincidence and should not necessarily be considered as direct borrowing from the treaties. But taking into account that the deuteronomic curses come into effect as a punishment for breaking the covenant, it would be quite reasonable to suppose that

passage in *VTE* threatens: 'May the great gods of heaven and earth who dwell in the world, as many as are named in this tablet, strike you, look fiercely at you, with a bitter curse may they curse you angrily.' The two passages differ in that the latter stresses the deity's role as executor of the disaster while the former intimates that it is the very power inherent in the curse that causes the destruction. On the difference in this respect between East- and West-Semitic curse formulation see S. Gevirtz, *Interpreter's Dictionary of the Bible*, I, 750.

[1] According to Frankena (*Oudtest. Studiën* 14, p. 132), ll. 519–25 belong originally to the sections 414–71.

[2] *Treaty Curses*, p. 40.

[3] So, for example, the curse of Bēlet-ilē in *VTE*, ll. 437–9 has its origin in the Epic of Irra, cf. Frankena, *Oudtest. Studiën* 14, pp. 129–30.

[4] Especially the Maqlu incantations, cf. Hillers, *Treaty Curses, passim.*

[5] Cf. above, p. 120.

these conform with the sanctions of the covenant and were therefore formulated intentionally in the manner of treaty curses.

Indeed the prophetic word of God which lies at the core of deuteronomic theology[1] is also formulated in legal phraseology similar to that met with in the covenant between God and Israel: it is said to be confirmed (הקים דבר 1 Kgs. 12: 15, etc.) just as the covenant is confirmed (הקים ברית 2 Kgs. 23: 3).[2] The Deuteronomist informs us that historical events of Israel have materialized in accordance with the word of God which preceded them—a concept which is also met with in contemporary Assyrian literature, for example, in the Aššurbanipal annals: 'The divine word, which they (the gods) had uttered in remote days, they then revealed for the coming generations.'[3]

1. Scholars have long recognized[4] that Nathan's punitive oracle in 2 Sam. 12: 10–12 is a late interpolation which interprets Absalom's rebellion and violation of his father's concubines (2 Sam. 16: 22) as the retributive punishment of David's adulterous act with Bathsheba.[5] The tendency of this interpolation appears to be

[1] Cf. above, pp. 15 ff.

[2] The opposite of confirming the word (literally: erecting) is נפל דבר 'the falling of the word', cf. above, p. 22.

[3] Streck, *Assurbanipal II*, p. 58, vi: 116–18 (compare K 3065: *η*, ibid., p. 216): *amāt qibīt ilūtišun ša ultu ūmē rūqūte iqbû, eninna ukalimmū nišē arkūti.* Compare 2 Kgs. 19: 25 (= Isa. 37: 26): הלא שמעת למרחוק אותה עשיתי למימי קדם ויצרתיה, עתה הבאתיה 'Have you not heard, long ago I made it, in ancient times I created it? now have I brought it to pass.'

[4] Verses 10–12 have been regarded as redactorial accretion since Wellhausen's time. It seems, however, that the entire address is deuteronomic. Though the prophecy itself may derive from pre-deuteronomic tradition, it was incorporated in the text and apparently redacted by the Deuteronomist, cf., e.g., the deuteronomic expression: 'to do evil in the sight of Yahweh' עשה הרע בעיני יהוה. The redaction, however, may be a composite one. Verses 11–12 appear to be a separate prophecy; note the recurrence of the introductory phrase 'Thus says the Lord' in v. 11 and the reference only to David's punishment for having committed adultery, whereas the prophecy in 7b–10 announces the punition of the 'sword' as the retribution for having killed Uriah with the sword (cf. L. Rost, *Die Überlieferung von der Thronnachfolge Davids*, 1926, pp. 92 ff.). The two sections of the prophecy nevertheless have one object: to give prophetic validity to the calamities that befell the Davidic house during and after David's lifetime. Cf. also Carlson, *Samuel*, ad loc.

[5] See H. W. Hertzberg, *Die Samuelbücher*², ATD, 1960, p. 258: 'So kommt Gottes Gerechtigkeit deutlich zum Vorschein und zwar in dem Sinne, wie die *deuteronomistische und die "Weisheits-literatur"* gern darstellen: in unmittelbarer Entsprechung'. This fact apparently suffices to determine the date and character of the prophecy and there is consequently no warrant for repudiating its lateness (*pace* Hertzberg).

similar to that encountered in 1 Kgs. 12: 15, where the division of the kingdom occurred against the background of natural and rational circumstances (excessive taxes) but the Deuteronomist added a religious reason, the fulfilment of Ahijah's word of God. Absalom's violation of his father's concubines is also explained in rational terms in 2 Sam. 16: 22 (the execution of Achitophel's counsel) but is interpreted by the Deuteronomist as the consequence of the word of God which foreordained it. The imprecation met with in this oracle is identical with the *VTE* imprecation quoted above:

2 Sam. 12: 11	*VTE*, ll. 428–9
Thus says the Lord . . . 'I will take your wives before your eyes and give them to another[1] and he shall lie with your wives in the sight of this sun.[2]	May Venus, the brightest of the stars, make your wives lie in the lap of your enemy[3] before your eyes.

2. 1 and 2 Kgs.	*VTE*
Who dies in the city the dogs shall eat (1 Kgs. 14: 11, 16: 4; 21: 24).	May dogs and swine eat your flesh (l. 451).[5]
And the dogs shall eat Jezebel in the *ḥeleq* of Jezreel and none shall bury her (2 Kgs. 9: 10; cf. 1 Kgs. 21: 23).[4]	May dogs and swine drag your corpses to and fro in the squares of Aššur; may the earth not receive (them) (ll. 483–4).[6]

[1] A. Schultz (*Die Bücher Samuel*, EH, 1920 II, 126) justifiably translates 'und sie einen andern als dir geben'. The Gesenius lexicon also renders the word רע in this context 'ein Anderer'. It must also be taken in this sense in 1 Sam. 15: 28 and in 28: 17. For the deuteronomic background of these verses, see above, p. 15 n. 5. The word רע occasionally connotes 'rival' (Exod. 2: 13; 2 Sam. 2: 16; Prov. 18: 17); however, the basic meaning of the word is simply 'the other person'.

[2] The mention of astral bodies (the sun, Venus) in both of these maledictions is perhaps a further analogy.

[3] LÚ KÚR which is Akk. *nakru*. The same logogram stands for *šanû* and *aḫû* (= foreigner). The Sumerian LÚ KÚR means, then, as the Hebr. רע, 'another man' sometimes with the connotation of an enemy. Compare also Hebr. זר, which may mean a man from another family or another group as also an enemy.

[4] For a discussion of the place of these verses in the deuteronomic history, see P. Ackroyd, 'The Vitality of the Word of God in the O.T.', *Annual of the Swedish Theological Institute*, 1 (1962), 7–23.

[5] Cf. also the annals of Aššurbanipal quoted below and also *ARu* 15: 61, 16: 61. (= Postgate, *Neo-Assyrian Royal Grants*, 9: 64 (p. 29), 10: 64 (p. 32).

[6] UR.KU ŠAH.MEŠ *ina re-bit Aššur li-in-da-ša-ru* LÚ.ÚŠ.MEŠ-*ku-nu*. KI-*tim a-a im-ḫur*. LÚ.ÚŠ.MEŠ-*ku-nu* is the object of *lindašarū* (cf. Streck, *Assurbanipal*, II, p. 24, iii: 9 and see Borger, *ZA* 20 ad loc.). *ina* IGI^{II}-*ku-nu* in l. 482 belongs to the previous sentence (Wiseman's division of the sentences in ll. 481–4 is therefore wrong).

Though the Biblical malediction, which is formulated in poetic metre, may be of pre-deuteronomic origin[1] and may perhaps even contain authentic north-Israelite prophetic idioms such as עצור ועזוב,[2] it was undoubtedly the Deuteronomist who converted it into a stereotyped curse on the dynasties of Jeroboam and Ahab, in conformity with his method of employing political imagery current at that time.[3] The similarity between the deuteronomic curse and its parallel in *VTE* is even greater in the LXX readings of 1 Kgs. 21: 19, 22: 38, which like the *VTE* also refer to both dogs and swine. So does Isa. 66: 3: 'He who sacrifices a lamb, like him who breaks a dog's neck; he who presents a cereal offering, like him who offers swine's blood'.[4] It is possible, therefore, that the LXX reading reflects the original wording which was tendentiously obscured in the Masoretic text.[5]

The same punishment is encountered in the annals of Aššurbanipal: 'With their dismembered bodies I fed dogs, swine, jackals, eagles (or vultures), the birds of heaven, and the fish of the deep'.[6]

[1] G. von Rad, *Studies*, pp. 82–3.

[2] Cf. the expression ואפס עצור ועזוב in the Song of Moses (Deut. 32: 36) which has also preserved other northern expressions. For the meaning of this phrase (= 'ruler and caretaker') cf. M. Held, *A. Neuman Festschrift*, 1962, p. 283 n. 8.

[3] On the Utopian character of these curses, see above, pp. 20 ff.

[4] The conjunction of dogs and swine occurs in the Mari letters (*ARM* II, 106: 16). Cf. also *EA* 84: 17 (according to the reading of W. L. Moran, 'A Syntactical Study of the Dialect of Byblos as Reflected in the Amarna Letters', Dissertation of Johns Hopkins University 1950, p. 157). Cf. also dogs and swine in the Hittite texts: *ANET*², pp. 207, i: 20; 398, iii: 16. Cf. also Matt. 7: 6.

[5] The MT in 1 Kgs. 22: 38 may perhaps still retain traces of the word 'swine'. The phrase 'and the harlots washed' והזנות רחצו creates difficulties which the Aramaic translators tried to overcome by seeing the Aramaic זינא in the word הזנות and thus translated 'and they washed his armour' as do some modern translators. The original text may, however, have read וחזרים רחצו which intentionally or unintentionally was corrupted to והזנות רחצו. The imagery of bathing swine alongside feeding dogs is also encountered in the proverb related in the Second Epistle of Peter (2: 22): 'The dog turns back to his own vomit, and the sow is washed only to wallow in the mire.' (Cf. S. Loewenstamm, art. 'חזיר' in *Encyclopedia Miqra'it* IV). If this conjecture is correct, then we may conclude that the LXX has preserved a conflated reading of both the original וחזרים and secondary והזנות versions (this conflated reading was later transferred to 1 Kgs. 21: 19). We may perhaps surmise that the reference to swine in this text which implies that they were bred and eaten in an Israelite city was unfavourably viewed by later Palestinian scribes and that they consequently altered the original reading (cf. BT Menahoth 64b on Hyrcanus' ruse in sending the besieged Aristobulus a pig instead of a clean animal for the daily temple sacrifice, which gave rise to the dictum: 'Cursed be the man who rears pigs').

[6] Streck, *Assurbanipal II*, p. 38, iv: 74–6: '*šērešunu nukkusūti ušākil kalbī*

3. 1 Kgs. 14: 15	*VTE*, l. 630
The Lord will smite (or shake)[1] Israel, as a reed is shaken in the water.	May they (the gods) shake you like a reed in water.[2]

It is difficult to regard the resemblance between the two as being only coincidental.

4. The sequel of the foregoing verse: '. . . and root up Israel out of the good land' derives from the phraseology of Deuteronomy which threatens Israel with destruction *from off the face of the earth* מעל פני האדמה (6: 15), annihilation and banishment *from the land* מעל הארץ (4: 26; 11: 17). This idea is literally met with in the *VTE* imprecations: 'may your name, your seed, and the seed of your sons and your daughters *perish from the land*'[3] (ll. 538–9); 'may your seed and the seed of your sons and your daughters *perish from the face of your ground*'[4] (ll. 543–4).

5. The true import of the punition described in the deuteronomic interpolation[5] concerning Ahab's blood spilling on to the

šahî zībī erî iṣṣūrāt šamê nūnī apsî. It is hard to believe that this reflects pure reality; we have rather here stereotypes used by the scribes of Aššurbanipal who wanted to stress the realization of the divine curse (*iṣṣūrāt šamê nūnī apsî* is the equivalent of עוף השמים ודגי הים which occurs in a prophetic admonition in Zeph. 1: 3). The rebels of Šamaššumukin, which are dealt with here, are also said to be 'caught by the net of the gods from which not one escapes', a conventional curse prevalent already in the third millenium B.C., see above, p. 73 n. 6.

[1] According to the following metaphor we would expect here והניד instead of והכה. Graetz (*Emendationes in V.T.*, 1892) actually replaced והכה by והניד. R. Kittel (*BH*³) adds the word והתנודדו before כאשר but the style can be explained as elliptical (see J. Montgomery, ICC, note ad loc.).

[2] *ki-i* GI.AMBAR (= *qan appari* and not GI.BUNIN = *buginnu*, as Wiseman reads) ina A.MEŠ *lu-ni-šu-u-ku-nu*, see *CAD*, vol. 1 (A II) p. 181, 2′.

A similar curse appears in the Hittite treaties (W2, Rs. 31, p. 52): *kī qanê liḫeṣṣiṣka* = 'may they break you like reeds', and also in the Esarhaddon inscriptions (R. Borger, *Die Inschriften Asarhaddons* 65: 33) and in the Irra Epic (F. Gössmann, *Das Era Epos*, 1956), iv: 67: *kī qanê tuḫtaṣṣiṣ*. However, the image of shaking is found only in *VTE* and in the book of Kings.

[3] *TA KUR l*[*iḫliq*], *ḫalāqu* is equated with Hebr. אבד, cf. *EA* 288: 52 where *ḫalqat* is glossed by *abadat*.

[4] [*ina*] UGU *pa-ni šá qaq-qa-ri*-[*ku-nu li-iḫ-liq*]. On the basis of duplicates 27 and X. 12, Wiseman restores: [TA] UGU *pa-ni šá qaq-qa-ri*-[*ku-nu ina* KUR *li-iḫ-liq*] = ['may be destroyed from the land] on the face of your ground'. But Borger justifiably doubts whether these two texts are really identical. Indeed it seems that one of them (27) read: [TA] UGU *pāni ša qaqqari liḫliq* = 'may be destroyed [from] the face of the ground', while the other (X. 12) read: *ina* KUR *liḫliq* = 'may be destroyed from the land', cf. l. 539.

[5] Cf. above, p. 20.

chariot and overflowing it in 1 Kgs. 22: 35 and 38 can also be understood in the light of the *VTE* imprecations:

1 Kgs. 22: 35 and 38	*VTE*, ll. 612–15
And the blood of his wound poured down into the base of the chariot . . . And it flooded the chariot.[1]	Just as this chariot with its base-board[2] is flooded[3] with blood, just so, in battle with your enemy, may they flood your chariots with your own blood.

It would appear therefore that the description of Ahab's death in 1 Kgs. 22: 35b, 38, also depicts the fulfilment of one of the conventional curses that appeared in the treaties of this period.

In the deuteronomic prophetic orations we meet with similes whose purpose was to portray graphically the magnitude of the punishment awaiting the transgressor of the covenant:

Behold . . . I will utterly consume the house of Jereoboam, *as a man burns up dung until it is gone* (1 Kgs. 14: 10).

The Lord will smite (or shake)[4] Israel, *as a reed is shaken in the water* (1 Kgs. 14: 15).

And I will wipe Jerusalem, *as one wipes a dish, wiping it and turning it upside down* (2 Kgs. 21: 13).

[1] The phrase שטף does not refer to the washing of the chariot, as is generally asserted, but refers to the blood which flooded (= the primary meaning of the verb שטף, see Dictionaries) the chariot in which Ahab stood, hence the use of the verb in singular. The interpretation that the dogs lapped the blood as it was being washed off with water or afterwards is implausible. It is more likely that the verse meant to say that the dogs lapped the blood that was on the chariot, and if so it is obvious that they were licking freshly spilt blood and not blood which had dried on the vehicle that was driven back from Ramoth-Gilead. It appears, in the light of the aforesaid, that the phrase 'by the pool of Samaria' was inserted here because of a misunderstanding resulting from the obscure conclusion of the verse (see p. 19 above). The reference to the bathing of the harlots and the washing of the chariot caused a misunderstanding of the true meaning of the verse and necessitated the removal of the verse from its original position after v. 35 (cf. Schultz, *Bücher Samuel*, ad loc.).

[2] *sassu* means the base or floor (of the chariot) = חיק הרכב. חיק in Ezek. 43: 14 and 17 denotes the base of the altar.

[3] *raḫāṣu* in Akkadian is equivalent to Hebr. שטף. Both denote 'flooding' and 'rinsing', cf. Wiseman, *VTE*, p. 89 n. 613, for discussion of *raḫāṣu*.

[4] See above, p. 133 n. 1.

Similes of this type are also employed in the descriptions of divine punishment in Deuteronomy:

And they chased you *as bees do* (1: 44).

And you shall grope at noonday, *as the blind gropes in the darkness* (28: 29).

The Lord will bring a nation against you from afar, from the end of the earth, *as swift as the eagle flies* (28: 49).

Now an entire series of such similes[1] is also found in the curses of the *VTE* and of the Aramaic Sefire treaty, where, as in deuteronomic literature, they are introduced with the word כאשר = *kī ša* in Akkadian and איך זי in Aramaic. The scribes drew their similes from all fields of life: from the world of flora and fauna and the inanimate world.[2] The similarity between these similes lay not only in the area from which they were drawn, but also in their subject-matter. We have already seen that the *VTE* simile of 'the shaken reed' occurs verbatim in the deuteronomic prophecy of Ahijah. A similar correspondence may be found between other similes. Thus, 'as the bees do' (Deut. 1: 44) is also met with in the Esarhaddon curse: 'just as the honeycomb is pierced with holes, so may they pierce your flesh . . .' (ll. 594–8). The simile of turning upside down employed in 2 Kgs. 21: 13 is also employed in the Sefire treaty: 'May the gods overturn that man and his house and all that is in it, and may they make its lower part its upper part.'[3]

This use of the simile, however, is not confined to Deuteronomy and deuteronomic literature but is also found in the admonitions of the classical prophets:[4]

I will press you down in your place, *as a cart full of sheaves presses down* (Amos 2: 13).

As the shepherd rescues from the mouth of the lion, etc. (Amos 3: 12).

As if a man fled from a lion and a bear met him . . . (5: 19).

I will shake the house of Israel . . . *as one shakes with a sieve* (9: 9).

Many prophetic maledictions were pronounced during a dramatic portrayal of the divine punishment which was symbolically

[1] *VTE*, ll. 526–668; Sefire I, A: 35–42.

[2] Cf. Wiseman, *VTE*, p. 26.

[3] I, C: 21–4.

[4] For treaty curses in classical prophecy, cf. especially C. Fensham, 'Malediction and Benediction in Ancient Near Eastern Treaties and the Old Testament', *ZAW* 74 (1962), 8 ff.; Hillers, *Treaty Curses*.

enacted by the seer.[1] Such dramatic enactments may have originated from the politico-judicial sphere of ancient Near-Eastern life. Several of the similes employed in the *VTE* and almost all of those in the Sefire treaty were actually dramatized during the treaty ceremony by means of animals and various inanimate objects:

Just as they burn an image (made) of wax in fire and dissolve one of clay in water, just so may your figure burn in the fire and sink in the water (*VTE*, ll. 608–11).

Just as this wax is burned by fire, so shall Matî[ʿel be burned by fi]re (Sefire I, A: 37–8).

Just as (this) bow and these arrows are broken, so may Anahita and Hadad break [the bow of Matîʿel] and the bow of his nobles (ibid. 38–9).

[Just as] this calf is cleft, so may Matîʿel be cleft and his nobles be cleft (ibid. 39–40).

[And just as] a [ha]r[lot is stripped naked],[2] so may the wives of Matîʿel be stripped naked and the wives of his offspring and the wives of [his] no[bles] (ibid. 40–1).

The simile of the broken bow which is very common in the treaty literature[3] is employed in Hosea (1: 5) and Jeremiah (49: 35),[4] and in Jeremian times we meet with a dramatization of a like simile in which the yoke is broken off from the neck of the prophet Jeremiah (Jer. 28: 10–11). The curse of nakedness, on the other hand, was dramatized by Isaiah: 'As my servant Isaiah has walked naked

[1] For discussion, see G. Fohrer, *Die symbolischen Handlungen der Propheten*, 1953.

[2] So Fitzmyer, *Sefîre*, following H. Bauer (*AfO* 8 [1932–3], 10) in the reading **ערר** and Hillers in the reading **זניה**. For **ערר** cf. Isa. 32: 11: **פשטה וערה** 'strip and make yourself bare'.

[3] Compare *VTE*, ll. 573–4: 'may they break your bow and cause you to sit beneath your enemy, may they reverse the direction of the bow in your hand' (so Borger, *ZA* 20, 193). Compare the parallel in the treaty of Esarhaddon with Baal (Borger, *Asarhaddon*, p. 109, iv: 18–19). For reversing the direction of the bow cf. 2 Sam. 1: 22: **קשת יהונתן לא נשוג אחור** 'the bow of Jonathan did not turn back' and also Hos. 7: 16, Ps. 78: 57: **קשת רמיה**. Cf. Jer. 21: 4: 'I will make the weapons in your hands turn (back)' **מסב את כלי המלחמה . . . בידכם**. Cf. also E. von Schuler, *Die Kaskaer*, 1965, p. 111, ii: 19–21; Ahiqar ix: 126 (Cowley, *Aramaic Papyri*, p. 216) (Ahiqar refer. by courtesy of S. Paul).

[4] Compare the prophecy to Aššurbanipal (K 2647, Streck, *Assurbanipal II*, p. 322): [*qaš*]*āte māt elamti ušabbirma qaštaka udannin* = 'I broke the bows of Elam and strengthened your bow.' Is it mere coincidence that a prophecy of Jeremiah and this Assyrian prophecy both speak about breaking the bows precisely of Elam? The Elamites were apparently known as good archers, cf. Isa. 22: 6 and see also Livy 37. 40 (*Elymaei sagittarii*).

and barefoot . . . so shall the king of Assyria lead away the Egyptian captives . . . naked and barefoot' (Isa. 20: 3–4). These dramatic enactments were performed against the background of political alignments which were then being formed (Jeremiah—when the formation of an anti-Babylonian coalition was in progress; Isaiah—when an Egyptian alliance was being considered) and their purpose was to portray graphically the imprecations which generally formed part of the treaty ceremony.

The maledictions were therefore either dramatized or graphically depicted by literary simile in Israelite prophecy, just as they were in ancient Near-Eastern treaties. As the maledictions were a sanction against breach of treaty, so the purpose of the prophetic threats was to portray the calamities that would follow as a consequence of the violation of Israel's covenant with Yahweh.[1] By their use of the malediction the classical prophets appear to be continuing an older popular prophetic tradition, diverging from it only in that the maledictions were pronounced against Israel instead of Israel's neighbours. In early Israelite prophecy these maledictions were pronounced before engagement in battle against a national enemy[2] and we may surmise that to a certain extent they correspond to the curses contained in the treaty violated by the nation against which war was going to be waged.[3]

The fact, then, that the curses of the type encountered in political treaties are especially met with in the prophetic oracles against foreign nations[4]—which contain ancient war oracles—points to the conclusion that these imprecations and threats derive from the treaties between Israel and Judah and the neighbouring countries. Amos's oracles against foreign nations are not based on the pattern of the Egyptian execration texts,[5] as A. Bentzen[6] argued. In the

[1] On the covenant-*rīb* in Israelite prophecy see H. B. Huffman, 'The Covenant Lawsuit in the Prophets', *JBL* 78 (1959), 258 ff.; J. Harvey, 'Le "*rīb*-pattern", Réquisitoire prophétique sur la rupture de l'alliance', *Biblica* 43 (1962), 172 ff.; G. E. Wright, 'The Lawsuit of God', *Israel's Prophetic Heritage*, 1962, pp. 45 ff.

[2] See I. L. Seeligmann, 'The Character and History of Israelite Prophecy', *EI* 3 (1954), 128 ff. (Hebrew).

[3] For a stimulating suggestion with respect to the oracle on Edom in Isa. 34, see Hillers, *Treaty Curses*, pp. 44 f.

[4] Cf. Hillers, op. cit., p. 78.

[5] See K. Sethe, *Die Ächtung feindlicher Fürsten*, etc. 1926; G. Posener, *Princes et Pays d'Asie et de Nubie*, 1940.

[6] 'The Ritual background of Amos I, 2–II, 16', *Oudtest. Studiën* 8 (1950), 85 ff. Against Bentzen's hypothesis see M. Weiss, *IEJ* 19 (1969), 150–7.

light of ancient Near-Eastern treaty curses they should rather be regarded as a dramatic symbolic enactment of the enemy's destruction. The word פשע employed in the Amos oracles seems to allude to the fact that these nations have violated their treaty with Israel and 'sinned' against her.[1] The prophetic allusion is, however, an ironic one, inasmuch as the principal purpose of the Amos oracles is to denounce Israel's sins and its violation of its covenant with Yahweh.[2]

However, while the prophetic treaty maledictions were pronounced in the context of concrete political circumstances and reflect the specific time and historical circumstances of the prophet who pronounced them, in deuteronomic literature the maledictions occur in stereotyped form and are applicable to any time and place. Their stereotyped nature is particularly apparent in the prose sermons in Jeremiah[3] which we shall discuss in the next section of this chapter.

(*c*) *Prose Sermons of Jeremiah*

In contrast to those in the poetic Jeremian prophecies which vary in simile and subject-matter, the maledictions in the prose passages of Jeremiah (see above, pp. 27 ff.) recur in the same stereotyped and monotonous formulations met with in the deuteronomic prophecies in the books of Kings. Thus, for example, both the poetic and the prose punitive oracles prophesy the horror of Israelite corpses being cast upon open ground and left unburied. But, while in the authentic prophecies we may sense a creative imagination freely expressing itself in rich and poetic simile, in the prose prophecies we meet with stereotyped and ossified formulations reflecting the dry, rational mentality of the scribes.

[1] Cf. Amos 1: 9: 'And did not remember the covenant of brotherhood', which refers to the treaty between Israel and Tyre in Solomonic times or thereafter. The Akkadian term for a parity treaty is *aḫūtum* (see Munn-Rankin, *Iraq* 18 (1956), 68 ff.) and cf. Hiram's designation of his ally Solomon as 'my brother' (1 Kgs. 9: 13). For פשע as denoting breach of treaty, cf. 1 Kgs. 12: 19, 2 Kgs. 1: 1; 3: 5, 7; 8: 20, 22.

[2] Amos 2: 9 ff. is to be understood against a covenant-*rīb* background. The treaty element in Amos is particularly apparent in 4: 6–11 which contains a series of treaty curses, see above, p. 125.

[3] See Hillers, *Treaty Curses*, p. 77: 'Of the prophetic books, Jeremiah contains by far the most numerous and impressive parallels to treaty curses.' We shall see below, however, that these curses are largely encountered in the deuteronomic prose sermons of Jeremiah and not in the authentic prophecies.

The poetic prophecies mention this divine punishment in three different passages, and in each instance it is depicted in different natural imagery:

The dead bodies of men shall fall (like dung)[1] upon the open field, like sheaves after the reaper and none shall gather them (9: 21).

With the burial of an ass he shall be buried, dragged and cast forth beyond the gates of Jerusalem (22: 19).

And his dead body shall be cast out to the heat by day and the frost by night (36: 30).

The same punishment is referred to six times in the deuteronomic sermons and is, in contrast, always worded in one of two stereotyped formulae: 'And the dead bodies . . . will be food for the birds of the heaven and for the beasts of the earth' והיתה נבלת . . . למאכל לעוף השמים ולבהמת הארץ (7: 33; 16: 4; 19: 7; 34: 20); 'And they shall not be gathered (or: they shall not be lamented) or buried, they shall be as dung on the surface of the ground' לא יאספו (לא יספדו) ולא יקברו לדמן על פני האדמה יהיו (8: 2; 16: 4; 25: 33).[2] The first formula, which is already met with in Deuteronomy, has its counterpart, as we have observed, in the Esarhaddon treaty.[3]

It is interesting to note, then, that almost all of the conventional maledictions in the book of Jeremiah have their counterparts in extra-Biblical texts dating from the ninth to seventh centuries B.C.

[1] The word כדמן does not suit the simile and mars the poetic metre of the verse (see Duhm, KHC; Volz, KAT^{2} and Rudolph, HAT^{2} ad loc.) and as it is a characteristic idiom of the deuteronomic maledictions (see below) it may be taken as an accretion. The inclusion of the word may have been influenced by the phrase על פני השדה which recalled the deuteronomic formula כדמן על פני השדה (2 Kgs. 9: 37). The accretion thus entailed the affixing of the *waw* to the word כעמיר (which is omitted in the Vaticanus version). It may be surmised, then, that the original text read: 'The dead bodies of men shall fall upon the open field like sheaves after the reaper and none shall gather them.'

[2] Jer. 25: 33 is a prose accretion, see Rudolph, HAT^{2} and M. Weiss, *Tarbiz* 34 (1965), 218–19. Cf. the more lifelike and descriptive formulation of this curse in an authentic prophetic passage: 'and their corpses were as refuse in the midst of the streets' ותהי נבלתם כסוחה בקרב חוצות (Isa. 5: 25). Though similar imagery is also encountered in non-deuteronomic passages, it always contains departures from the deuteronomic stereotype, cf. Ps. 79: 2 לחיתו ארץ instead of לבהמת ארץ; 1 Sam. 17: 46 לחית הארץ (not נבלה but פגר); Jer. 15: 3 contains the same formulation but has omitted the reference to נבלה.

[3] Above, p. 118.

This fact leads us to conclude that they were not the spontaneous utterances of the prophet, and that they do not reflect the geographical and social environment as do those in the authentic prophecies, but constitute the conventional motifs and formula-types employed in treaty maledictions. Some of these may actually have been proclaimed by the prophet himself, but they cannot be considered his genuine creation so much as conventional formulae prevalent in treaty literature of his time.[1]

We cite the following parallels as cases in point:

1. Following the malediction concerning the corpses which shall be devoured by the birds of heaven and beasts of the earth, we hear in a long prose sermon (7: 1–8: 3) of the following divine judgement:

> At that time, says the Lord, the bones of the kings of Judah . . . shall be brought out of their tombs and they shall be spread before the sun and the moon and all the host of heaven, which they have loved[2] and served, which they have gone after, and which they have sought and worshipped (8: 1–2).

In the annals of Aššurbanipal we read:

> The sepulchres of their former and later kings, who did not fear Aššur and Ištar, my lords . . ., I exposed to the sun.[3]

It is difficult to regard the resemblance between the malediction in Jeremiah and this passage in the annals as coincidental. It is more plausible to assume that the malediction in Jer. 8: 1–2 reflects

[1] It is also probable that the prophet reworked some of the prosaic formulae, adopted by him from the above-mentioned sources, into poetry. So, for example, Jer. 18: 16:

לשום ארצם לשמה שריקות עולם
כל עובר עליה ישם ויניד בראשו

seems to be a poetic version of the prosaic schematic curse (cf. 1 Kgs. 9: 8; Zeph. 2: 15b) occuring in Jer. 19: 8: ושמתי את העיר הזאת לשמה ולשרקה כל עבר עליה ישם וישרק על כל מכותיה (compare also 50: 13). See S. E. Loewenstamm, 'Remarks on stylistic patterns in Biblical and Ugaritic literatures', *Lešonenu*, 32 (1967–8) p. 30 (Hebrew).

[2] The word 'love' here, as in other deuteronomic contexts, means loyalty as may be inferred from the expressions employed in this verse synonymous with 'love', as 'serve', 'go after', 'seek', 'worship' (lit. 'bow down'), cf. above, pp. 83 f.

[3] Streck, *Assurbanipal II*, p. 56, vi: 70–3: *kimāḫḫi šarrānišunu maḫrûti arkûti lā pāliḫūti* ^{d}*Aššur u* ^{d}*Ištar bēlēia . . . ukallim* ^{d}*šamši*. Compare *OIP* II, 99: 46.

an Assyrian practice to which a religious Israelite interpretation had been added: the bones of all the kings who had worshipped the sun, the moon, and other heavenly bodies shall be exposed in open view of these same bodies.

2. Alongside the description of Judah's impending destruction and devastation we encounter in the prose strand of Jeremiah a malediction concerning the ceasing of 'the sound of joy and the voice of gladness, the voice of the bridegroom and the voice of the bride' (7: 34; 16: 9; 25: 10; 33: 10–11). A similar curse is encountered in the extra-Biblical texts of the same period. Thus, for example, in an Esarhaddon inscription:[1] 'No joyful man enters its streets, no musician is met.' The Aššurnirari V treaty contains a similar imprecation: 'His peasant in his field shall not raise his voice in song, may the green of the field not come forth',[2] as does the Sefire treaty: 'nor may the sound of the lyre be heard in Arpad',[3] and the Aššurbanipal annals: 'I deprived their fields of the noise of the people, the tread of oxen and sheep, the sound of the glad worksong'.[4] There is a parallel to the last passage in the consolation prophecy in Jer. 33: 10–12: 'in this place of which you say, "It is a waste without man or beast . . ." there shall be heard again the sound of joy and the voice of gladness . . . in this place . . . there shall again be habitations of shepherds resting their flocks.'

3. The oracle in Jer. 25: 10 concerning the end of joy and gladness also speaks of the cessation of 'the sound of the millstones and the light of a candle' קול רחים ואור נר. A parallel to this malediction is again encountered in the *VTE*: 'May the sound of the mill[5] and oven not be heard in your houses' (ll. 443–4). As the oven is a more probable counterpart to the millstones, the word נר in the Jeremian verse should perhaps be taken in the sense of oven (= תנור; cf.

[1] R. Borger, *Asarhaddon*, p. 107, Rand 1: *ina sūqēšu ḫadû ul iba'a ēpiš nigûti ul ipparrik.*

[2] *AfO* 8 (1932–3), Rs. iv: 19–20: *ikkaršu ina ṣēri aj ilsâ alāla, urqīt ṣēri lū lā uṣṣâ.*

[3] I, A: 29: ואל יתשמע קל כנר בארפד, cf. Ezek. 26: 13. In the Sefire treaty, as also in the Aššurnirari treaty, this curse and the curse that 'the green of the field may not come forth' (see above, p. 124 n. 3) are juxtaposed (but in reverse order).

[4] Streck, *Assurbanipal II*, pp. 56–8, vi: 101–3: *rigim amēlūti kibis alpī u ṣênī šisīt alāla ṭābi uzammâ ugarēšu.*

[5] *ik-kil* NA_4.HUR = the sound of the millstone, cf. Borger, *ZA* 20, ad loc.

conversely תנור in the sense of אור 'light' or fire, in Isa. 31: 9 אשר אור לו בציון ותנור לו בירושלם.

4. In deuteronomic descriptions of the destruction of cities we hear of their being overthrown הפך (Deut. 29: 22), burned שרף (ibid.; Josh. 8: 28; 9: 11), strewn with sulphur and salt (Deut. 29: 22), and being turned into desolate heaps (Deut. 13: 17; Josh. 8: 28; 1 Kgs. 9: 7 ff.), all these being the conventional methods of retaliation for breach of treaty in the ancient Near East.[1] In the prose strand of Jeremiah this description is accompanied by an additional motif: the conversion of the city into a habitation ground for animals, a 'jackals' lair' מעון תנים.[2] It occurs in form of a curse in Jer. 9: 10:[3] 'And I will make Jerusalem heaps, a lair of jackals (מעון תנים), and I will make the cities of Judah a desolation without an inhabitant' (compare 10: 22; 49: 33; 51: 37).[4]

This curse is also encountered in the Sefire treaty: 'And may Arpad become a mound to [house the desert animal]: the gazelle and the fox and the hare and the wild cat and the owl and the (...) and the magpie'.[5] A similar motif appears in the continuation of the passages of Esarhaddon[6] and Aššurbanipal, quoted above under 2: 'Foxes and hyenas made their homes there;[7] 'Wild asses, gazelles, and every kind of wild animal of the desert I caused to lie down there undisturbed.'[8]

The motif appears to have been prevalent in Judah during the sixth century B.C., the time of destruction and exile, hence its

[1] Cf. above, pp. 109 ff.

[2] The expression מעון תנים is found only in Jeremiah; Isa. 34: 13; 35: 7 has נוה תנים.

[3] Jer. 9: 10–15 is a deuteronomic accretion. In v. 9 it is the Deity who speaks, whereas in v. 10 it is the prophet speaking. There is no warrant for reading שאו instead of the MT אשא as many commentators do (following the LXX), e.g. Rudolph, *Jeremiah*[2], HAT, ad loc. Verse 16 is the authentic sequence of v. 9 and resumes its lament (cf. J. Bright, *Jeremiah*, Anchor Bible, p. 73).

[4] For the late character of Jer. 10: 22, see Volz, *Jeremia*, KAT, and cf. Rudolph, HAT on Jer. 49: 33. Chapters 50–51, as is well known, are not authentic prophecies of Jeremiah.

[5] I, A: 32–3: ותהוי ארפד תל ל[רבק צי ו]צבי ושעל וארנב ושרן וצדה ו... ועקה, see Fitzmyer, *Sefîre* ad loc.

[6] In *VTE* the curse of desolation (l. 492) is accompanied by the dwelling of demons: *še-e-du, ú-tuk-ku, ra-bi-ṣu lim-nu* É.MEŠ-*ku-nu li-ḫi-ru* = 'may demon, devil, and evil spirit select your houses' (l. 493); see also above, p. 113.

[7] R. Borger, *Asarhaddon*, p. 107, Rand l. 3: *šēlabu u būṣu iqnunū qinnu*.

[8] Streck, *Assurbanipal II*, p. 58, vi: 104–6: ***sirrimē ṣabâti, umām ṣēri mala bašû pargāniš ušarbiṣa qerebšun.***

occurrence in many of the anonymous Biblical prophecies of the time (Isa. 13: 21–2; 34: 11-15; Jer. 10: 22; 49: 33; 51: 37; cf. also Lam. 5: 18).

5. In the deuteronomic imprecation passages in Jer. 9: 10–15 and 23: 15[1] we meet with the malediction: 'Behold, I will feed this people (in 23: 15 the prophets) with wormwood לענה and give them poisonous water מי ראש to drink.' A parallel to this curse is encountered in the *VTE* (ll. 521–2): 'may Ea . . . give you deadly water to drink, may he fill you with dropsy.'[2] Though this same idea is expressed in a Jeremian poetical passage, it will be noted that it is not worded in stereotyped deuteronomical phraseology: 'For the Lord our God doomed us to perish and has given us poisoned water to drink' (8: 14).

The fact that this malediction in Jer. 9 appears in the framework of a series of stereotyped maledictions and motifs occurring in contemporary Mesopotamian literature, such as desolation and dwelling-place of animals (v. 10), self condemnation (vv. 11–13) (see above, pp. 114–15), and exile (v. 15) shows that it also belongs to the same pattern.

6. The prose oracles in Jer. 28–9 declare that the Judeans will have to expiate their sins by being a subject people to the king of Babylon for seventy years (28: 11–12; 29: 10). C. F. Whitley[3] contends that these oracles are *vaticinia ex eventu*, having their origin in the post-exilic period when the seventy years that elapsed between the destruction of the first temple (586 B.C.) and the dedication of the second in 516 B.C. were taken by Judeans to be the term of divine punishment suffered by Israel. This conception, claims Whitley, was given theological standing by the invention of prophecies based on this concept and their ascription to Jeremiah.

[1] On Jer. 9, 10–15 see above, p. 142 n. 3. Jer. 23: 15a and 9: 14 have the same subject-matter, are identical in formulation, and thus constitute the same stereotyped malediction of the deuteronomic type. There is consequently no warrant for regarding one of the verses as authentic and the other as literary imitation as Rudolph and Volz do (both holding opposite views as to which of the verses is authentic and which imitation). On the non-authentic character of 23: 15, see Volz's cogent remarks (ad loc.): 'Man erwartet hier zwischen inne auch noch kein Gerichtswort; das Gericht liegt unausgesprochen in der Verderbnis, die die Propheten anrichten und für die sie die Verantwortung tragen.'

[2] ^{d}*é-a* . . . A.MEŠ *la* TI.LA *liš-qi-ku-nu a-ga-nu-til-la-a li-mal-li-ku-nu.*

[3] C. F. Whitley, 'The Term "Seventy Years Captivity"', *VT* 4 (1954), 60–72.

A. Orr[1] justifiably argues, however, that the notion that the temple and land were to lie in ruins for seventy years is not implicit in the Jeremian prophecies, but was read into them in late second-commonwealth times (Zech. 1: 12; 7: 5; Dan. 9: 2; 2 Chron. 36: 21); the seventy years in Jeremiah refer not to the duration of the land's desolation and the destruction of the temple, but to the duration of Babylonian rule over Palestine, 605–539 B.C., a total of sixty-six years which was expressed by the round number seventy. Be this as it may, P. Ackroyd has shown[2] that the oracles need not be interpreted in chronological terms. In the ancient Near East seventy years was a typological figure commonly employed to denote a period of punishment, for example, in Isa. 23: 15–17: 'In that day Tyre will be forgotten for seventy years . . . (and) at the end of seventy years, the Lord will visit Tyre and she will return to her hire.' Though R. Borger[3] believes that this numerical typology is based on the view that a person's average lifespan is seventy years, it is more probable that the figure (at least in Jeremiah) denotes a period of three generations.[4] The Jeremian prophecy in 27: 5–7, for example, which specifies the amount of time during which Judah and her neighbours will be subject to Babylon, declares (in phraseology reminiscent of 25: 11–14) that: 'All the nations shall serve him and his son and his grandson, until the time of his own land comes; then many nations and great kings shall make him their slaves' (v. 7).[5]

The same seventy-years' motif occurs also in an Esarhaddon inscription,[6] where it refers to a seventy-year period in which Babylon shall lie destroyed. D. D. Luckenbill asked therefore whether the Assyrian text might not help in elucidating the nature of the seventy-year motif in these Biblical verses.[7] Now the use of

[1] A. Orr, 'The Seventy Years of Babylon', *VT* 6 (1956), 304–6.

[2] P. R. Ackroyd, 'Two Old Testament Historical Problems of the Early Persian Period', *JNES* 17 (1958), 23 ff.

[3] R. Borger, 'An Additional Remark on P. R. Ackroyd', *JNES* 18 (1959), 74.

[4] Cf. Rudolph, HAT[2]; Weiser, *Jeremia*, ATD[4], ad loc.

[5] Jer. 27: 7 may possibly not be specifically referring to a period of three generations, but to an indeterminable period of time, cf. Jer. 2: 9: 'Therefore I shall contend with you, says the Lord, and with your children's children, I will contend', which is to be taken in a superlative sense, i.e. 'I will greatly contend with you', and not as referring specifically to three generations. See M. Weiss, *The Bible and Modern Literary Theory*, 1962, pp. 74–7 (Hebrew).

[6] See R. Borger, *Asarhaddon*, Epis. 10, p. 15.

[7] D. D. Luckenbill, 'The Black Stone of Esarhaddon,' *AJSL* 42 (1924–5), 167.

the same numerical typology in the two passages need not imply that the motif was borrowed from Assyrian sources. But in view of the number of other Assyrian influences met with both in the Book of Deuteronomy and deuteronomic literature, and particularly in view of the divine wrath motif encountered in Deut. 29 and the Esarhaddon inscription,[1] we may legitimately suppose that in this case it substantially was. Compare the parallel passages in Jer. 29 and in the Esarhaddon inscription:

Jeremiah	Esarhaddon
This whole land shall become a *ruin and a waste* and these nations shall serve the king of Babylon *seventy years* . . . And I will bring upon that land all my words which I have pronounced against it, all that *is written in this book*[2] (25: 11–13).	*Seventy years as the period of its* (*Babylon's*) *desolation he* (*Marduk*) *wrote* . . .[3]
When the seventy years are (מלא) *completed* for Babylon I will visit you and I will fulfil to you my promise . . . *the plans I have for you* . . . *plans for welfare* (שלום) (29: 10).	*Until the time becomes* [*full* (*malû*) and the heart of the great lord] Marduk shall become quiet and with the land which he punished *he shall become reconciled* (*iršû salīmu*), *seventy years shall be completed* (*malû*).[4]

The occurrence in both passages of the same numerical motif expressed in identical phraseology and in contexts which refer to subjugation to a foreign power can hardly be accidental. It appears therefore that its use in connection with subjugation of Babylon was known in Judah in those days and that it had been employed by the Judaic scribes to express the temporary subjugation of Judah. Though it may very well be that the original

[1] See above, pp. 115–16.

[2] Verse 12 is an interpolation, see Commentaries. Verse 13 abα refers to the land of Judah (the interpolation caused the change of הארץ הזאת into הארץ ההיא as if it were referring to Babylon, see Rudolph, ad loc.), 13bβ אשר נבא ירמיהו על כל הגוים is the title of the section of prophecies against nations (chs. 46–51) which belong here before vv. 15 ff. (So LXX and see Commentaries.)

[3] R. Borger, *Asarhaddon*, p. 15, Epis. 10, Fass. a: 3: 70 *šanāti minūt nidûtišu išṭurma*.

[4] Ibid. c: 26: *adi ūmē im*[*lû libbi bēli rabê?*] *Marduk inūḫuma ana māti ša eninu iršû sali*[*mu*] 70 *šanāti im?*[*lû*].

Jeremian oracle referred to three generations of Israelite subjection to Babylon, the deuteronomic formulation has employed the conventional numerical typology of the period, which appears to have been particularly employed by Mesopotamian scribes.

The admonitions in the Jeremian prose sermons thus revolve about a set of recurring stereotyped imprecations, all of which have parallels in political documents of the ninth to seventh centuries B.C. These recurring imprecations invariably appear in groups[1] and impress one as being a mechanical conglomeration of literary formulae, not maledictions uttered in actual circumstances. Unlike the maledictions in the authentic Jeremian prophecies whose subject-matter and phraseology are in keeping with the social and historical circumstances of their context, the maledictions in the Jeremian prose sermons are applicable to any time and place and are indeed merely dry conventional formulae which seem to be adopted from the texts of treaties made between Assyrian and Babylonian kings and their vassals.

LAW-CODE VERSUS TREATY

We have seen that in both structure and content Deuteronomy is closely related to the ancient Near-Eastern treaties, especially those of the ninth to seventh centuries B.C. But while the comparison of judicial and stylistic elements such as the occurrence of identical curses in the Esarhaddon treaties and in Deuteronomy suggests that the treaty literature directly influenced Deuteronomy, the latter, unlike the treaties, does not present these elements in a fixed order as befits a legal document. Thus the historical prologue

[1] Jer. 7: 33 ff. contains the motifs of: the exposed dead being devoured by animals and fowl (v. 33), the cessation of joy and gladness (v. 34a), the devastation of the land (34b), the disinterment of the bones of the dead (8: 1–2a).

Jer. 9: 10 ff. contains the motifs of: the desolate land becoming a habitation ground for animals (v. 10), self-condemnation and the vindication of Israel's punishment (vv. 11–13), the drinking of poisonous water and the eating of wormwood (v. 14), and exile (v. 15).

Jer. 16: 4 ff.: dishonouring the dead (vv. 4–8), the cessation of joy (v. 9), self-condemnation and vindication of Israel's punishment (vv. 10–11), exile and subjugation (v. 13).

Jer. 19: 7 f.: the exposed dead being devoured by animals and fowl (v. 7), the astonishment and wonder of passers-by (v. 8), the children being eaten by their parents (v. 9).

Jer. 25: 9 ff.: destruction and desolation (v. 9), the cessation of joy (v. 10a), the sound of the millstone and oven (v. 10b). (See above, pp. 141–2.) Jer. 5: 19: self-condemnation and subjugation in exile.

in Deuteronomy is not pure history but is interspersed with injunctions and admonitions, a fact which has led some scholars to think that the book consists of several cycles of covenantal structures.[1] The witnesses to the covenant (heaven and earth), which regularly appear either at the very beginning of a treaty[2] or at its very end,[3] appear in the book of Deuteronomy in both the prologue and the epilogue[4]. Furthermore, while the witnesses appear in the treaties in a separate section, in Deuteronomy they are interwoven in the framework of an admonitory sermon (4: 1–40; 30: 15–20; 31: 27 ff.).

Deuteronomy's section of the Blessings and Curses similarly differs from the corresponding part of the treaties in that it is preceded by a series of anathemas (27: 15–26), which are to be proclaimed in a sacral ceremony and which actually bear the stamp of ban and excommunication[5] rather than the threat of physical calamity that characterizes the treaty curses as well as those in Deut. 28. In fact the Dodecalogue in ch. 27 constitutes a series of injunctions similar in its contents and formulation to the series of injunctions in the Covenant Code (Exod 21: 12–17; 22: 17–19)[6] which apparently reflects the religious-sacral background of the ancient tribal life.[7]

Close to this levitical ceremony comes the passage (vv. 11–14) ordaining the utterance of blessings and curses by the tribes on Mt. Gerizim and Mt. Ebal.

These two traditions, rooted in ancient celebrations at Shechem, have hardly anything to do with the maledictions of Deut. 28 which, as we saw, reflect a period late in the history of the monarchy

[1] See Baltzer, *Bundesformular*, pp. 41 f.; N. Lohfink, *Das Hauptgebot*, pp 111 ff.; McCarthy, *Treaty and Covenant*, pp. 110 ff.

[2] As in *VTE* and the Sefire treaty.

[3] As in the Hittite treaties but not without exception, see, e.g., E. von Schuler, *Kaskäer*, p. 117, where the witnesses appear at the end of the treaty. According to von Schuler this is only a draft.

[4] Cf. above, p. 62.

[5] Cf. Gen. 4: 11; Josh. 6: 26; Judg. 21: 18; 1 Sam. 14: 24 and 28.

[6] See A. Alt, 'Ursprünge', *KS* I, 308 ff.

[7] The brevity and absolute nature of these sentences seem to indicate that they were proclaimed in a cultic setting. The sacral confederation of the tribes had to purge itself from evildoers in order to avoid a national disaster (compare the story of Achan in Josh. 7). If the evildoer committed a capital crime which could be controlled by the community he had to be punished or executed (מות יומת) but if the crime was committed in secrecy like those in Deut. 27 (see below, pp. 276 f.) the congregation had to dissociate itself from the guilty party by proclaiming a ban on him, which would take effect through the community's confirmation by saying אמן. Cf. also G. von Rad, *Deuteronomium*, ATD, ad loc.

and belong to quite a different genre of literature. The author of Deuteronomy, however, considered these two kinds of ceremonial proclamations as embodying the kind of reward and punishment described in ch. 28 (cf. 11: 27–8 with 27: 12–13) and therefore joined them together in the epilogue.

The most important deviation of Deuteronomy from the treaty form is that its central part is dedicated to civil, cultic, and criminal law. While we may regard this section as functionally equivalent to the stipulatory section of a treaty, it is very different in substance, and this difference stems from the fact that the object of the treaty is to assure the partner's loyalty—as reflected in the section which we called the stipulation of allegiance—and not to impose upon him a system of laws as does the book of Deuteronomy. The convergence of treaty and law-code forms is one of the crucial problems not only in understanding the pattern of the deuteronomic covenant but also in comprehending the covenant between God and Israel as presented in Exodus. It is necessary therefore to analyse briefly the relationship between law and covenant in the ancient Near East. The analysis of this relationship may also serve as a point of departure for understanding the crystallization of the covenant form in the theology of ancient Israel.

In the structure of the Old Babylonian law-codes (principally those of Ur-Nammu, Lipit-Ištar, and Hammurabi) we can discern a framework very similar to that of the treaty: preamble, historical prologue, laws (the equivalent of the stipulations in the covenantal structure) and blessings and curses.[1] Scholars generally regard the historical introduction of the Hammurabi Code as an interpolated text which originally had nothing to do with a law-code. Driver and Miles,[2] for example, contend that Hammurabi's boastfulness about his victories and achievements in the prologue rightfully belongs in royal inscriptions and not in a code of laws. It must be admitted that it is not impossible, and there is even some evidence[3] for the supposition that the Code of Hammurabi was diffused without the prologue. However, even if we agree that the prologue was added later, no one would argue that this was done arbitrarily

[1] This has not been preserved in the Ur-Nammu code. [2] *BL* I. 40–1.

[3] J. J. Finkelstein published a text of the Hammurabi Code (BM 78944+78979) in which no prologue occurs (*JCS* 21 (1967)). It is nevertheless still possible that in the schools they sometimes used to copy only parts of the classical works for teaching purposes, so that this find cannot serve as a proof for the unauthenticity of the prologue (see Addenda).

by the scribes, since the two other codes, the predecessors of the Hammurabi Code, also have prologues. In those codes, since the prologues deal with the conditions which brought about the new legislation, it is inconceivable that they are not an organic part of the documents in which they were incorporated. If, then, these three most ancient codes have an identical structure, this reflects without doubt a traditional pattern. Indeed, this pattern goes back to a document of the third millenium B.C. which, although formally not a legal code, has the same subject-matter as the codes and seems to be a classic example of the way codes came into being[1]—the Urukagina reform.[2] Here the proclamation of the reform itself is preceded by a long historical introduction which, like those in the Ur-Nammu and the Lipit-Ištar codes,[3] describes the liberation of the people from oppression and slavery[4] by the proclamation of the law.

All this might suggest an analogy between Deuteronomy and the Mesopotamian law-codes rather than the political treaty. If we still cling to the analogy with the treaty it is because of the covenant which lies behind the Exodus and deuteronomic traditions. But it has not been stressed enough that the covenant in the ancient Near East was not limited to the sphere of political treaties. The reform of Urukagina, which—as we indicated—exemplifies the *Sitz im Leben* of the Sumerian and Old-Babylonian law-codes, is sanctified by a covenant or an agreement with the god Ningirsu.[5] Moreover, although no covenant or divine agreement is mentioned explicitly in the Hammurabi Code there are some implicit indications of its covenantal character. Like the copies of a treaty, the Hammurabi stele, on which the laws are engraved, was deposited in the sanctuary and placed before a statue of the deity.[6] The Hammurabi

[1] Codification in the Old-Babylonian period had been motivated by social reforms (= acts of *mīšarum*), the Urukagina reform being one and most outstanding of these, see J. J. Finkelstein, 'Ammiṣaduqa's Edict and the Babylonian "Law-Codes"', *JCS* 15 (1961), 101 ff.

[2] Thureau-Dangin, *SAKI*, pp. 52 ff.; see also M. Lambert, *RA* 50 (1956) 182 f.; 52 (1958), 12 f.

[3] See, e.g., Kramer, *The Sumerians*, pp. 83 ff.

[4] Cf. the motif of liberation from the house of slaves in Egypt at the beginning of the ten commandments and also in the historical introduction of Deuteronomy (4: 20; 5: 15; 6: 21 ff., etc.).

[5] Cone B xii: 26–8: nin-gir-su-da uru-ka-gi-na-ke$_4$ inim-bi *KA*-e-da-kéš. Whether it has to be interpreted in the sense of divine agreement to the reform (so M. Lambert, *RA* 50 (1956), 183) or as a covenant with Ningirsu (so E. Sollberger, *Système verbal*, § 177), one thing is clear: the rules of the reform had been put under the authority of the god.

[6] See D. J. Wiseman, 'The Laws of Hammurabi again', *JSS* 7 (1962), 166 f.

Code also resembles the ancient Near-Eastern treaty forms, and particularly the deuteronomic covenant, in the relationship between its blessings and curses: the blessings are brief and few, while the curses are verbose and manifold.[1] Typologically, then, the law-code and the treaty greatly overlap,[2] and one may therefore say that Deuteronomy follows the pattern of a law-code and not that of a treaty. Against the assumption that Deuteronomy follows the pattern of a law-code one might argue that the threefold structure —prologue, laws, blessings and curses—is not attested after the Old Babylonian period. On the other hand, although no later codes with such a structure have been preserved, the Hammurabi Code was considered classical and was copied in the schools for a thousand years.[3] Consequently it exerted great influence on the literature of the ancient Near East[4] and may not have been without influence on Israel.

It seems, indeed, that there may be an echo of the Code of Hammurabi in Deut. 4: 8: 'For what great nation is there that has laws and judgements so righteous (חוקים ומשפטים צדיקם) as all this law?' 'Righteous' צדיקם as an adjective describing a noun other than a person is met with only in this verse,[5] and its occurrence here may be by no means accidental. In view of the formal similarity between Deuteronomy and the Hammurabi Code we must ask if the exceptional expression 'righteous laws' (משפטים צדיקם) was not intentionally employed as a reflection of the cognate term in the Code of Hammurabi: *dīnāt mīšarim*,[6] which corresponds literally to the Biblical expression and which served to express Hammurabi's excellence in justice. It is legitimate to suppose that the author of Deuteronomy employed the expression to compare

[1] See M. Noth, *The Laws in the Pentateuch, etc.*, pp. 123 ff.

[2] The prologue in the Hammurabi Code implies the motive of inspiring loyalty to the king, who cares for the people, similar to the motive behind the prologue in the treaties. By the same token, the epilogue of the Hammurabi Code is concerned not only with conserving the monument, as McCarthy argues (*Treaty and Covenant*, p. 82 n. 8), but also with encouraging obedience to the laws, cf. CH xxv b: 64–72; xxvi b: 2–8, 18–22.

[3] See W. Eilers, *AO* 31 (1931), 3–4, p. 5.

[4] Cf. Borger, *Orientalia* 34 (1965), 168–9, for an example of a quotation in the treaty of Marduk-zākir-šumi and Šamsi-Adad V from the Hammurabi Code. See also R. H. Pfeiffer, 'The Influence of Hammurabi's Code Outside of Babylonia', *Akten des XXIV Internationalen Orientalisten-Kongresses* (München, 1957), pp. 148–9.

[5] Cf. W. Gesenius–F. Buhl, *Handwörterbuch über das AT*[17], 1915, *sub voce*.

[6] CH xxiv b: 1–2.

the *dīnāt mīšarim* of the *wise* Babylonian king[1] with the 'righteous laws' of the *wise* and perspicacious Israel. We do, indeed, find in this passage a pronounced competitive tone challenging the supremacy of the laws of the other peoples: 'For that will be your wisdom and your understanding in *the sight of the peoples*, who when they hear all these laws will say 'surely this great nation is a wise and understanding people' (4: 6). It may be surmised, then, that the expression 'righteous laws' was employed as a polemic note against the Hammurabi Code, which at that time was widely studied in the ancient Near East.

To return to the question whether Deuteronomy reflects the typology of the law-code or that of the treaty, it seems that the Israelite covenant and especially the deuteronomic version combined two patterns which originally had nothing to do with each other. The law-code demands the observance of manifold precepts concerned with every area of life, while the treaty simply commands loyalty to the great sovereign. Moses, like Urukagina, was the lawgiver *par excellence* who made a covenant with God stressing the observance of laws. This emphasis on laws as opposed to simple loyalty is especially clear in the oldest Sinaitic tradition (Exod. 24: 3 ff.), where no mention is made of a covenant establishing the special relationship between God and Israel as in Exod. 19: 4–6 and in P (Exod. 6: 7; Lev. 26: 12 and 45, etc.) and D (Deut.

[1] F. R. Kraus ('Ein zentrales Problem des altmesopotamischen Rechtes: was ist der Codex Hammurabi?', *Genava*, Musée d'art et d'histoire, Genève VIII (1960), 283 ff.) has demonstrated that the Code of Hammurabi bears the stamp of wisdom ideology and that the expression *emqum* by which Hammurabi is designated may be traced back to the vocabulary of the scribes. The Babylonian judge was never styled a 'wise man' but this, on the other hand, is the typical appellation of the scribe (see *CAD*, vol. 4 (D), p. 151). Kraus contends therefore that the scribes described Hammurabi, the judge and the lawgiver, as they would have liked to visualize him. The scribes who formulated and committed the laws to writing have projected the law-giving king in their own image.

It would appear that a similar identification of Wisdom and Law took place in Israel in the seventh century B.C., the period in which the class of the scribes–wise men began to take an active part in the composition of legal literature (see below, pp. 158 f.). The scribes–wise men who undertook the transcription of wisdom literature (Prov. 25: 1) and the laws of the Torah (Jer. 8: 8) during this period were those who, in their literary compositions (Deuteronomy and deuteronomic historiography) identified the Israelite laws with wisdom (see below, pp. 244 ff). Just as Hammurabi, the king and sage, took pride in his *dīnāt mīšarim*, the wise and perspicacious people of Israel take pride in their 'righteous laws' (משפטים צדיקם).

26: 17–19; 27: 9; 29: 12).[1] The primary theme in Exod. 24 is expressed by reference to the 'commands' דברים and the 'judgements' משפטים in connection with which the covenant is concluded: 'this is the blood of the covenant which the Lord now makes with you concerning all these commands' (Exod. 24: 8; cf. 34: 27). While the passage leaves no doubt that Moses did establish a new relationship between Yahweh and the people, it makes it equally obvious that the covenant as such is made with respect to the laws and commandments of the God whose sovereignty is already recognized. By contrast, Joshua's covenant (Josh. 24) concerns itself primarily with the establishment of an unequivocal relationship with Yahweh, while the law mentioned there (v. 25) has only secondary importance. Moses' legislative action is therefore to be compared with the reforms, the so-called *mīšarum* acts[2] (níg-si-sá in Sumerian), which we find for the first time in the Urukagina texts and which actually lie behind the Old Babylonian codes.[3] The terminology employed in connection with his giving of the law is also identical with that of the performance of *mīšarum*. The term *mīšaram šakānum*, which denotes the executing of the reform,[4] is the equivalent of שים משפט in Hebrew, an equation supported by the Mari letters, in which *šipṭam šakānum* is employed in connection with introducing a social-economic change.[5] The leaders to whom the action of שים משפט is ascribed are Moses (Exod. 15: 25; 21: 1) and Joshua (Josh. 24: 25) and—as we shall see later—also David, who undoubtedly organized the civil and religious life of Israelite society in times of great transition. We may therefore conclude that Moses' really authentic achievement was the crystallization of Israel's tribal society by means of a reform, the exact nature of which remains unclear but which, in the light of the

[1] The underlying formula in these texts is the judicial familial formula: והייתי לכם . . . ואתם תהיו לי (cf. above, pp. 80–81) which in Exod. 19: 4–6 and in Deut. 26: 18–19 is being combined with the sovereign–vassal pattern, cf. סגלה, ממלכה (see above, p. 69, n. 1), עליון על כל הגוים. Y. Muffs (in a private conversation) expressed the opinion that the familial formula, . . . והייתי לכם ואתם תהיו לי, i.e. the adoptive formula, is characteristic of the Priestly Code and this has been combined with the vassal–political formula in Deuteronomy.

[2] Cf. F. R. Kraus, *Ein Edikt des Königs Ammi-Ṣaduqa von Babylon*, 1958, pp. 194 ff.

[3] See p. 149 n. 1 above.

[4] See Kraus, *Edikt*.

[5] Cf. A. Malamat, 'The Ban in Mari and in the Bible', *Biblical Essays, Proceedings of the ninth meeting of Die Ou-Testamentiese Werkgemeenskap in Suid-Afrika*, 1966, p. 45.

mīšarum analogy, seems to have included among other elements the liberation of slaves (Exod. 21: 2 f.) and the year of release (Exod. 23: 10–11).[1] This legal reform, which Moses initiated, is especially stressed in the ancient poem of the Blessing of Moses (Deut. 33). There we read of Moses the lawmaker (מחקק) performing God's צדקה ומשפט with Israel in the presence of the leaders of the people (v. 21).[2] That the term עשה משפט וצדקה there employed is identical with שים משפט and that it likewise refers to the introduction of social reforms of the *mīšarum* type (this seems also to be indicated in vv. 3–4) may be deduced from 2 Sam. 8: 15–18, where we encounter a state document from the Davidic period, which, after informing us of David's enthronement, relates that David 'established justice and righteousness עשה משפט וצדקה for all his people.'[3]

The association of these two incidents, David's enthronement and his establishment of justice, is not without purpose. It is known that the kings of the Old-Babylonian period performed their remissive acts, their acts of *mīšarum*,[4] shortly after ascending the throne. David's establishment of משפט וצדקה 'justice and righteousness' is therefore to be understood as an analogue to

[1] In the light of the *mīšarum* material discovered and published in recent years (see F. R. Kraus, *Edikt*, and the articles of J. J. Finkelstein and F. R. Kraus in *B. Landsberger-Festschrift*, *AS* 16, 1965), the whole problem of *shemitta* and *Jôbel* in ancient Israel has to be reconsidered. The laws in Lev. 25 cannot be seen any more as post-exilic but, on the contrary, as reflecting very ancient tribal reality. See J. Lewy, 'The Biblical Institution of *derôr* in the light of Akkadian Documents', *EI* 5, (1958), 21–31 (see Addenda).

The year of Jubilee in which the דרור is proclaimed is said to be the year in which everybody returns to his family (Lev. 25: 10). This actually explains the figure of speech used by the Sumerians for 'freedom'. The Sumerian term for proclamation of freedom: ama-ar-gi$_4$ (Akk. *andurāru* = Hebr. דרור), means literally 'return to the mother'. (See S. N. Kramer, *The Sumerians*, p. 79.) It seems that the roots of this expression lie in the liberation of slaves which was the most prominent feature of the Mesopotamian reform. Slaves came usually from families who in time of need sold their children as slaves. No wonder, then, that freedom became associated with 'return to the mother' or 'to family'.

[2] Read with LXX: כי שם חלקת מחקק ויתאספון ראשי עם (cf. v. 5) 'For there was the portion of the leader where the heads of the people assembled'. In the Hebrew manuscript upon which our text is based the letters ויתא, which were apparently skipped by the scribe and were added later above the word ספון, have been misplaced. The portion חלקה of the leader where Moses acted before his death and was buried there (הר עברים, ראש הפסגה, נבו and cf. Num. 21: 16–20 (cf. במחקק in v. 18)) belonged to Gad. Though this region was included in the inheritance of Reuben (Josh. 13: 20), it was gradually absorbed in the inheritance of Gad, cf. the Mesha inscription, l. 10.

[3] See Addenda.

[4] See J. J. Finkelstein, *JCS* 15 (1961), 101 ff.

the Babylonian practice.[1] David apparently proclaimed a *mīšarum* act just after securing his position on the throne. As he thereby fulfilled the king's economic responsibilities to the populace, he acquired the reputation of a righteous and just king (cf. *šar mīšarim* in Hammurabi's Code), and he thus established the pattern that the kings of Judah were expected to follow.

It appears that the Judean monarchs described by the Deuteronomists as doing right (הישר) in the eyes of Yahweh 'as their father David' were those who also 'did justice and righteousness', i.e. issued remissive proclamations (acts of *mīšarum*),[2] as did their ancestor David.[3] References to such remissive acts of the

[1] The expression ויהי דוד עשה משפט וצדקה לכל עמו reminds us of the date formula of Ammi-ṣaduqa (F. R. Kraus, *Edikt*, p. 229): ᵈutu-gim kalam-ma-ni-šè zi-dè-eš im-ta-è-a un šár-ra-ba si-bí-íb-sá-sá-a = 'he rose like the sun for his country in truth, *for all its people established justice*' (which refers to the *mīšarum* act). Cf. also CH va: 4 ff.: *mušēṣi nūrim ana māt Šumerim u Akkadim . . . kittam u mīšaram ina KA mātim aškun* = '(the sun of Babylon) who makes the light rise on the land of Sumer and Akkad . . . I established right and justice throughout the land.' *kīttum u mīšarum* seems to be equivalent to משפט וצדקה and has to be understood in the sense of social justice implemented by a royal decree.

The association of social justice with light and sunshine is also to be found in connection with the implementation of משפט וצדקה in David's court, see 2 Sam. 23: 3–4, Ps. 72: 1–5. In the Biblical passages the image of rain and dew is added to that of sunshine.

[2] Cf. D. J. Wiseman, 'The Laws of Hammurabi Again', *JSS* 7 (1962), 167–8.

[3] The kings who are referred to as having followed in the path of their ancestor David are: Solomon (1 Kgs. 3: 3), Asa (15: 11), Jehoshaphat (22: 43), Hezekiah (2 Kgs. 18: 3), and Josiah (22: 2). It could be conjectured that the righteousness of these reformer-kings lay in the fact that they all eliminated the high places and established the divine worship exclusively in the chosen place—a matter which is of central interest to the Deuteronomist and which serves as his criterion in the assessment of the history of the Israelite monarchy. However, this supposition does not stand up under closer scrutiny for two reasons:

(*a*) The law of cult centralization came into effect only after the temple was built in Solomon's days, which is why in David's time the people were still offering sacrifices at the high places (1 Kgs. 3: 2). The Davidic period could not consequently serve as a model period with respect to the observance of the law of centralized worship.

(*b*) Some kings, such as Asa and Jehoshaphat, who like David did what was right in the sight of the Lord, nevertheless did not abolish the cult of the high places. The righteousness of these kings moreover did not find expression in their steadfast loyalty to the God of Israel, because Solomon whose wives led him to worship other gods (1 Kgs. 11: 4) is none the less said to have 'loved the Lord' 'walking in the statutes of David his father' (3: 3). Yet Jehoash and Amaziah, on the other hand, who purified the cult of syncretistic elements, were not said to have attained the same degree of righteousness as had their ancestor David (2 Kgs. 12. 3; 14: 3). It seems therefore that David's righteousness is to be seen in his performance of social justice which is linked, according to the

reformer-kings Hezekiah and Josiah are met with in the prophecies of their respective contemporaries Isaiah and Jeremiah. Isaiah regarded Hezekiah as the true successor of David, because he believed that the newly crowned king[1] would establish his monarchy with 'justice and righteousness' (משפט וצדקה) (Isa. 9:6; cf. 16:5; compare Prov. 16: 12; 20: 28; 25: 5). In a similar prophecy in which Isaiah envisages the advent of an ideal ruler from the house of David—which may perhaps be an allusion to Hezekiah[2]—the prophet depicts the king as saving[3] the poor with *righteousness* (ושפט בצדק דלים) and deciding 'with equity (במישור) for the meek of the earth' (9:4). The reference to saving the poor with righteousness and the meek with equity would allude then to the king's amelioration of the destitute socio-economic lot of the populace by a royal proclamation which in Mesopotamia was termed a *mīšarum* (act) or an *andurārum*.[4]

Jeremiah similarly attests that Josiah also 'did justice and righteousness' (עשה משפט וצדקה) and that he judged the cause of the poor and needy (Jer. 22: 15–16);[5] and like Isaiah (11: 1–5)[6] he foresees the enthronement of a crown-prince[7] of the house of David (the younger Zedekiah?)[8] who upon assuming the throne will execute justice and righteousness (23: 5–6).[9]

Deuteronomist, to the Torah. The way of the crystallization of the law-codes in Mesopotamia (see above, p. 149 n. 1) allows us to suppose that some of the proclamations of these reformer-kings have been incorporated in the Holiness Code and in the deuteronomic Code.

[1] See A. Alt, 'Jesaja 8, 23–9, 6, Befreiungsnacht und Krönungstag', *KS* II, 206–25. Y. Kaufmann contends (*HIR* III, 166) that the passage alludes to the public proclamation of Hezekiah as crown-prince (cf. 'and the government shall be on his shoulder').

[2] Cf. J. Klausner, *The Messianic idea in Israel*, 1955, pp. 103 ff. (Hebrew).

[3] On the overlapping of שפט and הושיע see above, pp. 119–20.

[4] Cf. J. Lewy, 'The Biblical Institution of *derôr* in the light of Akkadian Documents', *EI* 5 (1958), 30 ff.

[5] The expression דן דין is to be taken in the same sense as its Babylonian cognate *dīnam dânu* which occurs in the Hammurabi Code (xxvi b: 27) and means the 'pronouncement of legal edicts on behalf of the indigent populace', see F. R. Kraus, 'Ein zentrales Problem etc.', *Genava*, pp. 284 ff.

[6] See A. Weiser, *Jeremia*, ATD, on Jer. 23: 5–6.

[7] The expression צמח צדק occurs in a Phoenician inscription and means 'crown-prince', see H. Donner and W. Röllig, *KAI* 43: 10–11. Cf. also the term בן צדק there, 16: 1. See above, p. 91 n. 2.

[8] See J. Klausner, *Messianic idea*, pp. 103 f., and A. Malamat, 'Jeremiah and the last two Kings of Judah', *PEQ* 83 (1951), 86.

[9] The expressions לעשות משפט וצדקה בארץ (cf. Jer. 9: 23), לשים משפט בארץ (Isa. 42:4), are the literal equivalents of the Babylonian expression *mīšaram*

None of the above precludes the possibility that Moses was also responsible for the covenant of vassalship between God and Israel. In the light of the ancient Near-Eastern covenant typology, however, one must distinguish between the covenant of law, which is basically social and internal or national, and the covenant of vassalship, which is political and external or international. If we adhere to this distinction in our analysis of the ancient covenantal traditions of Sinai and Shechem, we must conclude that the Sinai covenant belongs to the former, the Shechem covenant to the latter type.

It seems that these two different covenants stem from two different *Sitz im Leben*s. The God, whose real name Moses revealed to the children of Israel, was not a new deity, but the God of their fathers, who established a new relationship with them by the act of redemption (Exod. 3: 13 ff.). The purpose of the Sinai-covenant was therefore not the acceptance of a new sovereign, but the acknowledgement of a new system of laws, which the liberation from slavery and the achievement of political independence made indispensable. The primary aim of the Shechem covenant, on the other hand, was to reaffirm loyalty to God, which was so strongly at stake as a result of Canaanite–Israelite amalgamation, of which Shechem turned out to be the main centre. An additional aim of the Shechem covenant was the introduction to the autochthonic population of a new faith, which had to be affirmed through the solemn obligation made in the covenant ceremony.

The vassalship covenant, like the covenant of law, contained

ina mātim šakānum which occurs in both Old- and neo-Babylonian documents (cf. the recurring formula in the Ammi-ṣaduqa edict, Kraus, *Edikt: aššum šarrum mīšarum ana mātim iškunu* = 'because the king administered righteousness in the land'. See also in the neo-Babylonian inscriptions: *mīšari ina mātim aštakan* = 'I administered righteousness in the land' (S. Langdon, *Die Neubabylonischen Königsinschriften*, 1912, p. 216, ii: 2)

The representation of the king as proclaiming a *mīšarum* act at the commencement of his reign was translated to the Deity in eschatological psalmodic literature. Upon ascending the throne a mortal king 'judges with equity (במישור) the meek of the earth' (Isa. 11: 4), i.e. he issues a *mīšarum* act on behalf of the indigent populace, whereas the Lord, king of the earth 'judges the peoples (of the earth) with equity (במישור)' (Ps. 67: 5), for which reason the nations rejoice and sing in exultation. It is not accidental, then, that we encounter the idea that God judges the nations with equity (במישרים) particularly in the enthronement psalms (96: 10; 98: 9; 99: 4). Like the mortal king, the Divine King also proclaims *mīšarum* acts when he assumes the throne: 'Say among the nations. "The Lord reigns!" . . . he will judge the peoples with *mêšarim*' (Ps. 96: 10). For the conceptual parallelism *to establish mêšarim*//*to execute justice and righteousness* and its association with the newly enthroned king compare Ps. 99: 1 ff.

injunctions but these were, like the treaty-stipulations, injunctions concerning loyalty, i.e. warnings against serving foreign gods. When law and covenant became indistinct, however, the stipulations concerning loyalty and the other commandments were so intermingled that it has become impossible for us to distinguish them. Thus, for example, in the Decalogue the first three commandments are of the vassal type while the remainder are of the legislative type. All of them together were nevertheless seen as a unity.

We see, then, that this mixture of covenant and law is pre-deuteronomic and that the author of Deuteronomy adopted this mixed pattern from the sources lying before him. Like his predecessors, however, he continued to develop the covenant tradition. He enriched the covenant theme by introducing all the elements of the vassal treaty, while he blurred the covenantal pattern by putting it into a homiletic setting. Unlike the treaty, Deuteronomy is not a legal document but an oration. The structure of the speech follows a legal pattern, but its style is that of a sermon. The author of Deuteronomy had in mind the covenantal pattern in the form in which it had been lying before him in the tradition and in the manner in which it was generally formulated in his time. Nevertheless he presented the materials in a style that is free from rigid adherence to formality.

III

THE SCRIBAL ROLE IN THE CRYSTALLIZATION OF DEUTERONOMY

1. THE SCRIBES AND THE 'BOOK OF THE TORAH'

IN Jer. 8: 8 the prophet is quoted as saying to the wise men: 'How can you say we are wise, and the *Torah of Yahweh* is with us? But, behold, the false pen of the scribes had made it into a lie.' The phrase 'the Torah of Yahweh' in the mouth of the wise men has long troubled Biblical scholars;[1] since Marti's time,[2] however, it has generally been taken to mean the book of Deuteronomy, a view that appears to have some justification. As Skinner observed, 'in Jeremiah's time Deuteronomy was the only written law which we can readily imagine to have been the object of such religious confidence as is described in the first half of the verse' (of Jer. 8: 8).[3] However, even if the equation of תורת יהוה with the book of Deuteronomy were to be rejected, it is none the less clear that in Jeremiah's time there existed a circle of חכמים סופרים[4] engaged in the composition of Torah literature, and as this period coincided with the discovery and diffusion of the book of Deuteronomy we may legitimately suppose that the Torah written by the pen of these scribes had much to do with Deuteronomy. We have no clear evidence about the identity of these scribes, but it seems quite reasonable to suppose that the scribe (= Shaphan), who was present at the discovery of the book and read it (twice) on the same occasion, may have been the one who was entrusted, along with his scribal family, to carry out the literary elaboration of Deuteronomy. For, although the exact extent of the book found in the

[1] For an exhaustive survey of the problem see J. P. Hyatt, 'Torah in the Book of Jeremiah', *JBL* 60 (1941), 382 ff.

[2] See K. Morfi, *Der Prophet Jeremiah von Anatot*, 1889, pp. 18 ff.

[3] J. Skinner, *Prophecy and Religion*, 1922, p. 103.

[4] The wise men and scribes referred to in this verse are identical (see Kaufmann, *HIR* IV, 278; P. A. H. de Boer, 'The Counsellor', Suppl. *VT* 3 (1955), 61 *et al.*, but against J. Lindblom, 'Wisdom in the O.T. Prophets', Suppl. *VT* 3, 196). It is quite likely, as de Boer contends, that the חכמים סופרים generally held ministerial offices (ibid.; cf. Jer. 36: 10 ff.)

Temple cannot be determined, it is nevertheless clear that it was not found in its present form, and no scholar would deny that it subsequently went through a process of literary development. Not only the double prologues and epilogues but also the parallel sections found in the code[1] and in the framework of the code[2] indicate constant rewriting and reworking of the book.[3] That Shaphan's scribal family was involved in the deuteronomic history writing has been surmised by Jepsen.[4] It is also probable that the deuteronomic sermons in the book of Jeremiah designated by Mowinckel as source C were composed by this circle,[5] with which Jeremiah was intimately acquainted and connected. Ahikam the son of Shaphan the scribe, who saved Jeremiah from near-death (Jer. 26: 24), and his son Gedaliah symbolized in Jeremiah's eyes the hope and future of the remaining inhabitants of Judah. It was the office of Gemariah, the son of Shaphan, which was selected for the reading of the Jeremian prophecies (36: 10), and it was Gemariah who interceded with the king not to burn the scroll (v. 25). Had it not been for the quick-witted action of Micaiah, the son of Gemariah, who informed the royal ministers of the nature of the prophetic scroll (vv. 11–13), Jeremiah and Baruch would not have escaped royal arrest (vv. 19 and 26). These God-fearing scribes and ministers seated in the chamber of Gemariah son of Shaphan heard the prophetic words of God with alarm and trepidation (v. 16), as did the ministers of the Josianic delegation hearing the prophetic pronouncement of Huldah the prophetess (2 Kgs. 22: 14). Jehoiakim and his confidants,[6] in contrast, were neither

[1] Cf., e.g., the repetitions in ch. 12: the permission of non-sacrificial use of meat is mentioned twice (15–16, 20–5); the commandment to bring all the offerings to the chosen place is stated thrice (6–7, 11–12, 18). Note also that vv. 2–12 are styled primarily in the plural while vv. 13–28 are worded for the most part in the singular. See G. A. Smith, *Deuteronomy*, CB, pp. 159–60.

[2] Cf. 6: 7–9 (sing.) with 11: 18–20 (plur.).

[3] The editing of the book might have taken place during the time of Josiah and must not be seen as a product of generations.

[4] A. Jepsen, *Die Quellen des Königsbuches*², 1956, pp. 94–5.

[5] S. Mowinckel alluded to the scribes as being the circle where the deuteronomic school arose and in which law and Torah tradition were composed, in his study *Prophecy and Tradition* (p. 63): 'Baruch was a scribe and belonged to the learned; that the Deuteronomists are also associated with the learned circles of scribes is obvious; already Jeremiah offers us a piece of evidence that the law, the Torah Tradition and the literary pursuit of it, belongs to the scribes (Jer. 8: 8).'

[6] S. Yeivin, 'Families and Parties in the Kingdom of Judah', *Tarbiz* 12 (1941/2), 241–67) contends that Judean leadership during this period was divided into pro-Babylonian and pro-Egyptian factions. The scribes of the Shaphan

alarmed nor rent their clothes upon hearing the message (Jer. 36: 24) as Josiah did in similar circumstances (2 Kgs. 22: 11).[1] The fact, then, that the deuteronomic school particularly chose to redact the book of Jeremiah alone of the prophetic works strengthens our supposition that the scribes of the Shaphan family were the leading exponents of this literary school.[2]

The book composed by this scribal circle must have undoubtedly won Jeremiah's personal support. Jeremiah fully identified himself with the religious ideology of the book of Deuteronomy[3] and also appears to have supported the Josianic reforms (Jer. 11: 1–8).[4] There is no evidence to support the view that Jeremiah regarded Deuteronomy as an invention and forgery, as many scholars contend.[5] The word שקר in Jer. 8: 8 does not mean 'forgery', but 'in vain', 'to no purpose' as in 1 Sam. 25: 21: 'Surely in vain (לשקר) have I guarded . . .'.[6] The prophet in our verse is not denouncing the book of Deuteronomy but condemning the חכמים סופרים for not observing the teaching that they themselves had committed to writing: the pen of the scribes has made (i.e. composed)[7] to no purpose, the scribes have written in vain.[8]

family in his opinion belonged to the pro-Babylonian party, whereas the high-ranking military officers of the Achbor family were pro-Egyptian. If his contention is correct then the ministers here described as having the confidence of the king were probably the military officers belonging to the pro-Egyptian party.

[1] See E. Nielsen, *Oral Tradition*, 1954, p. 69.

[2] This assumption of course raises the question why the deuteronomic historian did not mention Jeremiah in his work. We may, however, account for the fact by assuming that at the time of the deuteronomic redaction of the book of Kings (*c.* 600–560), Jeremiah had not as yet won popular national recognition and was not therefore considered a 'historical' prophet in contrast with 2 Chr. 36: 12.

[3] See C. H. Cazelles, 'Jérémie et le Deutéronome', *Recherches de Science Religieuse* 38 (1951), 28 ff.; A. Gelin, *Jérémie*, 1951, pp. 47 f.

[4] Cf. P. Volz, *Jeremia*², KAT, 1928, pp. xxviii ff., and W. Rudolph, *Jeremiah*², HAT, 1958, pp. 73 f.; G. W. Anderson, *A Critical Introduction to the Old Testament*², p. 128.

[5] For a discussion of the various views, see H. H. Rowley, 'Jeremiah and Deuteronomy', in *Studies in O.T. Prophecy*, 1950, pp. 157–74.

[6] Cf. Kimḥi, ad loc.

[7] Cf. the use of the verb in this sense in Eccles. 12: 12; Ps. 45: 2.

[8] The LXX took the word in the same sense and thus translated by εἰς μάτην, the only instance in which the word in the book of Jeremiah is thus rendered; in all other instances the LXX translated by either ἄδικος or ψεῦδος. Hyatt nevertheless here takes the word לשקר to mean 'falsely' rather than 'in vain', pointing out that 'in the great majority of cases (the word) connotes falsehood or lying rather than vanity' (*JBL* 60 (1941), 382 n. 4). This may be true of the word שקר but not of the term לשקר, cf. e.g., Jer. 3: 23 where it also connotes 'vanity'.

Neither is there any reason to assume that Jeremiah's support of the Josianic reforms and covenant was only temporary and that he subsequently dissociated himself from them.[1] He appears on the contrary to have remained an ardent supporter of them all his life, though he may have lamented the fact that the reforms were not received wholeheartedly: 'Yet for all this her false sister Judah did not return to me *with her whole heart*, but in pretence' (Jer. 3: 10), that is to say, Judah's repentance was a sham.[2]

Though we first hear of the literary activity of the scribes—wise men—in the reign of Josiah, it or its predecessors had doubtlessly already begun almost a century before, in the Hezekian period. Prov. 25: 1 states that the 'men' of Hezekiah had 'transferred'[3] Solomonic proverbs, and this appears to have been done, as Junker has observed, within the framework of a more extensive literary programme of compiling and resuscitating ancient traditions.[4] This was indeed no local phenomenon. During the Hezekian–Josianic period the entire ancient Near East seems to have experienced a general literary renaissance.[5] The prophecies of Isaiah, furthermore, testify to the emergence of the wise men as a distinct Israelite class during this period[6] (5: 21; 29: 14),[7] which reached the zenith of its power during Jeremian times.

It has already been recognized that the wise men do not appear as a class or profession before the Hezekian period, and

See Kaufmann, *HIR* III, 463 n. 4, and G. von Rad, *Das Gottesvolk in Deuteronomium*, 1929, p. 94 n. 4.

1 So Rudolph, *Jer.*, HAT., see Rowley, 'Jer. and Deut.', pp. 171 f.

2 And not that the reform itself was a false one, as Welch contends in his study, *Jeremiah, His Time and His Work*, 1928, ch. v. It is also possible that Jeremiah who stresses the covenant written on 'the heart' (31: 32) defies the reliance upon the written word in the book, though he accepts its contents.

3 Like Akkadian *šūtuqu* (cf. *CAD*, vol. 4 (E), 390 f.) so Hebrew העתיק has the meaning of 'to make pass on' or 'to transfer'. Prof. H. L. Ginsberg suggested (in a letter to me) that this has to do with the transferring of literary works from northern Israel to Judah after the fall of Samaria, cf. below, p. 366.

4 H. Junker, 'Die Enstehungszeit des Ps. 78 und das Deuteronomium', *Biblica* 34 (1953), 496 n. 1.

5 See W. F. Albright, *From the Stone Age to Christianity*, pp. 314–19.

6 See R. B. Y. Scott, 'Solomon and the Beginnings of Wisdom', *Suppl. VT* 3 (1955), 277. J. Fichtner ('Jesaya unter den Weisen', *ThLZ* 74 (1949), cols. 75–9) suggests that Isaiah himself might have belonged to the class of the 'wise men'.

7 Verses 14 ff. in Isa. 29 occur in the context of Isaiah's denunciation of various leading Israelite circles (cf. Fichtner, op. cit.). In 29: 9 ff. Isaiah assails leading spiritual circles (the prophets, the wise men) as Jeremiah did in his own time (Jer. 18: 18; 8: 8–10; cf. 6: 9–15).

consequently Hezekiah may be considered the historically true patron of *wisdom* literature. Since the literary programme undertaken during the Hezekian–Josianic period also embraced ancient religious traditions, we must suppose that his patronage included religious as well as wisdom literature.[1]

The חכמים סופרים of the Hezekian period and afterwards differed essentially from their predecessors in that they saw the didactic importance of setting compositions down in writing. Whereas the term סופר originally designated an administrative or clerical function (2 Sam. 8: 17; Ps. 45: 2, etc.), now its didactic connotation[2] became predominant. Israelite didactic activity was not, however, confined only to wisdom composition, as was the case among the neighbouring peoples, but also invaded the sphere of religious literary composition; and, as may be deduced from Jer. 8: 8, the wise men during this period were also engaged in the composition of the 'Torah of Yahweh'. The Israelite סופר was consequently equated with four types of functions: clerical, political, didactic, and religious. The first three of these were already performed by Mesopotamian and Egyptian scribes, but the fourth, in the Hezekian–Josianic period and afterwards, was peculiar to the Judean scribe.

Ezra's function as a 'Schriftgelehrter' therefore is not a new phenomenon in Israel's life,[3] but rather an intensification of the process already known from the time of Hezekiah–Josiah. It was the sanctification and publication of the 'book of the Torah' in the time of Josiah which gave rise to scribes with the ability and competence to handle the scripture. In a similar manner the canonization of the whole Pentateuch sponsored by Ezra the *scribe*[4] brought with it a new impetus to scribal activity which marked the beginning of a new period, the period of the law scribes. In the period of Ezra the Torah underwent an even greater transition, being transferred from the jurisdiction of the priest to the jurisdiction of the scribe and the sage. The men who possessed the authority to impart Torah were no longer priests but the חכמים and סופרים, as they are called in the Rabbinic literature. Although the

[1] Cf. B. Gemser, *Sprüche Salomos*, HAT², p. 93.

[2] See Y. Kaufmann, *HIR* IV, 275–8.

[3] As H. H. Schaeder, *Esra der Schreiber*, 1930, stated.

[4] In spite of being a priest he is named as a scribe and he performs his religious functions as such.

real turning-point in Torah teaching took place only in the period of the second Temple, it had its roots in the time of Josiah when the process of canonization of scripture started. The difference between the time of Josiah and that of Ezra is merely that in the former period the priest still kept authority in the field of ritual-judicial (oral) instruction (cf. Deut. 17: 9; 19: 17; 24: 8; Hag. 2: 11, etc.)—though in national, social, and military matters the written scribal Torah already prevailed—while in the latter period the priest had been almost stripped of his instructional authority so that his function was limited to the performance of rites in the Temple.

There is a further analogy between Josiah and Ezra–Nehemiah. Josiah enforced the law of the 'book of the Torah' both by his royal authority and by means of a pledge taken by the people (2 Kgs. 23: 1–3). Likewise in the period of Ezra and Nehemiah the law of Moses was enforced both on behalf of the Persian crown (Ezra 7) and on the authority of a pledge, to which the people had agreed in a formal ceremony (אמנה, Neh. 10).[1]

Royal intervention in matters of religion, and especially in its public aspects, appears to antedate the Josianic period. Hezekiah, for example, abolished the provincial holy places (2 Kgs. 18: 4 and 22), and according to the book of Chronicles, he also organized the celebration of Pesach in Jerusalem (2 Chr. 30). Even earlier King Asa and King Jehoshaphat had reorganized Judaic worship, although they did not seek to centralize the cult. If we accept the authenticity of 2 Chr. 17: 7–9, we find evidence for the involvement of royal officials[2] in 'Torah' instruction before the time of Josiah. This procedure may be analogous to the Assyrian custom of the king's officers' instructing people in matters of worship and loyalty to the king.[3]

[1] It is not altogether certain whether or not Ezra took part in this ceremony. What is very significant for our purpose is the fact that it was deemed necessary to draw up a written compact although the execution of the law could well have been enforced by the old covenant.

[2] Cf. Lam. 2: 9: מלכה ושריה בגוים אין תורה 'Her King and her officers are among the nations, there is no more Torah.'

[3] Cf. especially in the Sargon inscriptions the phrase: *ana šûḫuz ṣibitti palāḫ ili u šarri aklī šāpirī uma"iršunūti* = 'to teach them (the natives in Assyria) the teaching of fearing God and king, I sent officers and overseers'. (For *ṣibittu* cf. S. Paul, *JBL* 88 (1969), 73–4.) The phrase *šûḫuz ṣibitti* may be analogous to הורה תורה. *aḫāzu*, *ṣabātu* in Akkadian, and אחז, לקח in Hebrew cover the same range of meanings (compare: *iḫzu* = לקח, cf. the phrases: לקחת מוסר

In the light of these precedents it is plausible to assume that the kernel of the deuteronomic code stems from the earlier reforms, which may have been consolidated in the form of books like the book of Jehoshaphat.[1] But the most radical reform was that accomplished by Josiah, and it was this reform that left the clearest imprint on the book connected with it. Though the main kernel of the book presumably antedated Josiah and may have been crystallized in the time of Hezekiah, its literary form, its canonization in a public ceremony, and its consequent acceptance as the nation's written constitution were undoubtedly the outcome of the Josianic reform.

While it was the technique of Jehoshaphat and the Assyrian kings to publish and to teach the new law through royal officers, who were sent out to every town and hamlet, Josiah brought representatives of the populace to the capital, where they pledged observance of the law on behalf of all the people. It was in this way that the Torah became a written national constitution, obliging each citizen to comply with its stipulations.[2]

The use of writing for didactic purposes is first met with in the book of Deuteronomy. The early sources, of course, also mention writing, but only in an archival role[3] (commemoration of a victory, Exod. 17: 14), a covenant document (24: 4 and 7), covenant tables (34: 27–8), or statute documents to be deposited in the sanctuary (Josh. 24: 25–6; 1 Sam. 10: 25)), whereas in the Hezekian period and afterwards it served to promote popular education. The words of God are inscribed on the doorposts of houses (Deut. 4: 7–8; 11: 18–21), a copy of the Law is written for the king (17: 18–19), the Law is inscribed on stones (27: 2–3), Moses writes a law book for the people (31: 9), etc.

Of greater interest to our discussion is the deuteronomic prescription commanding the Israelites to inscribe the entire content of the Torah book on a group of stones shortly after they cross the Jordan (Deut. 27: 1–8). There is doubtless some connection

(Jer. *passim*), אחזי חרב מלמדי מלחמה (Cant. 3: 8); תֹּפֵשׂ = *ṣābitu*, in the sense of being skilled, see Gen. 4: 21; Amos 2: 15; and Jer. 2: 8: תֹּפשי התורה).

[1] So the organization of the high court by Jehoshaphat (2 Chr. 19) may be reflected in Deut. 17: 8–12.

[2] The diffusion of law by officials seems also to be indicated in Ezra 7: 25, see H. L. Ginsberg, *EI* 9, *Festschrift W. F. Albright*, p. 30 n. 14.

[3] See Y. Kaufmann, *HIR* I, 110–11.

between this passage and the narrative in Josh. 4 concerning the erection of stones in Gilgal.[1] However, while the stones erected by Joshua and the people were designed according to the latter tradition 'as a memorial to the children of Israel' (Josh. 4: 7), the book of Deuteronomy orders them to be erected so that the law may be inscribed upon them. The entire ceremony appears, moreover, to have been transformed by the author to bring it into harmony with the literary temper of his age. As one who generally based his material on ancient traditions, he inserted verbatim part of an Elohist Shechem tradition[2] describing an important part of the covenant ceremony (the erection of an altar and the offering of sacrifices, vv. 5–7),[3] but he set it within a framework which converted the ritual ceremony into an educational one. In the Elohist's description of the Sinai covenant scene (Exod. 24: 3–8) mention is made of twelve stone pillars erected beside the altar similar to those erected at Gilgal.[4] Josh. 24, which also appears to be an Elohist document, likewise describes a Shechem covenant scene in which a large stone is erected (v. 26) to serve as an eternal testimony of the important event. It may be assumed then that in the Mt. Gerizim ceremony, as in the Sinai ceremony,[5] the stones served an important sacral function, but that the author of Deuteronomy, who expressly prohibits the erection of pillars,[6] transformed the stones into a law document which was to serve the Israelites as a guide upon their entry into the promised land. By assigning a documentary role to the stones the author has in effect divested the ceremony of its original character by obscuring its essential details. In the Sinai and Shechem ceremonies the stones and the document play two distinct roles: the stones stand as mute

[1] See C. Steuernagel. *Das Deuteronomium*², HKAT, 1923, p. 347; G. Hölscher, 'Komposition und Ursprung der Deuteronomiums', *ZAW* 40 (1923), 218, and E. Nielsen, *Shechem*², 1959, pp. 295 ff.

[2] For extensive discussion see E. Nielsen, ibid.

[3] Cf. v. 5 with Exod. 20: 25 (= E).

[4] See K. Galling, *Biblisches Reallexicon*, 1937, col. 368. This tradition was apparently exclusively claimed by the rival sanctuaries of Shechem and Gilgal, see H. Gressman's review (*ZAW* 44 (1926) 309 f.) of M. Y. Ben-Gurion's study, *Sinai and Gerizim*. See also E. Nielsen, *Shechem*, ibid.

[5] Cf. E. Nielsen's comment, *Shechem*, p. 351: 'Ex. 24. 3 ff. may reflect that part of the Shechemite ritual which was omitted by the Deuteronomists when they adopted the Shechemite traditions.'

[6] See Deut. 16: 22. The Septuagint and Samaritan versions, however, altered the reading 'pillars' in Exod. 24 to 'stones' to harmonize it with the deuteronomic law.

testimony to the event, whereas the ספר[1] contained the stipulations of the covenant. In the book of Deuteronomy, however, the two elements have been fused into a lapidary document devoid of all ritual significance. The altar, which is the last surviving vestige of the ritual ceremony, has been long felt to be an anomalous feature of the text,[2] and the passage in which it is referred to does in effect disrupt the continuity between verses 4 and 8. The author, who apparently wished to preserve the ancient Shechem tradition at all costs,[3] inserted the passage in question in complete disregard of the context. The deuteronomic editor of Josh. 8, however, treated the whole section as an organic literary unit[4] and therefore found it necessary to remove the friction between the two traditions by describing the stones upon which the law was inscribed as those from which the altar was constructed.

The scribes who committed the book of the Torah to writing presented its prescriptions in a new form and brought them into harmony with the temper of the age. Their hand is particularly evident in the laws relating to the centralization of the cult, the organization of executive and judicial institutions, and military affairs. The scribes gave full expression to the religious national aims of Hezekiah and Josiah in the laws dealing with cult centralization and the extirpation of the foreign cult.[5] The severity with which Josiah executed his programme is echoed in the laws of Deut. 13, which, as we have seen,[6] reflect a typical revolutionary atmosphere. The stringent laws of the ban in Deuteronomy also reflect the same rigorous national course that characterized Josiah's own programme. The ban was, to be sure, also practised by

[1] ספר like Akkadian *ṭuppu* denotes a tablet or memorial document (Ex. 17: 14; Isa. 30: 8; Job 19: 23), a letter (1 Kgs. 21: 8–9 *et al.*) or any other written deed or document (Deut. 24: 1, 3; Jer. 32: 11).

[2] For a discussion of the subject see E. Nielsen, *Shechem*, pp. 52 ff.

[3] The reason for the insertion of the passage stems less from a desire to resuscitate 'amphictyonic' traditions than from a desire for a *rapprochement* with the northern tribes and their traditions (which accords with the Hezekian and Josianic policies).

[4] Cf. Nielsen's comment, *Shechem*, p. 78: 'That this copy is written on the stones of the altar is a conception which certainly differs from Dt. 27. Josh. 8 is in this respect nothing but a confusion of elements which in Dt. 27 are still separated.'

[5] The formation of these laws was apparently begun in the Hezekian period but crystallized finally only in Josianic times.

[6] Above, p. 100.

Israelites in earlier times (Josh. 6–7; 1 Sam. 15; Num. 21: 1–3), but in the earlier documents and so among the surrounding peoples[1] it figures only as an *ad hoc* measure and is characterized by a vow taken before battle was engaged (Num. 21: 1–3), whereas in Deuteronomy it takes the form of an automatic decree applying to the inhabitants of a whole land, whether engaged in war or not. This formulation could only have been created at the writing-desk and does not reflect any real circumstances.[2] That this law was not implemented may be seen from 1 Kgs. 9: 21, where we read that Solomon enslaved the Amorites whom the Israelites could not exterminate. It was only the Deuteronomist in the book of Joshua who tried to present the picture of a total extermination of the Canaanites (Josh. 10: 40; 11: 12–15)[3]—in accordance with Deut. 20—whereas, according to the older sources, it is quite clear that even after Joshua's death the Canaanites were still dwelling among the tribes of Israel (Judg. 1: 27 ff.).

The inclusion of the laws that deal with warfare and the military (chs. 20–1) also reflects Judah's political resurgence during the Josianic period. Though their spirit may be that of the wars of the

[1] Cf. the Mesha inscription and see A. Malamat, 'The Ban in Mari and in the Bible', 'Biblical Essays', *Proceedings of the 9th Meeting of Die Ou-Testam. Werkgemeenskap in Suid-Afrika* (1966), pp. 40–9. Cf. also C. H. W. Brekelmans, *De Ḥerem in het Oude Testament*, 1959.

[2] It rather reflects the ideal disposition of the Josianic regime, see S. R. Driver, *Deuteronomy*, ICC, p. xxxii. The very command 'not to let a soul remain alive' may be an ancient one and may have accompanied the warriors in old times. However, Deuteronomy and the Deuteronomist conceived it as a general principle applying to the extermination of the whole population of Canaan, no matter whether engaged in war or not. The justification of the covenant with the Gibeonites (Josh. 9) did not come out of the necessity to reconcile the making of the treaty with the already existent law of the total ban in Deut. 20, as argued by J. Liver (*JSS* 8 (1963), 242). The story comes rather to explain the existence of a foreign ethnic group within a territorial enclave in the midst of Benjamin, the tribe which seems to have been the *Sitz im Leben* of the traditions in Josh. 2–9. The Israelites were hesitant to conclude the treaty, not for fear of violating the law of the ban, but for fear of the danger in the commitment to preserve a foreign element in their very midst. Had an excuse been necessary for not observing the law of the total ban in Deut. 20, we would rather expect it in connection with the remainder of the Canaanites all over the land (1 Kgs. 9: 21) and not precisely with this group of Hivites.

[3] The descriptions of the ban in Josh. 10: 28–43; 11: 12–20 are based on the law of the ban in Deut. 20: 10 ff. and are formulated in distinct deuteronomic phraseology (cf. Deut. 2: 34–5; 3: 6–7; 7: 2; 13: 16–17; 20: 14–17). The reference to the removal of the hanging corpses of the Canaanite kings in Josh. 10: 27 is a deuteronomic accretion in the spirit of the law in Deut. 21: 23 (cf. Josh. 8: 29). For the whole problem see my article in *VT* 17 (1967), 93–113.

premonarchic period, as most scholars suppose[1] it was the circle of the חכמים סופרים, which formulated them and incorporated them in the 'book of the Torah'. These scribes have in fact incorporated the traditions of all the national-spiritual currents then represented in the Israelite regime. The book of Deuteronomy appears indeed to have the character of an ideal national constitution[2] representing all the official institutions of the state: the monarchy, the judiciary, the priesthood, and prophecy.[3] These institutions are successively referred to in Deut. 16: 18–18: 22 and are depicted not only in realistic terms but also in terms of the ideal at which this neutral circle of scribes was clearly aiming—a national regime which incorporated all the normative, spiritual, and religious circles of the period.

The scribal attitude toward the monarchy is a positive one: the deuteronomic law of the king commands the monarch to observe the law 'so that he may continue long in his kingdom, he and his children in Israel' (17: 20). If there is any negative tendency in the law of the king in Deuteronomy it is not directed towards the monarchy as such but against a specific king. Solomon's sins are echoed in this law. It was he who multiplied silver and gold (1 Kgs. 10: 21 and 27), increased the number of his wives (1 Kgs. 11: 1–3), and sustained horse trade with Egypt on a very broad basis (1 Kgs. 10: 26 and 28–9).[4] Now the only Judaic king who reveals a clear anti-Solomonic attitude is Josiah, who dared for the first time to destroy the altars built by Solomon for his foreign wives (2 Kgs. 23: 13). These altars had been in existence for about 300 years, and no king-reformer had ever touched them. Even Hezekiah did not dare to do so although he dared to destroy the so greatly admired Mosaic *Neḫuštan* (2 Kgs. 18: 5). It seems correct therefore to surmise that the negative attitude towards Solomon which

[1] See G. von Rad, *Der heilige Krieg im Alten Israel*, 1951, pp. 68–78.

[2] Cf. K. Galling: 'Josia beschliesst die Erhebung des "Buches der Lehre" zum Bundesbuch d.h. zum Statsgesetz', *Die israelitische Staatsverfassung in ihrer vorderorientalischen Umwelt*, 1929, pp. 57–8.

[3] That is to say, official cultic prophecy and not classical prophecy, cf. 2 Kgs. 23: 2: הכהנים והנביאים.

[4] The Deuteronomist arranges the historical traditions about Solomon in such a way as to emphasize the king's violation of the law of Deut. 17. To the Solomonic traditions, which, for the most part, depict Solomon's successes, the editor appends the details about the king's treasures, horses, and wives (1 Kgs. 10: 26–11: 8), which according to the Deuteronomist brought about the decline of Solomon's kingdom (11: 9 ff.).

lies behind the law of the king in Deut. 17 stems from the Josianic court. The commandments in this law may be ancient,[1] but the selection of the restrictions and the present arrangement point to an anti-Solomonic tendency.

The positive attitude towards monarchy is also shared by the Deuteronomist. The anti-monarchic sentiments expressed in the traditions in 1 Sam. 8–12 are by no means deuteronomic,[2] and the deuteronomic passages in the books of Kings, on the other hand, exhibit no anti-monarchic tendencies. On the contrary, the fact that the Davidic dynasty and its capital, Jerusalem, lay at the core of deuteronomic ideology shows the Deuteronomist's sympathy and esteem for the monarchy, provided that the kings remained faithful to Yahweh's laws. The scribes, moreover, regarded the institution of monarchy as essential for the proper functioning of society. The premonarchic period, the period of the judges, is depicted by the Deuteronomist as one of religious and political anarchy: the Israelites did not obey the judges, 'raised up' by God to save them when he 'was moved to pity (כי ינחם)[3] by their groaning', but continued in their perverse and corrupt ways (Judg. 2: 17–19). Kaufmann[4] is correct in asserting that the author of the introduction to Judg. 2 intentionally delineated the period in sombre colours so as to bring the positive aspects of the monarchy into greater relief. This sombre depiction of the period also finds expression in the formula 'In those days there was no king in Israel; every man did what was right in his own eyes' that recurs in the literary unit comprising chs. 17–21 of the book (17: 6; 18: 1; 19: 1; 21: 25).

M. Buber rightly sees in this refrain the hand of court scribes,[5]

[1] They may have been taken from an old collection of commands which contained many more instructions (compare 1 Sam. 10: 25), cf. above, p. 82 n. 3.

[2] See A. Weiser, 'I Samuel 7–12', *FRLANT* 81 (1962).

[3] Cf. Judg. 21: 6 and 15; Jer. 20: 16; Ezek. 24: 14; Ps. 90: 13; see also Y. Kaufmann, *The Book of Judges*, 1962, p. 18 (Hebrew).

[4] op. cit., p. 52.

[5] See his *Königtum Gottes*[3], 1956, p. 41. M. Noth postulates that 'the formulae in Jg. 19: 1a and 21: 25 have been taken over editorially from Jg. 17–18 where they once intrinsically belonged' ('The Background of Judges 17–18', In *Israel's Prophetic Heritage*, 1962, p. 79). This, however, is improbable. The formula 'In those days there was no king in Israel', etc. serves the same uniform purpose throughout chs. 17–21 to discredit the period of the judges and demonstrate Israel's essential need for a monarchy, the establishment of which is recounted in the following chapters (i.e. in the book of Samuel; the account of the period of the judges continues until 1 Sam. 12, cf. above, p. 13). Noth's contention that the same formula originally served a different purpose in chs. 17–18 is therefore implausible.

that is, as we have argued, deuteronomic scribes active during the monarchic period. For the view expressed in it is also given covert voice in the law of cult centralization in Deuteronomy: 'You shall not do according to all that we are doing here this day, *every man doing whatever is right in his own eyes*, for you have not as yet come to the rest and to the inheritance' (Deut. 12: 8–9). The rest and peaceful inheritance referred to were secured only after the establishment of the monarchy (2 Sam. 7: 1 and 11; 1 Kgs. 5: 18; 8: 56),[1] and only then did the law of cult centralization come into effect (1 Kgs. 3: 2).[2] The author of Deuteronomy thus equates the period wherein 'each man did whatever was right in his own eyes' with the pre-monarchaic period, as does the recurrent theme in Judg. 17–21.[3] There may indeed be some significance in the fact that the complete formula of the refrain ('In those days there was no king in Israel; every man did what was right in his own eyes') occurs only in those narratives that concern private or provincial sanctuaries (Micah's sanctuary in 17: 1–5; the sanctuaries of Beth-el, Mizpah, and Shiloh in 21: 1–24), while the abbreviated version referring only to the absence of the monarchy ('In those days there was no king in Israel') occurs only in contexts describing the prevailing socio-moral disorder in Israel (18: 1 ff.; 19: 1 ff.).

Moreover, it seems that the Deuteronomist could not conceive of the implementation of the moral law contained in the 'book of the Torah' in the absence of the monarchy or of a quasi-regal figure like Joshua (Josh. 1: 7–8; 8: 30–5; 22: 5; 23: 6). To his mind the Torah was the ideal legal constitution for a monarchic

[1] The Israelites, to be sure, also enjoyed a respite from their enemies in Joshua's time (Josh. 21: 42; 23: 1 = Dtr) but this was only temporary and was immediately followed by a period of oppression and affliction (cf. Judg. 2: 14 and the similar phraseology in the opposite sense in Josh. 21: 42) that continued until the Davidic–Solomonic period (cf. 2 Sam. 7: 10–11).

[2] Kings Asa and Jehoshaphat, who according to the Chronicler also centralized the cult, were also given 'rest round about' by the Lord (2 Chr. 15: 15; 20: 30) as the Lord gave 'rest round about' to David and Solomon according to the author of the books of Kings.

[3] The deuteronomic scribes may have disposed these chapters at the end of the book of Judges to demonstrate that the monarchy was the inevitable consequence of the anarchy that prevailed during that period. There is no warrant for regarding them as a post-deuteronomic accretion. The fact that they lack the customary pragmatic framework of the editor ('And they did evil in the sight of the Lord', etc.) and contain only brief editorial refrains may be due to the reason that the narratives treat of the misdeeds of a single family and tribe, not those perpetrated by the entire nation, and hence are not suited to a comprehensive national framework of the type encountered in chs. 2–16.

regime (1 Kgs. 2: 3), and David's greatness lay precisely in the fact that he was the first Israelite ruler after Joshua to implement its laws during his reign (1 Kgs. 3: 14; 9: 4; 11: 33 and 38; 14: 8, etc.). The fact that the Deuteronomist could not conceive of the implementation of the law in a non-monarchic regime can explain the difference between his conception of the sin of the period of the judges and that of the monarchic period. It may be recalled that the deuteronomic editor of the books of Kings attributes the sins of the period to the kings: it is the actions of the monarchs which determine the fate of the people for good or ill; the righteous kings cast glory on their reigns, while the wicked kings create a shadow over their period and cause their people to sin (1 Kgs. 14: 16; 15: 34; 2 Kgs. 21: 11 and 16, etc.). This is not the case, however, in the deuteronomic conception of the period of the judges: during this epoch it is the people's action which determines their fate and the fate of their judges. This striking contrast in the conception of the two epochs has led a number of scholars to doubt the homogeneity of the deuteronomic composition.[1] But we can see that it stems from the Deuteronomist's conception of the 'book of the Torah'. To his mind 'the written Torah of Moses' (= the book of Deuteronomy) was designed for kings and *quasi*-regal leaders, who alone were capable of enforcing its sway over the people. It is indeed only when referring to kings and leaders of a regal type (Moses and Joshua, David and Solomon, and other kings) that the Deuteronomist alludes to the 'book of the Torah', whereas in the anarchic period of the judges, when each man did 'as was right in his eyes', no mention is made of it because the 'book of the Torah' could be implemented only in a society governed by a centralized government, that is, a king.

2. RHETORICAL TECHNIQUE

The author of Deuteronomy has endowed the book with the typical features of an oration. The rhetorical technique is here fully developed. As is expected of a good orator the author directs his message to the heart and emotions[2] of his audience, enlivening and

[1] See Y. Kaufmann, *HIR* II, 364–5, who denies that there is a deuteronomic redaction in Joshua–Judges, and G. von Rad, *Theologie*, pp. 343–4, who postulates two different redactors (but both from deuteronomic circles).

[2] On the important role of the πάθη in the oration, see Aristoteles, *Rhetorica*, 1356ª14–17.

variegating the ancient traditions by retelling them in such a manner as to capture and maintain the interest of his listeners. The ancient traditions make no reference, for example, to the apparel of the desert generation or to the physical adversities of the journey; the author of Deuteronomy, on the other hand, to achieve the desired effect, adds with rhetoric colouring:[1] 'Your clothing did not wear out (לא בלתה) upon you, and your foot did not swell, these forty years' (Deut. 8: 4; cf. 29: 4).[2] In order to impress upon his listeners the greatness of the manna miracle, he adds: 'And he fed you with the manna, which you did not know, nor did your fathers know' (8: 3); and he does the same whenever he wishes to stress whatever was exceptional in the event (13: 7; 28: 36). He brings out vividly the contrast between the desert and the good land promised to the Israelites. The desert in which Israel wandered is described in exceptionally strong tones: 'a great and terrible wilderness, with its fiery serpents and scorpions, thirsty ground נחש שרף ועקרב וצמאון where there was no water . . .' (8: 15).[3] Against this he juxtaposes the goodness of the land Israel is to inhabit: 'For the Lord your God is bringing you unto a good land of brooks of water, of fountains and springs, flowing forth in valleys and hills, a land of wheat and barley, of vines[4] and fig-trees and pomegranates, a land of olive-trees and honey, a land in which you will eat bread without scarcity' (vv. 7–9). Though the description may be essentially correct, there is doubtless an element of exaggeration in it: it is, as S. R. Driver[5] notes, 'an eloquent and glowing description'. His comparison of the land of Egypt with Palestine is fanciful and

[1] Cf. S. R. Driver, *Deuteronomy*, ICC, p. 108: 'The terms of the description are *rhetorical* (emphasis added) and are not of course to be understood literally.'

[2] Cf. the Gilgamesh Epic XI: 244–6: 'Until he gets to his city (var.: to his land), until he finishes his journey, let not (his) cloak have a mouldy cast, let it be wholly new' (*tēdiqu šība aj iddima edēšu lidiš*). Cf. S. Paul, *VT* 18 (1968), 119 n. 3. בלה is paralleled with אכלו עש 'eaten by moths' (Isa. 50: 9; Job 13: 28) and thus is close in sense to *šība nadû* = 'mouldy cast' in Gilgamesh.

[3] Cf. the inscriptions of Esarhaddon: *mirīt* (*sic*) (see *CAD*, vol. 16 (Ṣ), p. 244) *nābali*. . *ašar ṣumāmi*. . . *ašar ṣēru* (*u*) *aqrabu* 'an arid pasture land. . a waterless region. . . where serpents and scorpions . . .' (R. Borger, *Asarhaddon*, 56, iv: 54–6); see also the annals of Aššurbanipal: *madbar ašar ṣummê kalkalti* . . . 'a desert, a place of thirst and hunger' (Streck, *Assurbanipal* II, p. 70, viii: 87–90, cf. ibid. 204, vi: 10–12).

[4] Compare the Panammuwa I inscription (*KAI* 214: 5–6): . . . ארק שערי ארק חטי . . . ארק וכרם 'a land of barley . . . a land of wheat . . . land and vineyard'.

[5] *Deuteronomy*, ICC, ad loc.

distorted. Egypt is depicted in the early Biblical sources as the choicest of countries: 'Like the garden of the Lord, the land of Egypt' (Gen. 13: 10); yet the author of Deuteronomy, bent on convincing his audience of the superiority of the land promised them, exaggerates its shortcomings, remarking disparagingly that the land of Israel 'is not like the land of Egypt . . . where you sowed your seed and watered it with your feet, like a garden of vegetables' (11: 10–12).[1]

The deuteronomic orator often employs rhetorical phrases such as: 'your eyes see' עיניכם הראות, 'you have seen' אתם ראיתם (11: 7; 29: 1 *et al.*) to implant in his listeners the feeling that they themselves have experienced the awe-inspiring events of the Exdous; and he repeats these phrases again and again as if to hypnotize his audience. The device of the rhetorical question is also used significantly and with purpose: 'Did a people ever hear the voice of a god . . .?' (4: 33).

Having chosen the oration as their literary medium, the deuteronomic authors put their speeches into the mouths of kings and political leaders,[2] who were of course accustomed to speaking before assemblies and large audiences. Indeed, the author of Deuteronomy describes Moses as speaking 'unto all Israel' (Deut. 1: 1; 5: 1; 29: 1), that is to a vast audience consisting of tribal chiefs, judges,[3] elders, officers, men, women, children, and even alien residents (Deut. 29: 9). Joshua delivers his valedictory address before the elders of the people, chieftains, judges, and officers (23: 2, compare 24: 1, a verse redacted by the Deuteronomist).[4] This emphasis on vast audiences in the oration scenes and the detailed enumeration of the various leading classes participating in them is peculiar to the book of Deuteronomy and deuteronomic literature.[5]

These assembly scenes in Deuteronomy are generally identified by scholars with the 'amphictyonic' assemblies;[6] but it is difficult to believe that this is truly the case. The יום הקהל 'the day of the

[1] For the theological significance of this comparison, see M. Buber, *Israel und Palästina*, 41 ff.

[2] Cf. the Sumerian proverb: 'The scribal art is the mother of orators and the father of scholars', *BWL* 259: 19.

[3] Cf. above, p. 101 n. 6.

[4] See M. Noth, *Josua*², HAT ad loc.

[5] See E. Nielsen, *Shechem*², 1959, p. 79. On the covenantal background of these gatherings see above, p. 101.

[6] A. Alt, 'Die Ursprünge des Israelitischen Rechts', *KS* I, 326 and also G. von Rad, *The Problem of the Hexateuch*, pp. 31 f.

assembly' (Deut. 9: 10; 10: 4; 18: 16) and the terms 'as this day' or 'today' in Deuteronomy, do not necessarily denote the day of an amphictyonic ceremony,[1] but rather the day on which the people gathered to hear the address of their leader or of the Deity. The 'day of the assembly', is correctly defined in Deut. 4: 10: 'Now on that day you stood before the Lord your God at Horeb, the Lord said to me "*Gather the people to me, that I may let them hear my word*" . . .'. The purpose of the assembly is therefore the hearing of the address and not the performance of a sacral rite. The recurring expressions 'today' and 'this day' are merely rhetorical idioms intended to lay greater stress on the solemn moment in which the people are gathered to hear the oration. In his address to the people who assembled for the occasion of Abimelech's coronation Jotham declared 'And ye are risen up against my father's house *this day* (היום) . . . if ye have dealt truly and sincerely with Jerubaal . . . *this day* (היום הזה)' (Judg. 9: 18 and 19); and it can hardly be supposed that the massacre of Jerubaal's seventy sons and Abimelech's coronation occurred on one and the same day. The expressions 'this day' and 'today' are not to be understood literally and must be taken in the extended sense,[2] 'now'—a word which is commonly employed in rhetorical contexts (see below). The phrase 'this day' reminded Nielsen of the 'day of the assembly' of Deuteronomy[3] and he tried to infer by analogy that Jotham's oration, like the orations in Deuteronomy, is pervaded with the divine element. But in fact the phrase derives from a rhetorical reality, and it was from this reality that the school of Deuteronomy adopted the phrase.

The largest concentration of these phrases (היום, היום הזה) is encountered in the speeches which the court scribes put into David's mouth: twice in David's address to Goliath the Philistine (1 Sam. 17: 46); quite frequently in the exchange of diplomatically phrased addresses between David and Saul (1 Sam. 24: 10, 18, 19; 26: 19, 21, 23, 24), and again in the conversation in which David expresses his gratitude to Abigail (1 Sam. 25: 32 and 33).

A variation of 'this day' is the phrase 'as this day' כיום הזה, and it too is a common rhetorical term and is frequent in the deutero-

[1] See, e.g., G. von Rad, *The Problem of the Hexateuch*, pp. 31 f.
[2] See Y. Kaufmann, *The Book of Judges*, 1962, p. 205 (Hebrew).
[3] *Shechem*, p. 146 n. 1.

nomical orations. The speakers employ this term when recalling past events with specific reference to their own present time—the 'as this day' of the speaker. I. L. Seeligmann has pointed out that in Deuteronomy the divine promise and covenant with the Patriarchs (4: 37–8; 8: 18), the Exodus (4: 20), and the victory over Sihon (2: 30), are all referred to for the one purpose of stressing their significance and application to the *present* reality, the 'this day' of the author.[1] The single instance in which this phrase occurs in JE is in the wisdom context of Gen. 50: 20,[2] where the *wise and discreet* Joseph (Gen. 41: 39), represented as a successful wise man in the court of Pharaoh,[3] decorates his address to his brothers (50: 20–1) with rhetorical expressions prevalent in court circles.

Among these we encounter another term found both in orations and letters: 'and now' ועתה. This expression is employed in the letters as a transition between the opening salutation and the subject-matter (cf. especially the Lachish Letters and 2 Kings 10: 1–3);[4] while in the oration it generally indicates a turning-point,[5] such as the transition from the parable to the moral lesson that is to be drawn from it. It occurs frequently in deuteronomic orations. Thus, describing the long journey of the Israelites from Horeb to the steppes of Moab in Deut. 1–3, the speaker reaches the principal point of his address—his enjoinder: '*And now*, O Israel, listen to the laws and judgements which I teach you' (4: 1). The word recurs after the historical survey of 9: 7–10: 11: '*And now*, Israel, what does the Lord your God require of you...?' (10: 12). Samuel in his farewell speech likewise passes from his historical survey of the past to the contemporary situation by means of the same transitional phrase 'and now' (1 Sam. 12: 13).

In Prov. 1–9, whose fluent rhetorical style is similar to that of Deuteronomy, the term occurs after a series of clearly depicted figures. The wise teacher, having described in very realistic colours the woman ensnaring the young man, passes to the moral lesson to be derived: '*And now*, O sons, listen to me and be attentive

[1] 'Aetiological Elements', *Zion* 26 (1961), 146.

[2] See G. von Rad, *Das erste Buch Mose*, ATD, 1961, pp. 383–4.

[3] On the wisdom background of the Joseph story see G. von Rad, 'The Joseph Narrative and Ancient Egyptian Wisdom', *The Problem of the Hexateuch*, pp. 292–300.

[4] Cf. *inanna* in the Mesopotamian letters and also וכעת, וכענת, the Aramaic equivalents of the Hebrew ועתה, in Ezra and in the Elephantine Papyri.

[5] See O. Eissfeldt, *Einleitung*[3], p. 17.

to the words of my mouth. Let not your heart turn aside to her ways . . .' (Prov. 7: 24–5). In contrast to the strange woman who is described as perpetrating deception in darkness and secret places, Wisdom, in the personification of an independent and divine being, is described as proclaiming her message in public. Concluding his description of the strange woman and the divine Wisdom, the wise teacher passes on to the point of his lesson in this manner: '*And now*, my sons, listen to me . . .' (Prov. 5: 7; 7: 24).

This form of the vocative approach (ועתה שמעו) is also characteristic of the deuteronomic orations: ועתה שמע ישראל (4: 1) or without 'and now': שמע ישראל (6: 4; 9: 1, etc.). This manner of rhetorical address in the book of Deuteronomy is not peculiar to those passages which concern the recitation of the laws but is also met with in the military speeches (Deut. 20: 3; 9: 1);[1] it is unnecessary therefore to identify the *Sitz im Lieben* of this phraseology with the recitation of laws.[2] The phrase appears to be no more than a typical didactic form. The expressions 'hear' שמע and 'see' ראה[3] interspersed throughout the book of Deuteronomy are just standard rhetorical terms which give the book the style of a didactic speech; this is especially apparent in the phrase 'Hear, O Israel'. Openings of this sort are, in fact, encountered both in Israelite and non-Israelite wisdom literature.[4]

Even the place in which the Mosaic discourse is delivered is in keeping with the rhetorical practice. Orators generally delivered their speeches from some elevated position such as a mountain-top, the heights of an acropolis, or a city wall. Jotham speaks standing on the summit of Mt. Gerizim (Judg. 9: 7);[5] David addresses Abner and Saul from a mountain-peak (1 Sam. 26: 13); Abner speaks to Joab and his men from a hilltop (2 Sam. 2: 25); Abijah, son of Rehoboam, delivers his speech from atop Mt. Zemaraim (2 Chr. 13: 7); and so on down to the time of the 'Sermon on the Mount'. The wise men, who were active in large cities, would speak 'from the highest places of the town' על גפי מרמי קרת

[1] See above, pp. 45 ff.

[2] As does A. R. Hulst, 'Der Name Israel in Deuteronomium', *Oudtest. Studiën* 9 (1951), 68 ff.

[3] See C. Steuernagel, *Deuteronomium*², 1923, p. 51.

[4] See chapter below on Deuteronomic Didacticism, p. 305.

[5] As opposed to the Levites who stood in the valley, and addressed the tribes atop Mt. Gerizim and Mt. Ebal (cf. Y. Kaufmann, *The Book of Joshua*, 1959, p. 129 (Hebrew)).

(Prov. 9: 3)[1] or from city walls: 'On top of the walls she cries out' בראש המיות תקרא (Prov. 1: 21; for המיות read with LXX: חמיות).[2] The position which Moses takes up in order to deliver his speech is in keeping, then, with oratorical practice. According to all indications, the speech begins only after he has gone up to the *Pisgah* of Mt. Nebo; it is only after he surveys the good land from the *Pisgah* and after his words of encouragement to Joshua (Deut. 3: 23–9) that he begins his farewell speech. This detail in Deuteronomy conforms with the other traditions. The Priestly document, which has preserved the account of Moses' death, tells of his ascent to Mt. *'Abarim* from where he surveys the land, of his prayer concerning the appointment of a leader to succeed him, the commissioning of Joshua, and finally of his death there (Num. 27: 12–23; cf. Deut. 32: 48–52 = P). Deuteronomy has retained the topographical features of this tradition (Mt. *'Abarim* = Mt. Nebo) and its principal themes; it has, however, reshaped the content of the tradition in the typical deuteronomic spirit. Moses' prayer regarding the appointment of a new leader is replaced by his personal supplication to be permitted to enter the promised land. Instead of Joshua's appointment which entailed the sacral act of Moses laying his hands upon the candidate and imparting his spirit to him, we encounter a brief Mosaic address giving Joshua encouragement. Finally comes the major theme—Moses' valedictory address to Israel before he renders his soul to God on the summit of the mountain. As we have seen from the examples cited above, the height of a mountain served as a convenient and natural place from which to deliver a speech. It is ludicrous to suppose that Moses descended the mountain to deliver his oration before the people and then reascended it to die there. The verse preceding the oration: 'So we remained in the valley opposite Beth-peor' (3: 29) identifies the place in which the Israelites were located at this moment and does not necessarily imply that Moses delivered his speech in the valley.

The authors of Deuteronomy and the deuteronomic school must be sought for, then, among circles which held public office, among persons who had at their command a vast reservoir of literary

[1] Albright translates: 'on the edge of the acropolis of the town', 'Canaanite–Phoenician Sources of Hebrew Wisdom', Suppl. *VT* 3 (1955), 9.

[2] Cf. *ḫumītu* in *EA* 141: 44 (gloss) and *ḫmyt* = *ḫāmiyātu* (plur.) in Ugarit (*UT* 2: 28) and in Phoenician חמית (pl.) (*KAI* 26, A i: 13, 17).

material, who had developed and were capable of developing a literary technique of their own, those experienced in literary composition, and skilled with the pen and the book: these authors must consequently have been the *sōferim-ḫakamim*.

PARTS TWO AND THREE

INTRODUCTION: THE RELATIONSHIP BETWEEN THE PRIESTLY AND DEUTERONOMIC DOCUMENTS

In Pentateuchal literature we meet with two schools of crystallized theological thought: that found in the Priestly strand and that reflected in the book of Deuteronomy. These schools were, to be sure, antedated by the Jahwist and Elohist documents. But J and E are merely narrative sources in which no uniform outlook and concrete ideology can as yet be discerned, and thus contrast strongly with P and deuteronomic literature, each of which embodies a complex and consistent theology which we may search for in vain in the earlier sources.

These two schools differ from each other in their concept of religion, their mental climate, and their mode of expression. Scholars of the Graf–Wellhausen school endeavoured to explain these differences in historical terms. The Priestly document, in their opinion, crystallized during the exilic period, when Israel was severed from its land and agricultural life, and consequently evolved a schematic religion of sacral *mores* devoid of a national-territorial setting. The book of Deuteronomy, on the other hand, having received its fixed form during the Josianic period, reflects a religion deeply rooted in the life of a people settled on their land and leading a natural agricultural and political existence. Y. Kaufmann[1] in opposing this view has convincingly called into question

[1] *HIR* I, 113 ff. One of the basic misconceptions in Wellhausen's theory is the assumption that the religion of Israel developed from a religion sprouting out of life and nature (= JED) to a sacral lore (= P) stripped of life and its natural setting. This very assumption is now being challenged by the ever-growing body of discoveries from the ancient Near East which point to an opposite tendency: from the sacral to the secular, see, e.g., W. von Soden, 'Religiöse Unsicherheit, Säkularisierungstendzen und Aberglaube zur Zeit der Sargoniden',

the hypothesis of P's lateness and its dependence on D; he did not, however, provide any explanations that would account for the differences existing between these two works.

It is here suggested that the divergencies between the two schools stem from a difference in their sociological background rather than from a difference in their chronological setting. The problem at hand concerns two different ideologies arising from two different circles but not necessarily from two distinct historical periods. We would therefore regard the literary compositions of these schools as concurrent rather than successive documents.[1] In support of this view we point to the fact that there are no significant ideological or linguistic ties between these two literary *corpora*. Had P been dependent on D—as Wellhausen assumed—then we should be able to discern this dependence in verbal and conceptual parallels, but no such dependence has yet been convincingly demonstrated.[2] Moreover, since the Priestly editor incorporated his own traditions in the earlier JE material, it would be fair to assume that he would similarly have incorporated his traditions in D as well if the deuteronomic material had antedated him. Yet all indications point to the fact that, on the contrary, it was the deuteronomic school that incorporated and redacted Priestly tradition. Whereas the book of Deuteronomy[3] and deuteronomic historiography show traces

Studia Biblica et Orientalia (Analecta Biblica 12), 1959, pp. 356 ff. The lack of reference to political matters in the priestly literature does not point to the time of the hierocracy of the second temple but, on the contrary, reflects the ancient reality of Israel as do most of the other laws in the Pentateuch. See M. Noth, *The Laws in the Pentateuch*. Similarly the presence of the feasts of the new year (יום תרועה) and the day of atonement (יום הכפורים) in P does not point towards 'the leaden pressure of sin and wrath' (Wellhausen, *Prolegomena*, p. 112) but to the character of the Code which gew out of the domain of sanctuary. These feasts—as we can learn now from similar feasts in Mesopotamia (cf. F. Thureau-Dangin, *Rituels accadiens*, 1921, pp. 38–9, 86 f., 136 ff.)—are typical temple-feasts on which occasions the people do not perform any rites or acts of celebration. Mention of these feasts is therefore limited to the literature of the priests who are directly concerned with their observance.

[1] This last statement does not apply to the legislature and the basic ideology of these two sources. As I try to demonstrate below, the law of P, and the theological conception underlying it, are much older than those of D. D changes and reworks the traditional institutions and attitudes of P. But this does not permit us to draw any conclusions as to the date of the crystallization of P as a literary whole. It may have been put in a fixed written form at the time of Hezekiah–Josiah by a conservative priestly circle whose aim was the collection of the sacral tradition of Israel regardless of its relevance to the royal policy of their time.

[2] For discussion see Kaufmann, *HIR* I.

[3] Thus ch. 4, for example, is studded with Priestly idioms: *male and female*

here and there (see below) of Priestly views and phraseology, the Priestly strand shows no contact whatever with the deuteronomic school. Josh. 22: 9–34, for example, which is a Priestly composition, shows no affinity with deuteronomic literature, though this would certainly be expected in a passage which according to many scholars presupposes a unified cult; while Josh. 23, in contrast, which is written in the deuteronomic spirit and idiom—and is thus held to be a deuteronomic composition—contains a quotation from a Priestly source (compare v. 13 with Num. 33: 55).[1] Deut. 32: 48–52 also appears to be a quotation from a Priestly source (Num. 27: 12–14) which had been revised by the author.[2] Deut. 34 similarly contains Priestly material reworked by a deuteronomic hand,[3] a fact which may be particularly significant since this passage closes the Pentateuch. In view of the scholarly consensus that P followed D and Dtr we would expect the last verses of the Pentateuch to come from the pen of the Priestly editor rather than of the deuteronomic editor.[4]

(זכר ונקבה) (v. 16), *winged bird* (צפור כנף) (v. 17), *pattern* (תבנית) (vv. 17 and 18), *creeping thing* (רמש) (v. 18), *beget* (הוליד) (v. 25), *God created* (ברא) (v. 32). Deut. 12: 23 drew on Priestly phraseology and attitudes from Gen. 9: 4 and Lev. 17: 11, and Deut. 14: 4–20 quotes from a Priestly source (Lev. 11). For detailed discussion see Driver, *Deuteronomy*, ICC, ad loc. and W. Moran, 'The Literary Connection between Lev. 11: 13–19 and Dt. 14: 12–18', *CBQ* 28 (1966), 271–7. The expression 'an ark of acacia wood' (ארון עצי שטים) in Deut. 10: 3 appears to have been taken from the Priestly tradition in Exod. 25: 10, and Deut. 10: 6–9 in general appears to be an amalgamation of Priestly traditions, though the wording is not entirely the same as P's (cf. Num. 33: 30–9; 20: 22–9 and the traditions about the tribe of Levi in Num. 3–4, 8, and 18). The expression 'and to their descendants after them' (לזרעם אחריהם) Deut. 1: 8; 4: 37; 10: 15, reflects the phraseology of P in Genesis (cf. above, p. 78). The priestly formula 'I will be your God and you shall be my people' is reflected in Deut. 26: 17–18; 27: 9, 29: 12, cf. above, p. 80.

[1] See Y. Kaufmann, *The Book of Joshua*, ad loc.

[2] Note particularly the expression 'Mount Nebo . . . opposite Jericho' (v. 49) and its occurrence in Deut. 34: 1, and v. 52 which is reminiscent of Deut. 3: 23 ff., see M. Noth, *Überbeliefer. Studien*, p. 191 n. 1.

[3] Cf. M. Noth, ibid., p. 213: '*Die Grundlage des zusammengesetzten Textes hat also Dtr. abgegeben, jedenfalls nicht P.*' The deuteronomic redaction can, in my opinion, be particularly discerned in v. 9 which describes Joshua as being 'full of the *spirit of wisdom*' (רוח חכמה), in contrast to the Priestly source, on which this verse is based, which describes Joshua as 'a man in whom is the spirit' (אשר רוח בו) (Num. 27: 18). When רוח חכמה occurs in the priestly literature it means technical wisdom (= skill), cf. Exod. 28: 3, and not judicial wisdom as in the deuteronomic literature. Verse 9 agrees therefore with Deuteronomy's conception of the required intellectual qualities of the leader. For a discussion of the deuteronomic and predeuteronomic conceptions of wisdom see below, pp. 244 ff..

[4] Deut. 34: 11–12 is universally held to be deuteronomic.

The redaction of the book of Joshua similarly points to P's preceding D. As it was the Deuteronomist who gave the book its frame (ch. 1 = introduction, ch. 23 = conclusion) we may infer that the Priestly material[1] was redacted by the deuteronomic editor and consequently antedated D.

Be that as it may, the fact that we meet with Priestly material in D and Dtr rather than the converse clearly demonstrates that the deuteronomic school was familiar with Priestly composition, while the Priestly school was not acquainted with D at the time of P's recension. Not only does the deuteronomic school appear to have been familiar with the Priestly document, but sources which the Deuteronomist incorporated in his work also appear to have made use of Priestly material. Thus the annalistic[2] passage in 2 Kgs. 16: 10–16, for example, is written entirely in the Priestly idiom and is pervaded with ritual expressions encountered only in P, e.g. the combination of: *burnt offering, cereal offering, and drink offering* (עולה, מנחה, נסך), *throwing blood upon the altar* (זרק דם על המזבח) . . . which was before the Lord (אשר לפני ה׳), *the north side of the altar* (ירך המזבח צפונה) (cf. Lev. 1: 11), *the morning burnt offering* (עלת הבקר), *model* (דמות), *pattern* (תבנית), and the like. The Priestly account treating of cult and temple affairs thus lay before the deuteronomic editor and must therefore date from an earlier time. The same is true of a similar annalistic passage in 2 Kgs. 12: 5–17, which also pertains to temple affairs (the repair of the temple) and also contains many Priestly terms, such as: *the money for which each man is assessed* (כסף נפשות ערכו) (v. 5; cf. Lev. 27), *guilt-offering* (אשם), *sin offering* (חטאת), (v. 17.)

1 Traces of the Priestly source are clearly evident in Josh. 14: 1–21: 40 not only in the terms and expressions employed (cf. 14: 1–5; 18: 1–10; 19: 49–51 and chs. 20–1) but also in the disposition of the material. The material in these chapters has been arranged in the same manner as was the Priestly tradition in Num. 26–36. The partition of the land in the presence of Joshua and Eleazar coupled with the underlying geographical lists in Josh. 14–19 corresponds to the charge of dividing the land and the related genealogical and geographical lists in Num. 26–7, 32–4; the assignment of the cities of refuge and the Levitical towns in Josh. 20–1 is the implementation of the related commands recorded in Num. 35. Josh. 14: 1–21: 40 in general appear to have been edited by a Priestly redactor and subsequently incorporated *en bloc* by a deuteronomic editor.

On the unconvincing attempts of M. Noth to disprove the Priestly origin of Num. 32–6 and Josh. 14–22 (ibid., pp. 182 ff.) see S. Mowinckel, 'Tetrateuch–Pentateuch–Hexateuch', *BZAW* 90 (1964), 51 ff.

2 Concerning the annalistic character of this passage see A. Jepsen, *Die Quellen des Königsbuches*[2], pp. 54 ff.

Further, from the fact that both Jeremiah[1] and Ezekiel,[2] whose ministries date from the latter part of the pre-exilic period, drew respectively on the book of Deuteronomy and the Priestly document we may infer that both these sources already existed in fixed literary form. It would be futile to say that these two documents drew upon two individual prophets rather than that two prophets were influenced by the legal literature prevailing in their times.

The possibility that P and D may have existed as concurrent documents had for some reason never occurred to Wellhausen, and he thus sought only for a chronological solution. This is quite clear from his remarks in the introduction to his *Prolegomena*: 'Deuteronomy is the starting-point, not in the sense that without it it would be impossible to accomplish anything, but only because, when its position has been historically ascertained, we cannot decline to go on, but must demand that the position of the Priestly Code should also be fixed by reference to history.'[3] It was this peculiar sensitivity to chronological order that dominated the thought of the Wellhausenian school and its precursors and thus precluded investigation of the alternative possibility that the documents might have existed concurrently.

Which circles then stand behind these two theological schools?

One of the greater literary documents of the Bible, whose authorship may easily be determined, is the work which we designate as P. All scholars acknowledge that it is the work of priests, and the name by which it is designated is evidence of this. The authors of this document were therefore the bearers of an important temple office and, as the literary maturity of the composition indicates, we may assert that they were priests of the central sanctuary in Jerusalem.[4]

[1] Many deuteronomic expressions are encountered in the poetic oracles of Jeremiah as well as in the prose sections. See below, pp. 359–60 and W. L. Holladay, *JBL* 79 (1960), 351–67. Of more significance to our discussion is the fact that Jeremiah's religious conception fits the deuteronomic ideology, see above, pp. 160–1.

[2] See W. Zimmerli, 'Die Eigenart der proph. Rede bei Ezechiel', *ZAW* 66 (1954), 1 ff. Zimmerli's conclusion, in effect, calls into question the commonly held view of the date of P. Yet Zimmerli, surprisingly enough, did not investigate the conclusions that follow from his thesis.

[3] *Prolegomena*, p. 13.

[4] I concur with Y. Kaufmann (*HIR* I) that P does not presuppose cult centralization in Jerusalem (as opposed to D). However, this does not preclude the possibility that P was composed in Jerusalem. Since the Jerusalem temple was the most important of all sanctuaries even before the centralization of the

It is somewhat more difficult to determine the identity of the circle from which D arose; however, in view of our earlier observations, it is likely that the work was composed by one of the scribal circles connected with the court, probably the scribal family of Shaphan.[1] If this basic premiss is correct, then we are here confronted with two literary schools representing two ideological currents, the provenance of one being the temple (P), and the provenance of the second the royal court (D).

The temple and the court, of course, were the centres of learning in the ancient world. The priests, ministrants of the temple, and the scribes, officials of the court, were alike considered to be men of learning, and they alone were engaged in the field of literary composition. The priests composed literature which treated of the sacral realm and divine worship, while the scribes wrote literature dealing predominantly with man and the mundane world. It is conceivable that the distinction of subject-matter was not an absolute one. It was not impossible that the priest might engage in mundane literary activity, nor unimaginable that the scribe would compose sacral literature, although this possibility is the more remote.[2] Broadly speaking, however, there was a basic demarcation between these two fields of composition. The priestly vocation required a comprehensive knowledge of ritual minutiae in which the priest was expected to be skilled and proficient. The scribal office entailed an extensive knowledge of state affairs and royal manners, of administrative and military matters, and of geographical, historical, and political questions, all of which demanded intensive specialization.[3] Any combination of such diverse and

cult, it is only natural that it would serve as a centre of Priestly composition. Hempel ('Priesterkodex' *RE* 22, 1954, Sp. 1943–67), on the other hand, regards the Hebron sanctuary as the birthplace of the Priestly document, but this is unlikely. It is possible, to be sure, that several Priestly traditions are to be traced back to Hebron, but it is difficult to accept his view that this provincial sanctuary, which is not heard of during the monarchic period, should have been the home of the final redaction of P. The description of the tabernacle in the Priestly document would also indicate that the Priestly strand received its final form in Jerusalem, though an earlier sanctuary may underlie this description (see M. Haran, 'Shiloh and Jerusalem, The Origin of the Priestly Tradition in the Pentateuch' *JBL* 81 (1962), 14–24).

[1] See above, pp. 158 ff.

[2] The ritual texts were preserved in utmost secrecy and it is improbable that they would be entrusted to anyone not belonging to the Priestly class. See M. Weinfeld, 'On the Conception of Law in Israel and outside it', *Beth Mikra*', 17 (1963), 58 ff (Hebrew).

[3] On the heterogeneous knowledge required of the Egyptian scribe see, 'A Satirical Letter', *ANET*², tr. J. A. Wilson, pp. 475 ff.

unrelated functions would have reduced the professional competence of the priest or scribe, and there is, indeed, no evidence, as far as is known, attesting to such an amalgamation of functions. At any rate, we have as yet not met with priests who composed royal annals nor court scribes who composed ritual texts. We may safely assume, then, that the subject-matter of the literature composed by priests and by scribes was essentially different. Priestly composition was grounded entirely on religion and belief in the supernatural in which all is subordinate to the divine factor, while scribal composition, on the other hand, was grounded on secular reality.

It is against the background of this typological distinction that we have to comprehend the character of Priestly and deuteronomic composition. The Israelite Priestly school, whose roots lay in the temple, drew its inspiration from the divine sphere, while the deuteronomic school which was rooted in court reality drew its inspiration from the political-national sphere. Both these schools are, of course, founded on religion and divine faith, but nevertheless their respective spiritual worlds were fashioned and crystallized each in its own distinct and individual manner. Thus the ideological realm of the Priestly document has a religious-theocentric orientation, while the deuteronomic world has a religious-anthropocentric orientation. The sacral and supernatural atmosphere of the Priestly document is not, therefore, the product of the exile. It originates from a compact circle of learned priests whose sole interest lay in the temple and all that pertained to it. Indeed, the bulk of the laws in the Priestly source centre on the divine tabernacle and all that relates to its construction and the ministrations performed in it. It is the pervading presence of God in the midst of Israel (viz. the sanctuary) that gives meaning to the Israelite scene. Remove the divine immanence, and the entire Priestly code collapses. Not only would the worship of God cease, but laws relating to the social sphere would become inoperative. The laws of asylum, for instance, are inconceivable without a high priest (Num. 35: 25), the laws of warfare are unimaginable without the participation of sacral persons who march forth with their holy trumpets in hand (Num. 31: 6; cf. 10: 9), the law of suspected conjugal infidelity cannot be implemented without a sanctuary (Num. 5: 11 ff.), military operations cannot be conducted without the presence of the high priest bearing the Urim (Num. 27: 21), and so forth. These laws do not presuppose the theocentric state of the post-exilic period—as Wellhausen believed—because post-exilic Judah did not conduct wars nor were its leaders appointed in the presence of the *congregation*. Neither can we speak of the presence of God in a temple at a time when the ark—upon which the Glory of God dwelled between the cherubim, and to which the ritual of the sanctuary was oriented[1]—was non-existent. The reality reflected in the Priestly code accords more with the ancient life of Israel, grounded on sacral dogma[2] and prescriptions which continued to mould the life of the Israelites even after the establishment of the monarchy.[3] The reality depicted in the ancient narratives, which recount their tales freely and untendentiously, is indeed similar to that reflected in the Priestly document. Thus, Saul and David conduct their military campaigns according to the instructions provided by the Urim, holy wars resound with the blasts of priestly trumpets and horns (Josh. 6; Judg. 7: 18 f.), the priestly class participates in military expeditions (Josh. 6; Judg. 20: 26–8; 1 Sam. 4), and the booty is brought to the house of God (Josh. 6: 24; 2 Sam. 8: 11; 2 Kgs. 12: 19; cf. Num. 31: 54).

The regime of holiness and taboo underlying the Priestly document is not the product of the theological ruminations of priests of the post-exilic period, but derives from the real conditions prevailing during the times of the judges and the monarchic period. The sacral institutions which occupy a central place in the Priestly theology are known to us from early Biblical literature. Thus the Sabbath,[4] for example, or the new-moon, the 'days of solemn rest' (שבתון), and the 'holy convocations' (מקרא קדש), are not characteristic only of P. The early sources also speak of days on which one refrained from work (Amos 8: 5), days on which one partook of holy meals (1 Sam. 20: 24–34), made pilgrimages to holy men (2 Kgs. 4: 23), gathered in sacral assemblies and holy convocations (Isa. 1: 13), offered sacrifices, and poured libations (Hos. 9: 4–5).

Matters affecting purity and defilement, concerning which the

[1] See below, pp. 191 f.

[2] Cf. G. von Rad: 'Wir müssen uns den geistigen Lebenskreis des alten vorköniglichen Israels noch als einen sakral geschlossenen vorstellen. Alle Lebensgebiete ruhten in einer letztlich vom Kultus her normierten Ordnung und hatten sich noch nicht eigengesetzlich verselbständigt' (*Theologie* I, 1957, p. 262).

[3] For discussion see M. Noth, *The Laws in the Pentateuch*, pp. 1–107.

[4] See my article in *Tarbiz* 37 (1968), Appendix on the Sabbath, pp. 127 f.

Priestly document provides detailed regulations, are also known to us from early Biblical literature. The participants in a sacral event must purify themselves and cleanse their garments (Gen. 35: 2; Exod. 19: 10; 1 Sam. 16: 5), Israelite warriors before departing for war must observe sexual separation and consecrate their utensils (1 Sam. 21: 6), women cleanse themselves of menstrual impurity (2 Sam. 11: 4), lepers are ejected from the city (2 Kgs. 7: 3 ff.), persons defiled by contact with the dead are forbidden to enter the house of the Lord (Hos. 9: 4).

The same is true of matters concerning the temple and holy taboos. The danger that ensues from approaching the divine sanctum, so frequently mentioned in the Priestly document, is also alluded to in the early sources (1 Sam. 6: 19–20; 2 Sam. 6: 6–9). These old sources, furthermore, contain regulations for sacrifices and offerings to the Deity, and describe cultic practices which also figure as an essential part of Priestly teaching (Exod. 23: 18; 34: 25; 1 Sam. 2: 15–17; 21: 7—the bread of the Presence לחם הפנים; Amos 4: 5, compare Lev. 7: 13). We have already alluded to the fact that the early sources also contain references to holy consecrations, communal sacrifices, and sin- and guilt-offerings. The Nazirite institution, which is one of the most ancient in Israel, is mentioned remarkably enough only in the Priestly document (Num. 6), but nowhere else in the Pentateuch. Non-sacrificial slaughter, which is prohibited by the Holiness Code (Lev. 17), and which is designated as '*eating on the blood*' (Lev. 19: 26), is mentioned in 1 Sam. 14: 32–5: 'Behold the people are sinning against the Lord, *by eating on the blood*', i.e. eating without first sprinkling the blood upon an altar.[1]

Most astonishing in the Priestly document is the marked absence of civil ordinances and regulations pertaining to conjugal life, which occupy so great a place in the book of Deuteronomy. Even when we do encounter laws dealing with such matters they are always presented in a ritual aspect. Thus incest, for example, is exposed as sin defiling the land and desecrating the holy name of God who dwells in the land (Lev. 18: 24–30; 20: 22–7). The incest prohibitions are set forth, moreover, in the same context as the prohibitions concerning menstrual uncleanness, bestiality, Molech worship (18: 19–23), mantological practices, clean and

[1] See below, pp. 213 f.

unclean animals (20: 5 and 25). Incest, then, is conceived as a distinctly sacral matter and not one which concerns civil law.

The Sabbatical year, which in the book of Deuteronomy has a patently social character, figures in P as a sacral institution: 'The land shall keep a sabbath to the Lord' (Lev. 25: 2); and, as we shall see below, it is P which preserves the original conception of this institution.

The Deuteronomic Code, on the other hand, rests on a distinctly secular foundation. Not only do we encounter institutions of a manifestly secular character such as the judiciary (16: 18–20; 17: 8–13), the monarchy (17: 14–20), the military (20) and civil and criminal laws which treat of the family and inheritance[1] (21: 10–21; 22: 13–29; 24: 1–4; 25: 5–10), loans and debts (15: 1–11; 24: 10–13), litigations and quarrels (25: 1–3 and 10–12), trespassing (19: 14) and false testimony (19: 15–21) and the like; but, as we shall see below, even institutions and practices which were originally sacral in character have here been recast in secularized forms. The absence of sacral institutions in the book of Deuteronomy is no less surprising than the absence of socio-legal institutions in the Priestly document. The very book which is so centrally concerned with 'the chosen place' has almost completely ignored the sacral institutions which the chosen place must necessarily imply and without which the conduct of sacral worship is unimaginable.

The holy ministrations which involve the presentation of the shewbread, the kindling of candles, the burning of incense, the offering of the suet, the daily and seasonal sacrifices, and the reception and disposal of the holy donations, in short the most essential charges and rites of the Israelite cultus, find no mention whatever in Deuteronomy. The exhortations regarding the awe and reverence[2] with which the sanctity of the temple must be respected, and the restrictions imposed to avert the desecration of the sanctum are familiar to us from early Israelite literature and figure prominently in the Priestly document, but are passed over completely in Deuteronomy.

[1] Inheritance laws appear in P only with respect to the ordinance of the *naḥalah* as a part of the holy land to be distributed by divine lot (cf. Num. 27: 1–11, and 36).

[2] Cf. the Holiness Code: 'You shall reverence my sanctuary' (Lev. 19: 30; 26: 2), and the passages which warn against the desecration and defilement of the sanctuary (Lev. 21: 23; Num. 19: 13, etc.).

Even if the author of Deuteronomy presupposed these regulations he could still have given some intimation of their existence when setting forth the ordinances concerning the *chosen place*. The fact that he did not allude to them implies that they were of no concern to him and may even have been in conflict with his purposes.

Before us, then, are two theological schools, one of which is characterized by its theocentric and the other by its anthropocentric approach. The humanistic vein distinguishing the book of Deuteronomy has its roots—as we shall demonstrate below—in wisdom teaching, which embodied the humanistic thought of the ancient Near East.[1] The doctrine of reward, which is the deuteronomic rationale for the observance of the Torah, serves also as the characteristic rationale in wisdom literature; and, as in wisdom literature, reward in Deuteronomy is conceived in distinctly eudaemonistic terms: long life, blessed offspring, material affluence, and the like. The concept of education, so pronounced in Deuteronomy, also derives from the ideology of the sapiential scribes who served as the nation's teachers and educators: it is no coincidence that the verb למד occurs only in Deuteronomy and in no other Pentateuchal book. Apart from these affinities we also meet with wisdom substrata in Deuteronomy and in deuteronomic literature; as we shall see below, the former even contains literal quotations from wisdom literature.

In the first part of our study we saw that the authors of Deuteronomy and deuteronomic composition were scribes. In the second and third sections of this work we shall deal with the community of thought of these scribes.

[1] See O. S. Rankin, *Israel's Wisdom Literature*[2], ch. i.

PART TWO

DEMYTHOLOGIZATION AND SECULARIZATION

EVER since de Wette published his study of the Josianic reform,[1] the problem has remained a subject of continued and repeated scholarly consideration. It is indeed a very significant one,[2] demanding a comprehensive study and clarification of all its aspects. But unfortunately up to the present the various works devoted to the subject have confined themselves to the problem of the cultic significance of the reform, without giving due attention to its theological implications. The fact is, however, that the reform revolutionized all aspects of Israelite religion. The centralization of the cult was in itself, of course, a sweeping innovation in the history of the Israelite cultus,[3] but its consequences were, as we shall see, decisively more revolutionary in nature, in that they involved the collapse of an entire system of concepts which for centuries had been regarded as sacrosanct. With the elimination of the provincial cultus Israelite religious life was completely wrested from the control of priest and temple.[4] It was freed from its ties to the cult and was transformed into an abstract religion which did not necessarily require any external expression. Indeed the very purpose of the book of Deuteronomy, as has been correctly observed, was to curtail and circumscribe the cultus and not to extend or enhance it.[5] The deuteronomic conception of the cult is, as we shall show, vastly different from that reflected in the other Pentateuchal sources; it represents a turning-point in the evolution of the religious faith of Israel.

[1] W. M. L. de Wette, *Dissertatio critico-exegetica*, 1805.

[2] Cf. E. Meyer: 'Dem Akt vom Jahre 621 stehen an Bedeutung wenig andere Begebenheiten der Weltgeschichte gleich' (*Gesch. d. Altertums III* (2), p. 158).

[3] See below.

[4] Cf. Y. Kaufmann, *HIR* II, 272.

[5] Cf. G. von Rad, *Das Gottesvolk in Deuteronomium*, *BZAW*, 1929, pp. 14–15.

I

THE CONCEPT OF GOD AND THE DIVINE ABODE

THE conception underlying the description of God and his place of habitation, as it had crystallized in Israelite Priestly theology, is patently an anthropomorphic one. The worship of God is delineated in the Priestly source and in the sources antedating it against a background in which the Divinity is personalized and depicted in the most tangible corporeal similitudes. God, who possesses, as it were, a human form,[1] has need of a house or a tabernacle.[2] Within the inner recesses of the tabernacle, removed and veiled from the human eye, sits the Deity ensconced between the two cherubim, and at his feet rests the ark, his footstool.[3] In an adjoining chamber the high priest, the most intimate of God's ministrants, attends to his essential needs. There he spreads the shewbread before him, loaves of bread on a table where cultic vessels stand to supply the need for food and drink.[4] He also kindles the lamps to

[1] See below, pp. 199 f.

[2] The passages which refer to the tabernacle as a place of meeting, such as Exod. 25: 22; 29: 42–3, do not prove that P conceived it as serving this purpose only, as von Rad contends ('The Tent and the Ark', *The Problem of the Hexateuch*, pp. 103–24 and in his *Studies in Deuteronomy*, pp. 39 ff.). The tabernacle did serve as a meeting-place for Moses, but otherwise it was the Deity's permanent place of habitation, a notion which finds articulation in Exod. 25: 8 ('And let them make me a sanctuary, that I may dwell in their midst'), 29: 45, and Num. 16: 3—passages which von Rad finds difficult to ignore (*Studies*, p. 40 n. 1). The 'Tent of Meeting' is, to be sure, a pre-Priestly term (E) denoting nothing more than a place of meeting, a sort of oracular pavilion (see M. Haran, 'The Nature of the "'Ohel Mo'edh" in Pentateuchal Sources', *JSS* 5 (1959), 50–65), and not the permanent domicile of the Deity (Exod. 33: 7–11; Num. 12: 4–5; Deut. 31: 14–15). In Priestly theology, however, it assumed a new meaning and henceforth denoted a *tabernacle*. Indeed, the Glory of God in P is inseparably associated with the Tent of the Meeting in which it manifests itself to all Israel. In one instance alone does the Glory of God manifest itself outside the tabernacle, and that is before the latter was constructed (Exod. 16: 10).

[3] See M. Haran, 'The Ark and the Cherubim', *IEJ* 9 (1959), 30–8, 89–98.

[4] Idem, 'The Complex of Ritual Acts Performed Inside the Tabernacle', *Scripta Hierosolymitana* VIII, 1961, 272–302. The need for drink, as it were, is symbolized by 'the flagons to pour libations' (Exod. 25: 29; 37: 16, הקשות אשר יסך בהן, compare Num. 4: 7), ibid., pp. 286–7. It should be said, however, that

furnish light, and burns incense mornings and evenings to raise aromatic fumes for the divine pleasure.[1] All these acts are performed 'before the Lord (לפני יהוה)', that is, in his presence.[2]

The presence of the Deity in the sanctuary demands a rigorous observance of all measures affecting holiness and purity, any laxity in which might incur the wrath of the Deity and thus invite disaster. The Divine seclusion must be respected; one must not intrude upon it. The priest alone, who ministers to the Lord, may approach the divine sanctum, whilst the layman who draws near must die (Num. 17: 28, etc.).[3] Drawing nigh to the Deity here signifies entrance into the actual sphere of the divine presence and for this reason is fraught with great physical danger. The Deity is enveloped by a screen of fire,[4] which destroys all who would draw near him. The 250 persons of Korah's party who dared to approach the divine tabernacle and burn incense within the holy precints were consumed by the fire which shot forth from the Lord (Num. 16: 35).[5] Nadab and Abihu, the sons of Aaron, were similarly struck down when they presented strange fire with their incense (Lev. 10: 1–2).[6] This same fire emanating from the Lord consumes the pieces of fat which are offered upon the altar, thereby signifying that the sacrifice is pleasing to him (Lev. 9: 24).[7]

This anthropomorphic theology is not the invention of the Priestly author, but derives from early sacral conceptions. The notion of God sitting enthroned upon the cherubim was prevalent in ancient Israel (1 Sam. 4: 4; 2 Sam. 6: 2; Ps. 80: 2; 2 Kgs. 19: 15 = Isa. 37: 16). The Bread laid out before the Lord ('the bread of the presence'), the lamp (candelabrum) kindled before him, the burning of sweet incense for his pleasure (ריח ניחח), offerings consumed by the divine fire, the danger that accrues from approaching the Divinity are all alluded to in the early historiographic narra-

in Aramaic נסך is related to bread, cf. Sefire III: 5, 7 (see above, p. 100, note) and compare Dan. 2: 46.

1 M. Haran, 'Complex of Ritual Acts', 276–7.

2 Ibid., p. 282.

3 For a thorough study on this problem see J. Milgrom, *Studies in Levitical Terminology, I*, 1970, 5 ff.

4 See below, pp. 201 f.

5 On this verse see B. Baentsch, *Exodus–Leviticus–Numeri* HKAT 1903, p. 149.

6 Cf. R. Gradwohl, *ZAW* 75 (1963), 288 f.

7 'And fire came forth from before the Lord and consumed the burnt offering', etc.... ותצא אש מלפני יהוה ותאכל על המזבח את העלה. Compare the wording in connection with Nadab and Abihu: 'and the fire came forth from before the Lord and consumed them, thus they died before the Lord' (Lev. 10: 2) ותצא אש מלפני יהוה ותאכל אתם וימתו לפני יהוה, cf. also 2 Kgs. 1: 10, 12, 14.

tives.[1] The difference is, that in Priestly circles these anthropomorphic features underwent schematization and dogmatization.

In contrast to this priestly anthropomorphism, the theological conceptions of the book of Deuteronomy and the deuteronomic school are abstract ones. Deuteronomy defines the sanctuary as 'the place where the Lord chose to cause *his name* to dwell there'. Von Rad has correctly observed that the expression 'to cause his name to dwell' (לשכן שמו) reflects a new theological conception of the Deity, and that the repeated employment of it by the author of Deuteronomy is intended to combat the ancient popular belief that the Deity actually dwelled within the sanctuary.[2]

The phrase שִׁכֵּן שם itself seems to be very ancient and is indeed found in the Jerusalemite letters from Tel El Amarna.[3] Originally, however, it had nothing to do with an abstract notion of God;[4] it was the deuteronomic school that endowed it with a specific theological meaning, In fact it is one of a whole set of phrases built up by the deuteronomic school in order to give expression to the new theology: viz. 'to put his name' שים שמו, 'that his name be there' היה שמו, 'to call his name upon' קרא שמו על, and in connection with the building of the temple 'to build for his name' בנה לשמו, and 'dedicate to his name' הקדיש לשמו.[5] The deuteronomic school used this phraseology in a very consistent manner and never made the slightest disgression from it. There is not one example in the deuteronomic literature of *God's dwelling* in the temple or the building of a house *for God*. The temple is always the *dwelling of his name*, and the house is always built *for his name*. This consistency

[1] Cf. 1 Sam. 21: 7 for the shewbread (לחם הפנים), 1 Sam. 3: 3 for the lamp (נר יהוה), 1 Sam. 26: 19 for the odour, compare Gen. 8: 21 = JE (ריח הניחח), 1 Kgs. 18: 38 and Judg. 6: 21 for the divine fire consuming the sacrifice, and 1 Sam. 6: 19–20, 2 Sam. 6: 6–7 for the danger involved in approaching the Divinity.

[2] Cf. *Studies*, pp. 38–9.

[3] See *EA* 287: 60–1: *šarri šakan šumšu ina māt Urusalim ana dāriš* = 'the king has established his name in the country of Jerusalem for ever', compare *EA* 288: 5–7. Cf. 2 Kgs. 21: 7.

[4] It belongs to the sphere of royal inscriptions, where it is mostly connected with erecting a stele, e.g. *narâja alṭur u šumī ana dāriš altakan* = 'I inscribed my stele and established my name for ever' (*KAH* II, 26: 10). For other examples and the name conception in general cf. F. R. Kraus, 'Altmesopotamisches Lebensgefühl', *JNES* 19 (1960), 128 f. שם in Hebrew, and similarly יד, mean also stele and inscription, cf. for שם: 2 Sam. 8: 13; Isa. 56: 5, and for יד: 1 Sam. 15: 12; 2 Sam. 8: 3 (read: להציב ידו according to the parallel in Chronicles), 18: 18, and Isa. 56: 5 (שם and יד as hendiadys).

[5] For the development of this phraseology see Appendix A, II and p. 4 above.

is seen most clearly when a deuteronomic text is interwoven with an earlier text which does not know the 'name theology'. Thus, for example, in the authentic part of Nathan's prophecy the main issue is the building of a house for God's dwelling (לשבתו) (2 Sam. 7: 5 and 7) while the Deuteronomist (v. 13a)[1] speaks about building a house for his name. Similarly the building account and the ancient story of dedication of the temple speak plainly about building a house for God (6: 1 and 2; 8: 13), while the Deuteronomist, whenever he mentions the building, describes it as being for the *name of God* (3: 2; 5: 17 and 19; 8: 17, 18, 19, 20, 44, 48).

R. de Vaux[2] rejects the notion of 'name theology' in Deuteronomy and argues that the phrase means 'to claim ownership'.[3] He is undoubtedly right in saying—as we have already indicated—that the expression does not necessarily have any abstract connotation. However, the question is whether Deuteronomy's introduction of this metaphor of ownership in place of the earlier, simpler notion of 'dwelling in the house' does not indicate a theological shift to a more abstract understanding of the abode of God.

De Vaux admits[4] that the Deuteronomist developed a 'name theology' and endowed the phrase 'establishing the name' with a new, more abstract meaning, but he believes that this is quite different from the original meaning of the phrase in Deuteronomy. This argument can hardly be sustained in view of the following considerations. First, 'X is the owner of a place', which is implied by the phrase in Deuteronomy, is tantamount to 'X's name is there' יהיה שמי שם, which the Deuteronomist uses in his 'name theology'. For the old notion of indicating possession by inscribing the name of the possessor, which lies behind the phrase 'establishing the name', already implies the idea of extension of one's name and presence which is so characteristic of the 'name theology'. Both expressions presuppose a symbolic presence of the owner by extension of his personality through 'establishing his name'. There is, consequently, no difference in meaning between Deuteronomy's

[1] Since Wellhausen this verse has been considered a subsequent insertion in the prophecy (see also S. R. Driver, *Notes on the Hebrew Text of the Books of Samuel*, 1913, p. 276 n. 1). The phrase יבנה בית לשמי is—according to our opinion—an additional clue to the deuteronomic nature of this verse.

[2] *Das ferne und nahe Wort, Festschrift L. Rost, BZAW* 105 (1967), 219–29.

[3] He also is of the opinion that the idea may be traced back to the custom of kings inscribing their names (upon slates and cylinders) in order to indicate the proprietorship of the territories which they conquered or of sanctuaries which they had built (ibid., p. 221).

[4] Ibid., pp. 225 f.

phrase 'the place where I put My name' and the Deuteronomist's phrase 'the place where My name shall be'.

Secondly, in view of the continuity in ideas and terminology from Deuteronomy to the Deuteronomist, and since the tendency towards rationalization and demythologization is very prominent in Deuteronomy itself, it is quite reasonable to suppose that the theological refinement in connection with the temple found in the Deuteronomist[1] and admitted by de Vaux[2] also has its roots in Deuteronomy.

The most definitive expression of this theology is to be found in the deuteronomic litany of Solomon in 1 Kgs. 8.[3] According to this prayer, in which the functions of the temple are elaborately defined, the temple is not God's place of habitation, but serves only as a house of worship in which Israelites and pagans alike may deliver their prayers and their oaths[4] to the Lord *who dwells in heaven*. The idea that God's habitation is in heaven is here articulated most emphatically in order to eradicate the belief that the Deity sat enthroned between the cherubim in the temple. Whenever the expression 'Your dwelling place' (מכון שבתך) is employed we find that it is invariably accompanied by the word 'in heaven' (vv. 30, 39, 43, 49). The deuteronomic editor is clearly disputing the older view implied by the ancient song that opens the prayer (vv. 12–13)[5] and designates the temple as God's 'exalted[6] house and a dwelling place (or pedestal) for ever'.[7] The word בשמים 'in heaven' is consistently appended to the expression מכון שבתך to inform us that it is heaven which is meant and not the temple as the ancient song implies.

In actual fact, however, the term 'Your dwelling place' in the early sources as well as in Solomon's song (vv. 12–13) denotes the sanctuary; it is the Deuteronomist who is here attempting to alter this meaning and thereby wrest the song from its natural sense.[8]

[1] Cf. below.

[2] Ibid., p. 226.

[3] On the deuteronomic phraseology in this prayer, see above, p. 36.

[4] On this function of the temple in a dedication document, see Landsberger-Balkan, *Belleten* 14 (1950), p. 229, ll. 46 f. I owe this reference to Dr. J. Tigay.

[5] See above, p. 35.

[6] For the connotations of זבל see M. Held, *JAOS* 88 (1968), 90 ff.

[7] Compare in the Assyrian inscriptions, for example, *bīta dāria ana Šamaš . . . eppuš* = 'I want to build an eternal house for Šamaš' (Langdon, *Neubabyl. Königsinschr.* 256, i: 35), cf. above, p. 35 n. 4.

[8] מכון לשבתך means actually 'a daïs for Your throne '(see Cross–Freedman,

This may be apprehended from the Song of the Sea (Exod. 15), in which the poet declares: 'You will bring them in and plant them in Your own mountain, the place, O Lord, which You made for Your abode (מכון לשבתך), the sanctuary, O Lord, which Your hands established (v. 17).[1] The Song of the Sea in all probability dates from Solomonic times, as scholars contend,[2] but whatever its date it is obvious that the expression מכון לשבתך here refers to the temple, as is clearly attested by the parallel colon: 'the sanctuary, O Lord, which Your hands established'. Indeed Isaiah, who visualizes God as seated upon a throne in the temple (ch. 6), designates the temple as the 'place (מכון) of Mount Zion' (4. 5) and elsewhere explicitly describes the Lord as dwelling on Mount Zion (השכן בהר ציון) 8: 18; cf. 31: 9). The expression 'a place to dwell in', or rather the concept of a permanent abode for the Deity, goes back to the period of the United Monarchy when the

'The Song of Miriam', *JNES* 14 (1955), 250) and is equivalent to the Sumerian *bára* = Akk. *parakku* in the Mesopotamian temple inscriptions, which actually means the throne daïs. Originally, then, מכון לשבתך may have referred to the ark with the cherubim as the throne of God, a conception unacceptable to Deuteronomy and the Deuteronomist, see below, pp. 208–9.

[1] Cf. the parallel in the Ugaritic literature *btk ǵry il ṣpn bqdš bǵr nḥlty* = 'in the midst of my mount, Godly Zaphon, in the sanctuary, mount of my portion' (see C. H. Gordon, *UT*, ʿnt iii: 26–7, p. 254, translation according to H. L. Ginsberg, *ANET*², p. 136) and also the expressions *ksu ṯbth//arṣ nḥlth* = 'the throne that he sits on//the land of his inheritance' (*UT* no. 51, viii: 12–14; no. 67, ii: 15–16; ʿnt vi: 15–16, p. 255). For a discussion of these phrases see Cross–Freedman, *JNES* 14 (1955), 250.

The statement that Yahweh has made a sanctuary does not eliminate the specific reference to the earthly structure. In Ps. 78: 68 f. the idea of God's building the sanctuary also comes to clear expression: 'He built his sanctuary like the heights [or heavens, read perhaps כמרומים, see *BH*], like the earth which he founded for ever' (v. 70). Compare the Mesopotamian inscriptions as, for instance, 'Esagila the temple whose foundations are as solidly established as heaven and earth' (CH xxivb: 67–9), compare Langdon, *Neubabyl. Köningsinschr.* 72, ll. 31–2; 256, ii: 1. The notion of a god building his sanctuary is found also in the Sumerian literature, see 'Enki and the World Order' in Kramer's *The Sumerians*, 1963, p. 176, cf. also A. Sjöberg, *Der Mondgott Nanna-Suen in der sumerischen Überlief*, p. 39). It is true, however, that the entire passage in Ex. 15: 13 ff. refers to the entrance of the Israelites into the holy land and not into the temple. The temple and the holy mountain only symbolize the holy land (cf. H. L. Ginsberg, *El* 9 (1969), 45 n. 4). On the interrelationship between the local sanctuary, the sacred mountain, God's land, and the cosmic abode of the Deity, see R. E. Clements, *God and Temple*, 1965, pp. 53–5.

[2] See W. Staerk, 'Zum Atlichen Erwählungsglauben', *ZAW* 37 (1955), 23 and H. Gressman, *Anfänge Israels*², 1922, p. 55, and others. Cf. also S. Loewenstamm, *The Tradition of the Exodus in its Development*, 1965, pp. 112 f. (Hebrew).

house of the Lord was first erected,[1] and constitutes an innovation in the Israelite conception of the Divinity. The psalms which extol Zion and Jerusalem, most of which are rooted in the court theology of the United Monarchy,[2] consistently stress the idea that Jerusalem and its house of worship are the place of God's domicile (Pss. 46: 5; 48: 9; 50: 2; 43: 3, etc.). Thus Ps. 132, which describes the transfer of the ark to Jerusalem, expressly declares that 'the Lord has chosen Zion, for he has desired it for his habitation (מושב)' (v. 13). It is in the temple of Jerusalem that God found, in a sense, his true place of rest; hence the psalmist declares in the name of the Lord: 'This is my resting place for ever, here will I dwell, for I have desired it' (v. 14).

This conception appears to have been first contested during the period of the Hezekian–Josianic reforms and in all probability by the circle which was then engaged in the final crystallization of Deuteronomy. It is interesting to note that the very book which elevates the chosen place to the highest rank of importance in the Israelite cultus should at the same time divest it of all sacral content and import. With remarkable consistency it resorts again and again to the phrase 'the place which he shall choose to cause his name to dwell there' (לשכן/לשום שמו) so as to emphasize that it is God's name and not himself who dwells within the sanctuary, as against the Priestly tradition which speaks of God's dwelling in the midst of the children of Israel (Exod. 29: 45; 25: 8; Lev. 26: 11; Num. 16: 3). Indeed all sacral activity performed in the tabernacle as described by the Priestly writings is, as we have pointed out, based on the assumption of God's actual immanence in the sanctuary.[3]

[1] Cf. particularly the oracle of Nathan in 2 Sam. 7. Nathan bases his objection to the construction of a house of God on an early and original tradition according to which God had 'gone from tent to tent' (cf. 1 Chr. 17: 5) and had no permanent dwelling-place.

[2] Concerning this theology (Hoftheologie) see M. Noth, 'Jerusalem und die israelitische Tradition', *Oudtest. Studiën* 13 (1950), 28–46 (= *The laws in the Pentateuch*, etc. pp. 132–44).

[3] The belief of the divine presence in the sanctuary did not, of course, preclude the belief in the Deity's heavenly abode. Israel appears to have shared this dialectical conception of the divine abode (cf. Ps. 20: 3 vs. 7) with other peoples of the Ancient East (see 'The significance of the temple in the Ancient Near East', *BA* 7 (1944), 41 ff.). This dialectical belief, however, is a non-deuteronomic conception and is completely rejected by the deuteronomic school (see G. E. Wright, 'The Temple in Palestine–Syria', *BA* 7. III (1944), pp. 75 f.) which regarded heaven as the exclusive place of God's abode.

This theological corrective occurs explicitly in Deuteronomy itself. In Deut. 26: 15 the Israelite entreats God: 'Look down from Your holy habitation (מעון קדשך) from heaven . . .'. The words 'from heaven' seem to be an explanatory appendage intended to prevent misconstruing the expression 'holy habitation' as referring to the sanctuary. This explanatory appendage here, then, is analogous to that encountered with reference to 'Your dwelling place' in 1 Kgs. 8. Indeed, the fact that the earlier conception prevailing was that God's habitation (מעון) was in Zion may be inferred from Ps. 76: 3: 'His abode has been established in Salem, his habitation (מעונתו)[1] in Zion.' A similar change in concept also occurred with respect to the meaning of the term 'zebul'. According to the ancient Song in 1 Kgs. 8: 13, Solomon built an exalted[2] house (בית זבל) *for God*; yet in Deutero- (or Trito-)Isaiah, on the other hand, the same term denotes God's *heavenly* abode: 'Look down from heaven and see from Your holy exalted (habitation) (מזבל קדשך)' (63: 15).

It appears then that it was the deuteronomic school that first initiated the polemic against the anthropomorphic and corporeal conceptions of the Deity and that it was afterwards taken up by the prophets Jeremiah and Deutero-Isaiah.[3] It is by no means coincidental that the only passages which reflect a *quasi*-abstract conception of the Deity and negation of his corporeality are to be found in Deuteronomy and Deutero-Isaiah: Deut. 4: 12: 'You heard the sound of words, but saw no form' תמונה (compare v. 15); and Isa. 40: 18: 'To whom will you liken God or what likeness compare to him?', and similarly in Isa. 40: 25, and 46: 5.[4]

These later conceptions then are diametrically opposed to the earlier views articulated in the JE and P documents and in the prophetic books antedating Deuteronomy. Thus in Exod. 24: 9–11 we read about the leaders, elders, etc. seeing God; in Exod. 33: 23 Moses is said to have *beheld God's back*, and Num. 12: 8 speaks even more strikingly of Moses as gazing upon 'the *form* (תְּמֻנַת) of the Lord'. Amos similarly sees the Lord 'standing beside the altar' (9: 1), and Isaiah beholds God sitting upon a throne with his train filling the temple (6: 1; compare 1 Kgs. 22: 19 f.).

The Deity is also described in the Priestly document as pos-

[1] For the early date of this psalm see H. Schmidt, *Die Psalmen*, HAT, p. 146.

[2] Cf. above, p. 195 n. 6.

[3] Not so Ezekiel, who continues the tradition of P.

[4] Cf. my article in *Tarbiz* 37 (1968), 124–5.

sessing a human form. God according to the Priestly conception 'created man in his own image' (Gen. 1: 27; cf. 5: 1; 9: 6). Though the account of man's creation in God's image in Gen. 1: 26–7 was subsequently elucidated in a more abstract vein by Hellenistic Jewry,[1] an explanation that has been taken up by some recent commentators,[2] scholars have proved this more abstract exegesis to be untenable.[3] J. Hehn[4] justifiably remarks with regard to these verses that although this sounds strange in the Old Testament, it is nevertheless in line with the concepts of the other ancient Near-Eastern peoples in the area. This anthropomorphic notion is encountered not only in Mesopotamian but also in Egyptian literature. In an Egyptian text which is similar in content and spirit to the creation account in Gen. 1 and which is styled by S. Hermann as 'die kleine Genesis'[5] we read:[6] 'He made heaven and earth . . . and he repelled the water monster (or chaos).[7] . . . He made the breath of life (for) their nostrils. They (i.e. men) who have issued from his body are *his images* . . . He made for them plants, animals, fowl, and fish to feed them.'

Some scholars[8] contend that the phrase בצלמנו כדמותנו, 'in our image, after our likeness' precludes the anthropomorphic interpretation that man was created in the divine image. The plural possessive employed in this verse which refers to the members of the divine suite signifies, to their mind, that man was created in the image of the sons of God, i.e. the celestial suite, but not in the image of God himself. However, the following verse (v. 27) states quite specifically and in the singular that 'God created man in his own image'.[9]

[1] Cf. The Wisdom of Solomon 2: 23 and Philo, *op. mund.* 69.

[2] See, e.g., A. Dillmann, *Genesis*, KeH, 1892, ad loc.

[3] Cf. the commentaries of Gunkel (HKAT), Skinner (ICC), and von Rad (ATD), pp. 44–6.

[4] 'Zum Terminus "Bild Gottes" ', *Festschrift E. Sachau*, 1915, p. 45.

[5] 'Die Naturlehre des Schöpfungsberichtes', *ThLZ* 86 (1961), 416 f.

[6] 'The Instruction of King Meri-Ka-Re', *ANET*², p. 417.

[7] Cf. A. Volten, 'Zwei altägyptische politische Schriften', *Analecta Aegyptiaca* 4 (1945), 73 f.

[8] L. Köhler, 'Die Grundstelle der Imago-Dei Lehre, Genesis i, 26', *ThZ* 4 (1948), 16 f., and G. von Rad, *Theologie* I², 1958, p. 149.

[9] There is no justification for deleting this colon as others suggest (cf. S. Hermann, 'Naturlehre etc.', n. 27). On the contrary, this verse, which is formulated in poetic style and which comprises a complete metrical unit (three lines of four beats each, see U. Cassuto, *A Commentary on Genesis, Part I, From Adam to Noah*, p. 57 [Hebrew]), has an ancient ring to it, and its purpose is to magnify the solemnity of man's creation, the crown of all creation.

The plural form in verse 26 is not employed in reference to either the 'image' or 'likeness' of man, but only to emphasize the solemnity of the act of man's creation. Before initiating such an act the divine assembly must be consulted; all the heavenly hosts are participants, as it were, in the exalted act of man's creation. Further instances of such consultation are recorded in some of the subsequent creation narratives,[1] generally at a time when a crucial decision must be made with regard to man. Man, being endowed with godly qualities, constitutes a potential threat to the sovereignty of God and the sons of God;[2] and, whenever man threatens to upset this order, the divine assembly convenes to decide on a proper course of action. When man eats of the tree of knowledge he arouses the celestial fear that he will also eat of the tree of life and thus become god-like. God accordingly turns to the divine council and speaks: 'Behold, the man has become like one of us, knowing good and evil; and now, lest he put forth his hand and take also of the tree of life and eat, and live for ever . . .' (3: 22). Men decide to make a name for themselves by constructing a tower reaching into the heavens; God accordingly descends to see what the men have built, and returns to his heavenly abode to report to the heavenly council the nature of man's activity and the threat it entails. Then the fateful decision is made: 'Come let us go down, and there confuse their language, that they may not understand one another's speech' (11: 7). Even the Priestly narrative, then, which succeeded in elevating itself above these folk conceptions propagates the view of the divine hosts who stand in God's attendance[3] and serve as his quasi-advisory council (cf. 1 Kgs. 22: 19–22 and Job 1).

Corporeal representation of the Deity in the Priestly document found its clearest expression in the conception of the 'Glory of God', against which the book of Deuteronomy promulgated its doctrine of 'God's Name'.

[1] In this and other respects the first eleven chapters of the book of Genesis have a certain uniformity. See Y. Kaufmann, *HIR* II, 494 ff.

[2] The tenor of the passage reveals the underlying motif of the gods' jealousy of man, common in ancient mythology. The motif, however, belongs to the mythical substratum of the section, and plays no perceptible role in the Israelite narrative.

[3] The fact that P does not explicitly mention angels does not necessarily prove (cf. the commentaries of Gunkel and Skinner) that P did not acknowledge their existence. Ezekiel presents a fully developed angelology and, as his theology is generally related to P, we may assume that his angelology stems from the same source.

The underlying imagery of the concept of God's Glory (כבוד יהוה), the '*Kabod* of Yahweh', embedded in Priestly tradition is drawn in corporeal and not abstract terms.[1] This is most clearly seen in the book of Ezekiel whose ideology is grounded on Priestly doctrine.[2] In Ezekiel ch. 1 the *Kabod* is described as having a human form which is enveloped by fire and brightness and is seated upon a throne of sapphire conveyed underneath by a chariot of beasts and wheels. From afar the apparition is like a blazing fire upon a great cloud swept by a storm wind. This description comprises all the elements of Israelite theophany, wind, cloud, fire, brightness, tumult, the heavenly hosts, and so forth (Exod. 19: 16; 20: 18; 24: 10 'sappir'; Isa. 6; Pss. 18: 8 ff.; 97: 2–6; Hab. 3, etc.); but its most singular feature is the anthropomorphic imagery, which is elsewhere encountered only in P. Thus the notion that God possesses a human form is, as we have already observed, clearly stated in Gen. 1: 26–7. Similarly the brightness 'like the appearance of the bow that is in the cloud on the day of rain' (Ezek. 1: 28) derives from the Priestly tradition in Gen. 9, which recounts that the divine bow (cf. Hab. 3: 9) was set in the cloud as a sign and token of the cessation of God's war with man.[3]

Ezekiel's systematic description of God's *Kabod* as a brilliant and radiant fire encased in a cloud is characteristic only of the Priestly writings. In the theophanies encountered in the other Biblical sources the cloud and fire are only the attendant signs of God's terrifying and overwhelming power (Exod. 19: 16–18; Ps. 97: 2–3, etc.), not component parts of the divine manifestation, nor indispensable features of the divine apparition. The account of the burning bush in Exod. 3, for example, lacks the cloud, in Exod. 34 the fire is missing, and in Exod. 24 both the fire and the cloud are wanting. In these sources the fire and cloud figure only as elements which minister to and execute the Deity's bidding (Ps. 104: 3–4): the fire consumes the adversaries of the Deity (Ps. 97: 3), and the cloud serves as a kind of divine chariot, the vehicle by which God descends to earth (Exod. 34: 5; Num.

[1] Even when employed in an abstract sense, the term כבוד יהוה is nevertheless still grounded on mythological corporeal imagery, cf. H. Kittel, *Die Herrlichkeit Gottes*, *ZNW* Beiheft 16 (1934), 138.

[2] See above, p. 183 n. 2. Concerning Ezekiel's dependence on P for his conception of the 'glory of God' see B. Stein, *Der Begriff 'Kebod Jahweh'*, 1939, p. 299.

[3] For discussion see below, p. 206.

11: 25; 12: 5; Deut. 31: 14–15). The imagery of the divine chariot-cloud motif is indeed of ancient origin and is met with in Ugaritic literature (*rkb ʻrpt*),[1] which appears to have influenced Biblical imagery (Ps. 68: 5; cf. Pss. 18: 11; 104: 3). This explains why the older sources employ the cloud motif only when describing the *approach* of the Deity, i.e. his dynamic state of manifestation but never when describing his static manifestation. In Priestly and Ezekielian literature, on the other hand, the fire and cloud are inseparable elements of the apparition of God's Glory. The *Kabod* is here conceived both in the psychic and physical sense as a ponderous complex of phenomena comprising both the Deity and his cloud.[2] *Kabod* literally means 'body'[3] or 'substance' ('the *kabod* of Jacob will be brought low, and the fat of his *flesh* will grow lean', Isa. 17: 4, compare 10: 16)[4] and particularly designates the weight and importance of a given substance, in this case that of the divine personality.[5]

The cloud in P and in Ezekiel is the divine envelope which screens the Deity from mortal view. God does not *descend* (ירד) in a cloud as in the earlier sources, but *manifests himself* (נראה) in a cloud (Exod. 16: 10; Num. 17: 7) so that man may not gaze upon him and die.

As opposed to the earlier sources, then, in which the cloud serves as either a guide (Exod. 13: 21), a shield protecting the people (14: 19 and 24), or a vehicle conveying the Deity, in P it serves only as a medium which envelops and screens the Deity from mortal view.[6] Only Moses, who converses with God face to face, may enter into the cloud[7] (Exod. 24: 18a = P). To the Israelites, however, God manifests himself only when covered by a cloud; unlike Moses,

[1] See, for instance, *UT* 51, iii: 11.

[2] Cf. B. Stein's comments (*Kebod Jahweh*, pp. 323–4): 'Alle Ableitungen von כבד sind letzlich auf die Bedeutung "schwer" zurueckzuführen. Das ist eine allgemeine anerkannte Tatsache.'

[3] This is the meaning of the word כבוד in the passage: הראני נא את כבדך (Exod. 33: 18), to which the Deity replies: 'You cannot see my face, for man shall not see me and live' (v. 20).

[4] Cf. H. L. Ginsberg, 'Gleanings in First Isaiah', *M. Kaplan Jubilee Vol.*, 1953, pp. 276–7.

[5] For discussion see B. Stein, *Kebod Jahweh*, pp. 323 ff.

[6] The expression 'pillar of cloud' (עמוד ענן) does not appear in the P document.

[7] The radiance of the Glory of God communicated itself to the face of Moses. This aroused the fear and awe of the Israelites who now feared to approach him, for which reason Moses was compelled to veil himself when he went forth among them (Exod. 34: 30–5).

they see only flames flashing forth (from the cloud) (Exod. 24: 17), they see no image. Once only does God manifest himself to Israel without his screen of cloud—on the day of the inauguration of the tabernacle (Lev. 9: 23), an event whose importance parallels the Sinaitic revelation in the JE source.

The cloud departs from the Deity only when he assumes another mode of concealment, viz. the tent of the meeting. When the Glory of God enters the tabernacle, the cloud remains outside and covers the tent. When the tabernacle is dismantled, the Glory of God leaves the tent enveloped once again by the cloud which awaits him and rises upwards (Num. 9: 15 ff.; cf. Ex. 40: 34–8, Num. 10: 11. 12).

Just as no man except Moses is permitted to enter into the screen of cloud, so may no man enter the place wherein the Deity resides. Even Aaron, when making his annual entrance into the Holy of Holies, is forewarned not to enter the inner sanctum without first raising up a cloud of smoke (Lev. 16: 13) from his incense-pan: 'For I will appear in the cloud upon the kapporeth' (v. 2). The cloud referred to in this verse is not that in which the Glory of God generally manifests itself, but the cloud of incense which Aaron raises from his pan.[1] If a cloud did continuously screen the seat of the Deity between the cherubim, there would be no need for Aaron to create an artificial one. The phrase 'lest he die'[2] which recurs in two verses of this passage (vv. 2 and 13) may indeed indicate that the purpose of the incense smoke is to conceal the divine form and thus prevent the certain death awaiting the high priest should his gaze fall upon the Deity.[3]

[1] See J. Morgenstern, 'Biblical Theophanies', *ZA* 25 (1911), 148, and B. Stein, *Kebod Jahweh*, pp. 96–7.

[2] This phrase ולא ימות is common in P and usually serves as a reminder that any deviation from the fixed sacral procedure would have fatal consequences (see Haran, 'The Complex of Ritual, etc.', 288). However, the fact that from among all the rules and regulations in this chapter only that about the incense is accompanied by the warning 'lest he die' points toward the danger involved in the encounter with God in the Holy of the Holies.

[3] See J. Z. Lauterbach's discussion (*HUCA* 4 (1927), 173 ff.) of the Sadducee belief that it *was* possible to see the Glory of God in the Holy of Holies. It was for this reason, he contends, that the Sadducees interpreted Lev. 16: 13 as obliging the high priest to throw the incense into the burning pan while still outside the curtain separating off the Holy of Holies, so as to produce a smoke screen which would prevent him from gazing upon the divine presence as he entered the inner sanctum, cf. Ibn Ezra, ad loc.

It must be said, however, that the simple reading of Lev. 16: 12–13 does not

The doctrine of the 'Glory of God' was evolved by the Jerusalemite priesthood; this is attested by the description of the temple's dedication in 1 Kgs. 8: 11: 'And when the priests came out of the holy place, a cloud filled the house of the Lord, so that the priests could not stand to minister because of the cloud; for the Glory of the Lord filled the house of the Lord.' The dedication of the desert tabernacle is also described in similar terms in Exod. 40: 34–5: 'Then the cloud covered the tent of the meeting, and the Glory of the Lord filled the tabernacle. And Moses could not enter the tent of the meeting, because the cloud abode upon it, and the Glory of the Lord filled the tabernacle.' The Glory of the Lord enters the tabernacle accompanied by the cloud as far as the Holy of Holies, during which time the priests or Moses may not remain inside, i.e. they were forbidden to remain inside.[1] Only after the cloud departs and the Glory of God arrives at its place between the cherubim can the priests re-enter the sanctuary. The resemblance between the two scenes may be attributed to the fact that the description of the dedication of the tabernacle is a retrojection of that of the Jerusalem temple.[2]

The imagery of the *Kabod* of God, however, derives from ancient traditions concerning divine manifestations. According to Exod. 33: 18–23, Moses entreats God 'to reveal his *Kabod* to him', הראני נא את כבדך (v. 18), and God grants the request but permits him to view only his back. 1 Sam. 4: 21 speaks of the departure of the *Kabod* from Israel after the ark has been captured by the Philistines. The 'Glory' that had departed is undoubtedly the 'Glory of God' that dwelled between the cherubim above the ark, and not the glory of Israel. The 'King of Glory' in Ps. 24 is also none other than the selfsame king who sits enthroned upon the ark and before whom the gates swing open as he is conveyed into the sanctuary.[3]

The Priestly document therefore also rests on ancient traditions as regards the conception of the Glory of God.[4] Though the JE source, as we have noted, also depicts the Glory of God as accompanied by cloud and smoke, in P the theophany has assumed a more static form. The cloud and fire in the Priestly document

support the interpretation of the Sadducees. On the whole problem see L. Finkelstein, *The Pharisees*[3], 1962, I, 118 f., II, 654 f.

[1] Cf. B. Stein, *Kebod Jahweh*, pp. 58–9, see also on the verb יכל above, pp. 2–3.

[2] See above, p. 183 n. 4.

[3] Cf. Gunkel's commentary on this psalm.

[4] See M. Noth, *Überlieferungsgeschichte des Pentateuchs*, 1948, p. 255.

are not part of the terrifying natural phenomena that accompany the theophany, such as thunder and lightning, hailstones and torrential rains (Pss. 18: 8–16; 77: 17–19; 97: 2–6, etc.) but supernatural and metaphysical apparitions which arouse the wonder and awe of the spectator. The theophany in JE is a convulsive and staggering experience, to be dreaded rather than desired (Exod. 19: 16; 20: 18–20), whereas in P it is a desirable experience and is received with joy and acclamations. On the eighth day of the installation ceremonies Moses commands the priests and the laity to prepare a cultic ceremony, and at its close, he assures them, 'the Glory of the Lord will appear' (Lev. 9: 6).[1] At the conclusion of the ritual ceremony (9: 23), the Glory of God appears, and 'when the people saw it, *they shouted in exultation* (וירנו)[2] *and fell on their faces*.'[3] The reaction to the theophany here is rejoicing and prostration, whereas JE, when describing the people's reaction to the Sinaitic revelation, employs almost identical language to describe a far different response: 'And *the people were afraid*,[4] *and stood far off*' (Exod. 20: 18), and elsewhere 'and all the people who were in the camp trembled' (19: 16). The difference between the Priestly conception of the Deity and that of the early sources is not in the essence of the conception but in the response which the divine apparition evokes. The corporeal imagery of a somewhat mythologically tinged Deity that characterizes the earlier sources is carried over into the Priestly theology, but in a systematized and glorified version befitting learned priests of a speculative bent of mind.

The motif of the Divine Bow encountered in the Priestly stratum of the Pentateuch (Gen. 9: 13 ff.) also illustrates P's corporeal conception of the Deity. The bow that appears in the cloud according to Gen. 9 originally represents the bow with which the

[1] See above, p. 203.

[2] For similar rejoicing in connection with the appearance of God compare Job 38: 7: 'When the morning stars acclaimed together (ברן יחד) and all the sons of God shouted for joy.' The divine Assembly resounds with joy upon God's manifestation of his omnipotence by the act of creation. Cf. also Deut. 32: 43 (LXX and Q): 'Acclaim (הרנינו), O heavens, before him and ascribe might (והבו עוז) to him, O sons of God' (cf. Ps. 29: 1). For the reconstruction of the original text see F. M. Cross, *The Ancient Library of Qumran*, 1961, pp. 182–3.

[3] Ezekiel also prostrates himself upon the appearance of the Glory of God (Ezek. 1: 28), cf. also Gen. 17: 3; Num. 20: 6, both P.

[4] Read with LXX and Samaritan version: ויירא instead of וירא, compare v. 20: אל תיראו.

Deity wages his battles, and its placing in the cloud is a sign to denote the cessation of God's warlike hostilities against man. This portrayal of God as waging war against his 'enemies' with weapons in hand is encountered in earlier Biblical literature. In the Song of the Sea (Exod. 15: 3) he is described as 'a man of war', and in an ancient theophany in Habakkuk the bow and arrows are mentioned explicitly: 'Bare did You strip Your bow' (3: 9), and 'by the light of Your arrows they move' (3: 11).[1]

In Priestly literature, however, the bow motif, like the cloud and fire, has been transfigured. The bow of the Deity has become part of the complex which constitutes the Glory of God that appears in the cloud (cf. Ezekiel 1: 28).[2] The bow, which according to ancient sources serves as the Deity's weapon against his enemies, has in P been transformed into a covenant sign. It no longer symbolizes the martial prowess of the Deity, but constitutes on the contrary the sign of the cessation of God's warlike activities against man.

In contradiction to this corporeal representation of the 'Glory of God' Deuteronomy promulgates the doctrine of 'Yahweh's Name'.[3] The Deity cannot be likened to any form whatever, and he cannot therefore be conceived as dwelling in a temple. He has caused the temple to *be called by his name* or has *caused his name to dwell* therein, but he himself does not dwell in it.

The expression כבוד, when occurring in Deuteronomy, does not denote the being and substantiality of God as it does in the earlier sources but his splendour and greatness: 'Behold, the Lord our God has shown his *glory* (כבדו) and greatness' (Deut. 5: 24). That the *glory* and the greatness (גדל) referred to here denote abstract and not corporeal qualities may be gathered from the deuteronomic account of the Sinaitic revelation. In contrast to the account in Exod. 19 of God's descent upon Mt. Sinai (19: 11 and 20) we read in Deut. 4: 36: 'Out of heaven he let you hear his voice,[4] that he

[1] Cf. *Enuma Eliš* iv: 35 ff. (*ANET*[2], p. 66).

[2] Compare the brilliance (*melammu*) of the weapons of the Assyrian gods which is identical, in our view, with the refulgence of the Priestly Glory of God. See *Tarbiz* 37 (1968), 131–2. The verse in Job 29: 20: '*My glory* fresh with me and *my bow* ever new in my hand' may also indicate the correspondence between the two terms.

[3] See G. von Rad, *Studies*, pp. 37 ff. This was briefly noted before by G. E. Wright *BA* 7 (1944), 75 and F. M. Cross, *BA* 10 (1947), 62 f.

[4] Though Exod. 20: 22 expresses the same idea: 'You have seen (אתם ראיתם) that I have *talked* with you *from heaven*', the verse is not an original part of the

might discipline you; and on earth he let you see his great fire and you heard his words out of the midst of the fire.' In other words, the commandments were heard from out of the midst of the fire that was upon the mount, but they were uttered by the Deity from heaven. Deuteronomy has, furthermore, taken care to shift the centre of gravity of the theophany from the visual to the aural plane. In Exod. 19 the principal danger confronting the people was the likelihood that they might 'break through to the Lord to gaze' (v. 21); it was to prevent this that there was need to 'set bounds for the people round about' (v. 12) and to caution them not to ascend the mountain. Indeed, the pre-deuteronomic texts always invariably speak of the danger of *seeing* the Deity: 'For man shall not see me and live' (Exod. 33: 20) and similarly in Gen. 32: 31: 'For I have seen God face to face, and yet my life is preserved' (cf. Judg. 13: 22, Isa. 6: 5). The book of Deuteronomy, on the other hand, cannot conceive of the possibility of seeing the Divinity.[1] The

passage and appears to be a deuteronomic accretion. See Holzinger, *Exodus*, KHC, and Baentsch, *Exodus*, HKAT, ad loc. The verse may, on the other hand, possibly derive from the Elohist source which also opposed corporeal conceptions of the Deity and may thus have been the ideological precursor of Deuteronomy.

The Rabbinic exegetes also sensed the conflict between Exod. 19: 20 and 20: 22 and attempted to reconcile them in various ways. Thus, for example, in the Mekilta of Rabbi Ishmael: 'One passage says: "That I have talked with you from heaven" and another passage says: "And the Lord came down upon Mount Sinai." How can both passages be maintained? The matter is decided by the third passage: "Out of heaven he made thee to hear His voice, that he might instruct thee; and upon earth He made thee to see His great fire" (Deut. 4: 36). These are the words of R. Ishmael. R. Akiba says: "Scripture teaches us that the Holy One, blessed be He, lowered the upper heavens of heaven down to the top of the mountain and thus actually still spoke to them from the heavens." And thus it says "He bowed to the heavens also, and came down; and thick darkness was under his feet" '. (Ps. 18: 10) (translation according to J. Z. Lauterbach. *Mekilta de-Rabbi Ishmael* II, 275–6).

The controversy between Rabbi Ishmael and Rabbi Akiba seems to reflect two different approaches to revelation (see A. J. Heschel, תורה מן השמים באספקלריה של הדורות (vol. I, 1962; vol. II, 1965), with regard to our point cf. vol. II, p. 58) which in a certain measure overlap the approaches of JEP and D respectively.

[1] A similar tendency is also met with in Jeremiah and in Deutero-Isaiah which, as we have already observed, propagate the conceptions of the deuteronomic school. As opposed to First Isaiah and Ezekiel, whose messages involve a *visio dei*, an oracle, and the physical touch of the Deity (Isa. 6: 7; Ezek. 2: 8), the visual element is lacking in the account of Jeremiah's appointment, and both the visual and tactual elements are lacking in the appointment of Deutero-Isaiah. (For a discussion of the nature of the scene in Isa. 40: 1–6 see F. M. Cross, 'The Council of Yahweh in Second Isaiah', *JNES* 12 (1953), 274–7.)

Israelites saw only 'his great fire' which symbolizes his essence and qualities (4: 24: 'For the Lord your God is a devouring fire, a jealous God', cf. 9: 3), whereas God himself remains in his heavenly abode. The danger threatening the people here, and the greatness of the miracle, is that of *hearing the voice* of the Deity: 'Did any people ever hear the voice of a god speaking out of the midst of the fire as you have heard, and survived?' (4: 32; cf. 5: 23).[1]

This attempt to eliminate the inherent corporeality of the traditional imagery also finds expression in Deuteronomy's conception of the ark.

The specific and exclusive function of the ark, according to the book of Deuteronomy, is to house the tables of the covenant (10: 1–5); no mention is made of the ark cover (כפרת) and the cherubim which endow the ark with the semblance of a divine chariot or throne (compare Exod. 25: 10–22 = P).[2] The holiest vessel of the Israelite cult performs, in the deuteronomic view, nothing more than an educational function: it houses the tablets upon which the words of God are engraved, and at its side the Book of the Torah is laid from which one reads to the people so that they may learn to fear the Lord (Deut. 31: 26; cf. vv. 12 and 13). The ark does not serve as God's seat upon which he journeys forth to disperse his enemies (Num. 10: 33–6), but only as the vessel in which the tables of the covenant are deposited. This becomes quite clear when we compare Deut. 1: 42–3 with Num. 14: 42–4, a tradition on which the deuteronomic account is based. In Num. 14: 44 we read that after the sinful incident of the spies '*the ark of the covenant of the Lord* . . . departed not out of the camp' and that this was the reason for the Israelites' defeat in their subsequent battle with the Amalekites and Canaanites. The deuteronomic account, on the other hand, completely omits the detail of the ark and ascribes the Israelite defeat to the fact that God was not in their midst without referring to the whereabouts of the ark.

The author of Deuteronomy similarly relates that it was God who went before the people to seek out new resting places (1: 33), whereas the earlier source, upon which Deuteronomy was dependent, relates that it was the ark which journeyed forth before the people to seek out new resting places for them (Num. 10: 33).[3]

[1] Cf. above, p. 38 n. 1.
[2] Cf. above, p. 191.
[3] Cf. J. Morgenstern, 'The Book of the Covenant', *HUCA* 5 (1928), 26.

The absence of the ark is especially striking in the deuteronomic law of warfare (23: 15). One would expect a passage which speaks of the presence of the Divinity within the military encampment to make some mention of the ark which accompanied the warriors on their expeditions, as in 1 Sam. 4: 6–7, 'And when they learned that the ark of the Lord had come to the camp . . . they said, the gods have come into the camp.' The deuteronomic law, however, speaks of the Lord as moving about the camp but does not make the slightest allusion to the ark or the holy vessels.[1]

A similar conception is encountered in the book of Jeremiah, for instance at 3: 16–17, 'They shall say no more, "The ark of the covenant of the Lord". It shall not come to mind . . . At that time Jerusalem shall be called the throne of the Lord.' In other words, the ark of the covenant shall no longer serve as God's seat,[2] as the people were previously accustomed to believe[3] but all of Jerusalem shall be 'the seat of Yahweh', that is in a symbolic sense. In another passage the prophet declares: 'Do I not fill heaven and earth? says the Lord' (23: 24), recalling the words of Deutero- (or Trito-)[4] Isaiah when he expressly repudiates the notion of the sanctuary as the place of God's habitation: 'Heaven is my throne and the earth is my footstool, what is the house which you build for me? and what is the place of my rest?' (66: 1). This view is also met with in the deuteronomic prayer of Solomon: 'Behold, heaven and the highest heaven cannot contain thee; how much less this house which I have built' (1 Kgs. 8: 27). The sanctuary is here conceived as a house of prayer and not as a cultic centre.[5] This tendency to minimize the cult is—as we shall point out in the next chapter—already manifest in the book of Deuteronomy and signifies a religious turning-point which occurred following the abolition of the high places and the provincial sanctuaries.

[1] See S. D. Luzatto, Commentary, ad loc., who rightly indicates that 'and turn away from you' (ושב מאחריך) cannot refer to the ark but to God himself.

[2] Cf. O. Eissfeldt, *Einleitung in das A.T.*[3], 1964, p. 90 n. 3.

[3] Cf. above, p. 191.

[4] Cf. above, p. 42 n. 2.

[5] Ibid.

II

SACRAL AND FESTAL OBSERVANCES

1. SACRIFICE AND HOLY DONATIONS

THE first thing that strikes our attention when endeavouring to grasp the significance of sacrifice in the book of Deuteronomy is that we do not find sacrifice practised for its own sake. The Deity, in the deuteronomic view, has no need of the ריח ניחח 'pleasing odour'[1] of sacrifice, and so we find no mention of those sacrifices which are offered 'by fire to the Lord' and which in the Priestly document are deemed to be the 'food of God' לחם אלהים.[2] Neither is there any mention of the sin and guilt[3] offerings designed to atone for involuntary sins, ritual impurity, perjury, theft, and deception (Lev. 4–5). The author's view seems to be that spiritual purification and repentance—consisting of confession and prayer—and not sacrificial offerings expiate sin. The sole instance in which the book of Deuteronomy does mention a rite analogous in character to the sin and guilt offering[4] is in the law of unsolved murder (Deut. 21: 1–9). Yet interestingly enough it is precisely this law which reflects Deuteronomy's special attitude towards sacrifice. The rite conducted here does not consist of a sacrificial offering complete with ceremonial slaughter and blood sprinkling,[5] but calls only for the breaking of the heifer's neck in an uncultivated valley. The priests are present during this act,[6] not

[1] Cf. Gen. 8: 21; 1 Sam. 26: 19; and the various formulae in P.

[2] Lev. 3: 16; 21: 6, 8, 17, etc.; cf. the shewbread לחם הפנים in 1 Sam. 21: 7; Exod. 25: 30, etc.

[3] The sin and guilt offerings were not the innovations of P, cf. 2 Kgs. 12: 17; Mic. 6: 7 and the guilt offering in 1 Sam. 6: 3, 8, 17, cf. R. de Vaux, *Studies in Old Testament Sacrifice*, 1966, 104–5.

[4] For discussion see Dillmann, *Numeri, Deuter., und Josua*, KeH, 1886, ad loc.

[5] The omission of these cultic rites is not to be attributed to the fact that the ceremony is here executed outside the sanctuary grounds. Cf. P's ceremony of the red heifer (Num. 19), which also takes place outside the camp but is nevertheless executed in accordance with cultic procedure; it is ritually slaughtered, its blood is aspersed, its remains burnt, etc. Note also P and D's identical stipulation with regard to the selection of a heifer 'upon which a yoke has never come'.

[6] Verse 5 of this passage, which refers to the priests, the sons of Levi, does not appear to be an original part of the early tradition of the law but a later

because they play any part in the execution of the ritual, for this is carried out entirely by the elders, but merely to guarantee the religious aspect of the ceremony by presiding over it.[1] The entire act has only a symbolic value:[2] the heifer's neck is broken at the scene of the crime, as it were, and the elders cleanse their hands only as a purificatory expression of their innocence (cf. Pss. 24: 4; 26: 6, 10;[3] 73: 13, etc.). There is no *miasma* here which hovers over the city and which must be ceremonially removed. There is no laying of the hands on the heifer nor a transference of the sin to it as in the case of the ritual scapegoat (Lev. 16: 21), because its beheading as such[4] does not atone for the sin; expiation is effected only by the confession and prayer uttered at the close of the ceremony (vv. 7–8). In this rite, God[5] absolves the sin himself without recourse to any intermediary, whereas in P all expiatory sacrifices are executed by the priests, whose mediation alone effects the expiation of the sin (cf. the common Priestly expression in the book of Leviticus: וכפר עליו הכהן 'and the priest shall make atonement for him'). In the deuteronomic law atonement is possible only through the confession of the elders of the city, who, as representatives of the guilty city, beseech absolution through prayers; in P expiation is effected only through ritual sacrifice and incense burning, which are not accompanied by confession or prayer on the part of the penitent.

Deuteronomic sacrifice consists primarily of offerings which are consumed by the offerer in the sanctuary and are designed to be shared with the poor, the Levite, the alien resident, the orphan, and the widow. The constant emphasis on the obligation to share the sacrificial repast with indigent persons creates the impression that the principal purpose of the offering is to provide nutriment for the

incorporation of the editor. However, we are here mainly concerned with the views of the editor rather than with the nature of the material upon which he drew.

[1] See Driver, *Deuteronomy*, ICC, p. 243.

[2] The ceremony is apparently based on early magical-animistic practice (cf. Y. Kaufmann, *HIR* I, 569, and A. Roifer, 'The Breaking of the Heifer's Neck', *Tarbiz* 31 (1961), 119 ff. (Hebrew, with English summary)). In the present version to the law, however, the rite has been freed of its magical associations; cf. above, p. 32.

[3] On this verse see H. Schmidt, *Psalmen*, HAT, 1934.

[4] Cf. the beheading in the covenant ceremony of Aššurnirari V and Mati'ilu of Bit Agusi, quoted above, p. 103.

[5] Cf. C. Steuernagel, *Deuteronomium*, HKAT, 1900, p. 78, and G. von Rad, *Theologie des A.T.* I, p. 269.

destitute elements of Israelite society. The author of Deuteronomy alludes to this himself when, after prescribing that the joyful nature of the festival be shared with the *personae miserabiles*, he goes on to say: 'You shall remember that you were a slave in Egypt; and you shall be careful to observe these statutes' (16: 12). It is indeed remarkable that the very book which promulgates the law of centralized worship at the 'chosen place' has not so much as a word to say about the presentation of communal sacrifices (the daily and seasonal offerings) which constituted the principal mode of worship at this exclusive sanctuary.[1]

Sacrifice, according to Deuteronomy, is not an institutional practice but a personal one, which has two principal objects: (*a*) humanitarian—to share the sacrificial repast with the poor, as noted above; (*b*) a private—to fulfil a religious obligation and express one's gratitude to the Deity by means of votive offerings (12: 6, 11, 17, 26; 23: 22–4). God has no need of the sacrifice itself; it is only an expression of gratitude to the Deity, and this constitutes its entire significance.[2] We may perhaps note in passing that the expression 'to pay a vow' שלם נדר is not found in any book of the Pentateuch except Deuteronomy (23: 22).

The same attitude is revealed in the only passage in Deuteronomy (12: 27) that describes the manner in which the sacrifice is to be offered. The verse differentiates between non-burnt offerings זבח and burnt offerings עֹלָה, and ordains that the flesh and blood of the burnt offering be offered up entirely on the altar, whereas the blood of the non-burnt offering is to be poured upon the altar and the meat eaten. It is most surprising that the author makes no mention of the burning of the suet, the fat piece which is set aside for God and which thus renders the meat permissible for priestly and lay consumption (1 Sam. 2: 15–17). The blood and fat were deemed to be the food of God (cf. Ezek. 44: 7), which is why P forbids the eating of the fat, just as it forbids the 'eating' of blood

[1] The daily burnt offering (*tamid*) and its concomitant cereal offerings and libations (Num. 28: 1–8) were part of the temple ritual during the pre-exilic period and are clearly attested to in 2 Kgs. 16: 13–15. This passage conflicts with the Wellhausenian thesis that the daily offerings were introduced only in post-exilic times (*Prolegomena*, Meridian Library, p. 79).

[2] Biblical wisdom literature also refers only to votive offerings (cf. Prov. 7: 14; Job 22: 27; Eccles. 5: 3–4, etc.). He who makes a sacramental pledge thereby expresses his implicit faith in God, and to place one's trust in God is one of the basic teachings of wisdom literature (on the relationship between the book of Deuteronomy and wisdom ideology, see below, Part III).

(Lev. 7: 22–7). Yet the author of Deuteronomy not only fails to mention the interdiction concerning the eating of the suet, but completely ignores the fact that the suet was to be offered upon the altar, the very reason for which the sacrifice had to be offered at the sanctuary. Ritual detail, then, is of no importance to the author of Deuteronomy, and it is possible that he deliberately ignored it because it did not accord with his own religious frame of mind.

The book of Deuteronomy, therefore, holds the view that sacrifice is only of subordinate importance and that the essential requisite for atonement is the sincere intentions of the worshipper; sacrifice alone cannot expiate sin. The cultic ceremonies described in Deuteronomy are always accompanied by prayers[1] and thanksgiving, in contrast to the rituals described in P, which are conducted in complete silence.[2] Thus the ceremony for unsolved murder, as we have already observed, is accompanied by a confession and prayer for absolution, the ceremonial deposit of the firstfruits at the chosen place by a prayer of thanksgiving (26: 1–11), and the presentation of the tithes by a negative confession whereby the Israelite affirms that he has not been negligent in carrying out the prescribed ordinances (26: 12–15).

Sacrifice, however, is not the only rite to be conceived differently by the book of Deuteronomy, for all laws pertaining to cult and ritual are here conceived more rationally than in the earlier sources. This is particularly evident in the laws contained in chs. 12–19, laws which are a direct consequence of the implementation of cult centralization and form the legal basis of the religious reformation. These laws clearly mirror the change in religious beliefs and attitudes which occurred in the wake of the reform.

Ch. 12 promulgates the law of centralized worship at the chosen place, but alongside this law, or as a result of it, we find the authorization permitting non-sacrificial slaughter. Whereas before the reform all slaughter—except that of game animals—was deemed to be a sacral act and was prohibited even for non-sacrificial purposes unless the blood was sprinkled upon the altar (Lev. 17: 1–7; cf. 1 Sam. 14: 32–5), it was now permissible to perform non-sacrificial slaughter without being obliged to sprinkle the blood

[1] See above, pp. 32 f.
[2] Cf. Kaufmann, *HIR* II, 476.

upon an altar (Deut. 12: 15, 16, 20–4).[1] It need hardly be said that the sanctioning of profane slaughter freed a significant aspect of Israelite daily life from its ties to the cultus. The more crucial import of the law, however, is that by sanctioning non-sacrificial slaughter it repudiates the hallowed Israelite dogma which ascribed a sacral quality to the blood and prohibited one from pouring it upon the ground. According to the Priestly document or, to be more precise, the Holiness Code, the blood of slaughtered animals potentially valid for sacrifice must be sprinkled upon the altar, whereas the blood of game animals—which are invalid for sacrifice—must be covered with dust (Lev. 17: 13): for all spilt blood, even of fowl and beasts of prey, cries out for vengeance and satisfaction, and if the shedding of blood cannot be atoned by offering it upon the altar, then it must be covered up. Uncovered blood begs, as it were, for an avenger (Job. 16: 18, 'O earth, cover not my blood . . .'; cf. Isa. 26: 21; Ezek. 24: 7–8), a role which, in the case of homicide, is assumed by the Deity. The author of Deuteronomy, on the other hand, declares that the blood of all animals slaughtered for non-sacrificial purposes may be poured upon the ground[2] like water (12: 16 and 24), thereby asserting that blood has no more a sacral value than water has. He does, to be sure, retain the interdiction on the eating of blood (compare Deut. 12: 23 with Gen. 9: 4; Lev. 17: 11), but he absolutely repudiates the concept that the spilt blood of animals requires satisfaction.

The book of Deuteronomy also contains a less sacral conception of the tithes than the other Pentateuchal sources. The tithe, which the Priestly document designates as 'holy to the Lord' (Lev. 27: 30–3), and which according to a second tradition accrues to the Levites (Num. 18: 21–32), remains by deuteronomic legislation the property of the original owner (14: 22–7).[3] Furthermore, it

[1] The prevailing Wellhausenian view dating the composition of D before that of the Priestly document has not succeeded in elucidating the evolution of three major sacral laws: the prohibition of non-sacrificial slaughter in P after it was sanctioned in D; the nomadic features of the paschal rite in P after they were eliminated by D (see below, pp. 216–17); the tithe and the firstlings as accruing to the Levites and the Priests respectively after the deuteronomic legislation decreed that it be consumed by the offerer. The Graf–Kuenen–Wellhausen theory founders, then, on these controversial points, as was demonstrated by Y. Kaufmann, *HIR* I.

[2] Cf. 1 Sam. 14: 32: 'And . . . slew them on the ground' (וישחטו ארצה), an act which was regarded as a cultic sin (v. 33).

[3] Cf. my article 'tithe' in the *Encycl. Judaica.*

may be secularized and employed for profane purposes on payment of its equivalent monetary value (without the addition of the fifth-part required by P (cf. Lev. 27: 31)).[1] This provision seems to be yet another expression of the liberation of the cultus from its intimate ties to nature.[2] The sanctity of the tithe is not conceived as an inherent quality of the grain or animal, as in the Priestly document (Lev. 27: 30–3); for it is man who consecrates it and may, if he wishes, secularize it through redemption. In the deuteronomic view, sanctity is not a taboo that inheres in things which by nature belong to the divine realm but is rather a consequence of the religious intentions of the person who consecrates it.

The wording of the deuteronomic law of firstlings makes this conception particularly clear. The author of Deuteronomy instructs the Israelite to consecrate (תקדיש) the firstborn of his animals to the Lord (Deut. 15: 19), a command which openly contradicts the injunction in Lev. 27: 26: 'But a firstling of animals, which as a firstling belongs to the Lord, *no man may consecrate* (לא יקדיש), whether ox or sheep; it is the Lord's.'[3] According to the Priestly law the sanctity inheres in the animal by virtue of its birth (cf. 'which as a firstling belongs to the Lord' (אשר יְבֻכַּר ליהוה); it is not man who makes it holy. Thus Num. 18: 17 expressly forbids the redemption of the firstling of clean animals: 'But the firstling of cattle . . . you shall not redeem; they are holy.' Man can neither make the firstling holy nor secularize it by redemption. The author of Deuteronomy, in contrast, by ordaining that the owners consecrate their firstlings with the alternative of redemption if they find it too difficult to bring them to Jerusalem (14: 23 ff.),[4] shows that he does not recognize automatic sanctity but only sanctity which derives from the express will of the consecrant.

Like the tithe, the firstling is also taken from the possession of the priest and is restored to the owner. According to JE (Exod. 22: 29; 34: 19) and P (Num. 18: 15–17) the firstling is 'holy to Yahweh' whether it is given to the Lord (Exod. 22: 29) or presented to his servants (i.e. the priests, according to P, Num. 18: 17–18), while

[1] Cf. Kaufmann, *HIR* I, 149.

[2] Cf. G. von Rad, *Das Gottesvolk im Deuter.*, p. 30.

[3] I wish to thank Mr. M. Freundlich for calling my attention to this contradiction. For the Rabbinic attempt to resolve the conflict cf. Mishnah Arakhin viii: 7.

[4] Ibn Ezra has endeavoured to reconcile the Priestly and deuteronomic law by explaining the expression 'and you shall turn it into money' as referring to the tithe only, but the interpretation is obviously a harmonistic one.

according to Deuteronomy it remains in the possession of its original owner, although he is obliged to consume it at the chosen place. Indeed, it is the law of the firstlings which informs us of the author's negative attitude towards holy taboo. In the earlier laws the regulations pertaining to the redemption of the firstlings of clean animals are always accompanied by regulations concerning the firstborn of humans and the firstlings of unclean animals (Exod. 13: 2, 12–16; 22: 28–9; 34: 19–20; Lev. 27: 26–7; Num. 18: 15–18). The book of Deuteronomy, however, omits the laws of the human firstborn and the firstlings of unclean animals, because these regulations in no way advance its humanitarian purposes (the participation of the *personae miserabiles* in the consumption of the firstlings), and because they are based on mythical and magical conceptions which the author of Deuteronomy does not share.[1]

The severance of these laws from the realm of myth and magic finds its clearest expression in the Deuteronomic ordinances concerning the paschal sacrifice. According to the JE and P[2] documents

[1] For the primitive and magical conception underlying the consecration of the firstborn, cf. Ezek. 20: 26; Mic. 6: 7, etc. It seems that Deuteronomy ignores the law of the human firstborn because of the possible identification of this rite with the rite of the consecration of first sons to foreign gods (= מלך), which flourished in those days. The worship of the 'molech' was introduced apparently through Assyrian influence. Indeed, the first king who passed his son through fire was Ahaz (2 Kgs. 16: 3) who opened the door to Assyrian influence through his treaty with Tiglath-Pileser (2 Kgs. 16: 7). New light on the problem of Molech has been shed recently by K. Deller (*Orientalia*, 35 (1966), 382–6) who argues very convincingly that to 'burn the first son' (*aplu rabiu šarāpu*) in a few neo-Assyrian documents is not to be taken literally but means 'consecrating to the God-King Adad'. The consecration was done by the means of a ceremony in which burning spices had taken an important place. The ceremony was usually conducted outside the city in a place called *ḫamru*, a word associated with the weather god Adad. Compare 2 Kgs. 17: 30: 'and the men of Sepharvaim burned their children in the fire to Adadmelech'. (For the reading Adadmelech instead of Adramelech see W. F. Albright, *Archaeology and the Religion of Israel*[3], 1953, pp. 162–4, and Deller, art. cit.) It seems to me that the *tophet* in the outskirts of Jerusalem bore the character of the *ḫamru* and that the burning of sons there was none other than consecration to the foreign god—King Adad (= Baal). Cf. Fifth World Congress of Jewish Studies, vol. I, Jerusalem, 1969, 37 ff..

[2] Wellhausen could not ignore the fact that P, which he dated later than D, preserves the old Pesach celebrated at home and not 'before Yahweh'. He explained that this was a remnant of the old custom, which shows itself as a peculiar conception (*Prolegomena*, p. 100). This peculiarity exists, however, only if we accept Wellhausen's view that P is dependent on D and that it takes centralization of worship for granted. As a matter of fact, as Kaufmann has shown, the idea of centralization is never expressed in P, and therefore there is nothing strange about the Pesach in P, nor about the prohibition of profane slaughtering in Lev. 17 (see above, p. 213 n. 3). Both reflect the pre-deuteronomic reality. In

the paschal sacrifice is a domestic celebration accompanied by apotropaic rites of an animistic nature: the paschal blood is daubed upon the lintel and doorposts (Exod. 12: 7 (= P), 22 (= JE)), the animal must be roasted together with its head, legs, and inner parts (v. 9), it may not be removed from the house, no bone may be broken (v. 46), and a special dress is prescribed for the celebrants (v. 11). In the deuteronomic law, however, not the slightest reminiscence of these magical prescriptions has been preserved. The paschal ritual has instead been converted into a communal sacrifice which must be offered up at the central sanctuary like all other sacrifices. The paschal offering—which is the most ancient sacrifice in Israel's tradition and which apparently originates from tribes' former nomadic life[1]—succeeded in preserving its early primitive character until it was here divested of its original import and recast in a form more consistent with the spirit of the times. Even the earliest features of the sacrifice, such as the requirement that it be selected only from sheep or goats, or that it be roasted by fire—which attest to the nomadic origin of the ritual—have been completely obscured by the deuteronomic law. The new provision allows the Israelite to select the animal from cattle as well as sheep and goats (Deut. 16: 2) and permits it to be cooked like any other ordinary sacrifice (v. 7).

2. THE FEASTS

The paschal sacrifice was not the only festive rite which underwent a metamorphosis in the book of Deuteronomy, for all the festivals were altered and freed of their ties to the ancient sacral ceremonies. The feast of unleavened bread and the feast of weeks marked the season of the harvest and firstfruits during which the first yield of the fields was brought to the sanctuary. This season was not the occasion for spontaneous rejoicing without fixed religious forms—as Wellhausen assumed—but was, on the contrary, a time which called for the performance of complex sacral rites (cf. Hos. 9: 4–5). At the beginning of the harvest season every farmer was obliged to bring his first sheaf to the priest, together with a male lamb which was to be sacrificed as a burnt offering to the Lord

the post-exilic period the Pesach was indeed sacrificed according to the principle of D, i.e. in the central sanctuary, but was eaten in the homes in line with P. Thus laws of different origin were combined. See Y. Kaufmann, *HIR* I, 122–3.

[1] See R. de Vaux, *Studies in O.T. Sacrifice*, pp. 1–26.

(Lev. 23: 10–14). At the close of the season he was required to present two loaves of bread baked from new wheat and two male lambs which were 'holy to the Lord for the priest' (vv. 15–21).[1] By means of these gifts he secured blessing for his crops and sacral permission to enjoy them (v. 14). Failure to present these gifts to the sanctuary rendered the new grain ritually unclean, as it were, for consumption.

The feast of booths which marks the season of the ingathering of crops was also characterized by religious ceremonies consisting of festive processions adorned with fruits and decorative plants (Lev. 23: 40). These took place in neighbouring sanctuaries located at not too great a distance from the booths in which the celebrants resided during the seven-day period of the festival (v. 42).[2] This, indeed, was the season for merry celebration (*hillūlim*, Judg. 9: 27; cf. Lev. 19: 24) when the Israelites were wont to bring their vintage crops and wines to the house of God (cf. Isa. 62: 9). The booths were apparently set up in the vineyards (cf. Isa. 1: 8), where festal dances took place (Judg. 21: 19–22).

Such ceremonies were possible only in provincial sanctuaries situated in the neighbourhood of the fields and vineyards of the celebrants. It is hard to believe that the first of the harvest sheaves or the two loaves of bread were brought to the capital city from settlements some three, or more, days' journey distant. It is likewise absurd to assume that at the feast of booths the farmer was required to bring willows and decorative flora which might

[1] Verses 10–22 and 39–44 describe undoubtedly the provincial (= pre-deuteronomic) celebrations of the harvest and gathering festivals, a fact which is clearly indicated by בכל מושבותיכם in v. 21 (cf. Kaufmann, *HIR* I, p. 124, and see K. Elliger, *Leviticus*, HAT, 1966, p. 317: 'Aus der Bemerkung dass es *an all euren Wohnsitzen* so gehalten werden solle, darf man schliessen, dass die Vorlage noch nicht an Kultzentralization gedacht hat.'). Verses 18–19a may have been incorporated by a later priestly editor, cf. Num. 28: 27–30, but it is also possible that they are an organic part of the unit referring to the local communal offerings in this local sanctuary.

[2] Cf. Hos. 12: 10, 'I shall make you dwell in tents as in the days of the feast' עוד אושיבך באהלים כימי מועד. ימי מועד may also mean the days of Meeting in the desert, and it is even possible that Hosea alludes here to the tradition of the 'Tent of Meeting' in the desert (= אהל מועד). Indeed, Lev. 23: 43 connects the feast of the booths with the tents of the desert, and it is not impossible that Hosea also makes this connection. אהל 'tent' and סֻכָּה 'hut' are overlapping (cf. סכת דוד in Amos 9: 11 with אהל דוד in Isa. 16: 5) and Hosea therefore could refer to both the huts of the feast of ingathering and the tents of the Israelites in the desert.

easily wither during the journey from areas located at a considerable distance from the chosen city. Moreover, one would naturally imagine the booths situated in a rustic and agricultural setting able to provide the necessary materials for their construction, rather than in a metropolis. In post-exilic times an attempt was, indeed, made to observe the law of the booths in the one city of Jerusalem, but the practice of erecting them on housetops, in courtyards, and in the streets (Neh. 8: 16) is manifestly an artificial one. The ritual purpose of the four species of flora[1] was, by that time, also forgotten, and they were thought to be the materials prescribed for the construction of the booths (v. 15).[2]

The feast of booths enjoyed the distinction of being the festival *par excellence*[3] and, as it marked the end of the ingathering of the crops and the commencement of the new year,[4] it was celebrated with a special magnificence and a display of decorative plants and goodly fruits. The altar, it seems, was decked with ornamental flora (Ps. 118: 27; cf. Jubilees 16: 31)[5] as the celebrants chanted prayers for rain.[6]

The book of Deuteronomy, following the law of cult centralization, ignores all these rituals whose very implementation predicates the existence of provincial sanctuaries, and re-establishes the festivals on the exclusive basis of ceremonial rejoicing and votive offerings. It does not prescribe a sheaf-waving ceremony or the donation of loaves of bread and offerings of lambs, nor does it contain any allusion to the four species of flora or to the festal purpose of the booths, notwithstanding the odd fact that the very names of the festivals, *weeks* (שבעות) and *booths* (סכות), still retain a reminiscence of these rites. The author of Deuteronomy has, to be

[1] For post-exilic references to this rite see 2 Macc. 10: 6 ff. and Flavius Josephus, *Antiquities*, III. X. 4.

[2] See W. Rudolph, *Esra–Nehemia*, HAT, 1949, p. 151.

[3] The feast of booths was designated as 'the feast of Yahweh' (Lev. 23: 39, Num. 29: 12) or simply 'the feast' (1 Kgs. 8: 2, 65; 12: 32–3; Ezek. 45: 25; Mishnah, *Rosh Hashanah* i: 2, etc.).

[4] Cf. Exod. 23: 16, 'the feast of the ingathering at the end of the year' בצאת השנה; 34: 22, 'the feast of the ingatherings at the turn of the year' תקופת השנה; for discussion see P. Volz, *Das Neujahrsfest Jahves*, 1912, p. 34.

[5] Jubilees elucidates Lev. 23: 40 in this interesting manner: the boughs and willows are to serve as materials for the construction of the booths, whereas the palm branches and the fruits were to be used to adorn the altar.

[6] The willows are a botanical symbolization of water; cf. the Rabbinic tradition attesting to water-pouring ceremonies as one of the rituals of this festival (cf. Mishnah, *Sukkah* iv: 9).

sure, preserved the festivals themselves and their prescribed times of celebration, but he has stripped them of their original sacral content. For instance, he prescribes the counting of seven weeks between the start of the harvesting and the festival of weeks, as does the Priestly document (Lev. 23: 15–16). In P, however, the counting has a specific and express purpose: the seven weeks constitute the forty-nine-day period which must elapse from the time of the presentation of the first harvest stalks until the presentation of the new cereal offering (v. 16); a sacral calendrical reckoning must be observed (7×7; cf. similarly Lev. 25: 8–9)[1] so that the sacral offerings may be presented at the sanctuary at the ordained time. The book of Deuteronomy retained the custom of this seven-week counting, but the sacral exigencies for the reckoning, such as the sheaf-waving ceremony or the new cereal offering, no longer existed.[2] The same is true of the feast of booths. Here again it is only the name of the festival that has been preserved, but no mention is made either of the four species of flora or of the festal purpose of the booths.

By removing the sacral basis of the festivals, Deuteronomy has also divested them of their distinctive character. The feast of unleavened bread still retains some distinctiveness because of the paschal sacrifice, but the feast of weeks and the feast of booths have been generalized to such an extent that they are hardly distinguishable from each other. Both these festivals in Deuteronomy involve rejoicing at the chosen place and the presentation of votive offerings at the sanctuary, whereas in P the feast of booths is singled out for rejoicing, and the feast of weeks as the occasion for the presentation of the firstfruits.

This metamorphosis of the Israelite festivals was accompanied by a change in the manner in which the poorer members of society

[1] The Cappadocian *ḫamuštum* means five days (see *CAD* s.v.) or a fifth of a month, i.e. a week (*AHw*) and not fifty days as it used to be translated. Nothing can therefore be deduced from this Old Assyrian term in regard to our problem. See also R. de Vaux, *Ancient Israel*, p. 180.

[2] It may be argued that the seven weeks in the book of Deuteronomy mark the duration of the harvest period and that this was later adopted as the basis for P's sacral reckoning. The supposition, however, is a highly improbable one. The duration of the harvest is determined by natural factors such as the ripening of grain and the like, and cannot be forced *a priori* into a mathematically fixed period of forty-nine days. Sacral religious factors, then, must be responsible for the reckoning, but these factors are no longer predicated by the book of Deuteronomy.

were to participate. The gifts which must be given to the poor according to Lev. 23 are mentioned in the same context as the sheaf-waving and the firstfruits, that is in connection with the harvest season. 'And when you reap the harvest of your land, you shall not reap your field to its very border, nor shall you gather the gleanings after your harvest; you shall leave them for the poor and for the stranger' (Lev. 23: 22; cf. 19: 9).[1] In Deuteronomy, on the other hand, the law which prescribes gifts for the poor accompanies the ordinances concerning the feast of weeks and the feast of booths. The nature of these charitable provisions has also been altered. In P the gifts given to the poor and the stranger consist of *naturalia*, i.e. crop leftovers and gleanings, whereas in Deuteronomy the charitable provisions are no longer dictated by the agrarian scene but are left free to be determined by the benefactor himself; in practice they generally took the form of direct participation in the festal repast held in the chosen city (16: 11 and 14; cf. 12: 12 and 18).

The character of the sacral donations was also altered in accordance with the new circumstances. In Lev. 23 these gifts have a fixed composition. At the start of the harvest ('on the morrow of the Sabbath') the farmer must bring the first stalks of his reaping to the priest and offer up a male lamb to the Lord, and at the end of the season (on the fiftieth day) he must bring two loaves of bread and two male lambs. Deuteronomy, on the other hand, ordains that each celebrant should bring whatever offering his means allow (16: 10 and 17) and in whatever form he sees fit. The law of the firstfruits, which was always intimately connected with this festival,[2] is thus in Deuteronomy completely severed from its festal associations and converted into an expression of thanksgiving whose composition and time of execution is left entirely to the discretion of the farmer (26: 1–11).[3]

[1] For the different types of indigent persons referred to in the two sources (i.e. the poor and the resident alien in P and the Levite, the resident alien, the orphan, and the widow in D) see above, p. 55 n. 1.

[2] According to the Book of the Covenant the harvest festival is also the festival of the firstfruits (Exod. 23: 16, 19; 34: 22, 26), which apparently were brought to the sanctuary during the feast of weeks, and not during the feast of unleavened bread, as H. Kosmala contends ('The So-Called Ritual Decalogue', *Annual of the Swedish Theological Institute* 1 (1962), 38 ff.). On the other hand, I accept his over-all assertion that Exod. 23: 18–19 and its counterpart in Exod. 34 reflect earlier festal ordinances.

[3] According to Mishnah Bikhurim i: 3, 6 the firstfruits could be offered during the whole summer, i.e. from the feast of weeks onwards.

The book of Deuteronomy also contains a divergent conception of the Sabbath. According to P (Gen. 2: 1–3; Exod. 31: 17) and the Decalogue in Exod. 20: 8–11, the rationale for the Sabbath is that God worked six days in creating the world and rested on the seventh. That is to say, that man, by his Sabbath rest, re-enacts, so to speak, God's rest on the seventh day of Creation—a point of view appropriate to the priestly circle, which, by means of its ritual in the sanctuary, re-enacts what takes place in the divine sphere. The author of Deuteronomy rejects this mythological rationale and replaces it with a social one: 'so that your manservant and your maidservant may rest as well as you' (Deut. 5: 14). The stress is thus shifted from cause to purpose (cf. למען): the purpose of the Sabbath is, to be sure, that man shall rest, but not because God himself rested on this day. The notion that God labours and rests was contrary to the view of this book and to its fundamental conception of the Divinity[1] and therefore had to be rejected by the author as the rationale of the Sabbath. Instead of relating the Sabbath to the mythological event of creation, the book of Deuteronomy associates its origin with an historical event: 'You shall remember that you were a servant in the land of Egypt . . . therefore the Lord your God commanded you to keep the Sabbath day' (5: 15). Thus in Deuteronomy the Sabbath recalls an historical occurrence whereas in P it commemorates a sacral one. It is not accidental that D has reformulated the exhortation: 'Remember (זכור) the Sabbath day' to read: 'Observe (שמור) the Sabbath day'. The earlier formulation bears sacral implications[2] (cf. 'remembrance' זכרון in P): by 'remembering' the Sabbath one redramatizes, as it were, the act of creation. But the deuteronomic 'observe' signifies no more than what its natural sense implies.

It is possible that the social motivation existed alongside the sacral and that they were both able to coexist. It is a fact that the Sabbath is given a social motivation in Exod. 23: 12. There is, however, significance in the fact that the author of P selected specifically the sacral reason and developed it in his own way while the book of Deuteronomy chose the social motivation and formulated it in its own unique way, that is, humanistically.

[1] See above, Chapter I, and my article in *Tarbiz* 37 (1968), 105–32.

[2] Cf. P. A. H. de Boer, *Gedenken und Gedächtnis in der Welt des Alten Testaments*, 1962, pp. 38 ff.; B. S. Childs, *Memory and Tradition in Israel*, 1962, pp. 55 and 66 ff.; W. Schottroff, '*Gedenken*' *im Alten Orient und im Alten Testament*², 1967, pp. 313 ff.

The law of the sabbatical year is also conceived in a unique manner in Deuteronomy. According to the Priestly document, in the seventh year 'the land shall observe a Sabbath to the Lord' (Lev. 25: 2), that is, it must remain fallow, as stipulated by the book of the Covenant (Exod. 23: 10–11), which prescribes that the land be abandoned and left uncultivated during the seventh year.[1] Before it can reabsorb the exiled Israelites the land must run its full course of the sabbatical years during which the Israelites did not permit it to rest (Lev. 26: 34–5).[2] The sabbatical year is, therefore, a taboo year, a year in which all agricultural work must cease.

This is not the case in Deuteronomy. It is not the 'release of land' that the deuteronomic law speaks of, but the 'release of debts'. The sabbatical year in Deuteronomy has only a social significance: 'so that there be not among you a poor man' (15: 4). The Priestly Code, however, even though it contains regulations about matters pertaining to loans,[3] seems to be entirely unacquainted with the law of the cancellation of debts. It appears, therefore, that Deuteronomy, by regarding the primary function of the sabbatical year as the cancellation of debts and by ignoring the provision for land release, has divested the law of what, according to pre-deuteronomic sources, was its original import.[4]

[1] There is a certain line of development from the Covenant Code to P. According to Exod. 23: 11, the owner of the field has no right at all to enjoy the fruits of his land in the Sabbatical year. For the owner, the land is a complete taboo, only the poor people may eat from the production; what is left is to be devoured by the animals but not to be touched by the owner. In Lev. 25, on the other hand, the product of the seventh year becomes ownerless property, which everybody may enjoy: the poor men, the animals, as well as the owner (v. 6). The two codes also differ with respect to the objects of the Sabbatical restrictions. According to Exod. 23: 11 the *shemittah* refers to fields, vineyards, and to olive-groves alike, while the P version limits the *shemittah* to grain and wine and omits mention of olives. The fact that the ancient law does not permit the owner to enjoy the fruit of his land even in the case when there are no poor men to avail themselves of it indicates that the provenance of the law of release of land is to be seen in the sacral domain rather than in the social one.

[2] Exile and desolation of lands were not invented by the neo-Assyrian empire but go back to the beginning of civilization. (Cf., e.g., the famous 'Lamentation over the destruction of Ur'. See S. N. Kramer, *The Sumerians*, 1963, pp. 142 f.) Nothing in the verse quoted supports the view that it reflects the time of the Exile of Judah.

[3] Lev. 25 is very much concerned with the commercial and financial implications of the sabbatical year and the Jubilee, and if the P author had presupposed remission of debts, he certainly would have included it in his law. See Y. Kaufmann, *HIR* I, 64.

[4] The original law of the sabbatical year consists of one succinct verse: 'At

It must be pointed out that as far as actual practice is concerned the two laws are not mutually exclusive: it is quite likely that both were observed or, at any rate, that both were regarded as obligatory and that there was some connection between them. But what is important for us is the way in which the two laws are taken in the sources under discussion. The Priestly author is interested only in the sacral aspect of the seventh year, while the author of Deuteronomy is interested solely in its social aspect and completely ignores the sacral side.

the end of every seven years you shall grant a release' (15: 1): the subsequent verses (2–11) introduced by 'and this is the manner of the release' constitute a reinterpretation in accordance with the author's social tendency. Release of debts itself cannot be a late institution (cf. the edict of Ammiṣaduqa in the Old Babylonian period, F. R. Kraus, *Edikt*, 1958, and J. J. Finkelstein, *JCS* 15 (1961), 101 ff.) but seeing that (rather than the release of the land) as the essential purpose of the Sabbatical year is an innovation of the deuteronomic Code.

III

PURITY AND IMPURITY IN THE DEUTERONOMIC CONCEPTION OF HOLINESS

IMPURITY, in the Priestly document, has a markedly ritual character and belongs to a realm that is essentially demonic in nature. Holiness prevails only within the camp, at the centre of which stands the tabernacle, whereas impurity lies 'outside the camp', where satyrs and demons abound. It is in the open field that one sacrifices to satyrs (Lev. 17: 5–7); it is to the wilderness that lies outside the bounds of human settlement that one dispatches the scapegoat bearing the sins and impurities of Israel (16: 10 and 22);[1] it is 'out of the city and into the open field' that one releases the lustral bird during the ceremony of the leper and the 'leprous house' (14: 7 and 53); and lepers, gonorrheics, and persons defiled by a corpse are all sent outside the camp (Num. 5: 1–4). P's over-all conception is that impurity is a kind of a palpable substance that spreads from object to object by physical contact. It can, moreover, even be transmitted to the land itself, for according to the Priestly conception *blood pollutes and defiles the land.* This conception becomes particularly evident when one contrasts the deuteronomic law of asylum with its legal analogue in Num. 35. The law in the book of Numbers closes with the exhortation (vv. 33–4) not to permit spilt blood to pollute and defile the *land*, whereas the deuteronomic law concludes with the warning not to allow innocent blood to be shed in the land lest the bloodguilt fall upon the *people* (19: 10).[2] A comparison between Deut. 21 and Num. 35 seems to reflect the same conception. Deut. 21: 8 reads: 'Forgive

[1] See Y. Kaufmann, *HIR* I, 543.

[2] We may, consequently, reject Bentzen's view (*Die Josianische Reform und ihre Voraussetzungen*, 1926, p. 56) that the exhortations against the spilling of innocent blood are of magical-ritual nature and belong to the area of purity and impurity. A distinction must be made between *innocent* blood and *pure* blood, a distinction which the German language is inherently incapable of making because it renders the Hebrew terms נקי and טהור by the same word: *rein.* It is possible that the linguistic inexactitude was the cause of this misunderstanding.

your people Israel', whereas in Num. 35: 33 we read: 'And *the land* can have no expiation'.

The book of Deuteronomy conceives impurity as an 'abomination' (תועבה), a repugnant and odious condition which a holy and noble people ought to avoid. The 'abomination' belongs to that category of things which the delicate find odious and abhorrent, which is why we find injunctions against such disparate practices as self-mutilation, head-shaving as a sign of mourning, and the eating of unclean animals or the remains of animals that died naturally (נבלה), all grouped together in one section (Deut. 14). The section opens and closes with the same statement: 'For you are a holy people to the Lord your God', that is to say, as a holy and noble people you must abstain from such repugnant practices. The deuteronomic notion of holiness does indeed seem to have more of a national than a cultic aspect. Holiness in Deuteronomy is a condition that derives from the relationship existing between the people of Israel and God.[1] Israel is holy because God has chosen and set Israel apart from all other nations: 'For you are a people holy to the Lord your God and the Lord has chosen you to be a people for his own possession[2] out of all the peoples that are on the face of the earth' (Deut. 14: 2). This rationale of Israel's holiness occurs twice in the book of Deuteronomy, each time in connection with the practices of foreign peoples unbecoming to the noble people of Israel (14: 2 and 21; 7: 6).

Holiness in the Priestly view is a condition that can be secured only by constant physical purification and sanctification, whereas in Deuteronomy it is the effect of a unique act of God—the divine election of Israel—and thus devolves automatically upon every

[1] Cf. H. Breit, *Die Predigt des Deuter.*, 1933, pp. 36–48.

[2] For the meaning of סגלה and its Akkadian equivalent *sikiltum* see M. Greenberg, *JAOS* 71 (1951), 172 ff. Cf. now *PRU* V, no. 60: 7, 12, where the Ugaritic vassal is called the *sglt* of his sovereign, which is rendered by C. Virolleaud as *propriété*. The *sglt* in the Ugaritic text elucidates now the סגלה in the Pentateuch. It seems that *sglt* and סגלה belong to the treaty and covenant terminology and that they are employed to distinguish a special relationship of the sovereign to one of his vassals. On the basis of the Ugaritic, Biblical, and also Alalaḫian evidence (cf. the seal impression in D. J. Wiseman, *Alalaḫ*, pl. iii, where the king is said to be the *sikiltum* of a goddess) we may be right in saying that the basic meaning of the root *sakālu* is to set aside a thing or certain property either with good intention (as Israel is set aside from all the other nations) or with an evil purpose as in the Hammurabi Code § 141 and in other Babylonian sources. See the discussion of M. Held in *JCS* 15 (1961), 11–12. For the Ugaritic text compare H. B. Huffmon–Parker, *BASOR* 184 (1966), 36 f. See also above, p. 69 n. 1.

Israelite, who consequently must not profane it by defilement. The Priestly document conceives holiness to be contingent upon physical proximity to the divine presence and the preservation of that proximity through ritual means. The priests are charged with observing particular regulations because of their physical closeness to the Deity and the divine abode. Thus, according to the Holiness Code, only the priests are forbidden to eat *nebelah* (Lev. 22: 8; cf. Ezek. 44: 31), whereas lay Israelites may eat it provided that they undergo ritual purification afterwards (Lev. 11: 39–40; cf. 17: 15).[1] Deuteronomy, on the other hand, makes no distinction between priests and laity in matters concerning holiness and therefore forbids *all* Israelites to eat *nebelah*. The reason for this divergency between the laws is that the Priestly document regards the priests as an essential part of the sanctuary or the divine sphere, who therefore must possess a greater degree of holiness than the lay Israelites and must accordingly be treated as holy persons (Lev. 21: 8). Deuteronomy, on the other hand, regards *all* the people of Israel as holy,[2] not by reason of their physical proximity to the tangible sanctity of the Deity but by virtue of their election by God.

One may even discern a polemic note in the book of Deuteronomy directed against the Priestly view. There is doubtless some significance in the fact that the rationale of 'a holy *people*' appears particularly in a context that deals with self-mutilation and the eating of *nebelah* (14: 1–2 and 21), transgressions which P and H stress especially in connection with the priests. The author of Deuteronomy surely wished to emphasize that these practices, previously forbidden only to priests because of their special degree of holiness, were henceforth prohibited to the entire people, since they were *all* 'holy'. It is not accidental, then, that the concept of a

[1] Cf. Lev. 7: 24, which warns against eating the suet of the *nebelah*; from this we may infer that the *nebelah* itself was not forbidden to lay Israelites.

[2] Exod. 19: 5–6 also speaks of Israel as a סגלה, 'a kingdom of priests and a holy nation' but the connotation there is quite different. The idea of election there does not serve as a motivation for keeping the obligations, as in Deuteronomy, but as a reward for being faithful to the covenant. As a reward for her loyalty Israel will in turn be God's most precious possession: she will be God's priesthood. Cf. Isa. 61: 6: 'And you shall be called the priests of Yahweh. You will be named servants of our God, you shall eat the wealth of the nations, and in their splendour you shall excel.' Cf. R. B. Y. Scott, *OTS* 8 (1950), 213–15. For a recent thorough discussion of this passage see W. L. Moran, 'A Kingdom of Priests', *The Bible in current Catholic thought*, 1962 (ed. J. McKenzie), pp. 7–20.

'holy *people*' that predominates in the theological system of Deuteronomy is completely absent in earlier Biblical sources. JE and P speak of 'holy men' (Exod. 22: 30) and of 'being holy' (Lev. 19: 2; 20: 7), but not of a 'holy people' עם קדוש.[1] The difference is not merely one of phraseology, it is also one of ideological import. When the non-deuteronomic sources speak of holy men or of being holy they mostly refer to a state of holiness that is achieved by observing purity. Thus we encounter in these sources such expressions as: 'And you *shall be* holy men unto Me ואנשי קדש תהיון לי: you must not eat flesh torn by beasts'; 'Sanctify yourselves and *be* you holy' והתקדשתם והייתם קדושים; 'You *shall be* holy' קדושים תהיו, that is to say, your holiness is dependent upon your observance of purity. Purity according to the book of Deuteronomy, however, is not the prerequisite of holiness, but rather an obligation which holiness imposes upon the Israelite: 'you shall not cut yourselves . . . you shall not eat anything that dies of itself *because you are* a holy people' (by divine election) כי עם קדוש אתה.[2]

An echo of this controversy concerning the scope of Israelite holiness may be found in the Priestly narrative of Korah's rebellion. Korah and his adherents demand an equal status for priests and Levites alike, a status which the book of Deuteronomy takes for granted (cf. the deuteronomic expression 'the Levitical priests' and Deut. 18: 6–8). Korah's contention, which is similar to that of the author of Deuteronomy, is that all the members of the Israelite congregation are equally holy (Num. 14: 3). Moses, on the other hand, claims that there exists an hierarchic system of holiness and asserts that the next day's ceremony of incense burning before the Lord will prove just whom the Lord has *chosen to be holy* (v. 7). Indeed, the verb בחר is employed by P only when speaking of priests; when referring to Levites and lay Israelites it only uses the verb הבדל (Num. 8: 14: 16: 9; Lev. 20: 26).

As opposed to the deuteronomic concept of the 'holiness of the people', P promulgates the concept of the 'holiness of the land'.

[1] Exod. 19: 6 speaks about גוי קדוש and not about עם קדוש—a fact which is not without significance. גוי וממלכה (so in Exod. 19 ממלכת כהנים וגוי קדוש) denote a large national conglomerate, united by royal government, whereas עם denotes a body of persons related by blood, cf. E. A. Speiser, 'People and Nation of Israel', *JBL* 79 (1960), 157–63. Besides, as we have shown in the previous note, the notion of a holy nation in Exodus has a quite different meaning. Compare W. L. Moran, op. cit., pp. 13, 17 n. 59.

[2] For further discussion compare my article in the 'Proceedings' of the *American Academy for Jewish Research*, 1969, 133 ff.

According to P, the western side of the Jordan is the land in which God's tabernacle dwells (Josh. 22: 19),[1] and consequently all the inhabitants of the land,[2] without distinction of status or ethnic affiliations, are subject to the sacral code.[3] The resident alien and the native Israelite alike are all required to observe the regulations of the Law, because it is a person's residence in the land that subjects him to its cultic ordinances. Residence in the land is deemed to be an automatic recognition of the god of the country on the part of the resident and thus also entails the obligation to worship him (cf. 2 Kgs. 17); conversely an Israelite who resides outside the land of Yahweh is deemed to dwell in an unclean land and be the worshipper of foreign gods (1 Sam. 26: 19; and cf. Josh. 22: 16–19 = P).[4] The resident alien and the native Israelite, therefore, both draw their sustenance from a common sacral source and both are consequently required to observe the code of holiness that it entails.

This is not the view of the book of Deuteronomy. According to Deuteronomy, the laws of the Torah apply only to the true Israelites, that is, members of the Israelite nation by blood and race,[5] whereas the resident alien is not deemed to be a true Israelite and is consequently not required to observe the sacral laws of the congregation even though he be willing to subject himself to them. Although he enjoys the full protection and the same political

[1] The land that was divided by lots before the Lord (Num. 34; Josh. 14: 1–5; 18: 1–10; 19: 49–51) comprises only Western Palestine. Ezekiel similarly includes only Western Palestine in his land-division programme (chs. 40–8).

[2] The Priestly phrase 'in all your dwellings' בכל מושבותיכם, which denotes the territorial bounds of the law's application, has a much wider meaning than the deuteronomic expression 'in your gates' בשעריכם which refers only to Israelite cities. P wishes to secure the observation of the law throughout all the inhabited areas of the land, while Deuteronomy is only concerned with the Israelite city.

[3] To a lesser extent, to be sure, than the priests whose duties brought them into the sacral presence of the Deity. This view accords with the concept of 'concentric circles' found in P. The lay Israelites are situated in the outer ring of the cities and their holiness is consequently of an inferior nature.

[4] Cf. Y. Kaufmann, *HIR* I, 619. This is one of the deep-rooted views of the ancient Israelite religion (cf. Hos. 9: 3; Amos 7: 17).

[5] The social polarity in Deuteronomy is גר–אח, whereas in P it is גר–אזרח. What distinctly characterizes the Israelite in P, therefore, is his ties to the land (cf. the expression אזרח הארץ, Exod. 12: 19 and 48; Num. 9: 14; for the meaning of the word אזרח cf. Ps. 37: 35: 'And spreading himself like a luxuriant tree in its native soil' (כאזרח רענן). In the book of Deuteronomy, on the other hand, the term אזרח is supplanted by the term אח which denotes mainly the consanguineous relationship.

and economic rights that all Israelites enjoy, he is still not a true Israelite and thus need not assume the special sacral obligations imposed upon the 'holy people'.

This distinction in Deuteronomy between the Israelite and the resident alien in all matters pertaining to religious obligations is evident in the rules concerning the eating of the *nebelah*. In Deut. 14: 21 we read: 'You shall not eat anything that dies of itself (נבלה): you may give it to the alien (גר) who is within your towns, that he may eat it, or you may sell it to a foreigner; for you are a people holy to the Lord your God . . .' The Holiness Code (Lev. 17: 15), on the other hand, ordains 'and every person that eats what dies of itself . . . whether he is a native or a alien (גר), shall wash his clothes, and bathe himself in water . . .'. The two passages thus stand in open contradiction to each other, and the source of the contradiction is to be found in the divergent viewpoints of the two documents. P is concerned only with the ritual problem of impurity involved: all who eat *nebelah*, whether Israelite or resident alien (גר), carry impurity upon them, and the land is unable to bear impurity, no matter who the carriers of the impurity may be (cf. 'lest the *land* vomit you out, when you defile it', Lev. 18: 25, 28). But Deuteronomy regards the prohibition only as a *noblesse oblige*. Israel must abstain from eating *nebelah* because it is an act unbecoming to a holy people, and not because it causes impurity from which one must purge oneself by ritual bathing (Lev. 11: 40; 17: 15). Therefore it does not impose this noble obligation upon those who are not of the holy people.

It is commonly asserted[1] that the *ger* in P, being subject to the the same laws as the Israelite, has a status similar to the one held by the proselytes during the post-exilic period. This view, however, is without foundation. The Priestly document imposes upon the *ger* only those obligations which affect the sanctity and purity of the congregation, such as regulations concerning sacrificial procedure (Lev. 17: 8, 10, 12, 13),[2] the prohibition of eating leaven, whose presence was forbidden in Israelite territory during the Matzoth festival (Exod. 12: 19), regulations concerning defilement by a corpse (Num. 19: 11), the impurity of incest, the impurity of *nebelah*

[1] See especially A. Bertholet, *Die Stellung der Israeliten und der Juden zu den Fremden*, 1896.

[2] In contrast to profane slaughter which is prohibited only to Israelites (Lev. 17: 2–7).

and Molech worship (Lev. 18: 26; 20: 2), the impurity of spilt blood (Num. 35: 15 and 34), blasphemy (Lev. 24: 16; Num. 15: 30), and regulations concerning abstinence on the Day of Atonement (Lev. 16: 29)—the day on which the sanctuary and the congregation, among whom God dwells, must be purged of all impurity (Lev. 16: 16 and 19; cf. Exod. 30: 10).[1] It does not require the *ger* to observe the regulations and ceremonies which are part of Israel's special religious heritage and which do not particularly involve ritual purity. For example, such 'covenant signs' of the Priestly document as the Sabbath and circumcision (Exod. 31: 16–17; Gen. 17: 10–11), the non-observance of which entails the *kareth* penalty (Exod. 31: 14; Gen. 17: 14), are not binding upon the *ger*. The latter must submit to circumcision only if he chooses to observe the paschal ritual, that is, if he wishes to take part in the distinctively Israelite ceremony (Exod. 12: 48; cf. Num. 9: 14); If he does not wish to do so he may remain uncircumcised. This implies that he is under no obligation to perform the paschal ritual, whereas the Israelite who fails to do so incurs the penalty of *kareth* (Num. 9: 13).

With respect to the festival of booths the law explicitly reads: 'All that are native (כל האזרח) in Israel shall dwell in booths' (Lev. 23: 42), from which we may infer that the law does not apply to the resident alien. Bertholet's[2] contention that the *ger* was accidentally omitted from the law is groundless. Whenever the Priestly law applies to both the native Israelite and the resident alien we find that they are coupled together in such formulations as: 'the native or the alien who sojourns among you' (Lev. 16: 29; 18: 26); 'for you and for the alien who sojourns with you' (Num. 15: 16); 'of the children of Israel and the aliens that sojourn in Israel' (Lev. 20: 2), etc. We should have to assume, therefore, that an entire clause was accidentally omitted, which is highly improbable. The real explanation for freeing the *ger* from dwelling in booths is that this is not a ritual regulation concerned with the purity or impurity of the land, but constitutes like the Sabbath, circumcision, and Pesach, a special duty commemorating events from Israel's special heritage. That this is so is evident from the rationale which follows the commandment of dwelling in booths: 'so that your descendants may

[1] The Day of Atonement, according to P, is distinctly a sanctuary festival (cf. Y. Kaufmann, *HIR* I, 217–18). Cf. above, p. 180 note.

[2] Ibid., p. 172.

know that I made the Israelites live in booths when I brought them out of the land of Egypt' (Lev. 23: 43). In view of the fact that such fundamental Israelite precepts as the Sabbath, circumcision, the paschal sacrifice, and the *sukkoth* celebrations do not apply to the resident alien, we must conclude that the regulations which the Priestly Code imposes upon him are not to be taken as a sign of his complete assimilation into the Israelite congregation.

The difference between the Priestly and deuteronomic attitudes toward the *ger* is not, then, a result of historical development, as is generally believed, but one of definition of status. The author of the Priestly Code, to whom sacral-ritual matters are of primary importance, is concerned with preserving the sanctity and purity of the congregation inhabiting the *holy land* and therefore takes steps to ensure that this sanctity be not profaned by the *ger*. The author of Deuteronomy, on the other hand, who is free of such sacral conceptions or indifferent to them, does not impose upon the *ger* the obligation of holiness, which is peculiar to the *people of Israel*.

IV

SECULAR TRENDS IN DEUTERONOMY

A SINGLE central sanctuary could not have performed all the functions originally discharged by the local sanctuaries; it is not surprising, therefore, that on the abolition of the provincial sanctuaries many institutions and practices were divorced from their original ties to the sanctuary in a manner that rendered them completely secular. The Book of the Covenant, for example, prescribes that the ear of the slave who refuses manumission be pierced at the house of God: 'Then his master shall bring him to God, he shall be brought to door . . .' (Exod. 21: 6).[1] The author of Deuteronomy, however, who predicates the existence of one exclusive sanctuary, deletes this detail of bringing the slave to God from his own slave law (though it is based on that in the Book of the Covenant) and thereby transforms the act into a purely secular one (Deut. 15: 17).

The secular aspect of the judicial function in Deuteronomy becomes especially clear when one compares Exod. 18: 19 with Deut. 1: 17. According to the former source, major disputes have to be brought to Moses, who brings them before God for final decision. In the latter the detail about the disputes being brought before God was omitted by Moses.[2]

1. THE JUDICIAL REFORM

The centralization of the cultus in one exclusive sanctuary necessarily brought judicial reforms in its wake. Before the religious reform the provincial sanctuaries also performed judicial functions. Civil or family suits which could not be settled by the elders because of the lack of witnesses or evidence were generally submitted to sacral jurisdiction, which decided them by the administration

[1] Legal transactions in Mesopotamia were also carried out at the gate of the temple, see *CAD* vol. 2 (B) *bābu*, p. 19, 4′.

[2] Cf. BT Sanhedrin 8*a* where it says (R. Josiah) that Moses was punished because of this: the law escaped his memory when the daughters of Zelophehad presented their case (Num. 27: 5).

of oaths (Exod. 22: 7, 10), sacral lot-casting (Exod. 22: 8; 28: 30; 1 Sam. 2: 25; Prov. 16: 33)[1] or trial by ordeal (Num. 5: 11 ff.). The abolition of the sacral courts created a judicial vacuum in the provincial cities, and the law providing for the appointment of state judges in every city was apparently designed to fill it (Deut. 16: 18–20). Guilt and innocence were no longer established through sacral media[2] but by human magistrates (cf. Deut. 25: 1 with Exod. 22: 8b). Thus the deuteronomic code refers all cases requiring a clear-cut verdict (such as the establishment of guilt or innocence, 25: 1–3; 19: 18) to the adjudication of the magistrates (שפטים), leaving only patriarchal and family litigation to be decided by the elders (זקנים) (19: 12; 21: 19–20; 22: 15 ff.; 25: 8–9). The elders functioned together with the magistrates only in instances when the crime affected the clan, the family, and the central authorities alike. A case of this type is met with in the law of unsolved murder (21: 1–9). The magistrates present at the ceremony of the heifer's beheading are the representatives of the state central authorities. Their task is to prevent overt friction between the two neighbouring cities and to guard against any discriminatory attempt to fix the responsibility on the wrong city—an eventuality which they seek to avert by personally supervising the precise measurement of the area surrounding the scene of the crime (v. 2). While the elders are responsible to the victim and his family, that is, their responsibility is to secure satisfactory compensation for the family of the deceased, the magistrates are state functionaries responsible for securing and maintaining proper judicial order throughout the land.

Though the institution of appointed magistrates and clerical officers had undoubtedly existed before the Josianic reforms, it came into full operative force only as a result of those reforms. It is by no means accidental, then, that this institution is heard of so frequently, particularly in the book of Deuteronomy and in the historical works inspired by it.[3]

[1] See B. Gemser, *Sprüche Salomos*², 1963, ad loc.

[2] Cf., e.g., the parallel accounts of the destruction of the golden calf in Exod. 32: 20 and Deut. 9: 21. Whereas the earlier narrative relates that Moses caused the Israelites to drink of the water in which he threw the dust of the idol, by which he undoubtedly meant to identify the sinners through trial by ordeal, the author of Deuteronomy completely omitted this detail. (Note also the similarity between the description of the destruction of the calf in Deuteronomy and Josiah's destruction of the idolatrous altars in 2 Kgs. 23: 12.)

[3] Cf. above, pp. 101, 173.

If the provincial magistrate was unable to render a decisive verdict[1] the litigation was submitted to the adjudication of the central tribunal in Jerusalem (17: 8–13). The central judiciary also dispensed with the sacral media of jurisdiction (lot-casting, ordeal) and conducted its proceedings through the mediation of purely human factors. It was a court of law in which priests and magistrates sat in judgement. This combination of priests and magistrates[2] (vv. 9, 12) constitutes such an innovation in the history of the Israelite judicial system that some scholars take the magistrates as a later interpolation,[3] while others assert that the priests are a later appendage.[4] Steuernagel, on the other hand, justifiably contends that the deuteronomic law reflects two judicial traditions which were originally independent of each other.[5] Indeed, the redundancies (vv. 10–11) and the twofold terminology occurring in this section (תורה || משפט, הורה || הגיד) would lead us to infer that two diverse judicial procedures have here been combined into one. Before the reform there had existed, on the one hand, the sacral judicial institution (the sanctuary) over which the priests presided, and, on the other hand, the civil judiciary (the city gate) in which the elders and judges officiated, whereas after the reform the two institutions were combined and the two previously distinct judicial circles now sat under one roof to constitute a supreme tribunal.[6] Even if we were to assume that such a body had already

[1] This situation is expressed by the verb פלא, which denotes something beyond one's power to apprehend and resolve, i.e. something beyond one's ken. Cf. Ps. 131: 1 ('things too marvellous for me' ובנפלאות ממני); Prov. 30: 18; Job 42: 3, etc., cf. below, pp. 258 f.

[2] The term 'judge' is in all probability employed as a *nomen unitatis*, cf. 19: 17: 'the priests and the judges who are in office in those days'; the same may be inferred from v. 11 of the passage here discussed: 'According to the judgement which *they* pronounce to you' which alludes to the *judges* (pl.) just as the phrase 'according to the instruction (תורה) which *they* give you' refers to the priests.

[3] e.g., Bertholet, *Deut.* KHC, 1899, ad loc., Hempel, *Die Schichten*, pp. 212–17; Horst, *Privilegrecht*, pp. 104 ff.

[4] E. König, *Deuter.*, KAT, 1917, ad loc.; Procksch, *Die Elohimquelle*, p. 269.

[5] *Deuteronomium*, HKAT², 1923, ad loc.

[6] Ehrlich (*Randglossen*) would divide the functions of the tribunal between the priests, who judge all sacro-ritual questions and the magistrates, who try all civil cases. But Deut. 19: 17 describes the 'parties to the dispute' (ריב) as appearing before the priests and the magistrates alike. Deut. 21 : 5, furthermore, attests to the non-division of functions in its reference to the priests, the sons of Levi: '*by their word every dispute* and every assault *shall be settled*'. For discussion see H. Breit, *Die Predigt des Deuteronomisten*, 1933, pp. 97–8, and Y. Kaufmann, *HIR* II, 466–7.

existed in Jerusalem before the deuteronomic reform,[1] the abolition of the provincial sanctuaries and the strengthening of judicial connections of the outlying districts with the Jerusalem temple must have necessitated its reorganization. Indeed, the law of the supreme tribunal body in Deut. 17 is set within a body of laws which predicate the doctrine of centralization, and it must therefore be interpreted in accordance with this context. The provision for the appointment of secular magistrates over matters which formerly lay within sacral jurisdiction implies, therefore, that the Israelite judiciary had undergone a process of secularization.[2]

2. THE LAWS OF ASYLUM

In early Israel the altar and sanctuary were the original places of asylum for the accidental manslayer (Exod. 21: 13–14),[3] and were supplanted in a subsequent period by temple cities in which members of the sacral class, the Levites, resided[4] (Num. 35; cf. Josh. 20–1).[5] The premiss underlying these laws of asylum is that the accidental manslayer must atone for the shedding of innocent blood and must therefore undergo the punishment of forced residence at a sacral domicile.[6] According to P the homicide is compelled to reside in a city of refuge until the death of the high priest[7]—the

[1] See W. F. Albright, 'The Judicial Reform of Jehoshaphat', in the *A. Marx Jubilee Volume*, 1950, pp 74 ff.

[2] A similar process is encountered in the Hammurabi reforms, see R. Harris, 'On the Process of Secularization under Hammurabi', *JCS* (1961), 117–20.

[3] The מקום 'place' in Exod. 21: 13 denotes a sanctuary as does the Arabic *maqām*; cf. the expression 'the *place* he shall choose'. Note also the term המקומות in 1 Sam. 7: 16 which are none other than the sanctuaries of Bethel, Gilgal, and Mizpah; compare the LXX readings of the verse. See S. Talmon, 'Synonymous Readings in the Old Testament', *Scripta Hierosolymitana* 8 (1961), 359–60.

[4] It is legitimate to suppose that the cities of refuge were actually temple cities (cf. M. Greenberg, 'The Biblical Conception of Asylum', *JBL* 78 (1959), 125 ff.). Hebron and Shechem (Josh. 20: 7) were temple cities and apparently so was the Galilean Kadesh. The sacral character of these cities may be inferred from the use of the verb ויקדישו in Josh. 20: 7. The verb הקרה employed in Num. 35: 11 also bears sacral implications (cf. Gen. 24: 12; Num. 23: 16, etc.).

[5] The institution of the cities of asylum in Num. 35 is an early one, see M. Loehr, *Asylwesen im A.T.*, *Schriften der Königsberger Gesellschaft* VIII. 3, 1930, pp. 127–72. On the Levitical cities see W. F. Albright, 'The List of the Levitic Cities', in the *L. Ginsberg Jubilee Volume*, 1945, pp. 43–73; M. Haran, 'Studies in the Account of the Levitical Cities', *JBL* 80 (1961), 45–54, 156–65.

[6] See M. Greenberg, *JBL* 78 (1959), 129.

[7] Kaufmann (*HIR* I, 140, and in the excursus to his commentary on the Book of Joshua) takes the verse to refer to the high priest of the manslayer's city. It is more probable, however, that it is the high priest of the city of asylum that

person who bears 'the iniquity of the holy offerings of the children of Israel'[1] and whose death alone might serve as the expiation of bloodguilt.[2] The city of refuge, according to this conception, does not necessarily perform the protective function of safeguarding the accidental manslayer from the avenger but serves as the place in which he atones for his sin.

The book of Deuteronomy, however, with the abolition of provincial altars and sanctuaries, removes the institution of asylum from sacerdotal jurisdiction. It retains the numerical principle of three cities of refuge on each side of the Jordan (Deut. 4: 41–3; 19: 1–10)[3] but strips it of its sacral character. The assignment of cities of refuge is no longer dependent upon sacral factors (temple cities = Levitical cities) but is decided by rational[4] and geographic considerations. The land must be measured[5] and subdivided equally into three sections and cities of refuge assigned at equidistant locations so that the fleeing manslayer may reach the place of asylum with the maximum speed. The asylum is not the place in which he serves his punishment, but the place which protects him from the vengeance of the blood redeemer: 'lest the avenger of blood in hot anger pursue the manslayer and overtake him, etc.' (Deut. 19: 6). Therefore, the deuteronomic law does not prescribe the period of time that the homicide must reside in asylum (i.e. until the death of the high priest)—he is to remain there until the rage of the avenger subsides.

is intended. For discussion see B. Z. Dinur, 'The Religious Character of the Cities of Refuge', *EI* 3 (1954), 135 ff. (Hebrew, with English summary).

[1] See Exod. 28: 38, and M. Greenberg, op. cit., p. 130.

[2] Cf. M. Greenberg, op. cit.: 'Only another human life can expiate the guilt of accidental slaying.'

[3] Deut. 19 provides for the appointment of three additional cities of asylum should God enlarge the borders of the land (v. 8). The verb refers to the completion of the conquest, which, according to the deuteronomic view, was to be undertaken after the death of Joshua, see Y. Kaufmann, *HIR* II, 382. No mention is made of providing the cities of refuge in the east of Jordan as these were already allocated by Moses himself according to 4: 41–3.

[4] In contrast to the priestly tradition, which uses in connection with the designating of the cities of refuge the verb קדש (see p. 236 n. 4), Deuteronomy uses the neutral הבדיל (set aside) for this purpose (4: 41; 19: 2, 7).

[5] תכין לך הדרך means: mark off the area by measurement (cf. Steuernagel's commentary). The roots כון and כול also imply measurement and counting, cf. Isa. 40: 12: 'Who has *measured* the waters in the hollow of his hand, and *marked off* (תכן) the heavens with a span, *enclosed* (וכל) the dust of the earth *in a measure*?' See also Exod. 16: 5 והכינו את אשר יביאו which means 'when they measure what they brought'. (Cf. A. Ehrlich, *Randglossen*, ad loc.)

3. THE LAWS OF WARFARE

The wars of Israel had always been the wars of Yahweh (Exod. 14: 14; 15: 3; Num. 21: 14, etc.); they were to be conducted, therefore, according to prescribed ritual formula.[1] Before departing for battle Israelite warriors were required to sanctify themselves and observe sexual separation (Josh. 3: 5; 1 Sam. 21: 6; 2 Sam. 11: 11); the holy vessels were brought into the battle with horns and trumpets (Num. 10: 9; 31: 6 [both P]; Josh. 6; cf. Judg. 7: 19–20; 2 Sam. 11: 11); and a portion of the war spoils was set aside as a gift for the Lord to be disposed of by the sanctuary (Num. 31: 50–4 = P; Josh. 6: 24; 2 Sam. 8: 11, etc.). According to P the returning warriors were required to purify themselves (Num. 31: 19 and 24) and cleanse their clothing and utensils (vv. 20–3).

The book of Deuteronomy contains numerous regulations for war, but these lack all the sacral features noted above. The ark and the holy vessels are not mentioned at all[2] nor is anything said of the sounding of Priestly horns or trumpets or of the spoils that must be dedicated to the sanctuary. There has clearly been a change in the conception of warfare. Thus, for instance, the warriors are enjoined to keep themselves from 'every evil thing' and doing 'anything indecent' ערות דבר within the camp, that is to keep from relieving bodily needs within the camp and to leave the camp in the event of nocturnal pollution.[3] The fact that the law specifies only these two matters[4] leads us to conclude that it is here providing for cleanliness of the camp not less than for its sacral purity; for there is no Biblical reference to the effect that human excrement defiles.

Further comparison between the deuteronomic and Priestly warfare is instructive. P, for example, ordains that in time of engagement in battle the priests are to sound their holy trumpets (Num. 10: 9), while D ordains that a priest is to go out and address the body of warriors (Deut. 20: 1–4). Whereas the sacerdotal trumpet blowing in P serves as a remembrance (זכרון) to God ('that you may be remembered before the Lord'),[5] the purpose

[1] G. von Rad, *Der heilige Krieg im alten Israel*, 1951.

[2] Cf. above, p. 209.

[3] Deut. 23: 10–15.

[4] Cf. Num. 5: 1–4 according to which the leper, one who suffers from a discharge, and anyone defiled by a corpse have to be removed from the camp. (That law does not refer to nocturnal pollution but to permanent discharge.) Cf. also Num. 31: 19, which is similarly ignored by Deuteronomy.

[5] Cf. above, p. 222, and note 2 there.

of the priest's address in D is only to fortify the spirits of the warriors.[1]

According to P, even captive enemy women and children must be slain in war, only the young virgins may be spared (Num. 31: 17–18; Judg. 21: 11–12 which underwent Priestly revision). D, on the other hand, permits enemy women and children to be taken captive in non-Canaanite wars and even prescribes humane treatment for female captives (21: 10–14).

According to D all the spoils of war accrue to the warriors (in contrast to Josh. 6: 17, 24, 1 Sam. 15: 3), and there is no need to consecrate any of them to the Lord: 'all its spoil you shall take as booty for yourselves' (20: 14).[2] This is at variance with P, which ordains that the Israelites must devote a portion of the spoils as an atonement for themselves (Num. 31: 50) and as a memorial before Yahweh (v. 54, cf. Josh. 6: 24).

The law prohibiting the destruction of fruit-bearing trees during war (20: 19–20) may also indicate the altered conception of war in Deuteronomy. During the campaign against Moab Elisha commanded by divine oracle that the Israelites fell every good tree, stop up all water-springs, and ruin every 'good' piece of land with stones (2 Kgs. 3: 19). Deuteronomy, however, expressly prohibits the use of fruit-bearing trees even for siege purposes; how much more, then, the wanton destruction of trees.

4. SIN AND PUNISHMENT

The concept of sin and punishment has also been transferred from the divine to the human sphere. The ancient Israelite apodictic[3] legal code, as it finds expression in the Book of the Covenant and in the Priestly Code, bears a distinctly sacral cast. In the series of legal proclamations which open with the active

[1] See above, p. 45.

[2] This applies also to Canaanite wars, according to the deuteronomic view, cf. Deut. 2: 35; 3: 7; Josh. 8: 2, 27; 11: 14.

[3] Alt's fundamental distinction between casuistic and apodictic style (A. Alt, 'Die Ursprünge des Israelitischen Rechts', *KS* I, 278 ff.) appears to be a valid one (especially so in the Book of the Covenant), although the participial clauses are closer to the casuistic than to the apodictic law. However, stylistic differences between legal formulae do not necessarily attest to different ethno-cultural origins as Alt claims, rather than the different contexts from which they arose. On the whole problem see M. E. Andrews's introduction to J. J. Stamm, *The Ten Commandments*², 1967.

participle and close with the phrase: 'he shall be put to death' מות יומת[1] we encounter laws that deal with murder (Exod. 21: 12), adultery (Lev. 20: 10),[2] and abduction (Exod. 21: 16), on the one hand, and laws concerning bestiality (Exod. 22: 18), blasphemy (Lev. 24: 16), and the profanation of the Sabbath (Exod. 31: 14), on the other. No distinction is made between offences committed against God and offences committed against man either in the formulation of the law or in the kind of punishment prescribed. Crimes committed against man are deemed to be a violation of sacral principle no less than sins committed against God. As we have noted above,[3] laws concerning incest, purity, and defilement, which are set forth in the same context and coupled with murder, are all conceived as sins which contaminate and pollute the land (Lev. 18: 28; Num. 35: 33–4).[4]

The book of Deuteronomy, on the other hand, not only lacks the ancient proclamations[5] but also fails to provide any regulations dealing with violations of sacral law (= *fas*). Blasphemy, for example, which in Israel was deemed to be an extremely grave offence and is mentioned in the Book of the Covenant (Exod. 22: 27) and the Priestly document (Lev. 24: 15–16; Num. 15, 30–1) as well as in ancient historical literature (1 Sam. 2: 30;[6] 1 Kgs. 21: 13), is left entirely unprovided for in the book of Deuteronomy. Bestiality, which according to the Book of the Covenant (Exod. 22: 18) and the Holiness Code (Lev. 20: 15–16; cf. 18: 23) also incurs the death penalty, is mentioned in the Dodecalogue in Deut. 27, but does not appear in the deuteronomic code proper. Magic, divination, and Molech worship, which according to the Book of the Covenant, the Holiness Code, and various allusions in the historical literature, all carry the death penalty (Exod. 22: 17; Lev. 18: 21; 20: 1–6 and 27; 1 Sam. 28: 3 and 9), are prohibited, it is

[1] Concerning the substance and nature of these announcements, see Alt, 'Ursprünge', 302 ff.

[2] Some of the apodictic proclamations have been slightly reworded. Thus, e.g., Lev. 20: 9 reads: 'For everyone who curses (כי איש איש אשר יקלל) his father or his mother shall be put to death' instead of: 'Whoever curses מקלל his father or his mother shall be put to death' (as in the Book of the Covenant). The formula underlying v. 10 is: 'Whoever commits adultery with a man's wife shall be put to death.' (Cf. Alt, 'Ursprünge', 312.)

[3] Above, pp. 187–8.

[4] See above, pp. 225–6.

[5] Cf. Alt, 'Ursprünge', 308. Alt noted the absence of these formulations in the book of Deuteronomy but failed to draw conclusions.

[6] M. Tsevat, 'Studies in the Book of Samuel, I', *HUCA* 32 (1961), 203.

true, by the deuteronomic code (18: 10–13) but without any specification of the penalty they entail.

The deuteronomic code, on the other hand, lists some capital offences that are not encountered in any other of the law *corpora*, such as contempt of the central tribunal (17: 12) or incitement to sin (13: 2–12). We have dwelt above[1] on the political nature of the law of incitement, and we need hardly point out that the law of judicial contempt also has political implications (insubordination to supreme judicial authority). The other deuteronomic offences carrying the death penalty are also found in the other Biblical codes, but they are predominantly those offences which constitute the basis of every criminal law-code, such as murder, adultery, abduction, and the law of the defiant son. The last of these graphically illustrates the metamorphosis that the judicial conception underwent in the book of Deuteronomy. The Book of the Covenant and the Holiness Code prescribe the death penalty for the cursing of parents (Exod. 21: 17; Lev. 20: 9), an offence conceived on the same plane as blasphemy and *lèse-majesté* (= prince: נשיא in Exod. 22: 27)[2] and implying insubordination to authority. The author of Deuteronomy, on the other hand, says nothing of the son cursing or striking (cf. Exod. 21: 15) his parents, but speaks only of an incorrigible son whose perversity is likely to bring ruin upon himself and his family[3] (cf. Prov. 23: 19 ff.).

The secular character of the judicial conception of the book of Deuteronomy is also apparent in the absence of those grave sacro-cultic offences which, according to P, incur the penalty of *kareth*, such as: the eating of blood and suet (Lev. 7: 22–7), the eating of ritual meat while in a state of impurity (7: 20–1), contamination of the sanctuary and its appurtenances (Num. 19: 13 and 20; Lev. 22: 3); non-circumcision (Gen. 17: 14), the eating of

[1] See above, p. 92; Ezekiel, who was inspired by the Priestly school, also alludes to the prophet who would incite to sin (14: 9–10), but the penalty specified is executed by divine and not human agency.

[2] Though the stem קלל also means 'to treat disrespectfully' or 'to abuse' (see Brichto, *Curse*), there is no warrant for taking the verb in this sense in the verses cited above as Brichto contends (ibid., pp. 132 ff. and 150 f.). The fact that the stem occurs as a parallel to ארר in Exod. 22: 27, where Brichto admits that it has the force of 'curse', 'spell' (ibid., p. 114), would infer that the stem here refers to a verbalism and is to be taken in the sense 'to revile' and not 'to treat with disrespect'.

[3] Cf. Mishnah Sanhedrin, viii: 5: 'A stubborn and rebellious son is tried on account of his ultimate destiny: let him die innocent and let him not die guilty.'

leavened bread during the Matzoth festival (Exod. 12: 15–19), and eating on the Day of Atonement (Lev. 23: 29). The penalty of *kareth* denotes death by divine intervention[1] and relates to the province of sacral law (= *fas*), whereas Deuteronomy is generally concerned with the province of the *jus* and is therefore not interested in offences of this sort. Since sacral offences and the *kareth* penalty which they entail are referred to in early Israelite literature and particularly in the Elides narratives[2] there is no basis for the assertion that the author of Deuteronomy was not familiar with them. It is more plausible to assume that the deuteronomic conception of sin differs from that encountered in the Priestly document and early Israelite literature. The earlier view reflected in these sources conceived sin as a sort of palpable substance (*miasma*) which rests upon the malefactor. The evildoer bears his sin until he is cut off from his people.[3] Should a group of persons commit a sin, then the sin is borne by the earth until it vomits them out (Lev. 18: 28) or swallows them (Num. 16: 28 ff.).[4] The punishment is conceived as the almost automatic consequence of the offence.

Contrary to this conception, which finds its clearest articulation in such expressions as 'and he will bear his iniquity' ישא עונו, 'that person shall be cut off from his people' ונכרתה הנפש ההיא מעמיה, we encounter a more rational view in the book of Deuteronomy which finds expression in the formula 'you shall purge the evil from among you' ובערת הרע מקרבך.[5] In the deuteronomic view sin does not act of its own accord, nor is the malefactor cut off from his people by the natural course of events: the people themselves must purge the evil from their midst so that the malefactor 'shall never again commit such evil' and 'not act presumptuously again' (cf. 13: 12; 17: 13). The Priestly document also lists offences which society is commanded to punish, but the manner in which the penalty is executed reveals the particular conception of sin and punishment

[1] M. Tsevat, 'Studies in the Book of Samuel, I', *HUCA* 32 (1961), 191 ff.

[2] Ibid.

[3] *Kareth* is the inevitable consequence of one who bears iniquity (נשא עון), cf. Lev. 19: 8; 20: 17; Num. 9: 13; 15: 31.

[4] Cf. M. Tsevat's discussion (ibid.) of Num. 16: 29 ('If these men die the common death of all men') with respect to the significance of the *kareth* penalty. The passage also resembles P with respect to the chthonian rule in the punishment of sin: according to both sources it is the earth which is represented as executing the punishment, except that in JE it acts by swallowing the evildoers, whereas in P it expels them.

[5] For the political background of this formula cf. below, p. 355, n. 2.

held by the Priestly source. The condemned malefactor must be brought outside the camp (Lev. 24: 14; Num. 15: 35) or the city (1 Kgs. 21: 13),[1] that is, to a place of impurity,[2] for the execution of the verdict. It was in this setting that the persons of the congregation would lay their hands upon the offender (Lev. 24: 14; cf. 2 Kgs. 11: 16) and thus transfer to him the sins of those who were contaminated by the crime (e.g. those who heard the cursing of God in Lev. 24: 14). Deuteronomy, on the other hand, prescribes that the verdict be executed at the gate of the city (17: 5; 21: 19; 22: 24), that is, at the place of judgement;[3] in the case of a betrothed maiden condemned for infidelity the verdict is even executed at the entrance of her father's dwelling (22: 21), so that all may know of her sin and of the reproach which she has brought upon her father's house. As in other instances (cf., e.g., above, p. 224) so also in this case the divergence between the Priestly law and the deuteronomic one is not one of practice but rather of the view involved. According to Deuteronomy, the death penalty does not serve a sacral need for the destruction of the malefactor who had defiled the holy state (cf. Lev. 20: 3), nor is it an object in itself, that is, the removal of impurity. It serves as a deterrent 'so that all may obey and fear' (13: 12; 17: 13; 19: 20; 21: 21).[4]

[1] Cf. Acts 7: 58; Heb. 13: 12.

[2] Concerning the area outside the camp see above, p. 225.

[3] 'The gate of the city' and 'outside the city' or 'camp' are not the same, *contra* Dillmann and Driver (on Deut. 17: 5). For the Rabbinic interpretation of the problem cf. D. Halivni (Weiss), 'The Location of the Beth Din in the Early Tannaitic Period', *Proceedings of the American Academy for Jewish Research*, 29 (1960–1), 181–91.

[4] Cf. below, p. 298.

PART THREE

DEUTERONOMIC LITERATURE AND WISDOM LITERATURE

I

WISDOM SUBSTRATA IN DEUTERONOMY AND DEUTERONOMIC LITERATURE

1. THE CONCEPT OF WISDOM

THE Mosaic appointment of a body of leaders and magistrates is recounted in three different passages of the Pentateuch: Exod. 18: 13–27, Num. 11: 11–30, and Deut. 1: 9–18. There are of course a number of divergences between the three traditions of the narrative,[1] but the most essential difference between them concerns the personal qualities ascribed to the appointed leaders and magistrates. In Exod. 18: 21 Jethro advises Moses to appoint '*capable men who fear God, trustworthy men who spurn ill-gotten gain*'. In Num. 11: 16–30 God endows the elders who were to aid Moses in governing the people, with a *divine spirit*. In Deut. 1: 13–17 Moses appoints 'wise men, and (men of) understanding and full of knowledge'[2] (חכמים ונבנים וידעים). According to Exod. 18, then, the qualities required of a magistrate are capability, integrity,

[1] Thus, e.g., in Exodus it is *Jethro* who conceives the idea of appointing the judges, in Deuteronomy it is *Moses* who suggests the plan, and in Numbers it is God who proposes it. For further divergences cf. the quasi-military function of the judiciary in Exodus and Deuteronomy ('the officers of the hundreds', 'the officers of the thousands') and the non-existence of this function in the book of Numbers. Numbers and Deuteronomy, on the other hand, refer to the *šōṭerim* as the assistants of the magistrates, whereas Exodus makes no mention of them.

[2] The LXX renders ידעים by *συνετούς*, a word which also translates נבנים, חכמים cf. Hatch–Redpath, *Concordance to the Septuagint*, s.v. Professor H. L. Ginsberg suggested to me that the original reading was יֹדְעים (particip.), which is supported by Eccles. 9: 11, which, like Deuteronomy, enumerates נבנים, חכמים, and יֹדְעים. Cf. also Job 34: 2 where יֹדְעים parallels חכמים. On the Canaanite סופר יודע 'the knowing scribe' as reflected in the Egyptian literature, see A. Rainey, *JNES* 26 (1967), 58–9.

and fear of God, and according to Num. 11 a leader must have charismatic qualities. But according to Deut. 1 magistrates and leaders must possess intellectual qualities: wisdom, understanding, and knowledge, traits which characterize the leader and magistrate in wisdom literature also. Thus, in Prov. 8: 15–16, Wisdom declares: 'By me kings reign and rulers decree what is just; by me princes rule, and nobles govern (read with LXX: ישפטו) the earth.'[1]

Moreover, Deut. 1: 9–18 interrupts the narrative of the expedition from Horeb to the Jordan and has been rightly seen as an intrusion but no satisfactory reason for it has been given.[2] It could, however, be explained by the strong predilection for wisdom[3] characterizing the scribes who were responsible for the composition of Deuteronomy.

A comparison between Deut. 16: 19 and Exod. 23: 8 brings this deuteronomic conception into greater relief. Thus while Exod. 23 reads: 'and you shall take no bribe, for a bribe blinds them that have sight' (פקחים), Deut. 16 reads: 'You shall not take a bribe, for a bribe blinds the *wise*' (חכמים); the author believes, that the prerequisite qualifications of a judge must be intellectual in character—he must, namely, possess *wisdom*.

The affinities to wisdom of the two passages dealing with the appointment of judges in Deuteronomy (1: 9–18; 16: 18–20) may be also recognized by their phraseology. Thus the phrase הכר פנים במשפט 'to respect persons in judgement'[4] is found again in the O.T. only in Prov. 24: 23; 28: 21 and the same concept occurs in Egyptian literature.[5] The term שמע 'hear' in connection with judgement, which we find in Deut. 1: 16–17, is very prominent in Egyptian literature[6] and also in Babylonian literature.[7]

[1] In language influenced by sapiential literature, Isaiah similarly says of the ideal king who 'shall judge the poor with righteousness ' that a 'spirit of wisdom and understanding' shall rest upon him' (Isa. 11 : 2). For the 'sapiential-psalmodic element in Isaian phraseology' cf. Y. Kaufmann, *HIR* III. Excursus II, p. 302.

[2] Cf. M. Noth, *Überliefer. Studien*, 15; N. Lohfink, 'Darstellungskunst und Theologie in Dtn. 1, 6–3, 29', *Biblica* 41 (1960), 107, n. 1; J. G. Plöger, *Literarkritische, formgeschichtliche und stilkritische Untersuchungen zum Deuteronomium*, 1967, p. 31.

[3] This was suggested to me by J. Tigay.

[4] Cf. below, p. 273.

[5] Cf. 'The Vizier of Egypt', *ANET*², 213, A: 37 f, B: 12 f.

[6] Cf. C. H. Cazelles, 'Institutions et Terminologie en Deut. I', *SVT* 15 (1966), 109–10, and the reference there for 'to hear between' (Deut. 1: 16) in Egyptian literature.

[7] Cf. C. H. Cazelles, ibid. 108 n. 1. Cf. Also *BWL* 112: 16: *dīn Bābilaya išmēma*, 'should he hear the case of a Babylonian'.

A conception similar to that of Deut. 1: 9–18 is met with in 1 Kgs. 3: 4–15, a passage which describes Solomon as entreating God to bestow wisdom on him so that he may judge the people competently. In this passage the tradition concerning the dream at Gibeon and Solomon's return to Jerusalem is an ancient and genuine one, as may be ascertained from parallel traditions which we shall discuss below. The content of the dream and its stylistic cast, however, are definitely of deuteronomic origin. The deuteronomic expressions that characterize this passage occur not only in vv. 6–8 as M. Noth contends,[1] but throughout the entire section. Thus the idom 'to hear the case' שמע משפט (vv. 9 and 11) is also found in Deut. 1: 16–17;[2] the phrase 'so that none like you has been . . . and none like you shall arise' (vv. 12–13) is peculiar to deuteronomic literature (cf. the deuteronomic assessment of the reigns of Kings Hezekiah and Josiah in 2 Kgs. 18: 5; 23: 25);[3] and it need hardly be said that all of v. 14 bears a deuteronomic stamp.[4] The deuteronomic character of the passage, however, is apparent not only in its stylistic features but also in its thought.

The principal theme is reminiscent of Deut. 1: 9–18 and may perhaps even derive from it. Moses complains of the burden of governing a people who are as '*the stars of heaven for multitude*' (Deut. 1: 9–10) and therefore seeks *wise and understanding* men to aid him in judging the people (vv. 12 ff.). Solomon, too, speaks of the difficulties of judging a great people '*that cannot be numbered nor counted for multitude*' (1 Kgs. 3: 8–9) and therefore entreats God to endow him with a לב שמע, i.e. with wisdom and understanding (vv. 9 and 12). Like the author of Deut. 1: 9–18, the deuteronomic editor of 1 Kgs. 3: 4–15 regards the possession of wisdom as the principal requisite for the competent functioning of the judiciary. Solomon's wisdom, furthermore, is conceived by the Deuteronomist as consisting largely of his 'understanding of judgement'. True wisdom, to the Deuteronomist's mind, is the

1 M. Noth, *Könige*, BK IX, 1, 1964, pp. 45 ff.

2 The idiom 'an attentive heart' לב שמע (v. 9) and the use of the verb 'hear' in a didactic sense is very prevalent in Egyptian and Israelite wisdom literature (see H. Brunner, *Altägyptische Erziehung*, 1957, pp. 110–12 and 156).

3 See also A. Šanda, *Die Bücher der Könige*, I, EH, 63, and cf. below, pp. 358–9.

4 M. Noth, BK IX, ad loc., regards v. 14a as a deuteronomic accretion and believes 14b to be the original sequel of the older narrative. However, longevity figures as one of the characteristic deuteronomic rewards for the observance of the Law (see Chapter IV below), and there is, consequently, no warrant in assigning the two sections of the verse to different strands.

intellectual faculty which enables man to distinguish between good and evil in the judicial sphere:[1] 'Give Your servant, therefore, an understanding heart to govern Your people, that I may discern between good and evil' (3: 9).

It will become apparent later that the Deuteronomist had reworked the content material of Solomon's dream at Gibeon, so as to make it conform with his own conceptions. He discarded the earlier dream material which he found objectionable and introduced a new content which was more consistent with his own views.[2] Is it possible, however, to ascertain the nature of the original content of Solomon's dream?

We may infer from Biblical and extra-Biblical texts of the ancient Near East that the founding of a new sanctuary first required a prophetic revelation in which divine approval of the project was granted. Moses, for example, begins the construction of the tabernacle after he is shown its plan in a divine vision on Mt. Sinai (Exod. 25: 9; 26: 30; cf. 1 Chr. 28: 19). Before David undertakes the building of a sanctuary he must first obtain divine approval. (In this case, however, the Deity discloses his disapproval in a nocturnal vision that appeared to the prophet Nathan—2 Sam. 7: 4 ff.) The Patriarchs found holy sites which were designed to serve holy sanctuaries after they too had received divine revelations[3] (Gen. 12: 7—Shechem; 26: 24–5— Beersheba; 28: 12–19—Bethel). According to one tradition Gideon erects an altar to Yahweh after having seen God in a dream (Judg. 6: 25), and according to a parallel tradition (vv. 11–24) after an angel of the Lord had visited him. The ἱερὸς λόγος of the Jerusalem sanctuary also figures in dual traditions of this type. According to 2 Sam. 7: 4 the revelation

[1] Cf. W. Malcolm Clark, 'A Legal Background of the Yahwist's use of "Good and Evil" in Genesis 2–3', *JBL* 88 (1969) 266 ff. I cannot agree, however, with Clark that 2 Sam. 14: 17 reflects a similar background. 'To hear the good and the evil' is altogether different from 'to discern between good and evil' (1 Kgs. 3: 9). Besides, 2 Sam. 14: 20, which—as Clark admits—corresponds to v. 17, speaks about 'knowing all which is on the earth' and it is this general understanding of human affairs which is linked there to wisdom (cf. below, p. 254) and not the supposed judicial understanding of v. 17.

[2] Verse 5 is difficult (cf. M. Noth, *Könige*, ad loc.). Verse 5a apparently belongs to a different literary strand from that of vv. 5b ff. (note the change in the divine name: Yahweh in v. 5a and Elohim in 5b). The textual irregularity may be due to an editorial deletion in the verse.

[3] In Israel as elsewhere in the ancient Near East a significant relationship existed between the theophany and the theological dream, cf. A. L. Oppenheim, *The Interpretation of Dreams in the Ancient Near East*, 1956.

concerning the Jerusalem sanctuary occurs in a nocturnal vision (בלילה ההוא; cf. the same expression in Judg. 6: 25); and according to 2 Sam. 24 David erects an altar on the threshing-floor of Araunah—the future site of the Jerusalem temple (1 Chr. 22: 1; cf. Gen. 28: 17)—after receiving a revelation from an angel of the Lord. It may be legitimately assumed, then, that the original dream of Solomon at Gibeon also was a prophetic vision whose purpose was to grant divine approval for the construction of a sanctuary, an undertaking which the Deity had previously rejected in the Nathan prophecy.

Of the similar extra-Biblical texts of the ancient Near East which treat of the foundation or construction of a sanctuary,[1] the most instructive for our purpose are the cylinders of Gudea, *ensi* of Lagash,[2] which contain an elaborate description of the building of the Ningirsu temple. During the night, so the inscription recounts, Gudea received a divine vision (A, i: 17–21). Unable to understand its meaning, he journeys to the sanctuary of the goddess Gatumdu and there offers up sacrifices to the goddess (A, ii–iv). The oracle-goddess of the sanctuary interprets his dream (A, v–vi) and among other things informs him that the tablet held by a hero which he saw in his dream contained none other than the plan of the sanctuary (A, vi: 5; cf. 1 Chr. 28: 19). Following the advice of the oracle-goddess, Gudea returns to Lagash and presents gifts to the god Ningirsu. Gudea prays and requests a second revelation (A, viii: 15–ix: 4), which he is granted in a dream (cf. 1 Kgs. 9: 2): the god promises him that his land will prosper and that he will succeed in his building enterprise (A, ix: 5–xii: 11). Gudea begins the construction, levies taxes upon the land, cuts cedars, quarries stones (cf. 1 Kgs. 5: 27–32), and assembles great quantities of silver, bronze, and gold, and multitudes of precious stones (A, xiv–xvi; cf. Exod. 35: 21 ff.) like the dust of the earth ((A, xvi: 18, cf. 1 Kgs. 10: 27). During the course of the work he permits himself neither rest nor sleep (A, xvii: 5–9; cf. Ps. 132: 3–4). Upon the completion of the temple Gudea solemnly declares that

[1] For a recent discussion on temple building in the ancient East, see A. S. Kapelrud, 'Temple Building, a Task for Gods and Kings', *Orientalia* 32 (1963), 56–62.

[2] F. Thureau-Dangin, *SAK* 140 ff.; G. A. Barton, *Royal Inscrip.* 205 ff. For discussion and analysis, see M. Lambert–R. J. Tournay, 'Le Cylindre A de Gudéa', *RB* 55 (1948), 403 ff.; 'Le Cylindre B de Gudéa', 520 ff.

he has constructed a domicile for Ningirsu and his consort, the goddess Bau (B, ii: 16–iii: 1; cf. 1 Kgs. 8: 12–13).[1] After the gods have been installed in the sanctuary, a seven-day feast is celebrated with great rejoicing (B, xvii: 18–xviii: 9; cf. 1 Kgs. 8: 65 ff.), and at its conclusion Gudea receives the blessing of the god, who promises him long life and success (B, xxiv).

There is a similar description in an Assyrian text that treats of the rebuilding of the Esagila temple by Esarhaddon.[2] After the Assyrian god vanquished all of Esarhaddon's enemies (Epis. 11: A, cf. 1 Kgs. 5: 17–18) and the divine omens proved favourable (Epis. 12) Esarhaddon is commanded to rebuild the temple (Epis. 14a). Fearing to begin construction until the appropriate time is divinely revealed to him, he kneels before his god and entreats him to disclose his will (Epis. 16). On receiving the divine approval through liver auguries (Epis. 17) he immediately begins the building of the sanctuary. Like Gudea and Solomon, Esarhaddon mobilizes corvée labour, including war captives, to fell trees and transport materials, commands cedars to be brought from the mountains of Amanus, and erects a temple the dimensions and appurtenances of which are listed in detail (cf. 1 Kgs. 6–7).[3] Upon its completion he proclaims an *andurāru*[4] (cf. 1 Kgs. 8: 66) and prays for the prosperity of his kingdom (Epis. 37, 39).[5]

A neo-Babylonian text similarly recounts that Nabonidus received divine approval to build the Eḫulḫul (the Sin temple in Harran) in two dream visions (H2 A, i: 11–14; iii: 1–3).[6] After building it he summoned the peoples of Akkad and Hatti land, installed the gods in their 'everlasting' sanctuary, poured generous libations and offered them gifts, and 'exceedingly gladdened the hearts of the people' (iii: 18–28).

In the Baal Epic of Ugarit[7] we hear of Baal making repeated requests to the god El to grant him permission to construct a sanctuary. El eventually complies, whereupon the mobilization of workers commences, 'wise' craftsmen are sent for from Egypt (cf. Exod. 31: 1 ff.; 1 Kgs. 7: 13 ff.), and cedar wood is brought from

[1] Cf. above, p. 35.
[2] See R. Borger, *Die Inschriften Asarhaddons*, 16 ff.
[3] Ibid., Epis. 18–36.
[4] Cf. above, p. 153.
[5] Cf. above, pp. 35 f.
[6] Cf. C. J. Gadd, 'The Harran inscriptions of Nabonidus', *Anatolian Studies* 8 (1958), 35–92.
[7] II, AB i–vi; for translation see H. L. Ginsberg, *ANET*², pp. 131–4.

Lebanon. The completion of the sanctuary is celebrated with great rejoicing and numerous sacrifices of cattle and sheep.

We find, then, a great similarity between these accounts and the tradition concerning the construction of the Solomonic temple. It is interesting to note, however, that the resemblance is confined to the pre-deuteronomic strand of the Biblical narrative (5: 16–8: 13; 8: 62–6), whereas the deuteronomic traditions (3: 5–14; 8: 14–61; 9: 3–9) present an entirely different picture. While Gudea, Esarhaddon, Nabonidus, and Baal await a prophetic dream or divine approval to signal the beginning of the construction,[1] Solomon's dream at Gibeon, according to the deuteronomic account, serves merely as the medium through which the Deity promises him judicial wisdom. While the purpose of Gudea's and Esarhaddon's prayers is to request the success of their building enterprise and reward for their religious undertakings, the prayer of Solomon according to the deuteronomic tradition in 1 Kgs. 8, as we have already observed, is no more than a liturgical articulation of the Deuteronomist's theological programme.[2] It appears, therefore, that the pre-deuteronomic source contained traditions similar to those found in the extra-Biblical accounts of sanctuary building cited above, but that they had been reworked by the Deuteronomist who wished to accommodate them to his own purposes. The dreams at Gibeon, where the great high place stood, seem originally to have pertained like Nathan's dream, the Patriarchal dreams, and those of Gudea and Nabonidus, to the building of the temple. The purpose of Solomon's journey to Gibeon apparently was to receive a revelation conveying divine permission to begin the construction of a temple; this is why he offers up a holocaust of a thousand sacrifices (χιλιόμβη) upon the altar and spends the night in the sanctuary (= incubation).[3] Having received the dream he returns to Jerusalem to present himself before the ark of the Lord, as Gudea had similarly journeyed to the sanctuary of Gatumdu.

S. Herrmann[4] has recently pointed out Egyptian analogies to the Solomonic traditions here discussed. He had discovered elements

[1] On the thematic similarity between ancient divine and royal temple building accounts, see Kapelrud, 'Temple Building'.

[2] Cf. above, pp. 35 f.

[3] See E. L. Ehrlich, *Der Traum im Alten Testament*, 1953.

[4] S. Herrmann, 'Die Königsnovelle in Ägypten und Israel', *Wissenschaftliche Zeitschrift der Karl Marx Universität, Leipzig*, Gesellschafts- und Sprachwissenschaftliche Reihe, 3. Jahrgang (1953–4), pp. 51 ff.

of the Egyptian *Königsnovelle* in 1 Kgs. 3 and in 2 Sam. 7, whose style, he believes, was adopted by the authors of Israelite court composition during the period of United Monarchy. There is a salient resemblance between the passage in 1 Kgs. 3: 4–15 and the *Königsnovelle* in the 'Sphinx Stele' of Thutmose IV.[1] The stele recounts that when Thutmose was still a prince he once sought refuge from noonday heat in the shade of the sphinx's shadow, whereupon he fell asleep and dreamt that the god of the sphinx spoke to him and promised him that he would some day ascend the throne of Egypt. The god also requested Thutmose to attend to the needs of his statue and clear it of the encroaching desert sands. Thutmose woke from his sleep, and without informing anyone of his dream ordered his men to proceed at once to the city sanctuary and offer sacrifices to the god.

But as with the Mesopotamian texts, the affinities between the Biblical tradition and the Egyptian account—a dream theophany within the precincts of a sacral area, secrecy concerning the experience, the journey to a sanctuary, and the presentation of sacrificial offerings[2]—are confined to the thematic material of the pre-Deuteronomic narrative (i.e. the dream at Gibeon, Solomon's return to Jerusalem) and are not present in the deuteronomic content of the dream. The content of Thutmose's dream, like that of Gudea's, treats of a sanctuary and a divine image, themes which generally figure as major motifs of the *Königsnovelle*.[3] The *Königsnovelle* of Sesostris I and Thutmose III, from which Herrmann adduces further analogies to 1 Kgs. 3: 4–15, also revolve about the theme of temple construction and cultic places.

The Egyptian parallels to 1 Kgs. 3: 4–15 may be found, then, only in the traditions concerning the dream at Gibeon and Solomon's return journey to Jerusalem, but not in the content of the dream. Though Herrmann does cite Egyptian parallels to the motifs occurring in the dream they are in truth not parallels at all. The election motif which appears in the *novelle* of Sesostris I and

[1] For translation see *ANET*², p. 449.

[2] Other typological features of the Egyptian *Königsnovelle* are the royal feast prepared for the king's officials and the assembly of the royal ministers before whom the king announces his programme, cf. E. Otto, *Handbuch der Orientalistik* I. 2 Ägyptologie, 1952, 143 ff.

[3] Cf. E. Otto, *Handbuch*, 140 ff., and Herrmann's comment in his study cited above: 'Am haüfigsten ist die Königsnovelle im Zusammenhang mit Bauwerken, insbesondere mit Tempeln und dessen Kultur' (p. 52).

Thutmose III[1] bears no resemblance whatever to Solomon's declaration that he is a mere child 'who knows not to go out and come in' (v. 7). The election from infancy (= predestination) is a motif that occurs in royal annals and inscriptions of Mesopotamia[2] and in Israelite prophetic literature.[3] Its purpose is to stress the importance of the person's election to office and the magnitude of the task which that office demands of him, a task for which he was elected when still in his mother's womb. Solomon, on the other hand, declares that he is still a child in order to heighten his unpreparedness[4] for the task he is called upon to perform, rather than to enhance the nature of his office. In the royal Egyptian *novelle*, moreover, the king speaks of his childhood only retrospectively, whereas Solomon refers to the *present* state of his 'immaturity'[5]. In this respect, then, there are no affinities between the compositions in question.

Herrmann also finds traces both of the Egyptian coronation ceremony in Solomon's remarks in v. 6 (' . . . and has given him a son to sit on his throne this day') and of royal title-giving (in the expressions: אמת, צדקה, ישרת לבב, חסד), motifs which he thinks have an important place in the *Königsnovelle* of Thutmose III. But this is unconvincing. The great and steadfast love (חסד) which Yahweh is said to have shown for David by giving him a son 'to sit on his throne . . . this day' is a typical deuteronomic theologumenon,[6] whose purpose is to bear witness to the greatness and continuity of the Davidic Dynasty which had materialized in consequence of the word of God uttered by the prophet Nathan in 2 Sam. 7; it has no reference whatever to an enthronement ceremony. The expression 'this day' is a stereotyped deuteronomic idiom employed to emphasize the fact that the ancient prophecies and divine promises

[1] See S. Herrmann, 'Königsnovelle', pp. 54–5.

[2] See S. Paul, 'Deutero-Isaiah and Cuneiform Royal Inscriptions', *JAOS* 88 (1968) and the sources quoted there on pp. 184–5.

[3] This motif is especially prevalent in the Deutero-Isaiah prophecies (44: 2 and 24; 49: 1) but appears for the first time in Jer. 1: 5; see Paul, op. cit.

[4] As does Jeremiah who declares his unpreparedness for the task imposed upon him in similar language: 'For I am only a youth' (1: 6). Regardless of the fact, God appoints him for the task by informing him that he had already been consecrated for it even before his birth (v. 5). There is, however, no suggestion of this in the Solomonic declaration.

[5] To support his thesis, Herrmann is compelled to render the phrase ואנכי נער קטן 'when I was still a small boy' (während ich noch ein kleiner Knabe war); his rendering is, however, gratuitous.

[6] Cf. 1 Kgs. 2: 4; 8: 20, 25; 9: 5.

have come to pass.[1] In the introductory section of the deuteronomic prayer of Solomon it too refers to the perpetuation of the Davidic dynasty: 'who have kept with Your servant David my father what You did declare to him; yea, You did speak with Your mouth and with Your hand have fulfilled it *this day*' (8: 24).[2]

The traits enumerated in v. 6 (truth, righteousness, and uprightness of heart) are not royal epithets assumed by the newly enthroned king, as is the case in the Egyptian texts and in Isa. 9: 5–6,[3] but describe rather the loyalty and faithfulness of David as a reward for which his dynasty was established for ever.[4] Contrary to Hermann, the qualities wisdom, understanding, righteousness, and equity mentioned in our Biblical passage do not signify[5] the *charismata* which the king acquires when he ascends the throne. To 'walk before Yahweh' means to 'serve Yahweh', and the expressions אמת, ישרת לבב, צדקה signify the loyalty and wholeheartedness constantly stressed in deuteronomic literature and ascribed particularly to David, the loyal king.[6] The 'wisdom and understanding' referred to in the passage are, on the other hand, the intellectual qualities requested by Solomon so that he might execute his judicial office completely. The two kinds of qualities are consequently not to be classed together, nor are they to be regarded as a series of titular epithets assumed by Solomon upon his succession to the throne.

Since we may infer from existing parallels between the Egyptian *Königsnovelle*, Mesopotamian sanctuary building texts, and Biblical traditions that the *ἱερὸς λόγος* motif bore a uniform stamp throughout the entire ancient Near East, it is plausible to assume that the tradition concerning Solomon's dream at Gibeon originally followed this pattern. The Deuteronomist who found theophanies of this type (i.e. *incubation* theophanies) conflicting with his own views[7] severed the Gibeon dream tradition from its connection with the building of the sanctuary and associated it with Solomon's request for judicial wisdom.[8] In his version neither

[1] See above, p. 174.
[2] Cf. above, p. 36 n. 2 (*g*).
[3] See A. Alt, 'Jesaja 8, 23–9, 6, Befreiungsnacht und Krönungstag', *KS* II, 206–25.
[4] Cf. above, pp. 77 f.
[5] 'Königsnovelle', pp. 55–6.
[6] See above, p. 77.
[7] M. Noth, *Könige*, p. 54 has similarly raised the question whether the irregularity in v. 5a may not be due to the deletion of an incubation tradition which the Deuteronomist did not find to his liking.
[8] See also Kapelrud, 'Temple Building'.

dream referred to the construction of the temple; the first (3: 5–14) was one in which Yahweh had promised to bestow wisdom on Solomon, and the second (9: 3–9) was a warning to him to observe the divine laws and precepts spoken of in the first.

It is quite possible that in the pre-deuteronomic version of the dream Solomon was, among other things, also promised the wisdom necessary to execute the construction of the temple, i.e. *technical* wisdom, the sense in which the term 'wisdom' occurs in the pre-deuteronomic strands of the Solomonic traditions (5: 21; 10: 4, etc.; see below). The Deuteronomist, however, has here employed it in a judicial and moral sense which has no connection whatever with the temple-construction theme, but which does indeed reflect a turning point in the Israelite conception of wisdom.

The author of Deuteronomy and the Deuteronomist conceive wisdom in an entirely novel manner. In the Tetrateuch and in pre-deuteronomic historical traditions 'wisdom' signifies native shrewdness (2 Sam. 13: 3; 1 Kgs. 2: 9)[1], persuasive speech (2 Sam. 14: 2; 20: 16),[2] artistic skill and craftsmanship (= τέχνη; Gen. 41: 8, 33, 39; Exod. 7: 11; 28: 3; 31: 6; 35: 25 and 26; 36: 1, etc.),[3] and general knowledge (2 Sam. 14: 20).[4]

These traits, especially the last, characterize Solomon in the pre-deuteronomic tradition (1 Kgs. 2: 5–9; 3: 16–27; 5: 9–14; 10: 1–10 and 23–4), where he is depicted as a cunning individual capable of outwitting the next fellow (2: 5–9; 3: 16–27), as possessing extraordinary knowledge of natural phenomena

[1] The last verse belongs to the pre-deuteronomic strand of the narrative, as opposed to vv. 3–4 which are of Deuteronomic origin. Cf. above, p. 11. Solomon is here depicted as an insidious person capable of finding the proper pretext to kill Shimei the son of Gera.

[2] The royal counsellors also belong to the category of the 'wise', since they owe their position to their gift of speech and rhetoric, see P. A. H. de Boer, 'The Counsellor', *SVT* 3 (1955), 42 ff.; W. McKane, *Prophets and Wise Men*, Studies in Biblical Theology, 44, 1965.

[3] Joseph is described as a wise and perspicacious person because of skill in interpreting dreams like the wise men of the Egyptian court (v. 8). However, his wisdom also finds expression in his exceptional ability in organizing food supplies during the famine years (vv. 33 and 39), cf. G. von Rad, 'The Joseph Narrative and the Ancient Wisdom', *The Problem of the Hexateuch*, 292–300.

The attribute חכם לב, characteristic of the Priestly code, denotes a person possessing superior artistic and creative skill. A similar expression also occurs in Assyrian texts, cf. *niklat libbi* in Sennacherib inscription K 4730 (verso l. 16) (H. Tadmor, *EI* 5, 1958, p. 156). Cf. also E. Weidner, *AfO* 18 (1957), 353: 77.

[4] See below, pp. 257 f.

(5: 9–14),[1] as a highly skilled artisan (10: 4),[2] and as a pragmatically successful ruler. Thus, whereas deuteronomic tradition describes Solomon as having proved himself worthy of being king over *all Israel* because of his display of judicial wisdom (3: 28), in pre-deuteronomic tradition he figures as a monarch who astounds *all the world* with his prodigious knowledge (5: 14; 10: 1[3] and 23–4) and extraordinary talents.

R. B. Y. Scott distinguishes between these two traditions concerning Solomon's wisdom in the books of Kings and regards 1 Kgs. 5: 9–14 and 10: 1–10 as post-deuteronomic accretions.[4] He is of the opinion that the sapiential image of Solomon was created during the Hezekiah period when the Israelite sapiential class first became prominent, and that it is reflected in the deuteronomic tradition in 1 Kgs. 3: 5–14, not in the tradition recorded in 5: 9–14 and 10: 1–10. In view of Alt's study,[5] however, there is no reason to repudiate the tradition in 1 Kgs. 5: 9–14, which in the light of onomastic analogues encountered in Egyptian and Mesopotamian literature appears to be of greater antiquity and authenticity than the deuteronomic. Thus the Hezekiah period, which marked the beginning of deuteronomic literary activity,[6] is not to be regarded as the period in which the traditions concerning Solomonic wisdom first crystallized, as Scott argues, but as one which marks a historical turning-point in the development of the Israelite conception of wisdom. During this period, which is marked by a resurgence of intellectual literary activity, the concept 'wisdom' had taken on a new meaning which accorded with the new temper of the times. The Deuteronomist no longer conceived of 'wisdom' as meaning cunning, pragmatic talent, or the possession of extraordinary knowledge, but held it to be synonymous with the knowledge and understanding of proper behaviour and with morality.

Until the seventh century Law and Wisdom existed as two separate and autonomous disciplines. Law belonged to the sacral sphere, whereas Wisdom dealt with the secular and the mundane.

[1] Cf. A. Alt, 'Die Weisheit Salomos', *KS* II, 90–9.

[2] For further remarks on this verse see J. A. Montgomery, *Kings*, ICC, p. 216.

[3] The ability to solve riddles also requires an accurate knowledge of flora and fauna, cf. Judg. 15: 12–18; Prov. 30: 15–31. Cf. O. Eissfeldt, *Einleitung*³, pp. 114–15.

[4] R. B. Y. Scott, 'Solomon and the Beginnings of Wisdom in Israel', *SVT* 3 (1955), 262 ff.

[5] Art. cit. in n. 1 above.

[6] Cf. above, pp. 161 f.

These two disciplines were amalgamated in the book of Deuteronomy, and the laws of the Torah were now identified with wisdom: '. . . for this is your wisdom and your understanding' (Deut. 4: 6).[1] This identification of Torah with wisdom is indeed somewhat paradoxical, for laws and statutes which were given by God are here regarded as being indicative of the wisdom and understanding of Israel. The verse undoubtedly reflects the difficulties which resulted from the sapiential desire to identify Torah with wisdom. The inherent contradiction was ultimately resolved only by identifying wisdom with Torah, as a result of which both were conceived together as a heavenly element which descended from heaven to take up its abode among the children of Israel (Ben-Sira 24).

Just as the author of the book of Deuteronomy identified law and judgement with wisdom, so the Deuteronomist regarded Solomon's judicial perspicacity, not his knowledge, as the major component of his unparalleled wisdom (1 Kgs. 3: 12). Until the seventh century Solomon's wisdom was conventionally understood: in terms of his pragmatic talents and prodigious knowledge on the one hand (1 Kgs. 5: 9–14; 10: 1–9 and 23–4), and on the other, in terms of his native shrewdness and acumen and his successful machinations (1 Kgs. 3: 16–27). The scribes of the seventh century in contrast began conceiving it in a judicial sense and in terms of his ability to discern between social good and evil. It was they who ascribed the *Lebensweisheit* proverbs, which they had begun collating during this period, to Solomon.

The Deuteronomist, however, not only projected Solomon as a sage and magistrate in the tradition of his own school, but also attempted to depict him in a similar light even in the earlier traditions in which he had originally figured as a cunning and knowledgeable person. Thus, for instance, the narrative in 1 Kgs. 3: 16–27, in which he is represented as cunning and shrewd (cf. 2: 9), was inserted by the Deuteronomist in a wider literary context which describes his judicial wisdom (3: 5–28), thereby altering the character of the episode and making it demonstrate Solomon's judicial intellect rather than the native shrewdness and machinations which were the original point of the episode.

The Deuteronomist has apparently conceived the tradition concerning Solomon's pragmatic successes and prodigious knowledge

[1] See above, pp. 150 f.

in a similar manner. These were not, in his view, manifestations of Solomon's wisdom, as assumed in the ancient tradition which the Deuteronomist inserted in his composition, but rather the divine reward bestowed upon him for his love of (judicial) wisdom. In wisdom literature we meet with the idea that he who chooses the path of wisdom will be rewarded with 'long life' ארך ימים and 'riches and honour' עשר וכבוד (Prov. 3: 16). In accordance with this axiom God promises Solomon unsurpassed 'riches and honour' גם עשר גם כבוד, and if he will walk in the path of the Lord he is assured that his days 'shall be lengthened' והארכתי את ימיך (1 Kgs. 3: 13–14). Wealth and honour are promised him as his reward for requesting wisdom, and he is assured of a long life if he observes its tenets (i.e. the laws of the Torah). The wealth which God promises Solomon is reflected, according to the Deuteronomist, in the splendour and magnificence of the Solomonic court (ch. 10), while the divine promise of honour is fulfilled in the universal fame enjoyed by the Israelite monarch (5: 9–14).

This development in the conception of wisdom led to an ideological conflict which has left traces in wisdom literature and the book of Deuteronomy. Thus, for example, the author of Job 28[1] repudiates the conventional sapiential view which identifies wisdom with the knowledge and understanding of nature's laws and asserts that the wisdom of cosmic creation and nature is possessed only by God and 'man knoweth not the way'[2] to it. Man's wisdom, the author declares, lies in his fear of God. 'Behold the fear of the Lord, that is wisdom; and to depart from evil is understanding' (v. 28). This view also underlies the divine reply to Job in chs. 38 ff. In a sarcastic vein, reminiscent of the queries put by the learned Egyptian scribe to the novice in the Anastasi Payprus 1,[3] God questions Job concerning nature and the cosmos. Von Rad[4] rightly contends

[1] Most scholars regard the chapter as an extraneous sapiential composition later incorporated in the book of Job. However, even those who regard it as having originally formed a part of the book are nevertheless of the opinion that it stands as an independent composition, cf., e.g., N. H. Tur-Sinai, *The Book of Job*, Jerusalem, 1957, pp. 394–5.

[2] The LXX renders דרכה for the MT's ערכה. The underlying idea of both versions is nevertheless the same: it is beyond man's capacity ever to comprehend the mysteries and marvels of nature and the cosmos.

[3] See *ANET*[2], pp. 475–9.

[4] G. von Rad, 'Job xxxviii and Ancient Egyptian Wisdom', *The Problem of the Hexateuch*, pp. 281–91.

that the subject-matter of these questions, as well as those in the Anastasi Papyrus, was taken from ancient onomastica which, among other things, contained detailed material on geographical and cosmological subjects. In the same manner in which scribal instructors were wont to test the knowledge of student scribes, God tests the knowledge of Job and castigates him for his ignorance. The difference lies only in that the questions put by the Egyptian scribes could easily have been answered by a novice who had studied his onomastic material properly, while those which God puts to Job concern matters beyond the scope of human comprehension and thus ridicule man's desire to acquire such knowledge. Indeed Job himself ultimately acknowledges this and declares: '. . . therefore have I uttered that which I did not understand, things too wonderful for me, which I did not know' לכן הגדתי ולא אבין נפלאות ממני ולא אדע (42: 3).

This polemic against the view that wisdom consists of universal knowledge seems also to underlie such gnomic dicta as 'The fear of the Lord is the beginning of wisdom' (Ps. 111: 10; Prov. 9: 10) and 'The fear of the Lord is the beginning of knowledge' (1: 7). The sapiential authors of these dicta apparently wished to say thereby that man's wisdom lies in his moral behaviour. They realized that the human mind could neither fathom the mysteries of creation nor acquire universal knowledge (cf. Ps. 139: 6; Ben-Sira 11: 4) and that the only wisdom man could aspire to was that which pertained to human affairs, i.e. *Lebensweisheit* and not *Naturweisheit*.

A similar note may be discerned in Deut. 30: 11–14: 'For this commandment which I command you this day *is not too wondrous* (נפלאת) *for you, neither is it far off* (רחקה). It is not in heaven, that you should say: "Who will go up for us to heaven, and bring it to us, that we may hear it and do it?" Neither is it beyond the sea, that you should say: "Who will go over the sea for us, and bring it to us, that we may hear and do it?" But the word is very near you; it is in your mouth and in your heart, so that you can do it.' Like the wisdom sources quoted above, the author of Deuteronomy asserts that his teaching may be comprehended by all who accept it. Unlike the cosmic knowledge of which Job says: '(It is) too *wonderful* (נפלאות) for me, (and) which I did not know' (42: 3), and unlike the wisdom of embryogeny (i.e. the secret of animate existence) concerning which the psalmodic poet says: 'Such knowledge is too *wonderful*

(פלאיה) for me; too high, I cannot attain it' (Ps. 139: 6), it is plain and intelligible to all. The expression נפלא ממני ולא אדע was apparently a conventional sapiential idiom employed in encyclopedic and onomastic compositions, principally in connection with riddles. In Prov. 30: 15–33 we meet with a group of numerical proverbs, most of which deal with natural, and particularly animal, life. Scholars have recognized that these proverbs belong to the same genre as those ascribed to Solomon in 1 Kgs. 5: 12–13.[1] One of the numerical proverbs in this collection opens as follows: 'three things are too *wonderful* (נפלאו) for me; four I do not understand (לא ידעתים)' (v. 18). Tur-Sinai[2] has correctly pointed out that this and other numerical proverbs of the same collection ultimately derive from riddle questions, such as: 'What things are insatiable?' or 'What things leave no traces after them?', and the like. The riddles with which the Queen of Sheba (1 Kgs. 10: 1) and Hiram, King of Tyre, (according to a tradition preserved by Josephus)[3] tested Solomon seem to have been of this sort.

As opposed to those things which are too *wondrous* for man to comprehend, the author of Deuteronomy describes his teaching to the reader as being 'not too wondrous (נפלאת) for you'. In contrast to that wisdom which is *remote* (רחק) and which no man can hope to acquire (Eccles. 7: 23),[4] he states that the wisdom of his teaching is not inaccessible (רחקה) to man.

Within the context of this polemic concerning the wondrous and inaccessible nature of wisdom the author of Deuteronomy declares, as we have observed above, that the wisdom of his teaching 'is not in heaven that (one) should say: "who will go up for us to heaven?" . . .' (v. 12). In a similar context, and in phraseology like that met with in the knowledge-testing questions of the Anastasi Papyrus and in Job 38–9 Agur son of Jakeh, after acknowledging the limitations of his intellectual capacity (Prov. 30: 1–3), asks 'Who has ascended to heaven and come down?' (v. 4).

A close parallel to Deut. 30: 11–14 is found in the 'Babylonian Theodicy'.[5] The eighth stanza of this wisdom poem conveys the idea that in contrast to the divine knowledge which is remote like

[1] See, e.g., O. Eissfeldt, *Einleitung*[3], pp. 114–15; A. Alt, *KS* II, pp. 90–9.

[2] משלי שלמה, Tel-Aviv, 1947, 62; cf. also Eissfeldt, *Einleitung*[3].

[3] *Antiquities* viii. 143–9.

[4] Cf. H. L. Ginsberg, קהלת, Jerusalem, 1961, p. 102.

[5] Cf. Lambert, *BWL*, 76, ll. 78–88. I am indebted to Professor J. J. Finkelstein (Yale University) for this reference.

the inner part of the heaven[1] the commands of the gods *are close at hand*[2] and are given for mankind to study properly. This passage can be correctly understood against the background of ll. 256–7 of this poem. There we read: 'The divine mind is as remote as the inner part of the heaven, knowledge of it is difficult, mankind does not know it.'[3]

We may conclude that the author of Deuteronomy has employed sapiential material of the same type in order to emphasize that the wisdom embodied in his teaching may be easily understood by all: 'For the word is very near you; it is in your mouth and in your heart, so that you can do it.'

2. WISDOM CONTENT IN DEUTERONOMY

The book of Deuteronomy contains laws which have almost literal parallels in both Israelite and non-Israelite wisdom literature. Several scholars have called attention to these parallels,[4] but they seem to have reversed the order of things by concluding that the Biblical wisdom literature was influenced by the book of Deuteronomy instead of the other way round. This conclusion is based on the presupposition current in Biblical scholarship during the early decades of this century that the book of Deuteronomy antedated the book of Proverbs. Its groundlessness has been proved by the discovery during the recent decades of wisdom compositions which clearly demonstrate that Israelite wisdom teaching is substantially of ancient origin[5] and consequently antedates the book of Deuteronomy.

The assertion that wisdom literature adopted material from the book of Deuteronomy is improbable also for other reasons:

1. Parallels to Deuteronomy are met with not only in Israelite

[1] *ki-i qi-rib šamê* (l. 82, compare p. 86, l. 256, and Lambert's comment on p. 309).

[2] *qé-ru-ub ṭé-en-ši-na* (l. 87). *ṭēmu* in this context is not 'reason' as Lambert translates but 'decision' or 'decree' (compare *qibīt pî* in l. 83, *kibsu* in l. 86).

[3] *BWL*, p. 86: *libbi ili kīma qirib šamê nesīma, lē'ûssu šupšuqatma nišê la lamdā*. *nesû* is equated with *rūqu* (cf. *AHw*, p. 781) = Heb. רחוק.

[4] See A. Robert, 'Les attaches littéraires bibliques de Prov. I–IX', *RB* 43 (1934), 42–68, 172–204, 374–84; 44 (1935), 344–65, 502–25; W. O. E. Oesterley, *The Wisdom of Egypt and the Old Testament*, 1927, pp. 76 f.; R. Pfeiffer, 'Edomitic Wisdom', *ZAW* 44 (1926), p. 17 n. 3; J. Fichtner, *Die altorientalische Weisheit in ihrer israelitisch-jüdischer Ausprägung*, 1933, pp. 26–7.

[5] See, for instance, W. Baumgartner, *Israelitische und altorientalische Weisheit*, 1933; W. F. Albright; 'Some Canaanite–Phoenician Sources of Hebrew Wisdom', *SVT* 3 (1955), 1–15.

wisdom literature but also in extra-Biblical wisdom literature. Are we to assume that the book of Deuteronomy also influenced Egyptian and Babylonian wisdom literature?

2. If deuteronomic thinking really had an impact on Israelite wisdom literature, how are we to account for the fact that the material supposedly drawn from the book of Deuteronomy does not contain the slightest suggestion of the religio-national concept that lay at the core of deuteronomic teaching?

Let us briefly consider the principal parallels between the book of Deuteronomy and Israelite wisdom literature:

'You shall not add to the word which I command, nor take from it' לא תוסיפו על הדבר אשר אנכי מצוה אתכם ולא תגרעו ממנו (Deut. 4: 2). 'All this that I command you you shall be careful to observe; you shall not add to it or take away from it' את כל הדבר אשר אנכי מצוה אתכם אתו תשמרו לעשות לא תסף עליו ולא תגרע ממנו (Deut. 13: 1; cf. Jer. 26: 2).

'All the word of God (כל אמרת אלוה) proves true . . . Do not add to his words (אל תוסף על דבריו) lest he rebuke you, and you be found a liar' (Prov. 30: 5–6). 'Whatever God does (כל אשר יעשה האלהים) endures for ever; nothing can be added to it; nor anything taken away from it' עליו אין להוסיף וממנו אין לגרע (Eccles. 3: 14; cf. Ben-Sira 18: 6; 42: 21).

Many scholars find a parallel to this exhortation in a passage of the Instruction of Ptahhotep[1] (*m iṯj md.t m inj.śj m rdj. k.t. m ś.t k.t*), which until recently has been translated as follows: 'Neither add a word nor detract, and exchange not one for another.'[2] The phraseology of this passage was found to be so similar to the verses in Deut. 4: 2 and 13: 1 that J. Leipoldt and S. Morenz[3] assumed that the deuteronomic phraseology had been influenced by Egyptian wisdom literature. However, a new translation has recently been suggested for this passage, 'say not first "thus" and afterwards "thus", and exchange not one thing for another',[4]

[1] *Papyrus Prisse*, 18, 7–8, cf. Z. Žába, *Les Maximes de Ptaḥḥotep*, 1956, p. 63: 608–9.

[2] Cf. A. Volten, *Studien zum Weisheitsbuch des Anii*, 1937, p. 8; Leipoldt–Morenz, *Heilige Schriften*, 1953, p. 56.

[3] Ibid., p. 56.

[4] Z. Žába, *Les Maximes de Ptaḥḥotep*, 1956, pp. 104, 169 f.; see also: S. Morenz, *Ägyptische Religion*, 1960, p. 235. Morenz contends that even if the new translation proves to be correct, later Egyptian and non-Egyptian (e.g. Israelite) scribes nevertheless interpreted the passage in the way in which modern Egyptologists had at first interpreted it, as referring to the literal obedience to

which makes the analogous character of the Egyptian passage rather doubtful.

However, we do encounter this formulation in Mesopotamian literature—though in a prophetic rather than in a speculative context. On stylistic grounds the Mesopotamian text has a greater affinity to the deuteronomic formulation than does the Egyptian passage in its hitherto accepted translation. It reads as follows: 'It was revealed to him in the night, and when he spoke in the morning he did not leave out a single line, nor did he add one to it.'[1] Unlike the formulation in the earlier translation of the Egyptian passage, in which the object added to or detracted from it occurs in the accusative case,[2] in the Mesopotamian as in the deuteronomic formulation it is in the dative case preceded by the preposition 'on' (*ana muḫḫi*).

This formulation is also encountered in the closing section of ancient Greek treaties,[3] and the question thus presents itself whether the deuteronomic formulation might not derive from the vocabulary of ancient treaty forms,[4] particularly when we consider that the frame of Deuteronomy is based on this pattern of ancient Near-Eastern treaty formulae. However, as it does not occur in the closing section of the covenant in the book of Deuteronomy and has no reference to the 'words of the covenant', it is difficult to regard it as a juristic formula.

Be the original character of the formula as it may, it is none the less true that it is employed as an admonition both in wisdom literature and in the book of Deuteronomy, and an investigation

the text. The expression *iṯj inj* literally means *to take and to bring*, an Egyptian idiom which may be interpreted in two ways: *to detract and to add* or *to act first in one manner and then in another*.

[1] *ina šāt mūši ušabrīšuma kî ša ina munatti idbubu ajamma ul iḫti ēda šuma ul uraddi ana muḫḫi*, cf. F. Gössmann, *Das Era Epos*, 1956, V: 43; W. G. Lambert, 'The Fifth Tablet of the Era Epic', *Iraq* 24 (1962), 122, ll. 43–4.

[2] See W. Herrmann, 'Zu Kohelet 3, 14', *Wissenschaftliche Zeitschrift der Karl Marx Universität*, Gesell. und Sprachwiss. Reihe, 3 (1953–4), p. 294.

[3] Cf. H. Bengston, *Die Staatsverträge des Altertums: Die Verträge der griechisch-römischen Welt von 700 bis 338 v. Chr.*, vol. II, 1962; *Die Verträge der griech.-röm. Welt von 338 bis 200 v. Chr.*, vol. III, 1969 (see Index). The phrase there is προστίθημι ἢ ἀφαιρέω, which is identical with the LXX translation of Deut. 4: 2, 13: 1, and Eccles. 3: 14. Cf. also Rev. 22: 18 f. and 1 Macc. 8: 30 (the treaty of Judas Maccabeus with the Romans).

[4] Cf. H. G. Güterbock, 'Mursili's accounts of Suppiluliuma's dealings with Egypt', *RHA* 66 (1960), 59–60, ll. 7 ff.: 'To this tablet I did not add a word nor did I take one out. O gods, my lords, look, I do not know whether any of those who were kings before (me) added [a word] or took one out.'

of the affinity between the formulae employed in these two sources may help us in determining which of them is the more natural and original context. Since we have already observed that there is no justification for assuming deuteronomic influence on wisdom literature, we need only consider the alternative hypothesis, that the deuteronomic formula was adopted from sapiential composition. This indeed appears to be the case. Prov. 30: 6, for example, occurs in a speculative context and articulates the idea that the wisdom of divine creation lies beyond the scope of human comprehension[1] and thus remains inscrutable and unattainable by man. The wisdom that does lie within man's reach is religio-moral wisdom (= the 'word of God', Prov. 30: 5) which, in contrast to cosmogonic knowledge, has been tried and demonstrated (cf. Ps. 13: 7)[2] and is consequently not to be doubted nor modified. This view which, as we have seen above,[3] lies at the core of Job 28 and underlies God's reply to Job (38–41) and the repeated dicta that the fear of God is the beginning of wisdom[4] was apparently developed further and assumed additional connotations in Biblical psalmodic literature and in later wisdom literature. Thus the 'word of God' in the Psalms signifies not only the word and command of God (Ps. 18: 31) but also his oracles and promises (12: 7);[5] in the Torah psalms the expression came to denote God's Torah as it does in the book of Deuteronomy, while in later Israelite wisdom literature it signifies God's conduct of human affairs (Eccles. 3: 14, Ben-Sira 18: 6; 42: 21). In any event it is evident that the formula substantially derived from sapiential thought and that it was developed along the lines of Torah ideology in the book of Deuteronomy and in later wisdom literature.

The phrase in question occurs therefore in a distinctly sapiential ideological context; and Herrmann's view[6] that the deuteronomic formula (which to his mind was adopted from the Instructions

[1] N. H. Tur-Sinai reads in Prov. 30: 1: לאיתי אל לאיתי אל ואכל 'I have wearied myself, O God, I have wearied myself, O God, and can I (endure any longer)?' משלי שלמה, 1947, p. 2 (Hebrew). Be it as it may, Prov. 30: 1–4 nevertheless expresses weariness and disappointment with conventional wisdom (= *Naturweisheit*), cf. above, pp. 257 f.

[2] See also Ps. 18: 31 (cf. Pss. 119: 140; 19: 8–10) in which the poet's intent is that God's way is perfect and his word is true and proven and one must therefore place his trust in God.

[3] p. 257.

[4] See N. H. Tur-Sinai, *Job*, ad loc.

[5] See Gunkel's commentary, HKAT, ad loc.

[6] 'Zu Kohelet 3, 14.'

of Ptahhotep)[1] influenced Prov. 30: 6, which in turn influenced the book of Ecclesiastes must be rejected. The converse is to be assumed, that wisdom literature had in this respect influenced the book of Deuteronomy. The formula in Proverbs and Ecclesiastes is best explained against the background of sapiential[2] rather than deuteronomic ideology, and thus appears to support our supposition that the phrase has a sapiential rather than a deuteronomic provenance. Furthermore, Herrmann published his views when the passage in the Egyptian composition was assumed to treat unequivocally of 'adding to or detracting from' the given counsel; now that it has been shown that the passage may be rendered otherwise, his view that the phrase is of Egyptian origin falls to the ground. It appears then that the author of Deuteronomy adopted the phrase from sapiential sources, just as he had adopted other sapiential expressions and values, except that in this instance he stripped the phrase of its speculative import and employed it simply as an exhortation.

It is to be noted moreover that traces of the former background and original context of the formula can still be discerned in the book of Deuteronomy. We have already observed[3] that the author of Deuteronomy contrasts his teaching, which may be easily comprehended, with the 'wondrous and remote' knowledge (30: 11–14) which can be neither comprehended nor attained by man, a notion which constitutes the deuteronomic rationale for the observance of the word of God as it was conveyed to Israel. However, whereas in Prov. 30: 1–6 the 'wondrous' concept of wisdom is still referred to in association with the concept of 'do not add', these two concepts were separated in the book of Deuteronomy. A slight trace of the original association of these two ideas may perhaps still be discerned in the proximity of Deut. 4: 6: 'Keep them and do

[1] Herrmann correctly observes (op. cit., p. 295 n. 21) that the deuteronomic commandment does not refer to strict obedience to the literal text: 'Schon das Dtn nimmt die Formel des Ptahhotep nicht genau in dem Sinne jenes Ägypters auf. Dem liegt tatsächlich an jeden einzelnen Wort, während man übereinstimmend der Meinung sein wird, dass die entsprechenden Stellen im Dtn die Gebote als ganze meinen'. But his observation did not appear to alter his opinion that the passage in Deuteronomy was influenced by the Ptahhotep composition.

[2] For an interesting interpretation of Deut. 13: 1 see M. Greenberg, 'Ezekiel XX and spiritual Exile', *'Oz le-David, Biblical Essays in honor of D. Ben-Gurion*, 1964, p. 437 n. 3 (Hebrew). However, his interpretation of that verse does not elucidate the meaning and background of Deut. 4: 2.

[3] Above, pp. 258 f.

them; for that will be your wisdom and your understanding' to verse 2 of the same chapter. The proximity of the two verses seems to convey the impression that the purpose of verse 6 is to declare that the defined and given Torah constituted true wisdom and consequently one should neither add to nor detract from it.

2. You shall not move your neighbour's landmark, set up by previous generations לא תסיג גבול רעך אשר גבלו ראשונים (Deut. 19: 14, cf. 27: 17).	Move not the ancient landmark set up by your fathers. אל תסג גבול עולם אשר עשו אבותיך (Prov. 22: 28). Do not move an ancient landmark[1] or enter the fields of the fatherless (Prov. 23: 10).
You shall not have in your bag alternate weights (אבן ואבן), larger and smaller. You shall not have in your house alternate measures (איפה ואיפה), a larger and smaller. A full and just weight (אבן שלמה) you shall have .... For all who do such things, all who act dishonestly, *are an abomination to the Lord* your God (Deut. 25: 13–16).	Alternate weights (אבן ואבן) and alternate measures (איפה ואיפה) are both alike *an abomination* to the Lord but a just weight (אבן שלמה) is his delight (11: 1). Alternate weights (אבן ואבן) are *an abomination to the Lord*; and false scales are not good (20: 23, cf. v. 10).

Removing landmarks and using false weights and measures are the themes of a great many exhortations in Israelite and non-Israelite[2] wisdom literature. This need not surprise us, for sapiential morality, which attempted to achieve its ends by persuasion and preaching, primarily treats of clandestine malefactions which cannot be effectively controlled by society. There is no warrant then for assuming that the book of Proverbs was influenced by Deuteronomy, particularly with respect to this subject. On the contrary, an examination of parallel passages in Proverbs, Deuteronomy, and the Teaching of Amenemope will demonstrate that the author of Deuteronomy was influenced in this respect by the school of wisdom rather than the converse.

The two exhortations in the book of Proverbs which treat of the removal of landmarks occur in the collection comprising chs. 22:

[1] In the light of the Egyptian parallel in the Teaching of Amenemope and the conventional biblical parallelism אלמנה, יתום, the word עולם in this verse has generally been emended to אלמנה. However, the reading עולים (= infants) was suggested as far back as 1860 by A. Geiger (*Hechalutz* V, 26) and has been adopted by more recent scholars, see Tur-Sinai, משלי שלמה, p. 52 and I. L. Seeligmann, 'Voraussetzungen der Midrashexegese', *SVT* 1 (1953), 165–7.

[2] See J. Fichtner, *Die altorient. Weisheit*, pp. 26–7.

17–23: 11, which as a whole parallels the Teaching of Amenemope.[1] The general consensus of opinion is that it was the Egyptian composition which had directly or indirectly influenced the Biblical collection. Even the small minority of scholars who argue for an Israelite influence on the Egyptian composition[2] must concur that the exhortations under discussion are not of Israelite origin, since they are also encountered in Egyptian sapiential compositions which antedate the Amenemope collection.[3] It may be assumed, then, that the exhortations in the book of Proverbs were formulated under the influence of Egyptian wisdom literature. Even if this supposition were also to be rejected it must none the less be conceded in view of the parallels in Israelite[4] and non-Israelite wisdom[5] literature that these exhortations possess a distinctly sapiential character. Now if some relationship between the exhortations in Deut. 19: 14 and Prov. 22: 28 does exist—as is plainly evident from their similar phraseology—we can only conclude that the author of Deuteronomy was influenced in this instance by sapiential literature and not the contrary.

Although the formula is substantially sapiential in character it was developed in its own distinct manner in the book of Deuteronomy. This may be inferred by contrasting it with its development in the book of Proverbs itself. Tur-Sinai has recognized[6] that the phrase 'Do not move the ancient landmark' originally constituted an independent and apparently ancient one-line aphorism, which was later expanded into a bi-colon or couplet—a common literary device in the book of Proverbs—in two different ways: (*a*) by the addition of a synthetic colon 'which your fathers have set' (22: 28) or (*b*) by the addition of a synonymous colon: 'or enter the fields of the fatherless' (23: 10), which is based on the reading עוּלִים (= *young children*) instead of עוֹלָם (= *ancient*).[7] The author of Deuteronomy, on the other hand, expanded the aphorism in the first of these two ways, but did so in his own characteristic manner and in accordance with the national orientations of his composition. He added the phrase: 'in the inheritance which you will hold in the land that the Lord your God gives you'

[1] For the parallel to our case compare the sixth chapter of Amenemope, *ANET*², 422.

[2] See below, p. 295 n. 1.

[3] See, e.g., 'The Protests of the Eloquent Peasant', *ANET*², 408; 100–75.

[4] See Job 24: 2 and compare 31: 38–9.

[5] Cf. Fichtner, *Die altorient. Weisheit*, pp. 26–7.

[6] משלי שלמה, p. 52.

[7] Cf. above, p. 265 n. 1.

etc., and accordingly altered the formula by replacing the phrase 'ancient (עולם) landmark' by the clause 'a landmark set up by the previous generations' (ראשנים), i.e. the landmark set by those who first settled the land (cf. Lev. 26: 45).[1]

The deuteronomic interdiction against the falsification of weights and measures is also dependent on sapiential teaching, as becomes particularly clear when one compares the deuteronomic law with its analogue in Lev. 19: 35–6. Thus we discover that the expressions used in the exhortations against the falsification of weights and measures in the book of Proverbs, the Teaching of Amenemope, and in Babylonian wisdom literature,[2] such as אבן שלמה, (אבני) כיס, איפה ואיפה, אבן ואבן, are also employed in the deuteronomic law, but are lacking in the parallel law in Lev. 19. Moreover, the deuteronomic law and the analogous sapiential exhortations are accompanied by the same rationale: 'for it is an abomination to Yahweh', an expression which is found only in the book of Deuteronomy and the book of Proverbs. The exhortation against the falsification of weights and measures in the Teaching of Amenemope[3] is provided with the same rationale: 'make not for yourself a bushel measure of two capacities . . . for the bushel is the eye of Re,[4] *its abomination* is he who detracts from it' (xviii: 21–xix: 1). The fact that the expression 'an abomination to God' is employed as the rationale of the exhortation against the falsification of weights and measures in the book of Deuteronomy, Proverbs, and the Teaching of Amenemope alike may indeed enable us to clarify its significance. The use of false weights and measures represents the classic example of deception and hypocrisy; and, as we shall presently see, the large majority of the interdictions accompanied by the rationale 'it is an abomination to God' concern practices which are fundamentally

[1] See Driver, *Deuteronomy*, ICC, ad loc. However, the use of the word ראשונים instead of the synonymous term עולם (cf. Isa. 61: 4) may be in keeping with general deuteronomic diction, cf., e.g., Deut. 4: 32 as opposed to 32: 7.

[2] Cf., e.g., the phrase *muš-te-nu-ú* [*a-b*]*a-an ki-i-si* 'he who uses two sets of weights' in the Šamas Hymn, W. G. Lambert, *BWL*, p. 132 l. 108, cf. also p. 319 n. 69.

[3] For the text, translation, and comments, cf. M. O. Lange, *Das Weisheitsbuch des Amenemope*, 1925. I wish to thank Dr. M. Gilula for putting at my disposal his (unpublished) work on the Teaching of Amenemope, on which I have based part of the present discussion.

[4] For the expression 'the eyes of Yahweh', cf. Deut. 11: 12; Prov. 5: 21; 15: 3; compare Pss. 11: 4; 94: 9–10. On its affinity to the expression the 'eyes of Re', see A. S. Yahuda, *The Language of the Pentateuch in its Relation to the Egyptian*, p. 62 n. 3.

hypocritical and deceptive in character. Let us review the passages in question and try to ascertain their common underlying character.

In the Teaching of Amenemope the expression 'an abomination of God' occurs four times: twice with respect to hypocrisy (xiv: 2–3; xiii: 15–16), once with respect to slander (xv: 20–1), and once with respect to the falsification of weights (xviii: 21–xix: 1). In the book of Proverbs the expression 'an abomination to Yahweh' occurs in connection with the perverse individual, as opposed to the upright (3: 32; 11: 20); the mendacious, as opposed to those who act in good faith (12: 22); the sacrifice of the wicked (15: 8); the way of the wicked, as opposed to the pursuit of righteousness (v. 9); the thoughts of the wicked, as opposed to the words of the pure (v. 26); the arrogant (16: 5); justification of the wicked and condemnation of the righteous (17: 15); and the falsification of weights and measures (11: 1; 20: 10 and 23). In the book of Deuteronomy it occurs in connection with idolatrous images (7: 25–6; 27: 15), child burning (12: 31), the sacrifice of blemished animals (17: 1), idolatrous mantic practices (18: 9–12); transvestite practices (22: 5), sacral offerings financed from the earnings of sacral prostitutions (23: 19), remarrying one's divorced wife (24: 4), and the falsification of weights and measures (25: 13–16).

As the expression 'an abomination to Yahweh' occurs, then, in connection with miscellaneous moral, religious, and cultic interdictions, an investigation of their subject-matter can be of little help in ascertaining its original significance. We shall learn more by investigating the general *nature* of the individual malefactions than from their specific *subject-matter*. Now the general feature common to them all is the two-faced or hypocritical attitude of the malefactor, the classic example being that of the falsifier of weights and measures. It is this two-facedness or false pretension assumed when dealing with one's fellow man or in the execution of one's sacrificial dues that is an abomination to God. In the book of Proverbs this expression occurs mainly in aphorisms pertaining to the individual's social conduct, i.e. with respect to his hypocritical or deceptive dealings with his fellow men.[1] In the one case in

[1] This applies to all the verses cited above. The maxim concerning the arrogant person also belongs to the category of aphorisms, as the person in question has unjustifiably assumed an overbearing attitude toward his fellow men.

I have cited only those proverbs in which the entire expression תועבת יהוה

which it is encountered in a cultic context, that pertaining to the sacrifice of the wicked (15: 8; cf. 28: 9), the point at issue is also the hypocritical attitude of the malefactor, in this case with respect to his relation to God: on the one hand he violates the precepts of God, yet on the other he offers sacrifice to the very author of these precepts.

Malefactions of the last type are the sort which predominate in the 'abomination' laws of the book of Deuteronomy. The introduction of idolatrous modes of worship into the cult of Yahweh (7: 25–6; 12: 31; 27: 15), the practice of idolatrous mantology to discover the word of Yahweh (18: 9–12), the offering of blemished animals as sacrifices (17: 1; cf. Mal. 1: 7–8)[1] and sacrifices financed by the earnings of sacral prostitution (23: 19) are all indicative of a certain religious vacillation on the part of the one whom the Teaching of Amenemope describes as the 'half-hearted'[2] as opposed to the 'whole-hearted' individual. The author of Deuteronomy after warning against the practice of such abomination enjoins the Israelite to be '*perfect* (תמים) before Yahweh' (18: 13), that is to be 'whole-hearted' and not act deceptively with the Lord. The term *whole-heartedness* (לב שלם) is indeed one of the basic expressions of deuteronomic historiography (1 Kgs. 8: 61; 11: 4; 15: 3 and 14; 2 Kgs. 20: 3) and was afterwards adopted by the Chronicler (1 Chr. 12: 38; 28: 9; 29: 9 and 19; 2 Chr. 16: 9; 25: 2).

Transvestism (Deut. 22: 5) appears to be an idolatrous practice[3] which fundamentally involves deceit and misrepresentation, while remarrying one's wife whom one had divorced after discovering an indecency in her (24: 1–4) constitutes, in essence, a lack of integrity and a hypocritical attitude toward the institution of marriage.[4]

occurs and not those which contain the word תועבה alone. The acts described as abominable in Prov. 6: 16–19 also involve pretence and deception. Thus, e.g., the shedding of 'innocent blood' (v. 17b) is generally committed by ambush and in concealed places (cf. Prov. 1: 11 and Ps. 10: 8–10). Actually the verse really refers to the practice of ensnaring a person into a detrimental position, the phrase 'innocent blood' being used only in a metaphoric sense; cf. 1: 19 and the comments of Gemser, *Sprüche*², on the cited verses.

[1] Cf. the Babylonian observation: 'the pig is not fit for a temple . . . an abomination to all the gods', Lambert, *BWL*, p. 215, ll. 15–16.

[2] 'His (god's) great abomination is the hypocrite (lit. split belly)' (xiv: 3).

[3] Cf. the Babylonian aphorism: 'an Amorite says to his wife: "You be the man, I will be the woman . . . I became a man . . . female" ', Lambert, *BWL*, p. 226, i: 1–6 and p. 230.

[4] ערות דבר means an 'indecent' or 'immodest' or 'improper act' (cf. Deut. 23: 15) and here suggests an act of infidelity or of sexual aberration committed by

3. When you make a vow to the Lord your God, you shall not be slack to pay it כי תדר נדר ליהוה אלהיך לא תאחר לשלמו; for the Lord your God will surely require it of you and it would be a sin in you (והיה בך חטא). But if you refrain from vowing it shall be no sin in you וכי תחדל לנדר לא יהיה בך חטא. You shall be careful to perform what has passed your lips . . . what you have promised with your mouth מוצא שפתיך תשמר ועשית . . . כאשר נדרת . . . אשר דברת בפיך (Deut. 23: 22–4).

Be not rash with your mouth nor let your heart be hasty to utter a word before God . . . אל תבהל על פיך ולבך אל ימהר להוציא דבר לפני האלהים . . . When you make a vow to God do not delay paying it כאשר תדר נדר לאלהים אל תאחר לשלמו, for he has no pleasures in fools. Pay what you vow. It is better that you should not vow than that you should vow and not pay. Let not your mouth lead you into sin. טוב אשר לא תדר משתדור ולא תשלם. אל תתן את פיך לחטיא את בשרך (Eccles. 5: 1–5).

It is a snare for a man to say rashly 'it is holy' and to reflect only after making his vows (Prov. 20: 25; cf. Ben-Sira 18: 22).

As may be gathered from the analogous exhortations in Prov. 20: 25 and Ben-Sira 18: 22, the subject-matter of the deuteronomic passage cited above is distinctly sapiential in character and we need not assume that the passage in Ecclesiastes is dependent upon it. It may be noted, moreover, that the exhortation in Ecclesiastes occurs in a distinctly sapiential context.[1] In Eccles. 4: 17–5: 6 the author warns his reader against reckless speech—a tendency which both Israelite and non-Israelite wisdom literatures very frequently treat of.[2] The author particularly warns against reckless speech in religio-cultic matters, as in prayer (5: 1)[3] or religious

the woman with the man whom she afterwards married—cf. the phrase 'after she has been defiled' (אחרי אשר הטמאה), 24: 4, cf. Lev. 18: 20, Num. 5: 13, 14, 20)—which is why the first husband is forbidden to remarry her (compare Jer. 3: 1), cf. also J. J. Rabinowitz, *JNES* 18 (1959), 73.

[1] Despite the lateness of the book it nevertheless contains a great deal of early material, compare, e.g., 9: 7–9 with the Old-Babylonian version of the Gilgamesh epic (*VAT* 4105, iii: 6–14, translated *ANET*², p. 90) and compare also the 'Song of the Harper' (*ANET*², p. 467). For a Mesopotamian parallel to Eccles. 4: 9–12, cf. A. Shaffer, *EI* 8 (1967), 247–50; 9 (1969), 159–60. For remarks and parallels see P. Humbert, *Recherches sur les sources égyptiennes de la littérature sapientiale d'Israël*, 1929, pp. 110 ff.

[2] See L. Dürr, *Das Erziehungswesen im Alten Testament und im Antiken Orient*, 1932, 42 ff., 139 ff.

[3] See the interpretation of Targum Jonathan which was taken up by both traditional and modern exegetes, cf., e.g., Hertzberg, KAT, and Zimmerli, ATD, ad loc.

vows and commitments (vv. 3–4) or other religious matters (v. 5).[1]

It is the sapiential view that a loquacious person or a person given to rash declarations is a fool who will only bring misfortune upon himself[2] or, as the author of Proverbs would say, he is certain to 'ensnare' himself (20: 25; 18: 7; cf. 12: 13).[3] Rather than make vows recklessly it is best not to vow at all and thus save oneself from possible misfortune. The motivation which urges the individual to adopt the advice is thus a distinctly utilitarian one, typical of sapiential literature. There is consequently no reason to seek Pentateuchal influence on this passage. The passage also exhibits an extremely reserved attitude toward the cult and divine worship, and H. L. Ginsberg is correct in observing that its 'frigidity almost bordering on antipathy' toward divine worship deviates from the normal Israelite attitude.[4] This attitude can hardly be a Pentateuchal one and is undoubtedly of sapiential origin. The style of the exhortation: 'It is better (טוב) that you should not vow than that you should vow and not pay' is also sapiential and is characteristic of the gnomic dicta which begin with the word 'better'.[5]

If any relationship does exist between the deuteronomical prescription and the sapiential exhortation, then it is evident that it is Deuteronomy which was dependent upon wisdom teaching rather than the contrary. Von Rad[6] is indeed quite correct when he asserts that this prescription is out of place in a legal code and that it rightfully and more suitably belongs in a sapiential homiletic context. Like wisdom literature, the prescription in Deut. 23: 22–4 strongly warns the Israelite to beware of the verbal commitments he makes:

[1] For a similar counsel by Babylonian wise men, compare: 'Beware of careless talk, guard your lips, do not utter solemn oaths while alone. For what you say in a moment will follow you afterwards', see Lambert, *BWL*, p. 104: 131–3 and his comments on p. 319.

[2] The root meaning of חטא is to 'miss the mark', hence 'to err, go wrong, be wanting' (cf., e.g., Job 31: 30). See H. L. Ginsberg, קהלת, 1961, pp. 6–18. The phrase לחטיא בשרך means therefore 'to cause the body to be wanting', i.e. to suffer; cf. also the phrase והעבר רעה מבשרך in Eccles. 11: 10.

[3] For the parallelism מוקש, חטא, cf. Exod. 23: 33; Isa. 29: 21.

[4] Ginsberg, קהלת, p. 26.

[5] On the טוב aphorisms in wisdom literature see W. Zimmerli, 'Zur Struktur der alttestamentlichen Weisheit', *ZAW* 51 (1933), 192–4. In Ecclesiastes these aphorisms are largely concentrated in ch. 7: 1–14.

[6] G. von Rad, *Deuteronomium*, ATD, 1964, p. 106.

'You shall be careful to perform . . . what you have promised with your mouth', the difference being only in the Torah phraseology in which the exhortation has been reworded so as to accommodate it to the religious aims of the book. In place of the neutral sapiential rationale: 'for (God) has no pleasure with fools', the author of Deuteronomy supplied it with a religious rationale: 'for the Lord your God will surely require it of you'. The term 'sin' (חטא) in the deuteronomic prescription is not used in the same sense as in the sapiential source, i.e., 'to bring misfortune upon oneself',[1] but in the religious sense of committing 'a religious wrong', as in Deut. 15: 9 and 24: 15. However, despite the fact that the exhortation has here been revised in a religious spirit, the original sapiential moment underlying the prescription may still be discerned.

4. You shall not turn over to his master a slave who seeks refuge with you from his master לא תסגיר עבד אל אדניו אשר ינצל אליך מעם אדניו (Deut. 23: 16).	Do not slander a servant to his master אל תלשן עבד אל אדניו (Prov. 30: 10).

This deuteronomic prescription also has a humanistic character and articulates a distinctly sapiential attitude.[2] It is rather strange to meet with a prescription of this sort in a law-code which by nature should be primarily concerned with stabilizing inter-class relations rather than prescribing laws which would tend to undermine them. Indeed, whereas ancient Near-Eastern law-codes[3] and state treaties[4] make special provisions for the extradition of fugitives, the book of Deuteronomy expressly forbids it. The deuteronomic prescription is not to be taken, then, as a legal ordinance but rather as an appeal to the conscience of the individual—of the type met with in wisdom literature—exhorting the free Israelite to give asylum to the fugitive slave who has fled from his oppressive master (cf. Gen. 16: 6).[5] Though the exhortation

[1] Cf. above, p. 271 n. 2.

[2] Cf. H. Ringgren, *Sprüche*, ATD, 1962, p. 116: 'Es ist ein kluger Rat rein menschlicher Weisheit.'

[3] See, e.g., CH, §§ 15–20; HL, §§ 22–4; and for this provision in legal contracts see Driver–Miles, *BL* I. 105–6.

[4] See, e.g., the treaty between Ḫatušiliš III and Ramses II (*ANET*², p. 203), the treaty between Idrimi and Piliya, and the treaty between Niqmepa of Alalaḫ and ÌR-IM of Tunip (D. J. Wiseman, *The Alalaḫ Tablets*, 1953, nos. 2 and 3).

[5] Slaves who were well treated did not flee from the masters; on the contrary, they would at times even refuse manumission, cf. Exod. 21: 5–6 and Deut. 15:

in Prov. 30: 10 treats of slander and not of surrendering a fugitive slave, the underlying humanistic incentive is the same (cf. Eccles. 7: 21–2), and its formulation identical with that of the deuteronomic ordinance; we may therefore legitimately assume that the deuteronomic prescription has its ultimate source in sapiential literature.[1]

5. You shall not be partial in judgement לא תכירו פנים במשפט (Deut. 1: 17; cf. 16: 19).	Partiality in judging is not good הכר פנים במשפט בל טוב (Prov. 24: 23b; cf. 28: 21).

This prescription is substantially also a gnomic aphorism belonging to the category of the '*tōb*' maxims[2] which had been incorporated by the author of Deuteronomy and reformulated in a Torah-legal style. It may not be fortuitous that this prescription occurs in two deuteronomic passages whose contexts refer to wise men (1: 13; 16: 19)[3] and that the analogous maxim in Prov. 24: 23b occurs near the superscription: 'These also are the sayings of the wise' (24: 23a).

6. Justice (צדק) and only justice you shall pursue (תרדף) that you may live (Deut. 16: 20).	He who pursues (רדף) righteousness (צדקה) . . . will find life (Prov. 21: 21).

The notion that the pursuit of justice and righteousness will preserve one's life is an intrinsic idea of Biblical wisdom literature (Prov. 11: 19; 12: 28; 16: 31; 10: 2; 11: 4) and appears to have its ultimate source in Egyptian wisdom teaching, in which we repeatedly meet with the concept that the practice of *maat*—'Justice'—preserves one's life.[4] In the Teaching of Amenemope, for example, we find 'Restore property to its (rightful) owners and seek life for yourself' (xxi: 17–18).

16–17. There is no evidence that the verse refers to a non-Israelite slave as many scholars contend (see G. von Rad, *Deut.*, ATD, p. 105). Israelite slaves who fled from their masters were apparently not returned to them. Had such an ordinance existed, the situation would not have grown to the proportions described in 1 Sam. 22: 2 and 25: 10.

[1] Cf. the colophon of the 'Instruction for Merikare' (ll. 144–50), where the scribe says about himself: 'the one who did not slander the servant to his master', see A. Scharff, 'Der historische Abschnitt der Lehre für König Merikare', *Sitzungsberichte der Bayerischen Akademie der Wissenschaften*, Phil.-histor. Abteilung, Jahrgang 1936, Heft 8, p. 6 n. 2. Compare also Amenemope xi: 6–7, though the meaning is not entirely clear, cf. M. Gilula in the study quoted above, p. 267 n. 3.

[2] Cf. above p. 271, n. 5.

[3] See above, p. 245.

[4] See *Handbuch der Orientalistik*, 1952, I. 2, pp. 93–5.

We have seen, therefore, that in all instances, in which deuteronomic passages have clear and literal parallels in wisdom literature, the wisdom prescriptions prove to be in a more natural and original context. We can only conclude that it was the book of Deuteronomy which adopted the thematic material in question from wisdom literature rather than the converse.

3. THE FEAR OF GOD

The fear of God, which in the wisdom literature (Prov. 1: 7; 9: 10; 15: 33; Job 28: 28; Ps. 111: 10) is synonymous with wisdom, is given particular emphasis in the book of Deuteronomy (Deut. 4: 10; 5: 26; 6: 2, 13, 24; 8: 6; 10: 12 and 20; 13: 5; 14: 23; 17: 19; 28: 58; 31: 12–13). It is true that the basic connotation of 'fear of God' in Deuteronomy is covenantal loyalty, i.e. observance of the stipulation of the covenant.[1] Indeed, ירא יהוה in Deuteronomy goes hand in hand with אהב, עבד, הלך אחרי, שמר מצות,[2] which, as we have seen, belong to the treaty terminology.[3] However, as with the covenantal structure,[4] so also with its formulations there is no rigid uniformity in Deuteronomy. Its author is not exclusively committed to the use of the covenantal pattern and covenantal conceptions; as a preacher and a scribe, he enriches his literary creation by drawing from different sources and traditions. Fear of God in Deuteronomy is, therefore, not mere loyalty to the covenant, as Becker contends,[5] but has also a meaning of general morality, as in the E source and in wisdom literature. Moreover—as we shall see later on—even the nomistic connotation[6] attested in the later post-exilic wisdom literature may be discovered here.

A classic example of יראת אלהים in the sense of general morality is Deut. 25: 18, where Amalek's unforgettable crime of cutting down all the stragglers in the rear is motivated by lack of fear of God: ולא ירא אלהים. The fear of God in this instance has no national limitations, as it is binding even upon a nation which has

[1] Cf. above, p. 83. This was also recognized by J. Becker, *Gottesfurcht im A.T.*, Analecta Biblica 25, 1965, pp. 85 ff., but he is unaware of the fact that the term appears also in Akkadian in treaty context, see above, p. 83 n. 6.

[2] Cf. especially 10: 12–13; 13: 5.

[3] Above, p. 83.

[4] Cf. above, p. 157.

[5] op. cit., pp. 85 ff.

[6] Ibid., pp. 262 ff.

no relationship to Yahweh. The meaning of יראת אלהים here is conscience, the human quality which deters a man from harming somebody even though there be no fear of punishment. Amalek, according to the deuteronomic presentation, was afraid to make a frontal attack and chose to attack the powerless stragglers, who would not be able to resist and protect themselves, thus violating elementary human conscience. The passage in Deut. 25: 17–19 is a genuine deuteronomic one[1] and actually revises the ancient tradition of the war with Amalek in accordance with the deuteronomic concept. According to Exod. 17: 8–17, Amalek came to fight with Israel and was defeated by Joshua. God commands that the memory of Amalek is to be blotted out, but no reason is given for this. The deuteronomic author, whose national conscience was highly developed, could not tolerate the notion that a nation should be wiped out just because of its having proclaimed a war.[2] He had therefore to supply an explanation[3] which changed the picture of the whole event. According to this reinterpretation Amalek had to be blotted out, not because he attacked Israel in war, but because he chose a cruel, inhuman way of doing so.

The same conception underlies the Elohistic passages in which יראת אלהים is mentioned. Thus Abraham (Gen. 20: 11) explained the concealing of his wife's identity by saying that he thought that there was no fear of God in that place and that people might kill him because of his wife. In other words, since he was a stranger and thus unprotected by the local law, his life would be at stake unless there was fear of God among the local inhabitants. Similarly Joseph as ruler of Egypt had the legal power to arrest all his brothers; what prevented him from doing so was the fear of God (Gen. 42: 18). The midwives in Pharaoh's court were commanded

[1] Becker (pp. 200–1) admits that the style of the passage is deuteronomic but nevertheless supposes that the phrase ולא ירא אלהים is taken from the *Vorlage*, i.e. the predeuteronomic tradition upon which Deuteronomy depends. But this supposition seems to be gratuitous; its sole aim is to maintain the argument that יראת אלהים in the general moral sense is not to be found in the deuteronomic literature.

[2] For other instances of deviation from the older tradition which may be explained by reasons of national pride and highly developed national conscience, see my article: 'The Awakening of National Conscience in Israel in the Seventh Century B.C.', *'Oz le-David, Biblical Essays in Honor of D. Ben-Gurion*, 1964, (Hebrew), pp. 412–14.

[3] For this he may be relying upon a tradition differing from that of Exod. 17 but the very selection of this argument reveals his tendency.

to kill the sons of the Hebrew women, but they violated the commandment because they feared God (Exod. 1: 17 and 21). In like vein Nehemiah explains in his memoirs (5: 15) that his predecessors in the office of commissioner had exploited the people by extorting food and money, etc., but that he did not do so because of יראת אלהים. In each of these cases the fear of God refers to the conscience of the individual as it does in the five admonitory formulae in the Holiness Code: 'You shall fear your God' ויראת מאלהיך (Lev. 19: 14 and 32; 25: 17, 36, 43). Cursing the deaf and putting a stumbling-block before the blind (19: 14), not showing deference to the old (19: 32), to wrong or deceive in business (25: 17), to exact interest from the poor (25: 36), and rule ruthlessly over the servant (25: 43)—all these are transgressions which cannot be controlled or punished by the authorities, and only fear of God, i.e. conscience, can deter a man from committing them.

This universal notion of 'fear of God' occurs in Deuteronomy only in connection with a foreign nation. When referring to the Israelites the author uses the term with its covenantal connotation. Like other conceptions[1] it seems to have undergone a process of nationalization, so that its original sense was preserved only with regard to foreign nations. Yet, even though Deuteronomy does not normally use the term in its general ethical sense, the general ethical attitude expressed by it nevertheless pervades the book.

The original conception of the 'fear of God' is grounded on the idea of divine providence according to which all of man's secret actions and thoughts lie exposed before the omniscience of God, and it thus deters man from committing malefactions surreptitiously. The eyes of God are everywhere,[2] and one must consequently be mindful not to sin even secretly. Indeed, both sapiential literature and the book of Deuteronomy frequently treat of matters whose observance is contingent upon the goodwill and conscience of the individual and not upon external pressure which can be brought to bear on him.[3] It is therefore by no means accidental that the Dodecalogue in Deut. 27: 15–26 has been preserved in Deuteronomy. The prohibitions in the Dodecalogue are of course of ancient origin and may perhaps originate from ancient

[1] See below, p. 308.

[2] See Prov. 15: 3; 5: 21; Job 34: 21; Pss. 11: 4; 94: 9–10; Zech. 4: 10; Ahiqar viii: 124 and see above, p. 267 n. 3. Compare Deut. 11: 12, although here in the sense of constant care.

[3] See Chapter II below.

premonarchic ceremonies,[1] but they were undoubtedly reworked[2] and incorporated in the book to serve the ideological purposes of the deuteronomic circle.[3] The Dodecalogue deals with the same clandestine transgressions as wisdom literature warns against when exhorting the pupil to fear God.[4] The section, indeed, abounds with affinities to wisdom literature. Verse 15, for example, which is generally considered to be a deuteronomic accretion because of its style,[5] and its unusual formulation,[6] treats of secret idol worship. This sin is also denounced in the confessions of Job (31 : 26–8): 'If I have looked at the sun when it shone, or the moon moving in splendour and my heart has been secretly enticed[7] and my mouth has kissed my hand; this would be an iniquity to be punished by the judges, for I should have been false to God above.'

The offence of dishonouring (מקלה) one's parents referred to in Deut. 27: 16 is also a clandestine one. As קלה and קלל are two distinct verbs (though there is some affinity between them) the prohibition against dishonouring (מקלה) parents is not to be confused with that against cursing (מקלל) parents. In the latter instance the malefaction is committed by speech,[8] whereas in the former it

[1] Cf. A. Alt, 'Ursprünge', *KS* I, 320.

[2] A. Alt (art. cit.) investigated the stereotyped formulations of these imprecations and found that like the apodictic ordinances in Exod. 21: 12 and 15–17 they also originally consisted of a formula comprising four strokes:

ארור מקלה אביו ואמו (v. 16)
ארור מסיג גבול רעהו (v. 17)
ארור משגה עור בדרך (v. 18)

The phrases which mar this metre are indeed couched in deuteronomic style. Thus in v. 15 תועבת יהוה and מעשה ידי חרש are outspoken deuteronomic expressions. תועבת יהוה has been dealt with already in the previous section, while מעשה ידי חרש is part of the deuteronomic polemic against idolatry, see below, pp. 324, 367. In v. 19 the words גר יתום ואלמנה are a deuteronomic cliché. It is likely that the original formula was ארור מטה משפט רעהו and has been changed in the spirit of Deut. 24: 17 to מטה . . . גר יתום ואלמנה or that ארור מטה משפט גר was the original to which יתום ואלמנה has been added in order to make it conform with the deuteronomic cast. כי גלה כנף אביו in v. 20 seems to be an imitation of Deut. 23: 1. In v. 25 דם נקי is a known phrase in the deuteronomic literature. Verse 26 is wholly a deuteronomic accretion.

[3] Cf. E. Nielsen, *Shechem*[2], 1959, p. 83.

[4] Cf. above, pp. 265 ff.

[5] See n. 2 above.

[6] In contrast to the simple one-clause formulation of the other prohibitions, this verse and v. 26 contain relative clauses.

[7] The same idiom פתה לב is also employed in Deut. 11: 16, in connection with idolatrous worship. See also below, p. 304.

[8] Cf. above, pp. 241 n. 2.

consists of the offender's attitude towards his parents. The substantive form of this stem is קלון which means 'shame', 'disgrace', and is often employed as a contrast to כבוד 'honour' (Prov. 3: 35; 12: 9; Hos. 4: 7; Hab. 2: 16). The stem קלה is encountered a second time in the book of Deuteronomy in the phrase ונקלה אחיך לעיניך (25: 3), where it again denotes 'contempt'. In the present context, which treats only of clandestine malefactions, it would hardly be apposite to exhort against cursing one's parents, an act which can be overheard by others, but it would be relevant to exhort against shaming and slighting parents,[1] an offence which is unperceived by others and cannot, therefore, be penalized. Exhortations of this sort against contemptuous behaviour toward parents abound in Israelite and non-Israelite wisdom literature,[2] and we need not dwell here on the subject.

Deut. 27: 17 curses the remover of landmarks, an act that is generally executed secretly and is frequently referred to in wisdom literature.[3] The prohibition against misleading a blind man on the road (v. 18) has its counterpart in 'You shall not . . . put a stumbling-block before the blind' (Lev. 19: 14) which occurs in a section that enjoins the Israelite to fear God.[4] Such interdictions are met with in Biblical and extra-Biblical wisdom literature alike.[5] Prov. 28: 10, in an analogous context, even employs the same verb (משגה): 'He who misleads the upright into an evil way will fall into his own pit.' The *hiphil* formation of the verb שגה is employed elsewhere only in wisdom literature (Job 12: 16; Ps. 119: 10 = a didactic psalm).

The concern which verse 19 shows for the just treatment of the alien resident, the fatherless and the widow, who have no patron to protect them, also conforms with the spirit of this section and is a well-known and widespread motif of wisdom literature.[6] Warnings against striking down a person in secret (v. 24) are also met with in Prov. 1: 10–19 and in Ps. 10: 8. Accepting bribery 'to slay an innocent person' or 'to acquit the one who sheds innocent blood' (v. 25) is explicitly mentioned in a psalm of didactic sapiential

[1] Cf. the exegesis of Rashi and Ibn Ezra on this verse.

[2] See, e.g., Prov. 15: 20; 23: 22; 30: 17, etc. For analogous exhortations in extra-Biblical wisdom literature see L. Dürr, *Erziehungswesen*, 32 ff. and 81 ff.

[3] See above, pp. 265 f.

[4] Cf. above, p. 276.

[5] Compare the instructions of Amenemope, ch. 25, *ANET*², 424; Prov. 17: 5, 28: 10.

[6] Cf. C. Fensham, *JNES* 21 (1962), 129 ff.

character (Ps. 15: 5)[1] and is a practice frequently denounced in wisdom literature (Job 15: 34; Prov. 17: 23; Eccles. 7: 7).[2] It need hardly be said that bribery is transacted in private (a point made in Prov. 21: 14). The deuteronomic rationale against the practice of bribery (16: 19; cf. Exod. 23: 8) stems apparently from some gnomic aphorism (cf. Eccles. 7: 7).[3]

The central passage of the Dodecalogue contains four imprecations concerning sexual offences (vv. 20–3), and some scholars have consequently styled the entire section the 'Sexual Dodecalogue'.[4] It may be surmised that, like the prohibition lists in Lev. 18 and 20, the imprecations against sexual offences were the original kernel of the section, and that the passages treating of moral transgressions were later appended by the editor of Deuteronomy, though taken from old sources.

The author of Deuteronomy asserts that God is to be feared 'all of one's days' כל הימים or 'as long as one lives on the earth' כל הימים אשר אתם/הם חיים על האדמה (4: 10; 5: 26; 14: 23; 31: 13; cf. the deuteronomic verses: Josh. 4: 24; 1 Kgs. 8: 40; Jer. 32: 39).[5] A similar idea is found in Prov. 23: 17: 'but with the fear of the Lord all the day' כי אם ביראת יהוה כל היום. The idea brought to expression here is that the fear of God must be the guiding principle in man's life and must remain uppermost in his mind at all times. This is expressed also by the idea of learning to fear God (Deut. 4: 10; 14: 23; 17: 19; 31: 12–13), a conception found also in Babylonian texts.[6] That fear of God is to be taught is found also in a wisdom text, Ps. 34: 12 'I will teach you the fear of the Lord' יראת יהוה אלמדכם, but there יראת יהוה refers to general moral behaviour, while in Deuteronomy it refers to the covenantal law.

Since the law is embodied in a book, learning of יראת יהוה is accomplished by reading and studying the book (17: 19; 31: 12–13).

[1] On the character of this psalm and the like, see Y. Kaufmann, *HIR* II, 518, 529, 674. [2] See J. Fichtner, *Die altorient. Weisheit*, pp. 25 ff. and 28 f.

[3] See B. Gemser, 'Motive Clauses in O.T. Law', *SVT* 1 (1953), 64; idem, *Sprüche Salomos*², HAT, p. 59.

[4] This was first suggested by H. Gressmann, *Mose und seine Zeit*, 1913, p. 473.

[5] Cf. *VTE* ll. 507–9: 'As long as we, our sons, our grandsons are alive (*ūmê ammar anīnu . . . balṭānini*), Aššurbanipal, the crown prince, shall verily be our king and our Lord.'

[6] See, e.g., S. Langdon, *Die neubabylonischen Königsinschriften* (VAB 4), 1912, p. 60, l. 18: *ša palāḫ ili u ištari litmudu ṣurruššu* = 'who is trained in his heart by the fear of gods and goddesses' (Nabopolassar).

As the fear of God has to be practised 'all the days', so also the Torah has to be studied all the time: 'and let him (the king) read it all his life' וקרא בו כל ימי חייו (17: 19). The Deuteronomist goes even further when in the commandment given to Joshua about observing the Torah he says: 'the book of the Torah shall not depart from your mouth and you will meditate והגית (literally: murmur) in it day and night' (Josh. 1: 8).

This brings us close to Psalm 1: 2: 'and in his Torah he will meditate (lit. murmur) day and night' (ובתורתו יהגה יומם ולילה). The deuteronomic prescriptions about reading the Torah seem indeed to mark the beginning of the nomistic conception of fear of God found in the didactic Torah-Psalms (1; 19: 8–15; 119). Becker[1] distinguishes sharply between the covenantal conception of יראת יהוה in the deuteronomic literature and the nomistic conception in the Psalms. But this radical distinction can hardly be maintained. As we have indicated, the covenant metaphor is not the only one in Deuteronomy and it does not by any means exclude the nomistic concept. Furthermore, the elements which make the Torah-Psalms nomistic—law as the absolute rule and the influence of wisdom—are already found in Deuteronomy itself. The idea of a written Torah as Israel's guide dominates Deuteronomy, and the connection of this book with wisdom literature is also clear. The only difference between the deuteronomic concept of יראת יהוה and the later nomistic one is that Deuteronomy directs itself to the nation as such while post-exilic nomistic literature addresses itself to the individual. This difference may, however, be explained by historical and social developments (the loss of national independence, etc.) and also by a more profound influence of the wisdom literature. It must be admitted that there is a difference between the deuteronomic and the post-exilic nomistic conception of the Law, but the difference is more in quantity and intensity than in quality.

Fearing God 'all the days' means constant awareness of God. No wonder, then, that the author of Deuteronomy exhorts the Israelite not to forget the Lord (6: 12; 8: 11, 14, 19).[2] The causes of such forgetfulness are the pride and arrogance which come with material wealth and satiety (6: 10–11; 8: 12–13; 17: 16–20; cf. 31: 20; 32: 13–15). The notion that affluence and satiety bring one to deny and forget God also belongs to wisdom ideology. Thus Agur Ben Jakeh declares in his supplication for life's golden mean (Prov.

[1] *Gottesfurcht*, pp. 87 ff. and 262 ff. [2] Cf. below, p. 368.

30: 8–9): 'Give me neither poverty nor riches . . . lest I be full and deny and say "Who is the Lord?" .' A similar articulation of this idea is met with in Job 21: 7–15; 22: 17–18 (cf. v. 13), in Ps. 73: 7–11,[1] in prophetic literature (Hos. 13: 6; Jer. 5: 27b–28), and in poetic compositions (Deut. 32: 13–15; Ps. 81: 11–17) inspired by wisdom literature.[2] In one such passage the author of Deuteronomy even uses phraseology identical with that employed in wisdom literature—the expression 'houses full of good things' ובתים מלאים כל טוב (Deut. 6: 11), which resembles Job 22: 18: 'Yet he filled their houses with good things' והוא מלא בתיהם טוב. Another motif generally encountered in such contexts is the exhortation against an overreliance on horses and chariots. This theme appears in a wisdom psalm which treats of divine providence (Ps. 33: 13–16): 'The Lord looks down from heaven, he sees all the sons of men; from where he sits enthroned he looks forth on all the inhabitants of the earth; he who fashions the hearts of them all, and observes all their deeds. A king is not saved by his great army; a warrior is not delivered by his great strength. The war-horse is a vain hope for victory (שקר הסוס לתשועה), and by its great might it cannot save.' The passages in which wisdom literature repudiates the notion that victory lies in the military supremacy of war-horses and chariots are numerous (Prov. 21: 31 'the horse is ready for the day of battle but the victory comes from God' סוס מוכן ליום מלחמה וליהוה התשועה; Pss. 20: 8; 147: 10, etc.), and the theme is not lacking in Deuteronomy: 'When you go forth to war against your enemies, and see horses and chariots (סוס ורכב) . . . you shall not be afraid of them . . . for the Lord your God is he that goes with you . . . to give you the victory' (להושיע אתכם) (Deut. 20: 1–4). It is for this reason that the author warns the king not to increase the number of his horses (17: 16).[3]

[1] See A. Roifer, 'Psalm LXXIII, 7', *Tarbiz* 32 (1962–3), 109–13 (Hebrew with English summary).

[2] That the motif is basically a didactic one may be learned from a Sumerian school text which sounds very similar to Deut. 32: 13–15 and Jer. 5: 27b–28: 'You have accumulated much wealth, have expanded far and wide, have become fat, broad, powerful, and puffed' (S. N. Kramer, *The Sumerians*, p. 245).

[3] A. Bentzen, *Die Josianische Reform*, 1926, pp. 59–60, is inclined to view the protests against reliance on war-horses and chariots as a distinctly Israelite attitude, and argues that the motif has been borrowed from psalmodic literature (Pss. 20: 8; 33: 16; 44: 7; 60: 13; 147: 10). However, as psalmodic literature has strong affinities to wisdom literature, it is more plausible to assume that the psalmodic compositions in question adopted the motif from wisdom literature rather than the contrary.

II

HUMANISM

BIBLICAL scholars have long recognized the moral and humanistic character of Deuteronomy. The book contains many ethical laws which have no counterpart elsewhere in the Pentateuch, and those which do have Pentateuchal parallels appear in Deuteronomy with divergent and more humanistic overtones. The example customarily cited in support of this observation is the slave law in Deut. 15: 12–18 in contrast to its analogue in the Book of the Covenant (Exod. 21: 2–11). The law in Exodus ordains that the slave must be set free after a six-year period of service, while the deuteronomic law adds that the manumitted slave must also be provided with gifts, apparently to help facilitate his return to private life. According to the slave law in Exodus the maidservant is not entitled to manumission after six years of service, while the deuteronomic law stipulates that both male and female slaves must be set free after six years.[1] More instructive still is the fact that the major and casuistic section[2] of the parallel slave law in the Book of the Covenant pertaining to the wife and children of the slave is completely lacking in Deuteronomy. The reason for this deletion may be ascribed to the change that took place in the attitude toward the slave. According to the deuteronomic view, the master has no command over the private life of the slave. He neither gives the slave a wife nor deprives him of one. The slave of Deuteronomy is regarded as a citizen, 'a brother' (אח v. 12), who only sells his

[1] Cf. Driver's comments, *Deuteronomy*, ICC, ad loc. It is true that the maidservant in Exodus enjoys the status of a concubine and that her situation is therefore better than the slave's. Her entering into concubinage, however, is not her own decision but the will of her father who sells her because of his financial distress, while in Deuteronomy the maidservant, like the manservant, sells herself: כי ימכר לך אחיך העברי או העבריה (v. 12). The subject of concubinage is avoided in Deuteronomy altogether because that book sees the servant as a free person, whose marital life is a private concern, which has nothing to do with his service (cf. below).

[2] The four conditional clauses of the law (vv. 3 a, b, 4a, 5a) introduced by the word אם (= Akk. *šumma*) make up four-fifths of the slave law in Exodus. For the casuistic style of Biblical law, cf. A. Alt, 'Ursprünge', *KS* I, 287–8.

service, but not his person, to the master. Hence, there is no mention of the master's providing the slave with a wife in order to increase his slaveholdings as in the case in the Book of the Covenant (21 : 4). As a citizen enjoying the same rights as his master, the slave conducts an independent family life free of his master's interference. Thus, while the slave in Exodus is described as refusing manumission because he is unwilling to leave behind the wife and children whom he loves ('I love my master, *my wife, and my children*', 21 : 5), in Deuteronomy his refusal to be set free is ascribed only to the love he has for his master and his master's household: 'Because he loves you and your household, since he is happy with you' (15: 16). His wife and children are his own private and personal affair, independent of his relationship to his master. It is moreover by no means accidental that the word 'master' (אדון) is not employed in the deuteronomic slave law. As the slave is deemed to be the 'brother' of the slave-owner, it would be inappropriate to describe the latter as his 'master'.

The expression 'you shall let (תשלחנו) him free' in the deuteronomic law (v. 12) is also indicative of the humanistic approach of the author. The law in Exodus establishes the right of the slave 'to go free': 'he shall *go out* (יצא) free' (v. 2)—whereas the deuteronomic law states that the slave-owner is *obliged* to manumit (שלח) his slave.[1] At the same time it exhorts him not to begrudge the slave's release: 'Do not feel aggrieved when you let him go free from you, for . . . he has given you double the service of a hired man.' (v. 18). The slave ordinance in fact reads more like a moral exhortation than the pronouncement of law.

The book of Deuteronomy does, indeed, mark the transition from the narrow casuistic and statutory law *corpus* to the humanistic law-code. Laws concerning civil damages, which make up almost the entire bulk of the casuistic section of the Book of the Covenant (Exod. 21: 18–22: 16) and which figure prominently in ancient Near-Eastern law *corpora*, are entirely lacking in the book of Deuteronomy. These laws deal with the protection of

[1] That the Covenant Code is aware of the difference in meaning between these two terms may be learned from vv. 27–8, where we find שלח instead of יצא. When dealing with regular manumission (Exod. 21 : 2–11), the right of the slave or the maidservant *to go out free* (יצא לחפשי) is stated; when dealing with liberation of the slave as a result of injury caused by the master, the duty of the master *to let the slave free* (שלח לחפשי) is stressed. I owe this observation to Professor M. Greenberg.

property (i.e. compensation for injury, property damages, theft, and custody) and are therefore not the concern of the deuteronomic legislator. His purpose was not to produce a civil law-book like the Book of the Covenant, treating of pecuniary matters, but to set forth a code of laws securing the protection of the individual and particularly of those persons most in need of it. It is in keeping with this purpose that the author of Deuteronomy incorporated in his legal *corpus* laws concerning the protection of the family and family dignity (22: 13–19) which are, significantly enough, not found elsewhere in the Pentateuch.[1]

It has been asserted,[2] that the family laws found in Deut. 22: 13 ff. once constituted part of a larger body of family laws originally included in an earlier version of the Book of the Covenant (henceforth BC) and that of these laws only that of the seduction of an unbetrothed virgin has survived in the present form of the BC (Exod. 22: 15–16). According to this view the present law originally stood at the end of the series of family laws, which also comprised legislation regarding the betrothed virgin and the married woman (cf. Deut. 22: 22–9). This supposition, however, fails to stand up under closer scrutiny. The casuistic section of the BC is devoted—as we have already said—to legislation affecting pecuniary matters. Now the law of the seduction of the virgin fits in well with this category of law, because the father has incurred the financial loss of his daughter's marriage-price (*mohar*).[3] This, however, is not true of the conjugal laws in Deuteronomy (22: 13 ff.), which deal essentially with the violation of family morality rather than with financial liability.[4] So the seduction law in the BC

[1] The laws themselves are undoubtedly ancient (though they have here been revised, see below, p. 287 n. 4), but the fact that only the author of Deuteronomy incorporated them in his code attests to the particular orientation of his composition.

[2] See A. Klostermann, *Der Pentateuch*, NF 1907, 512, and A. Alt, 'Ursprünge', p. 286. Cf. also A. Jirku, *Das weltliche Recht*, 1927, p. 49; J. Morgenstern, 'The Book of the Covenant', *HUCA* 7 (1930), 120 ff.

[3] Ancient Near-Eastern law attests to the practice of the bride's father returning the marriage-price to the bridegroom or the bridegroom's father (cf. Driver–Miles, *BL* I, 253 ff., and I. Mendelsohn, 'On marriage in Alalaḫ', *Essays on Jewish Life and Thought in honour of S. W. Baron*, 1959, pp. 352 ff.). However, we may infer from Gen. 34: 12 that in early Israelite legal practice—which of course is also reflected in the Book of the Covenant—the bride's father or guardians retained the marriage-price; otherwise Shechem's assurances would not have had any practical significance.

[4] In Assyrian law, the laws of adultery, rape, and seduction also appear in

conforms with the context and purpose of the legal section in which it is set, but when it is incorporated into the framework of Deuteronomy's conjugal laws it has to be revised to conform with the new context. Indeed, the divergencies between the deuteronomic law and its counterpart in the BC can be explained only in the light of the particular purposes of the author of Deuteronomy. The object of the author of the BC is to protect the financial interests of the virgin's father by prescribing compensation for the loss of his daughter's marriage-price which would have naturally accrued to him—and he receives that compensation even if he refuses to marry his daughter to her seducer. It need hardly be said that in such instances the continued presence of the maiden in her father's household may well have heightened her shame and ruined her future marriage prospects. But the author of the BC is not concerned with the personal plight of the maiden.

This is not true of the author of Deuteronomy. He is concerned with rectifying the moral and personal wrong committed against the maiden and not with the financial interests of the father. The man who violates a maiden's honour must take her as his wife and may never divorce her (as in the case of conjugal slander, 22: 19); the father does not figure here as a party to the case. The seducer, to be sure, must pay the father the sum of 50 shekels (22: 29), but it is paid as a fine (cf. v. 19) for violating the maiden and not as compensation for the father's loss of the marriage-price as in the BC. The *mohar* is the monetary price, or its equivalent,[1] which the bridegroom pays the bride's father for his daughter and is determined only after the two parties have agreed on the specific sum and not before.[2] The 50 shekels in the deuteronomic law, on the other hand, is a fixed sum which in character resembles a fine and not a *mohar* which must first be agreed on by the two parties. It is significant that the word *mohar* is nowhere employed in the deuteronomic law of seduction.

different legal categories. The former (A, §§ 12–16) figure in association with the law of murder (§ 10), the latter (§§ 55–6) in association with the marriage of a woman taken as surety for her father's debt (§ 48), inheritance (§ 49), and miscarriage due to injury (§§ 50–3), Cf. Driver–Miles, *The Assyrian Laws*, 1935.

[1] Cf. *UT* 77: 19–20.

[2] Cf. Gen. 34: 12: 'Ask of me a bride-price ever so high . . .'. The bride-price (*tirḫatum*) in Mesopotamia fluctuated between 1 silver shekel (cf. M. Schorr, *Urkunden des altbabylonischen Zivil- und Prozessrechts*, 1913, pp. 36–8) to 2 minas = 120 shekel (cf. M. David, *Die Adoption im altbabylonischen Recht*, pp. 115–16, iv: 44–5).

Some scholars contend[1] that the two analogous laws in the BC and the book of Deuteronomy treat of two different cases: the former with seduction, the latter with rape. This view, however, is unacceptable for the following reasons:

1. The phrase 'and they were found' (ונמצאו) in Deut. 22: 28[2] implies that both parties committed the act willingly and that the maiden was not forced. There is, indeed, nothing in the two verses of this law that necessarily points to rape. The word ותפשה means 'held' and not necessarily 'attacked'.[3] When dealing with rape the author of Deuteronomy employs the verb החזק (22: 25) and not תפש. The phrase תחת אשר ענה in verse 29 does not prove that the case deals with a maiden who was attacked. Verse 24 of the same chapter, which treats of the betrothed maiden *who did not cry out for help*, employs the same verb, ענה, though the maiden is assumed not to have been raped. Nor is the same phrase (תחת אשר עניתה) in Deut. 21: 14 to be understood as referring to rape, for the woman was taken sexually only after her marriage to the Israelite and after she had dwelled in his household for a month. We may note in passing that both Targum Jonathan and the Rashbam similarly read the phrase in Deut. 21: 14: 'because he had intercourse with her'.[4] When used in connection with women the verb ענה appears, then, to connote sexual intercourse in general rather than rape, and it is to be rendered accordingly in such verses as Gen. 34: 2; Judg. 19: 24; 2 Sam. 13: 12; Ezek. 22: 10–11.[5]

2. If we assume that the law of the BC deals with seduction and the book of Deuteronomy with sexual attack, it is difficult to

[1] See J. Morgenstern, *HUCA* 7 (1930), 118 ff. and Y. Kaufmann, *HIR* I, 57.

[2] ונמצאו denotes that the malefactors were apprehended (cf. Jer. 50: 24 נמצאת וגם נתפשת 'you were found and caught' and Prov. 6: 31, 'and if he is caught (ונמצא) he will pay sevenfold'). The LXX reads the verb in the singular: ונמצא, but there is no reason to prefer the Greek to the Masoretic version. The LXX may have understood the law as referring to rape as the Rabbis did, see below, p. 287 n. 2.

[3] Cf. particularly Jer. 40: 10: 'and live in the towns that you have held' ושבו בעריכם אשר תפשתם. Since the verse refers to the Judaeans who remained in the country after the destruction of Judah, the verb תפש surely cannot be rendered: 'which you have conquered' but 'which you have occupied, held as your own', see Ehrlich, *Randglossen*, ad loc., and at Isa. 41: 9.

[4] 'The plain meaning (of the phrase) is conjugal intercourse', Rashbam, ad loc.

[5] The verses may be interpreted more satisfactorily if we assume that they refer not strictly to rape, as Professor M. Greenberg suggested to me privately, but to other instances of sexual intercourse, which are innocent but which involve an element of imposition upon the woman. It might then still refer to seduction.

understand why the father's right to refuse his daughter in marriage is mentioned particularly in the law of seduction and not in the law of rape.[1] It is certainly more plausible to assume that the father would refuse to marry his daughter to a rapist but would consent to marry her to her seducer.[2]

3. Had the author of Deuteronomy referred only to rape and presupposed other legislation for cases of seduction, then he would have cited the laws of these alternative cases[3] just as he did in the preceding law of the betrothed maiden (22: 23–7).[4]

It appears, therefore, that the law in Deuteronomy is here dealing with the same case as its analogue in BC,[5] except that it has been revised—as we have observed—to fit the author's aims and views.

[1] According to Assyrian law, which apparently differentiated between cases of seduction and rape (though the question has not been entirely clarified, cf. Driver–Miles, *Assyrian Laws*, pp. 546), the father may refuse to marry his daughter in both instances (§§ 55 and 56).

[2] Rabbinic exegetes, who took the two laws to refer to seduction and rape respectively, concluded, by inferring *a minori ad maius*, that the father in the deuteronomic law (which in their view treats of rape) may also refuse to give his daughter in marriage to her violator: 'If in the case of seduction where (the seducer) only sinned against her father's wish he can keep her only if her father so wishes, but if her father wishes he must give her up, it is but logical that in the case of rape, where he sinned against her own wish and her father's wish, he should have to give her up if her father wishes it and keep her as his wife only if her father consents to it' (Mekilta to Exod. 22: 15–16; see Lauterbach, *Mekilta* III. p. 132).

[3] It appears, then, that the author of Deuteronomy does not differentiate between cases of seduction and rape with respect to an unbetrothed virgin and therefore refrains from using the term פתה employed in the parallel law in the Book of the Covenant. J. J. Finkelstein ('Sex Offenses in Sumerian Laws', *JAOS* 86 (1966), 368 ff.) has shown that in the Ancient East where the unmarried women were usually minors 'who would not seek sexual experience of their own initiative', the difference between rape and seduction was almost non-existent. Sexual relations with a young, even unbetrothed, girl had always been taken as coercive.

[4] The assertion that Deut. 22: 22 ff. and Exod. 22: 15–16 originally constituted one law and that the law differentiated between cases of seduction and rape with respect both to the betrothed and to the unbetrothed maiden (cf. the studies of Jirku and Morgenstern, above, p. 284 n. 2) is highly improbable. The legal formulation in Deut. 22: 22 ff. is an amalgamation of casuistic and apodictic style (the verdict in vv. 24 and 26 is formulated in the second person). Moreover, the background of these laws is distinctly Israelite (execution by stoning, religious justification for the condemnation: 'for he has defamed a virgin in Israel', v. 19; 'you will sweep away evil from Israel', v. 22). They are not, therefore, on the same level as the casuistic laws in the Book of the Covenant which are formulated in the conventional casuistic style of the ancient Near-Eastern law *corpora* and are devoid of any Israelite colouring (cf. Alt, 'Ursprünge', and his discussion of Exod. 21: 13–14 and 23b).

[5] See Driver, *Deuteronomy*, ICC, pp. ix and 258.

The law of the seduced virgin and the slave law are the only laws of the casuistic section of BC which the author of Deuteronomy incorporated in his legal code. He chose to incorporate these laws in particular because, aside from their civil economic content, which had been stressed in the casuistic law, they also possessed moral-humanitarian aspects[1] onto which he could throw emphasis in his new formulation.

The only two laws in the deuteronomic code which, properly speaking, deal with civil wrongdoings are the landmark law (19: 19) and the law of just weights and measures (25: 13–16).[2] These laws, however, also exhibit the particular tendency of the author of Deuteronomy. Unlike the laws of damages in the BC, which are designed for the judiciary, these laws are moral exhortations directed at the individual in a way characteristic of the book of Deuteronomy. Malefactions of this nature, which are committed in stealth and in a clandestine fashion, and which can be combated only by an appeal to the conscience of the individual, are accorded particular attention in the wisdom literature[3] of the ancient Near East whose teachings centre on moral comportment.[4] The subject-matter of these two laws, as well as their sapiential phraseology,[5] thus informs us of the source from which the book of Deuteronomy had adopted them.[6]

The humanistic tendency of the author of Deuteronomy becomes particularly evident when one compares the social laws of Deuteronomy with their counterparts in the BC. We cite the following laws in illustration, bearing in mind the conclusions that are to be drawn from the divergencies that emerge from the comparison:

1. Exod. 23: 4 ordains that a stray animal must be returned to its rightful owner.[7] The deuteronomic legislator, however, extends

[1] Deuteronomy regards the slave as a hired worker (see above), and thus any offence committed against him entails the same punishment as that committed against a free Israelite (i.e. *talio*). Hence, the author of Deuteronomy did not incorporate the laws of Exod. 21: 20–2 and 26–7, though they also possess humanistic aspects.

[2] See R. H. Pfeiffer, *Introduction to the Old Testament*, p. 238.

[3] See above, pp. 265 f.

[4] See L. Dürr, *Erziehungswesen*, etc., pp. 35 ff. and 83 f.

[5] See above, p. 265.

[6] We account in this manner for the presence of these laws in the book of Deuteronomy, as opposed to Pfeiffer, *Introduction*, p. 238.

[7] On the deuteronomic use of the term 'brother' in contradistinction to the

this law to garments and all types of lost articles (22: 3), and exhorts the finder not to ignore the lost object but to take it home with him and keep it until it is sought for by its owner (vv. 2–3).

2. The BC commands the creditor who has taken a debtor's garment as surety to restore it to the debtor at sundown so that he may cover himself with it at night (22: 25–6). According to the deuteronomic law, however, not only must the creditor return the garment at sunset, but he is denied the right to select what article he wishes as surety (24: 6 and 17) and is even forbidden to enter the debtor's house to collect it: 'You shall stand outside and the man to whom you make the loan shall bring the pledge out to you' (24: 11).

3. The BC forbids the Israelite to wrong or afflict the resident alien (22: 20–2;[1] 23: 9). The author of Deuteronomy, in contrast, not only enjoins the Israelite to refrain from discriminating against the resident alien, but also exhorts the Israelite to *love* him (10: 19) and to be solicitous for his welfare.

4. The BC ordains that what has been torn by beasts (= טרפה), which Israelites are forbidden to eat for sacral reasons, should be cast to the dogs (22: 30). The deuteronomic law, on the other hand, ever attentive to the needs of indigent persons, enjoins the Israelite to give the carcass (נבלה) to the resident alien (14: 21).[2] The humanistic tendency becomes clear in the light of the juxtaposition of the resident alien and the foreigner. The author enjoins the *giving* of the carcass to the resident alien, but the *selling* of it to the foreigner, who was usually involved in trade and commerce.[3]

term 'enemy' employed in the BC law, see my article: 'The Awakening of Israel's national consciousness in 7th century B.C.', '*Oz le-David*, 1964 (Hebrew), pp. 417–18.

[1] The LXX and Syriac translate the verbs תונה and תענה by the same words: κακώσετε in LXX, *thrwn* in Syriac. It is possible therefore that v. 20 originally read. 'You shall not afflict (תענה)' a supposition which may find support in the formulation of the exhortation in v. 22 which relates to v. 20. The root ינה is characteristic of the Priestly document (cf. Lev. 19: 33 (regarding the resident alien); 25: 14) and it may have been a factor which influenced the corrupt reading תונה in place of the original תענה.

[2] נבלה and טרפה are considered as one and the same, cf. Lev. 7: 24; 17: 15; 22: 8.

[3] See my article נכרי in the *Encyclopedia Miqra'it*, vol. 5.

5. The BC forbids a slave-owner to sell an undesirable *maid-servant* to a foreign kin (21: 8).[1] Deuteronomic law, however, not only precludes such an eventuality—since the law of six-year service applies to both male and female slaves—but also forbids the selling of a *captive woman* (21: 14) no longer desired by her warrior-husband who had brought her back from the wars.[2]

The humanistic vein of deuteronomic legislation is apparent not only in its socio-moral laws, but also in its distinctly cultic ordinances. The law of cult centralization, which opens the deuteronomic code (ch. 12), is punctuated with exhortations concerning the Levite, the slave, and the maidservant (vv. 12, 18, 19). Indeed, one gains the impression that the primary purpose of the festal repasts at the 'chosen place' is to provide nutriment for *personae miserabiles*. In the closing section of the law of cult centralization the legislator enjoins the celebrant: 'Take heed that you do not forsake the Levite as long as you live in your land' (v. 19). The laws of the tithes and firstlings have also assumed the cast of a social institution in Deuteronomy. The farmer brings his tithes and firstlings to the chosen place so that the destitute persons can partake of the festal repast with him. Every third year he must, moreover, give all of the tithes to these persons so that 'the Levite . . . and the stranger, the fatherless and the widow who are with you in your towns, shall come and eat and be filled' (14: 29). The Sabbatical year, as we have seen,[3] had also become a social institution whose purpose was to help the poor.

The festal pilgrimages and their joyful celebrations seem to be designed almost only for the benefit of the poor (16: 11 and 14). Indeed, the author of Deuteronomy states as much in his law of the festivals: 'You shall remember that you were a slave in Egypt, and you shall be careful to observe these statutes' (16: 12). The Sabbath law, as we have noted above,[4] also has a humanistic objective: 'that your manservant and your maidservant may rest *as well as yourself*' (5: 15), the temper of which is similar to that met with in Job 31: 15: 'Did not he who made me in the womb make him? And did not one fashion us in the womb?' (cf. Mal. 2: 10).

[1] The word עם occurs here in the archaic sense: 'kin' or 'family', cf. נאסף אל עמיו (Gen. 25: 8, 17; 35: 29), etc.

[2] For the resemblance between the exhortations against selling a captive woman and a Hebrew maidservant see E. Neufeld, *Ancient Hebrew Marriage Laws*, 1944, pp. 72–3.

[3] Above, p. 223.

[4] Above, p. 222.

The book of Deuteronomy shows a particularly humanistic attitude towards women. We have already noted the lack of distinction in its law between male and female slaves and its approach to the law of the seduced maiden. There are also a number of laws pertaining to conjugal life which have no counterpart in any other of the Pentateuchal books. They deal with such matters as the inheritance rights of an unloved woman's son (21: 15–17); the protection of a wife's honour and reputation as articulated in the law of conjugal slander (22: 13–19); consideration for a woman's intimate feelings (24: 5: 'he shall gladden his wife whom he has taken'); and the law of the female captive (21: 10–14). Though the laws themselves may be quite ancient, the fact that the author of Deuteronomy chose to incorporate them in his code attests to his humanistic orientation.

The attitude of the author of Deuteronomy towards man and woman finds its clearest expression in the passages which enumerate the participants in the covenant ceremonies. In contrast to the earlier Biblical sources, in which no mention is made of women and according to which the male participants must even separate themselves from their women before the ceremony (Exod. 19: 15), the author of Deuteronomy makes a particular point of mentioning that women, as well as men, participate (29: 10 and 17; cf. 31: 12). The same is true of the festivals and the festal repasts. On such occasions we meet with the Israelite's daughter as well as his son, and his maidservant as well as the manservant (12: 12 and 18; 16: 11 and 14). The wife, it is true, is not mentioned in these passages, but the very absence of all reference to the wife is indicative here of Deuteronomy's view regarding the equality of the sexes. The author of Deuteronomy certainly did not mean to imply that all the members of the Israelite household were expected to make the festal pilgrimage and that the wife alone was to remain at home and not participate in the celebration of the festival. She is not explicitly referred to in the list of festal participants because the word 'you' which opens the list refers equally to the husband and the wife,[1] who in Deuteronomy's view both enjoy the same prerogatives.

Thus, the views of the author of Deuteronomy are more progressive, in this respect, than those of the BC. According to the

[1] Cf. G. A. Smith, *Deuteronomy*, CB, ad loc.: 'wives are not mentioned for they are included in those to whom the law is addressed, *a significant fact*' (emphasis added).

BC law only males are obliged to make the pilgrimage to 'behold' the face of the Lord, whereas the author of Deuteronomy, who is familiar with this law and even cites it on one occasion (16: 16), has extended its application[1] to all members of the Israelite household, male and female alike (16: 11 and 12). This, of course, should not be considered a novelty in Israelite tradition. As we learn from 1 Sam. 1, the pilgrimage of the whole family to the sanctuary was customary in the time of Eli. Our purpose is only to put in relief the tendency of the deuteronomic legislator by contrasting it with a different tradition which is undoubtedly older.

Some of these humanistic laws have their parallels in the ancient Near-Eastern Codes but without the special overtones found in Deuteronomy. Especially salient in this respect are the affinities to the Assyrian laws, a fact which may not be without significance for the background of the composition of Deuteronomy.[2] Thus we find in the Middle-Assyrian laws a law (A, § 8) parallel to that of Deut. 25: 11–12, which prescribes a punishment, reflecting an Assyrian practice (cutting off a member of the body).[3] These two laws, however, differ enormously in that the Assyrian law punishes the woman for the crime of physical injury while the deuteronomic law concerns itself not with injury but with a breach of modesty.[4]

[1] Cf. G. A. Smith, *Deuteronomy*, CB ad loc.

[2] Unlike the other Biblical codes, Deuteronomy preserved a series of family laws similar to those in the Middle-Assyrian laws. Conspicuous similarities are to be found also in the style and language. Compare, e.g., in connection with slander: Deut. 22: 14: 'and makes up charges against her', ושם לה עלילות דברים, MAL, A, § 19: *ina muḫ ṭappā'i abāta iškun*, 'made up charges against his neighbour'; in connection with rape: 'but you shall do nothing to the girl' ולנערה לא תעשה דבר (Deut. 22: 26) and MAL, A, § 23: *mimma lā eppušū* = 'they will do nothing (to the adulterer); in connection with clearing of guilt: 'there is no sin of death' אין . . . חטא מות (Deut. 22: 26) and MAL, A, § 16: *ḫīṭu laššu* 'there is no sin' (cf. also *ḫīṭu yānu* in neo-Assyrian); in connection with punishing by flogging: 'he shall beat him 40 blows' ארבעים יכנו (Deut. 25: 3) and MAL, A, § 18: 40 *ina ḫaṭṭē imaḫḫuṣūš* = 'they will beat him 40 blows with rods' (note also the expression 'a month's time' ירח ימים in Deut. 21: 13 and MAL, A, § 18 *araḫ ūmāte*). Compare also the law against communal (familial) liability in Deut. 24: 16 with MAL, A, § 2b. Cf. also R. Yaron, *Biblica* 51 (1970), 549 ff.

[3] Dr. S. Paul called my attention to Ezek. 23: 24–5 where it is said that 'Oholiba (= Jerusalem) will be judged by the Assyrians according to their judgements (ושפטוך במשפטיהם) which is explained later: אפך ואזניך יסירו = 'they will remove your nose and your ear'. For this kind of punishment compare, for instance, MAL, A §§ 4–5. Cf. Borger, *Asarhaddon*, 106: 24. See, however, in Egyptian texts, *ANET*², 215, iv.

[4] S. Loewenstamm (*Encycl. Miqra'it*, vol. 4, art. מבושים) argues that in this case the Assyrian law also demands punishment, though it is more lenient. Loewenstamm interprets §§ 7–9 in MAL in the following way: § 7 deals with a

The case of a slandered woman, with which Deut. 22: 13 f. deals, is also encountered in the Mesopotamian law.[1] As in Deuteronomy, the punishment consists of flogging and paying a fine.[2] But the main concern of the deuteronomic legislator is to protect the woman from defamation while that of the Mesopotamian lawgivers is to deal with the problem of false accusation in conjugal matters.[3]

What then is the source of this unique humanism, which characterizes the book of Deuteronomy?

Many scholars ascribe its origin to the prophetic school, which, to their minds, left its stamp upon the book. S. R. Driver, for example, asserts that Deuteronomy is a 'prophetical law-book',[4] R. H. Pfeiffer that it was composed by a priest upon whom the prophetic school had a strong impact.[5] Indeed, most scholars incline to the view that Deuteronomy, because of its strong moral emphasis, is the literary product of the prophetic spirit.[6] This view, however, is without foundation. Y. Kaufmann has

woman 'putting forth her hand' (*qāta wabālu*, compare ושלחה ידה 'puts forth her hand' in Deut. 25: 11) towards the secret parts of a man, which is to be punished by a payment of 20 manehs of lead and flogging. A woman who crushes a man's testicle in an affray (§ 8), or a man 'putting forth his hand' towards the 'privates' of a woman (§ 9), is punished by having one finger cut off. According to this interpretation § 7 is parallel in its case to Deut. 25: 11–12, the difference being only in punishment. However, this interpretation, which in itself is quite logical, lacks real textual evidence. Section 7 does not mention secret parts at all and only speaks about a woman putting forth or laying her hand on a man, which might be understood simply as an assault. Similarly § 9 speaks about a man laying hand on a married woman and treating her as a young child (so G. R. Driver) or attacking her like a young rutting bull (*CAD*, vol. 2 (B), p. 324, reading: *kī būri ēpussi*) and no reference at all is made to the secret parts of a woman. The only clear parallel left is § 8 which, like Deut. 25: 11–12, speaks about an affray—which is not mentioned in § 7 —and grasping the 'privates', the difference being only the outcome of the assault and the measure of punishment.

The document from Nuzi brought by C. H. Gordon (*JPOS* 15 (1935), 29 ff.) as parallel to Deut. 25: 11–12 is also not clear enough to enable us to draw any conclusions (*aḫu* is not attested elsewhere in the sense of 'genitals').

[1] Cf. Lipit-Ishtar, § 33 (see M. Civil, *AS* 16, p. 4), Compare also CH, § 127, and MAL, A, § 18, both dealing with slander by a third party.

[2] Fine paying in Lipit-Ishtar and flogging in CH § 127. In the Middle-Assyrian law (§ 18) both flogging and paying a fine occur. Work for the king and castration, which are also mentioned there, are not to be conceived in Israelite law.

[3] Cf. J. J. Finkelstein, 'Sex Offenses', *JAOS* 86 (1966), 367. The law of slander in Deuteronomy also deals with the legal problem of false accusation (dealt with in Deut. 19: 19 f.), but, even so, its central theme is defamation: 'for the man has defamed a virgin in Israel' (22: 19).

[4] *Deuteronomy*, ICC, p. xxvi.

[5] *Introduction*, p. 180.

[6] H. Gressmann, *Die älteste Geschichtsschreibung und Prophetie Israels*, 1922, SAT, xvi–xvii; R. Kittel, *Geschichte des Volkes Israel*, 1917, II, 596.

demonstrated[1] that fundamental differences exist between Pentateuchal and prophetic view-points. The concept of the primacy of morality over the cult, for example, which constitutes the very heart of prophetic teaching, is absent from the Pentateuchal books and significantly so from Deuteronomy, despite its pronounced moral character. Although Deuteronomy contains a highly developed system of moral laws, it threatens with exile not those who disobey the moral law, but those who practise idolatry (4: 25 f.; 6: 14–15; 8: 19–20; 11: 16–17). In contrast, prophetic literature threatens exile precisely for those who disobey the moral law.

Kaufmann also pointed out other radical differences between Pentateuchal and prophetic views, especially with regard to the concept of eschatology. The eschatological ideas which are the heart and matter of the prophetic school find no mention in Deuteronomy, notwithstanding the fact that it treats of the restoration of Israel at the 'end of days' (4: 30; 30: 1–5). The concept of the 'end of days' in Deuteronomy contains not a trace of the splendour which surrounds it in prophetic literature.

The vision of the end of idolatry in the world which is so prominent in prophecy is completely missing from Deuteronomy. On the contrary, Deuteronomy states twice that God apportioned idolatry to the nations (4: 19; 29: 25), as this would constitute their natural allotment.

We must seek elsewhere, then, for the provenance of the humanism reflected in the book of Deuteronomy; and we find it in the school of wisdom, which scholars generally and rightly style the 'humanism' of the Ancient East.[2] The book of Deuteronomy is consequently a synthesis of Torah and sapiential thought and not of Torah and prophetic thought. It was influenced not by the prophetic school but by the school of wisdom.

W. O. E. Oesterley contends that Deuteronomy originated in prophetic-scribal circles, and that these ultimately transmitted their religious view to their colleagues, the sapiential scribes.[3] He even argues that the Instruction of Amenemope, whose pervasive temper resembles that of the book of Deuteronomy, is a product of Israelite-deuteronomic impact on Egyptian wisdom.

[1] *HIR* I. 24 f. (Compare the abridged English edition by M. Greenberg, Kaufmann, *The Religion of Israel*, 1960, 157 ff.)

[2] S. R. Driver, *An Introduction to the Literature of the O.T.*, p. 393; O. S. Rankin, *Israel's Wisdom Literature*, ch. i, 1936.

[3] W. O. E. Oesterley, *Wisdom of Egypt*, p. 76.

This is—as we have seen[1]—a highly implausible supposition. Oesterley also asserts that the social exhortations of the book of Proverbs, which deal with the poor, were adopted from prophetic teachings.[2] The recurring social demands of the prophets, to his mind, left a deep impression on sapiential thinking which would account for the particular concern which the book of Proverbs shows for the indigent. Rankin, however, has already remarked[3] that this was 'a case of placing the cart before the horse', since the social ideas of Proverbs are, properly speaking, distinctly sapiential ideas, based on the concept of the 'equality of men', which in turn derives from the sapiential concept of the 'Creator of man' predominating in wisdom literature.[4] We need not, therefore, look elsewhere for the origin of these ideas. Oesterley contends too that the concept of the primacy of morality over the cult in Proverbs is also the result of prophetic influence on the book. However, as this concept is also prevalent in extra-Biblical wisdom literature,[5] Rankin's observation would apply to this contention as well. It may very well be that the converse is true, that the social aspects of prophetic teaching derive from sapiential thought rather than the contrary. However, even if we were to reject this thesis[6] it is none the less clear that sapiential composition constituted a distinct and separate province of Israelite literature, which was dependent upon extra-Biblical sources. There was consequently no need for wisdom composition to resort to national sources with which it had nothing in common, when it could have drawn the same material from the sources that it was accustomed to draw upon. Israelite wisdom, moreover, dates back to early antiquity, as is now conceded by most scholars and attested by parallels from ancient Near-Eastern wisdom literature;[7] and since it is, therefore, much older than the

[1] This line of argument was recently defended by E. Drioton, 'Sur la Sagesse d'Amenemope', *Mélanges bibliques rédigés en l'honneur d'A. Robert*, 1957, pp. 254–80, and again in 'Proverbes et Amenemope', *Sacra Pagina* I, Bibl. Ephem. Theol. Lovan, XII, 1958, 229–41. However, the view has been rejected by R. J. Williams, 'The Alleged Semitic Original of the Wisdom of Amenemope', *JEA* 47 (1961), 100–6.

[2] *The Book of Proverbs*, Westminster Commentaries, p. 159.

[3] *Israel's Wisdom Literature*, p. 14.

[4] Cf. 'The Instruction of Amenemope', ch. 25, *ANET*², 424; Job. 21: 13–15 *et al.*

[5] Cf. 'The Instruction for Merikare', *ANET*², 417, ll. 128 f.: 'More acceptable is the character of one upright of heart than the ox of the evildoer.'

[6] See Y. Kaufmann, *HIR* II, 643–5.

[7] W. Baumgartner, *Israelitische und altorientalische Weisheit*, 1933.

prophetic school, it cannot have adopted its material from the latter. If Oesterley has indeed discovered numerous affinities between sapiential literature and the book of Deuteronomy, including a similar concern for the poor and destitute,[1] the true explanation is that Deuteronomy had taken its material directly from, or was directly influenced by, the sapiential school, and not the prophetic school.

Fichtner, on the other hand, though conceding that Egyptian wisdom had influenced the book of Proverbs, nevertheless asserts that the latter contains pronounced deuteronomic traces in a number of passages.[2] It is remarkable, however, that in Fichtner's opinion the author of Proverbs had to turn to Pentateuchal sources for such subjects in particular as the removal of landmarks and the use of false weights and measures, which constitute part of the classic content material of sapiential composition.[3] He, too, seems to be 'placing the cart before the horse' when he claims that the expression 'an abomination to Yahweh' (Prov. 20: 10) is taken from Deuteronomy (25: 13–16). Indeed, he unconsciously contradicts his own argument by citing Amenemope 29: 1, which contains the expression 'an abomination to Re'. In fact this is not the only instance in which we encounter the expression outside the Bible, for it is found scattered throughout Egyptian[4] and Babylonian[5] wisdom literature. Why must we assume, then, that the idiom originates from the book of Deuteronomy rather than the converse, that is, that it derives from the sapiential phraseology and that it found its way into Deuteronomy from wisdom literature, as did many other sapiential expressions (see below)?

Pfeiffer, who assigns the date of the composition of Proverbs to late post-exilic times, states that 'the teachings of the prophets and Deuteronomy, rejected by most Judeans before the Exile notwithstanding the reform of 621, have become commonplaces in Proverbs'.[6] This statement, to say the least, is astonishing. If Proverbs was composed in late post-exilic times, that is, in the

[1] *The Wisdom of Egypt*, pp. 22, 79.

[2] J. Fichtner, *Die altorient. Weisheit*, pp. 26–7.

[3] See L. Dürr, *Das Erziehungswesen*, pp. 35 f. and 83 f.

[4] See above, p. 267.

[5] See W. G. Lambert, *BWL*, p. 117 where he describes a sapiential composition in which over thirty ethical interdictions conclude with the phrase: *ikkib* ^{d}*Nammu* = 'an abomination to the god Nammu' (cf. Prov. 6: 16–19).

[6] *Introduction*, p. 655.

same period in which the Pentateuch was fixed, and if it had, as Pfeiffer maintains, assimilated Pentateuchal concepts, how are we to account for the fact that it does not contain the slightest suggestion of a distinctly national or Israelite idea? The book of Ben Sira, a wisdom composition of the period in question, is, for example, suffused with national and Pentateuchal concepts and even identifies Wisdom with Torah. Why, then, did Proverbs remain uncommitted to these fundamental concepts if they had already assumed crystallized form at the time of its composition?

The views just discussed seem all to be based on one presupposition, that the book of Deuteronomy antedates the book of Proverbs, a hypothesis which is completely groundless. It is more plausible to assume that the book of Deuteronomy was influenced by the ancient sapiential ideology that found expression in the book of Proverbs and the wisdom literature of the ancient Near East.

III

DIDACTICISM

THE book of Deuteronomy is known to possess a strong didactic temper (cf., e.g., 4: 9–10; 6: 2, 7, 20–5; 11: 19; 31: 10–13). In this respect it greatly resembles wisdom literature, the central concern of which is education. Sapiential writings played a significant role in the system of ancient Near-Eastern education; indeed it is because of the reproduction of these compositions for study and teaching purposes that such a large number of them have come down to us.[1] An examination of Deuteronomy will demonstrate that it, too, was composed with a pedagogical aim in mind. This is apparent even in its legal section, in the injunctions, for example, that all infractors of the law be punished so that 'all Israel shall hear and fear and never again do such evil things' (13: 12; 19: 20; cf. 17: 13; 21: 21).[2]

It must, however, be said that the didactic tendency is also found in the treaties of the ancient Near East[3] and that Deuteronomy as a 'Book of the Covenant' followed the treaty model in its educational imagery as in other features. Indeed, as we shall see, it is sometimes hard to say which is the origin of a certain education motif: the covenant or the wisdom.[4] We must therefore take into account influences from both spheres, though that of wisdom appears to have been the stronger. It seems that in order to strengthen the Israelite loyalty to the covenant the author of Deuteronomy not only relied on covenant typology but also employed modes of expression and imagery taken from the sapiential sphere.

The sapiential teacher regards the concept of 'the fear of God' as the essential content of his instruction, and the pupil is assured that his reward for fearing God will be a 'good life':[5] 'Come, O sons, listen to me, I will teach you the *fear of the Lord*. What man is there who desires *life* החפץ חיים *and covets many days, that he*

[1] See L. Dürr, *Das Erziehungswesen*, etc.

[2] See Y. Kaufmann, *HIR* I, 53.

[3] See below, pp. 302–3.

[4] It is even possible that the treaties themselves employed wisdom or school imagery.

[5] See below, pp. 307 f.

may enjoy good?' אוהב ימים לראות טוב (Ps. 34: 12–13). The father in Deuteronomy instructs his son in similar language: 'And the Lord commanded us to do all these statutes, *to fear the Lord our God, for our good always, that he might preserve us alive as this day*' לטוב לנו כל הימים לחיותנו כהיום הזה (6: 24).

Though the connotation of the 'fear of God' in the deuteronomic passage (observance of covenant obligations) differs from that in Ps. 34 (general morality), the motivation is identical in both passages: 'life' and 'good'. Both passages are framed as educational addresses of the father to his son,[1] the only stylistic difference being that in Ps. 34 'sons' is a metaphor for students, while in Deuteronomy 'son' means literally the father's son. That the address of the father to the son in Deuteronomy has much in common with the address of the teacher to his pupil in wisdom literature becomes particularly clear when we compare Deut. 6: 6–9; 11: 18–20 with Prov. 6: 20–2; 7: 3; 8: 34.

Deuteronomy	Proverbs
And these words . . . will be upon your heart. And you shall teach them diligently (ושננתם) to your children and you shall talk of them when you sit in your house and when you walk (בלכתך) by the way, and when you lie down (בשכבך) and when you rise. And you shall bind them (וקשרתם) for a sign (לאות) upon your hand and they shall be as frontlets (לטטפת) between your eyes (6: 7–8; cf. 11: 18–20).	My son, keep your father's commandments and forsake not your mother's teaching. *Bind them* (קשרם) upon your heart always; tie them about your neck. When you walk (בהתהלכך) they will lead you, when you lie down (בשכבך) they will watch over you, and when you awake they will talk to you (תשיחך) (6: 20–2; cf. 1: 9: 'For they are a fair garland for your head and pendants for your neck'; 3: 3; 4: 9).
	Bind them (קשרם) on your fingers, write them (כתבם) on the tablets of your heart (7: 3).
You shall write them (וכתבתם) on the doorposts of your house (מזוזות ביתך) and on your gates (6: 9; 11: 20).	Happy is the man . . . watching daily at my gates, waiting beside the posts of my doors (מזוזות פתחי) (8: 34).

As in Proverbs, so in Deuteronomy, constant awareness of the educational ideal is demanded from the son-student. The

[1] See above, p. 279.

commandments of the father and the mother in Proverbs and the commandments of God in Deuteronomy have to be tied to the body like binding ornaments (Proverbs) and binding אות and טטפת (Deuteronomy); just as amulets and ornaments are always attached to the person wearing them, so should the commandments always accompany the student.

The most valuable object attached to the body was the seal, usually tied to the arm or right hand (Jer. 22: 24; Hag. 2: 23; Cant. 8: 6)[1] or to the breast (על לבך, Cant. 8: 6). Next to it comes the diadem or the wreath on the head (Prov. 1: 9; 4: 9), the necklace, and the various breast ornaments (Prov. 1: 9; 3: 3 and 22; 6: 21). As all these objects were also used as amulets, it is hard to say where amulets are meant and where simply ornaments are implied. But since it is quite apparent that both in Proverbs and in Deuteronomy the author speaks of these objects not literally but figuratively the distinction is irrelevant for our purpose.

The idea of permanent attachment is also expressed by the simile of the girdle which is always attached to the body[2] and by that of the fringes of the dress (Num. 15: 37 f.).[3] A similar idea of permanence occurs in the priestly account of the tabernacle, according to which the diadem and the breastpiece of the high priest serve as permanent reminders before God concerning the sons of Israel (Exod. 28: 29–30, 38). But here of course we have to do with real holy objects and not with similes.[4]

The passage we are considering also expresses the notion that the student should always be conscious of his lore, regardless of the situation in which he finds himself—staying at home or being away, lying down and arising[5]—a notion which Deuteronomy also expresses in the phrase about writing them on the doorposts through which one enters and leaves, and which Proverbs expresses by the idea of watching daily at the gates of Wisdom.

[1] Cf. also the seal of Judah and the cords (for binding the seal) in Gen. 38 which constitute together with the staff the personal belongings always attached to its owner, given as a pledge to Tamar.

[2] Cf. Jer. 13: 11 and compare A. Ehrlich, *Randglossen* to Isa. 11: 5.

[3] See below, p. 302.

[4] For the notion of permanency תמיד and the idea of reminder זכרון in connection with the overgarments of the high priest, see M. Haran, 'The Complex of Ritual Acts', *Scripta Hierosolymitana* 8 (1961), 283 ff.

[5] Like 'coming and going' (Deut. 28: 6 and 19; Ps. 121: 8), 'sitting and standing' שבתך and קומך render the idea of permanency (see Isa. 37: 28, cf. Qumran version).

One must admit that the text in Deuteronomy is dependent upon Exod. 13: 9 and 16;[1] but, as in other instances, Deuteronomy has reworked and reshaped the ancient tradition in a didactic way characteristic of Wisdom. The differences between the two texts are instructive:

1. In contradistinction to Exod. 13, where the אות and טטפת refer to a specific rite, the dedication of the firstlings, in Deuteronomy the אות and טטפת refer in general to the words and commandments of God, as the injunctions in Proverbs also refer to instruction in general.

2. As in Proverbs (3: 1 f.; 4: 4 f.), so also in Deuteronomy (6: 6 f.; 11: 18 f.) the reference to the binding of amulets and ornaments is preceded by the injunction to take the words to heart and not to forget them (cf. Prov. 3: 1).[2] This injunction points to a figurative understanding of what follows it. That the binding of ornaments in Proverbs is not to be taken literally may be learned from 4: 9, where it is said of Wisdom: 'She will give to your head a chaplet of grace, a crown of glory will she bestow on you.'

3. As does Proverbs (3: 3; 6: 21; 7: 3), Deuteronomy employs the verbs 'bind' קשר and 'write' כתב in the context under discussion, while Exod. 13 uses the term 'to be as a sign' היה לאות, which usually occurs in a sacerdotal context (e.g. Gen. 9: 13; 17: 11; Exod. 12: 13; Num. 17: 3)[3] and which has the meaning of a real physical token.[4] These last two observations apply also to the term 'be as a reminder' היה לזכרון in Exod. 13: 9. It seems, therefore, that Exod. 13 speaks of actual apotropaic symbols[5] which also have an admonitory significance. This last implication is seen in the declared purpose of the 'sign' אות and the 'reminder' זכרון; they come 'in order that the teaching of the Lord may be in your mouth' (v. 90). This verse could hardly be understood were we to argue that the 'sign' and the 'reminder' are to be taken figuratively. The outcome of such an interpretation would be tautology: 'you

[1] On the relationship between these two texts, see M. Caloz, Exode XIII, 3–16 et son rapport au Deutéronome', *RB* 75 (1968), 5 ff.

[2] In Deuteronomy the warning not to forget immediately follows the passage discussed here, i.e. 6: 10–12.

[3] In Num. 15: 39 read also והיה לכם לאות instead of והיה לכם לציצת (see Comm.).

[4] See E. A. Speiser, 'Palil and Congeners: A Sampling of Apotropaic symbols', *AS* 16, 1965, 389–93.

[5] Ibid.

will always keep it in mind so that the teaching of the Lord may be in your mouth'. The reverse of it would be more understandable. But if we interpret the 'sign' and 'the reminder' as real amulets the verse has perfect sense.

In fact Deuteronomy preserves the notion of keeping God's words in the mouth by 'you will talk of them' ודברת בם (cf. 11: 19 לדבר בם), but here it occurs along with the 'sign' and *totaphot* as one of the admonitory devices, and not as in Exodus where the sign serves as the means to the end, which is keeping the Torah in the mouth. A phenomenon very similar to the 'sign' and the 'reminder' in Exod. 13 is the ציצת 'fringe'[1] in Num. 15: 37 f., which also is to be observed physically 'in order that you shall recall Yahweh's commandments' (v. 39). Interestingly enough this prescription is also preserved in Deuteronomy (22: 11), where, however, it is cited together with some other priestly prescriptions without the admonitory function ascribed to it in P. It seems that, unlike P, the author of Deuteronomy does not resort to the use of real reminders, and when mentioning them he refers to them as similes in order to further his educational aims. Deuteronomy and Proverbs may have been aware of the apotropaic and protective use of these symbols,[2] but when they speak of binding them they do so metaphorically as befits the wise teacher, and do not intend to impose the concrete observance of these precepts upon their students.

The similes expressing constant awareness are to be found also in treaty texts. Thus, we read in a Hittite covenantal text: 'As you wear a dress, so shall you carry with you these oaths'.[3] In *VTE* we find an idea similar to that of Deut. 6: 7; 11: 19; and Prov. 6: 22: '(if anyone makes an insurrection) whether by day or by night, whether on the way or within the city'.[4] The idea of impressing the words upon heart and soul (Deut. 6: 6; 11: 18) occurs several times in the Hittite treaties[5] and is also encountered in *VTE*, though in

[1] See p. 301 n. 3. The main symbol here is the פתיל תכלת 'a cord of blue'. Compare the cords of Judah in Gen. 38, see note above, p. 300 n. 1.

[2] In Prov. 3: 21 f.; 6: 20 f. the protective use of amulets is taken as an analogue of the protective attribute of wisdom.

[3] *KUB* XXVI. 25: 6′ ff., see translation by H. Otten, *MDOG* 94 (1963), 4.

[4] ll. 198–9: *lu ina kal* u_4*-me lu-u ina kal mu-ši lu-u ina* KASKAL *lu ina qap-si* KUR. *qapsu* is the inner part of an enclosure of city or region, see Wiseman, note ad loc.

[5] F3, § 21: 24, § 22: 23. The term there is ŠÀ-*ta tarna* 'to let into the heart', or ZI-*ni tarna* 'to let into the soul'.

the negative sense.[1] However, although these ideas are attested in treaty literature and may therefore be rooted in covenantal imagery, their formulation seems to reflect the didactic-sapiential sphere, as we shall see below.

The distinctive pedagogical consciousness of the book of Deuteronomy may be apprehended from its didactic vocabulary. We have already observed[2] that the verb למד 'teach' does not occur in the Pentateuch except in Deuteronomy. Its connotation is synonymous with that of the verb יסר 'discipline'[3] which, with its derivative מוסר, is also used in Deuteronomy (4: 36; 8: 5; 11: 2; 21: 18; 22: 18).[4] Furthermore, like Deuteronomy, Proverbs speaks not only of fatherly discipline (19: 18; 29: 17; 13: 1), but also of divine discipline: 'My son, despise not the chastening of the Lord (מוסר יהוה) . . . for whom the Lord loves he corrects' (3: 11–12); we may compare Job 5: 17: 'Happy is the man whom God corrects, do not despise the chastening (מוסר) of the Lord'. When Deuteronomy employs this term, it generally does so with reference to the nation as a whole: 'As a man disciplines his son, the Lord your God disciplines you' (8: 5; cf. 11: 2).

The gluttonous son זולל וסבא referred to in Deuteronomy (21: 18–21) is also met with in Proverbs (23: 20–1; 28: 7): 'Be not among drunkards בסבאי יין or among gluttonous eaters of meat בזללי בשר; for the drunkard and the glutton סבא וזולל will come to poverty, and drowsiness will clothe a man with rags',[5] and, as in Deuteronomy, the warning occurs in connection with the injunction to obey one's parents, as is attested by the following verses.[6] The gluttonous son is referred to in Deuteronomy as a 'wayward and defiant son' (סורר ומורה), an expression which seems to belong to the didactic vocabulary of Biblical literature.[7] The word סורר has a meaning

[1] *a-bu-tu la* SIG₅ *-tu . . . ina lìb-bi-ku-nu ta-ša-kan-a-ni* = 'if you set in your heart (Hebrew שים על לב) an evil word' (ll. 183–5). [2] Above, p. 189.

[3] The original meaning of the verb למד is actually 'to discipline', cf. Jer. 31: 17: כעגל לא למד 'like an untrained calf'; Hos. 10: 11: עגלה מלמדה 'a trained heifer', hence the term מלמד הבקר 'an ox-goad' (Judg. 3: 31).

[4] In the last two instances יסר has the sense of physical discipline: flogging.

[5] Sapiential writings also devote much space to commending the virtue of moderation and restraint, hence the exhortations against drunkenness, gluttony, and inordinate desire in general (Prov. 20: 1; 23: 1–8 and 29–35, etc.).

[6] Verse 23 disrupts the continuity of the passage and does not appear in the LXX version.

[7] Beside Deuteronomy it occurs in Ps. 78: 8 in the framework of the didactic introduction (see e.g. Kraus, *Psalmen*, BK ad loc.) and in Jer. 5: 23 (לב סורר ומורה) in a passage marked by its proverbial-didactic character.

approximate to that of the word סור[1] (cf. Jer. 6: 28), which in wisdom literature and also in deuteronomic literature denotes 'deviation from the proper path', or conversely 'to turn from the path of evil' or 'to turn from sin'.[2] The idiom 'to turn or to stray right or left' נטה/סור ימין ושמאל is a stock phrase of the author of Deuteronomy and the Deuteronomist (Deut. 5: 29; 17: 20; 28: 14; Josh. 1: 7; 23: 6; 2 Kgs. 22: 2, etc.) and is also employed in sapiential literature (Prov. 4: 27).[3] The path of righteousness is the golden path that is strewn with long life, riches, and honours (Prov. 3: 16).

He who turns others from the path of righteousness is styled a מדיח, i.e., 'one who leads astray' a term which occurs both in the book of Proverbs (7: 21) and in Deuteronomy (4: 19; 13: 6 and 11; 30: 17) and the deuteronomic literature (2 Kgs. 17: 21, [Qerê וידח] cf. 2 Chr. 21: 11; 13: 9). The expression פתה לב 'to be lured' also belongs to the didactic vocabulary common both to Biblical wisdom literature and the book of Deuteronomy (cf. Deut. 11: 16; Job 31: 9 and 27).[4] The idioms 'turn the heart' פנה לב (Deut. 29: 17; 30: 17), 'turn away the heart' נטה לב, and הטה לב[5] also belong to this category. The word 'heart' is used in a great number of variations:[6] idioms like 'obstinacy of the heart' שרירות לב, 'evilness of heart' רוע לבב, 'harden the heart' אמץ לבב, 'straightness of heart' ישר לבב, 'haughtiness of heart' רום לבב are stock expressions in the Psalms and wisdom literature, and they are also met with in the book of Deuteronomy and in deuteronomic literature.

The imperative שמע ('hear', 'listen'), which we have already discussed in another connection,[7] also belongs to the didactic vocabulary

[1] Actually it corresponds to the verb סור as does שובב to שוב.

[2] In the wisdom literature usually סור מרע and in the deuteronomic literature סור מחטאת (especially in the deuteronomic framework of the book of Kings). In the negative sense it occurs in the wisdom literature as נטה/סור מאמרי פי (Prov. 4: 5; 5: 7) and in the deuteronomic literature: סור מהדרך, סור מאחרי יהוה, סור מהתורה, סור מהדברים, and סור only (Deut. 11: 16; 1 Sam. 12: 21; 2 Kgs. 22: 2).

[3] Compare also the Assyrian texts in *VTE* ll. 632–6 and *ABL* 1110: 19; see R. Frankena, *Oudtest. Studiën* 14 (1965), 144.

[4] Cf. above, p. 277 n. 7. Compare also Hos. 7: 11: ויהי אפרים כיונה פותה אין לב.

[5] Compare 1 Kgs. 8: 58; 11: 2, 3, 4, 9 (= Dtr) with Prov. 2: 2; 21: 1. See also Josh. 24: 23; 2 Sam. 19: 15; Ps. 119: 36 and 112; 141: 4.

[6] Cf. W. O. E. Oesterley, *Proverbs*, Westminster Commentaries, pp. lxxii–lxxx, and J. Malfroy, 'Sagesse et loi dans le Deutéronome', *VT* 15 (1965), 54.

[7] Above, pp. 175 f.

bulary of the book of Deuteronomy. The expression essentially has its origin in the instructor's mode of address to his pupil: שמע בני (Prov., *passim*; cf. Ps. 34: 12: 'Come, O sons בנים, *listen to me* שמעו לי, I will teach you the fear of the Lord'). The use of שמע in the sense of 'to obey' is prevalent in wisdom literature, gnomic aphorisms, and notably in the instruction of Ptahhotep which strongly emphasizes the importance of obedience.[1] Biblical exegetes, especially those scholars who regard Deuteronomy as a composite of singular and plural strands, have been troubled by the use of the word שמע and particularly the phrase 'Hear, O Israel' שמע ישראל in the singular in a context which is ascribed to the so-called plural source (Deut. 4: 1; 5: 1). The present writer is inclined to regard שמע ('hear', 'listen') as a pedagogical expression with which the instructor or preacher generally begins his address; hence its use in the parenetic orations of Moses (4: 1; 5: 1; 6: 3; 9: 1; 27: 9) and in the priest's address to the Israelite warriors preparing to depart for battle (20: 3). The expression שמע ישראל in these passages recalls the phrase שמע בני with which the wise man commences his talk to his pupil, who is expected to absorb his master's teaching by listening.[2] The book of Deuteronomy regards Israel as one cohesive body and thus addresses the nation in the singular number: שמע ישראל and in the second person singular: אתה.

The didactic tendency of Deuteronomy can also be seen in its constant emphasis on the educational role of the father. In the Ancient East the father played a central role in education. Indeed, the very relationship between teacher and pupil is depicted as that between a father and his son. The expression 'my son', with which the teacher addresses the pupil, is prevalent not only in the book of Proverbs but in all ancient Near-Eastern wisdom literature.[3] However, not only the father, but also the mother, takes part in the educational process of the child. The book of Proverbs exhorts the child to obey the teaching of his mother as well as his father (1: 8; 6: 20) and regards her as contributing equally to the child's education (6: 20; 10: 1; 15: 20; 19: 26; 23: 22–5; 30: 17). The

[1] *ANET*², p. 414.

[2] See Gemser, *Sprüche*², p. 21, cf. also Malfroy, art. cit., pp. 57–8.

[3] In the schools of ancient Mesopotamia the teacher was styled 'father' and the pupil 'son'. Cf. B. Landsberger, *City Invincible*, a Symposium on Urbanization and Cultural Development in the Ancient Near-East conducted at the Oriental Institute of the University of Chicago, December, 4–7, 1958, pp. 95 f. See also Gemser, *Sprüche*², p. 21.

book of Deuteronomy also has the mother take an equal part in the education of the child. The child is disciplined by both his mother and his father (21: 18). Both the father and the mother bring their incorrigible son before the elders of the city, and both of them address the presiding judicial body (21: 18–21).[1] By the same token, in the case of the slandered bride both the father and the mother produce the evidence of the girl's virginity before the elders (22: 15).

[1] Cf. Prov. 23: 22–5.

IV

THE DOCTRINE OF REWARD

AT the core of deuteronomic literature lies the concept of national reward, the chief incentive employed by the deuteronomic school to induce the nation to observe its teaching. The concept of reward was indeed the dominating principle that governed wisdom teaching in the ancient Near East.[1] So that the pupil may derive the maximum benefit from life and attain true happiness he must be made cognizant of the principle on which life is based.[2]

Indeed all the distinctive features of the doctrine of reward met with in ancient Israelite wisdom teaching and in ancient wisdom teaching in general are encountered in the book of Deuteronomy. All the material benefits comprised under the heading of reward in wisdom literature, such as the good life, longevity, large families, prosperity, joy, and the 'possession of the land', are woven into the deuteronomic exposition, the difference being only that in Deuteronomy these features have undergone a process of nationalization.

I. LIFE AND GOOD

'Life' in the book of Deuteronomy, as in both Israelite and non-Israelite wisdom literature,[3] constitutes the framework of reward, and the concept is therefore employed in its broadest sense. 'Life' here denotes 'happiness',[4] that is to say, life in its fullest sense. Deuteronomy promises life and longevity to the obedient Israelites on all possible occasions, whether it be in connection with the observance of specific laws (16: 20; 22: 7; 25: 15) or the observance of the Torah in general (4: 1 and 40; 6: 24; 8: 1; 11: 9; 30: 6 and 15–20; 32: 47). The conception of life as a 'way' that man is to choose for himself is found in Deut. 30: 15–20 and accords, in

[1] See L. Dürr, *Erziehungswesen*, pp. 48 f.

[2] Cf. Ps. 34: 12–13; Deut. 6: 24, cited above, pp. 298–9.

[3] Cf. J. Fichtner, *Altorient. Weisheit*, p. 64.

[4] W. W. Graf Baudissin, 'Alttestamentliches *hayyim*, "Leben", in der Bedeutung von "Glück" ', *Festschrift* E. Sachau, 1915, pp. 143–61.

effect, with the doctrine of the 'path of life' or 'way of life'[1] which predominates in the book of Proverbs and is equally common in Egyptian wisdom literature.[2]

The author of Deuteronomy enjoins Israel to choose *life* and the *good* and to reject *death* and the *bad* (30: 15 and 19); Wisdom similarly avers that 'he who finds me finds *life* . . . all who hate me love *death*' (Prov. 8: 35–6). The author of Deuteronomy says of Law: 'For (it) means life to you and length of days' כי הוא חייך וארך ימיך (30: 20); the sages similarly say of Wisdom: 'For she is your life' כי היא חייך (Prov. 4: 13) or 'long life is in her right hand' ארך ימים בימינה (3: 16), the only difference being that in wisdom literature the Israelite is addressed as an individual whereas in Deuteronomy he is addressed as a member of the national body.[3] This motif ('for it is your life') is also encountered in Deuteronomy (32: 47) in a plural formulation: 'For it is your life (חייכם) and thereby shall you live long' (תאריכו ימים). Baudissin,[4] who was influenced by the scholarly consensus of his day which ascribed Biblical wisdom literature to post-exilic times, asserted that the sapiential concept of 'life' evolved from the prophetic concept of 'life' articulated in the book of Deuteronomy. We have seen,[5] however, that the view that wisdom ideology was inspired by Pentateuchal and prophetic teaching is completely groundless, and there is no need for us to reiterate the arguments here. The term 'life' is in point of fact employed in Deuteronomy and in Israelite and non-Israelite wisdom literature in exactly the same sense, as Baudissin himself had observed.[6]

The deuteronomic use of the term in the sense of happiness is not an innovation but a continuation of the older sapiential usage of the word. The addition of the word 'good' indicates the sense in which 'life' is employed in the book of Deuteronomy: it is the 'good life', i.e. a full life, in brief—a happy life. The humanistic ideology which characterizes sapiential teaching scrutinizes all

[1] See Prov. 2: 19; 5: 6; 6: 23; 10: 17; 15: 24; cf. also the expressions 'source of life' and 'tree of life' 3: 18; 10: 11; 13: 12; 16: 22. For discussion see L. Dürr, *Die Wertung des Lebens im A.T. und im antiken Orient*, 1926.

[2] See H. Brunner, *Handbuch der Orientalistik*, I. 2, Ägyptologie, 1952, p. 94. The 'way of life and the way of death' is explicitly mentioned in Jer. 21: 8, which was apparently reworked by the deuteronomic editor. See W. Rudolph, *Jeremia*², HAT, p. 125.

[3] See the remarks of G. von Rad, *Theologie*², I, pp. 441–2.

[4] 'Alttestamentliches *hayyim*'.

[5] Above, pp. 293 f.

[6] op cit., p. 148.

matters from the human point of view and consequently seeks those ends which will prove to be for 'man's good'. This particular concern of wisdom finds expression in the books of Proverbs and Ecclesiastes,[1] but it is no less pronounced in Deuteronomy. The expression 'that it may go well with you' למען ייטב לך is characteristic of, and peculiar to, the book of Deuteronomy,[2] as is evident from a comparison of the different rationales that accompany the parallel commandments to honour parents in the deuteronomic Decalogue (5: 16) and in the Decalogue in the book of Exodus (20: 12). The promise of reward in Deuteronomy is indeed generally expressed in terms of *life and the good* (4: 40; 5: 30; 6: 3; 22: 7, etc.).

In connection with the idea of the 'good life' we also encounter the reward of *longevity* (ארך ימים), a prevalent motif in both Biblical and extra-Biblical wisdom literature. The association of the idea of *life* with *longevity* was common among the scribal circles connected with the royal courts. This is attested by such expressions as ארך ימת ושנת, *ana balāṭi . . . ūmē arkūte* (= for life and the length of days) and the like, frequently encountered in the royal Phoenician and Mesopotamian inscriptions.[3]

The concept of retribution—death and the bad—is articulated in Deuteronomy and in Biblical wisdom literature in identical phraseology, except for the deuteronomic use of the verb אבד instead of מות (Deut. 7: 20; 8: 19; 28: 20 and 22, etc.; cf. Prov. 11: 10; 28: 28, etc.).[4] The verb נסח, which is used in Akkadian for 'to exile', is found, significantly enough, only in Deuteronomy and in Proverbs in the sense of ejection from the land (Prov. 2: 22; Deut. 28: 63).[5] The idiom שמר נפש 'to watch one's life' also belongs to the vocabulary in which this concept is expressed and occurs both in Deuteronomy and in Biblical wisdom literature, the fundamental idea being that observance of the commandments guarantees the preservation of one's life. Thus the author of Prov. 19: 16 declares: 'He who keeps the commandment keeps his life' (שמר נפשו). The author of Deuteronomy similarly enjoins the Israelite: 'Only take heed and watch yourself (ושמר נפשך)

[1] See W. Zimmerli, 'Zur Struktur der alttestamentlichen Weisheit', *ZAW* 51 (1933), 192–4. See also H. Gunkel, 'Psalm 133', *Budde Festschrift*, p. 70.

[2] Cf. the remark on p. 345, at VII. 4.

[3] On the Phoenician inscriptions see Donner–Röllig, *KAI* (cf. Index), and on the Mesopotamian inscriptions see, e.g., S. Langdon, *Die neubabylonischen Königsinschriften*, 1912, *passim*.

[4] See Zimmerli, 'Zur Struktur', p. 195.

[5] Cf. below, p. 316. The Akkadian verb is *nasāḫu*.

scrupulously lest you forget' . . . (4: 9, compare v. 15), when referring to the danger ensuing from forgetfulness of the sacred past. This idiom is also employed by the Deuteronomist (Josh. 23: 11) and in the deuteronomic sermons in the book of Jeremiah (17: 21).[1]

Other concomitant concepts of reward, such as affluence and satiety, also find prominent mention in the book of Deuteronomy and in wisdom literature. The blessing of overflowing barns met with in Deut. 28: 8 has its parallel in the sapiential dictum 'Honour the Lord with your substance . . . then your barns will be filled with plenty' וימלאו אסמיך שבע in Prov. 3: 10. Indeed these are the only two passages in the Bible in which the word אסם (= barn) appears.[2] The idiom employed in Deuteronomy to express the idea of economic prosperity is 'houses full of good things' בתים מלאים כל טוב (6: 11), which is also met with in wisdom literature: 'Yet he filled their houses with good things' והוא מלא בתיהם טוב (Job 22: 18). The righteous in receiving their just reward are blessed with plenty to enable them to lend generously to the poor. This idea is expressed, for example, in a sapiential psalm which describes the righteous as 'ever giving liberally and lending, and his children becoming a blessing' כל היום חונן ומלוה וזרעו לברכה (Ps. 37: 26). It occurs also in Ps. 112: 5: 'It is well with a man who deals generously and lends'; in Prov. 19: 17: 'He who is kind to the poor lends to the Lord' מלוה יהוה חונן דל; and in a Babylonian maxim[3] which reads: 'The man who sacrifices to his god is happy,[4] he is making loan upon loan.' The book of Deuteronomy also associates the idea of the reward of material plenty with the idea of being able to lend to the destitute, though in characteristically national terms: 'And you shall lend to many nations, but you shall not borrow' (15: 6; 28: 12; cf. v. 44).

[1] For this idiom in wisdom literature see Prov. 13: 3; 16: 17; 19: 16, 22: 5; compare Job 2: 6. It must be said, however, that in the deuteronomic literature the notion of 'caution and carefulness' in this phrase prevails over that of 'guarding' and 'preserving life'.

[2] It was recently found in an Israelite letter dating from the seventh century, the letter from Yavneh-Yam (see J. Naveh, 'A Hebrew Letter from the Seventh Century B.C.', *IEJ* 10 (1960), 129 ff. = *KAI* 200).

[3] For text and translation see W. G. Lambert, *BWL* (Dialogue of Pessimism), p. 146: 56–7. See also R. H. Pfeiffer, *ANET*², p. 438.

[4] Lambert (*BWL*, p. 326) observes that *libbašu ṭāb* is the usual phrase in Old-Babylonian business documents 'for expressing the satisfaction of the contracting parties with the term of the contract' and consequently renders the phrase in the present passage in the same vein: 'satisfied with the bargain'. His translation, however, does not suit the context and I find Pfeiffer's translation 'is happy' the preferable one. (Cf. Muffs, *Aramaic Legal Papyri*, p. 140 n. 1.)

The material blessing with which the righteous is rewarded is described in Deuteronomy in terms of the yield of his lands, the increase of his flock, and the fecundity of his wife (28: 4; 7: 13). The same threefold blessing is also met with in Babylonian literature: for instance: 'Bow down to Ištar, the goddess of your city, that she may grant you offspring; take thought for your livestock, remember the planting.'[1]

The idea that the righteous are blessed with many sons is frequently encountered in wisdom literature (cf. Job 5: 25; Ps. 128, etc.), where they are, moreover, assured that their sons too shall enjoy the beneficence of God (Pss. 25: 13; 112: 2; Job 21: 8). The book of Deuteronomy also promises that the descendants of those who observe the Torah shall partake of the reward enjoyed by their fathers: 'that you and your descendants may live' (30: 19); 'that it may go well with you and with your children after you' (12: 28); 'that your days and the days of your children may be multiplied' (11:21).[2] Thus the three ideal aspects of material reward: longevity, affluence, and blessed offspring, which epitomize the good life and are largely familiar to us from wisdom literature are also met with in our book, though they are not always referred to in connection with each other.[3]

The experience of a good life evokes joyousness within the heart of the individual. This sense or experience of joy is also one of the distinctive features of reward. Such passages as 'And you shall rejoice in all the good which the Lord your God has given you' (Deut. 26: 11), 'You shall rejoice before the Lord your God' (12: 18), 'You shall be altogether joyful' (16: 15) suggest the joyous feeling of the righteous and God-fearing who have received their just recompense from God.[4] A Babylonian sage similarly declares: 'the day for reverencing the god was a joy to my heart'.[5]

[1] See Lambert, *BWL*, p. 108: 13–14. There may be some relationship between the name Ištar in this passage and the parallel term עשתרת in Deut. 7: 13; 28: 4, which occur in a similar context.

[2] Cf. Prov. 13: 22; 14: 26; Pss. 25: 13; 37: 25.

[3] I. L. Seeligmann observes that these ideals have been dissociated in Eccles. 6: 2–3, cf. *Tarbiz* 27 (1958–9), p. 131, n. 15.

[4] Cf. also 12: 7 and 12; 14: 26; 16: 11 and 14; 28: 47, and in Psalmodic-sapiential literature: 68: 4; 100: 2; 105: 3; 119: 74; Prov. 29: 6, etc. Mark the JPS translation of the Torah (1967) at Deut. 12: 7: ושמחתם בכל משלח ידכם 'happy in all the undertakings' and at 16: 15: והיית אך שמח 'you shall have nothing but joy'.

[5] *ūmu palāḫ ilī ṭūb libbīya*, *BWL*, 38: 25.

In Deuteronomy the divine *blessing* is conceived in terms of national prosperity in which the Israelite who observes God's ways shares, as against the Israelite who does not walk in the ways of God and thus suffers want and privation. The divine *blessing* enjoyed by the individual is here conceived as the direct consequence of his own religious and moral acts, not as something attained through the agency of the sacral class or effected through cultic rites as in the Priestly document (Num. 6: 22–7; cf. Lev. 9: 22). For in Deuteronomy each and every Israelite may turn to God in prayer and entreat his blessing for the success of his own or the nation's enterprises (26: 15). The divine *blessing* is here conceived as the material beneficence which continuously emanates from the Godhead (12: 15, 16: 12, 28: 8), a concept prevalent also in the wisdom literature (Prov. 10: 22; 28: 20). According to Deuteronomy God's blessing brings about the success that accompanies the enterprises of the righteous ברך מעשה ידים/משלח יד,[1] a concept expressed in the same style in Job 1: 10: מעשה ידיו ברכת 'You have blessed the work of his hands'. This blessing which inheres in the work of the righteous is his reward for aiding the poor and the destitute, his compensation for having given up part of his own wealth for the welfare of others. Thus Deut. 14: 29 declares 'and the Levite . . . and the stranger, the fatherless, and the widow . . . shall come and eat and be filled, so that the Lord your God may bless you in all the enterprises you undertake' למען יברכך יהוה אלהיך בכל מעשה ידך אשר תעשה. In connection with lending to the poor the deuteronomic legislator says: 'Give to him readily and have no regrets when you do so, for in return the Lord your God will bless you in all your works and in all your undertakings' (15: 10). Similarly we read in 23: 21: 'You shall not charge interest upon loans to your brother . . . so that the Lord your God may bless you in all your undertakings' למען יברכך יהוה אלהיך בכל משלח ידך (cf. 15: 18), and in 24: 19: 'when you reap the harvest . . . and overlook a sheaf . . . do not turn back . . . it shall go to the stranger, the orphan, and the widow—in order that the Lord your God may bless you in all your undertakings'. This conception of reward conforms with that of the book of Proverbs. Thus Prov. 11: 25 states that 'a liberal man (נפש ברכה = soul of blessing) will be enriched, and one who waters (ומרוה) will himself be watered', and 22: 9 'He who has a bountiful eye will be blessed, for he shares his

[1] Cf. 2: 7; 14: 29; 15: 10 and 18; 16: 15; 23: 21; 24: 19; 28: 8 and 12.

bread with the poor.' Similarly in 28: 27: 'He who gives to the poor lacks nothing' (cf. Deut. 2: 7: 'you have lacked nothing') 'and one who disregards (the poor) is full of curses' (רב מארות).

מארה is the opposite of ברכה, and indeed the bestowal of blessing (ברכה, Deut. 28: 8) is contrasted with the sending of the curse (מארה, v 20). The מארה ומהומה which afflict the enterprises of Israel the transgressor (Deut. 28: 20) are also the instruments of punishment directed against the evildoer's property in Proverbs (3: 33; 15: 16).

2. THE POSSESSION OF THE LAND

The motif of possessing the land ירש הארץ, which runs through the entire book of Deuteronomy, also seems to have its ultimate source in wisdom ideology, though in Deuteronomy it has assumed a national cast. Let us first examine the import of this concept in wisdom literature.

In Ps. 37 the meek and righteous are promised that they shall 'possess the land' יירשו ארץ (vv. 11, 22, 29, 34; cf. 25: 13). Some scholars take the phrase to refer to the 'Israelite reconquest of the land that had become subject to foreign rule'[1] and to express the Israelite desire of absolute dominance over all of the promised land. Others take it in an eschatological sense on the basis of its occurrences in Isaiah 57: 13; 60: 21.[2]

It seems, however, to have escaped the attention of these scholars that the concept ירש ארץ is also expressed by another idiom: שכן ארץ (Ps. 37: 3, 27, 29), which is also employed in the book of Proverbs (2: 21–2; 10: 30), a book which, except for its monotheistic view, has no affinities with other national concepts. It cannot be plausibly assumed, then, that it refers to the Israelite reconquest of the land or that it has an eschatological sense;[3] since the idiom parallels שכן ארץ (cf. Ps. 37: 3 and 29) it must undoubtedly denote the same thing.

[1] 'die Widergewinnung des Israeliten des von Heiden beherrschten Landes', so H. Birkeland, *Die Feinde des Individuums in der israelitischen Psalmen-literatur*, 1933, p. 274.

[2] Cf. Mishnah Sanhedrin x: 1 and compare Matt. 5: 5.

[3] Scholars who contend that Prov. 1–9 is a post-deuteronomic composition may argue that Prov. 2: 21 was influenced by Deuteronomy. But how will they account for the concept in 10: 30 which is universally assigned to an early period?

Gunkel,[1] therefore, correctly sees in the phrase a reference to the farmers who count the fact that they can go on working their land and bequeath it to their sons as a blessing and divine favour. Munch[2] finds in the expression ענוי ארץ a reference to the poor and humble peasants to whom the psalmist promises the restoration of their lands from the hands of the iniquitous rich. He justifiably observes that the verb ירש means 'to conquer' or 'dispossess', but this does not necessarily mean that it always has this sense, nor does it preclude our taking the verb in this instance in its extended meaning 'to assume ownership over property'.

This motif also occurs in the book of Job which has a universal setting: 'The earth is given into the hand of the wicked ארץ נתנה ביד רשע; he covers the faces of the judges' (9: 24); or 'To (them) alone the land was given נתנה הארץ and no stranger passed among them' (15: 19) and similarly in 22: 8: 'The man with the power possessed the land, and the favoured man dwelt in it.' These verses demonstrate that the concept was a conventional motif in sapiential literature. Job here calls into question the notion of God's just government of the world by exposing the fact that it is not the righteous who possess the land, as is commonly asserted, but the iniquitous, who have acquired it by violence and who still continue to possess it. It is to this situation that Job refers when he insists that 'the land is given into the hand of the wicked; he covers the faces of its judges', that is, he succeeds in blinding the eyes of the judges—who are responsible for the maintenance of social order and justice—from beholding the perpetration of his theft. In contradistinction to the optimistic belief in Ps. 37: 17 that 'the arms of the wicked (זרועת רשעים) shall be broken', Job laments that 'the man with an arm (איש זרוע) possesses the land'. Not so Eliphaz, the friend of Job, who, convinced of the justness of divine government, asserts (15: 19) that 'the land was given to the righteous alone',[3] upon which they dwell in tranquillity enjoying its produce, as opposed to the wicked who wander about in search of bread (v. 23).[4] Those exegetes[5] who take the idiom ירש ארץ to refer to the reconquest of the land and dispossession of its alien

[1] H. Gunkel, *Die Psalmen*, 1926, p. 156.

[2] P. A. Munch, 'Das Problem des Reichtums in den Psalmen 37, 49, 73', *ZAW* 55 (1937), 36 ff.

[3] Cf. N. H. Tur-Sinai, *The Book of Job*, ad loc.

[4] See Ps. 37: 25: 'I have been young, and now am old; yet I have not seen the righteous forsaken nor his children begging bread.'

[5] See, e.g., G. Hölscher, *Das Buch Hiob*, HAT, 1952.

inhabitants delete Job 15: 19 on the assumption that it is a late gloss. Hölscher, who shares this view, remarks that apparently 'the glossator had forgotten that Job is not an Israelite'. We have already seen, however, that the notion that the righteous 'possess' the land is an integral part of the doctrine of divine reward characteristic of all wisdom literatures of the ancient Near East. The fact that Job, a non-Israelite, should voice this idea is therefore by no means extraordinary. The motif appears to have been originally connected with the recurring exhortations in wisdom literature against the removal of landmarks and apparently at first referred to the removal of 'ancient landmarks' or landmarks 'which the men of old have set' (Deut. 19: 14).[1]

There is no warrant, then, for seeing in the 'possession of the land' motif in wisdom literature the idea of conquest and dispossession. The converse is true: this idea is always set against the background of an idyllic scene in which the Israelite is depicted as dwelling tranquilly on his ancestral estate undisturbed by alien factors.

The idiom ירש ארץ is, to be sure, generally employed in the book of Deuteronomy in the sense of 'to conquer', 'to dispossess', as would be expected in an address delivered by Moses on the eve of the Israelite conquest (see above, p. 177). Nevertheless, the author does at times employ it in its sapiential sense of 'possession and perpetual inhabitation of the land'. For instance at 16: 20: 'Justice, justice shall you pursue, that you may live and occupy the land' וירשת את הארץ. It is evident that the verse does not refer to the conquest of the land but to the reward accruing to the Israelites, should they observe this prescription *after they had settled in the land* (v. 18). The idiom is apparently also to be rendered in the sense of 'possession and perpetual inhabitation of the land' in other contexts in Deuteronomy, and not always in the sense of conquering the land from the Canaanites.

The expression 'to lengthen (or multiply) one's days upon the land' which is frequently encountered in Deuteronomy (4: 25 and 40; 5: 30; 11: 9 and 21) also embraces the sapiential idea of 'possessing the land' except that in wisdom literature the promise relates to the individual, whereas in Deuteronomy it relates to the entire nation. In Deuteronomy the converse of 'to lengthen (or multiply) one's days upon the land' is 'to perish from the land or

[1] Cf. above, p. 265.

the earth' (4: 26; 11: 17; cf. Josh. 23: 13 and 16), this constituting the punishment for not observing the prescriptions of the Torah. In one such context in the book of Deuteronomy we meet with the expression 'to be plucked (נסח) from the land' (28: 63) which also occurs in wisdom literature (Prov. 2: 22; cf. 15: 25; cf. Ps. 52: 7) as the converse of inhabiting and striking roots in the land.[1]

3. THEODICY

A book in which the doctrine of reward and retribution occupies so significant a place cannot pass over the question of Good and Evil in silence.

The idea of divine providence which finds marked expression in wisdom literature must of necessity touch upon the question of the existence of Evil in the world. If God truly requites the deeds of each individual, why, then, do the righteous suffer and the wicked prosper? Wisdom literature solves this problem through the concept of the אחרית—'the latter end' or 'issue' of all phenomena—according to which the prosperity of the wicked and the suffering of the righteous are only transitory states. The decisive factor is the 'latter end': the righteous have a future, their hope shall not be cut off (Prov. 23: 18; 24: 14), whereas the future of the wicked shall be cut off (Pss. 37: 38; 73: 17, etc.). In psalmodic literature this concept is graphically conveyed in the natural simile of the withering of flowers in bloom (37: 2; 92: 8, etc.).

Wisdom literature also sought to explain the suffering of the righteous in educational terms: 'For the Lord reproves him whom he loves, as a father the son in whom he delights' (Prov. 3: 12). In the Psalter and in parts of the book of Job suffering is conceived as a blessing and a good, since it serves to discipline and instruct the righteous, just as the rod chastens and disciplines the wayward child so that he may correct his conduct (cf. Ps. 94: 12; Job 5: 17; 33: 27–30; and Ps. 119: 71: 'It is good for me that I was afflicted, that I might learn Your statutes').

The book of Deuteronomy provides the same two explanations, but since it again concentrates on the national aspect of the problem it uses them to account for Israel's affliction during the desert wandering. The educational explanation is formulated in phraseo-

[1] Cf. above, p. 309.

logy similar to that in Prov. 3: 12: 'as a man disciplines his son, the Lord your God disciplines you' (Deut. 8: 5). God fed the Israelites with manna, so that they might learn 'that man does not live by bread alone, but that man lives by everything that proceeds out of the mouth of the Lord' (v. 3).[1]

The other explanation also appears in connection with the manna. According to the earlier sources God fed the people with manna so that he might test their faith in him: 'that I may prove them, whether they will walk in my law or not' (Exod. 16: 4 = JE). Deuteronomy, in addition to this older rationale (8: 2), also cites a sapiential rationale according to which God's purpose was to purify and cleanse their faith through suffering so that he might reward and 'do them good in the end' להיטבך באחריתך (8: 16). In the earlier sources the divine test has only a theological significance: to test Israel's faith in God, to teach them the fear of God and to warn them of the consequences of little faith (Gen. 22: 1; Exod. 20: 20) In Deuteronomy a sapiential and anthropocentric motif is added which expresses the utilitarian benefit that accrues from this trial, which is 'a good end'.

The idea that the wicked have no אחרית is clearly stated in Deut. 7: 10: 'who instantly (אל פניו) requites with destruction those who reject him—never late (לא יאחר) with those who reject him, but requiting them instantly',[2] a notion which lies at the core of the sapiential doctrine of retribution and finds similar expression in Job 21: 19: '(You say) God stores up their iniquity for their sons? Let him recompense (ישלם) it to themselves, that they may know it.'[3]

The verse cited from Deut. 7: 10, which clearly and unequivocally expresses the principle of individual retribution (compare the deuteronomic liturgical sermon in Jer. 32: 19), occurs in the context of a larger formula which is also encountered in analogous versions elswhere in the Pentateuch (Exod. 20: 5b–6 = Deut. 5: 9b–10; Exod. 34: 6–7; Num. 14: 18). However, it has already been observed that the deuteronomic formula differs radically from its Pentateuchal parallels and that it arises from the concept of individual retribution which also finds expression in the prophecies of

[1] See G. von Rad, *Das erste Buch Mose*, ATD², p. 11 n. 1.

[2] Translated according to *The Torah*², JPS, 1967. The verb שלם in the sense of 'to requite, to recompense' is a sapiental usage (cf. Job 34: 11; Prov. 11: 31; 25: 22, etc.).

[3] The first half of this verse is to be read as a question, see Tur-Sinai, *Job*, ad loc.

Jeremiah and Ezekiel (Jer. 31: 28–9; Ezek. 14: 12–23; 18; 33: 1–20).[1] The phrase 'visiting the iniquity of the fathers upon the children' was intentionally deleted in the deuteronomic formula in 7: 9–10 and was replaced by a verse clearly contradicting the view articulated in the older formula: God does not visit the iniquity of the fathers upon the children but requites the sinners instantly (lit. *to their faces*).

In keeping with this conception the author of Deuteronomy revised the second commandment of the Decalogue.[2] In Exod. 34: 6–7 and Num. 14: 18 we read that God 'visits the iniquity of the fathers upon the children . . . to the third and fourth generation'. The deuteronomic editor, however, appended the word לשנאי ('that reject me'; cf. לשנאיו in Deut. 7: 10) to the Decalogue formula so as to make the passage state that God exacts punishment only from those children who 'reject' him, that is, those who propagate the evil ways of their fathers.[3] He also added the words 'to those who love me and keep my commandments' to the phrase 'but showing kindness to thousands' to make the passage state the converse idea that the descendants of the righteous will enjoy divine grace only if they themselves will observe God's precepts. These two motifs, the love of God אהב את יהוה and the observance of his precepts שמר מצות, are an integral part of deuteronomic theology.[4]

The conception that God requites the sins of the fathers on the children only if the latter propagate the evil ways of their fathers is, in effect, the underlying view of the concept of retribution in the deuteronomic history. Thus we have seen[5] that according to the

[1] We do not accept the Wellhausenian view that the concept of individual retribution evolved from the earlier idea of collective retribution (see M. Weiss, 'Studies in the Biblical Doctrine of Retribution', *Tarbiz* 31 (1962–3), 236 ff., Hebrew with English summary). I find J. Scharbert's interpretation more acceptable ('Formgeschichte und Exegese von Ex. 34, 6 f. und seiner Parallelen', *Biblica* 38 (1957), 130–50). He contends that the notion of individual retribution was always existent, but only in a latent form; in the 7th century B.C., however, it became explicit.

[2] As was observed by B. D. Eerdmans, *Alttestamentliche Studien*, III, 1910, pp. 8 and 131 ff.

I believe that the Decalogue was at first revised by the author of Deuteronomy alone and that in later times the Exodus version was corrected in accordance with the deuteronomic one. But only minor changes and corrections were inserted. Principal and lengthy statements like that on the motivation of Sabbath remained unchanged. Only this explanation seems to explain both the occurrence of deuteronomic phraseology in Exodus and the difference between the two versions.

[3] Cf. BT *Berakoth* 7a; *Sanhedrin* 27b.

[4] See Appendix A, pp. 333, 336.

[5] Above, p. 19.

reflection of this view in the books of Kings it is not the individual punishment that is transferred from royal ancestor to descendant as in the pre-deuteronomic strands, but the dynastic punishment; and even in the instances of the transference of dynastic punishment the Deuteronomist is careful to point out the role played by the principle of individual retribution. Thus the monarchs in whose reigns the dynasty was destroyed do not perish as a consequence of their fathers' sins but because they have adopted and propagated the evil ways of their fathers. We do not, indeed, hear of any king 'who did that which was just in the sight of the Lord' but was nevertheless destroyed in requital for the sins of his fathers.

Manasseh of Judah, and Jeroboam and Ahab of Israel overburdened the land with their sins and for this reason God had vowed to exile Israel and destroy Jerusalem. But had Jehoiakim and Zedekiah adopted the ways of their ancestor David, and had the kings of Israel not propagated the sins of Jeroboam, then God would not have executed his fateful decision in their days.

The deuteronomic turning-point in the conception of retribution is most evident in the Ahab pericope. According to the pre-deuteronomic narrative God transferred the punishment for Naboth's murder from Ahab to his son, who was eventually executed by Jehu.[1] The Deuteronomist, however, who professes the idea of individual retribution, cannot accept the earlier tradition of the transference of Ahab's personal punishment to another, and therefore interprets Ahab's fall in battle as his punishment for shedding the innocent blood of Naboth.[2] The death of his son Jehoram is interpreted as the fulfilment of the prophecy concerning the destruction of the dynasty; but Jehoram, needless to say, is also described as doing evil in the sight of the Lord and propagating the sins of his father (2 Kgs. 3: 1–3).

[1] See above, p. 18. [2] Above, p. 19.

APPENDIX A

DEUTERONOMIC PHRASEOLOGY[1]

I. THE STRUGGLE AGAINST IDOLATRY

A. *Warnings against foreign worship*

1. הלך אחרי אלהים אחרים 'to follow (lit. to go after) foreign gods'. For the idiom 'go after' in Akkadian see below, V. A. 1 (p. 332).

   Deut.: 6: 14, 8: 19, 11: 28, 13: 3, 28: 14.

   Dtr: Judg. 2: 12, 19; 1 Kgs. 11: 10, cf. 1 Kgs. 21: 26 (אחרי הגלולים), 2 Kgs. 17: 15 (אחרי ההבל), compare Jer. 2: 5 and see I. B. 5. (p. 323).

   Jer. C: 7: 6, 9, 11: 10, 13: 10, 16: 11, 25: 6, 35: 15.

   Cf. 1 Kgs. 18: 18, 21 (אחרי הבעל / הבעלים), Jer. 2: 23 (אחרי הבעלים), Deut. 4: 3 (אחרי בעל פעור).

2. עבד אלהים אחרים 'to worship (lit. serve) foreign gods'. For the idiom in Akkadian see below, V. A. 2 (p. 332).

   Deut.: 7: 4, 11: 16, 13: 7, 14, 17: 3, 28: 36, 64, 29: 25. Cf. 4: 19, 8: 19, 30: 17.

   Dtr: Josh. 23: 16; 1 Sam. 8: 8 (deuteronomic interpolation); 1 Kgs. 9: 6; 2 Kgs. 21: 21 (את הגלולים).

   Jer. C: 16: 13, 44: 3; cf. 8: 2.

   The phrase is already attested in pre-deuteronomic literature, and especially in the Elohistic source: Deut. 31: 20; Josh. 24: 2, 16; Judg. 10: 13, see also 1 Sam. 26: 19.

2a. עבד הבעל/ הבעלים והעשתרות/ האשרות 'to worship the Baal/Baalim and the Ashtaroth/ Asheroth'.

   Dtr: Judg. 2: 11, 13, 3: 7, 10: 6, 10; 1 Sam. 12: 10; 1 Kgs. 16: 31, 22: 54; 2 Kgs. 17: 16.

   Cf. 2 Kgs. 10: 18.

3. הלך ועבד אלהים אחרים / הלך אחרי אלהים אחרים ועבד (אתם) 'to follow foreign gods and to worship them/to go and worship foreign gods'.

   Deut.: 13: 3, 7, 14, 28: 14.

   Jer. C: 11: 10, 35: 15.

   Cf. 1 Sam. 26: 19.

[1] The parallel phrases in Chronicles are not listed.

4. השתחוה (לאלהים אחרים) ועבד (אתם)/ עבד (לאלהים אחרים) והשתחוה (להם) 'to worship (foreign gods) and to bow down (to them) / to bow down . . . and to worship'.

Dtr: Josh. 23: 7; 1 Kgs. 9: 9, 22: 54; 2 Kgs. 17: 35, 21: 3, 21.

Jer. C: 22: 9.

Cf. Exod. 20: 5 (= Deut. 5: 9), 23: 24, and in the secular context, that is, in reference to serving a nation or a king: Gen. 27: 29; Ps. 72: 11 (in parallel members).

5. הלך ועשה אלהים אחרים 'to go and make foreign gods'.

Dtr: 1 Kgs. 14: 9.

5a. הלך אחרי אלהים אחרים והשתחוו להם

Dtr: Judg. 2: 12.

6. הלך סר ועבד אלהים אחרים (הבעל/הבעלים) והשתחוה (להם) 'to go to worship foreign gods (the Baal/Baalim) and to bow down'.

Deut.: 8: 19, 11: 16, 29: 25.

Dtr: Josh. 23: 16; Judg. 2: 19; 1 Kgs. 9: 6, 16: 31.

Jer. C: 13: 10, 16: 11, 25: 6. Cf. in Jer. 44: 3: הלך קטר ועבד לאלהים אחרים 'to go, to burn incense and to worship foreign gods'.

7. נדח, השתחוה לאלהים אחרים ועבד 'to be lured, to bow down . . . and to worship'.

Deut.: 4: 19, 30: 17.

7a. הטה לבב אחרי אלהים אחרים 'turn away the heart after foreign gods'.

Dtr: 1 Kgs. 11: 2, 4.

8. (הלך/נדח) עבד/השתחוה/קטר (לשמש לירח ולכוכבים) לכל צבא השמים '(to go/to be lured) to worship/to bow down/to burn incense (to the sun, to the moon, and to the stars) to the whole heavenly host'.

Deut.: 4: 19, 17: 3.

Dtr: 2 Kgs. 17: 16, 21: 3, 5.

Jer. C: 8: 2, 19: 13.

Compare 2 Kgs. 23: 5; Zeph. 1: 5.

9. קטר לאלהים אחרים 'to burn incense to foreign gods'.

Dtr: 2 Kgs. 22: 17.

Jer. C: 1: 16, 19: 4, 44: 5, 8, 15.

Cf. 2 Chr. 28: 25.

10. קטר לבעל (לכל צבא השמים) 'to burn incense to Baal (the whole heavenly host)'.

Jer. C: 7: 9, 11: 13, 17, 19: 13, 32: 29.

Cf. 2 Kgs. 23: 5. Occurs for the first time in Hos. 2: 15 (though with the hiphʿil).

11. קטר על הגגות 'to burn incense on the roofs'.

Jer. C: 19: 13, 32: 29.

Cf. Zeph. 1: 5; Isa. 65: 3; see D. Conrad, *ZAW* 80 (1968), 232–4.

12. הסך נסכים לאלהים אחרים 'to pour libations to foreign gods'.

Jer. C: 7: 18, 19: 13, 32: 29, cf. 44: 17.

13. ירא אלהים אחרים 'to fear (= to worship) foreign gods'.

Dtr: 2 Kgs. 17: 7, 35, 37, 38.

14. אלהי העמים אשר סביבותיכם 'gods of the peoples around you'.

Deut. 6: 14, 13: 8.

Dtr: Judg. 2: 12.

15. על (כל) הר/גבעה (גבהה) ותחת כל עץ רענן 'on (every) mountain/(lofty hill) and under every luxuriant tree'.

Deut. 12: 2.

Dtr: 1 Kgs. 14: 23; 2 Kgs. 16: 4, 17: 10.

Cf. Jer. 2: 20, 3: 6, 17: 2; Ezek. 6: 13; Hos. 4: 13, which seems to be the origin of the phrase, see Holladay, *VT* 11 (1961), 170–6, and cf. below, p. 366.

Compare Jer. 3: 13; Isa. 57: 5.

16. שרף בנים (ובנות) באש 'to burn the sons (daughters) in fire'.

Deut.: 12: 31.

Jer. C: 7: 31, 19:5 (with עלות לבעל).

Cf. 2 Kgs. 17: 31.

17. העביר בן (ובת) באש 'to pass the son (and daughter) in fire'.

Deut.: 18: 10.

Dtr: 2 Kgs. 16: 3, 17: 17, 21: 6.

Cf. 2 Kgs. 23: 10 (with למלך); Ezek. 20: 31. In Lev. 18: 21 העביר זרע comes with למלך and not with באש. Jer. 32: 35 seems to be influenced by P.

18. בנה במות תופת/בעל 'to build high places of *tophet*/Baal'.

Jer. C.: 7: 31, 19: 5, 32: 35.

B. *The Polemic against idolatry*

1. תועבה '(idolatry as) abomination'.

Deut.: 7: 25, 26, 13: 15, 17: 4, 18: 9, 20: 18.

Dtr: 1 Kgs. 14: 24; 2 Kgs. 16: 3, 21: 2, 11, cf. 23: 13.

Jer. C: 32: 35, 44: 4, 22; cf. Jer. 16: 18.

Occurs frequently in Ezekiel. Compare also Isa. 41: 24, 44: 19 (in the framework of polemics against idolatry). Appears for the first time in Deut. 32: 16, which may reflect its origin (didactic poetry).

1a. תועבת יהוה 'Yahweh's abomination'.

Deut.: 7: 25, 12: 31, 17: 1, 18: 12, 22: 5, 23: 19, 25: 16, 27: 15.

See above, pp. 267 f. and cf. Prov. 3: 32, 11: 1, 20, 12: 22, 15: 8, 9, 26, 16: 5, 17: 15, 20: 10, 23.

2. תועבת הגויים 'abomination of the nations'.

Deut.: 18: 9.

Dtr: 1 Kgs. 14: 24; 2 Kgs. 16: 3, 21: 2.

3. שקוצים 'detestable things'.

Deut.: 29: 16, cf. 7: 26 (שקץ in P never refers to idolatry).

Dtr: 1 Kgs. 11: 5, 7; 2 Kgs. 23: 24. Cf. 2 Kgs. 23: 13.

Jer. C: 7: 30, 32: 34; cf. in Jeremian poetry: 4: 1, 13: 27, 16: 18.

Nahum 3: 6, Zech. 9: 7 do not refer to idols. Ezekiel adopted the deuteronomic usage (*passim*) and so Second Isaiah (66: 3). שקוצים in Hos. 9: 10, which is close there to בשת, may already reflect the deuteronomic sense, but the verse is not altogether clear.

4. גלולים 'fetishes'—seems to derive from גל, גלל 'dung' (Ezek. 4: 12, 15; Job 20: 7).

Deut.: 29: 16.

Dtr: 1 Kgs. 15: 12, 21: 26; 2 Kgs. 17: 12, 21: 11, 21, 23: 24.

Cf. Lev. 26: 30; Jer. 50: 2; Ezek. (*passim*).

5. תהו/הבל 'vanity, nothingness'.

Dtr: 1 Sam. 12: 21; 1 Kgs. 16: 13, 26; 2 Kgs. 17: 15 (seems to be a quotation from Jer. 2: 5).

The idiom is particularly frequent in genuine Jeremiah 2: 5, 8: 19, 14: 22, 10: 3, 15 (= 51: 18), 16: 19, and may be traced back to Deut. 32: 21: קנאוני בלא אל כעסוני בהבליהם. The latter seems to have influenced Jer. 8: 19b: הכעיסוני בפסליהם בהבלי נכר. Compare also Ps. 78: 58: ויכעיסוהו בבמותם ובפסיליהם יקניאוהו.

6. אלהים (אחרים) אשר לא ידעת(ם)/ידעום '(foreign) gods whom you have/ they had never known'. For the interpretation of this phrase in the light of Hosea 13: 4: ואנכי יהוה אלהיך מארץ מצרים ואלהים זולתי לא תדע ומושיע אין בלתי 'Ever since the land of Egypt, only I Yahweh have been your God; beside me *you have never known* a God, other than Me you have never had a Helper' cf. H. L. Ginsberg, art. 'Hosea, The Book of; C' in the *Encyclopaedia Judaica.*

Deut.: 11: 28, 13: 3, 7, 14, 28: 64, 29: 25.

Jer. C: 7: 9, 19: 4, 44: 3.

The idiom may have its roots in the didactic religious poetry, cf. Deut. 32: 17, אלהים לא ידעום.

7. (אלהים) מעשה ידים/ידי אדם/חרש (עץ ואבן) 'man-made/craftsman's/ hand-made (gods) (of wood and stone)'.

Deut.: 4: 28, 27: 15; cf. 28: 64, 31: 29.

Dtr: 1 Kgs. 16: 7; 2 Kgs. 19: 18 (= Isa. 37: 19), 22: 17.

Jer. C: 1: 16, 25: 6, 7, 32: 30, 44: 8.

Cf. Isa. 2: 8; Hos. 14: 4; Mic. 5: 12; see below, p. 367.

II. CENTRALIZATION OF WORSHIP— THE CHOSEN PLACE AND THE 'NAME' THEOLOGY

1. המקום אשר יבחר 'the site that the Lord will choose'.

Deut.: 12: 5, 11, 14, 18, 21, 26, 14: 23, 24, 25, 15: 20, 16: 2, 6, 7, 11, 15, 16, 17: 8, 10, 18: 6, 26: 2, 31: 11.

Dtr: Josh. 9: 27.

1a. העיר/ירושלם אשר בחר 'the city/Jerusalem that the Lord has chosen'.

Dtr: 1 Kgs. 8: 16, 44, 48, 11: 13, 32, 36, 14: 21; 2 Kgs. 21: 7, 23: 27.

2. הבית/העיר אשר נקרא שמי עליו 'the house/city which my name is called upon'.

Dtr: 1 Kgs. 8: 43.

Jer. C: 7: 10, 11, 14, 30, 25: 29, 32: 34, 34: 15.

Cf. Dan. 9: 18, 19. The same term is applied to the election of Israel (see below). The expression קרא שם על (in the sense of ownership and protection (cf., e.g. S. R. Driver, *Deuteronomy*, ICC, p. 306) is itself ancient (2 Sam. 6: 2, 12: 28; Isa. 4: 1; Ps. 49: 12) and as such cannot be considered to be deuteronomic. It is the application to Israel on the one hand and the application to city and temple on the other that makes the term deuteronomic.

3. (המקום אשר יבחר) לשכן שמו שם '(the site that the Lord will choose) to make his name dwell there'.

Deut.: 12: 11, 14: 23, 16: 2, 6, 11, 26: 2; cf. also 12: 5 and the next paragraph.

Jer. C: 7: 12

Cf. Neh. 1: 9; Ezra 6: 12.

For the meaning of the phrase and its implications see above, pp. 193 f.

4. לשום שמו שם 'to put his name there'.

Deut.: 12: 5, 21, 14: 24.

Dtr: 1 Kgs. 9: 3, 11: 36, 14: 21; 2 Kgs. 21: 4, 7.

Deut. 12: 5 contains a conflated version לשום שמו and לשכן שמו, originally read לשום שמו שם לְשַׁכְּנוֹ, but was later altered to read לְשִׁכְנוֹ, which has been attached to the second part of the verse (see A. Geiger, *Urschrift und Übersetzungen der Bibel*, 1857, p. 322). For a general discussion of conflated readings in Biblical literature, see S. Talmon, 'Double Readings in the Massoretic Text', *Textus* I (1960), 144–84.

5. להיות שמו שם 'that his name be there'.

Dtr: 1 Kgs. 8: 16, 29 (but compare 2 Chr. 6: 20, לשום); 2 Kgs. 23: 27.

6. בנה בית לשם יהוה 'to build a house for the name of the Lord'.

Dtr: 2 Sam. 7: 13; 1 Kgs. 3: 2, 5: 17, 18, 19, 8: 17, 18, 19, 20, 44, 48, see pp. 193 f.

7. הקדיש בית לשם יהוה 'to dedicate a house for the name of the Lord'.

Dtr: 1 Kgs. 9: 7.

8. מעון קדשך / (מקום) מכון שבתך . . . השמים 'your holy abode / daïs, the heavens'.

Deut.: 26: 15.

Dtr: 1 Kgs. 8: 30, 39, 43, 49.

See above, pp. 195 f.

9. זִבֵּחַ בבמות / זִבֵּחַ וקִטֵּר בבמות 'to sacrifice and burn incense at the high places'.

Dtr: 1 Kgs. 3: 2, 3 (מקטיר), 22: 44; 2 Kgs. 12: 4, 14: 4, 15: 4, 35, 16: 4.

Cf. 1 Kgs. 11: 8 (idolatry); Hos. 4: 13, 14, 11: 2, 12: 12 (read לשדים זבחו; compare Deut. 32: 17, יזבחו לשדים).

Though the verbs do not necessarily imply illegitimate worship (cf. M. Haran, *VT* 10 (1960), 160 ff.), a negative vein is implicit in them. All the occurrences except 1 Kgs. 8: 5 have something more or less admonitory in them. In Jer. 44: 21, 23 קטר without any object is sufficient to indicate illegitimacy (J. Bright, *Jeremiah*, Anchor Bible, ad. loc., translates אשר קטרתם 'offered *these* sacrifices' and adds: 'Hebrew does not express *these*'; the addition of 'these', however, is not necessary). It may not be without significance that זִבֵּחַ וקִטֵּר, which seems to be a hendiadys, occurs for the first time in Hosea (4: 13, 11: 2) and again in Hab. 1: 16 in a passage attacking idolatry.

10. הבמות לא סרו 'the high places were not removed'.

Dtr: 1 Kgs. 22: 44; 2 Kgs. 12: 4, 14: 4, 15: 4, 35; cf. 1 Kgs. 15: 14.

III. EXODUS, COVENANT, AND ELECTION

1. פדה (ממצרים/מבית עבדים) 'to ransom (from Egypt / from the house of bondage)'.

Deut.: 7: 8, 9: 26, 13: 6, 15: 15, 21: 8, 24: 18.

Dtr: 2 Sam. 7: 23.

Cf. Mic. 6: 4. Elsewhere גאל, see Exod. 6: 6 (= P), 15: 18; Pss. 74: 2, 77: 16, 78: 35, and very frequently in Second Isaiah. On the difference between פדה and גאל, see S. R. Driver, *Deuteronomy*, on Deut. 7: 8.

2. בית עבדים 'the house of bondage'.

Deut.: 5: 6, 6: 12, 7: 8, 8: 14, 13: 6, 11.

Jer. C: 34: 13.

Cf. Exod. 13: 3, 14, 20: 2; Josh. 24: 17; Judg. 6: 8; Mic. 6: 4. Its origin is perhaps Elohistic.

3. וזכרת כי עבד היית בארץ מצרים 'Remember that you were a slave in the land of Egypt'.

Deut.: 5: 15, 15: 15, 16: 12, 24: 18, 22; cf. also 7: 18, 24: 9, 16: 3.

4. מכור הברזל 'from the iron-furnace'.

Deut.: 4: 20.

Dtr: 1 Kgs. 8: 51.

Jer. C: 11: 4.

Compare Isa. 48: 10: בכור עוני 'in the furnace of affliction'.

5. בחר 'to choose' (of Israel).

Deut.: 4: 37, 7: 6, 7, 10: 15, 14: 2.

Dtr: 1 Kgs. 3: 8.

Jer. C: 33: 24.

Cf. Pss. 33: 12, 78: 68 (of Judah); Isa. 14: 1; Ezek. 20: 5; Isa. 41: 8, 9, 43: 10, 44: 1, 2, 49: 7.

6. היה לו לעם 'to be a people to him'.

Deut.: 4: 20, 7: 6, 14: 2, 26: 18, 27: 9.

Jer. C: 7: 23, 11: 4, 13: 11, 24: 7, 30: 22, 25, 31: 32, 32: 38. Cf. Lev. 26: 12; Ezek. 11: 20, 14: 11, 36: 28, 37: 23, 27; Zech. 2: 15, 8: 8; 2 Kgs. 11: 17.

The phrase is rooted in marriage–adoption terminology, cf. above, pp. 80 f.

6a. הקים/עשה/כונן לו לעם 'to establish as a people to him'.

Deut.: 28: 9, 29: 12.

Dtr: 2 Sam. 7: 23, 24; 1 Sam. 12: 22.

7. קרא שם על (ישראל) 'to call his name upon (Israel)'.

Deut.: 28: 10.

Cf. Jer. 14: 9, 15: 16 (referring to the prophet); Amos 9: 12; Isa. 63: 19; 2 Chr. 7: 14; see II. 2 (p. 325).

8. לשם לתהלה ולתפארת 'in fame, renown, and glory'.

Deut.: 26: 19.

Jer. C: 13: 11, 33: 9 (לשם ששון לתהלה ולתפארת).

Expresses the superiority of the people in the sight of other nations.

9. עם סגולה 'treasured people'.

Deut.: 7: 6, 14: 2, 26: 18.

Cf. Exod. 19: 5 (והייתם לי סגולה), see also Ps. 135: 4. For סגלה in the general sense compare Mal. 3: 17; Eccles. 2: 8; 1 Chr. 29: 3.

For the meaning, cf. Akkadian *sikiltu* and especially in suzerain–vassal relationship, e.g. *PRU* V, no. 60: 7, 12; see above, p. 226 n. 2.

10. עם קדוש 'holy people'.

Deut.: 7: 6, 14: 2, 21, 26: 19, 28: 9.

In Exod. 19: 6 גוי קדוש. Cf. also אנשי קדש 'holy men' in Exod. 22: 30. On the difference between עם קדוש and גוי קדוש see above, p. 228 n. 1.

11. עמך ישראל 'your people Israel'.

Deut.: 21: 8, 26: 15.

Dtr: 2 Sam. 7: 23, 24; 1 Kgs. 8: 33, 34, 38, 43, 52.

Jer. C: 32: 21.

Cf. Isa. 10: 22. All the deuteronomic occurrences appear in a liturgical context.

12. עם נחלה / עם ונחלה 'a people of inheritance'.

Deut.: 4: 20, 9: 26, 29.

Dtr: 1 Kgs. 8: 51, 53.

13. אהב/חשק באבות/בישראל 'to love/desire the Patriarchs/Israel'.

Deut.: 4: 37, 7: 7, 8, 13, 10: 15, 23: 6.

Dtr: 1 Kgs. 10: 9.

A basic concept in the theology of Hosea (3: 1, 9: 15, 11: 1, 4, 14: 5, cf. Jer. 31: 2). (The erotic undertone may also be hidden in Deuteronomy in the verb חשק which occurs in this book in reference to the captive woman (21: 11), cf. above, p. 290, and see also Appendix B, pp. 366 f.

Cf. also Isa. 41: 8, 43: 4; Ps. 47: 5 (אהב גאון יעקב); 2 Chr. 20: 7.

14. יד חזקה וזרע נטויה 'a strong hand and outstretched arm'.

Deut.: 4: 34, 5: 15, 7: 19, 11: 2, 26: 8.

Dtr: 1 Kgs. 8: 42.

Jer. C: 21: 5 (inverted order), 32: 21 (אזרע).

Cf. Ezek. 20: 33, 34; Ps. 136: 12. 'Strong hand' alone appears in Deuteronomy and also in older sources (Deut. 3: 24, 6: 21, 7: 8, 9: 26, 34: 12; Josh. 4: 24 (= Dtr); Exod. 3: 19, 6: 1 (of Pharaoh), 13: 9, 32: 11; Num. 20: 20 (of Edom). 'Outstretched arm' alone appears in P (Exod. 6: 6) and in D (9: 29). For חֹזֶק יד cf. Exod. 13: 3, 14, 16.

'Strong hand' and 'strong arm' in reference to the great king occurs often in the Amarna letters and especially those of Abdi-Ḫepa from Jerusalem (*qāt* ŠU *zuruḫ šarri dannu* or *zuruḫ šarri dannu*) cf. *EA* 286: 12, 287: 27, 288: 14, 34. It seems to belong to Egyptian royal typology, cf., for example, *JEA* 55 (1969), 86, fig. 5 A C.

15. בכח גדול ובזרע נטויה 'with great might and outstretched arm'.

Deut.: 9: 29.

Dtr: 2 Kgs. 17: 36.

Jer. C: 32: 17, cf. 27: 5.

In Exod. 32: 11 בכח גדול וביד חזקה 'with great might and *strong* hand'.

Cf. Neh. 1: 10.

16. גודל ויד חזקה 'greatness and strong hand'.

Deut.: 3: 24, 11: 2, cf. 9: 26.

'Greatness' alone (5: 21) is found elsewhere (Deut. 32: 3; Ps. 150: 2).

17. גדולות ונוראות 'great and awesome deeds'.

Deut.: 10: 21.

Dtr: 2 Sam. 7: 23.

17a. ראה/ידע מעשה יהוה הגדל אשר עשה 'to see the great deed that Yahweh performed'.

Deut.: 11: 7.

Dtr: Josh. 24: 31 = Judg. 2: 7; cf. Judg. 2: 10.

18. אתות ומופתים 'signs and portents'.

Deut.: 4: 34, 6: 22, 7: 19, 26: 8, 29: 2, 34: 11.

Jer. C: 32: 20, 21.

Cf. Pss. 78: 43, 105: 27, 135: 9; Neh. 9: 10. The phrase is rooted in the tradition of the plagues in Exod. 4: 21 (מופתים only), 7: 3 (אתתי ומופתי = P), 10: 1, 2 (אתות only), 11: 9, 10 (מפתים only = P); Num. 14: 11, 22 (אתותי).

19. המסות 'the trials'.

Deut.: 4: 34, 7: 19, 29 : 2.

20. במורא גדל / במוראים גדלים 'with great terror(s)'.

Deut.: 4: 34, 26: 8, 34: 12.

Jer. C: 32: 21.

P uses in the context of the Exodus a similar set of phrases yet different, cf. שפטים גדלים, זרע נטויה, אתות ומופתים (Exod. 6: 6, 7: 3–5).

21. שמר הברית והחסד 'who keeps the gracious covenant'.

Deut.: 7: 9, 12.

Dtr: 1 Kgs. 3: 6, 8: 23.

Cf. Ps. 89: 29 לעולם אשמר לו חסדי ובריתי נאמנת לו. The phrase occurs as a liturgical formula in the post-exilic literature: Dan. 9: 4; Neh. 1: 5, 9: 32.

The equivalent expression in P is זכר ברית 'to remember the covenant', see Gen. 9: 15; Exod. 2: 24, 6: 5; Lev. 26: 42; compare Ezek. 16: 60 (see my articles in *JAOS* and *Lešonenu*, both in press).

Liturgical terms

22. התנפל לפני יהוה 'to throw oneself before Yahweh'.

Deut.: 9: 18, 25.

Cf. Ezra 10: 1.

23. תפלה, תחנה 'prayer, supplication'.

Dtr: 1 Kgs. 8: 28, 30, 38, 45, 49, 52, 54, 9: 3.

Cf. נפל/הפל תחנה 'to make fall a supplication' in Jer. 36: 7, 37: 20, 38: 26, 42: 2, 9; Dan. 9: 20.

24. רנה ותפלה 'exultation and prayer'.

Dtr: 1 Kgs. 8: 28.

Jer. C: 7: 16, 11: 14.

Cf. Pss. 17: 1, 61: 2, 88: 3.

IV. THE MONOTHEISTIC CREED

1. וידעת/לדעת כי יהוה הוא האלהים 'you shall know / to know that Yahweh alone is God'.

   Deut.: 4: 35, 39, 7: 9, cf. 10: 17.

   Dtr: Josh. 2: 11; 1 Kgs. 8: 60.

   Cf. 1 Kgs. 18: 39 (twice).

2. בשמים ממעל ועל הארץ מתחת 'in the heaven above and on earth below'.

   Deut.: 4: 39.

   Dtr: Josh. 2: 11; 1 Kgs. 8: 23.

   Cf. Exod. 20: 4; Deut. 5: 8 (in the context of idolatry).[1]

3. האל הגדול הגבור (והנורא) 'the great, mighty and (awesome) God'.

   Deut.: 10: 17, cf. 7: 21, 28: 58 (השם הנכבד והנורא).

   Jer. C: 32: 18.

   Cf. Dan. 9: 4; Neh. 1: 5, 4: 8, 9: 32; Ps. 99: 3 (שם גדול ונורא).

4. (יהוה הוא האלהים) אין עוד '(Yahweh alone is God) there is no other'.

   Deut.: 4: 35, 39.

   Dtr: 1 Kgs. 8: 60.

   Cf. Isa. 45: 5, 6, 14, 18, 21, 22, 46: 9; Joel 2: 27 (see above, p. 42 n. 2).

5. אין כמוך (ואין אלהים זולתך) 'there is none like you (and no God besides you)'.

   Dtr.: 2 Sam. 7: 22; 1 Kgs. 8: 22.

   Jer. C: 10: 6, 7.

   Cf. Ps. 86: 8; Isa. 45: 5. (כי אין בלתך in 1 Sam. 2: 2 is a gloss, see Commentaries.)

6. אתה . . . האלהים לבדך 'You alone . . . are the God'.

   Dtr: 2 Kgs. 19: 15, 19 (= Isa. 37: 16, 20); compare Deut. 4: 35.

   Cf. Pss. 83: 19, 86: 10; Neh. 9: 6.

7. אתה עשית את השמים ואת הארץ 'You made heaven and earth'.

   Dtr: 2 Kgs. 19: 15.

   Jer. C: 32: 17.

   Cf. Neh. 9: 6; 2 Chr. 2: 11; see also 1 Chr. 29: 11; 2 Chr. 20: 6.

[1] The phrase seems to be of deuteronomic origin. For deuteronomic revision of the Decalogue in both its versions, see above, p. 318.

V. OBSERVANCE OF THE LAW AND LOYALTY TO THE COVENANT

A. *Loyalty*

1. הלך אחרי יהוה 'to follow (lit. to go after) Yahweh'. Cf. Akkadian *alāku arki* in a political context (*EA* 136: 11 f., 149: 46, 280: 20).

   Deut.: 13: 5.

   Dtr: 1 Kgs. 14: 8; 2 Kgs. 23: 3.

   Already attested in predeuteronomic literature, cf. 1 Kgs. 18: 21; Hos. 11: 10; see also Jer. 2: 2. See above, p. 83 n. 2.

2. עבד את יהוה 'to serve Yahweh'. Cf. Akkadian *arādu* in a political context, in the El-Amarna letters. See above, p. 83 n. 4.

   Deut.: 6: 13, 10: 12, 20, 11: 13, 13: 5, 28: 47.

   Dtr: Josh. 22: 5; 1 Sam. 12: 14, 20, 24; cf. Josh. 24: 14a (reworked by Dtr).

   It occurs very often in predeuteronomic literature. However, there it stands by itself and has predominantly the meaning of cultic worship, whereas in the deuteronomic literature it is always accompanied by other expressions of devotion, such as אהב 'to love', ירא 'to fear', הלך אחרי ה׳ 'to follow the Lord', שמע בקול ה׳ 'to hearken to Yahweh's voice', etc., or by adverbs such as בכל לב 'wholeheartedly', בתמים, באמת 'sincerely', which point towards the understanding of the verb as loyalty.

3. ירא את יהוה 'to fear Yahweh' (in the sense of serving). Cf. Akk. *palāḫu* in the treaties. See above, p. 83 n. 6.

   Deut.: 4: 10, 5: 26, 6: 2, 13, 24, 8: 6, 10: 12, 20, 13: 5, 14: 23, 17: 19, 28: 58, 31: 12, 13.

   Dtr: Josh. 4: 24; 1 Sam. 12: 14, 24; 1 Kgs. 8: 40, 43; 2 Kgs. 17: 32, 33, 34, 39, 41.

   Jer. C: 32: 39.

3a. למד ליראה את יהוה 'to learn to fear Yahweh'. Cf. *ša palāḫ ili litmudu* in the neo-Assyrian and neo-Babylonian royal inscriptions; see above, p. 279.

   Deut.: 4: 10, 14: 23, 17: 19, 31: 12, 13.

   Like עבד, ירא in the deuteronomic literature is always attached to phrases such as הלך בדרכיו, שמע בקולו, עבד באמת, שמר לעשות, and therefore has to be understood as loyal service and piety. The only exception is 2 Kgs. 17: 32 ff., where it means sole worship (cf. especially vv. 35, 36, where it is coupled with sacrificing and prostrating) which is natural when referring to the Samaritans.

3b. ירא את יהוה כל הימים / כל ימי חייך 'to fear Yahweh all the days / as long as you live', cf. X. 16 (p. 358).

Deut.: 4: 10, 6: 2, 5: 26, 14: 23, 31: 13.

Dtr: Josh. 4: 24; 1 Kgs. 8: 40.

Jer. C: 32: 39.

4. אהב את יהוה 'to love Yahweh'. Cf. Akkadian *ra'āmu* in the treaties, see Moran, *CBQ* 25 (1963), 77 ff.

Deut.: 6: 5, 10: 12, 11: 1, 13, 22, 13: 4, 19: 9, 30: 6, 16, 20, cf. 7: 9.

Dtr: Josh. 22: 5, 23: 11; 1 Kgs. 3: 3.

Cf. Exod. 20: 6 = Deut. 5: 10 (see above, p. 318); Judg. 5: 31; Isa. 56: 6 (with שם ה'); Pss. 5: 12 (with שם ה'), 31: 24, 69: 37 (with שם ה'), 97: 10, 119: 132 (with שם ה'), 145: 20. (Neh. 1: 5 and Dan. 9: 4 are taken from Deut. 7: 9.)

Characteristic of Deuteronomy is love which can be commanded, i.e. loyalty (see below, p. 368). The very concept of love of God may be early, as one can learn from Judg. 5: 31.

5. דבק ביהוה ' to cleave to Yahweh'.

Deut.: 4: 4, 10: 20, 11: 22, 13: 5, 30: 20.

Dtr: Josh. 22: 5, 23: 8; 2 Kgs. 18: 6.

Cf. Pss. 63: 9 (דבק אחר יהוה), 119: 31 (דבק בעדות).

6. הלך בדרך/בדרכי יהוה 'to walk in the way/ways of Yahweh'.

Deut.: 8: 6, 19: 9, 26: 17, 28: 9, 30: 16.

Dtr: Judg. 2: 22, 1 Kgs. 2: 3, 3: 14, 11: 33, 38.

Cf. 1 Sam. 8: 3, 5 (in the ways of Samuel); in a negative sense = in the way of Jeroboam/kings of Israel: 1 Kgs. 15: 26, 34, 16: 2, 19, 22: 53; 2 Kgs. 8: 18, 27, 16: 3.

Cf. Hos. 14: 10; Ps. 81: 14; Zech. 3: 7. In Exod. 18: 20 the phrase appears in a neutral sense ('the way they are to walk') and is not a theological term.

6a. הלך בכל הדרך / בכל דרכיו 'to walk in *all* his way/ways'.

Deut.: 5: 30, 10: 12, 11: 22.

Dtr: Josh. 22: 5; 1 Kgs. 8: 58; 2 Kgs. 21: 21. Cf. 1 Kgs. 22: 43 (בכל דרך אסא); 2 Kgs. 22: 2 (דרך דוד). In the negative sense: 2 Kgs. 21: 21.

Jer. C: 7: 23.

7. הלך בתורת יהוה 'to walk in the law of Yahweh'.

Dtr: 2 Kgs. 10: 31.

Jer. C: 9: 13, 26: 4, 32: 23, 44: 10, 23.

Cf. Pss. 78: 10, 119: 1; Dan. 9: 10; Neh. 10: 30; 2 Chr. 6: 16. Exod. 16: 4 refers to general instruction and not to the specific 'Law'.

8. הלך לפני יהוה בתום לבב ובישר / בכל לב / באמת ובצדקה 'to walk before Yahweh with wholeheartedness and integrity / with all the heart / in truth and righteousness' (for the Akkadian parallels, cf. above, pp. 76 f.).

Dtr: 1 Kgs. 2: 4, 3: 6, 8: 23, 25, 9: 4, always referring to the king and the dynasty.

Elsewhere the phrase is: התהלך לפני, Gen. 17: 1, 24: 40, 48: 15; 2 Kgs. 20: 3 (= Isa. 38: 3); Pss. 56: 14, 116: 9. Compare התהלך את יהוה but only in the Priestly literature: Gen. 5: 22, 24, 6: 9 and in reference to prediluvian figures (Enoch and Noah).

9. בכל לב ובכל נפש (ובכל מאד) 'with all the heart and all the soul (and all the might)'. Cf. Akk. *ina kul libbi*, *ina gummurti libbi* in a covenantal context. Mostly as an adverb to שמר מצות יהוה / דרש את יהוה / הלך אחרי יהוה / הלך לפני יהוה / הלך בתורת יהוה / שוב אל יהוה / עבד את יהוה / לשמר ולעשות / אהב את יהוה

Deut.: 4: 29, 6: 5, 10: 12, 11: 13, 13: 4, 26: 16, 30: 2, 6, 10.

Dtr: Josh. 22: 5, 23: 4; 1 Kgs. 2: 4, 8: 48; 2 Kgs. 23: 3, 25 (the full phrase as in Deut. 6: 5 and referring to Josiah).

Jer. C: 32: 41 (God speaking of himself).

9a. בכל לב/לבב 'with all the heart'.

Dtr: 1 Sam. 12: 20, 24; 1 Kgs. 8: 23, 14: 8; 2 Kgs. 10: 31.

Jer. C: 24: 7, 29: 17.

Cf. 1 Sam. 7: 3; Jer. 3: 10; Joel 2: 12; Ps. 119: 10, 34, 69; Prov. 3: 5. Unlike 9 this phrase is attested outside the deuteronomic literature.

10. שלם (לב) 'perfect (of the heart)'.

Dtr: 1 Kgs. 8: 61, 11: 4, 15: 3, 14. Cf. 2 Kgs. 20: 3 (= Isa. 38: 3).

It seems to be equivalent to תמים (לב) and תום (לב) (cf. 1 Kgs. 9: 4 and see Ps. 119: 80). On this concept in Assyrian literature see above, p. 76.

11. שוב אל יהוה בכל לב 'to return to Yahweh with all the heart'.

Deut.: 30: 10.

Dtr: 1 Kgs. 8: 48; 2 Kgs. 23: 25.

Jer. C: 24: 7

Cf. Jer. 3: 10.

12. שים דברי יהוה על לב 'to put the words of Yahweh upon the heart'.

Deut.: 11: 18 (compare 6: 6 היה על לב), 32: 46.

On this expression in Mesopotamian literature see above, pp. 302–3.

13. לב ליראה את ה׳ 'a heart to fear Yahweh'.

Deut.: 5: 26.

Jer. C: 32: 39, 40.

14. שמר משמרת ה׳ 'to keep the charge of Yahweh'.

Deut.: 11: 1.

Dtr: Josh. 22: 3; 1 Kgs. 2: 3.

Cf. Mal. 3: 14. The original meaning is guarding in the physical sense[1] (2 Kgs. 11: 5, 6, 7 and in the Priestly literature (*passim*)). In the abstract sense it is also found in Gen. 26: 5; Lev. 18: 30. The same applies to the Akk. *naṣāru maṣṣartu*, see above, pp. 75–6.

15. עשה הישר (והטוב) בעיני ה׳ 'to do that which is right (and which is good) in the eyes of Yahweh'.

Deut.: 6: 18, 12: 25, 28, 13: 19, 21: 9.

Dtr: 1 Kgs. 11: 33, 38, 14: 8, 15: 5, 11, 22: 43; 2 Kgs. 10: 30, 12: 3, 14: 3, 15: 3, 34, 16: 2, 18: 3, 22: 2.

Jer. C: 34: 15.

Elsewhere only in Exod. 15: 26 (Deuteronomic reworking?). 'To do what is right in the eyes of *somebody*' in Deut. 12: 8; Judg. 17: 6, 21: 25; Josh. 9: 25; Jer. 26: 14, may also be of deuteronomic origin.

[1] i.e. 'keeping watch', cf. J. Milgrom, *Studies in Levitical Terminology* I, 8 ff.

16. שמר מצוה/מצות/חוקים/עדות/משפטים 'to keep the commandment(s)/ statutes/testimonies/judgements'. Cf. Akk. *naṣāru amāt* (*šarrūti*) see p. 77 above (n. 6).

Deut.: 23 times.

Dtr: Josh. 22: 5; 1 Kgs. 2: 3, 3: 14, 9: 4, 6, 8: 58, 61, 11: 11, 34, 38, 14: 8; 2 Kgs. 17: 13, 19, 18: 6, 23: 3.

Cf. Gen. 26: 5; Exod. 13: 10 (החוקה הזאת), 15: 26, 16: 28, 20: 6 (= Deut. 5: 10); Lev. 18: 4, 5, 26, 19: 19, 20: 8, 22: 31, 26: 3; 1 Sam. 13: 13; 1 Kgs. 6: 12; 13: 21 (= P); Pss. 78: 7 (נצר), 56, 89: 32, 105: 45, 119: 5, 8, 60; Amos 2: 4; Mal. 3: 7; Eccles. 12: 13; Neh. 1: 7, 9.

In wisdom literature שמר מצוה occurs in a neutral sense (= command of parents). Prov. 4: 4, 6: 20 (נצר), 7: 2, 19: 16; Eccles. 8: 5; cf. also 1 Kgs. 2: 43; Jer. 35: 18.

17. שמר (עשה) כל המצוה / כל מצותי/מצותיו 'to keep, (to do) the whole commandment / all the (my/his) commandments'.

Deut.: 5: 26, 6: 25, 11: 8, 22, 13: 19, 15: 5, 19: 9, 26: 18, 27: 1, 28: 1, 15.

Cf. 1 Kgs. 6: 12; Neh. 10: 30.

17a. שמר ועשה / שמר לעשות 'to keep and to do / keep to do'. Cf. Akk. *amātē naṣāru/epēšu* (*CAD* vol. 2 (A, ii), p. 37).

Deut.: 27 times.

Dtr: Josh. 1: 7, 8, 22: 5, 23: 6; 2 Kgs. 17: 37, 21: 8.

Cf. Ezek. 11: 20, 36: 27, 37: 24; Neh. 10: 30; 1 Chr. 22: 13. P uses זכר ועשה 'to keep in mind (recall) and to do' (Num. 15: 39, 40).

17b. שמר/עשה כל דברי התורה / את כל הכתוב בספר התורה הזה 'to keep/ do (all) the words of this Torah/ whatever is written in this Torah'.

Deut.: 17: 19, 28: 58, 29: 28, 31: 12, 32: 46.

Dtr: Josh. 1: 7, 23: 6.

It seems that the usage of שמר דברי התורה הזאת, etc. suppressed the vague expression שמר תורה, which is found only once in the deuteronomic literature (Jer. 16: 11, cf. Ps. 119: 34 (נצר), 44, 55, 136; 1 Chr. 22: 12). It is found, however, in wisdom literature, where it occurs in the neutral sense like שמר מצוה (no. 16 above), see Prov. 28: 4, 7 (נצר), 29: 18. By the same token the term שמר ברית, which is quite common in other sources (Gen. 17: 9, 10; Exod. 19: 5; Deut. 33: 9 (נצר); Pss. 78: 10, 103: 18, 132: 12), is attested only once in the deuteronomic literature (1 Kgs. 11: 11). The variety of concrete forms available, such as: שמר, מצות, חוקים, משפטים, עדות, etc. apparently caused the disuse of this general term. This may also have been the reason for the disuse of שמר דרך יהוה 'to keep the way of Yahweh', which occurs only once in the deuteronomic literature (Judg. 2: 22), but appears often in the older sources (Gen. 18: 19; 2 Sam. 22: 22 = Pss. 18: 22, 37: 34; Job 23: 11).

18. שמע (אל) מצות יהוה 'to keep (lit. to listen to) the commandments'.

Deut.: 11: 13, 27, 28, 28: 13.

Dtr: Judg. 2: 17, 3: 4.

Cf. Neh. 9: 16, 29, and Jer. 35: 14, 18 in the more neutral sense.

18a. שמע בקול יהוה 'to hearken to Yahweh's voice'.

Very frequent in deuteronomic literature (see J. Bright, *JBL* 70 (1951), Appendix A, no. 46), but already a cliché in JE.

19. מלא אחר יהוה 'to fill up after' (to follow with loyalty/perfection).

Deut.: 1: 36; cf. Num. 14: 24, 32: 11, 12.

Dtr: Josh. 14: 8, 9, 14; 1 Kgs. 11: 6.

Seems to have its origin in the tradition of the grant to Caleb (see my article in *JAOS* 90 (1970), 200).

20. סור (מאחרי) מחטא(ת) 'to depart from (behind) the sin'.

Dtr: 2 Kgs. 3: 3, 10: 29, 31, 13: 2, 6, 11, 14: 24, 15: 9, 18, 24, 28, 17: 22.

21. חקים ומשפטים 'statutes and judgements'.

Deut.: 4: 1, 5, 8, 14, 5: 1, 11: 32, 12: 1, 26: 1.

Dtr: 1 Kgs. 9: 4; 11: 33 (חקות ומשפטים).

Cf. Mal. 3: 22; 1 Chr. 22: 13; Ps. 147: 19.

In P and in Ezekiel: חקות ומשפטים. 1 Kgs. 6: 12 is P and not Dtr.

21a. חקים ומצות / מצות וחקים 'statutes and commandments'.

Deut.: 4: 40, 27: 10, 28: 15, 45, 30: 10, 16.

Dtr: 1 Kgs. 3: 14, 8: 61 (as parallel member).

Cf. Exod. 15: 26 (as parallel members); Ezra 7: 11.

21b. חקות ומצות / מצות וחקות.

Deut.: 6: 2, 10: 13, 28: 15, 45, 30: 10.

Dtr: 1 Kgs. 9: 6, 11: 34, 38; 2 Kgs. 17: 13.

Cf. 2 Chr. 7: 19.

21c. המצוה/המצות החקים והמשפטים.

Deut.: 6: 1, 5: 28, 7: 11.

Dtr: 1 Kgs. 8: 58.

Cf. Neh. 1: 7; 2 Chr. 19: 10.

21d. מצות עדות וחקים 'commandments, testimonies, and statutes'.

Deut.: 6: 17.

Dtr: 2 Kgs 23: 3.

Cf. 1 Chr. 29: 19.

21e. העדות החקים והמשפטים.

Deut.: 4: 45, 6: 20.

21f. מצות משפטים וחקות/חקות משפטים ומצות / חקים מצות ומשפטים.

Deut.: 8: 11, 11: 1, 26: 17, 30: 16.

Dtr: 1 Kgs. 2: 3 (חקות מצות משפטים ועדות).

21g. התורה והמצוה / המצוה והתורה.

Dtr: Josh. 22: 5; 2 Kgs. 17: 34, 37.

Cf. 2 Chr. 14: 2, 31: 21; see Exod. 24: 12.

21h. החקים והמשפטים והתורה והמצוה.

Dtr: 2 Kgs. 17: 37.

21i. ברית וחקות/חקים ברית ועדות 'covenant and testimonies'.

Dtr: 1 Kgs. 11: 11; 2 Kgs. 17: 15.

21j. תורת יהוה וחקותיו / תורת יהוה חקותיו ועדותיו.

Jer. C: 44: 10, 23.

Unlike JE (Gen. 26: 5; Exod. 18: 16, 20; cf. Ps. 105: 45) and P (Exod. 16: 28; Lev. 26: 46, compare Ezek. 44: 24), Deuteronomy and the deuteronomic literature never use תורות but always תורה in the singular, in compliance with the notion of a canonized Torah. On the other hand, P and JE never combine עדות with חקים, etc. P uses עֵדֻת (in the singular) only in connection with the tabernacle and the tablets: משכן העדת / אהל העדת, לחות העדת. Cf. above, p. 65.

22. המצוה הזאת 'this commandment'.

Deut.: 6: 25, 11: 22, 15: 5, 19: 9, 30: 11.

23. התורה הזאת / ספר התורה הזאת (הזה), ספר התורה 'this law' / 'this book of law'.

Deut.: 19 times.

Dtr: Josh. 1: 8; 2 Kgs. 22: 8, 11.

24. תורת משה / ספר תורת משה 'the law of Moses' / 'the book of the law of Moses'.

Dtr: Josh. 8: 31, 32, 23: 6; 1 Kgs. 2: 3; 2 Kgs. 14: 6.

B. *Disloyalty*

1. עשה הרע בעיני יהוה 'to do that which is evil in the eyes of Yahweh'.
Deut.: 4: 25, 9: 18, 17: 2, 31: 29.

Dtr: Judg. 2: 11, 3: 7, 12, 4: 1, 6: 1, 10: 6, 13: 1, and over 40 times in Kings.

Jer. C: 7: 30, 18: 10, 32: 30.

Cf. Num. 32: 13; 1 Sam. 15: 19; 2 Sam. 12: 9 (Dtr?); Isa. 65: 12, 66: 4.

2. סור 'to turn away' (in the sense of apostasy).

Deut.: 11: 16.

Dtr: 1 Sam. 12: 21.

Cf. Jer. 5: 23 (compare סורר ומורה in this verse with Deut. 21: 18 and Ps. 78: 8), 6: 28; Dan. 9: 11.

2a. סור מן הדרך 'to turn aside from the way'.

Deut.: 9: 12, 16, 11: 28, 31: 29.

Dtr: Judg. 2: 17; 1 Kgs. 22: 43.

Cf. Exod. 32: 8; Mal. 2: 8.

2b. סור מאחרי יהוה 'to turn away from Yahweh'.

Dtr: 1 Sam. 12: 20; 2 Kgs. 18: 6.

Jer. C: 32: 40.

2c. סור . . . ימין ושמאל 'to turn right or left'.

Deut.: 5: 29, 17: 11, 20, 28: 14.

Dtr: Josh. 1: 7, 23: 6; 2 Kgs. 22: 2.

Cf. Prov. 4: 27 (with נטה), and in the literal sense: Deut. 2: 27; 1 Sam. 6: 12.

3. השחית 'to act wickedly'.

Deut.: 4: 16, 25, 31: 29.

Dtr: Judg. 2: 19.

Cf. Isa. 1: 4; Jer. 6: 28; Ezek. 16: 47; 2 Chr. 26: 16, 27: 2. In predeuteronomic sources שחת: Exod. 32: 7 = Deut. 9: 12; Deut. 32: 5; Hos. 9: 9, 13: 9; cf. Gen. 6: 11.

4. לעבור בריתי(ו) 'to transgress my/his covenant'.

Deut.: 17: 2.

Dtr: Josh. 23: 16; Judg. 2: 20; 2 Kgs. 18: 12.

Cf. Hos. 8: 1. Josh. 7: 11, 15 refer to the violation of the law of *ḥerem* and not to the law in general.

5. החטיא את הארץ/ישראל/יהודה 'to bring sin upon the land/Israel/Judah'.

Deut.: 24: 4.

Dtr: Kings (18 times).

Jer. C: 32: 35.

Cf. Exod. 23: 33; Isa. 29: 21; Neh. 13: 26.

6. כעס/הכעיס את יהוה 'to vex Yahweh'.

Deut.: 4: 25, 9: 18, 31: 29.

Dtr: Judg. 2: 12; Kings (17 times)

Jer. C: 7: 18, 19, 11: 17, 25: 6, 7, 32: 29, 30, 32, 44: 3, 8.

Cf. Deut. 32: 16, 21; Isa. 65: 3; Hos. 12: 15; Jer. 8: 19 (see above, p. 324); Ezek. 8: 17, 16: 26; Pss. 78: 58, 106: 29; Neh. 3: 37.

7. הלך בחטאת/בחטאות / אחר חטאות 'to go in/after the sin/sins of . . .'.

Dtr: 1 Kgs. 15: 3, 26, 34, 16: 19, 26, 31; 2 Kgs. 13: 2, 17: 22.

8. הלך בשרירות לב / אחרי שרירות לב 'to go in/after the stubbornness of the heart'.

Deut.: 29: 18.

Jer. C: 3: 17, 7: 24, 9: 13, 11: 8, 13: 10, 16: 12.

Cf. Ps. 81: 13; Jer. 23: 17.

8a. עשה שרירות לבו.

Jer. C: 18: 12.

9. הקשה עורף 'to stiffen the neck'.

Deut.: 10: 16.

Dtr: 2 Kgs. 17: 14.

Jer. C: 7: 26, 17: 23, 19: 15.

Cf. Prov. 29: 1; Neh. 9: 16, 17, 29; 2 Chr. 30: 8, 36: 13.

10. התמכר לעשות הרע 'to sell oneself to do evil'.

Dtr: 1 Kgs. 21: 20, 25; 2 Kgs. 17: 17. For the form התמכר cf. Deut. 28: 68.

10a. הדיח / מן הדרך / מעל יהוה 'to lead you astray / from the way / from the Lord'.

Deut.: 13: 6, 11, 14.

Dtr: 2 Kgs. 17: 21.

Cf. Prov. 7: 21; 2 Chr. 21: 11; compare Pss. 5: 11, 62: 5.

11. דבק בגויים 'cling to the nations'.

Dtr: Josh. 23: 12; 1 Kgs. 11: 2

12. (ממרים/מכעיסים) מן/למן היום אשר יצאו/יצאת ממצרים ועד היום הזה ('rebel/vex) from the day that you/they left Egypt until this day'.

Deut.: 9: 7.

Dtr: 1 Sam. 8: 8 (מיום העלותי); 2 Kgs. 21: 15.

Jer. C: 7: 25; cf. 32: 31.

13. ואמרו . . . על מה עשה ה׳ ככה / על מה דבר ה׳ עלינו . . . הרעה . . . ואמרו/ואמרת . . . על אשר עזבו את ברית ה׳ '. . . and they will ask (lit. say) "why did Yahweh do thus / decree such evil?" and they/ you will answer (lit. say): "because they forsook the covenant of Yahweh".'

Deut.: 29: 23–4.

Dtr: 1 Kgs. 9: 8–9.

Jer. C: 16: 10–11, 22: 8–9; cf. 9: 11–12, 5: 19.

For the Assyrian parallel cf. above, p. 115.

VI. INHERITANCE OF THE LAND

1. אשר יהוה אלהיך נתן לך (ל)נחלה (לרשתה) 'which Yahweh, your God, is giving you as an inheritance (to possess it)'.

Deut.: 4: 21, 15: 4, 19: 10, 20: 16, 21: 23, 24: 4, 26: 1: 25: 19.

Dtr: 1 Kgs. 8: 36.

The completion 'as an inheritance (to possess it)' makes the phrase deuteronomic. The completion in P is לאחזה (Lev. 14: 34; Num. 32: 5; Deut. 32: 49, all P—never in D) and always without לרשתה.

2. ובאת(ם) וירשת(ם) את הארץ/ארצם, הארץ אשר אתה בא שמה לרשתה/לרשת אותם / לרשת ארצם 'the land whither you come in to possess it' / 'to possess them (the nations)' / 'to possess their land'.

Deut.: 4: 1, 5, 6: 18, 7: 1, 8: 1, 9: 1, 5, 11: 8, 10, 29, 31, 12: 29, 28: 21, 63, 30: 16.

Dtr: Josh. 1: 11, 18: 3.

Jer. C: 32: 23.

Cf. Judg. 18: 9; Neh. 9: 24. In P 'to come into the land' without 'to possess it'. Compare especially Lev. 14: 34, 23: 10, 25: 2; Num. 15: 2, (כי תבואו) with Deut. 17: 14, 26: 1.

3. הארץ אשר אתם עברים / אתה עבר שמה לרשתה 'the land whither you pass over (Jordan) to possess it'.

Deut.: 4: 14, 22, 26, 6: 1, 9: 1, 11: 8, 11, 31, 30: 18, 31: 13, 32: 47.

Dtr: Josh. 1: 11.

Cf. Num. 33: 51, 35: 10 (both P) where the phrase 'you pass over the Jordan to the land of Canaan' occurs without 'to possess it'.

4. יְרֻשָּׁה 'possession'.

Deut.: 2: 5, 9, 12, 19, 3: 20.

Dtr: Josh. 1: 15, 12: 6, 7 (cf. 2 Chr. 20: 11).

In P (Exod. 6: 8) and Ezekiel (*passim*): מורשה. In ancient poetry: יְרֵשָׁה, יָרֵשָׁה (Num. 24: 18; Deut. 33: 23).

5. הוריש גויים 'to dispossess nations'.

Deut.: 4: 38, 7: 17, 9: 3, 4, 5, 11: 23, 18: 12.

Dtr: Josh. 23: 5, 9, 13; Judg. 2: 21, 23 (with מהר); 1 Kgs. 14: 24; 2 Kgs. 16: 3, 17: 8, 21: 2.

Cf. Exod. 34: 24; Ps. 44: 3. In JE and P this verb is mostly associated with אמורי, the Canaanites, and the יושב(י) הארץ 'the inhabitants of the land' (Num. 21: 32; Judg. 11: 23, 24; Num. 33: 52, 53, 55 = P, 1 Kgs. 21: 26 might be an old cliché though embedded in a deuteronomic stratum). גרש 'drive out', which is very common in JE in the context of conquest, never occurs in D.

6. הגויים האלה / הגויים ההם 'these nations' or 'those nations'.

Deut.: 7: 17, 22, 9: 4, 5, 11: 23, 12: 30, 18: 9, 14, 20: 15, 16 (העמים האלה), 31: 3.

Dtr: Josh. 23: 3, 4, 12, 13; Judg. 2: 23, 3: 1 (cf. 2 Kgs. 17: 41).

In previous sources the prevalent term is יושבי הארץ 'the inhabitants of the land' (cf. no. 5 above) and might be limited to the population of Palestine only (Exod. 23: 31, 34: 12, 15; Num. 13: 28, 32: 17, 33: 52, 55 = P); Josh. 7: 9, 9: 24, 24: 18; Judg. 1: 32, 2: 2, cf. 2 Chr. 20: 7.

See recently F. Langlamet, *RB* 76 (1969), 330 f.

7. ירש/הוריש/נשל גויים רבים (גדולים) ועצומים ממך/מכם 'to dispossess nations larger and mightier than you'.

Deut.: 4: 38, 7: 1, 9: 1, 11: 23.

Dtr: Josh. 23: 9.

8. להניח (מכל אויב מסביב) 'to give you rest (from all enemies around you)'.

Deut. 3: 20, 12: 10, 25: 19.

Dtr: Josh. 1: 13, 15, 21: 42, 22: 4, 23: 1; 1 Kgs. 5: 18.

Cf. 2 Sam. 7: 1 (Dtr?), 11 and 1 Chr. 22: 18, 23: 25; 2 Chr. 14: 5, 6, 15: 15, 20: 30. (Cf. above, p. 170 n. 2.) Exod. 33: 14 (והניחתי לך) is different, and means 'quietening'.

9. מנוחה (ונחלה) 'rest (and/of inheritance)'.

Deut.: 12: 9.

Dtr: 1 Kgs. 8: 56; cf. Ps. 95: 11.

10. הארץ/האדמה הטובה 'the good land/ground'.

Deut.: 1: 35, 3: 25, 4: 21, 22, 6: 18, 8: 10, 9: 6, 11: 17.

Dtr: Josh. 23: 13, 15, 16; 1 Kgs. 14: 15.

In Dtr האדמה הטובה = 'good ground', except Josh. 23: 16, which is a quotation from Deut. 11: 17; cf. 1 Chr. 28: 8.

Conquest—Military

11. חזק ואמץ 'Be strong and resolute'.

Deut.: 3: 28 (חזקהו ואמצהו), 31: 6, 7, 23.

Dtr: Josh. 1: 6, 9, 18, 10: 25. In Josh. 1: 7 the term is applied to observance of the Torah, cf. above, p. 5.

Cf. 1 Chr. 22: 13, 28: 20; 2 Chr. 32: 7.

12. אל/לא תירא ואל/לא תחת 'Fear not and be not dismayed'.

Deut.: 1: 21, 31: 8.

Dtr: Josh. 8: 1, 10: 25.

Cf. (in parallel members) Isa. 51: 7; Jer. 30: 10, 46: 27; Ezek. 2: 6, 3: 9; For deuteronomic phrasing but in various contexts, cf. 1 Chr. 22: 13, 28: 20; 2 Chr. 20: 15, 17, 32: 7. Compare also 1 Sam. 17: 11 (in inverted order); Jer. 23: 4. For the equivalent Assyrian expressions cf. above, pp. 50–1.

13. לא תערץ/תערצו 'Have no dread'.

Deut.: 1: 29, 7: 21, 20: 3, 31: 6.

Dtr: Josh. 1: 9.

Cf. Isa. 8: 12, 13.

14. לא יתיצב איש בפניך(כם) 'no man shall stand up to you'.

Deut.: 7: 24, 11: 25.

Dtr: Josh. 1: 5.

Cf. Job 41: 2.

14a. לא יעמד איש בפניך(כם).

Dtr: Josh. 10: 8, 21: 42, 23: 9; cf. Judg. 2: 14.

Cf. 2 Kgs. 10: 4; Jer. 49: 19; Pss. 76: 8, 147: 17; Prov. 27: 4; Dan. 8: 4; Esther 9: 2.

15. נמס/המס לב 'to melt the heart'.

Deut.: 1: 28, 20: 8.

Dtr: Josh. 2: 11, 5: 1, 14: 8.

Cf. Josh. 7: 5; 2 Sam. 17: 10; Isa. 13: 7, 19: 1; Ezek. 21: 12; Nahum 2: 11; Ps. 22: 15.

16. לא השאיר שריד 'left no survivor'.

Deut.: 2: 34.

Dtr: Josh. 10: 28, 30, 37, 39, 40.

16a. עד בלתי השאיר לו שריד.

Deut.: 3: 3.

Dtr: Josh. 10: 33, 11: 8; cf. 2 Kgs. 10: 11.

Cf. Num. 21: 35; Josh. 8: 22 (שריד ופליט).

17. לא חִיה/השאיר/נותר כל נשמה 'left/spared no soul'.

Deut.: 20: 16.

Dtr: Josh. 10: 40, 11: 11, 14; cf. 1 Kgs. 15: 29.

For the Assyrian equivalents to nos. 16 and 17, cf. above, p. 51 n. 3.

VII. RETRIBUTION AND MATERIAL MOTIVATION

1. האריך ימים 'days to be long' or 'to prolong days'.

Deut.: (a) man as subject of prolonging days: 4: 26, 40, 5: 30, 11: 9, 17: 20, 22: 7, 30: 18, 32: 47. (b) days as subject: 5: 16 (= Exod. 20: 12), 6: 2, 25: 15.

Dtr: 1 Kgs. 3: 14 (with God as subject as in the Phoenician and Aramaic inscriptions, cf. *KAI* 4: 3, 6: 2, 7: 4, 10: 9, 226: 3).

Cf. Isa. 53: 10; Prov. 28: 16; Eccles. 8: 13.

2. כי ברך יברכך ה׳ / כאשר יברכך ה׳ / כי ה׳ אלהיך ברכך / וברך את עמך ישראל ואת האדמה וגו׳ 'in order that Yahweh may bless you / as Yahweh has blessed you / so that Yahweh will bless you / and bless your people Israel and the land, etc'.

Deut.: 12: 7, 14: 24, 15: 6, 14, 16: 10, 26: 15, 30: 16.

2a. ברך מעשה ידים / משלח יד 'to bless the enterprise of'.

Deut.: 2: 7, 14: 29, 15: 10, 18, 16: 15, 23: 21, 24: 19, 28: 8 (צוה ברכה), 12, (30: 9) cf. Job 1: 10.

2b. ברך פרי בטנך ופרי אדמתך (שגר אלפיך ועשתרות צאנך) 'to bless the issue of the womb and the produce of the soil (the calving of the herd and the lambing of the flock)'.

Deut.: 7: 13, 28: 4, 11, 30: 9, and the opposite in 28: 53.

The same idea is expressed differently in Exod. 23: 25–6.

3. למען תחיה/תחיו 'to live' (in the sense of 'prosper').

Deut.: 4: 1, 5: 30, 6: 24, 8: 1, 16: 20.

Cf. Amos 5: 14; Jer. 35: 7.

3a. חיים 'life' in the sense of 'prosperity and happiness' (cf. above, pp. 307 ff.).

Deut. 30: 6, 15, 19, 20, 32: 47.

Cf. Proverbs (*passim.*)

4. למען/אשר ייטב לך/לכם 'so that it may be well with you'.

Deut.: 4: 40, 5: 16, 26, 6: 3, 18, 12: 25, 28, 22: 7.

Jer. C: 7: 23, 42: 6.

Cf. Gen. 12: 13, 40: 14; Ruth 3: 1; Jer. 38: 20, 40: 9, in the neutral sense and not as motivation to obedience.

4a. וטוב/לטוב לך/לכם/לנו.

Deut.: 5: 30, 6: 24, 10: 13, 19: 13.

Cf. the opposite term in Jer. 7: 6, 26: 7 (both C): לרע לכם.

5. שמח לפני ה׳ 'to rejoice before Yahweh (your God)'.

Deut.: 12: 12, 18, 16: 11, 27: 7; cf. 14: 26, 26: 11.

Cf. Lev. 23: 40. Always in connection with a sacred meal.

5a. שמח בכל משלוח יד 'happy in all the undertakings'.

Deut.: 12: 7, 18.

6. למען תשכיל בכל אשר תעשה 'that you may succeed in all that you undertake'.

Deut.: 29: 8.

Dtr: Josh. 1: 7; 1 Kgs. 2: 3.

Cf. in a wisdom context: Ps. 111: 10 and Prov. 17: 8: אל כל אשר יפנה ישכיל. The expression seems to be rooted in wisdom literature.

7. נתן לפניך (כם)...(את דרך) החיים (ואת דרך) המות 'I set before you ...life and death'.

Deut.: 30: 15, 19.

Jer. C: 21: 8.

8. שיש עליך לטוב/להיטיב אתכם 'to be delighted in making you prosperous' (speaking of God).

Deut.: 28: 63, 30: 9.

Jer. C: 32: 41.

Punishment

9. התאנף 'was incensed'.

Deut.: 1: 37, 4: 21, 9: 8, 20.

Dtr: 1 Kgs. 11: 9; 2 Kgs. 17: 18; cf. 1 Kgs. 8: 46 (אנף). אנף is attested elsewhere: Isa. 12: 1; Pss. 60: 3, 79: 5, 85: 6, 2: 12; Ezra 9: 14; cf. also the Mesha inscription.

10. אבד/האביד/השמיד/כלה/נתש/נסח/הכרית מעל פני האדמה (מעל הארץ) 'to destroy / perish / put an end / to uproot / out of / from the face of the earth (or land)'.

Deut.: 4: 26, 6: 15, 11: 17, 28: 21, 63, 29: 27.

Dtr: Josh. 23: 13, 15, 16; 1 Kgs. 9: 7, 13: 34, 14: 15.

Jer. C: 12: 14, 24: 10.

Cf. Amos 9: 8, 15 (late accretions?); 2 Chr. 7: 20. Other instances, as Gen. 4: 14 (with גרש), 6: 7, 7: 4 (with מחה); Exod. 32: 12; 1 Sam. 20: 15; Zeph. 1: 3, apply to 'the earth' in the universal sense, in contrast to the deuteronomic literature where 'the earth' is the land of Israel, as may be deduced from the complementary phrases: 'which Yahweh is giving you', 'whither you come in to possess it', etc.

11. שלח מעל פני יהוה 'to dismiss from before the face of Yahweh'.

Dtr: 1 Kgs. 9: 7 (in the parallel verse in 2 Chr. 7: 20: השליך).

Cf. Jer. 15: 1.

11a. השלך מעל פני יהוה 'to cast away from before the face of Yahweh'.

Dtr: 2 Kgs. 13: 23, 17: 20, 24: 20 (= Jer. 52: 3).

Jer. C: 7: 15; cf. Ps. 51: 13.

11b. הסיר מעל פני יהוה 'to remove from before the face of Yahweh'.

Dtr: 2 Kgs. 17: 18, 23, 23: 27, 24: 3.

Jer. C: 32: 31.

11c. נטש מעל פני יהוה 'to cast off from before the face of Yahweh'.

Jer. C: 23: 39.

12. אבד/האביד/השמיד/הוריש מהר 'to destroy/perish/dispossess *quickly*'.

Deut.: 4: 26, 7: 4, 22, 9: 3, 11: 17, 28: 20.

Dtr: Josh. 23: 16; Judg. 2: 23.

13. מחה/האביד שם מתחת השמים 'to blot out / to cause to be lost the name from under heaven'.

Deut.: 9: 14, 25: 19 ('memory' instead of 'name' by influence of its source in Exod. 17: 14), 29: 19.

Dtr: 2 Kgs. 14: 27.

Cf. *Sefire* II, B: 7 ולאבדת אשמהם.

14. הפיץ בעמים/בגויים 'to scatter among the nations/peoples'.

Deut.: 4: 27, 28: 64, 30: 3.

Jer. C: 9: 15, 30: 11; cf. Ezek. (*passim*); Neh. 1: 8.

15. נדח/הדיח שמה 'be driven there'.

Deut.: 30: 1, 4.

Jer. C: 8: 3, 16: 15, 23: 3, 8, 24: 9, 29: 14, 18, 32: 37, 40: 12, 43: 5.

Cf. Jer. 27: 10, 15 (without שמה), 46: 28 (compare in the parallel passage 30: 11 הפיצתיך); Ezek. 4: 13; Dan. 9: 7.

16. ונצתה חמתי 'my anger will be kindled'.

Dtr: 2 Kgs. 22: 13, 17 (the parallel verses in 2 Chr. 34: 21, 25 ונתכה חמתי 'will be poured out' were probably influenced by Jeremiah, see S. Japhet, *Lešonenu* 31 (1967), 264–5).

The idea is expressed elsewhere by: תצא כאש (Jer. 4: 4, 21: 12), אש קדחה/קדחתם באפי (Deut. 32: 22; Jer. 15: 14, 17: 4.).

17. נתך אף וחמה 'anger with wrath to be poured out'.

Jer. C: 7: 20, 42: 18, 44: 6.

Cf. Nahum 1: 6; 2 Chr. 12: 7, 34: 21, 25 (see previous paragraph).

The phrase elsewhere is שפך חמה, compare *imta ṭabāku* in Akkadian.

18. באף ובחמה ובקצף גדול 'with anger, fury, and great wrath'.

Deut.: 29: 27.

Jer. C: 21: 5, 32: 37.

19. נתן/היה לזעוה לכל ממלכות הארץ 'to become a horror to all the kingdoms of the earth'.

Deut.: 28: 25.

Jer. C: 15: 4, 24: 9, 29: 18, 34: 17. *Ketib* in all these verses זועה, cf. Isa. 28: 19.

The word זעוה occurs in Ezek. 23: 46 and in 2 Chr. 29: 8 (*Ket.* זועה), but not in the framework of the given phrase.

20. היה למשל ולשנינה 'to become a proverb and a byword'.

Deut.: 28: 37.

Dtr: 1 Kgs. 9: 7.

Jer. C: 24: 9.

21. נתן/שים/היה לשמה, שרקה, חרבה,[1] חרפה, קללה, אלה, משל, שנינה

[1] This threat expresses the derision of Israel by other peoples and has therefore no place for חרבה 'desolation' in its context. It seems that חרבה is a scribal error for חרפה (cf. LXX to Jer. 25: 9) and especially since חרבה and חרפה

(בכל העמים) 'to become an astonishment, hiss, desolation, reproach, curse, oath, proverb, and byword (to all the nations)'. It is the opposite of היה לשם, תהלה ותפארת (cf. III. 8).

Deut.: 28: 37.

Dtr: 2 Kgs. 22: 19.

Jer. C.: 19: 8, 24: 9, 25: 9, 11, 18, 26: 6, 29: 18, 42: 18, 44: 8, 12, 22.

It occurs in a series of two, three, four, five, and six words in question. Cf. also Jer. 49: 13.

Ezekiel has different combinations: חרבה וחרפה (5: 14, never together in Jeremiah); חרפה וגדופה מוסר ומשמה (5: 15), חרפה וקלסה (22: 4), זעוה ובז (23: 46), שמה ושממה (23: 33).

Cf. 2 Chr. 29: 8.

22. והיתה נבלתך (נבלת העם) למאכל לעוף השמים ולבהמת הארץ 'your corpse shall be food for the birds of the heaven and the beasts of the earth'.

Deut.: 28: 26.

Jer. C: 7: 33, 16: 4, 19: 7, 34: 20.

Cf. Pss. 79: 2, and see above, p. 139 n. 2. For the phrasing of this curse in Dtr see VIII. A. 11.

22a. לדמן על פני השדה/האדמה '(the corpse) shall be dung on the face of the earth'.

Dtr: 2 Kgs. 9: 37.

Jer. C: 8: 2, 16: 4, 25: 33. For 9: 21 see above, p. 139.

Cf. Ps. 83: 11.

23. אכל/האכיל בשר בנים ובנות . . . במצור ובמצוק 'to eat / make eat the flesh of sons and daughters . . . because of the desperate straits'.

Deut.: 28: 53.

Jer. C: 19: 9, see above, pp. 127 f.

24. קרא אתם/אתכם (כל) הרעה (הזאת) 'to make misfortune (lit. evil) befall you'.

Deut.: 31: 29.

Jer. C: 32: 23, 44: 23.

never occur together in a series. The error was caused by misunderstanding of שמה: 'desolation' instead of 'astonishment'. שמה is mostly combined with חרבה (25: 9, 11, 18, 44: 22, 49: 13), and this combination contributed to the misunderstanding.

VIII. THE FULFILMENT OF PROPHECY

A. *All the branches of deuteronomic literature*

1. הקים דבר יהוה 'establish (lit. erect) the word of Yahweh'.
   Deut.: 9: 5.
   Dtr: 1 Kgs. 2: 4, 8: 20, 12: 15.
   Jer.C: 29: 10, 33: 14.
   Cf. Num. 23: 19; 1 Sam. 1: 23, 3: 12; 2 Sam. 7: 25; 1 Kgs. 6: 12 (priestly passage). In the deuteronomic literature it occurs always in connection with the fulfilment of a divine promise of a national nature.

1a. נאמן דבר יהוה 'the word of Yahweh to be validated' (cf. above, p. 87 n. 2).
   Dtr: 1 Kgs. 8: 26.
   Compare 1 Chr. 17: 23 (יאמן) and its parallel in 2 Sam. 7: 25 (הקם), and on the other hand 1 Chr. 17: 14 (והעמדתיהו) with 2 Sam. 7: 16 (ונאמן). See S. Japhet, *Lešonenu* 31 (1967), 265–6 (Hebrew).

2. מלא דבר יהוה 'to fulfil the word of Yahweh'.
   Dtr: 1 Kgs. 2: 27, 8: 15, 24 (דבר בפיו ובידו מלא 'has spoken with his mouth and fulfilled with his hand').

3. לא נפל דבר 'not a word has fallen' (cf. above, p. 130 n. 2).
   Dtr: Josh. 21: 43, 23: 14; 1 Kgs. 8: 56; 2 Kgs. 10: 10 (with ארצה).
   Cf. 1 Sam. 3: 19 in hiphʿil and with ארצה.

4. כיום הזה 'as at this day'.
   Deut.: 2: 30, 4: 20, 38, 6: 24 (כהיום), 8: 18, 10: 15, 29: 27.
   Dtr: 1 Kgs. 3: 6, 8: 24, 61.
   Jer. C: 11: 5, 25: 18, 32: 20, 44: 6, 22, 23.
   Cf. Gen. 50: 20 (cf. above, p. 175); 1 Sam. 22: 8, 13 (in a neutral context). Dan. 9: 7, 15; Ezra 9: 7, 15; Neh. 9: 10; 1 Chr. 28: 7 are influenced by the deuteronomic usage.

5. הנני/הנה אנכי מביא רעה על 'Behold, I will bring evil upon'.
   Dtr: 1 Kgs. 14: 10, 21: 21, (29); 2 Kgs. 21: 12, 22: 16, (20); cf. 1 Kgs. 9: 9.
   Jer. C: 11: 11, 19: 3, 15, 35: 17.
   Cf. Jer. 4: 6, 6: 19, 45: 5 and compare 11: 23, 23: 12, 32: 42, 39: 16, 49: 37, 51: 64. J. Bright (*JBL* 70 (1951), Appendix A, no. 40) lists הנני/הנה אנכי מביא without רעה, which is pointless.

6. אשר כל שמעה/שמעיו תצלנה שתי אזניו 'at which the two ears of him who hears of it shall tingle'.

Dtr: 2 Kgs. 21: 12.

Jer. C: 19: 3.

Cf. 1 Sam. 3: 11.

7. שוב (איש) מדרך הרעה 'turn (everyone) from the evil way'.

Dtr: 1 Kgs. 13: 33; 2 Kgs. 17: 13.

Jer. C: 18: 11, 25: 5, 26: 3, 35: 15, 36: 3, 7, all of them with איש, which indicates a development of Dtr, cf. above, p. 7, note.

Cf. Jonah 3: 8 (with איש), 10; Ezek. 13: 22, 33: 11; Zech. 1: 4; 2 Chr. 7: 14. Jer. 23: 14 might be the prototype for Jer. C, see Holladay, 'Prototype and copies', 355 and cf. also Jer. 23: 22.

8. בער/הבעיר אחרי 'to exterminate utterly'.

Dtr: 1 Kgs. 14: 10, 16: 3, 21: 21.

9. עבדי/עבדיו הנביאים 'my/his servants the prophets'.

Dtr: 2 Kgs. 9: 7, 17: 13, 23, 21: 10, 24: 2.

Jer. C: 7: 25, 25: 4, 26: 5, 29: 19, 35: 15, 44: 4.

Cf. Amos 3: 7; Zech. 1: 6; Ezra 9: 11; Dan. 9: 6, 10; compare Ezek. 38: 17.

10. כנע מפני יהוה 'to humble oneself before Yahweh'.

Dtr: 1 Kgs. 21: 29; 2 Kgs. 22: 19.

Cf. 2 Chr. 33: 12, 23 (with מלפני instead of מפני), and כנע alone in 2 Chr. 7: 14, 12: 7, 12, 30: 11, 32: 26, 33: 19. See also 2 Chr. 36: 12 (כנע מלפני ירמיהו). כנע in the religious sense appears for the first time in Lev. 26: 41, and compare Ps. 107: 12. Cf. S. Japhet, *VT* 18 (1968), 359.

11. המת . . . בעיר יאכלו הכלבים והמת בשדה יאכלו עוף השמים 'him who dies . . . in the city shall the dogs eat and him who dies in the country shall the birds of the heaven eat'.

Dtr: 1 Kgs. 14: 11, 16: 4, 21: 24; see above, p. 131.

11a. הכלבים יאכלו את איזבל בחל/בחלק יזרעאל 'the dogs shall eat Jezebel in the rampart/portion of Jezreel'.

Dtr: 1 Kgs. 21: 23; 2 Kgs. 9: 10, 36; see above, p. 21.

12. והכרתי ל(פלני) משתין בקיר עצור ועזוב בישראל 'I shall cut off him belonging to PN who pisses against the wall עצור ועזוב in Israel'.

Dtr: 1 Kgs. 14: 10, 21: 21; 2 Kgs. 9: 8; cf. 1 Kgs. 16: 11; 2 Kgs. 14: 26.

The components of this curse are attested in ancient sources: 1 Sam. 25: 22, 34; Deut. 32: 36. Cf. above, p. 132.

B. *Clichés characteristic of the Jeremian Sermons*[1]

1. השכם ודבר/ושלח/ולמד 'rising up early and speaking/sending/teaching'.

Jer. C: 7: 13, 25, 11: 7, 25: 3, 4, 26: 5, 29: 19, 32: 33, 35: 14, 15. Cf. 2 Chr. 36: 15, referring to the period of Jeremiah (see v. 12 there).

2. היטיבו דרכיכם ומעלליכם 'amend your ways and your doings'.

Jer. C: 7: 3, 5, 26: 13.

2a. (שובו נא איש מדרכו הרעה) ומרע מעלליכם '(turn every man from his evil way) and from the evil of your doings'.

Jer. C: 25: 5 (for the phrase in brackets see above, VIII, A. 7). Cf. Jer. 23: 22.

2b. (שובו נא איש מדרכו הרעה) והיטיבו מעלליכם '(turn every man from his evil way) and amend your doings'.

Jer. C: 18: 11, 35: 15.

3. מפני רע / מרע מעלליכם 'because of the evil of their doings'.

Jer. C: 25: 5, 26: 3, 44: 22.

Cf. Jer. 4: 4, 21: 12, 23: 2, 22 and Deut. 28: 20. Compare Isa. 1: 16; Hos. 9: 15; Ps. 28: 4.

4. לקח מוסר 'to learn discipline'.[2]

Jer. C: 17: 23, 32: 33, 35: 13.

Cf. Jer. 2: 30, 5: 3, 7: 28; Zeph. 3: 2, 7. It seems to be rooted in the didactic sphere, cf. Prov. 1: 3, 8: 10, 24: 32.

5. ולא הטו את אזנם 'they did not incline the ear'.

Jer. C: 7: 24, 26, 11: 8, 17: 23, 25: 4, 34: 14, 35: 15, 44: 5.

Cf. Prov. 5: 13. It is also a didactic term.

[1] Most of them are rooted in Jeremiah's genuine prophecy but copied and reworked by the deuteronomic circle. See W. L. Holladay, 'Prototypes and Copies: a new approach to the poetry–prose problem in the Book of Jeremiah', *JBL* 79 (1960), 351 ff.

[2] For this phrase see above, p. 163 n. 3.

6. פנים ולא ערף/אחור (פנה) 'to turn backwards and not forwards'.

Jer. C: 7: 24, 32: 33.

Cf. 2: 27, 18: 17, which might have influenced (especially 2: 27) the prose verses. See Holladay, 'Prototypes', 355, no. 5.

7. וצוה דבר (שלח) 'to (send) speak and command'.

Jer. C: 7: 22, 19: 5, 26: 2.

Cf. Jer. 1: 7, 17, 14: 14, 29: 23 and 23: 32. The phrase is found in the Pentateuch in P (Exod. 7: 2, 25: 22, 34: 34) and in D (Deut. 18: 20), which seems to have influenced Jer. 1: 7, 17, (compare נתתי דברי בפיך in Jer. 1: 9 with ונתתי דברי בפיו Deut. 18: 18).

8. אשר לא צויתי ולא עלתה על לבי 'which I did not command nor did it even enter my mind'. Cf. יסק על לבבך in Sefire III: 14.

Jer. C: 7: 31, 19: 5, 32: 35, always in connection with the Molech.

For the phrase עלה על לב 'enter the mind', see Jer. 3: 16, 44: 21, 51: 50; Ezek. 14: 3, 4, 7; Isa. 65: 17.

9. איש יהודה וישבי ירושלם 'the men of Judah and the rulers of Jerusalem' (for the meaning of יושב, see above, p. 88 n. 2.)

Jer. C: 11: 2, 9, 17: 25, 18: 11, 32: 32, 35: 13.

Cf. Jer. 4: 4, 36: 31; 2 Kgs. 23: 2; Dan. 9: 7.

10. בערי יהודה ובחוצות ירושלם 'in the cities of Judah and the streets of Jerusalem'.

Jer. C: 7: 17, 34, 11: 6, 33: 10, 44: 6, 9, 17, 21.

Cf. above, p. 7 note, and see Holladay, 'Prototypes', 356, no. 9.

11. הבאים בשערים האלה 'that enter these gates'.

Jer. C: 7: 2, 17: 20, 22: 2, cf. 22: 4: ובאו בשערי הבית הזה. שערי ירושלם 'gates of Jerusalem' by itself is too general a phrase and cannot be considered a cliché as Holladay, 'Prototypes', 354 suggests.

12. לא יאספו ולא יקברו / ולא יספדו להם 'they shall not be gathered, nor buried / nor lamented'.

Jer. C: 8: 2, 16: 4, 6, 25: 33; cf. above, p. 139.

13. (והשבתי) קול ששון וקול שמחה קול חתן וקול כלה '(I will banish) the voice of mirth and the voice of gladness, the voice of the bridegroom and the voice of the bride'.

Jer. C: 7: 34, 16: 9, 25: 10, 33: 11 (the last one in the positive sense).

14. מביא(ם) תודה בית יהוה 'who bring thank-offerings to the house of Yahweh'.

Jer. C: 17: 26, 33: 11.

15. שלח/משלח את החרב אחריהם/בם/בינתם 'to send the sword after them / upon them / among them.'

Jer. C: 9: 15, 24: 10, 25: 27, 29: 17; cf. 49: 37.

The equivalent in Ezekiel is הביא עליהם חרב 'to bring upon them the sword' (5: 17, 11: 8, 14: 17, 33: 2), which is taken from P (Lev. 26: 25), as are the two other expressions there: הריק חרב 'to draw out the sword' (Ezek. 5: 2, 12, 12: 14, compare Lev. 26: 33) and חרב תעבר 'the sword will pass' (Ezek. 14: 17, compare Lev. 26: 6).

16. (ונתתי את ירושלים) לגלים מעון תנים (שממה) '(I will make Jerusalem) rubble, a jackal's lair (an awesome/eternal waste)'.

Jer. C: 9: 10, 10: 22; cf. 49: 33, 51: 37.

Cf. נוה תנים in Isa. 34: 13, 35: 7; see above, p. 142. It is a stereotypic covenantal curse, which might have been used by Jeremiah himself.

IX. THE DAVIDIC DYNASTY

1. למען דוד (אביך) עבדי/עבדו 'for the sake of David (your father) my/his servant'.

Dtr: 1 Kgs. 11: 12, 13, 32, 34; 2 Kgs. 8: 19, 19: 34, 20: 6; cf. 1 Kgs. 15: 4.

2. נתן/היות ניר לדוד 'to give/be a lamp for David'.

Dtr: 1 Kgs. 11: 36, 15: 4; 2 Kgs. 8: 19 (cf. Ps. 132: 17).

3. בחר בדוד / את דוד 'to choose David'.

Dtr: 1 Kgs. 8: 16, 11: 34.

Cf. Ps. 78: 30.

4. הרימתיך מתוך העם / מן העפר 'I exalted you from among the people/from the dust'.

Dtr: 1 Kgs 14: 7, 16: 2.

Cf. Ps. 89: 20.

5. (הלך) בכל דרך דוד; ככל אשר עשה דוד; עשה הישר כדוד / לא כדוד 'did that which is right . . . as David / not as David'; '(walked) in all the way of David'.

Dtr: 1 Kgs. 15: 11; 2 Kgs. 14: 3, 16: 2, 18: 3, 22: 2.

6. ישב על כסא דוד / לדוד על כסאו 'sitting upon the throne of David'.

Jer. C: 13: 13, 17: 25, 22: 2, 4.

Cf. 29: 16, 36: 30, and 22: 30.

7. (מלכים ושרים ישבים על כסא דוד) רכבים ברכב ובסוסים 'kings and princes (sitting upon the throne of David) riding in chariots and on horses'.

Jer. C: 17: 25, 22: 4.

8. לא יכרת לך/לדוד איש (מלפני, ישב) מעל כסא ישראל 'there shall not be cut off a man from you (from before me) from the throne of Israel'.

Dtr: 1 Kgs. 2: 4, 8: 25, 9: 5.

Jer. C: 33: 17 (כסא בית ישראל). A similar phrase is used in reference to the priests the Levites (33: 18) and to Jonadab the son of Rechab (35: 19).

For the idiom, compare in Akk.: *ištu pāni parāsu* 'to cut off from the presence of PN' (*VTE*, 343).

9. ואתנך נגיד על עמי ישראל 'I appointed you a leader over my people Israel'.

Dtr: 1 Kgs. 14: 7, 16: 2.

The idiom in the previous sources is: **לצוות נגיד** (1 Sam. 13: 14, 25: 30; 2 Sam. 6: 21), **להיות נגיד** (2 Sam. 5: 2, 7: 8; 1 Kgs. 1: 35), **משח לנגיד** (1 Sam. 9: 16, 10: 1).

10. קרע ממלכה מעל 'to tear the kingdom from . . .'.

Dtr: 1 Kgs. 11: 11, 13, 31, 14: 8; 2 Kgs. 17: 21.

Cf. 1 Sam. 15: 28, 28: 17; see above, p. 15 n. 5.

X. RHETORIC AND PARENETIC PHRASEOLOGY

1. שמע ישראל / (ועתה) ישראל שמע 'Hear, O Israel'.

Deut.: 4: 1, 5: 1, 6: 4, 9: 1, 20: 3, 27: 9.

See above, pp. 175–6, 305.

2. ובערת הרע מקרבך/מישראל 'thus you shall exterminate the evil from your midst / from Israel'.

Deut.: 13: 6, 17: 7, 12, 19: 19, 21: 21, 22: 21, 22, 24, 24: 7.

Cf. Judg. 20: 13; 2 Sam. 4: 11.

Compare the idioms in the royal Mesopotamian and Phoenician inscriptions: *ina mātišu ragam u ṣēnam lissuḫ* 'may he (= the future ruler) remove the wicked man and the evildoer from his land' (*CH* xxv b: 91–2), cf. Langdon, *Neubabyl. Königsinschriften*, 112. i: 27, 124, ii: 28; ותרק אנך כל הרע אש כן בארץ 'I removed all the evil that was in the country' (*KAI* 26 A, I: 9).

3. וכל ישראל/העם ישמעו ויראו (ולא יוסיפו לעשות כדבר הרע הזה בקרבך) 'and all Israel / all the people will hear and be afraid (and will not do again such evil things in your midst)'.

Deut.: 13: 12, 17: 13, 19: 20, 21: 21.

4. שפך/נתן/מלא / דם נקי 'pour / lay upon / fill with innocent blood'.

Deut.: 19: 10, 21: 8; cf. 27: 25.

Dtr: 2 Kgs. 21: 16, 24: 4 (שפך and מלא).

Jer. C: 7: 6, 22: 3, 19: 4 (דם נקיים apparently by influence of Jer. 2: 34).

Cf. Jer. 22: 17, 26: 15; Isa. 59: 7; Ps. 106: 38; Prov. 6: 17; Joel 4: 19; Jonah 1: 14. דם נקי by itself is an ancient phrase, cf. 1 Sam. 19: 5; Ps. 94: 21.

4a. בער דם נקי 'remove innocent blood'.

Deut.: 19: 13, 21: 9.

5. והיה בך חטא 'you will incur guilt'.

Deut.: 15: 9, 23: 22, 23 (with 'not'), 24: 15; cf. 21: 22.

The equivalent phrase in P is נשא עון 'to bear guilt'.

6. גר יתום ואלמנה 'stranger, orphan, and widow'.

Deut.: 10: 18, 14: 29, 16: 11, 14, 24: 17, 19, 20, 21, 26: 12, 13, 27: 19 (see above, p. 277 n. 23).

Jer. C: 7: 6, 22: 3.

Cf. Exod. 22: 20–1 (in separate sentences) and Ezek. 22: 7 (in separate clauses).

7. אשר אנכי מצוך / מצוה אתכם (היום) 'which I command you (this day)'.

Deut.: 4: 2 (twice), 40, 6: 6, 7: 11, 8: 1, 11, 10: 13, 11: 8, 13, 22, 27, 28, 12: 11, 14, 28, 13: 1, 19, 15: 5, 19: 9, 27: 1, 4, 10, 28: 1, 13, 14, 15, 30: 2, 8, 11, 16.

Cf. Exod. 34: 11, but the subject there is God, and not Moses as in Deuteronomy (with the exception of Deut. 11: 13). See F. Langlamet, *RB* 76 (1969), 329–30.

8. על כן אנכי מצוך 'therefore I command you'.
Deut.: 15: 11, 15, 19: 7, 24: 18, 22.

9. וידעת/וידעתם היום, וידעת עם לבבך 'know therefore (this day)', 'know it in heart'.
Deut.: 4: 39, 7: 9, 8: 5, 9: 3, 6, 11: 2; cf. 29: 3.
Dtr: Josh. 23: 14.
Jer. C: 24: 7 (לב לדעת).

10. השיב אל לב 'to turn it to heart'.
Deut.: 4: 39, 30: 1.
Dtr: 1 Kgs. 8: 47.
Cf. Isa. 44: 19, 46: 8; Lam. 3: 21.

11. אשר ראו עינך 'which your eyes have seen'.
Deut.: 4: 9, 7: 19, 10: 21, 29: 2.
Cf. 1 Sam. 24: 10; Josh. 24: 7 (both in the framework of an oration).

11a. עיניכם הראת 'your eyes have seen'.
Deut.: 3: 21, 4: 3, 11: 7.

12. השמר לך פן תשכח את יהוה 'Take care lest you forget Yahweh'.
Deut.: 4: 9, 23, 6: 12, 8: 11. See below, p. 367.

13. השמר בנפש/לנפש 'watch your soul(s)'.
Deut.: 4: 15; cf. 4: 9.
Dtr: Josh. 23: 11.
Jer. C: 17: 21.

14. לא ידעו(ם) (המה ואבותם) / אשר לא ידעתם (אתם ואבותיכם) / אשר לא ידעת ולא ידעון אבתיך 'which you did not know, nor your fathers had ever known / which they did not know (nor their fathers)', referring to foreign gods (cf. I, B. 6), peoples, lands, desert, manna, etc.
Deut.: 8: 3, 16, 11: 28, 13: 3, 7, 14, 28: 33, 36, 64, 29: 25.
Jer. C: 7: 9, 9: 15, 16: 13, 19: 4, 44: 3.
Cf. Deut. 32: 17, Jer. 15: 14, 17: 4, 22: 28; Ezek. 32: 9. Compare Akk. *lā idû* in reference to lands, peoples (enemies) (cf. *CAD* vol. 7 (I), p. 29).

15. למען ידעון/דעת (וראו) כל עמי הארץ 'so that all the peoples of the earth will see/know'.

Deut.: 28: 10.

Dtr: Josh. 4: 24; 1 Kgs. 8: 43, 60.

16. כל הימים אשר אתם/הם חיים על האדמה 'as long as you/they live on the earth'. Cf. V. A. 3b (p. 33).

Deut.: 4: 10, 12: 1, 31: 13.

Dtr: 1 Kgs. 8: 40.

Cf. 1 Sam. 20: 31 in a neutral sense.

Compare the neo-Assyrian phrase *ūmê ammar anīnū . . . balṭānini* = 'as long as we live' in the context of covenantal loyalty (*VTE* 507–9).

The phrase כל הימים 'all the days' also belongs to the rhetorical clichés of Deuteronomy (see Driver, *Deuteronomy*, p. lxxxi, no. 41) but is too common to be considered as peculiarly deuteronomic, cf., e.g., 1 Sam. 2: 32, 35; 1 Kgs. 5: 15, 12: 7.

17. מקצה השמים/הארץ ועד קצה השמים/הארץ 'from one end of the heaven/earth to the other'.

Deut.: 4: 32, 13: 8, 28: 64; cf. 30: 4.

Cf. Jer. 12: 12, 25: 33.

18. המדבר הגדול והנורא 'the great and terrible desert'.

Deut.: 1: 19, 2: 7, 8: 15.

19. שמלתך (ונעלך) לא בלתה ורגלך לא בצקה 'your clothes (sandals) did not wear out nor did your feet swell'.

Deut.: 8: 4, 29: 4; cf. above, p. 172 n. 2 for a Mesopotamian parallel.

Cf. Neh. 9: 21.

20. ערים גדלות ובצרות בשמים 'large cities (with walls) sky-high' (lit. fenced into heaven).

Deut.: 1: 28, 9: 1.[1]

Cf. Jer. 33: 3 (גדלות ובצרות).

21. ולא קם . . . עוד כ(משה) ; כמוך/כמוהו לא היה/יהיה לפניך/לפניו ואחריך/ אחריו לא קם/יקום כמוך/כמוהו 'Never again did there arise . . . like

[1] Cf. the Tiglath–Pileser III inscriptions, in connection with Azariau from Judah: '(his fortresses reaching) sky-high' *ana šamê šaqû* (P. Rost, *Die Keilschrifttexte Tiglat–Pilesers III*, 1893, p. 18 line 106).

(Moses)'; 'there was no one like him/you before, and after him/you none arose / will arise like him/you'.

Deut.: 34: 10.

Dtr: 1 Kgs. 3: 12; 2 Kgs. 18: 5, 23: 25; cf. 1 Kgs. 14: 9 (מכל אשר היו לפניך).

Cf. Exod. 10: 14 (in connection with the locust in Egypt).

This superlative evaluation refers to Moses, Solomon, Hezekiah, and Josiah. In the case of Solomon it appears as a promise on conditions. Similar superlatives are found in the Mesopotamian and Phoenician royal inscriptions, as for example: *ša ina kal sarrāni abbêšu māḫira la išû* 'among all the kings his ancestors there was none like him (lit. had been no opponent)' (*AfO* 1 (1923), 19: 5–6, and similar phrases in the annals of the neo-Assyrian kings); בל ען כל המלכם אש כן לפני ; ובל פעל הלפני(ה)ם 'which the kings who were before me had not subdued/built' (*KAI* 26 A, I: 19; 24: 5).

XI. THE INFLUENCE OF DEUTERONOMY UPON GENUINE JEREMIAH[1]

A. *Affinities in idioms*

	Deuteronomy	Jeremiah
1.	ודבר אליהם את כל אשר אצונו (18: 18)	ואת כל אשר אצוך תדבר (1: 7)
2.	ונתתי דברי בפיו (18: 18)	הנה נתתי דברי בפיך (1: 9)
3.	המוציאך מארץ מצרים . . . המוליכך במדבר . . . אשר אין מים (8: 14–15)	המעלה אתנו מארץ מצרים, המוליך אתנו במדבר . . . בארץ ציה (2: 6–7)
4.	כי יקח איש אשה . . . וכתב לה ספר כריתת ונתן בידה ושלחה . . . והלכה והיתה לאיש אחר . . . לא יוכל . . . לשוב לקחתה . . . ולא תחטיא את הארץ (24: 1–4)	הן ישלח איש אשתו והלכה . . . והיתה לאיש אחר . . . הישוב אליה . . . הלוא . . . תחנף הארץ . . . ואתן את ספר כריתתיה . . . (3: 1, 8)
5.	ומלתם את ערלת לבבכם (10: 16) ומל יהוה . . . את לבבך (30: 6)	המלו ליהוה . . . ערלות לבבכם (4: 4) ערלי לב (9: 25)

[1] Cf. Y. Kaufmann, *HIR* III, 613 ff., though one must be aware of the fact that unfortunately he does not distinguish between the authentic and unauthentic parts of Jeremiah.

	Deuteronomy	Jeremiah
6.	ישא יהוה עליך גוי מרחוק . . . גוי אשר לא תשמע לשנו (28: 59)	הנני מביא עליכם גוי ממרחק . . . גוי לא תדע לשונו ולא תשמע מה ידבר (5: 15)
7.	שעריך . . . חמתיך הגבהת והבצרות אשר אתה בטח בהן (28: 62)	ערי מבצרך אשר אתה בטח בהנה (5: 17)
8.	ונתתי מטר . . . בעתו יורה ומלקוש (11: 14) לתת מטר ארצך בעתו (28: 12)	הנותן גשם ויורה ומלקוש בעתו (5: 24)
9.	הנביא . . . לדבר . . . בשמי את אשר לא צויתיו לדבר (18: 20)	הנביאים נבאים בשמי . . . ולא צויתים ולא דברתי אליהם (14: 14)
10.	לא תתגדדו ולא תשימו קרחה (14: 1)	ולא יתגדד ולא יקרח (16: 7)
11.	הוא תהלתך (10: 20)	תהלתי אתה (17: 14)
12.	וישלכם אל ארץ אחרת (29: 27)	והטלתי אתך . . . על הארץ אחרת . . . והשלכו על הארץ אשר לא ידעו (22: 26, 28)
13.	שלום יהיה לי . . . בשררות לבי אלך (29: 18)	שלום יהיה לכם, וכל הלך בשררות לבו (23: 17)
14.	את כל הדבר אשר אנכי מצוה אתכם . . . ולא תגרע ממנו (13: 1)	את כל הדברים אשר צויתיך . . . אל תגרע דבר (26: 2)
15.	ואל תתן דם נקי (21: 8)	דם נקי אתם נתנים (26: 15)
16.	ונתתי על ברזל על צוארך (28: 48)	על ברזל נתתי על צואר . . . (28: 14)
17.	יומת, כי דבר סרה על יהוה (13: 6) לא תדרש שלמם (23: 6)	אתה מת, כי סרה דברת אל יהוה (28: 16) כי סרה דבר על יהוה (29: 32) ודרשו את שלום העיר . (29: 7)
18.	לדבר דבר בשמי את אשר לא צויתיו (18: 20)	וידברו דבר בשמי . . . אשר לא צויתים (29: 23)

B. *Deuteronomic clichés in the poetry of Jeremiah*

1. על כל הר גבה/גבעה גבהה/גבעות גבהת, תחת כל עץ רענן (2: 20, 3: 6, 17: 2, cf. 3: 13. Cf. I. A. 15 and Hosea 4: 13.
2. שקוצים (4: 1, 13: 27, 16: 18). Cf. I. B. 3 and Hosea 9: 10.
3. הבל (2: 5, 8: 19, 10: 3, 15 (51: 18), 14: 22, 16: 19). Cf. I. B. 5 and Deut. 32: 21.
4. קרא שם על (ישראל) (14: 9). Cf. III. 7.
5. אהב (ישראל) (31: 2). Cf. III. 13 and Hosea (*passim*).
6. הלך אחרי יהוה (2: 2). Cf. V. A. 1 and Hosea 11: 10.
7. בכל לב/לבב (3: 10). Cf. V. A. 9a.
8. שוב אל יהוה בכל לב (3: 10). Cf. V. A. 11.
9. סרו, סורר ומורה (5: 23, 6: 28). Cf. V. B. 2 and Ps. 78: 8.
10. משחיתים (6: 28). Cf. V. B. 3 and Deut. 32: 5; Hos. 9: 9, 13: 9.
11. הכעיסוני (בפסיליהם) (8: 19). Cf. V. B. 6, Deut. 32: 16, 21; Hos. 12: 15; Ps. 78: 58.
12. הלך בשרירות לב (23: 17). Cf. V. B. 8 and compare Ps. 81: 13.
13. שוב איש מרעתו (23: 14). Cf. VIII. A. 7.
14. ומרע מעלליהם (שוב מדרך הרעה) (23: 22). Cf. VIII. B. 2a.
15. מפני רע מעלליהם (4: 4, 21: 12, 23: 22). Cf. VIII. B. 3 and Hos. 9: 15.
16. לקח מוסר (2: 30, 5: 3, 7: 28). Cf. VIII. B. 4 and XII. 12.
17. שפך דם נקי (22: 17, 26: 15). Cf. X. 4 and Prov. 6: 17.

C. *The influence of Deut. 32 upon Jeremiah*

	Deuteronomy 32	Jeremiah
1.	אי אלהימו . . . יקומו ויעזרכם (37–8)	ואיה אלהיך . . . יקומו אם יושיעך (2: 28)
2.	חלק יהוה עמו יעקב חבל נחלתו (9)	חלק יעקב . . . וישראל שבט נחלתו (10: 16)
3.	כעסוני בהבליהם (21)	הכעיסוני . . . בהבלי נכר (8: 19)
4.	כי אש קדחה באפי ותיקד עד . . . (22)	כי אש קדחה באפי עליכם תוקד (15: 4) כי אש קדחתם באפי עד עולם תוקד (17: 4)

XII. PROTOTYPES IN WISDOM LITERATURE

1. תועבת יהוה (Prov. 3: 32, 11: 1, 20, 12: 22, 15: 8, 9, 26, 16: 5, 17: 15, 20: 10, 23. Cf. I. B. 1a.
2. בכל לב (Prov. 3: 5). Cf. V. A. 9a.
3. שמר מצוה (Prov. 4: 4, 6: 20 נצר, 7: 2, 19: 16; Eccles. 8: 5). Cf. V. A. 16. and compare Ps. 78: 7.
4. שמר תורה (Prov. 28: 4, 7 נצר, 29: 18). Cf. V. A. 17b.
5. נטה ימין ושמאל (Prov. 4: 27). Cf. V. B. 2c.
6. הקשה ערף (Prov. 29: 1). Cf. V. B. 9.
7. הדיח (Prov. 7: 21). Cf. V. B. 10a.
8. האריך ימים (Prov. 28: 16; Eccles. 8: 13). Cf. VII. 1.
9. ברך מעשה ידים (Job 1: 10). Cf. VII. 2a.
10. חיים 'life' (in the sense of 'happiness') (*passim*). Cf. VII. 3a.
11. השכיל 'to succeed' (in all undertakings) (Ps. 111: 10; Prov. 17: 8). Cf. VII. 6.
12. לקח מוסר (Prov. 1: 3, 8: 10, 24: 32). Cf. VIII. B. 4.
13. לא הטה אזן (Prov. 5: 13). Cf. VIII. B. 5.
14. שפך דם נקי (Prov. 6: 17). Cf. X. 4, XI. B. 17.
15. חכמים נבנים וידעים (Eccles. 9: 11, Job 34: 1). Cf. Deut. 1: 13, 15, and see above, p. 244.
16. הכר פנים במשפט (Prov. 24: 23, 28: 21). Cf. Deut. 1: 17, 16: 19, and see above, p. 273.
17. ארך ימים . . . עשר וכבוד (Prov. 3: 16). Cf. 1 Kgs. 3: 13–14 (= Dtr), see above, p. 257.
18. נפלא ממני/ממך (Prov. 30: 18; Job 42: 3; Ps. 131: 1). Cf. Deut. 30: 11, see above, pp. 258–9.

18a. רחקה היא 'remote' (beyond reach in reference to wisdom) (Eccles. 7: 23). Cf. Deut. 30: 11, see above, pp. 258–9.

19. עליו אין להוסיף וממנו אין לגרע; אל תוסף על דבריו (Prov. 30: 6; Eccles. 3: 14, cf. BS 18: 6, 42: 21). Cf. Deut. 4: 2, 13: 1. See also XI. A. 14.

20. אל תסג גבול עולם אשר עשו אבותיך (Prov. 22: 28, cf. 23: 10). Cf. Deut. 19: 14; cf. 27: 17, and see above, pp. 265 f.

21. אבן ואבן, איפה ואיפה תועבת יהוה (גם שניהם) (Prov. 20: 10, cf. 20: 23). Cf. Deut. 25: 13–16, see above, pp. 265 f.

21a. אבן שלמה (Prov. 11: 1). Cf. Deut. 25: 15.

22. כאשר תדר נדר לאלהים... אל תאחר לשלמו (Eccles. 5: 3, cf. Prov. 20: 25). Cf. Deut. 23: 22, see above, pp. 270 f.

23. אל תלשן עבד אל אדניו (Prov. 30: 10). Cf. Deut. 23: 16, see above, p. 272.

24. רדף צדקה . . . ימצא חיים (Prov. 21: 21, cf. 15: 9). Cf. Deut. 16: 20, see above, p. 273.

25. נפתה לבי; ויפת לבי (Job 31: 9, 27). Cf. Deut. 11: 16 (compare Hos. 7: 11) and see above, p. 304.

26. משגה ישרים בדרך רע (Prov. 28: 10). For משגה cf. Job 12: 16; Ps. 119: 10. Cf. Deut. 27: 18, see above, p. 278.

27. כי אם ביראת יהוה כל היום (Prov. 23: 17). Cf. V. A. 3b.

28. יראת יהוה אלמדכם (Ps. 34: 12). Cf. V. A. 3a.

29. והוא מלא בתיהם טוב (Job 22: 18). Cf. Deut. 6: 11, see above, p. 310.

30. החפץ חיים אוהב ימים לראות טוב (Ps. 34: 12–13). Cf. Deut. 6: 24, see above, pp. 298–9.

31. בהתהלכך (תנחה אתך) בשכבך (תשמר עליך) והקיצות (היא תשיחך) (Prov. 6: 20–2). Cf. Deut. 6: 7, 11: 19, see above, p. 299.

32. קשרם על אצבעותיך; כי לוית חן הם לראשך (Prov. 1: 9, 7: 3, compare 3: 3, 22, 4: 9). Cf. Deut. 6: 8, 11: 18, see above, pp. 299 f.

33. לשקוד על דלתתי יום יום לשמר על מזוזת פתחי (Prov. 8: 34). Cf. Deut. 6: 9, 11: 20, see above, p. 299.

34. מוסר יהוה בני אל תמאס כי את אשר יאהב יהוה יוכיח וכאב את בן ירצה (Prov. 3: 11–12; Job 5: 17) Cf. Deut. 8: 5 (see also 11: 2), see above, pp. 303, 316.

35. סבא וזולל (Prov. 23: 21). Cf. Deut. 21: 20.

36. כי היא חייך (Prov. 4: 13). Cf. Deut. 30: 20, 32: 47, see above, p. 308.

37. יצפן לבניו אונו) ישלם אליו וידע) (Job 21: 19). Cf. Deut. 7: 10, see above, p. 317.

XIII. PROTOTYPES IN HOSEA, DEUT. 32, AND PSALM 78

A. *In Hosea*

1. הקטיר לבעל (2: 15). Cf. I. A. 10.
2. על ראשי ההרים . . . ועל הגבעות . . . תחת אלון ולבנה ואלה (4: 13). Cf. I. A. 15, XI. B. 1, and p. 336 below.
3. שקוצים (9: 10). Cf. I. B. 3, XI. B. 2.
4. (אלהינו) מעשה ידינו (14: 4, cf. 8: 6 (והוא חרש עשהו), 13: 2 (מעשה חרשים). Cf. I. B. 7.
5. זִבֵּח וקִטֵּר (4: 13, 11: 2). Cf. II. 9.
6. (ישראל) אהב (3: 1, 9: 15, 11: 1, 4, 14: 5). Cf. III. 13 and XI. B. 5.
7. הלך אחרי יהוה (11: 10). Cf. V. A. 1 and XI. B. 6.
8. הלך בדרכי יהוה (14: 10). Cf. V. A. 6.
9. שחתו (9: 9, cf. 13: 9). Cf. V. B. 3.
10. הכעיס (12: 15). Cf. V. B. 6.
11. על רע מעלליהם (9: 15). Cf. VIII. B. 3 and XI. B. 15.
12. עברו בריתי (8: 1). Cf. V. B. 4.
13. שבעו וירם לבם על כן שכחוני (13: 6). Cf. Deut. 8: 12 f., see below, pp. 367–8.
14. המה מצרים ישובו; לא ישוב אל ארץ מצרים (8: 5, 11: 5). Cf. Deut. 17: 16, 28: 68. See below, p. 369.
15. ובקשו פני בצר להם ישחרנני . לכו ונשובה אל יהוה (5: 15–6: 1). Cf. Deut. 4: 29–30 (Jer. 29: 13); Prov. 1: 27–8. See below, p. 369.

B. *In Deut. 32*

1. תועבות (= idolatry) (v. 16). Cf. I. B. 1.
2. הבל (= idolatry) (v. 21). Cf. I. B. 5 and XI. B. 3.
3. אלהים לא ידעום (v. 17). Cf. I. B. 6.
4. שחת 'act wickedly' (v. 5). Cf. V. B. 3, XI. B. 10, and XIII. A. 9.
5. כעסו; הכעיסו (vv. 16, 21). Cf. V. B. 6, XI. B. 11, XIII. A. 10.

C. *Parenetic terms in Psalm 78* (deuteronomic prototypes?)

1. סורר ומורה (v. 8). Cf. V. B. 2 and XI. B. 9.
2. ויכעיסהו // ויקניאהו (v. 58). Cf. V. B. 6, XI. B. 11, XIII. A. 10, XIII. B. 5.
3. אתות ומופתים (v. 43). Cf. III. 18.
4. הלך בתורת יהוה (v. 10). Cf. V. A. 7.
5. נצר מצות יהוה (v. 7). Cf. V. A. 16, XII. 3.
6. שמר עדות יהוה (v. 56). Cf. V. A. 16.
7. בחר בדוד (v. 70). Cf. IX. 3.

APPENDIX B

HOSEA AND DEUTERONOMY

SCHOLARS usually point to affinities between Hosea and Deuteronomy. Indeed, there are points of contact between Deuteronomy and Hosea, as there are between Jeremiah and Hosea. It seems that this contact reflects a current of northern thought flowing down to Judah, following the fall of Samaria.[1] The tradition of Ebal and Gerizim ceremonies, which serves as a kind of envelope for the code of Deuteronomy (11: 26–32, 27: 1–26), seems also to support this view (cf. above, p. 166 n. 3).

It is especially significant that the affinities are to be found in matters with which Deuteronomy is mostly concerned, such as the condemnation of idolatrous and syncretistic ways of worship on the one hand and the establishment of sincere relationship with God on the other. The verbal resemblances are particularly convincing.

Deuteronomy condemns the worship on the high places in a language which is very similar to that of Hosea. Hosea says: 'They sacrifice upon the tops of the mountains and burn incense upon the hills under the oak . . . the terebinth because their shade is good' על ראשי ההרים יזבחו ועל הגבעות יקטרו תחת אלון ולבנה ואלה כי טוב צלה (4: 13). Deuteronomy states in closely similar terms: '(You must destroy all the sites at which the nations worshipped their gods) whether on lofty mountains and on hills or under any luxuriant tree' על ההרים הרמים ועל הגבעות ותחת כל עץ רענן (12: 2).[2] Ezekiel seems to combine[3] the two versions while concluding the prophecy against the 'mountains of Israel': 'upon every lofty hill, on all the tops of the mountains, under every luxuriant tree and every leafy terebinth' אל כל גבעה רמה בכל ראשי ההרים ותחת כל עץ רענן ותחת כל אלה עבתה (6: 13).

Hosea speaks frequently about the sin of increasing altars מזבחות, pillars מצבות, and high places במות (8: 11, 10: 1, 8, 12: 12). As no indica-

[1] See, e.g., A. Alt, 'Die Heimat des Deuteronomiums', *KS* II, 270 ff.

[2] For רענן see D. Winton Thomas, 'Some Observations on the Hebrew Word רענן' *Hebräische Wortforschung, W. Baumgartner Festschrift* 1967, pp. 387–97.

[3] אלה . . . תחת and ראשי ההרים reflect Hosea's version whereas תחת כל עץ רענן and רמה (גבעה) reflects the deuteronomic one. In addition to these Hoseanic–deuteronomic phrases Ezekiel incorporates also Priestly vocabulary as ריח ניחח in our verse. Verses 3–8 are based on Lev. 26: 30–3, which describe the destruction of cultic sites. Cf. also Isa. 57: 5 where אלה stands in opposition to עץ רענן. Jeremiah uses the deuteronomic cliché (but with גבה instead of רמה), see Jer. 2: 20, 3: 6. See also Appendix A, p. 322, no. 15; 360, XI. B. 1.

tion is given that these are pagan in character, we may suppose that Hosea attacks the high places in general, thus siding with Deuteronomy in its struggle against the high places. Chronologically Hosea is close to Hezekiah, who was first to abolish the high places.

Like Deuteronomy, Hosea indulges in polemics with idolatry. The idol is the craftsman's handiwork מעשה חרשים (13: 2, cf. 8: 6), a term related to idols in Deut. 27: 15[1] and in Jer. 10: 3, 9. As in Deuteronomy (4: 28, compare 28: 36, 64, 31: 29) and the deuteronomic literature,[2] so in Hosea the idols are described as man-made gods מעשה ידי אדם (14: 4). They are mocked as being produced of wood and stone עץ ואבן (Deut. 4: 28, 28: 36, 64, cf. 29: 16; cf. 2 Kgs. 19: 18; see above, p. 324), an idea hinted at in Hosea 4: 12[3] and apparently taken over by Jeremiah (2: 27). The man-made gods are mentioned also in Isa. 2: 8 and Mic. 5: 12, that is, in the period which stands between Hosea and Deuteronomy. It seems therefore that the polemics with idolatry that started at the time of Hosea and Isaiah had been developed by the deuteronomic scribes and had reached their apogee in Deutero-Isaiah.

The idea that God's covenant is based on the Torah, which is so salient in Deuteronomy, is also given clear expression in Hos. 8: 1: 'because they have transgressed my covenant and trespassed against my law' יען עברו בריתי ועל תורתי פשעו (cf. 6: 7 and compare 8: 12). Moreover the expression for violating the covenant is the same as in the deuteronomic literature: עבר ברית (cf. Hos. 6: 7, 8: 1, and Deut. 17: 2, Josh. 23: 16, Judg. 2: 20, 2 Kgs. 18: 12).[4] Abandoning the covenant is tantamount to forgetting it and its sponsor God.[5] No wonder, then, that we meet with this idea in both Hosea and Deuteronomy.[6] In both it is the same cause, satiety, that makes men forget God.[7] Furthermore, even the language in which this idea is couched is the same, a fact which may point towards direct dependence, or—which seems more likely—to the use of a common source. Thus, we read in Deut. 8: 12 f.: 'lest when you have eaten

[1] See above, p. 277 n. 2.

[2] 1 Kgs. 16, 7; 2 Kgs. 19: 18, 22: 17; Jer. 1: 16, 25: 6–7, 32: 30, 44: 8 (= C). Cf. also Pss. 115: 4, 135: 15.

[3] Cf. Hos. 8: 6.

[4] These verses refer to the violation of the Torah, whereas the same expression in Josh. 7: 11, 15 refers to the violation of a specific law, namely the חרם. Cf. above, p. 340, no. 4.

[5] For 'forgetting the covenant' in an Akkadian text see S. A. Strong, 'On Some Oracles to Esarhaddon and Ašurbanipal', *Beiträge zur Assyriologie* 2 (1894), 628–9, col. iii: 6–10: 'You speak in your heart: "Ištar is powerless"; you go among your cities, your districts, eat and forget this treaty'.

[6] Hos. 2: 15, 8: 14, 13: 6, compare 4: 6 (ותשכח תורת אלהיך); Deut. 6: 12, 8: 11, 14, 19, compare 4: 23, 31, (שכח ברית); see also Jer. 2: 32, 3: 21, 13: 25, 17: 10, 18: 15, 23: 27. For 'forgetting God' in Dtr, see Judg. 3: 7; 1 Sam. 12: 9; 2 Kgs. 17: 38 (שכח ברית); cf. also Ezek. 22: 12, 23: 35.

[7] See pp. 280 f. on the sapiential character of this motif.

your fill . . . and your silver and gold have increased . . . your heart grow haughty and you forget the Lord your God' . . . [1]פן תאכל ושבעת וכסף [1]וזהב ירבה לך . . . ורם לבבך ושכחת את יהוה אלהיך and in Hos. 13: 6: 'they were filled and their heart grew haughty, therefore they forgot me' שבעו וירם לבם על כן שכחוני.

'Forgetting God' means actually reliance upon oneself and one's power, a thing which comes to clear expression in the continuation of the passage in Deut. 8: 12 f.: 'and you forget the Lord your God[2] . . . and you say to yourselves, "My own power and the might of my hand have won this wealth for me." Remember that it is the Lord your God who gives you the power to get wealth.' This idea has special relevance in connection with over-reliance on horses and military prowess, as may be seen from an Assyrian text in which Tirhakah, King of Egypt, who rebelled against Assyria, is being blamed by Aššurbanipal that 'he forgot the might of Aššur . . . and trusted in his own strength'.[3] Indeed, Deuteronomy and Hosea, which frequently mention the 'forgetting of God', also bring up the deliverance of God ישועת יהוה *vis-à-vis* horses and military power (Deut. 20: 1–4, cf. 17: 16; Hos. 1: 7; cf. 14: 4).[4]

The most prominent point of contact between Deuteronomy and Hosea is in their treatment of the love between God and Israel. It should be admitted that there is a fundamental difference between the conception of love in Deuteronomy and that of Hosea. 'Love of God' in Deuteronomy is, as has already been indicated, predominantly the loyalty of Israel, the vassal, to God, the sovereign, whereas in Hosea and Jeremiah the love has an affectionate connotation as in love between husband and wife.[5] But this is true only with regard to the love of Israel towards God; where the love of God towards Israel is concerned there is almost no difference between Hosea and Deuteronomy. The love of God towards Israel in Deuteronomy is certainly not loyalty, and although no connotation of conjugal love can be ascribed to it, it has without doubt the meaning of affectionate love. This may be inferred from three passages in Deuteronomy which describe the Israel–Yahweh relationship as one between father and son (1: 31, 8: 5, 14: 1,[6] cf. Exod.

[1] Cf. Deut. 17: 17, 20. Verses 18–19 are interpolated, see above, p. 5 n. 1.

[2] The participial clauses describing the greatness of God (from המוציאך in verse 14 to the end of verse 16) have to be put in parenthesis. Cf., for example, the translation of the JPS, 1962.

[3] Streck, *Assurbanipal II*, p. 6, i: 56–7. See also *AfO* 20, p. 94, l. 108.

[4] Cf. above, p. 281. The idea occurs also in Isa. 31: 1, but the key-verb ישע which accompanies the text in Deuteronomy and Hosea and in the sapiential texts mentioned above, p. 281 (compare also Zech. 10: 5–6) is missing there.

[5] Cf. above, p. 82 note.

[6] Of these three passages in Deuteronomy which describe the Yahweh–Israel relationship as one between father and son, only the last may be regarded as having an actual treaty setting (the relationship between the vassal and

4: 22).[1] Paternal love is actually mentioned in Hosea 11: 1–4 (compare Jer. 31: 8, 19), a passage which expresses the same idea as Deut. 1: 31. In Deut. 1: 31 and Hosea 11: 1–4 the image is that of a father tenderly carrying his son, in contradistinction to Exod. 19: 4 and Deut. 32: 11 where the image is that of an eagle carrying its young.

A minor point of contact between Deuteronomy and Hosea is the menace of returning to Egypt, expressed in a similar language.

Deuteronomy	Hosea
And he shall not send the people back to Egypt ולא ישיב את העם מצרימה (17: 16). The Lord will send you back to Egypt והשיבך יהוה מצרים (28: 68).	They will go back to Egypt המה מצרים ישובו (8: 13). He will not go back to Egypt לא ישוב אל ארץ מצרים (11: 5, cf. 9: 3).

The idea of return to God is likewise similarly expressed in Deuteronomy and in Hosea.

When you search there for Yahweh your God, you will find him, if you seek him with all your heart and soul; *when you are in distress* because all these things have befallen you . . . *return to Yahweh your God.*[2] ובקשתם משם את יהוה אלהיך ומצאת כי תדרשנו בכל לבבך ובכל נפשך. בצר לך ומצאוך כל הדברים האלה . . . ושבת עד יהוה אלהיך (Deut. 4: 29–30).	'They will seek my face, in *their distress* they will search for me: "come let us *return to* Yahweh".[2] ובקשו פני בצר להם ישחרנני. לכו ונשובה אל יהוה (Hos. 5: 15–6: 1).

The assertion, however, that the book of Deuteronomy resembles Hosea in its negative attitude toward the monarchy is groundless. Not even Hosea repudiates the monarchic institution;[3] and far from Deut. 17 reflecting a negative attitude towards the monarchy, Deuteronomy

the overlord was expressed in terms of son–father relationship: *mārūtum–abbūtum*, see J. M. Munn-Rankin, *Iraq* 18 (1956), 68 ff., and cf. 2 Kgs. 16: 7 בנך אני). McCarthy supposed that all three passages have a treaty background (*CBQ* 27 (1965), 144–7). But even in Deut. 14: 1 we cannot be sure that the image is taken from the treaty sphere.

[1] See S. E. Loewenstamm, *The Tradition of the Exodus in its Development*, 1965, p. 24 (Hebrew with English summary).

[2] Compare Prov. 1: 27–8: 'When distress and trouble come upon you, then they will call me but I will not answer, they will search for me but they shall not find me' בבא עליכם צרה וצוקה אז יקראנני ולא אענה ישחרנני ולא ימצאנני.

[3] See Kaufmann, *HIR* III, 137–8.

shows a positive concern for its welfare.[1] The purpose of the law of the king is to prevent the royal house from bringing ruin upon itself, so that its reigning representative 'may continue long in his kingdom, he and his children in Israel' (17: 20).

[1] See above, pp. 168 f.

SELECT BIBLIOGRAPHY

ALBRIGHT, W. F., *From the Stone Age to Christianity* (2nd edn.), Baltimore: Johns Hopkins Press, 1946.

—— *Archaeology and the Religion of Israel* (3rd edn.), Baltimore: Johns Hopkins Press, 1953.

—— 'Some Canaanite–Phoenician Sources of Hebrew Wisdom', *SVT* 3 (1955), 1–15.

ALP, S., 'Military Instructions of the Hittite King Tutḫaliya IV. (?)' Türk Tarih Kurumu, *Belleten* 11 (1947), 383–414.

ALT, A., 'Die Ursprünge des Israelitischen Rechts', *KS* I, Munich: C. H. Beck, 1953, pp. 278–332, originally appeared in *Berichte über die Verhandlungen der Sächsischen Akademie der Wissenschaften zu Leipzig* (Philologisch-historische Klasse, Bd. 86, Hft. 1), Leipzig: S. Hirzel, 1934.

—— 'Die Weisheit Salomos', *KS* II, Munich: C. H. Beck, 1953, 90–9, originally appeared in *Theologische Literaturzeitung* 76 (1951), 139–44.

—— 'Die Heimat des Deuteronomiums', *KS* II, Munich: C. H. Beck, 1953, 250–75.

ANDERSON, G. W., *A Critical Introduction to the Old Testament* (2nd edn.), London: G. Duckworth, 1960.

BAENTSCH, B., *Exodus–Leviticus–Numeri* (HKAT), Göttingen: Vandenhoeck & Ruprecht, 1903.

BALTZER, K., *Das Bundesformular* (Wissenschaftliche Monographien zum Alten und Neuen Testament, 4), Neukirchen: Neukirchener Verlag, 1960.

BARTON, G. A., *The Royal Inscriptions of Sumer and Akkad* (American Oriental Society—Library of Ancient Semitic Inscriptions, 1), New Haven: Yale University Press, 1929.

BAUDISSIN, W. W. G., 'Alttestamentliches *hayyim* "Leben" in der Bedeutung von "Glück"', *Festschrift E. Sachau*, Berlin: G. Reimer, 1915, pp. 143–61.

BAUMGARTNER, W., *Israelitische und altorientalische Weisheit*, Tübingen: J. C. B. Mohr, 1933.

BECKER, J., *Gottesfurcht im Alten Testament* (Analecta Biblica 25), Rome: Pontifical Biblical Institute, 1965.

BENTZEN, A., *Die Josianische Reform und ihre Voraussetzungen*, København: P. Haase & Søns, 1926.

BERTHOLET, A., *Die Stellung der Israeliten und der Juden zu den Fremden*, Freiburg: J. C. B. Mohr, 1896.

—— *Deuteronomium* (KHC), Freiburg: J. C. B. Mohr, 1899.

BORGER, R., *Die Inschriften Asarhaddons*, *AfO* Beiheft 9, 1956.

BORGER, R., 'Zu den Asarhaddon-Verträgen aus Nimrud', *ZA* 20, NF (1960), 173–96.

BREIT, H., *Die Predigt des Deuteronomisten*, Munich: Chr. Kaiser, 1933.

BRICHTO, H., *The Problem of the Curse in the Hebrew Bible* (*JBL* Monograph Series, 13), Philadelphia: Society of Biblical Literature and Exegesis, 1963.

BRIGHT, J., 'The Date of the Prose Sermons of Jeremiah', *JBL* 70 (1951), 15–35.

—— *Jeremiah* (Anchor Bible), Garden City, New York: Doubleday & Co., 1965.

—— 'The Prophetic Reminiscence: its Place and Function in the Book of Jeremiah', *Proceedings of the ninth meeting of Die Ou-Testamentiese Werkgemeenskap in Suid-Afrika* (1966), pp. 11–39.

BRUNNER, H., *Altägyptische Erziehung*, Wiesbaden: O. Harrassowitz, 1957.

—— 'Die Weisheitsliteratur', *Handbuch der Orientalistik*, Leiden: E. J. Brill, 1957, Bd. 1, Hft. 2, pp. 90–110.

BUBER, M., *Israel und Palästina*, Zurich: Artemis-Verlag, 1950.

—— *Königtum Gottes* (3rd edn.), Heidelberg: Schneiden, 1956.

BUDDE, K., 'Dtn. 13, 10 und was daran hängt', *ZAW* 36 (1916), 187–97.

—— *Das Lied Moses*, Tübingen: J. C. B. Mohr, 1920.

CARLSON, R. A., *David, the chosen King; a traditio-historical approach to the Second Book of Samuel*, trans. E. J. Sharpe and S. Rudman, Uppsala: Almqvist & Wiksell, 1964.

CAVAIGNAC, E., 'Daddassa-Dattasa', *RHA* 10 (1933), 65 ff.

CAZELLES, C. H., 'Jérémie et le Deutéronome', *Recherches de Science Religieuse* 38 (1951), 5–36.

—— 'Institutions et Terminologie en Deut. I', *SVT* 15 (1966), 97–112.

—— 'Passages in the singular within discourses in the plural of Dt. 1–4', *CBQ* 29 (1967), 207–19.

CHILDS, B. S., *Memory and Tradition in Israel* (Studies in Biblical Theology), Naperville, Illinois: A. R. Allenson, 1962.

—— 'Deuteronomic Formulae of the Exodus Traditions', *Hebräische Wortforschung, Festschrift for W. Baumgartner*, *SVT* 16 (1967), 30–9.

CLEMENTS, R. E., *God and temple*, Oxford: Blackwell, 1965.

—— *Abraham and David* (Studies in Biblical Theology, 2nd series, 5), Naperville, Illinois: A. R. Allenson, 1967.

COWLEY, A., *Aramaic Papyri of the Fifth Century B.C.*, Oxford: Clarendon Press, 1923.

CROSS, F. M., 'The Tabernacle', *BA* 10 (1947), 45–68.

—— *The Ancient Library of Qumran and Modern Biblical Studies* (rev. ed.), Garden City, N.Y.: Anchor Books, 1961.

—— and FREEDMAN, D. N., 'The Song of Miriam', *JNES* 14 (1955), 237–50.

DE BOER, P. A. H., 'The Counsellor', *SVT* 3 (1955), 42–71.

—— *Gedenken und Gedächtnis in der Welt des Alten Testaments*, Stuttgart: Kohlhammer, 1962.

DELCOR, M., 'Les attaches littéraires, l'origine et la signification de l'expression biblique "Prendre à témoin le ciel et la terre" ', *VT* 16 (1966), 8–25.

DE VAUX, R., *Ancient Israel*, London: Darlon, Longman & Todd, 1961.

—— *Studies in Old Testament Sacrifice*, Mystic, Connecticutt: Verry, 1966.

—— 'Le roi d'Israel, vassal de Yahvé', *Mélanges E. Tisserant*, I Studi e testi, Vatikan 1964, 119–33.

—— 'Le lieu que Yahvé a choisi pour y établir son nom', *Das Ferne und Nahe Wort, Festschrift L. Rost, BZAW* 105 (1967).

DE WETTE, W. M. L., *Dissertatio critico-exegetica, qua Deuteronomium a prioribus Pentateuchi libris diversum, alius cuiusdam recentioris auctoris opus esse monstratur*, 1805; reprinted in his *Opuscula*, Berlin, 1833.

DILLMANN, A., *Numeri, Deuteronomium und Josua* (KeH), Leipzig, 1886.

DONNER, H., and RÖLLIG, W., *Kanaanäische und Aramäische Inschriften*, 3 vols., Wiesbaden: O. Harrassowitz, 1962–4.

DRAFFKORN, A., 'Was King Abba-AN of Yamḫad a Vizier for the King of Ḫattuša?', *JCS* 13 (1959), 94–7.

DRIVER, G. R., and MILES, J. C., *The Assyrian Laws*, Oxford: Clarendon Press, 1935.

—— *The Babylonian Laws*, 2 vols., Oxford: Clarendon Press, 1952.

DRIVER, S. R., *Deuteronomy* (ICC), Edinburgh: T. & T. Clark, 1895.

—— *An Introduction to the Literature of the Old Testament* (8th edn.), Edinburgh: T. & T. Clark, 1909.

—— *Notes on the Hebrew Text and the Topography of the Books of Samuel* (2nd edn.), Oxford: Clarendon Press, 1913.

DUPONT-SOMMER, A., *Les Inscriptions araméennes de Sfiré*, Paris: Imprimerie Nationale, 1958.

DÜRR, L., *Die Wertung des Lebens im Alten Testament und im antiken Orient*, Münster in Westf.: Aschendorff, 1926.

—— *Das Erziehungswesen im Alten Testament und im antiken Orient* (*MVÄG*, Bd. 36, Hft. 2), Leipzig: J. C. Hinrichs, 1932.

EERDMANS, B. D., *Alttestamentliche Studien*, 4 vols., Giessen: A. Töpelmann, 1908–12.

EHRLICH, A., *Randglossen zur hebräischen Bibel*, 7 vols., Leipzig: J. C. Hinrichs, 1908–14.

EHRLICH, E. L., *Der Traum im Alten Testament, ZAW* Beiheft 73 (1953).

EISSFELDT, O., *Erstlinge und Zehnten im Alten Testament* (Beiträge zur Wissenschaft von Alten Testament, ed. Rudolf Kittel, Hft. 22), Leipzig: J. C. Hinrichs, 1917.

—— 'Die Bücher der Könige', *Heilige Schrift des Alten Testaments*, ed. Kautzsch, hrsg. von Bertholet, Tübingen. 4. Aufl. 1922/3.

—— *Einleitung in das Alte Testament* (3rd edn.), Tübingen: J. C. B. Mohr, 1964.

EMERTON, J. A., 'Priests and Levites in Deuteronomy', *VT* 12 (1962), 129–38.

Encyclopaedia Miqra'it I–V, Jerusalem: Bialik Institute, 1950–68.

ERMAN, A., *Die Literatur der Ägypter*, Leipzig: J. C. Hinrichs, 1923.

FALKENSTEIN, A., and VON SODEN, W., *Sumerische und akkadische Hymnen und Gebete*, Zürich: Artemis-Verlag, 1953.

—— 'Fluch über Akkade', *ZA* NF 23 (1965), 43–124.

FENSHAM, C., 'Malediction and benediction in Ancient Near Eastern treaties and the Old Testament', *ZAW* 74 (1962), 1–9.

FICHTNER, J., *Die altorientalische Weisheit in ihrer israelitisch–jüdischer Ausprägung, ZAW*, Beiheft 62 (1933).

FINKELSTEIN, J. J., 'Ammiṣaduqa's Edict and the Babylonian "Law-Codes"', *JCS* 15 (1961), 91–104.

—— 'Sex Offenses in Sumerian Laws', *JAOS* 86 (1966), 355–72.

FINKELSTEIN, L., *The Pharisees* (3rd edn.), 2 vols., Philadelphia: The Jewish Publication Society, 1962.

FITZMYER, J. A., *The Aramaic Inscriptions of Sefîre* (Biblica et Orientalia 19), Rome: Pontifical Biblical Institute, 1967.

FRANKENA, R., 'The Vassal Treaties of Esarhaddon and the Dating of Deuteronomy', *Oudtest. Studiën* 14 (1965), 122–54.

FRANKFORT, H., *Kingship and the Gods, a study of ancient Near Eastern religion as the integration of society and nature*, Chicago, University of Chicago Press, 1948.

FRIEDRICH, J., 'Der hethitische Soldateneid', *ZA* NF 1 (1924), 161–92.

—— *Staatsverträge des Hatti Reiches, MVÄG* 31, 1 (1926); *MVÄG* 34, 1 (1930).

—— *Hethitisches Wörterbuch*, Indogermanische Bibliothek, Zweite Reihe: Wörterbücher, Heidelberg, Carl Winter Universitätsverlag, 1952.

GADD, C. J., LEGRAIN, L., and SMITH, S., *Ur Excavation Texts I* (Publication of the Joint Expedition of the British Museum and the University Museum, University of Pennsylvania to Mesopotamia), London: British Museum, 1928.

GARSTANG, J. and GURNEY, O. R., *The Geography of the Hittite Empire*, London: British Institute of Archaeology at Ankara, 1959.

GEIGER, A., *Urschrift und Übersetzungen der Bibel*, Breslau: J. Hainauer, 1857.

GELB, I., Review of D. J. Wiseman, *The Vassal Treaties of Esarhaddon, BO* 19 (1962), 159–62.

GEMSER, B., *Sprüche Salomos* (2nd edn., HAT), Tübingen: J. C. B. Mohr, 1963.

—— 'The Importance of the Motive Clauses in OT Law', *SVT* 1 (1953), 50–66.

GESENIUS, W., *Hebrew Grammar* (as ed. and enlar. E. Kautzsch. 2nd Eng. edn. trans. and rev. in accordance with 28th German edn. (1909), A. E. Cowley), Oxford: Clarendon Press, 1910.

GEVIRTZ, S., 'Jericho and Shechem. A Religio–Literary Aspect of City Destruction', *VT* 13 (1963), 52–62.

GINSBERG, H. L., קהלת, Tel Aviv/Jerusalem: M. Newman Publishing House Ltd., 1961.
—— 'Hosea's Ephraim, More Fool than Knave, A New Interpretation of Hosea 12: 1–14', *JBL* 80 (1961), 339–47.
GOETZE, A., *Madduwattaš* (*MVÄG*, Bd. 32, 1927, Hft. 1), Leipzig: J. C. Hinrichs, 1928.
—— *Kizzuwatna and the Problem of Hittite Geography*, YOS Researches 22, New Haven: Yale University Press, 1940.
—— 'State and Society of the Hittites', *Historia, Zeitschrift für alte Geschichte*, Einzelschriften 7 (1964), 32 ff.
GORDON, C. H., *Ugaritic Textbook*, Rome: Pontifical Biblical Institute, 1965.
—— 'A New Akkadian Parallel to Deut. 25: 11–12', *Journal of the Palestine Oriental Society* 15 (1935), 29–34.
GÖSSMANN, F., *Das Era Epos*, Würzburg: Augustinus-Verlag, 1956.
GRAY, J., *I and II Kings* (OTL), London: SCM Press, 1964.
GREENBERG, M., 'Hebrew segulla: Akkadian sikiltu', *JAOS* 71 (1951), 172–4.
—— 'The Biblical Conception of Asylum', *JBL* 78 (1959), 125–32.
GREENFIELD, J., 'Stylistic Aspects of the Sefire Treaty Inscriptions', *Acta Orientalia* 29 (1965), 1–18.
—— 'Three notes on the Sefire inscriptions', *JSS* 11 (1966), 98–105.
GRESSMANN, H., *Die älteste Geschichtsschreibung und Prophetie Israels*[2] (SAT), Göttingen: Vandenhoeck & Ruprecht, 1921.
—— *Mose und seine Zeit*, Göttingen: Vandenhoeck & Ruprecht, 1913.
—— *Die Anfänge Israels*[2] (SAT), Göttingen: Vandenhoeck & Ruprecht, 1922.
GRIFFITH, F. Ll., 'The Teaching of Amenophis, the son of Kanekht', *JEA* 12 (1926), 191–231.
GROSS, K., 'Die literarische Verwandtschaft Jeremias mit Hoseas' (unpublished Berlin Theological Dissertation), 1930.
—— 'Hoseas Einfluss auf Jeremias Anschauungen', *NKZ* 42 (1931), 241–65, 327–43.
GUNKEL, H., *Genesis* (3rd edn., HKAT), Göttingen: Vandenhoeck & Ruprecht, 1910.
—— *Psalmen* (HKAT), Göttingen: Vandenhoeck & Ruprecht, 1926.
GÜTERBOCK, H. G., *Siegel aus Bogazköy*, *AfO* Beiheft 5, 1940.

HARAN, M., 'The Ark and the Cherubim: their Symbolic Significance in Biblical Ritual', *IEJ* 9 (1959), 30–8, 89–94.
—— 'The Nature of the "'Ohel Mo'edh" in Pentateuchal Sources', *JSS* 5 (1960), 50–65.
—— 'The Complex of Ritual Acts Performed Inside the Tabernacle', *Scripta Hierosolymitana* (publ. of the Hebrew University, Jerusalem), 8 (1961), 272–302.
HARVEY, J., 'Le "rîb-pattern", Réquisitoire prophétique sur la rupture de l'alliance', *Biblica* 43 (1962), 172–96.

HEMPEL, J., *Die Schichten des Deuteronomiums* (Beiträge zur Kultur- und Universalgeschichte, 33 Hft.), Leipzig: R. Voigtländer, 1914.

—— 'Priesterkodex', *RE* 22, Stuttgart: Alfred Druckenmüller, 1954, cols. 1943–67.

HERRMANN, S., 'Die Königsnovelle in Ägypten und Israel', *Wissenschaftliche Zeitschrift der Karl Marx Universität, Leipzig* (Gesellschafts- und Sprachwissenschaftliche Reihe, 3. Jahrgang, 1953–4), 51–62.

HERRMANN, W., 'Zu Kohelet 3: 14', *Wissenschaftliche Zeitschrift der Karl Marx Universität, Leipzig* (Gesellschafts- und Sprachwissenschaftliche Reihe, 3. Jahrgang, 1953–4), 293–5.

HERTZBERG, H. W., *Der Prediger* (2nd edn., KAT). Gütersloh: Gerd Mohn, 1963.

HILLERS, D. R., *Treaty Curses and the O.T. Prophets* (Biblica et Orientalia, 16), Rome: Pontifical Biblical Institute, 1964.

HILPRECHT, H. V., *The Babylonian Expedition of the University of Pennsylvania*, Series A, I, Philadelphia: Dept. of Archaeology, the University of Pennsylvania, 1893.

HINZ, W., 'Elams Vertrag mit Naram-Sin von Akkade', *ZA* 24 (1967), 66–96.

HOFFMANN, D., *Deuteronomium* I–II, Berlin: M. Poppelauer, 1913, 1922.

HOLLADAY, W. L., 'Prototype and Copies: A new approach to the poetry–prose problem in the Book of Jeremiah', *JBL* 79 (1960), 351–67.

HÖLSCHER, G., 'Komposition und Ursprung der Deuteronomiums', *ZAW* 40 (1923), 161–225.

HOLZINGER, H., *Exodus* (KHC), Tübingen: J. C. B. Mohr, 1900.

HORST, F., *Gottes Recht, Gesammelte Studien zum Recht im Alten Testament* (Theologische Bücherei, Bd. 12), Munich: C. Kaiser, 1961, originally appeared as *Das Privilegrecht Jahwes* (*Rechtsgeschichtliche Untersuchungen zum Deuteronomium* FRLANT, NF 28 Hft., Göttingen: Vandenhoeck & Ruprecht, 1930.

L'HOUR, J., 'Une legislation criminelle dans le Deutéronome', *Biblica* 44 (1963), 1–15.

HUFFMON, H. B., 'The Covenant Lawsuit in the Prophets', *JBL* 78 (1959), 285–95.

HUMBERT, P., *Recherches sur les sources égyptiennes de la littérature sapientiale d'Israël* (Memoires de l'Université de Neuchâtel, 7), Neuchâtel: Secretariat de l'Université, 1929.

HYATT, J. P., 'Torah in the Book of Jeremiah', *JBL* 60 (1941), 381–96.

JEPSEN, A., *Die Quellen des Königsbuches* (2nd edn.), Halle (Saale): M. Niemeyer, 1956.

JIRKU, A., *Die älteste Geschichte Israels in Rahmen lehrhaften Darstellung*, Leipzig: A. Deichert, 1917.

JUNKER, H., 'Die Entstehungszeit des Ps. 78 und das Deuteronomium', *Biblica* 34 (1953), 487–500.

KADUSHIN, M., *Worship and Ethics: A Study in Rabbinic Judaism*, Northwestern University Press, U.S.A. 1964.

KAUFMANN, Y., תולדות האמונה הישראלית I–IV, Jerusalem: The Bialik Institute, Tel Aviv: The Dvir Co. Ltd., 1937–56 (Hebrew) [= *HIR*].
—— *The Religion of Israel*, trans. and abr. M. Greenberg, Chicago: University of Chicago Press, 1960.
—— *The Book of Joshua*, Jerusalem: Kiryat Sepher Ltd., 1959 (Hebrew).
—— *The Book of Judges*, Jerusalem: Kiryat Sepher Ltd., 1962 (Hebrew).
KING, L. W., *The Annals of the Kings of Assyria* I, London: The British Museum, 1902.
—— *Babylonian Boundary Stones and Memorial Tablets in the British Museum*, London: The British Museum, 1912.
KLOSTERMANN, A., *Der Pentateuch* (NF), Leipzig: A. Deichert, 1907.
KOHLER, J., and UNGNAD, A., *Assyrische Rechtsurkunden*, Leipzig: Pfeiffer, 1913.
KÖNIG, E., *Deuteronomium* (KAT), Leipzig: A. Deichert, 1917.
KOROŠEC, V., *Hethitische Staatsverträge* (Leipziger rechtswissenschaftliche Studien, Hft. 60), Leipzig: T. Weicher, 1931.
—— 'Einige Juristische Bemerkungen zur Šaḫurunuva-Urkunde', *Münchener Beiträge zur Papyrusforschung und antiken Rechtsgeschichte* 35 (1945), 191–222.
KRAMER, S. N., *The Sumerians*, Chicago & London: University of Chicago Press, 1963.
KRAUS, F. R., *Ein Edikt des Königs Ammi-Ṣaduqa von Babylon* (Studia et Documenta ad Iura Orientis Antiqui Pertinentia, 5), Leiden: E. J. Brill, 1958.
—— 'Ein zentrales Problem des altmesopotamischen Rechtes: was ist der Codex Hammurabi?', *Genava*, Musée d'art et d'histoire, Nouvelle Série– Tome VIII, 1960, 283–96.
KRAUS, H. J., *Psalmen* (2nd edn., BK), Neukirchen: Neukirchener Verlag, 1960.

LAMBERT, W. G., *Babylonian Wisdom Literature*, Oxford: Clarendon Press, 1960.
LANGDON, S., *Die neubabylonischen Königsinschriften* (Vorderasiatische Bibliothek IV), Leipzig: J. C. Hinrichs, 1912.
LANGE, H. O., *Das Weisheitsbuch des Amenemope*, Det Kgl. Danske Videnskabernes Selskab., Historisk-filologiske Meddelelser XI, 2, København, 1925.
LAROCHE, E., 'Un point d'histoire: Ulmi-Teshub', *RHA* 48 (1948), 40–8.
LAUTERBACH, J. Z., *Mekilta de-Rabbi Ishmael* I–III, Philadelphia: Jewish Publication Society, 1935 (2nd imp., 1949).
LEWY, J., 'The Biblical Institution of *derôr* in the Light of Akkadian Documents', *EI* 5 (1958), 21–31.
LIE, A. G., *The Inscriptions of Sargon II King of Assyria. Part I: The Annals*, Paris: Geuthner, 1929.
LOEWENSTAMM, S. E., *The Tradition of the Exodus in its Development*, Jerusalem, The Magnes Press, 1965 (Hebrew with English Summary).
—— 'Zur Traditionsgeschichte des Bundes zwischen den Stücken,' *VT* 18 (1968), 500–6.

LOHFINK, N., *Das Hauptgebot, Eine Untersuchung literarischer Einleitungsfragen zu Dtn. 5–11* (Analecta Biblica, 20), Rome: Pontifical Biblical Institute, 1963.

—— 'Der Bundesschluss im Land Moab', *BZ* NF 6 (1962), 32–56.

—— 'Darstellungskunst und Theologie in Dtn. 1, 6–3, 29', *Biblica* 41 (1960), 105–34.

LUCKENBILL, D. D., *The Annals of Sennacherib*, The Oriental Institute Publications, vol. 2, Chicago, 1924 (= *OIP*).

LUZATTO, S. D., *Commentary to the Pentateuch* (ed. P. Schlesinger), Tel-Aviv: The Dvir Co., Ltd., 1965 (Hebrew).

MALFROY, J., 'Sagesse et loi dans le Deutéronome', *VT* 15 (1965), 49–65.

MCCARTHY, D. J., *Treaty and Covenant* (Analecta Biblica 21), Rome: Pontifical Biblical Institute, 1963.

MEISSNER, B., *Babylonien und Assyrien* I–II, Heidelberg: C. Winter, 1920, 25.

MENDENHALL, G. E., 'Covenant Forms in Israelite Tradition', *BA* 17 (1954), 49–76.

MEYER, G., 'Zwei neue Kizzuwatna Verträge', *MIO* 1 (1953), 108–24.

MILGROM J., *Studies in Levitical Terminology* I, University of California Press, Berkeley and Los Angeles, 1970.

MONTGOMERY, J. A., *Kings* (ICC), Edinburgh: T. & T. Clark, 1951.

MORAN, W. L., 'The Ancient Near Eastern Background of the Love of God in Deuteronomy', *CBQ* 25 (1963), 77–87.

—— 'The End of the Unholy War and the Anti-Exodus', *Biblica* 44 (1963), 333–42.

—— 'A Note on the Treaty Terminology of the Sefire Stelas', *JNES* 22 (1963), 173–6.

MORENZ, S., *Ägyptische Religion* (Die Religionen der Menscheit, Bd. 8), Stuttgart: W. Kohlhammer, 1960.

MOWINCKEL, S., *Zur Komposition des Buches Jeremia*, Kristiania: J. Dybwad, 1914.

—— *Prophecy and Tradition*, Oslo: J. Dybwads, 1946.

MUFFS, Y., *Studies in the Aramaic Legal Papyri from Elephantine* (Studia et Documenta ad Iura Orientis Antiqui Pertinentia, 8), Leiden: J. Brill, 1969.

MUNN-RANKIN, J. M., 'Diplomacy in Western Asia in the Early Second Millenium B.C.,', *Iraq* 18 (1956), 68–110.

NIELSEN, E., *Oral Tradition* (Studies in Biblical Theology, no. 11), Chicago: A. R. Allenson, 1955.

—— *Shechem* (2nd edn.), Copenhagen: G. E. C. Gads, 1959.

NOTH, M., *Überlieferungsgeschichtliche Studien* (Schriften der Königsberger Gelehrten Gesellschaft, Geisteswissenschaftliche Klasse, 18 Jahr, Hft. 2), Halle (Saale): M. Niemeyer, 1943.

—— *Überlieferungsgeschichte des Pentateuchs*, Stuttgart: W. Kohlhammer, 1948.

—— *Das Buch Josua* (2nd edn., HAT), Tübingen: J. C. B. Mohr, 1953.

—— *Könige* (BK) Neukirchen-Vluyn: Neukirchener Verlag des Erziehungs-Vereins, Band IX/1–2, 1964–5.
—— *The Laws in the Pentateuch and Other Studies*, trans. D. R. Ap Thomas, Edinburgh, London: Oliver & Boyd, 1966.
NÖTSCHER, F., *'Das Angesicht Gottes Schauen' nach biblischer und babylonischer Auffassung*, Würzburg: C. J. Becker, 1924.

OESTERLEY, W. O. E., *The Wisdom of Egypt and the Old Testament*, London: Society for Promoting Christian Knowledge, 1927.
—— *The Book of Proverbs* (Westminster Commentaries), London: Methuen & Co. Ltd., 1929.
OPPENHEIM, A. L., *The Interpretation of Dreams in the Ancient Near East* (Transactions of the American Philosophical Society, N.S. v. 46, pt. 3), Philadelphia: American Philosophical Society, 1956.
ORMANN, G., 'Die Stilmittel im Deuteronomium', *Leo Baeck Festschrift* 1938, 39–53.
OTTEN, H., 'Neue Quellen zum Ausgang des Hethitischen Reiches', *MDOG* 94 (1963), 1–23.

PARKE, H. W., and WORMELL, D. E. W., *The Delphic Oracle, I–II*, Oxford: Basil Blackwell, 1956.
PAUL, S., *Studies in the Book of the Covenant in the Light of Cuneiform and Biblical Law, SVT* 18, Leiden: J. Brill, 1970.
PFEIFFER, R. H., *State Letters of Assyria* (American Oriental Series, v. 6), New Haven: American Oriental Society, 1935.
—— *Introduction to the Old Testament*, New York: Harpers, 1957.
PLÖGER, J. G., *Literarkritische, formgeschichtliche und stilkritische Untersuchungen zum Deuteronomium* (Bonner Biblische Beiträge, 26), Bonn, 1967.
POSENER, G., *Princes et Pays d'Asie et de Nubie*, Brussels: Fondation égyptologique reine Elisabeth, 1940.
POSTGATE, J. N., *Neo-Assyrian Royal Grants and Decrees*, Studia Pohl: Series Maior 1, Pontifical Biblical Institute, 1969.
PROCKSCH, O., *Das nordhebräische Sagenbuch, die Elohimquelle übersetzt und untersucht*, Leipzig: J. C. Hinrichs, 1906.

RANKIN, O. S., *Israel's Wisdom Literature* (2nd edn.), Edinburgh: T. & T. Clark, 1936.
REINER, E., *Šurpu, a Collection of Sumerian and Akkadian Incantations*, *AfO* Beiheft 11, 1958.
REVENTLOW, H. G., *Liturgie und Prophetisches Ich bei Jeremia*, Gütersloh: Gerd Mohn, 1963.
RINGGREN, H., *Sprüche* (ATD), Göttingen: Vandenhoeck & Ruprecht, 1962.
ROBERT, A., 'Les attaches littéraires bibliques de Prov. I–IX', *RB* 43 (1934), 42–68, 172–204, 374–84; 44 (1935), 344–65, 502–25.
ROST, L., *Die Überlieferung von der Thronnachfolge Davids*, Stuttgart: W. Kohlhammer, 1926.

ROWLEY, H. H., 'The Prophet Jeremiah and the Book of Deuteronomy', *Studies in O.T. prophecy presented to T. H. Robinson*, New York: Scribner, 1950, pp. 157–74.

RUDOLPH, W., *Esra und Nehemia samt 3. Esra* (HAT), Tübingen: J. C. B. Mohr, 1949.

—— *Chronikbücher* (HAT), Tübingen: J. C. B. Mohr, 1955.

—— *Jeremia* (2nd edn., HAT), Tübingen: J. C. B. Mohr, 1958.

SAGGS, H. W. F., 'Assyrian Warfare in the Sargonid Period', *Iraq* 25 (1963), 145–54.

ŠANDA, A., *Die Bücher der Könige*, 2 vols. (EH), Münster i. Westf.: Aschendorffsche Verlagsbuchhandlung, 1911–12.

SCHAEDER, H. H., *Esra der Schreiber* (Beiträge zur historischen Theologie, 5), Tübingen: J. C. B. Mohr, 1930.

SCHARFF, A., 'Der historische Abschnitt der Lehre fur König Merikarê', *Sitzungsberichte der Bayerischen Akademie der Wissenschaften*, Phil.-histor. Abteilung, Jahrgang 1936, Heft 8, pp. 5–64.

SCHMIDT, H., *Die Psalmen* (HAT), Tübingen: J. C. B. Mohr, 1934.

SCHORR, M., *Urkunden des altbabylonischen Zivil- und Prozessrechts* (Vorderasiatische Bibliothek, 5), Leipzig: J. C. Hinrichs, 1913.

SCOTT, R. B. Y., 'Solomon and the Beginnings of Wisdom in Israel', *SVT* 3 (1955), 262–79.

SEELIGMANN, I. L., 'Voraussetzungen der Midrashexegese', *SVT* 1 (1953), 150–81.

—— 'Aetiological Elements in Biblical Historiography', *Zion* 26 (1961), 114–69 (Hebrew with English Summary).

SETHE, K., *Die Ächtung feindlicher Fürsten, Völker und Dinge auf altägyptischen Tongefässcherben des Mittlern Reiches*, Berlin: Verlag des Akademie der Wissenschaften, 1926.

SKINNER, J., *Prophecy and Religion, Studies in the Life of Jeremiah*, Cambridge: Cambridge University Press, 1922.

—— *Genesis* (2nd edn., ICC), Edinburgh: T. & T. Clark, 1930.

SMITH, G. A., *Deuteronomy* (CB), Cambridge: Cambridge University Press, 1918.

SMITH, S., *The Statue of Idrimi*, London: British Institute of Archaeology in Ankara, 1949.

SOLLBERGER, E., *Le Système verbal dans les inscriptions 'royales' présargoniques de Lagaš*, Geneva: E. Droz, 1952.

—— *Corpus des inscriptions 'royales' présargoniques de Lagaš*, Geneva: E. Droz, 1956.

STAMM, J. J. and ANDREWS, M. E., *The Ten Commandments in Recent Research* (2nd edn., Studies in Biblical Theology, 2nd ser. no. 2), London: SCM Press, 1967.

STEIN, B., *Der Begriff 'Kebod Jahweh'*, Emsdetten i. Westf.: H. & J. Lechte, 1939.

STEINMETZER, F. X., *Die babylonischen Kudurru (Grenzsteine) als Urkundenform* (Görres-Gesellschaft. Studien zur Geschichte und Kultur des Altertums, Bd. 11, Hft. 4–5), Paderborn: F. Schöningh, 1922.

STEUERNAGEL, C., *Deuteronomium und Josua* (HKAT), Göttingen: Vandenhoeck & Ruprecht, 1900.
—— *Deuteronomium* (2nd edn., HKAT), Göttingen: Vandenhoeck & Ruprecht, 1923.
STRECK, M., *Assurbanipal I–III* (Vorderasiatische Bibliothek, 3), Leipzig: J. C. Hinrichs, 1916.
SZEMERÉNYI, O., 'Vertrag des Hethiterkönigs Tudḫalija IV mit Ištarmūwa von Amurru', *Acta Societatis Hungaricae Orientalis* 9 (1945), 113–29.

TALMON, S., 'Synonymous Readings in the Old Testament', *Scripta Hierosolymitana* 8 (1961), 335–83.
THOMPSON, R. C., *The Prisms of Esarhaddon and Ashurbanipal found at Nineveh, 1927–28*, London: The British Museum, 1931.
—— *The Epic of Gilgamish*, Oxford: Clarendon Press, 1930.
THUREAU-DANGIN, F., *Die sumerischen und akkadischen Königsinschriften* (Vorderasiatische Bibliothek, 1), Leipzig: J. C. Hinrichs, 1907 [= *SAK*].
—— *Rituels accadiens*, Paris: E. Leroux, 1921.
—— 'Un acte de donation de Marduk-zākir-šumi', *RA* 16 (1919), 117–56.
The Torah—The five books of Moses, Philadelphia: The Jewish Publication Society, 1962.
TSEVAT, M., 'Studies in the Book of Samuel, I', *HUCA* 32 (1961), 191–216.
—— 'Studies in the Book of Samuel, III', *HUCA* 34 (1963), 71–82.
TUR-SINAI (TORCZYNER), N. H., משלי שלמה, Tel-Aviv: Debir, 1947.
—— *The Language and the Book*, I–III, Jerusalem: The Bialik Institute, 1948–55 (Hebrew).
—— *The Book of Job*, Jerusalem: Kiryath Sepher, 1957.

VOLTEN, A., *Studien zum Weisheitsbuch des Anii* (Danske Vid. Selskab. 23, 3), København: Levin & Munksgaard, 1937.
VOLZ, P., *Das Neujahrsfest Jahwes*, Tübingen: J. C. B. Mohr, 1912.
—— *Jeremia* (2nd edn., KAT), Leipzig: A. Deichert, 1922.
VON RAD, G., *Das Gottesvolk im Deuteronomium* (Beiträge zur Wissenschaft vom Alten und Neuen Testament, 3 Folge, Hft. 11), Stuttgart: W. Kohlhammer, 1929.
—— *Der heilige Krieg im Alten Israel*, Zurich: Zwingli-Verlag, 1951.
—— *Studies in Deuteronomy* (Studies in Biblical Theology no. 9), trans. D. Stalker, London: SCM Press, 1953.
—— *Genesis* (ATD), Göttingen: Vandenhoeck & Ruprecht, 1958.
—— *Theologie des Alten Testaments* (2 vols.), Munich: C. Kaiser, 1957–60.
—— *Deuteronomium* (ATD), Göttingen: Vandenhoeck & Ruprecht, 1964.
—— *The Problem of the Hexateuch and Other Essays*, trans. E. W. Dicken, Edinburgh, London: Oliver & Boyd, 1966.
VON SCHULER, E., *Hethitische Dienstanweisungen*, *AfO*, Beiheft 10, 1957.
—— 'Die Würdenträgereide des Arnuwanda', *Orientalia* 25 1956), 209–40.
—— *Die Kaskäer, Ein Beitrag zur Ethnographie des alten Kleinasien* (Erganzungsbände zu *ZA* NF 4 (1965).
VON SODEN, W., *Herrscher im alten Orient*, Berlin: Springer, 1954.

WATERMAN, L., *Royal Correspondence of the Assyrian Empire* (4 vols.), Ann Arbor: University of Michigan Press, 1930–6 [= *RCAE*].

WEIDNER, E. F., *Politische Dokumente aus Kleinasien, Die Staatsverträge in akkadischer Sprache aus dem Archiv von Boghazköi* (*BoSt*, 8–9), Leipzig: J. C. Hinrichs, 1923.

—— 'Der Staatsvertrag Aššurniraris VI von Assyrien mit Mati'ilu von Bit Agusi', *AfO* 8 (1932–3), 17–27.

—— 'Der Vertrag Šamši-Adads V mit Marduk-zākir-šumi I', *AfO* 8 (1932–3), 27–9.

—— 'Der Vertrag Asarhaddons mit Ba'al von Tyrus', *AfO* 8 (1932–3), 29–34.

—— *Die Inschriften Tukulti-Nimurtas I und seiner Nachfolger*, *AfO* Beiheft 12, Graz 1959.

—— 'Hochverrat gegen Nebukadnezar II', *AfO* 17 (1954–6), 1–9.

—— 'Hof- und Harems-Erlasse assyrischer Könige aus dem 2 Jahrtausend v. Chr.', *AfO* 17 (1954–6), 257–93.

WEINFELD, M., 'The awakening of national consciousness in Israel in the seventh century B.C.,' *'Oz le-David, Biblical Essays in honor of D. Ben-Gurion*, Jerusalem: Kiryath Sepher, 1964, pp. 396–420 (Hebrew).

—— 'Cult Centralization in Israel in the Light of a neo-Babylonian Analogy', *JNES* 23 (1964), 202–12.

—— 'The Period of the Conquest and of the Judges as Seen by the Earlier and the Later sources', *VT* 17 (1967), 93–113.

—— 'The Covenant of Grant in the Old Testament and in the Ancient Near East', *JAOS* 90 (1970), 184–203.

—— 'God the Creator in Gen. 1 and in the Prophecy of Second Isaiah', *Tarbiz* 37 (1968), 105–32.

WEISBERG, D. B., *Guild Structure and Political Allegiance in Early Achaemenid Mesopotamia*, New Haven: Yale University Press. 1967.

WEISER, A., *I Samuel 7–12*, *FRLANT* 81 (1962).

WEISS, M., *The Bible and Modern Literary Theory*, Jerusalem: Bialik Institute 1962 (Hebrew).

WELCH, A. C., *Jeremiah, his Time and his Work*, London: Oxford University Press, 1928.

WELLHAUSEN, J., *Die Composition des Hexateuchs und der historischen Bücher des Alten Testaments* (3rd edn.), Berlin: Georg Reimer, 1899.

—— *Prolegomena to the History of Ancient Israel*, transl. by Black–Menzies, New York: The Meridian Library, 1957.

WIDENGREN, G., *Sakrales Königtum im A.T. und im Judentum*, Stuttgart: W. Kohlhammer, 1955.

WISEMAN, D. J., 'Abban and Alalah', *JCS* 12 (1958), 124–9.

—— *The Alalakh Tablets*, Occasional Publications of the British Institute of Archaeology at Ankara 2, London 1953.

—— *The Vassal Treaties of Esarhaddon*, *Iraq* 20 (1958), 1–99.

WRIGHT, G. E., 'The Temple in Palestine–Syria', *BA* 7 (1944), 66–77.

—— 'The Levites in Deuteronomy', *VT* 4 (1954), 325–30.

—— *Shechem, the Biography of a Biblical City*, New York: McGraw Hill, 1965.

WÜRTHWEIN, E., *Der ʿam haʾareṣ im Alten Testament*, Stuttgart: W. Kohlhammer, 1936.

ŽÁBA, Z., *Les Maximes de Ptaḥḥotep, Texte, Traduction et Commentaire*, Éd. de l'Acad. Tchécoslovaque des Sciences, Prague, 1956.

ZIMMERLI, W., 'Zur Struktur der alttestamentlichen Weisheit', *ZAW* 51 (1933), 177–204.

—— *Der Prediger* (ATD), Göttingen: Vandenhoeck & Ruprecht, 1967.

ADDENDA

p. 87 n. 2: On the whole problem see my article in *Lešonenu* 36 (1971).

p. 91 n. 1: See my article in *Lešonenu* 36 (1971), 5 f.

p. 102 n. 11: Cf. 'Supplementary Notes' to that article (forthcoming issue).

p. 103: On covenantal sacrifices in Greece see P. Stengel, *Die Griechischen Kultusaltertümer*, 1920, 119 n. 17; 137.

p. 148 n. 3: That the prologue with the code together were circulating in the Old Babylonian period has been clearly shown by the tablet published by J. Nougayrol, *RA* 45 (1951), 67 ff. Cf. J. J. Finkelstein, ibid. (Addenda), p. 48.

p. 153 n. 1: For other connections between the *mīšarum*/*andurārum* and *shemiṭṭa* and *Jôbel*, see my article in *Beth-Mikra* 44/1 (1970), 15–16 (Hebrew).

p. 153, in reference to 2 Sam. 8: 15: The verse should be translated: 'And David was enthroned over all Israel and David became the establisher of justice for all his people.' 'ויהי with the particip. expresses at once origination and continuance' (so S. R. Driver, *Notes on the Hebrew Text of Samuel* on 1 Sam. 18: 9), compare Gen. 4: 2 ('Abel became a shepherd'), 4: 17, 21: 20b; Judg. 16: 21, 19: 1; 1 Sam. 18: 9; 2 Kgs. 15: 5. For עשה (משפט וצדקה) in the sense of 'establishing' and not 'doing' or 'executing' cf. A. B. Ehrlich, *Randglossen* on Jer. 9: 23.

p. 163 n. 3: The observance of the law of God along with the observance of the law of the king appears in Ezra's commission (7: 26).

p. 175 n. 5: Cf. also A. Laurentin, *Biblica* 45 (1964), 168–97, 413–32.

p. 193 n. 2: Cf. most recently S. Dean McBride, 'The Deuteronomic Name Theology', Dissertation of Harvard University 1969, and the discussion there on the relationship of Hebrew שָׁכֵן to Akkadian *šakānu*.

p. 231 in reference to Ex. 12: 48: The perfect consecutive וְעָשָׂה expresses a wish, cf. P. P. Joüon, *Grammaire de L'Hébreu Biblique*², 1947, § 119, w (p. 334) '"si un étranger habite avec toi *et veut faire* ועשה la pâque" (très clairement)'.

p. 234: For the elders in ancient Israel cf. my article 'Elder' in the *Encyclopaedia Judaica*.

p. 245 n. 5: See also R. O. Faulkner, 'The Installation of the Vizier', *JEA* 41 (1955), 22: 3, 12.

p. 259 n. 3: For an evaluation of this tradition of Josephus, cf. H. J. Katzenstein, *Beth-Mikra* 28 (1966), 28 ff. (Hebrew).

p. 262 n. 3: For the Greek treaty formulae and their oriental origin see my forthcoming article in *Lešonenu*.

p. 305 n. 2: Cf. Z. Žába, *Ptaḥḥotep*, 71: 49, 100: 534–7, 101: 546 f., 102: 575.

p. 340 no. 3: add 3a השחית/הרע מאבות/מכל . . . אשר לפניו *Dtr*: Judg. 2: 19; 1 Kgs. 16: 25, 30; 2 Kgs. 21: 11. *Jer. C*: 16: 12.

p. 366 n. 1: Cf. most recently H. L. Ginsberg, 'Hosea', *Encyclopaedia Judaica*.

GLOSSARIES

I. HEBREW

ואמר הדור האחרון/ ואמרו כל הגויים 115
אמרת אֱלוֹהַ 261
אמת/באמת 12, 77, 84, 93, 252–3, 332, 334
אנף/התאנף 345
אנשי המלחמה 48
אנשי קדש 228, 328
אסם 310
אסף/האסף 139, 290, 353
אף ואזן 292
אף וחמה 348
ארבה 124
ארבעים (יכנו) 181
ארון הברית 65
ארון העֵדֻת 65
ארון עצי שטים 181
ארור 277
ארך/האריך ימים 5, 257, 308–9, 345
האריך ימים על הממלכה 5
(ה)ארץ 133, 214, 313, 340, 341–3, 346, 348, 358
ארר 241
אֵש 192, 322, 348
אָשָׁם 182
אֲשֵׁרוֹת 320
אשת חיקך 98

בא (אל הארץ) 342
בא בשערים 353
בדל/הבדיל 228
בהל 270
בהמה 6, 139
בהמת הארץ 139, 349
בחר 4, 5, 23, 36, 42–3, 228, 324, 327, 354
בחר בנו מכל העמים ונתן לנו תורתו 43
הבוחר בעמו ישראל באהבה 43
בטח (על שקר) 6
בין/נבון 244, 258
בית/הבית (בית ה׳) 4, 299, 325, 354
(בקרב) ביתי 76
בית זבל 198
בית עבדים 326
בכור 112
בכל מקום אשר תראה 5
בְּכַר 215
בלה 172, 358
בלהות 113
בליעל 93
במה/במות 5–6, 323–4, 326, 366
בן אמך 98
בן/בנים 11, 48, 69, 98, 305, 368
(היה לו) לבן 79, 80
בנה 193, 323, 325
בני חיל 48
היה לבן חיל 11
בנים לה׳ 69
בעל(ים) 6, 320–3
בער/הבעיר 18, 242, 351, 355–6
בצקה 358
בצר לך/להם 369
בְּצָרוֹת 358
בקש נפש 7
בקש פני ה׳ 358
ברא 181
ברזל 327
ברית 62, 65, 76, 77, 79, 86, 87, 111, 115, 130, 330, 336, 338, 340, 341, 357, 367
ברית ואָלָה 63, 67
ברית כהונת עולם 76
ברית עולם 80
ברית(י) שלום 76
בֵּרַךְ 312, 345
ברכה 310, 310–13
בשר 270–1
בשר בנים ובנות 349
בשת 31, 323

גאון יעקב 328
גאל 37, 326

גבה(ה) 8, 322, 366
גבול 265, 277
גבול עולם 265
גבור 48, 331
גבורי חיל 48
גבעה/גבעות 8, 322, 326
גג/גגות 322
גדול (ים)/ גדלות 34, 40–1, 329, 330–1, 343, 358
גדופה 349
גדל 2, 37, 206
גדלה וגבורה 39
גדל שם 80
גוזל 73
גוי/גויים 112, 163, 228, 323, 341, 342–3, 347
גוי קדוש 228, 328
גלה אזן 99
גלול(ים) 125, 320, 323
גלים 354
גלל/גל 323
גפי מרומי קרת 176
גר 55, 229–30, 277, 356
גרב 117
גרע 261
גרש 47, 342, 347

דבק 8, 83, 333, 341
דֶּבֶר 6, 124, 125
דִּבֵּר 302, 352, 353
דִּבֵּר דָּבָר 91
דָּבָר (divine word) 15, 16, 21–2, 36(g), 77, 98, 125, 130, 350
דבר (ים) (commandments) 65, 152, 261, 304, 336
דִּבֵּר סָרָה 99
דִּבֵּר שקר 6
דגי הים 133
דוד עבדי/עבדו 7, 354
דור אחרון 115
(ל) דור/דרתם 78
דל(ים) 155, 310
דמות 182, 199
דֹּמֶן 139, 349

דם נקי/נקיים 277, 356
דן דין 155
דרור 153
דרך/דרכים 7, 8, 257, 277, 299, 304, 332–4, 339, 341, 351, 352, 354
דרש את ה׳ 334, 369

הביא חרב 354
הבל 320, 232–42
הגד 235, 258
הגד תגידנו/ונגידנו 94–6, 97
(ו)הגית בו 5, 280
(ובתורתו) יהגה 280
הורה תורה 163
החזיק 286
היטב 2
היום 174, 341, 356, 357
היום הזה 174, 341
הכה תכה 99, 133
הכיר פנים 245, 273
הכעים 17–18, 324, 340–1
הלך אחר 5, 77, 83, 247, 320–1, 332, 334
הלך אחרי הגלולים/ההבל/הבעל(ים))/בעל פעור 320
הלך בדרך 8, 23, 36, 299, 332–3, 354
הלך בחטאת 340
הלך בשלום ובמישור 76
הלך בתורת ה׳ 334
הלך ועבד/עשה/קטר 5–6, 320–1
הלך לפני ה׳ 76, 77, 334
הלך/התהלך בתום 76
התהלך 299
התהלך לפני ה׳/את ה׳ 76, 77, 334
הַמִּיּוֹת 177
הסגיר 272
הסיג גבול 265
הסך (נסך) 6, 322

העביר (למֹלֶך) 322
העתיק 161
הפך 111, 142
הפר ברית 115
הצדיק 36(h)
הציב יד 193
הקהיל 65
הקטיר 326
הקים 77, 130, 327
הקניא 324
הרג (תהרגנו) 94, 95
הקרה 236
הר(ים) 322, 366
הרימתיך מעם/ מעפר 354
הריק חרב 354
הר העברים 153
הר ציון 196
הרשיע 36(h)
(ו)השיגוך 109
השכיל 346
השכם (ודבד) 7, 352
השמיד 2
השתחוה 6, 321
התנפל 330

זבח 212
זִבַּח וקטר 326, 366
זְבֻל 195, 198
זולל וסבא 303
זונה/זונות 126, 132
זכר 41–2, 76, 77, 222, 327
זכר ברית 77, 330
זכרון 222, 300–1
זכר ונקבה 181
זכר ועשה 336
זללי בשר 303
זנה 82, 83
זעוה 348, 349
זעוה ובז 349
זקנים 234
זר 131
זֵרָה 114
זרוע 314
זרע נטויה 39, 41, 329, 330
זֶרַע 76, 78, 181, 310, 322
(ל)זרעו אחריו/ לזרעך אחריך 76, 78, 181
(ל)זרעך עד עולם 78
זרק 118, 182
זרק דם 182

חוח 110
חוס 2
חוצות 6, 139, 353
חוצות ירושלם 353
חוק/חוקים 65, 150, 336–8
חוקה/חוקות 336–8
חקות ומשפטים 337
חזיר 132
חֲזַק 343
חזק/התחזק/נתחזק 11, 46
חֲזָקָה 329
חֹזֶק יד 329
חטא/החטיא 17, 18, 270–1, 340
חטא/חטאת 17, 51, 111, 270, 271–2, 304, 337, 340, 356
חטאת ירבעם 17
חיה (רעה)/חית הארץ 124, 139
חַיָּה 299, 345
חיים 76, 279, 289, 308–9, 345, 346, 358
(כל ימי) חייו 280, 333
חיק 98, 134
חכם/חכמים 158, 160, 162, 168, 244, 245, 254
חכמה 181
חכמים ונבנים וידעים 244
חכם לב 254
חל/חלק יזרעאל 351
חלוצים 48
חֹלֶם חֲלוֹם 98
חלף עבדתם 78
חֶלְקָה 153
חֵמָה 348
חֲמֹר 110
חנן 310
חסד 39, 77, 252, 330

מות יומת 147, 239
וימתו לפני ה׳ 192
מזבח/מזבחות 182, 192, 366
מזוזות 299
מחה 347
מחנה 48
מחקק 153
מחשבה 105
מטה משפט 277
מטר 36(h)
מי כמוכה 43
מישור 76, 155, 156
מישרים 156
מכון 326
מכון שבתך 35, 195
מַכּוֹת 140
מָכַר 282, 341
מָלֵא 145
מְלֵא (בתיהם טוב)/ אסם 281, 310
מִלֵּא אחר ה׳ 78, 337
מִלֵּא דבר ה׳ 350
(בתים) מְלֵאִים (כל טוב) 281
מלאך 34
מַלְוֶה 310
(ארץ) מלחה 111
מלחמה 48, 164
מלך/מלכות 4, 43, 84, 163
מלכה ושריה בגוים אין תורה 163
מלמד הבקר 303
מלמדי מלחמה 164
ממלכת כהנים 228
ממלכה/ממלכות 152, 348, 355
(שמים) ממעל 331
מנוחה 343
מנחה 182
מנקיות 191
מסות 330
מסיג גבול 277
מסר ביד (השטן) 95
מעון קדשך 198, 326
מעון תנים 142, 354
מעלליהם 7, 352
מעשה ידים/ידי אדם 312, 324, 345, 366
מעשה ה׳ 329
מעשה חרשים 367
מעתה ועד עולם 114
מצא את ה׳ 369
נמצא 286
מצבה/מצבות 366
מצוה/מצות 77, 318, 334, 336–8
מצור ומצוק 113, 127–8, 349
מצרים 326, 327, 341, 369
(ה)מקום 4–5, 236, 324–5, 326
מקרא קדש 186
מקלה 277
מרה/המרה 303–4, 339, 341
מרום 196
משחית 200
משח לנגיד 355
משכן העדות 388
מָשָׁל 348
משלח יד 311, 345, 346
מְשַׁמָּה 349
משפטים צדיקים 150–1
משפט וצדקה/ צדקה ומשפט 91, 153, 154, 155
משפטים 65, 91, 150–3, 155, 235, 338, 245, 273, 336–8
משתין בקיר 252
מֵת 351
(הארץ) מתחת 331

נִבָּא 6, 145
נִבָּא שקר 6
נְבוֹ 153
נבון(ים) 244
נביא(ים) 6, 7, 98, 168, 351
נבלה 139, 226–30, 289, 349
נגיד 355
נדח/הדח 24, 304, 321, 341, 348
נדר 212, 270
נוד/התנודד 133, 140
נוה תנים 142, 354

עין הארץ	124
לעיניך	122, 278
(ב)עיני ה׳	8, 335, 339
(ה)עיר	4, 140, 324, 325, 351
עלה	182, 192, 212, 322
עלה/העלה	48, 124, 341
עלה על לב	353
עלילות (דברים)	292
עליון	152
עם/עמים	228, 242, 290, 322, 327, 328, 343, 347, 349, 354
היה לעם	80, 82, 152
עם הארץ	55, 87, 88, 90
עם המלחמה	48
עם יהודה	88, 90
עם קדוש	228
עמד בפני	334
עמד/העמיד	350
עמד לפני ה׳	77
עמוד ענן	202
עמי הארץ	358
עמיר	139
עִנָּה	286, 289
עָנָה	84, 369
עָנִי	55
ענוי (ארץ)	314
עפר	354
עצה	106
עץ ואבן	39, 324, 367
עצום	343
עצור ועזוב	132, 352
עצי שטים	181
עץ (רענן)	8, 322, 366
עצר שמים	36(h)
עקרב	172
ערץ	344
עֹרָה	136
ערוד	121
ערי יהודה	6, 353
ערים	111, 358
עֵרֶךְ	182, 257
עֹרֶף	353
עָשׁ	172
עשב	124
עשה דבר	292
עשה הטוב/הרע	335, 339, 341
עשה הישר	335, 354
עשה חסד לאלפים	39
עשה (לו לעם)	327
עשה משפט וצדקה	153, 155
עשה שמים וארץ	331
עשר וכבוד	257
עשתרות	6, 311, 320
עשתרות צאנך	311, 345
(ו)עתה	175, 176
פגר(ים)	125, 139
פדה	326
(פה) פיו	350
פי חרב	99
(פיץ) הפיץ	347, 348
פלא/נפלא	234, 258, 259
פָּנָה	83, 304, 346, 353
פנים	245, 273, 353
פנים/פניו	34, 187, 192, 210
פסגה	153
פסלים	324
פקד על	6
פקחים	245
פרי	114, 345
פרי אדמה	345
פרי בטן	345
פשׁתָה	136
פשע	138, 367
פתה	277, 278, 304
פתה לב	277
פֶּתַח	299
פתיל (תכלת)	302
צאת השנה	219
צבא השמים	321
ה׳ צבאות	6
צדיק(ים)	36(h), 91, 150, 155
צדק/צדקה	77, 91, 153, 155, 252–3, 273, 334
צוה	261, 353, 356–7
צוה ברכה	345
צוה נגיד	355
צוק	128

ציון 142, 196
ציץ 110
צִיצִת 301–2
צלם (אלהים) 199
בצלמנו כדמותנו 199
צלמות 113
צלע 112
צלצל 124
תצלנה (אזניו) 351
צמאון 172
צמח צדיק/צדקה 91, 155
צנוק 128
צעדות 86
צפונה 182
צפור כנף 181
צַר 113
צָר 34
צרה וצוקה 369

קבר/נקבר 139, 353
קדוש(ים) 228, 328
קדח כאש 348
קדמונים 114
קדש/הקדיש/התקדש 4, 186, 193, 198, 215, 228, 236
קדשך 326
קחל 174
קול ה׳ 332, 337
קול רחים ואור נר 141
קום/הקים 77, 104, 130, 350
יקומו מאחריכם 105
קומך 300
קוצים 111
(מ)קטן עד גדול 101
קטר 321–2, 326, 366
קלה 277, 278
קלון 278
ונקלה אחיך לעיניך 278
קלל 109, 239, 241, 277
קללה 51, 348
קללת אלהים 51
קלסה 349
קמוש 110
קַנָּא 81
קַנּוֹא 81
קִנְאָ 324

קצה השמים/הארץ 358
קצף 348
קרא 177, 193, 369
וקרא בו כל ימי חייו 280
קֶרֶב 2
קרה/הקרה 236
קרע (ממלכה) 355
קרת 176
(ה)קשה ערף 341
קשות הנסך 191
קשר 299, 301
קשת 136
קשת רמיה 136

ראה (טוב) 299
ראה/ידע 176, 207, 329, 358
ראה/נראה/הראה כבוד ה׳ 202, 204
ראה (עינים) 357
ראש (poison) 91, 143
ראש הפסגה 153
ראשונים 265, 267
ראשית תבואתה 31
רב/רבים 343
רבץ 109
רגל 358
רדף 109, 273
רדף צדקה 273
רוה/הרוה 312
רוח חכמה 181
רום לבב 304, 367–8
רוע (לבב) 304
רחים 141
רחץ 132
רחק/רחקה 36(h), 258, 259, 260
ריב 70, 235
ריח ניחח 192, 210, 366
רכב 134, 281, 355
רמש 181
רנה 330
רנן 205
רעך אשר כנפשך 98 n.
רֵעַ 98, 131, 265, 277
רֹעַ 352

(הָ)רָע 8, 18, 130, 242, 304, 339, 341, 355, 356
(הַ)רָעָה 7, 271, 350, 351
רענן 8, 229, 322, 366
רשע 36(h), 314

שאל בדבר האלהים 98 n.
שאל 40, 92, 98, 100
שאל לו בה׳ 100 n.
(שאר) השאיר 344
שבטיכם 101, 173
שָׁבַע 2, 310, 367–8
(שבע) נִשְׁבַּע 62, 84
שָׁבֻעוֹת 219
(שבת) השבית 353
שבתון 186
שגה 278
משגה 277–8
שגר אלפיך 345
שָׂדֶה 139, 349, 351
שֵׁדִים 326
שוב אל ה׳ 334–5, 369
שוב/השיב מצרימה 369
שוב/שובב/השיב 304, 351, 357
שוט/שוטט 125
שופט(ים) 120, 173, 234
שחט 214
שחין 117, 118, 121
שחת/השחית 111, 340
שחר את ה׳ 369
שִׂיד 111
(שִׂיח) תשׂיחך 299
שִׂים משפט 152, 153, 155
שִׂים שֵׁם 193, 325
שִׂישׂ 346
שכב 299
שכח ברית ה׳ 357, 367–8
שָׁכַן 196
שָׁכַן (ארץ) 313
שִׁכֵּן (שם) 4, 193, 325
שלום 76, 105–6, 145
שלח 352, 353
שַׁלַּח (מעל פני) 347
שִׁלַּח חרב 354

שָׁלַח יד 293
תְּשַׁלְּחנו 283
(שלך) השליך 347
שלל 7
שָׁלֵם 269, 335
שִׁלֵּם 317
שִׁלֵּם נדר 212, 270
שֵׁם 80, 328, 347, 349
שם ה׳ 4, 193, 325, 331, 333
(שמד) השמיד 346, 347
שַׁמָּה 140, 348, 349
שמח 311, 346
שמחה 7, 353
שמים 39, 195, 321, 326, 331, 347, 349, 358
שמים וארץ 39, 331, 349
שמלה/שלמה 358
שׂמם 113
שׂם על לב 303
שְׁמָמָה 349, 354
(תפלת) שמנה עשרה 44
שמע 92, 97, 245, 246
שְׁמַע/שִׁמְעוּ 176, 304, 355
שמע בקול ה׳ 12, 75, 84, 332, 337
שמע וירא 356
שמע מצות 337
שמע משפט 246
שמע קול ה׳ 38
שמר/השמר 76, 222, 357
שמר ברית 38, 336
שמר דרך ה׳ 337
שמר ועשה/לעשות 261, 336
שמר חסד 330
שמר מצוה 77, 318, 334, 336–7, 274
שמר משמרת 75–6, 335
שמר נפש 309
שמר תורה 336
שֶׁמֶשׁ 321
(ל)שׂנאיו 318
שְׁנִינָה 348
שני תולעת 73

II. DEUTERONOMIC PHRASEOLOGY

אשר אתה/אתם עבר(ים) שמה לרשתה	342
אשר ה׳ אלהיך נתן לך נחלה לרשתה	341
אשר כל שמעה/שמעיו תצלנה (שתי) אזניו	282, 351
אשר לא ידעת(ם) ידעו(ם)	28, 116, 122, 357
אשר לא צויתי ולא עלתה על לבי	353
אשר נתת . . . לאבתינו/לאבתם	36(d)
אשר ראו עיניך	357
אתה האלהים לבדך	39, 331
אתה עשית את השמים ואת הארץ	39, 331
אתות ומופתים	33, 37, 39–41, 330
אתם ראיתם	173, 207
בחר (בדוד)	5, 36, 354
בחר (בישראל)	42–3, 327
בחר בעיר (ירושלם)	23, 36, 324
בית עבדים	326
בנה בית לשם ה׳	36(a), 193, 194, 325
בנה במות תפת/בעל	323
בער דם נקי	356
בער/הבעיר אחרי	18, 351
(ו)בערת הרע מקרבך/מישראל	242, 355
ברית וחוקות	338
ברך יברכך ה׳ אלהיך	345
ברך מעשה ידים/משלוח יד	312, 345
ברך פרי בטנך ופרי אדמתך	345
(האל) הגדול הגבור (והנורא)	40–1, 331
גדלות ונוראות	37–8, 41, 329
גדלך, ידך החזקה	37, 329
(ה)גויים האלה/ההם	343
גויים (גדולים) רבים ועצומים	49, 343
גלה כנף אביו	277
גלולים	323
גלים מעון תנים	354
גר יתום ואלמנה	277, 356
דבק בגויים	341
דבק בה׳	8, 83, 333
דבר בפיו ובידו מלא	36, 350
(שלח) דבר וצוה	353
דברי התורה (הזאת)	65, 336
(ל)דמן על פני השדה/האדמה	139, 349
דרך דוד (אביו)	334
דרך החיים ודרך המות	346
האביד שם מתחת השמים	347
הבאים בשערים האלה	7, 353
הבל/תהו	323–4
הבמות לא סרו	326
הדיח מן הדרך/מעל ה׳	341, cf. 304
הוריש גויים	342
החטיא את הארץ/ישראל/יהודה	340
(לא) הטה אזן	352
הטה לב(ב) אחרי אלהים אחרים	321
היה בך חטא	270, 356
היה ה׳ לאלהים... היה לו לעם	38, 152, 327
היה לזועה לכל ממלכות הארץ	348
היה למשל ולשנינה	348
היה לשמה, שרקה, חרבה, קללה, אלה, משל ושנינה בכל העמים	348–9
היה שמו שם	36(a), 193–4, 235
היטיבו דרכיכם ומעלליכם	7, 352
הכלבים יאכלו את איזבל	351
הכעיס את ה׳	17–18, 340–1

הכרית ישראל מעל פני האדמה	346
(ו)הכרתי . . . משתין בקיר עצור ועזוב בישראל	352
הלך אחרי ה׳	77, 274, 332, 334
הלך בדרכי ה׳/בדרכיו	8, 23, 332–3
הלך בכל דרך דוד (אביו)	354
הלך בכל הדרך/בכל דרכיו	36, 333
הלך לפני ה׳ בתום לבב ובישר/בכל לב/באמת ובצדקה	36, 77, 334
הלך בחטאת/אחרי חטאת	340
הלך בתורת ה׳	334
הלך אחרי אלהים אחרים	5–6, 83, 320
הלך אחרי אלהים אחרים והשתחוה	5–6, 321
הלך, עבד אלהים אחרים והשתחוה	5–6, 321
הלך, עשה אלהים אחרים	321
הלך ועבד אלהים אחרים/הלך אחרי אלהים אחרים ועבד (אתם)	320
הלך, קטר ועבד לאלהים אחרים	321
הלד בשרירות לב/אחר שרירות לב	105, 340
המקום אשר יבחר	4, 324
המת . . . בעיר יאכלו הכלבים והמת בשדה יאכלו עוף השמים	17, 131, 351
המיס לב	344
המרה את ה׳	341
הניח מכל אויב מסביב	343
הנני/הנה אנכי מביא רעה על	18, 24, 28, 350
הסיר מעל פני ה׳	347
הסך נסכים לאלהים אחרים	6, 322
העביר בן ובת באש	322
העיר (ירושלים) אשר בחר	23, 324
הפיץ בעמים/בגויים	347
הקדיש בית לשם ה׳	4, 193, 325
הקים דבר ה׳	36(g), 77, 350
הקים לו לעם	327
הקשה עורף	341
הרימתיך מן העם/מן העפר	354
(לא) השאיר (כל) נשמה	51, 344
(לא) השאיר שריד	51, 344
השחית	340
השיב אל לב	36, 42, 357
השכיל בכל אשר עשה	346
השכם ודבר/ושלח/ולמד	7, 352
השמיד מהר	347
השמיד מעל פני האדמה	346
השמר(ו) בנפשך/בנפשתיכם	357
השמר לך פן תשכח את ה׳/ברית ה׳	357
השתחוה לאלהים אחרים ועבד (אתם)	321
השתחוה לשמש לירח ולכוכבים/לכל צבא השמים	321
התאנף	346
התמכר לעשות הרע (בעיני ה׳)	18, 341
התנפל לפני ה׳	330
זִבַּח (וְקִטֵּר) בבמות	5, 6, 326, 366
זכור תזכור	41, 42
(ו)זכרת כי עבד היית בארץ מצרים	327
חזק ואמץ	5, 45, 49, 343

(לא) חיה כל נשמה 344
חיה/חיים 298, 308–9, 345
חקים מצות ומשפטים 23, 36, 336–8
(ה)חקים והמשפטים התורה והמצוה 338
חקים ברית ועדות 338
חשק באבתיך 328

טוב/ייטב לך 299, 309, 345–6

יד חזקה וזרע נטויה 33–4, 36–7, 41, 329
ידע מעשה ה׳ הגדול אשר עשה 14, 329
ידע/לדעת כי ה׳ הוא האלהים 331
וידעת עם לבבך 357
וידעת(ם) היום 42, 357
ירא את ה׳ 12, 83, 274, 332–3, 335
ירא אלהים אחרים 322
ירא את ה׳ כל הימים/ימי חייך 36(e), 333
יְרֻשָּׁה 342
ירש ארץ 342
ישב על כסא דוד/ ישב לדוד על כסאו 7, 355
ישב על כסא ישראל 25, 36(b), 355
ישרת לב 77

כונן לו לעם 38, 327
כור הברזל 36(c), 327
כח גדול וזרע נטויה 39, 329
כיום הזה 299, 350
כלה מהר 347
כלה מעל האדמה 346
כל הימים אשר אתם/הם חיים על האדמה 36(h), 358
כל הימים/ימי חייך 333
(ב)כל לב(ב) (ובכל נפש) 12, 17, 36(e), 77, 332, 334–5, 369
(ב)כל נפש 36(e), 334
כמוהו לא היה ואחריו לא יקום 358
כנע מפני ה׳ 24, 251
(ה)כתוב בספר התורה 107, 109, 336

לב לדעת 357
לב ליראה את ה׳ 335
לב שלם 77, 335
למד ליראה את ה׳ 332
לקח מוסר 6, 352
לא השאיר (כל) נשמה 51, 344
לא השאיר שריד 51, 344
לא יאספו ולא יקברו/ולא יספדו להם 139, 353
לא יוסיפו לעשות כדבר הרע הזה 356
לא יכרת לדוד איש (מלפני, ישב) מעל כסא ישראל 5, 36(b), 335
לא יעמוד איש בפניך 344
לא יתיצב איש בפניך 46, 344
לא/אל תירא ולא תחת 45, 50, 344
לא נותר כל נשמה 344
לא תערץ/תערצו 45, 51, 344
לא תסיג גבול רעך אשר גבלו ראשונים 265
לא תסיפו על הדבר . . . ולא תגרעו ממנו 261
למען דוד עבדי/ עבדו 17, 23, 354
למען ידעון/דעת כל עמי הארץ 358

(ה)מדבר הגדול והנורא 358
מביאי(ם) תודה בית ה׳ 354
מורא גדל/ מוראים גדולים 33–7, 38, 330
מחה שם מתחת השמים 25, 347

מכון שבתך . . . השמים	326
מעון קדשך השמים	326
מקום שבתך . . . השמים	326
מלא דם נקי(ים)	28, 356
מלא אחר ה׳	337
מלא דבר ה׳	350
מן היום אשר יצאו ממצרים ועד היום הזה	341
ממלכות הארץ	39
מנוחה (ונחלה)	36(d), 343
(ה)מסות (הגדולות)	37, 41, 330
מעשה חרש (עץ ואבן)	324, 367
מעשה ידים/ידי אדם	39, 277, 324, 367
מעשה ה׳ הגדול	14, 42, 329
מעשיך וגבורתיך	37
המצוה הזאת	338
(ה)מצוה והתורה	338
מצות משפטים וחקות	338
מצות חקים ומשפטים	338
מצות עדות וחוקים	338
(ב) מצור ובמצוק (אשר יציק לך)	28, 349
נטש מעל פני ה׳	347
נתש מעל האדמה	17, 346
נדח/הדיח שמה	348
נצתה חמה	348
נתך אף וחמה	348
נבלת . . . למאכל לעוף השמים ולבהמת הארץ	28, 139, 349
נכרי . . . בא מארץ רחקה	36
ניר לדוד	23, 354
נתן נגיד על עמי ישראל	355
נתן לשמה, שרקה, חרבה, חרפה, קללה, אלה, משל, שנינה (בכל העמים)	348
נתן דם נקי	356
(לא) נפל דבר	23, 36(g), 130, 350
ספר התורה הזה/הזאת	107, 109, 336, 339
ספר תורת משה	339
סר	339
סר מן הדרך	339
סר מאחרי ה׳	339
סר ימין ושמאל	339
סר ועבד אלהים אחרים/הבעל(ים) והשתחוה להם	321
סר (מאחרי) מחטא(ת)	337
עבדי/עבדיו הנביאים	351
עבד את ה׳	5, 6, 12, 274, 332, 334
עבד אלהים אחרים	82, 320
עבד באמת (את ה׳)	332
עבד הבעל(ים) העשתרות/האשרות	320
עבד לאלהים אחרים והשתחוה (להם)	321
עבד (לשמש לירח ולכוכבים) לכל צבא השמים	321
(כל) עבר ישם וישרוק	28
עבר ברית	340, 367
עובר שמה לרשתה	342
עֵדוֹת	65, 79, 111, 336–8
העֵדוֹת החוקים והמשפטים	338
עד בלתי השאיר לו שריד	344
עיניכם הראות	42, 173, 357
על כן אנכי מצוך	357
על מה עשה/דבר ה׳ . . . על אשר עזבו . . .	341

על כל הר/גבעה (גבהה) ותחת כל עץ רענן	322, 366
עם סגולה	328
עם קדוש	328
עמך ישראל	32, 37, 44, 328
עם נחלה/עם ונחלה	36(d), 328
עמד איש בפניו	344
עצר שמים ולא יהיה מטר	36(h)
(ב)ערי יהודה וחוצות ירושלים	6, 353
ערים גדולות ובצרות בשמים	358
(ככל אשר) עשה דוד	354
עשה הישר כדוד	354
עשה הישר (והטוב) בעיני ה׳	8, 17, 23, 25, 335
עשה הרע (בעיני ה׳)	8, 18, 130, 339, 341
עשה לו לעם	12, 327
עשה שמים וארץ	39
עשה שרירות לבו	340
פדה לעם	38
פדה ממצרים/מבית עבדים	32, 37, 326
פנה ערף/אחור ולא פנים	353
קול ששון וקול שמחה קול חתן וקול כלה	7, 353
קטר לאלהים אחרים	28, 321
קטר לבעל (לכל צבא השמים)	322
קטר לכל צבא השמים	321
קטר על הגגות	322
קרא אתכם הרעה הזאת	349
קרא/נקרא שם ה׳ עליו	4, 36(a), 193, 325, 327
קרע ממלכה (מעל)	15, 17, 23, 355
(מ)קצה השמים/ והארץ ועד קצה השמים/הארץ	358
רָאָה	176
ראה מעשה ה׳ הגדול אשר עשה	14, 42, 329
(ו)ראו כל עמי הארץ	358
רכבים ברכב ובסוסים	355
רנה ותפלה	330
רע מעללים	352
שוב איש מדרך הרעה	7, 351, 352
שוב עד/אל ה׳ (בכל לב)	335, 369
שים דברי ה׳ על לב	307, 335
שים לשמה, שרקה, חרבה, חרפה, קללה, אלה, משל ושנינה (בכל העמים)	28, 348
שים שמו שם	193, 197, 325
שיש עליך/כם להיטיב/לטוב	346
שכח את ה׳/ברית ה׳	357, 367
שכן שמו שם	4, 193, 197, 325
שלח את החרב אחריהם/בם/בינתם	354
שלח מעל פני ה׳	347
שלם עם ה׳	77, 78
(ה)שם הנכבד והנורא	331
(ל)שם לתהלה ולתפארת	328, 349
שמח בכל משלח יד	346
שמח לפני ה׳	346
(ב)שמים ממעל ועל הארץ מתחת	36(f), 38, 40, 331
(ה)שמים ושמי השמים	41
שמלתך לא בלתה ורגלך לא בצקה	358
שממה, מעון תנים	354
שמע בקול ה׳	332, 337

III. AKKADIAN

bītu: ana ḫarbāti . . . târu, 126
bīt ippušu libêl šanumma, 123
bīt redūti, 87
bubūtu, 127, 128
buginnu, 123
bukru, 112
būru (hunger): ana būri . . . šēr mārē . . . akālu, 114, 127
būru (young bull), kī būri epēšu, 293
būṣu, 142

dabābu, 91, 93
dibbatu dabābu, 91
mušadbibūt liḫšu, 91
dabab surrāte) dababti sarrāti, 99
dagālu, dāgil iṣṣūrē, 101
dannu, dunnunu: ṭuppu dannu, 87
māmītu danna, 87
adê dunnunu, 87
riksāte dunnunu, 87
dânu dīnu, 155
dīnu šemû, 245
dīnāt mīšarim, 150, 151
dāru/dārītu: (šubat) dārāti, 35
adi dārīti, 78
ana dāriš, 78
dibbu ibaššu, 92
dibbu šemû, 92
dikkuldu/dikuggallu, 120
dummuqu, 69
dumqu ša šarri, 69
dūru, 113

edēlu: ummu eli mārtiša bābša lēdil, 127
edēšu, 172
ēdu amēla la īzib, 51
ēdu šuma ul iraddi, 262
ēdu ul ipparšid, 51
egirrû, 98
elēṣu: ulṣi rīšāte, 87
emqum, 151
emūqu: (ana) emūq ramānišu ittakilma, 85
enēnu, 145
enēšu: unnušu, 133
enzum see ḫazzum
epēšu: adê, 87
ana marūti, 69, 79
bartam, 92
bīta, 123, 195
ēpiš nigūti, 141
epru, 118
erû, 132

etēqu: māmītu, 108
šūtuqu, 161
ezēbu: amēlu, 51
napištu, 51
ezēzu: ezziš likkilmešu, 109

gapāsu: igpuš libbu, 85
garābu, 117
guḫlu, 73
gullultu, 51
gummurtu: ina gummurti libbi, 104, 334
gummuru: libbašu gummuru, 68, 75, 77

ḫadû: ḫadû rubê, 87
ḫadû ul iba'a, 141
ḫalāpu, 121
ḫalāqu, 133
ḫamru, 216
ḫamuštum, 220
ḫarābu-šuḫrubu, 110
ḫarbāte, 126
ḫasāsu, 76, 77
ṭābtam ḫasāsu, 77
ḫattu puluḫtu, 50, 51
ḫaṭṭu: ina ḫaṭṭē maḫāṣu, 292
ḫaṭû: ayamma ul iḫṭi, 262
ina adê ḫaṭû, 115
ḫazzum (ḫanzum/enzum), 102
ḫepû: mātkunu ana ḫapê, 126
ḫiāru, 142
ḫidāte rišāte, 87
ḫiṭītu: ḫiṭītu u gullultu, 51
ḫīṭu: ša ḫ. ušabsû, 51
ḫullu (= nīru), 84
ḫumītu, 177
ḫuṣṣuṣu: kī qanê tuḫtaṣṣiṣ, 133
ḫayaram qatālum, 102

iḫzu, 163
ikkaršu ina ṣēri ay ilsâ alāla, 141
ikkil erê (NA_4.ḪUR), 141
ilāni maššūte, 119
(ana) ili qullulum, 51
immeru (ṭabāḫu), 102
imta ṭabāku, 348
inanna, 175
iṣṣūrāt šamê, 132, 133
ištu pāni . . . parāsu, 355
ittu, idāte, 98

kal mūši, 302
kal ūmē, 302
kalbu, 132

kalkaltu, 172
kânu, 93
  kunnu šeriktu, 77
karāšu, 87
kasāsu kurussu, 114
kašādu: *errētim dannātim arḫiš likšudāšu*, 108
  māmīt ilāni rabûti ša ētiqu ikšudanni, 108
kēnu/kittu, 84, 93
kī ša, 135
kibsu, 260
  kibis alpī u ṣênī, 141
kimaḫḫu, 140
kinūnu, 102
kišādu: *kišād immeru iṭbuḫ*, 102
  (*nīra ubbalušu*) *ana kišādiya*, 84
kittu, 84, 93
  ina kināti uzuzzu, 75, 77
  ina kitti ša libbi, 84
  kittu šalimtu, 84
  kittu u mīšaru, 154
kudimmu, 110 f.
kudurru, 61, 71, 76, 121, 122
kullumu: *ukallim šamši*, 140
kurussu, 114
kussû: *ina kussî šarrūte šūšubu*, 86

lamādu, *šulmudu*, 104, 260, 279
lemnu, 142
ē'ûssu šupšuqat, 260
libbu: *gummurti libbi*, 104, 334
  libbašu gummuru, 68, 75, 77
  libbasu ṭāb, 310
  libbi ili, 260
  libbu . . . inūḫuma, 145
liḫšu, 93
lū awīlāt, 11

mā, 94, 115
madbaru, 172
maḫāru, 131
maḫḫu, 98
  šipir maḫḫê, 98
māhiru: *māḫira la išû*, 359
maḫru: *ina maḫrīya uzuzzu*, 75, 77
maḫrû: *maḫrûti arkûti*, 140
māmīt ilāni rabûti, 108
māmītu, 63, 66, 67, 87, 102, 106, 107, 108
mār šarri, 87
mār šarrūti, 87
mār šipri luṣamma, 92
maraṣu: *maruṣ qaqqadišu ubta''i*, 89
marūtum, 369
  ana māruttiya eppuškami, 69, 79
maṣṣartu, 68, 76, 335
mašāru, 95
mašiktu bašû, 93
mašmašê, 101
maššūte, 119
mātu(m), 123, 126
  mātu ana tūšari turru, 126
  mātu ana ḫapê, 126
  ina mātišu raggam u ṣēnam lissuḫ, 356
melammu, 206
mēsu: *adê mēsu*, 111
mimma lā ēpušu, 292
minūt nidûtišu, 145
mirīt nābali, 172
mīšaru(m), 149, 152 f.
  mīšaram ina mātim šakānum, 155, 156
  mīšaram šakānum, 152
  šar mīšarim, 154
  dīnāt mīšarim, 150, 151
miṭṭu, 86
munattu, 262
muššuru, 95

nabalkutu, 93
nadānu, 75
  nadānu ana šalāli, 126
  nadānu ana mārēšu . . . adi dārīti, 78
nadû, 118
  šiba nadû, 172
nagê, 110
nâḫu, 145
naḫalaptu, 121
nakāru, 92, 108
nakru, 131
narû: *narâya alṭur*, 193
nasāḫu, 309
  raggam u ṣēnam lissuḫ, 356
nasāku: *anāku ul anassukka*, 69
naṣāru, 65, 68, 76, 335
  naṣāru maṣṣarti šarrūtiya, 68, 76, 335
nāṣir amāt šarrūti, 77, 83, 336
našû: *abšāna našû*, 84
nesû, 260
nidûtu, 145
nigûtu: *ēpiš nigûti*, 141
niklat libbi, 254
niqê, 102
niqittu la taraššu, 51

nīru: *emēdu*, 84
  (*w*)*abālu*, 84
nišē, 101, 126
  nišē lā lamdā, 260
nišu: *nīš ilāni šuzkuru*, 87
niṭil ēnī, 123
nukurtu, 93
nukussūti, 132
nūnī apsî, 132, 133

palāḫu, 51, 83, 140, 332
  palāḫ ili (*u šarri*), 163, 311
  palāḫ ili litmudu, 279, 332
palāsu, *naplusu*: *ana qaqqad bēlīšu ippalas*, 89
pāliḫu, 77, 83, 84, 140
paqādu, 68
parakku, 196
parāku: *ēpiš nigūti ul ipparrik*, 141
parāsu: *ištu pāni . . . parāsu*, 355
pargāniš, 142
pašāqu, *šupšuqu*, 260
pašāṭu, 108
paṭāru, 83
petû (*uznu*), 99
puḫḫuru: *upaḫḫir nišē māt Aššur*, 87, 101
puluḫtu, 51
puzzuru, 97
  la tupazzaršu, 97

qabû, 95, 97, 115
  la taqabbāni, 97
qibītu: *qibīt ilūti*, 130
  qibit pî, 260
qanû: *kī qanê tuḫtaṣṣiṣ*, 133
  qan appari, 133
qapsu: *ina qapsi māti*, 302
qaqqadu, 89
qaqqaru: *ina eli pāni sa qaqqari liḫliq*, 133
  ina māti liḫliq, 133
qaštu, 136
  šebēru, 136
  dunnunu, 136
qatālum, 103
qātu: *qāt šarri dannu*, 329
  qāta wabālu, 293
qēpu, 93
  amēl qīpti, 93
qereb šamê, 260
qerūb ṭemšina, 260
qinnu qanānu, 142

qullulu ana ili, 51

ra'āmu, 333
rabāṣu, *šurbuṣu*, 142
rābiṣu lemnu, 142
raggam u ṣēnam nasāḫu, 356
rāgimu, 98
raḫāṣu, 134
rigmu: *rigim amēlūti*, 141
riḫṣu, 126
riksu (*u māmītu*), 66 f., 106 f.
  riksāte dunnunu, 87
  riksātim dannātim, 87
rēši, 89
rišāte, 87

saḫāru ana, 83
saḫlû, 110 f.
sakālu, 226
salīmu rešû, 145
sapāḫu, *suppuḫu*: *ṭābta* (*šam*) *saḫlê usappiḫa ṣīruššun*, 110
sassu, 134
sikiltu, 226, 328
sirrimu, 121, 142
sunqu, 128
sūqu, 141
surrāte/*sarrāte*, 99

ṣabātu, 163
ṣābitu, 164
ṣabītu, *ṣabâte*, 142
ṣâlu, 70
ṣēru (snake), 172
ṣēru: *umām ṣēri*, 142
ṣibittu, 163
ṣiddu u birtu, 116
ṣiḫir u rabi, 87, 101
ṣīpu, 110 f.
ṣumāmu/*ṣummê*: *ašar ṣummê kalkalti*, 172

ša'ālu, 92
šā'ilu: *šā'ili amāt ilī*, 98
  šaḫu, 132
šakānu: *mīšaram*, 152 ff.
  šipṭam, 152
  šuma(*m*), 192 f.
šalālu: *ana šalāli nadānu*, 126
šamê: *ana šamê šaqû*, 358
šanû, 131
šapāru: *ana niṭli ēnīšu massu lišpur*, 123
šarāpu: *aplu rabiu šarāpu*, 216

šarru dannu, 329
šarrum u šērīšu adi ḫamšīšu ina kussim uššab, 25
šattu, *šanāti*: 70 *šanāti minūt nidûtišu išṭurma*, 145
šaṭāru, 107 f., 145
  arrāti mala ina adêšunu šaṭrā, 107
  narâya alṭur, 193
šēdu, 142
šemēru, 86
šeriktu: *ukîn šeriktašu*, 77
šērtu rabītu, 120, 121
šēru: *akālu*, 127
šība nadû, 172
šisīt alāla ṭābi, 141
šubat dārāti, 35
šumu: *damqu*, 75
  šakānu, 193
  šaṭru (*pāšaṭu*), 108
šumu (= line), 262
šuttu, 98
  ina šāt mūši, 262

tappû: *ina muḫ tappā'īšu abāta iškun*, 292
târu: *amātu ša ina pīšu uṣṣu ana kutallišu ul itâr*, 79
tēdiqu: *tēdiqu šība ay iddima*, 172
tilu, *tilê*, 126
tirḫatu, 285
tūšaru, 126

ṭabāḫu, 102
ṭābtu (salt), 110 f.
ṭūb libbi, 311
ṭuppu, 67, 107, 108, 166
  dannu, 87
  ša ina libbi ṭuppi annīti šaṭrat, 107
  ša riksi/rikilti, 67
ṭupšarru, 101, 108

ugaru, 141
ulṣi rīšāte, 87
umām ṣēri, 142
ūmu, *ūmē*: (*adi*)*ūmē malû*, 145
  ūmē ammar anīnu . . . balṭānini, 279, 358
urqīt ṣēri, 124, 141
utukku, 142
uzna petû, 99
uzuzzu: *maḫar*, 77
  ina pāni, 77

(*w*)*âru*- *mu''uru*, 163
wašāru, 131
wuššuru, 95

zakāru, 76
  šuzkuru, 87
zerû, 110, 114
zību, 132
ša ziqni, 89
zumru, 120
zuruḫ šarri dannu, 329

IV. ARAMAIC

אח 89
אחו 126
איך זי 135
ארבה 124
ארנב 142
ארק שערי/חטי 172
ארקה 124
אשר – באשרה 83, 105
יסקן באשרה 105
תפנו באשרה 83

אתר – באתרה 105

בנוה 105
בניכי אחריכי 78
(ושבע) בנתה יהכן
  בשט לחם ואל
  יהרגן 125
בעה – יבעה ראשי
  להמתתי 89
בר 89

בתרה 105

דם 89

הפך 111
הרג 125

זחל – אל תזחל 45
זניה 125
זרע – ויזרע . . .
הדד מלח ושחלין 110

חזה – וליתחזי ירק 124
חצר 124

יומא – מן יומא זנה
ועד עלם 78
יקד – תקד... באש 110
ירק 124
ישמן – [יש]תחט
לישמן 126

כנר – קל כנר 141

לחם 125
(מלין) לחית 93, 96

מלח 110
מלין לחית 93, 96
מלכו 105
מסר 95

נגד 89
נוס – תהנס 108
נכה תכוה בחרב 99
נסך – ותסך להם
לחם 100
נפק – ואל יפק חצר 108
נסח – יסחו 108
נצר 108
נקם – ותקם דמי מן
יד שנאי 89

סכר – הסכר
תהסכרהם 95
סלק – יסקן באשרה 105
[יס]ק תוי 124
ספרא 107, 125

סקאה 124

עדן – עדי, עדיא 65, 86, 107, 111,
125
עדיא זי בספרא זנה 107
עין – ובעיני מחזה
אנה בני רבע 25
עלם – עד עלם 78
עקה 142
עקר 89
ערר – כן יערר͏ן נשי
מתעאל 136

ופגר ארבא מעל
פגר 125
פנה – ואל תפנו
באשרה 83
פקד 89

צי 142
צבי 142
צדה 142

קום – תקום מלכו 105
קריה 99
[רבק צי] 142
קתל – יקתל מן
יקתל 106

שחט (שחת) –
[יש]תחט לישמן 126
שחנא באישא 121
שחלין 110
שט – בשט לחם 125
שלט – אנתי שליטה
בה 78
שמע – יתשמע קל
כנר 141
שעותא 110
שעל 142
שקרתם בעדיא זי
בספרא זנה 125
שרן 142

תוי 124
תולעה 124
תל 125, 142

V. PHOENICIAN

ארך ימת ושנת 309
בן צדק 91, 155
בעל צמד 108
בעל שמם 108
חמית 177
מח שם 108
כון – אל יכן לם
שרש למט ופר
למעל 114
צמח צדק 91, 155
שחת – ישחת הספר
ז ישחת ראש 108
תרק – ותרק אנך
כל הרע אש כן
בארץ 356

VI. UGARITIC

arṣ nḥlth, 196
ǵr nḥlty, 196
ǵry il, 196
ksu ṯbth, 196
mhr, 285
qdš, 196
rkb ʿrpt, 202
sglt, 226

VII. SUMERIAN

ama-ar-gi$_4$, 153
inim, 149
kalam, 154
kešda: KA-e-da-kéš, 149
kú, 73
lugal ni-sig$_{10}$-ga-ra, 73
nig-si-sá, 152
NINDÁ+GUD, 73
si-sá, 152, 154
šár, 154
šim/šimbi, 73
šušgal, 73
^{d}utu-gim, 154
zi-dè-eš, 154

VIII. HITTITE

genzu ḫar(k)-, 97
idālaueš-, 93
idāluš memii̯aš, 93, 96
mema-, 95
memii̯aš ašant-, 93
paḫš-, 65
parḫ-, 65
šarā išpart-, 93
šullāi-, 70
(ZI-ni)tarna-, 303
(ŠÀ-ta)tarna-, 303
taštaši̯a-, 93
tuzzi-, 100
u̯ašta-, 79
zamurāi-, 93

IX. GREEK

ἄδικος, 160
διαθήκη, 11
ἱερὸς λόγος, 247, 253
κακώσετε, 289
(εἰς) μάτην, 160
προστίθημι ἢ ἀφαιρέω, 262
συνετούς, 244
τέχνη, 254
χιλιόμβη, 250
ψεῦδος, 160

INDEX OF SOURCES

I. CUNEIFORM

II. WEST SEMITIC

III. EGYPTIAN

IV. CLASSICAL

V. RABBINIC

INDEX OF SCRIPTURE REFERENCES

SUBJECT INDEX

Monarchy, 4, 13, 147, 154 n., 168, 169, 170, 188, 369
united, 80, 197
anti-, 82 n., 169, 369
pro-, 169, 170
Monotheistic (creed), 1, 36 f., 38, 40, 313, 331
Moses:
written Torah of, 171
as law-maker/lawgiver, 151 ff.
valedictory address of, 10 ff., 171 ff.
blessing of, 10, 153
death of, 177
prayer of, 37, 177
Song of, 10, 132 n.
Mother–son relationship, 300 f., 305 f.
Mountain(s):
high/lofty, 322, 360, 366
height, 176–7
sacred, 196 n.
of Israel, 366
Mourning (rites), 226
Mt. Ebal, 65, 147, 176 n.
Mt. Gerizim, 147, 176 n.
ceremony, 165
Mt. Nebo, 177, 181 n.
Murder, 239, 240 f., 285 n.
law of unsolved, 32, 210, 234
rite of unsolved, 210 f.
Muršiliš II, 69, 70, 71, 72, 79, 107 n.
treaty, 93, 107

Nabonidus, 249, 250
Naboth, 18 ff., 319
Name, 38 n., 80
God's (Yahweh), 4, 193 ff., 201, 206
to make/cause to dwell, 4, 193 f., 197, 206, 325
to put his, 4, 193 f., 325
to build for his, 4, 193, 325
to consecrate/dedicate to his, 4, 193, 325
(to) blot out, 347
greatness of, 10 f., 38 n., 80
'Name theology', 193, 194 f.
Naram-Sin, treaty, 102
Nathan, 197, 247
oracle, 130, 197 n., 247 f.
prophecy, 194
National, 261, 274 f.
prosperity, 312
resurgence, 50
consciousness (feelings), 50, 275, 275 n.
holiness, 226
Nationalization, 276, 307, 313, 315, 316
Naturweisheit, 258, 263 n.
Nebelah, *see* Carcass
Nebo, Mt., 177, 181 n.
Nehemia, 42, 263, 276
Neḫuštan, 168
Nerab inscription, 25 n., 108
Netherworld, 112 n., 113 n.
New year festival, 180 n., 219 n.
Ningirsu (god), 149
temple of, 35, 248
Ninlil, 119
curse of, 119 n.
Noah, 76, 80, 334
Nob (priestly city), 99 n.
Nocturnal pollution, 238
vision, 247 f.
Nomistic, 274 f., 280
Northern tradition, 57, 161, 166 n., 366 f.

Oak, 366
Oath:
oath-imprecation, 61–3, 64 n., 66, 67, 91, 100 ff.
sworn, 62–3
double, 88
loyalty of, 94, 96, 97, 99 n.
violation of, 51 n., 106, 108
Obedience, 77, 78, 150 n.
Observance, 36, 246 n., 264, 274
of the law, 1, 5, 11, 23, 45 n., 77, 81, 164, 168, 246 n., 309, 318, 332, 343
Offences, capital, 240 f.
Offering, 187, 211, 215, 218, 249
burnt, 182, 212, 217, 237
cereal, 182, 212 n., 220
daily, 212
drink, 182
guilt/sin, 182, 187, 210
non-burnt, 212
of suet, 188
paschal, 216–17
seasonal, 212
votive, 212, 219, 220
Officers, 101, 163, 164, 173, 244 n.
Official(s), 98, 99
Assyrian, 96, 97
Hittite, 96, 97